Learning Deep Learning

Learning Deep Learning

THEORY AND PRACTICE OF NEURAL
NETWORKS, COMPUTER VISION, NATURAL
LANGUAGE PROCESSING, AND
TRANSFORMERS USING TENSORFLOW

MAGNUS EKMAN

✦✦Addison-Wesley

Boston • Columbus • New York • San Francisco • Amsterdam • Cape Town
Dubai • London • Madrid • Milan • Munich • Paris • Montreal • Toronto • Delhi • Mexico City
São Paulo • Sydney • Hong Kong • Seoul • Singapore • Taipei • Tokyo

For information about buying this title in bulk quantities, or for special sales opportunities (which may include electronic versions; custom cover designs; and content particular to your business, training goals, marketing focus, or branding interests), please contact our corporate sales department at corpsales@pearsoned.com or (800) 382-3419.

For government sales inquiries, please contact governmentsales@pearsoned.com.

For questions about sales outside the U.S., please contact intlcs@pearson.com.

Visit us on the Web: informit.com/aw

Library of Congress Control Number: 2021937264

Cover image: R.Eva Robot design by Gavriil Klimov and Gregor Kopka

Figures P-4, 8-8, 8-10, 16-1, 16-6, 16-7, B-1, J-1, J-2: Magnus Ekman

ISBN-13: 978-0-13-747035-8
ISBN-10: 0-13-747035-5

157 2024

For my wife Jennifer, my children Sebastian and Sofia, my dog Babette, and my parents Ingrid and Krister

Contents

6 FULLY CONNECTED NETWORKS APPLIED TO REGRESSION 153

7 CONVOLUTIONAL NEURAL NETWORKS APPLIED TO IMAGE CLASSIFICATION 171

8   DEEPER CNNs AND PRETRAINED MODELS   205

9   PREDICTING TIME SEQUENCES WITH RECURRENT
NEURAL NETWORKS   237

CONTENTS

Foreword

Artificial intelligence (AI) has seen impressive progress over the last decade. Humanity's dream of building intelligent machines that can think and act like us, only better and faster, seems to be finally taking off. To enable everyone to be part of this historic revolution requires the democratization of AI knowledge and resources. This book is timely and relevant toward accomplishing these lofty goals.

Learning Deep Learning by Magnus Ekman provides a comprehensive instructional guide for both aspiring and experienced AI engineers. In the book, Magnus shares the rich hands-on knowledge he has garnered at NVIDIA, an established leader in AI. The book does not assume any background in machine learning and is focused on covering significant breakthroughs in deep learning over the last few years. The book strikes a nice balance and covers both important fundamentals such as backpropagation and the latest models in several domains (e.g., GPT for language understanding, Mask R-CNN for image understanding).

AI is a trinity of data, algorithms, and computing infrastructure. The launch of the ImageNet challenge provided a large-scale benchmark dataset needed to train large neural networks. The parallelism of NVIDIA GPUs enabled the training of such large neural networks. We are now in the era of billion, and even trillion, parameter models. Building and maintaining large-scale models will soon be deemed a prerequisite skill for any AI engineer. This book is uniquely placed to teach such skills. It provides in-depth coverage of large-scale models in multiple domains.

The book also covers emerging areas such as neural architecture search, which will likely become more prevalent as we begin to extract the last ounce of accuracy and hardware efficiency out of current AI models. The deep learning revolution has almost entirely occurred in open source. This book provides convenient access to code and datasets and runs through the code examples thoroughly. There is extensive program code available in both TensorFlow and PyTorch, the two most popular frameworks for deep learning.

I do not think any book on AI will be complete without a discussion of ethical issues. I believe that it is the responsibility of every AI engineer to think critically about the societal implications around the deployment of AI. The proliferation of harassment, hate speech, and misinformation in social media has shown how poorly designed algorithms can wreak havoc on our society. Groundbreaking studies such as the Gender Shades project and Stochastic Parrots have shown highly problematic biases in AI models that are commercially deployed at scale. I have advocated for banning the use of AI in sensitive scenarios until appropriate guidelines and testing are in place (e.g., the use of AI-based face recognition by law enforcement). I am glad to see the book cover significant developments such as model cards that improve accountability and transparency in training and maintaining AI models. I am hoping for a bright, inclusive future for the AI community.

—*Dr. Anima Anandkumar*
Bren Professor, Caltech
Director of ML Research, NVIDIA

Foreword

By training I am an economist. Prior to my work in technical education, I spent years teaching students and professionals well-developed frameworks for understanding our world and how to make decisions within it. The methods and skills you will discover in *Learning Deep Learning* by Magnus Ekman parallel the tools used by economists to make forecasts and predictions in a world full of uncertainty. The power and capabilities of the deep learning techniques taught in this book have brought amazing advances in our ability to make better predictions and inferences from the data in the world around us.

Though their future benefits and importance can sometimes be exaggerated, there is no doubt the world and industry have been greatly affected by deep learning (DL) and its related supersets of machine learning (ML) and artificial intelligence (AI). Applications of these technologies have proven durable and are profound. They are with us everywhere: at home and at work, in our cars, and on our phones. They influence how we travel, how we communicate, how we shop, how we bank, and how we access information. It is very difficult to think of an industry that has not or will not be impacted by these technologies.

The explosion in the use of these technologies has uncovered two important gaps in knowledge and areas of opportunity for those who endeavor to learn. First is the technical skillset required to develop useful applications. And second, importantly, is an understanding of how these applications can address problems and opportunities in the world around us. This book helps to address both gaps. For these reasons, *Learning Deep Learning* has arrived in the right place at the right time.

As NVIDIA's education and training arm, the Deep Learning Institute exists to help individuals and organizations grow their understanding of DL and other computing techniques so they can find creative solutions to challenging problems. *Learning Deep Learning* is the perfect addition to our training library. It is accessible to those with basic skills in statistics and calculus, and it doesn't require the reader to first wade through tangential topics. Instead, Ekman focuses on the building blocks of DL: the perceptron, other artificial neurons, deep neural networks (DNNs), and DL frameworks. Then he gradually layers in additional concepts that build on each other, all the way up to and including modern natural language processing (NLP) architectures such as Transformer, BERT, and GPT.

Importantly, Ekman uses a learning technique that in our experience has proven pivotal to success—asking readers to think about using DL techniques in practice. Simple yet powerful coding examples and exercises are provided throughout the book to help readers apply their understanding. At the same time, explanations of the underlying theory are present, and those interested in deepening their knowledge of relevant concepts and tools without getting into programming code will benefit. Plenty of citations with references for further study of a specific topic are also provided.

For all these reasons, *Learning Deep Learning* is a very good place to start one's journey to understanding the world of DL. Ekman's straightforward approach to helping the reader understand what DL is, how it was developed, and how it can be applied in our ever-changing world is refreshing. He provides a comprehensive yet clear discussion of the technology and an honest assessment of its capabilities and its limitations. And through it all, he permits the reader to dream, just a bit, about where DL may yet take us. That is exciting. It is why this economist finds this book so timely and important, and why I think you will too.

—Dr. Craig Clawson
Director, NVIDIA Deep Learning Institute

Preface

Deep learning (DL) is a quickly evolving field, which has demonstrated amazing results in performing tasks that traditionally have been performed well only by humans. Examples of such tasks are image classification, generating natural language descriptions of images, natural language translation, speech-to-text, and text-to-speech conversion.

Learning Deep Learning (this book, hereafter known as LDL) quickly brings you up to speed on the topic. It teaches how DL works, what it can do, and gives you some practical experience, with the overall objective of giving you a solid foundation for further learning.

In this book, we use green text boxes like this one to highlight concepts that we find extra important. The intent is to ensure that you do not miss key concepts. Let us begin by pointing out that we find **Deep Learning** important.

You will learn about the perceptron and other artificial neurons. They are the fundamental building blocks of deep neural networks that have enabled the DL revolution. You will learn about fully connected feedforward networks and convolutional networks. You will apply these networks to solve practical problems, such as predicting housing prices based on a large number of variables or identifying to which category an image belongs. Figure P-1 shows examples of such categories and images.

You will also learn about ways to represent words from a natural language using an encoding that captures some of the semantics of the encoded words. You will then use these encodings together with a recurrent neural network to create a neural-based natural language translator. This translator can automatically translate simple sentences from English to French or other similar languages, as illustrated in Figure P-2.

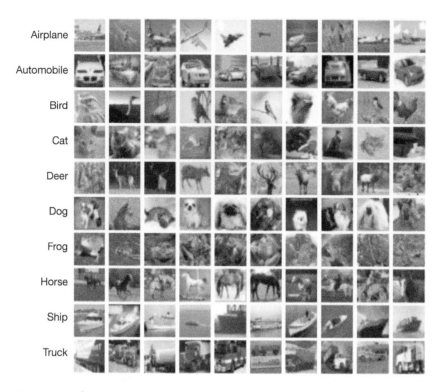

Figure P-1 Categories and example images from the CIFAR-10 dataset (Krizhevsky, 2009). This dataset will be studied in more detail in Chapter 7. (Image source: https://www.cs.toronto.edu/~kriz/cifar.html)

Figure P-2 A neural network translator that takes a sentence in English as input and produces the corresponding sentence in French as output

Finally, you will learn how to build an image-captioning network that combines image and language processing. This network takes an image as an input and automatically generates a natural language description of the image.

What we just described represents the main narrative of LDL. Throughout this journey, you will learn many other details. In addition, we end with a medley of additional important topics. We also provide appendixes that dive deeper into a collection of the discussed topics.

What Is Deep Learning?

We do not know of a crisp definition of what DL is, but one attempt is that *DL is a class of machine learning algorithms that use multiple layers of computational units where each layer learns its own representation of the input data. These representations are combined by later layers in a hierarchical fashion.* This definition is somewhat abstract, especially given that we have not yet described the concept of layers and computational units, but in the first few chapters, we provide many more concrete examples of what this means.

A fundamental part of DL is the deep neural network (DNN), a namesake of the biological neuron, by which it is loosely inspired. There is an ongoing debate about how closely the techniques within DL do mimic activity in a brain, where one camp argues that using the term *neural* network paints the picture that it is more advanced than it is. Along those lines, they recommend using the terms *unit* instead of *artificial neuron* and just *network* instead of *neural network*. No doubt, DL and the larger field of artificial intelligence (AI) have been significantly hyped in mainstream media. At the time of writing this book, it is easy to get the impression that we are close to creating machines that think like humans, although lately, articles that express some doubt are more common. After reading this book, you will have a more accurate view of what kind of problems DL can solve. In this book, we choose to freely use the words *neural network* and *neuron* but recognize that the algorithms presented are more tied to machine capabilities than to how an actual human brain works.

In this book, we use red text boxes like this one when we feel the urge to state something that is somewhat beside the point, a subjective opinion or of similar nature. You can safely ignore these boxes altogether if you do not find them adding any value to your reading experience.

Let us dive into this book by stating the opinion that it is a little bit of a buzz killer to take the stance that our cool DNNs are not similar to the brain. This is especially true for somebody picking up this book after reading about machines with superhuman abilities in the mainstream media. To keep the illusion alive, we sometimes allow ourselves to dream a little bit and make analogies that are not necessarily that well founded, but to avoid misleading you, we try not to dream outside of the red box.

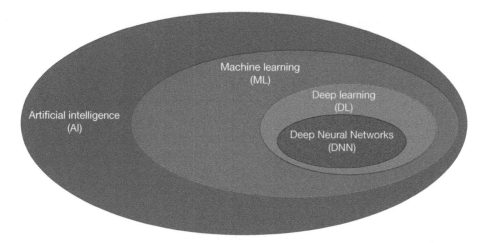

Figure P-3 Relationship between artificial intelligence, machine learning, deep learning, and deep neural networks. The sizes of the different ovals do not represent the relative size of one field compared to another.

To put DL and DNNs into context, Figure P-3 shows how they relate to the machine learning (ML) and AI fields. DNN is a subset of DL. DL in turn is a subset of the field of ML, which in turn is a subset of the greater field of AI.

> **Deep neural network (DNN)** is a subset of DL.
>
> DL is a subset of **machine learning (ML)**, which is a subset of **artificial intelligence (AI).**

In this book, we choose not to focus too much on the exact definition of DL and its boundaries, nor do we go into the details of other areas of ML or AI. Instead, we focus on details of what DNNs are and the types of tasks to which they can be applied.

Brief History of Deep Neural Networks

In the last couple of sections, we loosely referred to networks without describing what a network is. The first few chapters in this book discuss network architectures in detail, but at this point, it is sufficient to think of a network as an opaque system that has inputs and outputs. The usage model is to present something, for example, an image or a text sequence, as inputs to the network, and the network will produce something useful on its outputs, such as an interpretation of what the image contains, as in Figure P-4, or a natural language translation in a different language, as was shown in Figure P-2.

As previously mentioned, a central piece of a neural network is the artificial neuron. The first model of an artificial neuron was introduced in 1943 (McCulloch and Pitts, 1943), which started the first wave of neural network research. The McCulloch and Pitts neuron was followed in 1957 by the Rosenblatt perceptron (Rosenblatt, 1958). A key contribution from the perceptron was its associated automated learning algorithm that demonstrated how a system could learn desired behavior. Details of how the perceptron works are found in Chapter 1. The perceptron has some fundamental limitations, and although it was shown that these limitations can be overcome by combining multiple perceptrons into a multilayer network, the original learning algorithm did not extend to multilayer networks. According to a common narrative, this resulted in neural network research falling out of fashion. This is often referred to as the first AI winter, which was allegedly caused by a book by Minsky and Papert (1969). In this book, they raised the absence of a learning algorithm for multilayer networks as a serious concern.

We note that in the days of Rosenblatt's publications, they were certainly not shy about comparing their work with the human brain. In reading about the Rosenblatt perceptron (Rosenblatt, 1958), we see that the first paper he references is called "Design for a Brain."

This topic and narrative are controversial. Olazaran (1996) has studied whether the statements of Minsky and Papert had been misrepresented. Further, Schmidhuber (2015) pointed out that there did exist a learning algorithm for multilevel networks (Ivakhnenko and Lapa, 1965) four years before the book by Minsky and Papert was published.

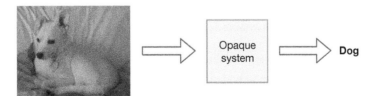

Figure P-4 A deep neural network as an opaque system that can take an image as an input and then output an indication of what type of object is in the image

The second wave of neural network research was initiated in the 1980s. It was heavily influenced by a paper that described the backpropagation algorithm for automatic training of multilayer networks (Rumelhart et al., 1986). Rumelhart and colleagues showed that this algorithm could be used to overcome the limitations of the perceptron. In the study, they explicitly pointed out that they believed this addressed the concerns raised by Minsky and Papert. Rumelhart and colleagues popularized the backpropagation algorithm in the context of neural networks, but it was not the first occurrence of the algorithm in the literature. The algorithm was applied to a similar problem domain in 1970 (Linnainmaa, 1970). Werbos (1981) described it in the context of neural networks in 1981.

Details of how this algorithm works are found in Chapter 3. An important outcome of this second wave of neural network research was the development of LeNet in 1989. It was a convolutional neural network (CNN), which was shown to be able to recognize handwritten zip codes (LeCun et al., 1990). It built on Fukushima's *Neocognitron* (Fukushima, 1980), which we believe is the first published CNN.

An enhanced version of LeNet was later used by major US banks to read handwritten checks, and it thereby became one of the first big commercial applications of neural networks. Convolutional neural networks are described in detail in Chapter 7. Despite the progress, neural networks fell out of fashion yet again, partly because the limited computational capability at the time prevented the networks from scaling to larger problems and partly because other traditional ML approaches were perceived as better alternatives.

The third wave of neural network research was enabled by a combination of algorithmic progress, availability of massive datasets, and the ability to use graphics processing units (GPU) for general purpose computing. From an outsider perspective, all this came together in 2012. At that point, the field had been rebranded as DL and was popularized in large part due to AlexNet (Krizhevsky et al., 2012), which was a CNN that scored significantly higher than any other participant in a computer vision competition known as the ImageNet challenge.

In reality, this third wave was enabled by persistent research groups who had continued to perform neural network research in the 1990s and first decade of the 2000s. These insiders started using the term *deep networks* in 2006. Further, the ImageNet challenge was not the first competition in which neural networks, some of which were GPU accelerated, beat more traditional techniques.

For example, Graves and colleagues (2009) won competitions in handwriting recognition with a neural network in 2009. Similarly, Ciresan and colleagues (2011) used a GPU accelerated network for image classification in 2011.

This work was shortly followed by similar breakthroughs in other fields, which have led to the DL boom that is still ongoing as of the writing of this book. The rest of this book will describe some of these key findings and how they can be applied in practice. For a more detailed description of the history of DL, we recommend Schmidhuber's (2015) overview.

Is This Book for You?

There are already many books on this topic, and different people like to approach subjects in different ways. In this book, we try to cut to the chase while still providing enough background to give you a warm fuzzy feeling that you understand why the techniques work. We decided to *not* start the book with an overall introduction to the field of traditional ML. Although we believe that anybody who wants to get serious about DL needs to also master traditional ML, we do not believe that it is necessary to first learn about traditional ML before learning the basics of DL. We even believe that having to first get through multiple chapters that do not directly discuss DL can be a barrier to entry for many people.

In this book, we use yellow text boxes like this one to highlight things that we otherwise do not discuss or explore in detail but nonetheless think are important for you to learn at some point. We believe that an important part of learning about a new topic is to not only acquire some basic skills but also get some insights into what the next steps are. We use the yellow boxes to signal to you that at this point it is perfectly fine to ignore a certain topic, but it will be important to learn as a next step.

Let us now begin by stating that it is important to know about **traditional ML** if you want to get serious about DL, but you can wait to learn about traditional ML until you have gotten a taste of DL.

Not starting the book with traditional ML techniques is an attempt to avoid one of the buzz killers that we have found in other books. One very logical, and therefore typical, way of introducing DL is to first describe what ML is and, as such, to start with a very simple ML technique, namely, linear regression. It is easy, as an excited beginner, to be a little disheartened when you expect to learn about cool techniques to classify cat images and instead get stuck reading a discussion about fitting a straight line to a set of random data points using mathematics that seem completely unrelated to DL. We instead try to take the quickest, while still logical, path to getting to image classification to provide you with some instant satisfaction, but you will notice that we still sneak in some references and comparisons to linear regression over time.

Apart from deciding whether to include traditional ML as a topic, any author of a book on DL needs to take a position on whether to include code examples and how deeply to dive into the mathematics. Our view is that because DL is an applied field, a book on this topic needs to contain a good mix of theory and practice, so code examples are necessary. We also believe that many topics in DL are inherently mathematical, and it is necessary to include some of the mathematics to provide a good description of how things work. With that background, we try to describe certain concepts from different angles using a good mix of elements:

- Figures

- Natural language (English) descriptions

- Programming code snippets

- Mathematical formulas

Readers who master all of the preceding might find some descriptions redundant, but we believe that this is the best way of making the book accessible to a large audience.

This book does not aim to include details about all the most recent and advanced techniques in the DL field. Instead, we include concepts and techniques that we believe are fundamental to understanding the latest developments in the field. Some of the appendixes describe how some major architectures are built on these concepts, but most likely, even better architectures will emerge. Our goal is to give you enough knowledge to enable you to continue learning by reading more recent research papers. Therefore, we have also decided to sprinkle references throughout the book to enable you to follow up on topics that you find extra interesting. However, it has been our intention to make the book self-contained so that you should never need to look up a reference to be able to follow the explanations in the book. In some cases, we include references to things that we do not explain but mention only in passing. In those cases, we try to make it clear that it is meant as future reading instead of being a central element of the book.

> The references in the book are strictly for future reading and should not be necessary to read to be able to understand the main topics of the book.

Is DL Dangerous?

There are plenty of science fiction books and movies that depict AI as a threat against humanity. Machines develop a form of consciousness and perceive humans as a threat and therefore decide to destroy us. There have also been thought experiments about how an AI accidentally destroys the human species as a side effect of trying to deliver on what it is programmed to do. One example is the paperclip maximizer (Bostrom, 2003), which is programmed with the goal of making as many paper clips as possible. In order to do so, it might kill all human beings to free up atoms needed to make paper clips. The risk that these exact scenarios will play out in practice is probably low, but researchers still see future powerful AIs as a significant risk.

More urgently, DL has already been shown to come with serious unintended consequences and malignant use. One example is a study of a commercially available facial recognition system (Buolamwini and Gebru, 2018) used by law enforcement. Although the system achieved 99% accuracy on lighter-skinned men, its accuracy on darker-skinned women was only 65%, thereby putting them at much greater risk of being incorrectly identified and possibly wrongly accused of crimes. An example of malignant use of DL is fake pornography (Dickson, 2019) whereby the technology is used to make it appear as if a person (often a celebrity) is featured in a pornographic video.

DL learns from data created by humans and consequently runs the risk of learning and even amplifying human biases. This underscores the need for taking a responsible approach to DL and AI. Historically, this topic has largely been neglected, but more recently started to receive more attention. A powerful demonstration can be found on the website of the Algorithmic Justice League (Buolamwini, n.d.) with a video showing how a face detection system fails to detect the face of a dark-skinned woman (Buolamwini) until she puts on a white mask.

Another example is the emergence of algorithmic auditing, where researchers identify and report human biases and other observed problems in commercial systems (Raji and Buolamwini, 2019). Researchers have proposed to document known biases and intended use cases of any released system to mitigate these problems. This applies both to the data used to create such systems (Gebru, et al., 2018) and to the released DL model itself (Mitchell et al., 2018). Thomas suggests a checklist of questions to guide DL practitioners throughout the course of a project to avoid ethical problems (Thomas, 2019). We touch on these topics throughout the book. We also provide resources for further reading in Chapter 18.

Choosing a DL Framework

As a practitioner of DL, you will need to decide what DL framework to use. A DL framework provides functionality that handles much of the low-level details when implementing DL models. Just as the DL field is rapidly evolving, so are the different frameworks. To mention a few, Caffe, Theano, MXNet, Torch, TensorFlow, and PyTorch have all been influential throughout the current DL boom. In addition to these full-fledged frameworks, there are specialized frameworks such as Keras and TensorRT. Keras is a high-level API that makes it easier to program for some of these frameworks. TensorRT is an inference optimizer and runtime engine that can be used to run models built and trained by many of the mentioned frameworks.

As of the writing of this book, our impression is that the two most popular full-fledged frameworks are TensorFlow and PyTorch, where TensorFlow nowadays includes native support for the Keras API. Another significant framework is MXNet. Models developed in either of these frameworks can be deployed using the TensorRT inference engine.

Deciding on what DL framework to use can be viewed as a life-changing decision. Some people would say that it is comparable to choosing a text editor or a spouse. We do not share that belief but think that the world is big enough for multiple competing solutions. We decided to provide programming examples in both TensorFlow and PyTorch for this book. The TensorFlow examples are printed in the book itself, but equivalent examples in PyTorch, including detailed descriptions, can be found on the book's website. We suggest that you pick a framework that you like or one that makes it easy to collaborate with people you interact with.

The programming examples in this book are provided in a TensorFlow version using the Keras API (printed in the book) as well as in a PyTorch version (online). Appendix I contains information about how to install TensorFlow and PyTorch, as well as a description of some of the key differences between the two frameworks.

Prerequisites for Learning DL

DL combines techniques from a number of different fields. If you want to get serious about DL, and particularly if you want to do research and publish your findings, over time you will need to acquire advanced knowledge within the scope of many of these skillsets. However, we believe that it is possible to get started with DL with little or partial knowledge in these areas. The sections that follow list the areas we find important, and in each section, we list the minimum set of knowledge that we think you need in order to follow this book.

STATISTICS AND PROBABILITY THEORY

Many DL problems do not have exact answers, so a central theme is probability theory. As an example, if we want to classify objects in an image, there is often uncertainty involved, such as how certain our model is that an object of a specific category, such as a cat, is present in the picture. Further, we might want to classify the type of cat—for example, is it a tiger, lion, jaguar, leopard, or snow leopard? The answer might be that the model is 90% sure that it is a jaguar, but there is a 5% probability that it is a leopard and so on. This book does not require deep knowledge in statistics and probability theory. We do expect you to be able to compute an arithmetic mean and understand the basic concept of probability. It is helpful, although not strictly required, if you know about variance and how to standardize a random variable.

LINEAR ALGEBRA

As you will learn in Chapter 1, the fundamental building block in DL is based on calculating a weighted sum of variables, which implies doing many additions and multiplications. Linear algebra is a field of mathematics that enables us to describe such calculations in a compact manner. This book frequently specifies formulas containing vectors and matrices. Further, calculations involve

- Dot products

- Matrix-vector multiplications

- Matrix-matrix multiplications

If you have not seen these concepts in the past, you will need to learn about them to follow the book. However, Chapter 1 contains a section that goes through these concepts. We suggest that you read that first and then assess whether you need to pick up a book about linear algebra.

CALCULUS

As you will learn in Chapters 2 and 3, the learning part in DL is based on minimizing the value of a function known as a *loss function* or *error function*. The technique used to minimize the loss function builds on the following concepts from calculus:

- Computing the derivative of a function of a single variable

- Computing partial derivatives of a function of multiple variables

- Calculating derivatives using the chain rule of calculus

However, just as we do for linear algebra, we provide sections that go through the basics of these concepts. These sections are found in Chapters 2 and 3.

NUMERICAL METHODS FOR CONSTRAINED AND UNCONSTRAINED OPTIMIZATION

In DL, it is typically not feasible to find an analytical solution when trying to minimize the loss function. Instead, we rely on numerical optimization methods. The most prevalent method is an iterative method known as *gradient descent*. It is helpful if you already know something about iterative methods and finding extreme points in continuous functions. However, we do not require prior knowledge of gradient descent, and we describe how it works before using it in Chapter 3.

PYTHON PROGRAMMING

It is hard to do anything except specific DL applications without some knowledge about programming in general. Further, given that the most popular DL frameworks are based on Python, it is highly recommended to acquire at least basic Python skills to enable trying out and modifying code examples. There are many good books on the topic of programming, and if you have basic programming skills, it should be relatively simple to get started with Python by just following tutorials at python.org. It is possible for nonprogrammers to read this book and just skip the coding sections, but if you intend to apply your DL skills in practice, you should learn the basics of Python programming.

You do not need to learn everything about Python to get started with DL. Many DL applications use only a small subset of the Python language, extended with heavy use of domain-specific DL frameworks and libraries. In particular, many introductory examples make little or no use of object-oriented programming constructs. A specific module that is used frequently is the *NumPy* (numerical Python) module that, among other things, provides data types for vectors and matrices. It is also common to use *pandas* (Python Data Manipulation Library) to manipulate multidimensional data, but we do not make use of pandas in this book.

The following Python constructs are frequent in most of the code examples in the book:

- Integer and floating point datatypes

- Lists and dictionaries

- Importing and using external packages

- NumPy arrays

- NumPy functions

- If-statements, for-loops, and while-loops

- Defining and calling functions

- Printing strings and numerical datatypes

- Plotting data with matplotlib

- Reading from and writing to files

In addition, many of the programming examples rely on constructs provided by a DL framework (TensorFlow in the book and PyTorch provided online). There is no need to know about these frameworks up front. The functionality is gradually introduced in the descriptions of the code examples. The code examples become progressively harder throughout the book, so if you are a beginner to coding, you will need to be prepared to spend some time honing your coding skills in parallel with reading the book.

DATA REPRESENTATION

Much of the DL mechanics are handled by highly optimized ML frameworks. However, your input data first needs to be converted into suitable formats that can be consumed by these frameworks. As such, you need to know something about the format of the data that you will use and, when applicable, how to convert it into a more suitable format. For example, for images, it is helpful to know the basics about RGB (red, green, blue) representation. Similarly, for the cases that use text as input data, it is helpful to know something about how characters are represented by a computer. In general, it is good to have some insight into how raw input data is often of low quality and needs to be cleaned. You will often find missing or duplicated data entries, timestamps from different time zones, and typos originating from manual processing. For the examples in this book, this is typically not a problem, but it is something you need to be aware of in a production setting.

About the Code Examples

You will find much overlap between the code examples in this book and code examples found in online tutorials as well as in other DL books (e.g., Chollet 2018; Glassner, 2018). Many of these examples have evolved from various published research papers in combination with publicly available datasets. (Datasets are described in more detail in Chapter 4.) In other words, we want to stress that we have not made up these examples from scratch, but they are heavily inspired by previously published work. However, we have done the actual implementation of these examples, and we have put our own touch on them to follow the organization of this book.

The longer code examples are broken up into smaller pieces and presented step by step interspersed throughout the text in the book. You should be able to just copy/paste or type each code snippet into a Python interpreter, but it is probably better to just put all code snippets for a specific code example in a single file and execute in a noninteractive manner. The code examples are also available for download both as regular Python files and as Jupyter notebooks at https://github .com/NVDLI/LDL/. See Appendix I for more details.

> We were tempted to not provide downloadable versions of the code examples but instead force you to type them in yourself. After all, that is what we had to do in the 1980s when typing in a code listing from a computer magazine was a perfectly reasonable way of obtaining a new game. The youth of today with their app stores simply do not know how lucky they are.

In most chapters, we first present a basic version of a code example, and then we present results for variations of the program. We do not provide the full listings for all variations, but we try to provide all the necessary constructs in the book to enable you to do these variations yourself.

> Modifying the code is left as an exercise for the reader. Hah, we finally got to say that!
>
> Seriously, we do believe that modifying existing code is a good way of getting your hands dirty. However, there is no need to exactly recreate the variations we did. If you are new to programming, you can start with just tweaking existing parameter values instead of adding new code. If you already have more advanced coding skills, you can consider defining your own experiments based on what you find extra interesting.

DL algorithms are based on stochastic optimization techniques. As such, the results from an experiment may vary from time to time. That is, when you run a code example, you should not expect to get exactly the same result that is shown in the book. However, the overall behavior should be the same.

Another thing to note is that the chosen format, where we intersperse code throughout the book and explain each snippet, results in certain restrictions, such as minimizing the length of each program, and we have also tried to maintain a linear flow and to not heavily modularize the code into classes and functions in most cases. Thus, instead of using sound coding practices to make the code examples easy to extend and maintain, focus is on keeping the examples small and readable.

That is a lame excuse for writing ugly code, but whatever works...

Another thing to consider is what kind of development environment is needed to follow this book. In our opinion, anybody who wants to do serious work in DL will need to get access to a hardware platform that provides specific acceleration for DL—for example, a suitable graphics processing unit (GPU). However, if you do not have access to a GPU-based platform just yet, the code examples in the first few chapters are small enough to be run on a somewhat modern central processing unit (CPU) without too much pain. That is, you can start with a vanilla setup using the CPU for the first few chapters and then spend the resources needed to get access to a GPU-accelerated platform[1] when you are getting to Chapter 7.

Medium term, you should get access to a GPU accelerated platform, but you can live with a standard CPU for the beginning of the book.

Instructions on how to set up a machine with the necessary development environment can be found in Appendix I, which also contains links to the code examples and datasets used in this book.

How to Read This Book

This book is written in a linear fashion and is meant to be read from beginning to end. We introduce new concepts in each chapter and frequently build on and refer back to discussions in previous chapters. It is often the case that we try to avoid introducing too many new concepts at once. This sometimes results in logically similar concepts being introduced in different chapters. However, we do sometimes take a step back and try to summarize a group of related techniques once they have all been introduced. You will see this for hidden units in Chapter 5,

---

1. Nothing prevents you from running all programming examples on a CPU, but in some cases, you might need to do it overnight.

output units in Chapter 6, and techniques to address vanishing and exploding gradients in Chapter 10.

Readers who are complete beginners to neural networks and DL (the core target audience of the book) will likely find the first four chapters more challenging to get through than the remainder of the book. We introduce many new concepts. There is a fair amount of mathematical content, and we implement a neural network from scratch in Python. We encourage you to still try to get through these four chapters, but we also think it is perfectly fine to skim through some of the mathematical equations if you find them challenging. In Chapter 5, we move on to using a DL framework, and you will find that it will handle many of the details under the hood, and you can almost forget about them.

APPENDIXES

This book ends with a number of appendixes. Appendixes A through D could have been included as regular chapters in the book. However, we wanted to avoid information overload for first-time readers. Therefore, we decided to put some of the material in appendixes instead because we simply do not think that you need to learn those concepts in order to follow the narrative of the book. Our recommendation if you are a complete beginner to ML and DL is to read these appendixes last.

If you feel that you already know the basics about ML or DL, then it can make sense for you to read the first four appendixes interspersed among other chapters during your first pass through the book. Appendix A can be read after Chapter 3. Appendix B logically follows Chapter 8. Appendix C naturally falls after Chapter 13. Finally, Appendix D extends topics presented in Chapter 15.

Alternatively, even if you are a beginner but want to learn more details about a specific topic, then do go ahead and read the appendix that relates to that topic in the order just presented.

Appendixes E through H are shorter and focus on providing background or additional detail on some very specific topics. Appendix I describes how to set up a development environment and how to access the programming examples. Appendix J contains cheat sheets that summarize many of the concepts described throughout the book.[2]

_____

2. Larger versions of these cheat sheets can be downloaded from http://informit.com/ title/9780137470358.

GUIDANCE FOR READERS WHO DO NOT WANT TO READ ALL OF THIS BOOK

We recognize that some readers want to read this book in a more selective manner. This can be the case if you feel that you already have some of the basic skills or if you just want to learn about a specific topic. In this section, we provide some pointers for such readers, but this also means that we use some terminology that has not yet been introduced. If you are not interested in cherry picking chapters to read, then feel free to skip this section.

Figure P-5 illustrates three different envisioned tracks to follow depending on your interests. The leftmost track is what we just described, namely, to read the book from beginning to end.

If you are very interested in working with images and computer vision, we suggest that you read Appendix B about object detection, semantic segmentation, and instance segmentation. Further, the last few chapters of the book focus on natural language processing, and if that does not interest you, then we suggest that you skip Chapters 12 through 17. You should still skim Chapters 9 through 11 about recurrent neural networks. This track is shown in the middle of the figure.

If you want to focus mostly on language processing, then you can select the rightmost track. We suggest that you just skim Chapter 8 but do pay attention to the description of skip connections because it is referenced in later chapters. Then read Chapters 9 through 13, followed by Appendix C, then Chapters 14 and 15, and conclude with Appendix D. These appendixes contain additional content about word embeddings and describe GPT and BERT, which are important network architectures for language processing tasks.

Overview of Each Chapter and Appendix

This section contains a brief overview of each chapter. It can safely be skipped if you just want to cut to the chase and get started with LDL!

CHAPTER 1 – THE ROSENBLATT PERCEPTRON

The perceptron, a fundamental building block of a neural network, is introduced. You will learn limitations of the perceptron, and we show how to overcome

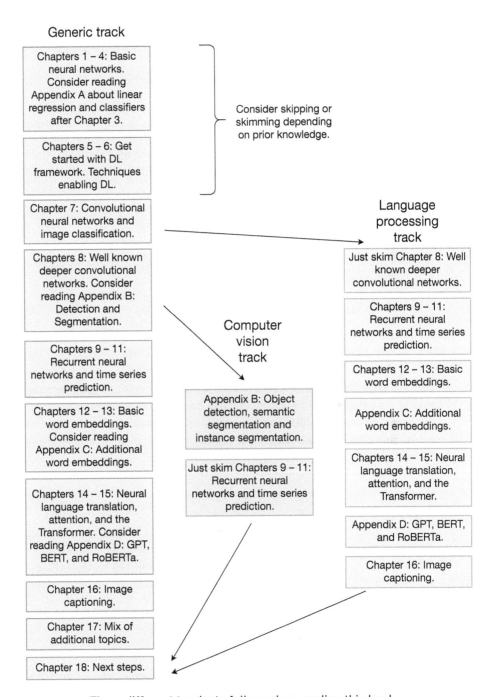

Figure P-5 Three different tracks to follow when reading this book

these limitations by combining multiple perceptrons into a network. The chapter contains some programming examples of how to implement a perceptron and its learning algorithm.

CHAPTER 2 – GRADIENT-BASED LEARNING

We describe an optimization algorithm known as *gradient descent* and the theory behind the perceptron learning algorithm. This is used as a stepping-stone in the subsequent chapter that describes the learning algorithm for multilevel networks.

CHAPTER 3 – SIGMOID NEURONS AND BACKPROPAGATION

We introduce the backpropagation algorithm that is used for automatic learning in DNNs. This is both described in mathematical terms and implemented as a programming example used to do binary classification.

CHAPTER 4 – FULLY CONNECTED NETWORKS APPLIED TO MULTICLASS CLASSIFICATION

This chapter describes the concept of datasets and how they can be divided into a training set and a test set. It also touches on a network's ability to generalize. We extend the neural network architecture to handle multiclass classification, and the programming example then applies this to the task of classifying handwritten digits. This programming example is heavily inspired by an example created by Nielsen (2015).

CHAPTER 5 – TOWARD DL: FRAMEWORKS AND NETWORK TWEAKS

The example from the previous chapter is reimplemented using a DL framework. We show how this framework vastly simplifies the code and enables us to model many variations on our network. Chapter 5 also introduces many techniques that are needed to enable training of deeper networks.

CHAPTER 6 – FULLY CONNECTED NETWORKS APPLIED TO REGRESSION

In this chapter, we study how a network can be used to predict a numerical value instead of classification problems studied in previous chapters. We do this with a programming example in which we apply the network to a regression problem where we are trying to predict sales prices of houses based on a number of variables.

CHAPTER 7 – CONVOLUTIONAL NEURAL NETWORKS APPLIED TO IMAGE CLASSIFICATION

You will learn about the one type of network that initiated the DL boom in 2012, namely, the convolutional neural network, or just convolutional network. A CNN can be used in multiple problem domains, but it has been shown to be especially effective when applied to image classification/analysis. We explain how it works and walk through a programming example that uses a CNN to classify a more complex image dataset. In this example, instead of just distinguishing between different handwritten digits, we identify more complex object classes such as airplanes, automobiles, birds, and cats.

CHAPTER 8 – DEEPER CNNs AND PRETRAINED MODELS

Here we describe deeper CNNs such as GoogLeNet, VGG, and ResNet. As a programming example, we show how to download a pretrained ResNet implementation and how to use it to classify your own images.

CHAPTER 9 – PREDICTING TIME SEQUENCES WITH RECURRENT NEURAL NETWORKS

One limitation of the networks described in the previous chapters is that they are not well suited to handle data of different input lengths. Important problem domains such as text and speech often consist of sequences of varying lengths. This chapter introduces the recurrent neural network (RNN) architecture, which is well suited to handle such tasks. We use a programming example to explore how this network architecture can be used to predict the next data point in a time series.

CHAPTER 10 – LONG SHORT-TERM MEMORY

We discuss problems that prevent RNNs from learning long-term dependencies. We describe the long short-term memory (LSTM) technique that enables better handling of long sequences.

CHAPTER 11 – TEXT AUTOCOMPLETION WITH LSTM AND BEAM SEARCH

In this chapter, we explore how to use LSTM-based RNNs for longer-term prediction and introduce a concept known as *beam search*. We illustrate it with a programming example in which we build a network that can be used for autocompletion of text. This is a simple example of natural language generation (NLG), which is a subset of the greater field of natural language processing (NLP).

CHAPTER 12 – NEURAL LANGUAGE MODELS AND WORD EMBEDDINGS

The example in the previous chapter is based on individual characters instead of words. In many cases, it is more powerful to work with words and their semantics instead of working with individual characters. Chapter 12 introduces the concepts language models and word encodings in a vector space (also known as *embedding space*) that can be used to capture some important relationships between words. As code examples, we extend our autocompletion example to work with words instead of characters and explore how to create word vectors in an embedding space. We also discuss how to build a model that can do sentiment analysis on text. This is an example of natural language understanding (NLU), which is yet another subfield of NLP.

CHAPTER 13 – WORD EMBEDDINGS FROM word2vec AND GloVe

In this chapter, we discuss two popular techniques for creating word embeddings. We download a set of existing embeddings and show how they capture various semantic relationships between words.

CHAPTER 14 – SEQUENCE-TO-SEQUENCE NETWORKS AND NATURAL LANGUAGE TRANSLATION

At this point, we introduce a network known as a sequence-to-sequence network, which is a combination of two recurrent neural networks. A key property of such a network is that its output sequence can be of a different length than the input sequence. We combine this type of network with the word encodings studied in the previous chapter. We build a natural language translator that takes a word sequence in one language (e.g., French) as an input and outputs a word sequence in a different language (e.g., English). Further, the output might be a different number of words and in a different word order than the input word sequence. The sequence-to-sequence model is an example of an architecture known as *encoder-decoder architecture*.

CHAPTER 15 – ATTENTION AND THE TRANSFORMER

In this chapter, we describe a technique known as *attention*, which can improve the accuracy of encoder-decoder architectures. We describe how it can be used to improve the neural machine translator from the previous chapter. We also describe the attention-based Transformer architecture. It is a key building block in many NLP applications.

CHAPTER 16 – ONE-TO-MANY NETWORK FOR IMAGE CAPTIONING

We describe in this chapter how a one-to-many network can be used to create textual descriptions of images and how to extend such a network with attention. A programming example implements this image-captioning network and demonstrates how it can be used to generate textual descriptions of a set of pictures.

CHAPTER 17 – MEDLEY OF ADDITIONAL TOPICS

Up until this point, we have organized topics so that they build on each other. In this chapter, we introduce a handful of topics that we did not find a good way of including in the previous chapters. Examples of such topics are autoencoders, multimodal learning, multitask learning, and neural architecture search.

CHAPTER 18 – SUMMARY AND NEXT STEPS

In the final chapter, we organize and summarize the topics discussed in earlier chapters to give you a chance to confirm that you have captured the key concepts described in the book. In addition to the summary, we provide some guidance to future reading tailored according to the direction you want to take—for example, highly theoretical versus more practical. We also discuss the topics of ethical AI and data ethics.

APPENDIX A – LINEAR REGRESSION AND LINEAR CLASSIFIERS

The focus of this book is DL. Our approach to the topic is to jump straight into DL without first describing traditional ML techniques. However, this appendix does describe very basic ML topics so you can get an idea of how some of the presented DL concepts relate to more traditional ML techniques. This appendix logically follows Chapter 3.

APPENDIX B – OBJECT DETECTION AND SEGMENTATION

In this appendix, we describe techniques to detect and classify multiple objects in a single image. It includes both coarse-grained techniques that draw bounding boxes around the objects and fine-grained techniques that pinpoint the individual pixels in an image that correspond to a certain object. This appendix logically follows Chapter 8.

APPENDIX C – WORD EMBEDDINGS BEYOND word2vec AND GloVe

In this appendix, we describe some more elaborate techniques for word embeddings. In particular, these techniques can handle words that did not exist in the training dataset. Further, we describe a technique that can handle cases in which a word has a different meaning depending on its context. This appendix logically follows Chapter 13.

APPENDIX D – GPT, BERT, AND RoBERTa

This appendix describes architectures that build on the Transformer. These network architectures have resulted in significant improvements in many NLP tasks. This appendix logically follows Chapter 15.

APPENDIX E – NEWTON-RAPHSON VERSUS GRADIENT DESCENT

In Chapter 2, we introduce a mathematical concept technique known as *gradient descent*. This appendix describes a different method, known as *Newton-Raphson*, and how it relates to gradient descent.

APPENDIX F – MATRIX IMPLEMENTATION OF DIGIT CLASSIFICATION NETWORK

In Chapter 4, we include a programming example implementing a neural network in Python code. This appendix describes two different optimized variations of that programming example.

APPENDIX G – RELATING CONVOLUTIONAL LAYERS TO MATHEMATICAL CONVOLUTION

In Chapter 7, we describe convolutional neural networks. They are based on, and named after, a mathematical operation known as *convolution*. This appendix describes this connection in more detail.

APPENDIX H – GATED RECURRENT UNITS

In Chapter 10, we describe a network unit known as *long short-term memory* (LSTM). In this appendix, we describe a simplified version of this unit known as *gated recurrent unit* (GRU).

APPENDIX I – SETTING UP A DEVELOPMENT ENVIRONMENT

This appendix contains information about how to set up a development environment. This includes how to install a deep learning framework and where to find the code examples. It also contains a brief section about key differences between TensorFlow and PyTorch, which are the two DL frameworks used for the code examples in this book.

APPENDIX J – CHEAT SHEETS

This appendix contains a set of cheat sheets that summarize much of the content in this book. They are also available for download in a different form factor: http://informit.com/title/9780137470358.

Register your copy of *Learning Deep Learning* on the InformIT site for convenient access to updates and/or corrections as they become available. To start the registration process, go to informit.com/register and log in or create an account. Enter the product ISBN (9780137470358) and click Submit. Look on the Registered Products tab for an Access Bonus Content link next to this product, and follow that link to access any available bonus materials. If you would like to be notified of exclusive offers on new editions and updates, please check the box to receive email from us.

Acknowledgments

I am incredibly grateful for all help I have received in the process of writing this book. I would like to extend my warmest gratitude to all of you:

- Eric Haines for reading this book front to back and providing guidance and feedback throughout the whole process. Having had you as a sounding board and discussion partner was invaluable.

- Ankit Patel and Amanda Lam for believing in me. Without any prior interaction with me, you worked extra hours to figure out how to make this book happen. Thank you for finding the perfect publisher, and thanks to Jenny Chen for working out the agreement. Being represented by a professional team allowed me to focus solely on the content of the book.

- Nick Cohron, Orazio Gallo, Boris Ginsburg, Samuli Laine, Ryan Prenger, Raul Puri, Kevin Shih, and Sophie Tabac for providing expert feedback on the material. All of your comments greatly improved the book.

- Aaron Beddes and Torbjörn Ekman for reading an early manuscript and providing valuable feedback, which gave me confidence to engage all the people above.

- Anders Landin, Feihui Li, Niklas Lindström, Jatin Mitra, Clint Olsen, Sebastian Sylvan, and Johan Överby for pointing out various issues, both in the manuscript and in the code examples.

- Andy Cook for your vision of how to tie the book to efforts within the NVIDIA Deep Learning Institute, as well as your involvement in the cover art proposal, together with Sandra Froehlich and Chris Strach. Sandra and Chris also contributed with other aspects of style and branding. The original image of the R.Eva Robot was designed by Gavriil Klimov and Gregor Kopka.

- Anima Anandkumar and Craig Clawson for writing the forewords.

- All people who Pearson involved in the publishing process, in particular Debra Williams Cauley, Carol Lallier, Julie Nahil, Chuti Prasertsith, and Chris Zahn.

- Darrell Boggs for providing your support when I first introduced the idea of starting this project. Further, the following NVIDIA colleagues all played a role in making this happen by supporting the project or connecting me with the right people: Tomas Akenine-Möller, Anima Anandkumar, Jonathan Cohen, Greg Estes, Sanja Fidler, David Hass, Brian Kelleher, Will Ramey, and Mohammad Shoeybi.

- The research community and other authors. This book does not contain original ideas. Its focus is on describing published work from multiple sources in a common framework. This would not have been possible without the original publications as well as multiple books on the topic. I have done my best to list all these sources in the bibliography.

Finally, I am grateful to my wife, Jennifer, and my children, Sebastian and Sofia, for being understanding and enabling me to spend the time required to write this book. I also want to give credit to our dog, Babette, and late cat, Stella, because I used their pictures in various object classification examples.

About the Author

Magnus Ekman, PhD, is a Director of Architecture at NVIDIA Corporation. His doctorate is in computer engineering, and he holds multiple patents. He was first exposed to artificial neural networks in the late 1990s in his native country, Sweden. After some dabbling in evolutionary computation, he focused on computer architecture and relocated to Silicon Valley, where he lives with his wife, Jennifer, children, Sebastian and Sofia, and dog, Babette. He has previously worked with processor design and R&D at Sun Microsystems and Samsung Research America and has been involved in starting two companies, one of which (Skout) was later acquired by The Meet Group, Inc. In his current role at NVIDIA, he leads an engineering team working on CPU performance and power efficiency for chips targeting markets ranging from autonomous vehicles to data centers for artificial intelligence (AI).

As the deep learning (DL) field exploded in the past few years, fueled by NVIDIA's GPU technology and CUDA, Dr. Ekman found himself in the midst of a company expanding beyond computer graphics and becoming a DL powerhouse. As a part of that journey, he challenged himself to stay up to date with the most recent developments in the field. He considers himself an educator, and in the process of writing *Learning Deep Learning* (LDL) he partnered with the NVIDIA Deep Learning Institute (DLI), which offers hands-on training in AI, accelerated computing, and accelerated data science. He is thrilled about DLI's plans to add LDL to its existing portfolio of self-paced online courses; live, instructor-led workshops; educator programs; and teaching kits.

Chapter 1

The Rosenblatt Perceptron

This chapter describes the Rosenblatt perceptron and shows how it can be used. Chapters 3 and 5 describe how the perceptron has been modified over time to enable more advanced networks. The perceptron is an artificial neuron, that is, a model of a biological neuron. Therefore, it makes sense to first briefly describe the parts of a biological neuron, as shown in Figure 1-1.

A biological neuron consists of one cell body, multiple dendrites, and a single axon. The connections between neurons are known as synapses. The neuron receives stimuli on the dendrites, and in cases of sufficient stimuli, the neuron fires (also known as getting activated or excited) and outputs stimulus on its

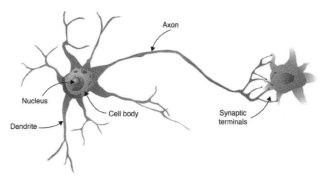

Figure 1-1 A biological neuron (Source: Glassner, A., Deep Learning: From Basics to Practice, The Imaginary Institute, 2018.)

axon, which is transmitted to other neurons that have synaptic connections to the excited neuron. Synaptic signals can be excitatory or inhibitory; that is, some signals can prevent a neuron from firing instead of causing it to fire.

The perceptron consists of a computational unit, a number of inputs (one of which is a special *bias input,* which is detailed later in this chapter), each with an associated input weight, and a single output. The perceptron is shown in Figure 1-2.

The inputs are typically named $x_0, x_1, \ldots, x_n$ in the case of n general inputs (x_0 being the bias input), and the output is typically named y. The inputs and output loosely correspond to the dendrites and the axon. Each input has an associated weight (w_i, where $i = 0, \ldots, n$), which historically has been referred to as *synaptic weight* because it in some sense represents how strong the connection is from one neuron to another, but nowadays it is typically just called weight or *input weight*. For the perceptron, the output can take on only one of two values, −1 or 1, but this constraint will be relaxed to a range of real values for other types of artificial neurons discussed in later chapters. The bias input is always 1. Each input value is multiplied by its corresponding weight before it is presented to the computational unit (the dashed rectangle with rounded corners in Fig. 1-2), which loosely corresponds to the cell body of a biological neuron.[1] The computational unit computes the sum of the weighted inputs and then applies a so-called activation function, $y = f(z)$, where z is the sum of the weighted inputs. The activation function for a perceptron is the sign function, also known as the signum function,[2] which evaluates to 1 if the input is 0 or higher and −1 otherwise. The sign function is shown in Figure 1-3.

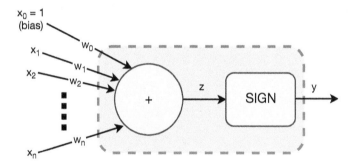

Figure 1-2 **The perceptron**

1. Hereafter, we do not discuss biological neurons, so any future reference to a neuron refers to an *artificial* neuron. Further, we often refer to a perceptron as a neuron because the perceptron is just a special type of neuron, and we often prefer the more generic name neuron except for when we detail properties that apply only to the perceptron.
2. The signum function should not be confused with the sigmoid function that is used for other neurons than perceptrons, as described in later chapters.

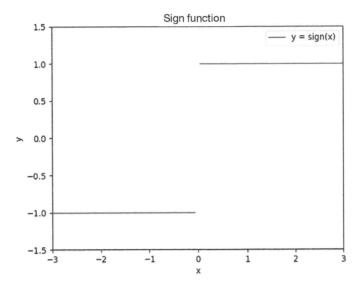

Figure 1-3 Sign (or signum) function. The figure uses variable names typically used for generic functions (y is a function of x). In our perceptron use case, the input to the signum function is not x but the weighted sum z.

A **perceptron** is a type of **artificial neuron.** It sums up the inputs to compute an intermediate value z, which is fed to an **activation function**. The perceptron uses the **sign function** as an activation function, but **other artificial neurons use other functions.**

To summarize, the perceptron will output −1 if the weighted sum is less than zero, and otherwise it will output 1. Written as an equation, we have the following:

$$y = f(z), \text{ where}$$

$$z = \sum_{i=0}^{n} w_i x_i$$

$$f(z) = \begin{cases} -1, & z < 0 \\ 1, & z \geq 0 \end{cases}$$

$$x_0 = 1 \text{ (bias term)}$$

We note how the bias term x_0 is special in that it always is assigned the value 1. Its corresponding weight w_0 is treated just like any other weight. Code Snippet 1-1 implements this function programmatically in Python. The first element of x represents the bias term and thus must be set to 1 by the caller of the function.

Code Snippet 1-1 Python Implementation of Perceptron Function

```
# First element in vector x must be 1.
# Length of w and x must be n+1 for neuron with n inputs.
def compute_output(w, x):
    z = 0.0
    for i in range(len(w)):
        z += x[i] * w[i] # Compute sum of weighted inputs
    if z < 0: # Apply sign function
        return -1
    else:
        return 1
```

We said in the preface that you should learn Python, so if you have not yet, now is a good time for you to start going over that Python tutorial.

At this point, the special bias input might seem odd, but we show later in this chapter how varying the bias weight is equivalent to adjusting the threshold at which the perceptron changes its output value.

Example of a Two-Input Perceptron

A simple example provides an idea of how the perceptron works in practice. Let us study a perceptron with two inputs in addition to the bias input. Without any justification (at this point), we set the weights to $w_0 = 0.9$, $w_1 = -0.6$, and $w_2 = -0.5$. See Figure 1-4.

Now let us see how this perceptron behaves for all input combinations assuming that each of the two inputs can take on only the values −1.0 and 1.0. If you want to get your hands dirty, you can paste Code Snippet 1-1 into a Python interpreter

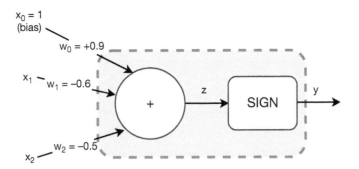

Figure 1-4 Perceptron with two inputs (in addition to the bias input) and defined weights

window (see Appendix I) and then call the function with the chosen weights and different *x*-input combinations. Remember that the first *x*-input should always be 1.0 because it represents the bias term. You should end up with the following if you call the function four times with all different combinations of *x*-inputs:

```
>>> compute_output([0.9, -0.6, -0.5], [1.0, -1.0, -1.0])
1
>>> compute_output([0.9, -0.6, -0.5], [1.0, -1.0, 1.0])
1
>>> compute_output([0.9, -0.6, -0.5], [1.0, 1.0, -1.0])
1
>>> compute_output([0.9, -0.6, -0.5], [1.0, 1.0, 1.0])
-1
```

To explore this behavior in more detail, we show the four different combinations in Table 1-1.

The table shows the inputs and the outputs, the intermediate values after applying the weights, as well as the sum before applying the activation function. Note what happens if we interpret the inputs and outputs as Boolean values, where −1 represents False and +1 represents True. The perceptron with these specific weights implements a NAND gate! Paraphrasing Nielsen, this is comforting because we know that by combining multiple NAND gates, we can build any logical function, but it is also kind of disappointing because we thought that neural networks were going to be something much more exciting than just Boolean logic (Nielsen, 2015).

Table 1-1 Behavior of a Perceptron with Two Inputs*

X_0	X_1	X_2	$W_0^*X_0$	$W_1^*X_1$	$W_2^*X_2$	Z	Y
1	−1 (False)	−1 (False)	0.9	0.6	0.5	2.0	1 (True)
1	1 (True)	−1 (False)	0.9	−0.6	0.5	0.8	1 (True)
1	−1 (False)	1 (True)	0.9	0.6	−0.5	1.0	1 (True)
1	1 (True)	1 (True)	0.9	−0.6	−0.5	−0.2	−1 (False)

*The values of the inputs and output can also be interpreted as Boolean values.

> We said in the Preface that we would avoid starting with traditional machine learning techniques in favor of jumping straight to the more recent stuff, and now we start talking about basic binary logic gates instead. Not cool! Seems like an epic fail, but bear with us. At least we are already talking about neurons, and we will soon move on to more impressive ways of using them.

As we soon will see, it turns out that neural networks are different from Boolean logic. This difference becomes clear in later chapters, where we demonstrate the amazing things that neural networks can achieve. Meantime, we can list some specific differences:

• Perceptron inputs are not limited to Boolean values. In addition, although perceptrons are limited to outputting only one of two values, other neuron models can output a range of real numbers.

• In our simple example, the perceptron has only two inputs and implements a basic logical function. In the networks we study later in the book, each neuron has many more inputs, often more than what is typical for a logic gate. Each neuron can also implement more complex functions than AND and OR.

• We know of a learning algorithm that can be used to automatically design neural networks by learning from examples. Curiously, the resulting networks tend to generalize and learn behavior that makes sense for not-yet-observed examples (this statement may seem fairly abstract, but the next section introduces the perceptron learning algorithm, and Chapter 4, "Fully Connected Networks Applied to Multiclass Classification," discusses generalization).

The Perceptron Learning Algorithm

In the previous example, we somewhat arbitrarily picked the three weights, and we ended up with a perceptron that behaves like a NAND gate if we view the inputs as Boolean values. By inspecting Table 1-1, it should be fairly easy to convince yourself that the chosen weights are not the only ones that result in this outcome. For example, you can see that the z-value is far enough from zero in all cases, so you should be able to adjust one of the weights by 0.1 in either direction and still end up with the same behavior. This raises the questions of how we came up with these weights in the first place and whether there is a general approach for determining the weights. This is where the perceptron learning algorithm comes into play.

We first describe the algorithm itself and apply it to a couple of problems. These experiments provide some understanding of how the algorithm works but also reveal some of the limitations of the perceptron. We then show that it is possible to overcome these limitations and examine the perceptron from other angles. In Chapter 2, "Gradient-Based Learning," we describe a somewhat more formal reasoning behind what the algorithm does.

The perceptron learning algorithm is what is called a *supervised learning algorithm*. The notion of supervision implies that the *model* that is being trained (in this case, the perceptron) is presented with both the input data and the desired output data (also known as *ground truth*). Think of it as a teacher presenting the question and answer to the model with the expectation that the model will learn that a certain input is associated with a corresponding output. The opposite of supervised learning is unsupervised learning in which the learning algorithm is responsible for finding patterns in the data by itself. An example of this concept is an algorithm that can find structure in natural language text. We study this concept in more detail in Chapter 11, "Text Autocompletion with LSTM and Beam Search," where we train a model to do autocompletion of text.

The term **model** is often used as a synonym for a **network.** That is, when we talk about training a model, it is the same thing as coming up with weights for a network consisting of one or more neurons.

In our example, we have four sets of input/output data, each corresponding to one row in Table 1-1. The algorithm works as follows:

1. Randomly initialize the weights.

2. Select one input/output pair at random.

3. Present the values $x_1, \ldots, x_n$ to the perceptron to compute the output y.

4. If the output y is different from the ground truth for this input/output pair, adjust the weights in the following way:

    a. If $y < 0$, add ηx_i to each w_i.

    b. If $y > 0$, subtract ηx_i from each w_i.

5. Repeat steps 2, 3, and 4 until the perceptron predicts all examples correctly.

The perceptron has certain limitations to what it can predict, so for some sets of input/output pairs, the algorithm will not converge. However, if it is possible to come up with a set of weights that enables the perceptron to represent the set of input/output pairs, then the algorithm is guaranteed to converge by finding these weights. The arbitrary constant η is known as the *learning rate*[3] and can be set to 1.0, but setting it to a different value can lead to faster convergence of the algorithm. The learning rate is an example of a *hyperparameter,* which is not a parameter that is adjusted by the learning algorithm but can still be adjusted. For a perceptron, the weights can be initialized to 0, but for more complex neural networks, that is a bad idea. Therefore, we initialize them randomly to get into that habit. Finally, in step 4, it might seem like all the weights will be adjusted by the same amount, but remember that the input x_i is not limited to take on the two values −1 and 1. It could well be 0.4 for one input and 0.9 for another, so the actual weight adjustment will vary.

We now walk through a Python implementation of this algorithm and apply it to our NAND example. Code Snippet 1-2 shows the initialization code where we first import a library for randomization and then initialize variables for the training examples and perceptron weights.

---

3. Some descriptions of the perceptron learning algorithm do not include the learning rate parameter, but since learning rate is an important parameter for the learning algorithm used for more complicated networks, we choose to introduce it here.

Code Snippet 1-2 Initialization Code for Our Perceptron Learning Example

```
import random

def show_learning(w):
    print('w0 =', '%5.2f' % w[0], ',  w1 =', '%5.2f' % w[1],
          ',  w2 =', '%5.2f' % w[2])

# Define variables needed to control training process.
random.seed(7) # To make repeatable
LEARNING_RATE = 0.1
index_list = [0, 1, 2, 3] # Used to randomize order

# Define training examples.
x_train = [(1.0, -1.0, -1.0), (1.0, -1.0, 1.0),
    (1.0, 1.0, -1.0), (1.0, 1.0, 1.0)] # Inputs
y_train = [1.0, 1.0, 1.0, -1.0] # Output (ground truth)

# Define perceptron weights.
w = [0.2, -0.6, 0.25] # Initialize to some "random" numbers

# Print initial weights.
show_learning(w)
```

Note how each input example consists of three values, but the first value is always 1.0 because it is the bias term. Code Snippet 1-3 restates the perceptron output computation that was shown in Code Snippet 1-1.

Code Snippet 1-3 Perceptron Function as Shown in Code Snippet 1-1

```
# First element in vector x must be 1.
# Length of w and x must be n+1 for neuron with n inputs.
def compute_output(w, x):
    z = 0.0
    for i in range(len(w)):
        z += x[i] * w[i] # Compute sum of weighted inputs
    if z < 0: # Apply sign function
        return -1
    else:
        return 1
```

Code Snippet 1-4 contains the perceptron training loop. It is a nested loop in which the inner loop runs through all four training examples in random order. For each example, it computes the output and adjusts and prints the weights if the output is wrong. The weight adjustment line contains a subtle detail that makes it look slightly different than how we described the algorithm. Instead of using an `if` statement to determine whether to use addition or subtraction to adjust the weights, the adjustment value is multiplied by y. The value of y will either be −1 or +1, and consequently results in selecting between addition and subtraction for the update. The outer loop tests whether the perceptron provided correct output for all four examples and, if so, terminates the program.

Code Snippet 1-4 **Perceptron Training Loop***

```
# Perceptron training loop.
all_correct = False
while not all_correct:
    all_correct = True
    random.shuffle(index_list) # Randomize order
    for i in index_list:
        x = x_train[i]
        y = y_train[i]
        p_out = compute_output(w, x) # Perceptron function

        if y != p_out: # Update weights when wrong
            for j in range(0, len(w)):
                w[j] += (y * LEARNING_RATE * x[j])
            all_correct = False
            show_learning(w) # Show updated weights
```

If we paste the three snippets together into a single file and then run it in a Python interpreter, the output will look something like the following:

```
w0 =  0.20 , w1 = -0.60 , w2 =   0.25
w0 =  0.30 , w1 = -0.50 , w2 =   0.15
w0 =  0.40 , w1 = -0.40 , w2 =   0.05
w0 =  0.30 , w1 = -0.50 , w2 =  -0.05
w0 =  0.40 , w1 = -0.40 , w2 =  -0.15
```

* In this code snippet, *y* refers to ground truth and is a different notation than in the numbered list on page 8.

Note how the weights are gradually adjusted from the initial values to arrive at weights that produce the correct output. Most code examples in this book make use of random values, so your results might not exactly match our results.

In addition to the described Python implementation, we also provide a spreadsheet that performs the same calculations. We find that directly modifying weights and input values in a spreadsheet is often a good way to build intuition. The location from which to download the spreadsheet can be found in the programming examples section in Appendix I.

Now that we have seen that this algorithm can learn the NAND function, we will explore a little bit more in depth what it learned. Up until now, we have restricted ourselves to making each input take on just one of two values (either −1 or 1). However, there is nothing that prevents us from presenting any real number on the two inputs. That is, we can present any combination of two real numbers to the perceptron, and it will produce either −1 or 1 on its output. One way to illustrate this is to make a chart of a 2D coordinate system where one axis represents the first input (x_1), and the other axis represents the second input (x_2). For each point in this coordinate system, we can write a "+" or a "−" depending on what value the perceptron outputs. Such a chart is plotted in Figure 1-5.

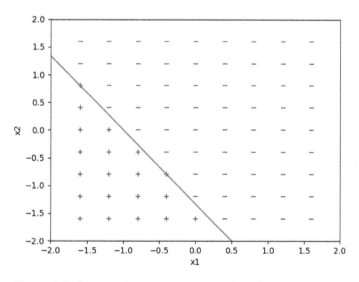

Figure 1-5 Output of a perceptron as a function of two inputs x_1 and x_2

This chart is different than plotting the function $y = f(x_1, x_2)$ in a traditional manner. A traditional plot of a function that takes two values as inputs and produces one value as an output would produce a 3D chart where some kind of surface is plotted as a function of the two inputs (this is shown later under "Geometrical Interpretation of the Perceptron"). Figure 1-5 is different in that instead of plotting the output value on its own axis (the z-axis in a 3D chart), we simply show the numeric values as symbols (+ and –) on the chart, which is simple to do because there are only two possible values (–1 and 1), and they also happen to fall in a nice simple pattern.

As you can see from the figure, the perceptron divides the 2D space into two regions, separated by a straight line, where all input values on one side of the line produce the output –1, and all input values on the other side of the line produce the output +1. A natural question is how we came up with the chart in the first place. One brute-force way of doing this is to test all combinations of (x_1, x_2) pairs and record the output from the perceptron. For the purpose of this discussion, this would be a fine way to do things, but if you are interested, it is simple to derive the equation for the line that separates the two regions. We know that the line represents the boundary between negative and positive output values of the perceptron. This boundary is exactly where the weighted sum of the inputs is zero, because the sign function will change its value when its input is zero. That is, we have

$$w_0 x_0 + w_1 x_1 + w_2 x_2 = 0$$

We want to rewrite this equation so that x_2 is a function of x_1, because x_2 is plotted on the y-axis, and normally when plotting a straight line, we do $y = f(x)$. We insert 1 for x_0, solve the equation for x_2, and arrive at

$$x_2 = -\frac{w_1}{w_2} x_1 - \frac{w_0}{w_2}$$

In other words, it is a straight line with slope $-w_1/w_2$ and a y-intercept of $-w_0/w_2$.

Now that we are familiar with this type of chart, we can look at the learning process in more detail. We replace the initialization code in our program by the extended version shown in Code Snippet 1-5. In this code snippet, we have extended the `show_learning()` function to produce a plot like the one described previously. In addition to the changes in Code Snippet 1-5, we need to add the following code line at the end of the program:

```
plt.show()
```

We do not describe details of the plot routine because it is uninteresting and is not built upon later in the book.

Code Snippet 1-5 **Extended Version of Initialization Code with Function to Plot the Output**

```
import matplotlib.pyplot as plt
import random

# Define variables needed for plotting.
color_list = ['r-', 'm-', 'y-', 'c-', 'b-', 'g-']
color_index = 0

def show_learning(w):
    global color_index
    print('w0 =', '%5.2f' % w[0], ', w1 =', '%5.2f' % w[1],
          ', w2 =', '%5.2f' % w[2])
    if color_index == 0:
        plt.plot([1.0], [1.0], 'b_', markersize=12)
        plt.plot([-1.0, 1.0, -1.0], [1.0, -1.0, -1.0],
                 'r+', markersize=12)
        plt.axis([-2, 2, -2, 2])
        plt.xlabel('x1')
        plt.ylabel('x2')
    x = [-2.0, 2.0]
    if abs(w[2]) < 1e-5:
        y = [-w[1]/(1e-5)*(-2.0)+(-w[0]/(1e-5)),
             -w[1]/(1e-5)*(2.0)+(-w[0]/(1e-5))]
    else:
        y = [-w[1]/w[2]*(-2.0)+(-w[0]/w[2]),
             -w[1]/w[2]*(2.0)+(-w[0]/w[2])]
    plt.plot(x, y, color_list[color_index])
    if color_index < (len(color_list) - 1):
        color_index += 1

# Define variables needed to control training process.
random.seed(7) # To make repeatable
LEARNING_RATE = 0.1
index_list = [0, 1, 2, 3] # Used to randomize order
```

```
# Define training examples.
x_train = [(1.0, -1.0, -1.0), (1.0, -1.0, 1.0),
           (1.0, 1.0, -1.0), (1.0, 1.0, 1.0)] # Inputs
y_train = [1.0, 1.0, 1.0, -1.0] # Output (ground truth)


# Define perceptron weights.
w = [0.2, -0.6, 0.25] # Initialize to some "random" numbers


# Print initial weights.
show_learning(w)
```

The resulting plot is shown in Figure 1-6, where the four input points are shown as three plus signs and one minus sign. The red line corresponds to the initial set of weights that do not correctly divide the chart between the plus and minus signs. For each weight update, we plot another line in the following color order: magenta, yellow, cyan, and blue. The blue line correctly divides the chart with all plus signs on one side and the minus sign on the other side, so the learning algorithm terminates.

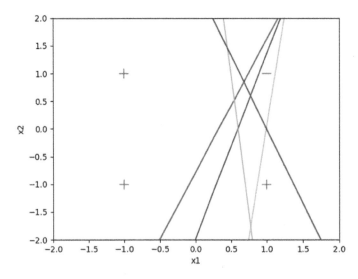

Figure 1-6 Learning process progressing in the following order: red, magenta, yellow, cyan, blue

We have now shown that the perceptron can learn to do a simple classification task, namely, to determine if a two-value input pair belongs to one class or another. It is not as advanced as distinguishing between a dog and a cat, but we need to learn to walk before we can run.

Limitations of the Perceptron

In Chapter 2, we look at the learning algorithm in more detail to justify why it works. However, you might have noticed[4] that we just ran into a big limitation of the perceptron. Let us take a moment to understand this limitation and its implications.

We saw that the two-input perceptron learns how to draw a straight line between two groups of data points. That is exciting, but what happens if a straight line cannot separate the data points? We explore this scenario using a different Boolean function, namely, the exclusive OR, also known as XOR. Its truth table is shown in Table 1-2.

Figure 1-7 shows these four data points on the same type of chart that we studied before, illustrating how the algorithm tries to learn how to draw a line between the plus and minus signs. The top chart shows what it looks like after 6 weight updates and the bottom chart, after 30 weight updates—where we have also run out of colors and the algorithm never converges.

It is trivial to solve the problem with a curved line but is not possible with a straight line. This is one of the key limitations of the perceptron. It can solve

Table 1-2 Truth Table for a Two-Input XOR Gate

X_0	X_1	Y
False	False	False
True	False	True
False	True	True
True	True	False

---

4. It is perfectly fine if you did not notice this. It is far from obvious when you see it the first time.

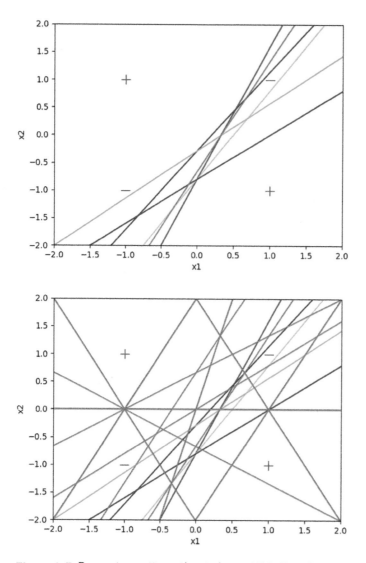

Figure 1-7 Perceptron attempting to learn XOR. Top: After 6 weight adjustments. Bottom: After 30 weight adjustments.

classification problems only where the classes are linearly separable, which in two dimensions (two inputs) means that the data points can be separated by a straight line. Thus, it seems we need to either come up with a different model of a neuron or combine multiple of them to solve the problem. In the next section, we explore the latter solution.

Combining Multiple Perceptrons

As shown previously, a single perceptron can separate the chart into two regions, illustrated by drawing a straight line on the chart. That means that if we add another perceptron, we can draw another straight line. Figure 1-8 shows one such attempt: One line separates one of the minuses from all other data points. Similarly, the other line separates the other minus also from all other data points. If we somehow can output 1 only for the data points between the two lines, then we have solved the problem.

Another way to look at it is that each of the two perceptrons will fire correctly for three out of four data points; that is, both of them almost do the right thing. They both incorrectly categorize one data point, but not the same one. If we could combine the output of the two, and output 1 only when both of them compute the output as a 1, then we would get the right result. So, we want to do an AND of their outputs, and we know how to do that. We just add yet another perceptron that uses the outputs of the two previous perceptrons as its inputs. The architecture of this two-level neural network and the weights are shown in Figure 1-9. (The chosen weights in Figure 1-9 will result in two lines of somewhat different slope and orientation but that also fall in-between the pluses and minuses in Figure 1-8.)

Table 1-3 shows the output of each of the three neurons. Looking at x_1, x_2, and y_2, it is clear that the neural network implements the XOR function.

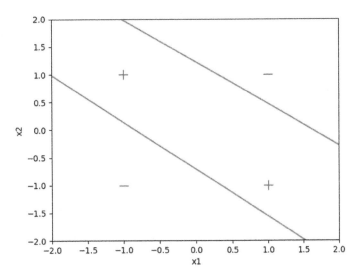

Figure 1-8 XOR output values isolated by two lines

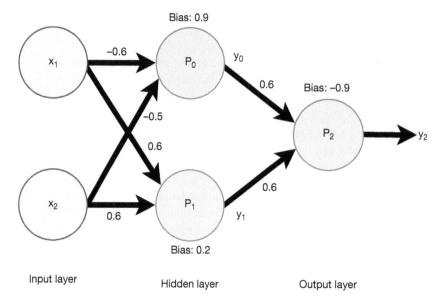

Figure 1-9 Two-level feedforward network implementing XOR function

Table 1-3 Input and Output Values Showing That the Network Implements the XOR Function

X_0	X_1	X_2	Y_0	Y_1	Y_2
1	−1 (False)	−1 (False)	1.0	−1.0	−1.0 (False)
1	1 (True)	−1 (False)	1.0	1.0	1.0 (True)
1	−1 (False)	1 (True)	1.0	1.0	1.0 (True)
1	1 (True)	1 (True)	−1.0	1.0	−1.0 (False)

This neural network is one of the simplest examples of a fully connected feedforward network. *Fully connected* means that the output of each neuron in one layer is connected to all neurons in the next layer. *Feedforward* means that there are no backward connections, or, using graph terminology, it is a directed acyclic graph (DAG). The figure also highlights the concept of layers. A multilevel neural network has an input layer, one or more hidden layers, and an output layer. The input layer does not contain neurons but contains only the inputs themselves; that is, there are no weights associated with the input layer. Note that the single perceptron we looked at also had an input layer, but we did not explicitly draw it. In Figure 1-9, the output layer has only one neuron, but in general, the output layer can consist of more than one neuron. Similarly, the network in the figure has only a single hidden layer (with two neurons), but a deep neural network (DNN) has more than one hidden layer and typically many more neurons in each layer. The weights (including bias) in the figure are spelled out, but in most cases, it is just assumed that they are there, and they are not shown. A feedforward network is also known as a *multilevel perceptron* even when it is built from neuron models that are not perceptrons, which can be somewhat confusing.

> In a **fully connected network,** a neuron in one layer receives inputs from all other neurons in the immediately preceding layer. A **feedforward network** or **multilevel perceptron** has no cycles. The **input layer** has no neurons. The outputs of neurons in a **hidden layer** are not visible (they are hidden) outside of the network. DNNs have **multiple hidden layers.** The **output layer** can have multiple neurons.

This XOR example is starting to get close to our definition of deep learning (DL): *DL is a class of machine learning algorithms that use multiple layers of computational units where each layer learns its own representation of the input data. These representations are combined by later layers in a hierarchical fashion.* In the preceding example, we did have multiple (two) layers. The neurons in the first layer had their own representation (the output from the hidden layer) of the input data, and these representations were combined hierarchically by the output neuron. A missing piece is that *each layer learns its own representation.* In our example, the network did not learn the weights, but we came up with them. A valid question is how we came up with all these weights. The answer is that we picked them carefully. The weights for the first perceptron already implemented a NAND function. We then picked weights for the second perceptron in the first layer to implement an OR function, and finally we picked the weights for the perceptron in the second layer to implement an AND function. By doing this, we arrived at the Boolean function for XOR*:

$$\overline{(A \cdot B)} \cdot (A + B)$$

* Notation for this equation: The letters *A* and *B* correspond to the two inputs, the dot symbol corresponds to *AND*, the plus symbol corresponds to *OR*, and the line above the first term corresponds to *NOT* (inverse).

Although we are just assuming −1 and +1 as input values in this discussion, the neural network that we have created can take any real numbers as inputs, and it will output 1 for all the points between the two lines in Figure 1-8. We chose the weights carefully to make the neural network behave the way we wanted, which was possible for this specific example but is nontrivial for the general case. Is there such an algorithm for a multilevel neural network? As described in the Preface, Minsky and Papert (1969) did not think so. However, it turns out that history proved the doubters wrong. The back-propagation algorithm was applied to various problem types from at least 1970 (Linnainmaa, 1970) and was popularized for neural networks in 1986 (Rumelhart, Hinton, and Williams, 1986). We cover this algorithm in detail in Chapter 3, "Sigmoid Neurons and Back-Propagation," but first we explore the perceptron a little bit more.

Implementing Perceptrons with Linear Algebra

Knowledge of linear algebra is handy when working with neural networks. We now introduce some basic concepts and describe how they relate to the perceptron and why this knowledge is useful. In particular, we show how we can describe the input examples and perceptron weights as vectors and matrices and how parts of the perceptron calculations are equivalent to dot products, matrix-vector multiplications, and matrix multiplications. Computing dot products, matrix-vector multiplications, and matrix multiplications efficiently is important in many scientific fields, so much effort has been spent on creating efficient implementations of these operations. For example, if you program in Python, there is a package known as NumPy, which is used for scientific computations. It has specific functions for the above-mentioned operations. Under the hood, NumPy makes use of the Basic Linear Algebra Subprograms (BLAS), which is heavily optimized to run as fast as possible on the platform where it is run. Further, if you have a graphics processing unit (GPU) capable of running CUDA, there is the CUDA BLAS (cuBLAS) library that enables NumPy to perform these operations efficiently on the GPU,[5] which can give you orders of magnitude speedup compared to running on a CPU.

---

5. Modern DL frameworks make use of a library known as cuDNN, which is specifically developed to accelerate neural network computations by offloading them to the GPU.

Specifying mathematical problems in **vector** or **matrix form** enables you to take advantage of efficient mathematics library implementations, and in particular to **offload computations to the GPU.**

If you already know linear algebra, you will find that much of this section describes basic mathematical concepts. If this is the case, you should focus on how the perceptron weights and inputs map to these basic concepts. If you have some linear algebra knowledge but have not used these skills for a while, we think this section will serve as a good refresher. If you have never seen linear algebra before, then we recommend that you start with reading this section. This is likely sufficient for many readers, whereas others might want to pursue more in-depth descriptions of the topic.

VECTOR NOTATION

In the previous sections, we saw examples of a large number of variables, such as multiple inputs (x) and corresponding weights (w) for each neuron, intermediate representations (z), and outputs (y). Common for all these variables is that they consist of a single value, which also is known as a *scalar variable*. It is often the case that we have a number of variables that kind of belong together, such as all the input variables $x_0, x_1, \ldots, x_n$ for a single neuron. One way to look at things is that each of these individual variables is only one component of the overall input. A more compact notation to use in this case is to arrange these scalar values into a vector variable:

$$x = \begin{pmatrix} x_0 \\ x_1 \\ \vdots \\ x_n \end{pmatrix}$$

We start variable subscripts at 0 because that is how it is done in most programming languages. The typical convention in linear algebra is to start indexing at 1, but we will continue using 0 to stay consistent and avoid any confusion when translating formulas into code.

Similarly, we can arrange the weight variables into a single weight vector variable:

$$\mathbf{w} = \begin{pmatrix} w_0 \\ w_1 \\ \vdots \\ w_n \end{pmatrix}$$

We use lowercase **bold italic** letters to denote vectors in this book.

If you are a programmer, then a vector should be a familiar concept, although it is typically known as an array. The vectors shown so far are also known as *column vectors*, because they are arranged vertically as a column. We can also arrange the elements horizontally into a *row vector*. We use the *transpose* operation to convert a column vector into a row vector. The vector **x** and its transpose are shown here:

$$\mathbf{x} = \begin{pmatrix} x_0 \\ x_1 \\ \vdots \\ x_n \end{pmatrix}, \qquad \mathbf{x}^T = \begin{pmatrix} x_0 & x_1 & \cdots & x_n \end{pmatrix}$$

In the field of linear algebra, mathematical operations have been defined for vectors and other related structures. One example is vector addition, which can be used to add one vector to another vector with the same number of elements. Vector addition is an element-wise operation. Element 0 of both vectors are added together to form element 0 of the output vector, element 1 of both vectors are added together to form element 1 of the output vector, and so on:

$$\mathbf{a} = \begin{pmatrix} a_0 \\ a_1 \\ \vdots \\ a_n \end{pmatrix} \quad \mathbf{b} = \begin{pmatrix} b_0 \\ b_1 \\ \vdots \\ b_n \end{pmatrix} \quad \mathbf{a} + \mathbf{b} = \begin{pmatrix} a_0 + b_0 \\ a_1 + b_1 \\ \vdots \\ a_n + b_n \end{pmatrix}$$

All of this enables a compact way of describing operations on the elements in the vectors. This is just an abstraction. We hide the individual elements when writing down the equations, but when we need to perform the computations, we are still working on each individual value (although, as previously mentioned, some hardware implementations can do the operations efficiently in parallel).

DOT PRODUCT

Another important operation on two vectors is the *dot product*. The dot product is defined only if the two vectors are of equal length, just like vector addition. It is computed by multiplying element 0 of the two vectors, then multiplying element 1 of the two vectors and so on, and finally adding all of these products:

$$\boldsymbol{w} \cdot \boldsymbol{x} = w_0 x_0 + w_1 x_1 + \ldots + w_n x_n = \sum_{i=0}^{n} w_i x_i$$

These computations might seem familiar. It is exactly how we compute the weighted sum z in our perceptron. That is, assuming that we have arranged the inputs into a vector $\boldsymbol{x}$ (where the first element is 1) and the weights into a vector $\boldsymbol{w}$ (where the first element is the bias weight), then we can write the perceptron equation as

$$y = sign(\boldsymbol{w} \cdot \boldsymbol{x})$$

It is almost as if the dot product was invented to implement perceptrons. Just as with the vector addition, the dot product did not eliminate any of the computations but only simplified the notation. However, in practice, it also enabled us to call an efficient library implementation of the computation instead of a loop-based implementation of the weighted sum. Code Snippet 1-6 shows how we can write our perceptron function using the NumPy dot-product functionality. We also changed the code to use the NumPy sign function instead of implementing it with an `if` statement.

Code Snippet 1-6 Our Perceptron Function Rewritten Using Vector Notation

```
import numpy as np
def compute_output_vector(w, x):
    z = np.dot(w, x)
    return np.sign(z)
```

EXTENDING THE VECTOR TO A 2D MATRIX

The vector concept is a special case of the more general concept of a multidimensional structure where the dimension of a vector is 1. A multidimensional structure in two dimensions is known as a *matrix* and is described next. An example of a matrix A with $m+1$ rows and $n+1$ columns is shown here:[6]

$$A = \begin{pmatrix} a_{00} & a_{01} & \cdots & a_{0n} \\ a_{10} & a_{11} & \cdots & a_{1n} \\ \vdots & \vdots & \ddots & \vdots \\ a_{m0} & a_{m1} & \cdots & a_{mn} \end{pmatrix}$$

We use italic uppercase letters to denote matrices in this book.

The numbering of elements in a matrix is somewhat different than if you refer to coordinates in a 2D coordinate system (an *xy* chart). In particular, the elements in the vertical direction are numbered in increasing order going downward in a matrix, whereas an increasing *y*-value in an *xy* chart is increasing going upward. In addition, in an *xy* chart, we state the horizontal coordinate (*x*) first and the vertical coordinate (*y*) second, whereas for a matrix, we state the row first and the column second. As an example, element a_{01} is the top element second from the left in a matrix, and the coordinate (*x*=0, *y*=1) is the leftmost element and second from the bottom in an *xy* chart.

Why do we want to use this 2D structure when working with neurons? It is seldom the case that we work with a single neuron or a single input example. We just saw how the weights (**w**) for a single neuron can be represented by a vector. This means that we can represent the weights for *n* neurons with *n* vectors by arranging them in a matrix. Similarly, we seldom work with a single input example (**x**), but we have a whole set of input examples. Just as for multiple neurons, we can represent a set of input examples as a set of vectors that can be arranged in a matrix structure.

Just as we can transpose a vector, we can also transpose a matrix. We do this by flipping the matrix along its diagonal; that is, element *ij*, where *i* is the

---

6. Just as we do for vectors, in this book we start with a subscript of 0 for matrices to keep it consistent with programming in Python. The convention in mathematical texts on the topic is to start with a subscript of 1.

column and j is the row, becomes element ji. An example for a 2×2 matrix is shown here:

$$A = \begin{pmatrix} 1 & 2 \\ 3 & 4 \end{pmatrix} \qquad A^T = \begin{pmatrix} 1 & 3 \\ 2 & 4 \end{pmatrix}$$

Now that we know the basics of the matrix, we are ready to move on to some important matrix operations.

MATRIX-VECTOR MULTIPLICATION

Using the preceding concepts, we are now ready to define *matrix-vector multiplication*:

$$y = Ax = \begin{pmatrix} a_{00} & a_{01} & \cdots & a_{0n} \\ a_{10} & a_{11} & \cdots & a_{1n} \\ \vdots & \vdots & \ddots & \vdots \\ a_{m0} & a_{m1} & \cdots & a_{mn} \end{pmatrix} \begin{pmatrix} x_0 \\ x_1 \\ \vdots \\ x_n \end{pmatrix} = \begin{pmatrix} a_{00}x_0 + a_{01}x_1 + \ldots + a_{0n}x_n \\ a_{10}x_0 + a_{11}x_1 + \ldots + a_{1n}x_n \\ \vdots \\ a_{m0}x_0 + a_{m1}x_1 + \ldots + a_{mn}x_n \end{pmatrix}$$

It is defined only for cases where the number of columns in the matrix matches the number of elements in the vector. It results in a vector with the same number of elements as there are rows in the matrix. The elements in this resulting vector are defined as

$$y_i = \sum_{j=0}^{n} a_{ij} x_j$$

We recognize the sum as the dot product between two vectors, as previously described; that is, a slightly different view of the matrix is to consider each of the $m+1$ rows of the matrix as row vectors (a transposed vector). In that case, the matrix-vector multiplication can be viewed as doing $m+1$ dot products of the matrix rows and the x-vector, as shown here:

$$y = Ax = \begin{pmatrix} \mathbf{a}_0^T \\ \mathbf{a}_1^T \\ \vdots \\ \mathbf{a}_m^T \end{pmatrix} \begin{pmatrix} x_0 \\ x_1 \\ \vdots \\ x_n \end{pmatrix} = \begin{pmatrix} \mathbf{a}_0^T \cdot \mathbf{x} \\ \mathbf{a}_1^T \cdot \mathbf{x} \\ \vdots \\ \mathbf{a}_m^T \cdot \mathbf{x} \end{pmatrix}$$

Now let us look at how to use matrix-vector multiplication in the context of perceptrons. Assume that we have $m+1$ perceptrons, each having n inputs plus the bias input. Further, we have a single input example consisting of $n+1$ values, where the first element in the input vector is 1 to represent the bias input value. Now assume that we arrange the vectors for the perceptrons' weights into a matrix W, so we have

$$W = \begin{pmatrix} \mathbf{w}_0^T \\ \mathbf{w}_1^T \\ \vdots \\ \mathbf{w}_m^T \end{pmatrix}$$

where each $\mathbf{w}_i$ is a multielement vector corresponding to a single neuron. We can now compute the weighted sums for all $m+1$ perceptrons for the input example $\mathbf{x}$ by multiplying the matrix by the vector:

$$\mathbf{z} = W\mathbf{x}$$

The vector $\mathbf{z}$ will now contain $m+1$ elements, where each element represents the weighted sum for a single neuron presented with the input example.

MATRIX-MATRIX MULTIPLICATION

Let us now introduce *matrix-matrix multiplication* of two matrices, A and B:

$$C = AB =$$

$$\begin{pmatrix} a_{00} & a_{01} & \cdots & a_{0n} \\ a_{10} & a_{11} & \cdots & a_{1n} \\ \vdots & \vdots & \ddots & \vdots \\ a_{m0} & a_{m1} & \cdots & a_{mn} \end{pmatrix} \begin{pmatrix} b_{00} & b_{01} & \cdots & b_{0p} \\ b_{10} & b_{11} & \cdots & b_{1p} \\ \vdots & \vdots & \ddots & \vdots \\ b_{n0} & b_{n1} & \cdots & b_{np} \end{pmatrix} = \begin{pmatrix} c_{00} & c_{01} & \cdots & c_{0p} \\ c_{10} & c_{11} & \cdots & c_{1p} \\ \vdots & \vdots & \ddots & \vdots \\ c_{m0} & c_{m1} & \cdots & c_{mp} \end{pmatrix}$$

The number of columns in the first matrix A must match the number of rows in the second matrix B. The elements of the resulting matrix C are defined as

$$c_{ij} = a_{i0}b_{0j} + a_{i1}b_{1j} + \ldots + a_{in}b_{nj}$$

or, alternatively,

$$c_{ij} = \sum_{k=0}^{n} a_{ik} b_{kj}$$

Again, we recognize this sum as a dot product. That is, if we view each of the $m+1$ rows of matrix A as a row vector and each of the $p+1$ columns of matrix B as a column vector, then the matrix multiplication results in $(m+1) \times (p+1)$ dot products. In other words, we compute all the dot products between all row-vectors in matrix A and all column-vectors in matrix B. To make this abundantly clear, we can write the definition in a slightly different form. We state the two matrices A and B as being collections of vectors, and the elements of the resulting matrix are computed as dot products between these vectors:

$$C = AB = \begin{pmatrix} \boldsymbol{a}_0^T \\ \boldsymbol{a}_1^T \\ \vdots \\ \boldsymbol{a}_m^T \end{pmatrix} \begin{pmatrix} \boldsymbol{b}_0 & \boldsymbol{b}_1 & \cdots & \boldsymbol{b}_p \end{pmatrix} = \begin{pmatrix} \boldsymbol{a}_0 \cdot \boldsymbol{b}_0 & \boldsymbol{a}_0 \cdot \boldsymbol{b}_1 & \cdots & \boldsymbol{a}_0 \cdot \boldsymbol{b}_p \\ \boldsymbol{a}_1 \cdot \boldsymbol{b}_0 & \boldsymbol{a}_1 \cdot \boldsymbol{b}_1 & \cdots & \boldsymbol{a}_1 \cdot \boldsymbol{b}_p \\ \vdots & \vdots & \ddots & \vdots \\ \boldsymbol{a}_m \cdot \boldsymbol{b}_0 & \boldsymbol{a}_m \cdot \boldsymbol{b}_1 & \cdots & \boldsymbol{a}_m \cdot \boldsymbol{b}_p \end{pmatrix}$$

All of this can be somewhat heavy to get through if you are not well versed in linear algebra, but familiarity with these notations will be very helpful for your future work with DL.

Similarly, to what we did with matrix-vector multiplication, we can use matrix-matrix multiplication in the context of perceptrons. Assume that we have $m+1$ perceptrons, each having n inputs (+ bias input) just as in the previous example. Further, we have $p+1$ input examples, each consisting of $n+1$ values. As always, we assume that the first element in each input vector is 1 to represent the bias input value. Now assume that in addition to the matrix W, which represents the perceptrons' weights, we arrange the vectors for the input examples into matrix X:

$$W = \begin{pmatrix} \boldsymbol{w}_0^T \\ \boldsymbol{w}_1^T \\ \vdots \\ \boldsymbol{w}_m^T \end{pmatrix} \quad , \quad X = \begin{pmatrix} \boldsymbol{x}_0 & \boldsymbol{x}_1 & \cdots & \boldsymbol{x}_p \end{pmatrix}$$

In this example, both $\mathbf{w}_i$ and $\mathbf{x}_i$ refer to multielement vectors. We can now compute the weighted sums for all $m+1$ perceptrons for all $p+1$ input examples by multiplying the two matrices:

$$Z = WX$$

The matrix Z will now contain $(m+1) \times (p+1)$ elements, where each element represents the weighted sum for a single neuron presented with a single input example. To make this more concrete, matrix W corresponds to the two neurons in the first layer of our XOR network previously shown in Figure 1-9. Matrix X contains all four input examples. The resulting matrix WX contains the weighted sum for the two neurons for all four input examples:

$$W = \begin{pmatrix} w_{00} & w_{01} & w_{02} \\ w_{10} & w_{11} & w_{12} \end{pmatrix} = \begin{pmatrix} 0.9 & -0.6 & -0.5 \\ 0.2 & 0.6 & 0.6 \end{pmatrix}$$

$$X = \begin{pmatrix} x_{00} & x_{01} & x_{02} & x_{03} \\ x_{10} & x_{11} & x_{12} & x_{13} \\ x_{20} & x_{21} & x_{22} & x_{23} \end{pmatrix} = \begin{pmatrix} 1 & 1 & 1 & 1 \\ -1 & -1 & 1 & 1 \\ -1 & 1 & -1 & 1 \end{pmatrix}$$

$$WX = \begin{pmatrix} 2 & 1 & 0.8 & -0.2 \\ -1 & 0.2 & 0.2 & 1.4 \end{pmatrix}$$

The computation resulting in the value 2 for the upper left element in the resulting matrix is

$$w_{00}x_{00} + w_{01}x_{10} + w_{02}x_{20} = (0.9)(1) + (-0.6)(-1) + (-0.5)(-1) = 2$$

The other values can be computed following the same pattern. We simply compute the dot products between row vectors in W and column vectors in X.

SUMMARY OF VECTOR AND MATRIX OPERATIONS USED FOR PERCEPTRONS

The preceding discussion described how linear algebra operations map to various combinations of input examples and number of perceptrons. Table 1-4 summarizes the mappings.

None of the preceding exercises have simplified or eliminated any computations, but the notation enables computations to be computed efficiently in parallel on a GPU.

Table 1-4 Combinations of Perceptrons and Input Examples and the Corresponding Linear Algebra Operation

NUMBER OF PERCEPTRONS	NUMBER OF INPUT EXAMPLES	LINEAR ALGEBRA OPERATION
One	One	Dot product
Multiple	One	Matrix-vector multiplication
Multiple	Multiple	Matrix-matrix multiplication

DOT PRODUCT AS A MATRIX MULTIPLICATION

Before moving on from matrices and vectors, we want to introduce one more common notation. We note that a vector can be viewed as the special case of a matrix with a single column. This implies that we can formulate our dot product of two vectors as a matrix multiplication. Assume that we have vectors a and b as follows:

$$a = \begin{pmatrix} a_0 \\ a_1 \\ \vdots \\ a_n \end{pmatrix}, \quad b = \begin{pmatrix} b_0 \\ b_1 \\ \vdots \\ b_n \end{pmatrix}$$

$$a \cdot b = \sum_{i=0}^{n} a_i b_i = \begin{pmatrix} a_0 & a_1 & \cdots & a_n \end{pmatrix} \begin{pmatrix} b_0 \\ b_1 \\ \vdots \\ b_n \end{pmatrix} = a^T b$$

That is, if we transpose vector a so it becomes a matrix with a single row, we can now do matrix multiplication between a^T and b and thereby omit the dot product operator. This is a common notation with which it is good to be familiar.

EXTENDING TO MULTIDIMENSIONAL TENSORS

Vectors and matrices are special cases of the more generalized concept of a tensor, which is equivalent to the programming concept of a multidimensional array. In other words, if we extended a matrix to another dimension, we would call the resulting entity a 3D tensor. Tensors can show up in cases where the input data itself is multidimensional, such as in a color image. It consists of a 2D array of pixel values, and each pixel consists of three components (red, green, and blue, or RGB for short). That is, the input data itself is 3D, and if we have a collection of images as input values, then we can organize all of these as a 4D tensor. This can be tricky at first and often takes some time to get used to. The greatest challenge is to keep track of all the indices correctly. In the end, all the computations are typically reduced to a large number of dot products.

Geometric Interpretation of the Perceptron

Previously in this chapter, we visualized the decision boundary created by a two-input perceptron. In that type of chart, we identified all the coordinates where the perceptron would output −1 and all the coordinates where the perceptron would output +1. Another way of visualizing what the perceptron does is to plot z as a function of x_1 and x_2. This takes the form of a 3D chart, as shown in Figure 1-10.

We can see that the z-value in the perceptron forms a plane. The actual output (y) of the perceptron will take on the value of −1 for any point on the plane that is less than 0, whereas it will be +1 for any point that is greater than or equal to 0. If you look at this chart from above and draw a line where the z-value of the plane

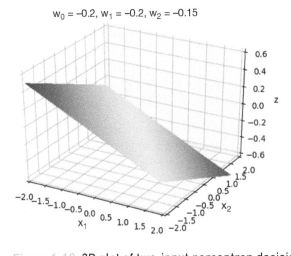

$w_0 = -0.2, w_1 = -0.2, w_2 = -0.15$

Figure 1-10 3D plot of two-input perceptron decision surface

is 0, you will end up with the same type of chart that we previously looked at in Figure 1-5.

The positioning and the orientation of the plane are determined by the three weights. The bias weight (w_0) determines where the plane will cross the z-axis at the point where both x_1 and x_2 equal 0; that is, changing w_0 causes the plane to move up or down on the z-axis. This is shown in the two upper charts in Figure 1-11, where the left chart is the same as in Figure 1-10, but in the right chart, we changed w_0 from −0.2 to 0.0. The two other weights (w_1 and w_2) determine the slope of the plane in the two different dimensions. If the weights are 0, then the plane will be parallel to the x_1 and x_2 axes, while a positive or negative value will cause the plane to tilt. This is shown in the two lower charts

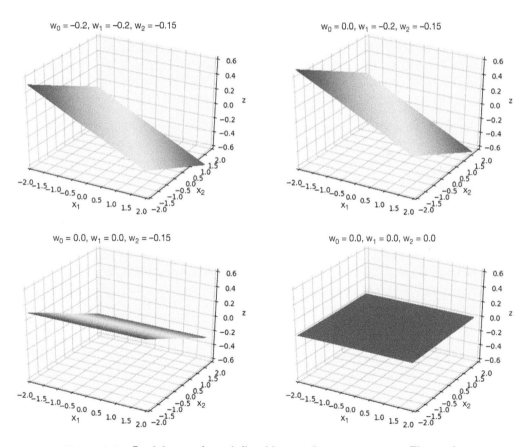

Figure 1-11 Decision surface defined by two-input perceptron. The surface orientation changes as the weights are modified.

in Figure 1-11, where in addition to setting w_0 to 0, we set w_1 to 0 in the lower left chart and all weights to 0 in the lower right chart and end up with a level plane.

This whole discussion has been centered on a perceptron with two inputs (in addition to the bias input) because it makes it possible to visualize the function. Adding more inputs is straightforward, but visualizing it is much harder because humans are inherently bad at visualizing more than three dimensions. The trick is to not even try to visualize but instead try to understand it from a mathematical point of view.

An example of this is that, as previously mentioned, the perceptron has the restriction that it can distinguish between two classes only if they are linearly separable, which for a two-input perceptron (two dimensions) means that they can be separated by a straight line. For a three-input neuron (three dimensions), it means that they can be separated by a plane. We do not delve into details here, but for readers who are already familiar with linear algebra, we point out that for the general case of a perceptron with n inputs (n dimensions), two classes are linearly separable if they can be separated by an $n{-}1$ dimensional hyperplane. This is a fairly abstract discussion, but do not worry if you have a hard time following it. Knowing about hyperplanes is not required to be able to understand the rest of the book.

Finally, there is also a geometric interpretation of the computation performed by the perceptron. The perceptron computes a dot product between the two vectors w and x, and we then apply the sign function to the result. Instead of implementing the dot product as a weighted sum, the dot product of the two vectors can also be computed as

$$w \cdot x = |w|\ |x|\ cos(\theta)$$

where θ is the angle between the vectors w and x. Since both $|w|$ and $|x|$ are positive, the angle between the two vectors will determine the output of the perceptron (an angle greater than 90 degrees will cause -1, and an angle less than 90 degrees will cause $+1$ as output).

It turns out that we can use the geometric definition of the dot product to reason about what weights will maximize the weighted sum for a given input, but you can safely ignore this for now if it is the first time you have seen this definition of the dot product.

Understanding the Bias Term

Our description of the perceptron includes the use of a bias term that we did not justify further. In addition, taking a closer look at our equations for the perceptron, a couple of things stick out:

$$y = f(z), \text{ where}$$

$$z = \sum_{i=0}^{n} w_i x_i$$

$$f(z) = \begin{cases} -1, & z < 0 \\ 1, & z \geq 0 \end{cases}$$

$$x_0 = 1 \text{ (bias term)}$$

In particular, the output values of −1 and 1 and the threshold of 0 seem like they have been chosen somewhat arbitrarily. If you are familiar with digital electronics, it might feel more natural if the output values were 0 and 1, and you might also feel that a threshold of 0.5 is more appropriate. We will get back to that in Chapter 3, but for now, we focus on the threshold, which is often denoted by θ (Greek letter theta). We could make our perceptron more general by replacing the activation function with the following, where the threshold is simply a parameter θ:

$$f(z) = \begin{cases} -1, & z < \theta \\ 1, & z \geq \theta \end{cases}$$

Looking more closely at the condition that needs to be fulfilled for the output to take on the value 1, we have

$$z \geq \theta$$

This can be rewritten as

$$z - \theta \geq 0$$

That is, as long as we subtract the threshold from z, we can keep our implementation that uses 0 as its threshold. Looking carefully at our original description of the perceptron, it turns out that we were a little bit sneaky and did this all along by including the bias term x_0 in the sum that computes z. That is, the rationale for the bias term in the first place was to make the perceptron implement an adjustable threshold value. It might seem like we should have subtracted the bias, but it does not matter because we have the associated weight w_0, which can be both positive and negative. That is, by adjusting w_0, our perceptron can be made to implement any arbitrary threshold θ. To be crystal clear, if we want the perceptron to use a threshold of θ, then we set w_0 to be $-\theta$.

Finally, if we ignore the activation function for a moment, we can consider how the bias term affects just the weighted sum z. We saw in the previous section how changing w_0 resulted in the plane sliding up and down along the z-axis. To make it even simpler, consider the lower-dimensional case where we have a straight line instead of a plane. The bias term is simply the intercept term b in the equation for a straight line:

$$y = mx + b$$

What we just described in this section does not change how we use the perceptron. It is just a justification for why we implemented it the way we did in the first place. It is also helpful to know when reading other texts that might use an explicit threshold instead of a bias term.

Concluding Remarks on the Perceptron

In this chapter, we introduced the perceptron and looked at it from a couple of different angles. We showed how it can be used to implement a logical function, starting with NAND. A key reason for starting by using the perceptron to implement logical functions is that it quickly leads to one of the perceptron's limitations, as we saw when trying to implement the XOR function. This then explained the need for connecting multiple perceptrons into a network.

In reality, when working with neural networks and DL, we typically do not think about the perceptron or other neurons in terms of logical gates. A perhaps more common view of looking at the perceptron is as a binary classifier. We feed the perceptron an input example consisting of a vector of input values. The perceptron classifies this input example as belonging to one of two classes. The vector of input values typically contains many more variables than two. For example, in a medical setting, the values in the vector might represent data about a patient, such as age, sex, and various laboratory results. The task for the perceptron is to classify whether the input values indicate that the patient has a specific medical condition. In reality, because of the limitations of the perceptron, this classifier would likely not be very good. Instead, just as for the XOR example, it is likely that a network of neurons would do better. We will see plenty of examples of such networks in the remainder of this book.

We also introduced the perceptron learning algorithm and showed how it learns a simple task. However, we never described *why* it works. That is the main topic of Chapter 2, which will also serve as a steppingstone for describing the backpropagation algorithm used to train multilevel networks in Chapter 3.

Chapter 2

Gradient-Based Learning

In this chapter, we describe how the perceptron learning algorithm works, which we then build upon in Chapter 3, "Sigmoid Neurons and Backpropagation," by extending it to multilevel networks. These two chapters contain more mathematical content than other chapters in this book, but we also describe the concepts in an intuitive manner for readers who do not like reading mathematical formulas.

Intuitive Explanation of the Perceptron Learning Algorithm

In Chapter 1, "The Rosenblatt Perceptron," we presented and used the perceptron learning algorithm, but we did not explain why it works. Let us now look at what the learning algorithm does. To refresh our memory, the weight adjustment step in the perceptron learning algorithm is first restated in Code Snippet 2-1, where

Code Snippet 2-1 Weight Update Step of Perceptron Learning Algorithm

```
for i in range(len(w)):
    w[i] += (y * LEARNING_RATE * x[i])
```

w is an array representing the weight vector, x is an array representing the input vector, and y is the desired output.

If an example is presented to the perceptron and the perceptron correctly predicts the output, we do not adjust any weights at all (the code that ensures this is not shown in the snippet). This makes sense because if the current weights already result in the correct output, there is no good reason to adjust them.

In the cases where the perceptron predicts the outputs incorrectly, we need to adjust the weights as shown in Code Snippet 2-1, and we see that the weight adjustment is computed by combining the desired y value, the input value, and a parameter known as LEARNING_RATE. We now show why the weights are adjusted the way they are. Let us consider three different training examples where x_0 represents the bias input that is always 1:

Training example 1: $x_0 = 1$, $x_1 = 0$, $x_2 = 0$, $y = 1$

Training example 2: $x_0 = 1$, $x_1 = 0$, $x_2 = 1.5$, $y = -1$

Training example 3: $x_0 = 1$, $x_1 = -1.5$, $x_2 = 0$, $y = 1$

We further know that the z-value (the input to the signum function) for our perceptron is computed as

$$z = w_0 x_0 + w_1 x_1 + w_2 x_2$$

For training example 1, the result is

$$z = w_0 1 + w_1 0 + w_2 0 = w_0$$

Clearly, w_1 and w_2 do not affect the result, so the only weight that makes sense to adjust is w_0. Further, if the desired output value is positive ($y = 1$), then we would want to increase the value of w_0. On the other hand, if the desired output value is negative ($y = -1$), then we want to decrease the value of w_0. Assuming that the LEARNING_RATE parameter is positive, Code Snippet 2-1 does exactly this when it adjusts w_i by adding a value that is computed as y * LEARNING_RATE * x[i], where x_1 and x_2 are zero for training example 1 and thus only w_0 will be adjusted.

Doing the same kind of analysis for training example 2, we see that only w_0 and w_2 will be adjusted, both in a negative direction because y is −1 and x_0 and x_2 are positive. Further, the magnitude of the adjustment for w_2 is greater than for w_0 since x_2 is greater than x_0.

Similarly, for training example 3, only w_0 and w_1 will be adjusted, where w_0 will be adjusted in a positive direction and w_1 will be adjusted in a negative direction because y is positive and x_1 is negative.

To make this even more concrete, we compute the adjustment value for each weight for the three training examples, with an assumed learning rate of 0.1. They are summarized in Table 2-1.

We make a couple of observations:

- The adjustment of the bias weight depends only on the desired output value and will thus be determined by whether the majority of the training examples have positive or negative desired outputs.[1]

- For a given training example, only the weights that can significantly affect the output will see a significant adjustment, because the adjustments are proportional to the input values. In the extreme, where an input value is 0 for a training example, its corresponding weight will see zero adjustment.

This makes much sense. In a case where more than 50% of the training examples have the same output value, adjusting the bias weight toward that output value will make the perceptron be right more than 50% of the time if all other weights are 0. It also makes sense to not adjust weights that do not have a big impact on a given training example, which will likely do more harm than good because the weight could have a big impact on other training examples.

In Chapter 1, we described how the z-value of a two-input (plus bias term) perceptron creates a plane in a 3D space (where x_1 is one dimension, x_2 the second, and the resulting value z is the third). One way to visualize the perceptron learning algorithm is to consider how it adjusts the orientation of this plane. Every

Table 2-1 Adjustment Values for Each Weight for the Three Training Examples

	W_0 CHANGE	W_1 CHANGE	W_2 CHANGE
Example 1	1*1*0.1 = 0.1	1*0*0.1 = 0	1*0*0.1 = 0
Example 2	(−1)*1*0.1 = −0.1	(−1)*0*0.1 = 0	(−1)*1.5*0.1 = −0.15
Example 3	1*1*0.1 = 0.1	1*(−1.5)*0.1 = −0.15	1*0*0.1 = 0

---

1. Only training examples that are incorrectly predicted will cause an adjustment. Thus, a case with many training examples with positive outputs can still result in a negative bias weight if many of the positive training examples already are correctly predicted and thus do not cause any weight adjustments.

update will adjust the bias weight. This will push the overall plane upward for positive training examples and downward for negative training examples.

For example, close to the z-axis (x_1 and x_2 are small), the bias weight is all that counts. For cases that are further away from the z-axis, the angle of the plane becomes a more significant lever. Thus, for mispredicted learning examples where the x_1 value is big, we make a big change to the weight that determines the tilt angle in the x_1 direction, and the same applies for cases with big x_2 values but in the orthogonal direction. A point on the plane that is located directly on the x_2 axis will not move as we rotate the plane around the x_2 axis, which is what we do when we adjust the weight corresponding to the x_1 value.

An attempt at illustrating this is shown in Figure 2-1, with $w_0 = 1.0$, $w_1 = -1.0$, and $w_2 = -1.0$, which are weights that we could imagine would result from repeatedly applying the weight adjustments from Table 2-1.

Looking at the plane, we can now reason about how it satisfies the three training examples. Because $w_0 = 1.0$, the output will be positive when x_1 and x_2 are close to zero ($z = 1.0$ when x_1 and x_2 are 0), which will ensure that training example 1 is correctly handled. We further see that w_1 is chosen so that the plane is slanted in a direction that z increases as x_1 decreases. This ensures that training example 3 is taken care of because it has a negative x_1 value and wants a positive output. Finally, w_2 is chosen so that the plane is slanted in a direction (around its other axis) that z increases as x_2 decreases. This satisfies training example 2 with its positive x_2 input and desired negative output value.

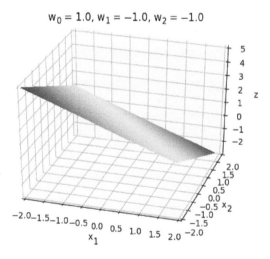

$w_0 = 1.0, w_1 = -1.0, w_2 = -1.0$

Figure 2-1 Example of weights that correctly predicts all three training examples

We believe that the reasoning is sufficient to give most people an intuitive idea of why the learning algorithm works the way it does. It also turns out that for cases that are linearly separable (i.e., cases where a perceptron has the ability to distinguish between the two classes), this learning algorithm is guaranteed to converge to a solution. This is true regardless of the magnitude of the learning rate parameter. In other words, the value of this parameter will only affect how quickly the algorithm converges.

To prepare ourselves for the learning algorithm for multilevel networks, we would now like to arrive at an analytical explanation of why we adjust the weights the way that we do in the perceptron learning algorithm, but we will first go through some concepts from calculus and numerical optimization that we will build upon.

Derivatives and Optimization Problems

In this section, we briefly introduce the mathematical concepts that we use in this chapter. It is mostly meant as a refresher for readers who have not used calculus lately, so feel free to skip to the next section if that does not apply to you. We start by briefly revisiting what a derivative is. Given a function

$$y = f(x)$$

the derivative of y with respect to x tells us how much the value of y changes given a small change in x. A few common notations are

$$y', \ f'(x), \ \frac{dy}{dx}$$

The first notation (y') can be somewhat ambiguous if y is a function of multiple variables, but in this case, where y is only a function of x, the notation is unambiguous. Because our neural networks typically are functions of many variables, we will prefer the two other notations.

Figure 2-2 plots the value of an arbitrary function $y = f(x)$. The plot also illustrates the derivative $f'(x)$ by plotting the tangent line in three different points. The tangent to a curve is a straight line with the same slope (derivative) as the curve at the location where the line touches the curve.

We can make a couple of observations. First, the derivative at the point that minimizes the value of y is 0 (the tangent is horizontal). Second, as we move further away from the minimum, the derivative increases (it decreases if we move in the other direction). We can make use of these observations when solving an

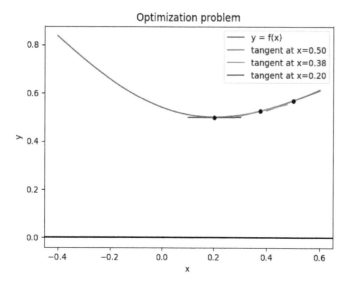

Figure 2-2 Plot showing a curve $y = f(x)$ and its derivative at the minimum value and in two other points

optimization problem in which we want to find what value of the variable x will minimize[2] the value of the function y. Given an initial value x and its corresponding y, the sign of the derivative indicates in what direction to adjust x to reduce the value of y. Similarly, if we know how to solve x for 0, we will find an extreme point (minimum, maximum, or saddle point)[3] of y.

As we saw in Chapter 1, we typically work with many variables. Therefore, before moving on to how to apply these concepts to neural networks, we need to extend them to two or more dimensions. Let us assume that we have a function of two variables, that is, $y = f(x_0, x_1)$, or alternatively, $y = f(\mathbf{x})$, where $\mathbf{x}$ is a 2D vector. This function can be thought of as a landscape that can contain hills and valleys,[4] as in Figure 2-3.

We can now compute two partial derivatives:

$$\frac{\partial y}{\partial x_0} \quad and \quad \frac{\partial y}{\partial x_1}$$

---

2. We assume that the optimization problem is a minimization problem. There are also maximization problems, but we can convert a maximization problem into a minimization problem by negating the function we want to maximize.

3. We worry only about minima in this book. Further, it is worth noting that these extreme points may well be local extremes. That is, there is no guarantee that a global minimum is found.

4. It can also contain discontinuities, asymptotes, and so on.

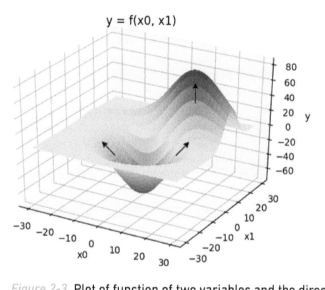

$y = f(x0, x1)$

Figure 2-3 Plot of function of two variables and the direction and slope of steepest ascent in three different points

A partial derivative is just like a normal derivative, but we pretend that all but one of the variables are constants. The one variable that we want to compute the derivative with respect to is the only variable that is not treated as a constant. A simple example is if we have the function $y = ax_0 + bx_1$, in which case our two partial derivatives become

$$\frac{\partial y}{\partial x_0} = a$$

$$\frac{\partial y}{\partial x_1} = b$$

If we arrange these partial derivatives in a vector, we get

$$\nabla y = \begin{pmatrix} \dfrac{\partial y}{\partial x_0} \\[2ex] \dfrac{\partial y}{\partial x_1} \end{pmatrix}$$

which is called the *gradient* of the function—that is, the gradient is a derivative but generalized to a function with multiple variables. The symbol ∇ (upside-down Greek letter delta) is pronounced "nabla."

The gradient has a geometric interpretation. Being a vector, the gradient consists of a direction and a magnitude.[5] The direction is defined in the same dimensional space as the inputs to the function. That is, in our example, this is the 2D space represented by the horizontal plane in Figure 2-3. For our example gradient, the direction is (a, b). Geometrically, this *direction* indicates where to move from a given point (x_0, x_1) in order for the resulting function value (y) to increase the most. That is, it is the direction of the steepest ascent. The *magnitude* of the gradient indicates the slope of the hill in that direction.

The three arrows in Figure 2-3 illustrate both the direction and the slope of the steepest ascent in three point. Each arrow is defined by the gradient in its point, but the arrow does not represent the gradient vector itself. Remember that the direction of the gradient falls in the horizontal plane, whereas the arrows in the figure also have a vertical component that illustrates the slope of the hill in that point.

There is nothing magic about two input dimensions, but we can compute partial derivatives of a function of any number of dimensions and create the gradient by arranging them into a vector. However, this is not possible to visualize in a chart.

Solving a Learning Problem with Gradient Descent

One way to state our learning problem is to identify the weights that, given the input values for a training example, result in the network output matching the desired output for that training example. Mathematically, this is the same as solving the following equation:

$$y - \hat{y} = 0$$

where y is the desired output value and $\hat{y}$ (pronounced "y hat") is the value predicted by the network. In reality, we do not have just a single training example (data point), but we have a set of training examples that we want our function

---

5. This explanation assumes that you are familiar with the direction and magnitude of vectors. The magnitude can be computed using the distance formula that is derived from the Pythagorean theorem. Details of this theorem can be found in texts about linear algebra.

to satisfy. We can combine these multiple training examples into a single error metric by computing their mean squared error (MSE):[6]

$$\frac{1}{m}\sum_{i=1}^{m}\left(y^{(i)} - \hat{y}^{(i)}\right)^2 \qquad (\textit{mean squared error})$$

The notation with a superscript number inside parentheses is used to distinguish between different training examples. It is not an indication to raise y to the power of i. Looking closer, it seems like using MSE presents a problem. For most problems, the MSE is strictly greater than 0, so trying to solve it for 0 is impossible. Instead, we will treat our problem as an optimization problem in which we try to find weights that *minimize the value* of the error function.

In most deep learning (DL) problems, it is not feasible to find a closed form solution[7] to this minimization problem. Instead, a numerical method known as *gradient descent* is used. It is an iterative method in which we start with an initial guess of the solution and then gradually refine it. Gradient descent is illustrated in Figure 2-4, where we start with an initial guess x_0. We can insert this value into

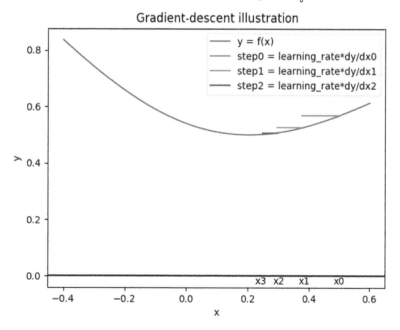

Figure 2-4 Gradient descent in one dimension

---

6. We will later see that MSE is not necessarily a great error function for some neural networks, but we use it for now because many readers are likely familiar with it.

7. A closed form solution is a solution found by analytically solving an equation to find an exact solution. An alternative is to use a numerical method. A numerical method often results in an approximate solution.

$f(x)$ and compute the corresponding y as well as its derivative. Assuming that we are not already at the minimum value of y, we can now come up with an improved guess x_1 by either increasing or decreasing x_0 slightly. The sign of the derivative indicates whether we should increase or decrease x_0. A positive slope (as in the figure), indicates that y will decrease if we decrease x. We can then iteratively refine the solution by repeatedly doing small adjustments to x.

Gradient descent is a commonly used learning algorithm in DL.

In addition to indicating in what direction to adjust x, the derivative provides an indication of whether the current value of x is close to or far away from the value that will minimize y. Gradient descent makes use of this property by using the value of the derivative to decide how much to adjust x. This is shown in the update formula used by gradient descent:

$$x_{n+1} = x_n - \eta f'(x_n)$$

where η (Greek letter eta) is a parameter known as the *learning rate*. We see that the step size depends on both the learning rate and the derivative, so the step size will decrease as the derivative decreases. The preceding figure illustrates the behavior of gradient descent using a learning rate (η) of 0.3. We see how the step size decreases as the derivative gets closer to 0. As the algorithm converges at the minimum point, the fact that the derivative approaches 0 implies that the step size also approaches 0.

If the learning rate is set to too large a value, gradient descent can also overshoot the solution and fail to converge. Further, even with a small step size, the algorithm is not guaranteed to find the global minimum because it can get stuck in a local minimum. However, in practice, it has been shown to work well for neural networks.

If you have encountered numerical optimization problems before, chances are that you have used a different iterative algorithm known as the *Newton-Raphson* or *Newton's method*. If you are curious about how it relates to gradient descent, you can find a description in Appendix E.

GRADIENT DESCENT FOR MULTIDIMENSIONAL FUNCTIONS

The preceding example worked with a function of a single variable, but our neural networks are functions of many variables, so we need the ability to minimize multidimensional functions. Extending it to more dimensions is straightforward. As described in the section "Derivatives and Optimization Problems," a gradient is a vector consisting of partial derivatives and indicates the direction in the input space that results in the steepest ascent for the function value. Conversely, the negative gradient is the direction of steepest descent, or the direction of the quickest path to reducing the function value. Therefore, if we are at the point $x = (x_0, x_1)$ and want to minimize y, then we choose our next point as

$$\begin{pmatrix} x_0 \\ x_1 \end{pmatrix} - \eta \nabla y$$

where ∇y is the gradient. This generalizes to functions of any number of dimensions. In other words, if we have a function of n variables, then our gradient will consist of n partial derivatives, and we can compute the next step as

$$x - \eta \nabla y$$

where both x and ∇y are vectors consisting of n elements. Figure 2-5 shows gradient descent for a function of two input variables. The function value y gradually decreases as we move from point 1 to point 2 and 3.

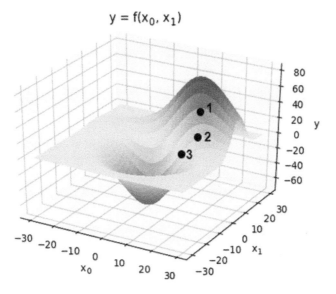

Figure 2-5 Gradient descent for a function of two variables

It is worth noting again that the algorithm can get stuck in a local minimum. There are various ways of trying to avoid this, some of which are mentioned in later chapters but are not discussed in depth in this book.

We are now almost ready to apply gradient descent to our neural networks. First, we need to point out some pitfalls related to working with the multidimensional functions implemented by neural networks.

Constants and Variables in a Network

A key idea when applying gradient descent to our neural network is that we consider input values (x) to be constants, with our goal being to adjust the weights (w), including the bias input weight (w_0). This might seem odd given our description of gradient descent, where we try to find input values that minimize a function. At first sight, for the two-input perceptron, it seems like x_1 and x_2 would be considered input values. That would be true if we had a perceptron with fixed weights and a desired output value and the task at hand was to find the x-values that result in this output value given the fixed weights. However, this is not what we are trying to do with our learning algorithm. The purpose of our learning algorithm is to, given a fixed input (x_1, x_2), adjust the weights (w_0, w_1, w_2) so that the output value takes on the value we want to see. That is, we treat x_1 and x_2 as constants (x_0 as well, but that is always the constant 1, as stated earlier), while we treat w_0, w_1, and w_2 as variables that we can adjust.

> During **learning,** not the inputs (x) but the **weights (w) are considered to be the variables** in our function.

To make it more concrete, if we are training a network to distinguish between a dog and a cat, the pixel values would be the inputs (x) to the network. If it turned out that the network incorrectly classified a picture of a dog as being a cat, we would not go ahead and adjust the picture to look more like a cat. Instead, we would adjust the weights of the network to try to make it correctly classify the dog as being a dog.

Analytic Explanation of the Perceptron Learning Algorithm

Now we have the tools needed to explain why the perceptron learning algorithm is defined the way it is. Starting with the two-input perceptron, we have the following variables:

$$ \mathbf{w} = \begin{pmatrix} w_0 \\ w_1 \\ w_2 \end{pmatrix}, \qquad \mathbf{x} = \begin{pmatrix} x_0 \\ x_1 \\ x_2 \end{pmatrix}, \qquad y $$

The weight vector $\mathbf{w}$ is initialized with arbitrary values. This is our first guess at what the weights should be. We also have a given input combination $\mathbf{x}$ (where x_0 is 1) and its desired output value (y), also known as the ground truth. Let us first consider the case where the current weights result in an output of +1 but the ground truth is −1. This means that the z-value (the input to the signum function) is positive and we want to drive it down toward (and below) 0. We can do this by applying gradient descent to the following function:[8]

$$ z = x_0 w_0 + x_1 w_1 + x_2 w_2 $$

where x_0, x_1, x_2 are constants and the weights are treated as variables. First, we need to compute the gradient, which consists of the three partial derivatives with respect to w_0, w_1, and w_2. Remember that when computing a partial derivative, all the variables except for the one that we are taking the derivative with respect to are constants, so the gradient simply turns out to be

$$ \nabla z = \begin{pmatrix} \dfrac{\partial z}{\partial w_0} \\ \dfrac{\partial z}{\partial w_1} \\ \dfrac{\partial z}{\partial w_2} \end{pmatrix} = \begin{pmatrix} x_0 \\ x_1 \\ x_2 \end{pmatrix} $$

---

8. In this description of the single perceptron case, we do not formally define an error function that we want to minimize but instead simply identify that we want to reduce the z-value to get the desired output and then use gradient descent to accomplish this. We will use an error function in the next chapter.

Given the current weight vector $\boldsymbol{w}$, and the gradient ∇z, we can now compute a new attempt at $\boldsymbol{w}$ that will result in a smaller z-value by using gradient decent. Our new $\boldsymbol{w}$ will be

$$\boldsymbol{w} - \eta \nabla z$$

which expands to the following for each component of the vector $\boldsymbol{w}$:

$$\begin{pmatrix} w_0 - \eta x_0 \\ w_1 - \eta x_1 \\ w_2 - \eta x_2 \end{pmatrix}$$

This is exactly the update rule for the perceptron learning algorithm. That is, the perceptron learning algorithm is equivalent to applying gradient descent to the perceptron function.[9]

If the learning case we considered instead had a ground truth of +1 and our current weight results in −1, then we can multiply all terms by −1 to still make it a minimization problem, and the only difference will be that the gradient will have a different sign, which again makes gradient descent equivalent to the perceptron learning algorithm.

At this point, it is worth pointing out that what we have described so far is an algorithm known as *stochastic gradient descent* (SGD). The distinction between stochastic and true gradient descent is that, with true gradient descent, we would compute the gradient as the mean value of the gradients for all individual training examples, whereas with SGD, we approximate the gradient by computing it for only a single training example. There are also hybrid approaches in which you approximate the gradient by computing a mean of some, but not all, training examples. This approach is studied more in later chapters, but for now we will continue using SGD.

> **Gradient descent** requires you to compute the gradient for **all input examples** before updating the weights, but **stochastic gradient descent** only requires you to compute the gradient for **a single input example**.

We stated the gradient descent algorithm for this problem in vector form. This form applies to any number of dimensions (i.e., it can be used for perceptrons with any number of inputs).

---

9. This statement is not strictly correct: There are some subtleties with respect to the perceptron function not being differentiable in all points, but for the purpose of this discussion, we can ignore that.

Geometric Description of the Perceptron Learning Algorithm

Finally, we offer a geometric explanation to how the perceptron learning algorithm works for readers who think visually. Given that we are limited to three dimensions when plotting, we can only visualize a function with two adjustable parameters. This corresponds to a single-input perceptron, which has w_0 and w_1 as adjustable parameters. Given a specific input example (x_0, x_1), where $x_0 = 1.0$ as always, our weighted sum z is now a function of the two weights w_0 and w_1. The independent variables w_0 and w_1 together with the resulting variable z will define a plane oriented in a 3D space. All points on this plane with a positive z-value will result in an output value of $+1$ for the given input values (x_0, x_1), whereas a negative z-value will result in an output value of -1 for the given input.

Let us assume that with the current input values and weights, the z-value is positive, but the ground truth is negative. The perceptron learning algorithm will simply adjust the weights w_0 and w_1 so that the z-value moves to a different point on this plane, and the point that we move to will be in the direction that the plane is tilted. You can envision that if we place a ball on the point corresponding to (w_0, w_1) and let it roll, it will roll straight toward the point that the perceptron learning algorithm will end up with in the next iteration. This is illustrated in Figure 2-6.

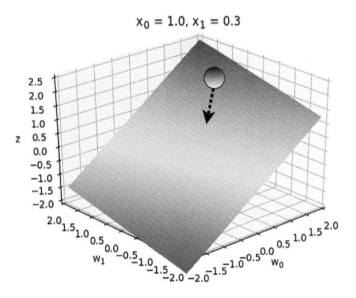

Figure 2-6 Visualization of weight adjustment for a perceptron when desired output is −1

Revisiting Different Types of Perceptron Plots

At this point, we have introduced a number of different plots using two and three dimensions. In some cases, we treated the perceptron inputs (x) as independent variables, and in some cases, we instead switched to making the plot a function of the weights (w). To avoid confusion, we revisit four charts in Figure 2-7 and explain how they relate to each other. The perceptron is presented with an input vector x and produces a single output y. Internally, it has a weight vector w and

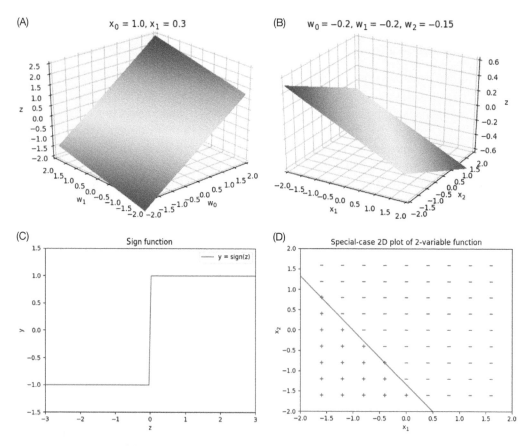

Figure 2-7 (A) Weighted sum z as function of weights w_0, w_1 for one-input perceptron. (B) Weighted sum z as function of inputs x_1, x_2 for two-input perceptron. (C) Perceptron output y as function of weighted sum z. (D) Decision boundary for two-input perceptron acting as a binary classifier.

computes a weighted sum of x and w. We call the weighted sum z and use it as input to a sign function that produces the output y.

Figure 2-7(A) shows the weighed sum z as a function of two weights w_0 and w_1. This type of chart is used to understand how the perceptron behavior will change if we adjust its *internal weights* (w). The chart assumes a specific input vector x ($x_0 = 1.0$, $x_1 = 0.3$). The weight w_0 is the bias weight, and x_0 is not a true input but is always set to 1.0. That implies that this chart represents a single-input perceptron. We cannot plot this type of chart for perceptrons with two or more inputs.

Figure 2-7(B) shows the weighted sum z as a function of two inputs x_1 and x_2. This type of chart is used to understand how a perceptron behavior will change when different *input values* (x) are presented to its inputs. The chart assumes a specific set of weights ($w_0 = -0.2$, $w_1 = -0.2$, $w_2 = -0.15$). Both x_1 and x_2 are real inputs, so the chart represents a two-input perceptron. That is, when we plot z as a function of the inputs, we can represent a perceptron with more inputs than can be done when we plot z as a function of the weights. This naturally follows from the fact that the bias input x_0 is always 1.0 (treated as a constant), whereas the bias weight w_0 is adjustable (treated as a variable).

Charts A and B visualize the weighted sum z. The two remaining charts visualize the output y as a dependent variable. Figure 2-7(C) simply shows the output y as a function of the weighted sum z. This chart applies to all perceptrons regardless of their weights or number of inputs. As such, the chart might seem somewhat uninteresting, but we see in Chapter 3 how we can replace the sign function by a different function to create a different type of artificial neuron.

Finally, Figure 2-7(D) visualizes the output y as a function of two inputs x_1 and x_2. At a first glance, this can be confusing when comparing to Figure 2-7(B), which also represents a two-input perceptron. Why must one chart be 3D when another chart can get away with being 2D? The explanation is that the 2D chart exploits the fact that the output has only two possible values (−1 and +1), and the regions that take on these two different values are clearly separated. Instead of plotting the output value on its own dimension, we indicate the output value for each point with plus and minus signs. We further draw a line representing the boundary between the two regions. The equation for this line can be derived from the perceptron function. This type of plot is very common when looking at any binary classification problem. The perceptron is just one out of many techniques for binary classification. It belongs to a class of techniques known as *linear classifiers*. Appendix A describes some other linear classifiers and uses the same type of chart to describe their behavior.

This is about as far as we can get in terms of visualizing the behavior of a perceptron. In reality, we often work with many more dimensions, so the attempts at visualizing the process break down. Instead, we will need to trust the mathematics and the formulas we have introduced.

Using a Perceptron to Identify Patterns

Before moving on to extending the learning algorithm to multilevel networks, we will sidetrack a little and look at a different use case for the perceptron. So far, we have studied cases in which the perceptron implements simple two-input logical functions. That is, the perceptron was used to classify data points as belonging to one of two classes, as long as the classes are linearly separable. This is an example of binary classification. An important case for this is to use the perceptron to identify a specific pattern. In such a case, we use the perceptron to classify inputs as either belonging to a specific class of interest or not belonging to that class. That is, we are still doing binary classification, but the other class is "everything else." Along these lines, we could envision a perceptron that works as a cat identifier. If we present an image of a cat to the perceptron, it will fire, but if we present any other image to the perceptron, it will not fire. If the perceptron does not fire, the only thing we know is that the image was not of a cat, but that does not mean we know what it is. It could be a dog, a boat, a mountain, or anything else. Now, before getting too excited about creating our cat-detecting perceptron, we point out that given the severe limitations of a single perceptron, it is not possible to build a good cat identifier from a single perceptron. We need to combine multiple perceptrons, as we did to solve the XOR problem, and that is something we will do in future chapters. For now, let us consider just a single perceptron and use it to identify some simpler image patterns.

In this example, we analyze a small part of a larger image. We arbitrarily choose to just look at 9 pixels that are arranged in a 3×3 grid. Further, to keep things simple, we assume that a pixel can take on only one of three intensities: white (1.0), gray (0.0), or black (−1.0). This is done to limit the number of training examples. Further, a training example will only consist of combinations of black and white pixels or black and gray pixels. There are no training examples with a combination of gray and white pixels or with black, gray, and white pixels. That is, we have $2^9 = 512$ examples that are black and white and $2^9 = 512$ examples that are black and gray. These two sets overlap at only one place: each contains an image of all-black pixels. So, to be precise, we end up with 1,023 unique training examples.

The task for the perceptron is to signal +1 as output for the specific example that we want it to be able to identify and to signal −1 for all others. To illustrate this, we trained five perceptrons. Each perceptron was trained to identify a specific pattern. The training process consisted of repeatedly presenting all input patterns in random order to the perceptron. We used a ground truth of +1 for the pattern that we wanted the perceptron to learn to identify and −1 for all other examples. Figure 2-8 shows the results.

The five columns correspond to the five different perceptrons. The top row in the figure shows the pattern that we wanted each perceptron to identify. The score under each pattern is the input value to the sign function in the perceptron after it had been trained (i.e., the weighted sum of the inputs when we present the target

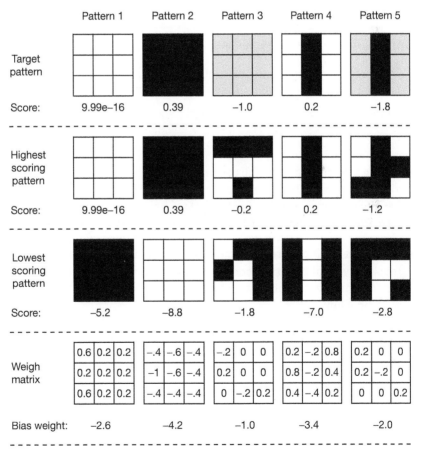

Figure 2-8 Five example patterns, the resulting weights, and highest- and lowest-scoring patterns

pattern to the trained perceptron). The second row shows the highest scoring pattern (we simply presented all combinations to the trained neuron and recorded which patterns resulted in the highest score) and its score. If the highest-scoring pattern is identical to the target pattern, then that means that our classifier is successful at identifying the target pattern. This does not necessarily mean that it does not make any mistakes. For example, a perceptron could output a high score on all patterns, in which case it signals many false positives. The third row shows the lowest-scoring pattern and its score. The bottom row shows the weights after training, including the bias weight.

> We can formalize the discussion about **false positives** and introduce the two concepts **precision** and **recall**. This is described in Appendix A.

We make the following observations:

- The perceptron is successful at identifying the black-and-white patterns (1, 2, and 4). Looking at the weights for these cases, they kind of mimic the pattern. Intuitively, this makes much sense if you think about it. If a pixel is white (1.0), you want to multiply it by a positive value to end up with a high score, and if a pixel is black (−1.0), you want to multiply it by a negative value to end up with a high score.

- For the all-white case, the target example barely brings the score above 0. This also makes sense because it implies that other examples that have many, but not all, white pixels will still not be able to get above 0; that is, the number of false positives is limited.

- Even if the input pattern is perfectly symmetric (e.g., all white or all black), the resulting weight pattern is not necessarily symmetric. This is a result of the random initialization of the weights and the algorithm finding one out of many working solutions.

- We see that the perceptron is not successful in perfectly identifying cases in which some of the pixels are gray. In these cases, the algorithm never converged, and we stopped after a fixed number of iterations. Apparently, these are not linearly separable[10] from the other examples. To identify such patterns, we will need to combine multiple neurons as we did for the XOR problem.

---

10. We have mentioned linear separability a fair number of times, which might give the impression that it is a very important concept to understand. However, the remainder of this book focuses on multilevel networks, which do not suffer from the limitation related to linear separability. Therefore, you do not need to worry much about this concept for the remainder of the book.

- From these examples, it starts getting clear that the perceptron is more powerful than a simple NAND gate. In particular, it can work with real-valued inputs, and we can change its behavior by applying a training algorithm.

  In Chapter 1, we briefly described how the dot product can be stated in terms of the angle between the two vectors. For two vectors of a given length, the dot product is maximized when the angle between the two vectors is 0. That is, if the two vectors are of the same length, the dot product is maximized if the two vectors are identical. Therefore, it makes total sense that the weight vector mimics the input pattern.

This concludes our experiment with the perceptron as a pattern (also known as *feature*) identifier, but we use these pattern identifiers as building blocks in future chapters for more advanced image analysis in multilevel networks.

Concluding Remarks on Gradient-Based Learning

This chapter continued to focus on the individual perceptron. We discussed more details of how the perceptron learning algorithm works, from both an intuitive perspective and a more mathematical perspective. As a part of the mathematical description of the perceptron learning algorithm, we introduced how to minimize a function with gradient descent. In addition to describing the learning algorithm, we explored how to use the perceptron as a pattern detector.

It is now time to shift focus from the single perceptron to multilevel networks. The key topic in the next chapter is how to extend the learning algorithm to such networks. The algorithm used to train multilevel networks is based on gradient descent and builds nicely on what you have learned in this chapter.

Chapter 3

Sigmoid Neurons and Backpropagation

In this chapter, we describe the basic learning algorithm, which virtually all neural-network learning algorithms are variations of. This algorithm is based on a technique known as *backpropagation* (or just *backprop*) and was introduced in the context of neural networks in the mid-1980s. It was a significant step on the path to deep learning (DL). Our impression is that even to many DL practitioners, this algorithm can be a little bit of a mystery because much of it is hidden under the hood of modern DL frameworks. Still, it is crucial to know the basics of how the algorithm works.

At the highest level, the algorithm consists of three simple steps. First, present one or more training examples to the neural network. Second, compare the output of the neural network to the desired value. Finally, adjust the weights to make the output get closer to the desired value. It is as simple as that! It is exactly what we did in the perceptron learning algorithm, and we used gradient descent to determine how much to adjust the weights. For a single perceptron, computing the partial derivatives was trivial. For a multilevel network with multiple neurons per layer, it can be hairy. This is where backprop comes to the rescue. It is a simple and efficient way to compute partial derivatives with respect to weights in a neural network.

Before describing how it works, it is worth pointing out a terminology inconsistency that can be confusing. Our description states that we use backprop to compute the partial derivatives that are needed by gradient descent to train the network. An alternative naming convention is to refer to the overall training algorithm as the *backpropagation algorithm.* Regardless of which terminology we use, the overall process consists of the following passes:

- The forward pass, where we present a learning example to the network and compare the network output to the desired value (the ground truth).

- The backward pass, where we compute the partial derivatives with respect to the weights. These derivatives are then used to adjust the weights to make the network output get closer to the ground truth.

The **backpropagation** algorithm consists of a **forward pass** in which training examples are presented to the network. It is followed by a **backward pass** in which weights are adjusted using **gradient descent.** The gradient is computed using the **backpropagation** algorithm.

Throughout this chapter, we build up the description of how the learning algorithm for a multilevel network works, and in the final section, we present a code example for implementing it to solve the XOR problem.

Modified Neurons to Enable Gradient Descent for Multilevel Networks

When we applied gradient descent to the perceptron, we sort of ignored the activation function, that is, the sign function that is applied to the z-value to arrive at the y-value. We did this by using gradient descent to drive z in the desired direction, which we knew would implicitly affect y. That trick cannot be used when working with a multilayer network where the outputs from the activation functions in one layer are used as inputs to the next layer. This is one reason that it was nontrivial to extend the perceptron learning algorithm to multilayer networks.

A key requirement to be able to apply gradient descent is that the function that it is applied to is differentiable, because we need to compute the gradient. The sign function does not fulfill that requirement due to its discontinuity at zero. Rumelhart, Hinton, and Williams (1986) addressed this when they presented the backpropagation algorithm for multilevel networks. They replaced the sign function with an S-shaped function. One example of such a function is shown in Figure 3-1, which shows the hyperbolic tangent (tanh) function.

The reason that such a function was chosen is obvious when comparing its shape to the sign function. Its shape mimics the sign function, but it is a continuous function and thereby differentiable everywhere. It seems like it is the best of both worlds because the sign function works well for perceptrons, but differentiability is needed for learning.

Another S-shaped function that is important to DL is the *logistic function,* shown in Figure 3-2. To avoid confusion, we should point out something about terminology. Strictly speaking, both tanh and the logistic function belong to a class of functions known as *sigmoid* functions. In older texts on neural networks, *sigmoid function* is commonly used to refer to either the tanh function or the logistic function. However, nowadays the DL field uses *sigmoid function* to refer only to the logistic function. In this book, we interchangeably use the terms logistic function, sigmoid function, and logistic sigmoid function when referring to said function, and we call out tanh separately. The scales of the axes are different for the charts of the tanh

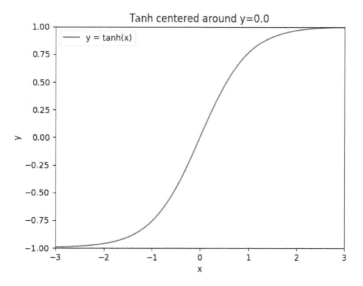

Figure 3-1 Hyperbolic tangent (tanh) function. Note how it is symmetric around 0 on both axes.

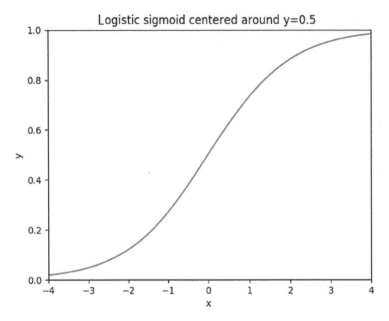

Figure 3-2 Logistic sigmoid function. Note how it is symmetric around 0 on the x-axis and around 0.5 on the y-axis. The scale of both the x-axis and the y-axis is different than in Figure 3-1.

function and the logistic function, so although the curves look similar, they are different.

Before discussing these two functions in more detail, we first introduce their mathematical definitions:

$$Hyperbolic\ tangent:\ \tanh(x)=\frac{e^x-e^{-x}}{e^x+e^{-x}}=\frac{e^{2x}-1}{e^{2x}+1}$$

$$Logistic\ sigmoid\ function:\ S(x)=\frac{1}{1+e^{-x}}=\frac{e^x}{e^x+1}$$

Each function can be stated in a couple of different forms, and you may well run into all of them in other texts on the subject. At a first glance, these definitions might look scary, and it seems magical that anybody could come up with the idea to use these functions when simulating neurons. However, the mathematical definition is less important, and it is the shape that was the driving force. If you study the asymptotes (the output value when x goes to the extreme), it is fairly easy to convince yourself[1] that as x approaches infinity, the tanh function approaches +1, and as x approaches negative infinity, the tanh function approaches −1, just like the sign function. If we do the same exercise for the logistic sigmoid function, we see that it also approaches +1 as x approaches infinity, whereas it instead approaches 0 as x approaches negative infinity.

We note that both functions are combinations of exponential functions. The shape of an exponential function is similar to a half S as shown in Figure 3-3. If you think about it a little bit, it seems intuitive that it is possible to combine exponential functions to create an S-shape. In particular, an exponential taking x as an argument will dominate for positive x but will be close to 0 for negative x. On the contrary, an exponential taking $−x$ as an argument will exhibit the opposite behavior.

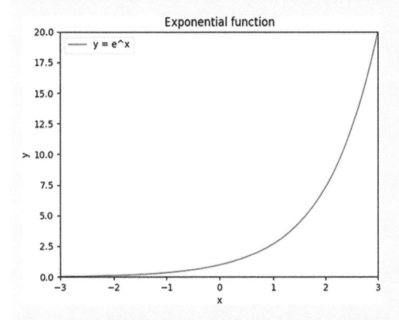

Figure 3-3 Exponential function shaped like the lower half of an S

1. One way of doing this is to play with a spreadsheet and insert different values of x, then look at how the values vary for the various exponential functions and the result of combining them.

We mentioned earlier that the two S-shaped functions are differentiable. Before going into more details of the functions themselves, let us first present their derivatives:

$$\text{Derivative of hyperbolic tangent}: \ tanh'(x)=1-tanh^2(x)$$

$$\text{Derivative of logistic sigmoid function}: \ S'(x)=S(x)(1-S(x))$$

One key property for both of these functions is that their derivatives can be computed from the function values even if the x-values are not available. Specifically, *tanh'(x)* is a function of *tanh(x)*, and similarly, *S'(x)* is a function of *S(x)*. To make it more concrete, for tanh, if we have computed $y = tanh(x)$ for a specific x, then the derivative of the tanh function for that same x can easily be computed as $1 - y^2$. We will make use of that property later in this chapter.

Let us now look closer at the differences between tanh and the logistic sigmoid function. Figure 3-4 shows both functions plotted in the same chart. We noted that the tanh function is more similar to the sign function in that it approaches −1 as x approaches negative infinity, whereas the logistic function bottoms out at 0. We also noted in Chapter 1, "The Rosenblatt Perceptron," that if you have a background in digital electronics, it might feel more comfortable to use a function with the output range 0 to 1 instead of −1 to +1. Another observation is that a range from 0 to 1 can make more sense if we want to interpret the output as a

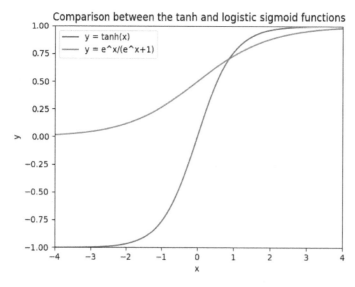

Figure 3-4 Chart comparing the tanh function and the logistic sigmoid functions

probability—for example, how probable it is that the input to the network is a picture of a cat.

In addition to the output range, there are some subtle differences to consider, namely, the different threshold values (i.e., where the function is centered in the x-direction). Table 3-1 shows three different combinations of threshold value and output range.

From Figure 3-4 and Table 3-1, we can see that both the tanh and logistic sigmoid functions are symmetric around 0 on the x-axis, so their threshold is 0. For the case where the output range is 0 to 1, you may think that a threshold of 0.5 (which we call *symmetric digital*) is more intuitive. To illustrate why, consider what happens if you connect multiple neurons after each other. Further assume that the input to the first neuron is close to its threshold value, and therefore the output of the neuron will fall in the middle of the output range. For both the tanh and symmetric digital neuron, this means that the subsequent neuron will get an input that is close to its threshold value, and again, its output will be in the middle of the output range. On the other hand, in the case of the logistic sigmoid function, the second neuron will get an input that is well above its threshold. Therefore, at a first glance, it seems like a neural net based on neurons using the logistic sigmoid function would be biased toward outputting +1.

The reasoning above ignores two important details. First, the weights can be both positive and negative. Thus, if we have initialized the weights randomly and each neuron is fed by the output from multiple neurons, then even if all the inputs to a neuron in a subsequent layer are close to 0.5, their weighted sum (the input to the activation function) will be close to 0 because about half of the inputs will be multiplied by a negative weight and half will be multiplied by a positive weight. That is, in practice, the symmetric digital function will be biased toward outputting 0, whereas the logistic sigmoid function would be close to the middle of its output range. Note that tanh works the same either way. The second

Table 3-1 Three Alternative Activation Functions

	SIGN/TANH	LOGISTIC SIGMOID	SYMMETRIC DIGITAL
Max output	1	1	1
Min output	−1	0	0
Threshold	0	0	0.5

detail to consider is the bias input. Let us assume a case where all the weights are positive. Even in this case, it is possible to set the bias weight for the logistic sigmoid function to a value at which the output from the previous layer, combined with the bias, will result in an input to the activation function that is close to the threshold value. As described in Chapter 1, changing the bias term is equivalent to picking a threshold. This means that as long as the bias weight is initialized (or learned) properly, this entire threshold discussion is moot. Neither of the neurons has a fixed threshold, but the threshold can be adjusted by changing the bias weight.

Which Activation Function Should We Use?

This discussion has taken for granted that the activation function should be fairly similar to the sign function but should be differentiable. This is all influenced by history and the all-or-nothing activation (either the neuron fires or it does not fire) described by both McCulloch-Pitts (1943) and Rosenblatt (1958). Rosenblatt mentioned that there were other ideas as well, and it turns out that there are other powerful activation functions that are much different from the sign function. Some of them are not even differentiable in all points even though that was assumed to be a strict requirement in 1986 when the learning algorithm for multilevel networks was introduced. Various examples of these more modern activation functions are introduced in Chapter 5, "Toward DL: Frameworks and Network Tweaks," and Chapter 6, "Fully Connected Networks Applied to Regression," but for now we limit ourselves to the logistic sigmoid function and tanh, and an obvious question, then, is which one to pick. As you will see later in this book, this is just one of many similar questions, and there are multiple alternative implementations to choose among. In general, there are no right or wrong answers, but the solution is to experiment and pick whatever method is best for the specific problem that you are working on. However, there are often heuristics that can point you in the right direction as a starting point for these experiments.

When using an S-shaped function as an activation function, we recommend starting with tanh for hidden layers because their output will be centered around 0, which coincides with the threshold of the next layer.[2] For the output layer, we recommend using the logistic sigmoid function so it can be interpreted as a

---

2. Assuming that the bias weight is initialized to 0 or randomly with an average of 0.

probability. We will also see that this function works well with a different type of loss function introduced in Chapter 5.

There exist a large number of activation functions where **some, but not all,** are S-shaped functions. Two popular choices are tanh and the logistic sigmoid function. When picking between the two, choose **tanh for hidden layers** and **logistic sigmoid for the output layer.**

The discussion about input and output ranges and their relationships to threshold values focused on the behavior during the forward pass. It turns out that these design choices also influence how easy it is for the backpropagation algorithm to adjust the weights to their desired values. We do not go into details about this, but some further discussions about the difference between the logistic sigmoid function and tanh and how they affect the network training process can be found in a paper by LeCun, Bottou, Orr, and Müller (1998).

Function Composition and the Chain Rule

A central theme in the backpropagation algorithm is to compute the derivative of a *composite function* using the chain rule. In this section, we provide a brief introduction to composite functions and the chain rule. As with the section about partial derivatives and optimization problems in Chapter 2, "Gradient-Based Learning," this section mainly targets readers who feel rusty with respect to these topics, so feel free to skip to the next section if that does not apply to you.

Function composition is used to combine two or more functions into a new function by using the output value of one function as input value to the next function. Assume that we have two functions:

$$f(x), \text{ and } g(x)$$

Further assume that we use the output of function $g(x)$ as an input to function $f(x)$. Then we can combine them into the composite function

$$h(x) = f(g(x))$$

A common alternative notation is to use the composition operator:

$$h(x) = f \circ g(x), \text{ or just } h = f \circ g$$

The notation with the composition operator is generally preferrable when composing multiple functions to avoid all the nested parentheses. In most cases, we use this notation for function composition.

The reason that we bring up function composition is that a multilayer neural network can be written as a composite function. We will see details of that in the next section, but before that, we also need to describe how to compute the derivative for composite functions. The derivative will be needed when applying gradient descent to a multilevel network. The *chain rule* states how we can compute the derivative of a composition of functions. If we have

$$h = f \circ g$$

then the derivative is

$$h' = (f' \circ g)g'$$

Stated differently, if we have

$$z = f(y) \quad \text{and} \quad y = g(x), \quad \text{so} \quad z = f \circ g(x)$$

then

$$\frac{\partial z}{\partial x} = \frac{\partial z}{\partial y} \cdot \frac{\partial y}{\partial x}$$

which is also known as *Leibniz's notation*. We will use this notation when applying the chain rule.

In these examples, we only used functions of a single variable. When applying these concepts to neural networks, we will generally work with functions with multiple variables. As an example, assume two input variables for both our functions $g(x_1, x_2)$ and $f(x_3, x_4)$. Further assume that the output of g is used as the second argument to function f. We get the composite function

$$h(x_1, x_2, x_3) = f \circ g = f\left(x_3, g(x_1, x_2)\right)$$

Just as we did in the Chapter 2, we want to compute partial derivatives of this resulting multivariate function. This is done by treating all other variables as constants, as described in the previous chapter. For the function h that we just described, this implies that we will need to use the chain rule to compute the partial derivatives with respect to variables x_1 and x_2. When computing the partial derivative with respect to x_3, g is treated as a constant and we only need to consider the derivative of function f. Detailed examples of this are found in the next section where we do these computations for a neural network.

Using Backpropagation to Compute the Gradient

It is now time to explore how to apply gradient descent to a multilevel network. To keep it simple, we begin with one of the simplest multilevel networks that we can think of, with only a single neuron in each layer. We assume two inputs to the first neuron. The network is shown in Figure 3-5.

We have named the two neurons G and F, where G has three adjustable weights, and F has two adjustable weights. In total, we have a network with five adjustable weights. We want a learning algorithm to automatically find values for these weights that result in the network implementing the desired functionality. The figure also contains something that looks like a neuron to the very right, but this is not a part of the network. Instead, it represents a function needed to determine how right or wrong the network is, which is needed for learning. (This is described in more detail shortly).

We use a weight-naming convention whereby the first letter in the subscript represents the source layer and the second letter represents the destination layer (the layer that the weight is a part of). The digit represents the input number, where 0 is the bias input. That is, w_{xg2} means input number 2 to the g-neuron, which receives its input from layer x. For consistency, we use the same naming

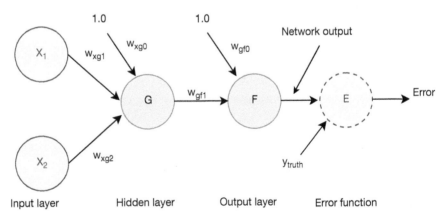

Figure 3-5 Simple two-layer network used to explain backpropagation. The last unit (dashed) is not a part of the network but represents the error function that compares the output to ground truth.

convention for the bias term as for the other terms, although technically it does not have a source layer.

The perceptron studied in Chapter 2 used the sign function as its activation function. As already noted, the sign function is not differentiable in all points. In this chapter, we use activation functions that are differentiable in all points. Neuron G uses tanh as an activation function, and neuron F uses S (the logistic sigmoid function). This means that a small change to any of the five weights will result in only a small change to the output. When we used a sign function, a small change in a weight would not change anything until the change was big enough to make one perceptron flip, in which case all bets were off because it could easily flip dependent neurons as well.

Taking a step back, our neural network implements the following function:

$$\hat{y} = S\left(w_{gf0} + w_{gf1}\tanh\left(w_{xg0} + w_{xg1}x_1 + w_{xg2}x_2\right)\right)$$

We know of an algorithm (gradient descent) that can be used to minimize a function. To make use of this algorithm we want to define an *error function*, also known as a *loss function,* which has the property that if it is minimized, then the overall network produces the results that we desire. Defining and minimizing error functions is not unique to neural networks but is used in many other contexts as well. One popular error function that comes to mind is the mean squared error (MSE), which we introduced in Chapter 2, and you might already have been familiar with because it is used for linear regression. The way to compute it is to, for each learning example, subtract the predicted value from the ground truth and square this difference, or stated as a mathematical formula:

$$MSE = \frac{1}{m}\sum_{i=1}^{m}(y^{(i)} - \hat{y}^{(i)})^2$$

We promised in the preface to not start the book with linear regression, but sometimes we still have to mention it. At least we waited until Chapter 3. For the purpose of this chapter, there is no need to know anything about linear regression, but if you are interested, then you can read more in Appendix A.

Remember that **error function** and **loss function** are two names for the same thing.

There are multiple loss functions to choose among. We use MSE for historical reasons in this section, but in reality, it is not a good choice in combination with a sigmoid activation function.

In other words, MSE is the *mean* (sum divided by *m*) of the squared error $(y - \hat{y})^2$ for all *m* training examples. In Chapter 5, we will learn that using MSE as an error function with this type of neural network is not optimal, but we will use it for now just to keep things familiar and simple. That is, assuming a single training example, we want to minimize our loss function $(y - \hat{y})^2$, where $\hat{y}$ was defined above and *y* is a part of the training example. The following equation combines the formula for MSE with the network function to arrive at the expression of the error function that we want to minimize for a single learning example:

$$Error = \left(y - S\left(w_{gf0} + w_{gf1}\tanh\left(w_{xg0} + w_{xg1}x_1 + w_{xg2}x_2\right)\right)\right)^2$$

We know that we can minimize this function using gradient descent by computing the gradient of the loss function ($\nabla Error$) with respect to our weights **w**, then multiplying this gradient by the learning rate (η), and then subtract this result from the initial guess of our weights. That seems straightforward enough, except that computing the gradient of our loss function seems a little bit scary.

A key thing to remember here is that because we want to adjust the weights, we view the **weights *w* as variables,** and we view the **inputs *x* as constants;** that is, the gradient is computed with respect to **w** and not with respect to **x**.

One brute-force way to solve this problem would be to compute the gradient numerically. We could present an input example to the network and compute and record the output. Then we add Δw to one of the weights and compute the new output and can now compute Δy. An approximation of the partial derivative is now $\Delta y / \Delta w$. Once we have repeated this procedure for all weights, we have computed the gradient. Unfortunately, this is an extremely computationally intensive way of computing our gradient. We need to run through the network *n*+1 times, where *n* is the number of weights in the network (the +1 is necessary because we need the baseline output without any adjustments to the weights).

The backpropagation algorithm solves this problem in an elegant way by computing the gradient analytically in a computationally efficient manner. The starting point is to decompose our equation into smaller expressions. We start with a function that computes the input to the activation function of neuron G:

$$z_g\left(w_{xg0},\ w_{xg1},\ w_{xg2}\right)=w_{xg0}+w_{xg1}x_1+w_{xg2}x_2$$

Next is the activation function for neuron G:

$$g\left(z_g\right)=tanh\left(z_g\right)$$

It is followed by the input to the activation function of neuron F:

$$z_f\left(w_{gf0},\ w_{gf1},\ g\right)=w_{gf0}+w_{gf1}g$$

This in turn is followed by the activation function of neuron F:

$$f\left(z_f\right)=S\left(z_f\right)$$

Finally, we conclude with the error function:

$$e(f)=\frac{\left(y-f\right)^2}{2}$$

Looking closely at the formulas, you might wonder where the 2 in the denominator of the error (e) came from. We added that to the formula because it will simplify the solution further down. This is legal to do because the values of variables that will minimize an expression do not change if we divide the expression by a constant.

Overall, the error function that we want to minimize can now be written as a composite function:

$$Error\left(w_{gf0},w_{gf1},w_{xg0},w_{xg1},w_{xg2}\right)=e\circ f\circ z_f\circ g\circ z_g$$

That is, e is a function of f, which is a function of z_f, which is a function of g, which is a function of z_g. Function z_f is not only a function of g but also of the two variables w_{gf0} and w_{gf1}. That was already shown further up in the definition of z_f. Similarly, z_g is a function of the three variables w_{xg0}, w_{xg1}, and w_{xg2}.

Again, note that this formula contains neither *x* nor *y* because they are not treated as variables but as constants for a given training example.

Now that we have stated our error function as a composition of multiple functions, we can make use of the chain rule. We use that to compute the partial derivative of the error function e with respect to the input variables w_{gf0}, w_{gf1}, w_{xg0}, w_{xg1}, and w_{xg2}. Let us start with the first one: We compute the partial derivative of e with respect to the variable w_{gf0}. We do this by simply regarding the other variables as constants, which also implies that the function g is a constant, and we then have a function

$$Error = e \circ f \circ z_f \left(w_{gf0} \right)$$

Applying the chain rule now yields:

$$\frac{\partial e}{\partial w_{gf0}} = \frac{\partial e}{\partial f} \cdot \frac{\partial f}{\partial z_f} \cdot \frac{\partial z_f}{\partial w_{gf0}} \tag{1}$$

Doing the same exercise, but with respect to w_{gf1}, yields

$$\frac{\partial e}{\partial w_{gf1}} = \frac{\partial e}{\partial f} \cdot \frac{\partial f}{\partial z_f} \cdot \frac{\partial z_f}{\partial w_{gf1}} \tag{2}$$

Moving on to w_{xg0}, w_{xg1}, and w_{xg2} results in expressions with two more functions in the composite function because the functions g and z_g are no longer treated as constants:

$$Error = e \circ f \circ z_f \circ g \circ z_g$$

The resulting partial derivatives are

$$\frac{\partial e}{\partial w_{xg0}} = \frac{\partial e}{\partial f} \cdot \frac{\partial f}{\partial z_f} \cdot \frac{\partial z_f}{\partial g} \cdot \frac{\partial g}{\partial z_g} \cdot \frac{\partial z_g}{\partial w_{xg0}} \tag{3}$$

$$\frac{\partial e}{\partial w_{xg1}} = \frac{\partial e}{\partial f} \cdot \frac{\partial f}{\partial z_f} \cdot \frac{\partial z_f}{\partial g} \cdot \frac{\partial g}{\partial z_g} \cdot \frac{\partial z_g}{\partial w_{xg1}} \tag{4}$$

$$\frac{\partial e}{\partial w_{xg2}} = \frac{\partial e}{\partial f} \cdot \frac{\partial f}{\partial z_f} \cdot \frac{\partial z_f}{\partial g} \cdot \frac{\partial g}{\partial z_g} \cdot \frac{\partial z_g}{\partial w_{xg2}} \tag{5}$$

One thing that sticks out when looking at the five partial derivatives is that there are a whole lot of common subexpressions. For example, the first two factors are the same in each of the five formulas, and three of the formulas share yet another two factors. This provides some intuition for why the backpropagation algorithm is an efficient way of computing the gradient. Instead of being recomputed over and over, these subexpressions are computed once and then reused for each partial derivative where they are needed.

Now let us attempt to compute one of the partial derivatives in practice. We start with number (1) above.

$$\frac{\partial e}{\partial f} = \frac{\partial \frac{(y-f)^2}{2}}{\partial f} = \frac{2(y-f)}{2} \cdot (-1) = -(y-f)$$

$$\frac{\partial f}{\partial z_f} = \frac{\partial (S(z_f))}{\partial z_f} = S'(z_f)$$

$$\frac{\partial z_f}{\partial w_{gf0}} = \frac{\partial (w_{gf0} + w_{gf1}g)}{\partial w_{gf0}} = 1$$

Note the **negative sign** for $-(y - f)$. Some texts simply flip the position of the two terms to get rid of it. In addition, some code implementations of the algorithm omit it and later compensate by using + instead of − when adjusting the weights further down.

Combining the three together, we get

$$\frac{\partial e}{\partial w_{gf0}} = -(y-f) \cdot S'(z_f)$$

There are three key observations here. First, we have all the values y, f, and z_f because y comes from the training example and the others were computed when doing the forward pass through the network. Second, the derivative of S is possible to compute because we consciously chose S as an activation function. This would not have been the case if we had stuck with the sign function. Third, not only can we compute the derivative of S but, as we saw earlier in this chapter, the derivative is a function of S itself. Therefore, we can compute the derivative from the value f that was computed during the forward pass. We revisit these three observations later in the chapter in a numerical example.

Let us now compute the partial derivative with respect to w_{gf1}, that is, number (2) presented earlier. The only difference compared to (1) is the third factor, which becomes

$$\frac{\partial z_f}{\partial w_{gf1}} = \frac{\partial (w_{gf0} + w_{gf1}g)}{\partial w_{gf1}} = g$$

Combining this with the first two factors yields

$$\frac{\partial e}{\partial w_{gf1}} = -(y-f) \cdot S'(z_f) \cdot g$$

This is the same as we had for w_{gf0} but multiplied by g, which is the output of neuron G that we already computed during the forward pass.

We can do similar exercises for the remaining three partial derivatives and arrive at all five derivatives that the gradient consists of (Equation 3-1).

$$\frac{\partial e}{\partial w_{gf0}} = -(y - f) \cdot S'(z_f) \tag{1}$$

$$\frac{\partial e}{\partial w_{gf1}} = -(y - f) \cdot S'(z_f) \cdot g \tag{2}$$

$$\frac{\partial e}{\partial w_{xg0}} = -(y - f) \cdot S'(z_f) \cdot w_{gf1} \cdot tanh'(z_g) \tag{3}$$

$$\frac{\partial e}{\partial w_{xg1}} = -(y - f) \cdot S'(z_f) \cdot w_{gf1} \cdot tanh'(z_g) \cdot x_1 \tag{4}$$

$$\frac{\partial e}{\partial w_{xg2}} = -(y - f) \cdot S'(z_f) \cdot w_{gf1} \cdot tanh'(z_g) \cdot x_2 \tag{5}$$

Equation 3-1   All five partial derivatives of the gradient

The derivative of tanh, like the derivative of S, is also simple to compute. Looking at the preceding equations, we can see a pattern. We start with the derivative of the error function and then multiply that by the derivative of the activation function for the output neuron. Let us call this product the error for the output neuron (neuron F). Now, the partial derivative with respect to an input weight for that neuron is obtained by multiplying the neuron error by the input value to that weight. In the case of the bias weight, the input value is 1, so the partial derivative is simply the neuron error. For the other weight, we multiply the neuron error by the output of the preceding neuron, which is the input to the weight.

Moving to the next (preceding) layer, we take the error for the output neuron, multiply it by the weight connecting to the preceding neuron, and multiply the result by the derivative of the activation function for the preceding neuron. We call this the error of the preceding neuron (neuron G). These computations *propagate the error backward* from the output of the network toward the beginning of the network, hence the name *backpropagation algorithm*. The full learning algorithm is shown in Figure 3-6.

So, as described, we start by applying the input example to the network to compute the current error. This is known as the *forward pass*. During this pass,

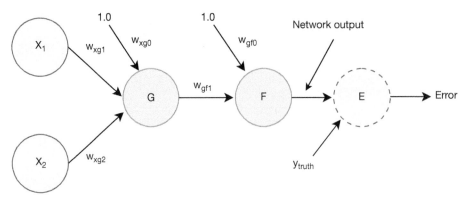

1. Forward pass: Compute and store activation function output (y) for each neuron and finally the error

Resulting stored variables: y_g y_f *Error*

2. Backward pass: Compute the derivative $e'(y_f)$ of the error function. Compute (*back propagate*) the error for each neuron by multiplying the error from the subsequent neuron (that it feeds) by the weight to that neuron and then multiply by the derivative of its own activation function. (e.g. the error for neuron G is $error_g = error_f$ * w_{gf1} * $g'(z_g)$ *where* $g'(z_g)$ is the derivative of the activation function for neuron G). This derivative can be computed from the stored output of the activation function.

Resulting stored variables: $error_g$ $error_f$ $e'(y_f)$

3. Update weights: For each weight, subtract (*learning_rate* * *input* * *error*) where input is the input value to that weight (from network input or output from preceding neuron) and error is the error term for the neuron the weight belongs to (e.g., for weight w_{gf1} the adjustment will be $-(learning\_rate * y_g * error_f)$ where y_g is the output of neuron G).

Figure 3-6 Network learning algorithm based on gradient descent using backpropagation to compute gradient

we also store the outputs (y) for all neurons because we will use them during the backward pass. We then start the backward pass during which we propagate the error backward and compute and store an error term for each neuron. We need the derivative to compute this error term, and the derivative for each neuron can be computed from the stored output (y) for the neuron. Finally, we can use this error term together with the input values to the layer to compute the partial derivatives that are used to adjust the weights. The input values to a hidden layer are the output values from the preceding layer. The input values to the first layer are simply the x-values from the training example.

Backpropagation consists of the following steps:

Compute the derivative of the error function with respect to network output, and call this the **output error**. Multiply this output error by the **derivative of the activation function** of the output neuron, and call this the **error term** for that neuron. The partial derivative with respect to any weight of that neuron is the **error term** times the **input value to the weight.** The error term for the preceding neuron is the **error term for the current neuron** times the **weight between the two neurons** times the **derivative of the activation function** of the preceding neuron.

Looking at the formula for a single component of the gradient, we can see that there are a number of things that determine how much to adjust the weight when the gradient is later used for gradient descent:

- The overall error—this makes sense in that a big error should lead to a big adjustment.

- All the weights and derivatives on the path from the weight in question to the error in the end of the network—this makes sense because if one or more weights or derivatives on this path will suppress the effect of this weight change, then it is not helpful to change it.

- The input to the weight in question—this makes sense because if the input to the weight is small, then adjusting the weight will not have much of an effect.

The current value of the weight to adjust is not a part of the formula. Overall, these observations make intuitive sense for how to identify which weights should get significant adjustments.

To make this more concrete, we now walk through a numerical example for the forward pass, backward pass, and weight adjustment for a single training example:

$Initial\ weights: w_{xg0} = 0.3; w_{xg1} = 0.6; w_{xg2} = -0.1; w_{gf0} = -0.2; w_{gf1} = 0.5$

$Training\ example: x_1 = -0.9; x_2 = 0.1; y_{truth} = 1.0$

$Learning\ rate = lr = 0.1$

FORWARD PASS

We compute the output of neuron G by applying the *tanh* activation function to the weighted sum of the inputs, namely the bias term and the two *x*-values:

$$y_g = \tanh\left(w_{xg0} + w_{xg1}x_1 + w_{xg2}x_2\right)$$

$$= \tanh\left(0.3 + 0.6\cdot(-0.9) + (-0.1)\cdot 0.1\right) = -0.24$$

We then compute the output of neuron F by applying the logistic activation function to the weighted sum of the inputs to this neuron, which is simply the bias term and the output from neuron G:

$$y_f = S\left(w_{gf0} + w_{gf1}y_g\right) = S\left(-0.2 + 0.5\cdot(-0.25)\right) = 0.42$$

We conclude the forward pass with computing the MSE between the desired output and the actual output to see how well the current weights work, but we will not use this computation for the backward pass.

$$MSE = \frac{\left(y - y_f\right)^2}{2} = \frac{\left(1.0 - 0.42\right)^2}{2} = 0.17$$

BACKWARD PASS

We start the backward pass with computing the derivative of the error function:

$$MSE' = -\left(y - y_f\right) = -\left(1.0 - 0.42\right) = -0.58$$

We then compute the error term for neuron F. The general way of doing this is to multiply the just-computed error term (for the layer that follows the current neuron) by the weight that connects this error to the current neuron and then multiply by the derivative of the activation function for the current neuron. This last layer is a little bit special in that there is no weight that connects the output to the error function (i.e., the weight is 1). Thus, the error term for neuron F is computed as

$$Error\ term\ f = MSE'\cdot y_f' = -0.58\cdot 0.42\cdot(1 - 0.42) = -0.14$$

In this formula, we computed the derivative of the logistic sigmoid function as $S\cdot(1-S)$.

We then move on to do the same computation for neuron G, where we now multiply the just-computed error term for neuron F by the weight that connects neuron F to neuron G and then multiply by the derivative of the activation function for neuron G:

$$Error\ term\ g = Error\ term\ f \cdot w_{gf1} \cdot y'_g = -0.14 \cdot 0.5 \cdot \left(1 - (-0.24)^2\right) = -0.066$$

In this formula, we computed the derivative of the tanh function as $(1 - tanh^2)$.

WEIGHT ADJUSTMENT

We are now ready to adjust the weights. We compute the adjustment value for a weight by multiplying the learning rate by the input value to the weight and then multiply by the error term for the neuron that follows the weight. The input values to the bias weights are 1. Note that for the weight connecting G to F, the input value is the output of neuron G (−0.25):

$$\Delta w_{xg0} = -lr \cdot 1 \cdot Error\ term\ g = -0.1 \cdot 1 \cdot (-0.066) = 0.0066$$

$$\Delta w_{xg1} = -lr \cdot x_1 \cdot Error\ term\ g = -0.1 \cdot (-0.9) \cdot (-0.066) = -0.0060$$

$$\Delta w_{xg2} = -lr \cdot x_2 \cdot Error\ term\ g = -0.1 \cdot 0.1 \cdot (-0.066) = 0.00066$$

$$\Delta w_{gf0} = -lr \cdot 1 \cdot Error\ term\ f = -0.1 \cdot 1 \cdot (-0.14) = 0.014$$

$$\Delta w_{gf1} = -lr \cdot y_g \cdot Error\ term\ f = -0.1 \cdot (-0.25) \cdot (-0.14) = -0.0035$$

We included a negative sign in the deltas above, so the updated weights can now be computed by simply adding the deltas to the existing weights:

$$w_{xg0} = 0.3 + 0.0066 = 0.3066$$

$$w_{xg1} = 0.6 - 0.0060 = 0.5940$$

$$w_{xg2} = -0.1 + 0.00066 = -0.0993$$

$$w_{gf0} = -0.2 + 0.014 = -0.1859$$

$$w_{gf1} = 0.5 - 0.0035 = 0.4965$$

Figure 3-7 shows the network annotated with key values computed during the forward and backward passes. The green and red arrows indicate the direction (green = positive, red = negative) and magnitude (wider is greater) of the resulting weight adjustments.

We can gain some intuition by looking at the magnitude and direction of the weight adjustments. Considering neuron G, we see that the weights for the bias term and the x_1 input are adjusted by an order of magnitude more than the weight for x_2 (0.0066 and −0.0060 for the bias and x_1 weights vs. 0.00066 for

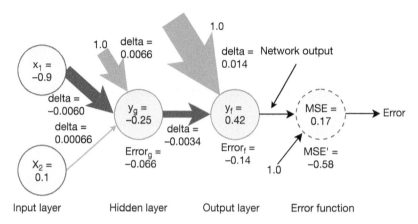

Figure 3-7 Network annotated with numbers computed during forward and backward passes. A green arrow represents a positive weight adjustment, and red represents a negative adjustment. The width of the arrow indicates the magnitude of the adjustment. Note that the actual weights are not shown in the figure; only the adjustment value (delta) is shown.

the x_2 weight). This makes sense because the magnitude of the bias input and x_1 is greater than the magnitude for x_2, and thus these two weights are more significant levers. Another observation is that the output is less than the desired output, so we want to increase the output of the network. This property, together with the sign of the input values that feed each weight, will determine the direction that the weight is adjusted. For example, the bias weight is increased, whereas the weight corresponding to input x_1 is decreased because the x_1 input is a negative value.

Just as for the perceptron learning algorithm, we provide a spreadsheet that replicates the computations. In addition, this spreadsheet contains multiple iterations of the algorithm. We recommend playing with that spreadsheet to get a better understanding of the computations and gain some intuition. The location of the spreadsheet can be found under "Programming Examples" in Appendix I.

The number of computations needed to compute the entire gradient is about the same as the number of computations that are needed for one forward pass. There is one derivative per neuron in the network and one multiplication per weight. This can be compared with the $N+1$ times the forward pass that would have been needed if we computed the gradient numerically using the brute-force method that we envisioned before describing the backpropagation algorithm. This makes it clear that the backpropagation algorithm is an efficient way of computing the gradient.

Backpropagation with Multiple Neurons per Layer

The network in the previous example was simple in that there was only a single path from each weight to the output of the network. Let us now consider networks that are a bit more complex with more layers, more neurons per layer, and even multiple outputs. These kinds of networks are shown in Figure 3-8.

The only difference for backpropagation in such networks is that when computing the error term for a neuron, we need to add up the weighted errors from all subsequent neurons instead of just a single weighted error term, as we did in our previous example. To clarify, for the leftmost network in Figure 3-8, when computing the error term for neuron M, we add together the weighted errors from O and P. Similarly, for the network in the middle, we add together the weighted errors from O, P, and Q. Finally, in the rightmost network, the network has two output neurons (R and S). The error function will need to be a function of both of these outputs to be able to compute error terms for both R and S. Then we use the weighted errors for R and S when computing the error terms for O, P, and Q. We will see examples of multioutput networks in Chapter 4, "Fully Connected Networks Applied to Multiclass Classification," but first we go over a programming example in which we apply backpropagation to a single-output network.

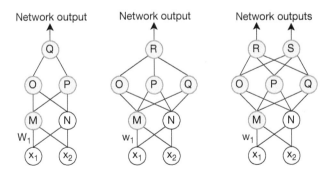

Figure 3-8 More complex networks. In this figure, the inputs are at the bottom, and layers are stacked vertically instead of horizontally. This is a common way to draw neural networks.

Programming Example: Learning the XOR Function

Now we have gotten to the point where it is time to check if the learning algorithm for multilevel feedforward networks works in practice. We use it to solve the XOR problem presented in Chapter 1, and we use the same three-neuron network that we used when we manually came up with a solution for the XOR problem. The network in Figure 3-9 shows neurons N_0, N_1, and N_2. We have omitted the bias inputs and not stated the weights in the figure. We use tanh as an activation function for N_0 and N_1 and the logistic sigmoid function as an activation function for the output neuron N_2, and we use MSE as the loss function.

The initialization code in Code Snippet 3-1 is similar to what we did for the perceptron example in Code Snippet 1-2. One thing to note is that we have started to use NumPy arrays so that we can make use of some NumPy functionality. The same holds for our random number generator (we call np.random.seed instead of just random.seed).

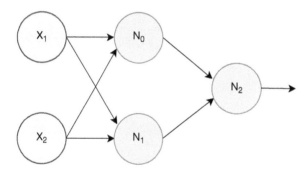

Figure 3-9 Network used to learn XOR problem.

Code Snippet 3-1 Init Code for XOR Learning Example

```
import numpy as np

np.random.seed(3) # To make repeatable
LEARNING_RATE = 0.1
index_list = [0, 1, 2, 3] # Used to randomize order

# Define training examples.
x_train = [np.array([1.0, -1.0, -1.0]),
```

```
        np.array([1.0, -1.0, 1.0]),
        np.array([1.0, 1.0, -1.0]),
        np.array([1.0, 1.0, 1.0])]
y_train = [0.0, 1.0, 1.0, 0.0] # Output (ground truth)
```

For the training examples, we have now changed the ground truth to be between 0.0 and 1.0 because, as previously described, we have decided to use the logistic sigmoid function as an activation function for the output neuron, and its output range does not go to −1.0 as the perceptron did.

Next, we declare variables to hold the state of our three neurons in Code Snippet 3-2. A real implementation would typically be parameterized to be able to choose number of inputs, layers, and number of neurons in each layer, but all of those parameters are hardcoded in this example to focus on readability.

Code Snippet 3-2 Variables Needed to Track State of Neurons

```
def neuron_w(input_count):
    weights = np.zeros(input_count+1)
    for i in range(1, (input_count+1)):
        weights[i] = np.random.uniform(-1.0, 1.0)
    return weights

n_w = [neuron_w(2), neuron_w(2), neuron_w(2)]
n_y = [0, 0, 0]
n_error = [0, 0, 0]
```

These are all the state variables that we need for each neuron for both the forward pass and the backward pass: weights (n_w), output (n_y),[3] and error term (n_error). We arbitrarily initialize the input weights to random numbers between −1.0 and 1.0, and we set the bias weights to 0.0. The reason to randomly initialize the input weights is to break the symmetry. If all neurons start with the same initial weights, then the initial output of all neurons in a layer would also be identical. This in turn would lead to all neurons in the layer behaving the same during backpropagation, and they would all get the same weight adjustments.

---

3. In our mathematical formulas, y refers to the ground truth, and $\hat{y}$ refers to the output of the network. By contrast, in our code examples, y (and variations thereof, such as n_y in this case) will generally refer to the network output. The ground truth is typically called y_train or sometimes train_label.

That is, we do not get any benefit from having multiple neurons in a layer. The bias weight does not need to be randomly initialized because it is sufficient to randomize the regular input weights to break the symmetry.

Initializing **bias weights** to **0.0** is a common strategy.

Code Snippet 3-3 starts with a function to print all the nine weights of the network (each `print` statement prints a three-element weight vector). The forward_pass function first computes the outputs of neurons 0 and 1 with the same inputs (the inputs from the training example) and then puts their outputs into an array, together with a bias value of 1.0, to use as input to neuron 2. That is, this function defines the topology of the network. We use tanh for the neurons in the first layer and the logistic sigmoid function for the output neuron.

Reading all this code can be pretty dull. We forgive you if you quickly skim it, as long as you pay attention to two things. First, not that much code is required to build a simple neural network. When we later move on to using a DL framework, amazing things can be done with even less code.

Code Snippet 3-3 Helper Functions for Backpropagation

```
def show_learning():
    print('Current weights:')
    for i, w in enumerate(n_w):
        print('neuron ', i,  ': w0 =', '%5.2f' % w[0],
                ', w1 =', '%5.2f' % w[1], ', w2 =',
                '%5.2f' % w[2])
    print('-----------------')
def forward_pass(x):
    global n_y
    n_y[0] = np.tanh(np.dot(n_w[0], x)) # Neuron 0
    n_y[1] = np.tanh(np.dot(n_w[1], x)) # Neuron 1
    n2_inputs = np.array([1.0, n_y[0], n_y[1]]) # 1.0 is bias
    z2 = np.dot(n_w[2], n2_inputs)
    n_y[2] = 1.0 / (1.0 + np.exp(-z2))
```

```python
def backward_pass(y_truth):
    global n_error
    error_prime = -(y_truth - n_y[2]) # Derivative of loss-func
    derivative = n_y[2] * (1.0 - n_y[2]) # Logistic derivative
    n_error[2] = error_prime * derivative
    derivative = 1.0 - n_y[0]**2 # tanh derivative
    n_error[0] = n_w[2][1] * n_error[2] * derivative
    derivative = 1.0 - n_y[1]**2 # tanh derivative
    n_error[1] = n_w[2][2] * n_error[2] * derivative

def adjust_weights(x):
    global n_w
    n_w[0] -= (x * LEARNING_RATE * n_error[0])
    n_w[1] -= (x * LEARNING_RATE * n_error[1])
    n2_inputs = np.array([1.0, n_y[0], n_y[1]]) # 1.0 is bias
    n_w[2] -= (n2_inputs * LEARNING_RATE * n_error[2])
```

The backward_pass function starts by computing the derivative of the error function and then computes the derivative of the activation function for the output neuron. The error term of the output neuron is computed by multiplying these two together. We then continue to backpropagate the error to each of the two neurons in the hidden layer. This is done by computing the derivatives of their activation functions and multiplying these derivatives by the error term from the output neuron and by the weight to the output neuron.

Finally, the adjust_weights function adjusts the weights for each of the three neurons. The adjustment factor is computed by multiplying the input by the learning rate and the error term for the neuron in question.

With all these pieces in place, the only remaining piece is the training loop shown in Code Snippet 3-4, which is somewhat similar to the training loop for the perceptron example in Code Snippet 1-4.

Code Snippet 3-4 Training Loop to Learn the *XOR* Function with Backpropagation

```python
# Network training loop.
all_correct = False
while not all_correct: # Train until converged
    all_correct = True
```

```
np.random.shuffle(index_list) # Randomize order
for i in index_list: # Train on all examples
    forward_pass(x_train[i])
    backward_pass(y_train[i])
    adjust_weights(x_train[i])
    show_learning() # Show updated weights
for i in range(len(x_train)): # Check if converged
    forward_pass(x_train[i])
    print('x1 =', '%4.1f' % x_train[i][1], ', x2 =',
          '%4.1f' % x_train[i][2], ', y =',
          '%.4f' % n_y[2])
    if(((y_train[i] < 0.5) and (n_y[2] >= 0.5))
            or ((y_train[i] >= 0.5) and (n_y[2] < 0.5))):
        all_correct = False
```

We pick training examples in random order, call the functions forward_pass, backward_pass, and adjust_weights, and then print out the weights with the function show_learning. We adjust the weights regardless whether the network predicts correctly or not. Once we have looped through all four training examples, we check whether the network can predict them all correctly, and if not, we do another pass over them in random order.

We want to point out a couple of issues before running the program. First, you might get a different result than our example produces given that the weights are initialized randomly. Similarly, there is no guarantee that the learning algorithm for a multilevel network will ever converge, and there are multiple reasons for this. It could be that the network itself simply cannot learn the function, as we saw in Chapter 2 when trying to learn XOR with a single perceptron. Another reason convergence might fail is if the parameters and initial values for the learning algorithm are initialized in a way that somehow prevents the network from learning. That is, you might need to tweak the learning rate and initial weights to make the network learn the solution.

Now let us run the program and look at the output. Here are the final printouts from our experiment:

```
Current weights:

neuron  0 : w0 =   0.70 , w1 =   0.77 , w2 =   0.76
```

```
neuron  1 : w0 =  0.40 , w1 = -0.58 , w2 = -0.56

neuron  2 : w0 = -0.43 , w1 =  1.01 , w2 =  0.89

- - - - - - - - - - - - - - -

x1 = -1.0 , x2 = -1.0 , y = 0.4255

x1 = -1.0 , x2 =  1.0 , y = 0.6291

x1 =  1.0 , x2 = -1.0 , y = 0.6258

x1 =  1.0 , x2 =  1.0 , y = 0.4990
```

The last four lines show the predicted output y for each x1, x2 combination, and we see that it implements the XOR function, since the output is greater than 0.5 when only one of the inputs is positive, which is exactly the XOR function.

Just as for the example that described backpropagation, we provide a spreadsheet that includes the mechanics of backpropagation for solving this XOR problem so that you can gain some insight through hands-on experimentation.

We did it! We have now reached the point in neural network research that was state-of-the art in 1986!

This was two years after the release of the first *Terminator* movie where a thinking machine was traveling back in time. Meanwhile, the research community is solving XOR, and we can conclude that more complicated AI was still science fiction at the time.

Network Architectures

Before moving on to solving a more complex classification problem in Chapter 4, we want to introduce the concept of network architectures. *Network architecture* is simply a name for how multiple units/neurons are connected when we build more complex networks.

Three key architectures are fundamental in most contemporary neural network applications:

- *Fully connected feedforward network.* We introduced this type of network when we solved the XOR problem. We learn more about fully connected feedforward networks in the next couple of chapters. As previously mentioned, there are no backward connections (also known as *loops* or *cycles*) in a feedforward network.

- *Convolutional neural network (CNN).* The key property of convolutional networks is that individual neurons do not have their own unique weights; they use the same weights as other neurons in the same layer. This is a property known as *weight sharing.* From a connectivity perspective, a CNN is similar to the fully connected feedforward network, but it has considerably fewer connections than a fully connected network. Instead of being fully connected, it is sparsely connected. CNNs have been shown to excel on image classification problems and therefore represent an important class of neural networks. The feature identifier described in Chapter 2 that recognized a pattern in a 3×3 patch of an image plays a central role in CNNs.

- *Recurrent neural network (RNN).* As opposed to the feedforward network, the RNN has backward connections; that is, it is not a directed acyclic graph (DAG), because it contains cycles. We have not yet shown any examples of recurrent connections, but they are studied in more detail in Chapter 9, "Predicting Time Sequences with Recurrent Neural Networks."

Figure 3-10 shows illustrations of the three network types.

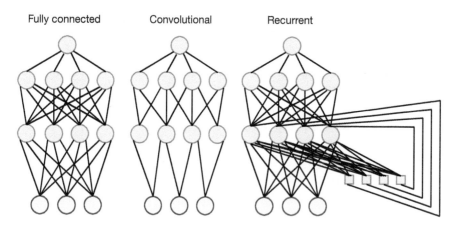

Figure 3-10 Three types of network architectures. Neurons in a convolutional network do not have unique weights but use the same weights (weight sharing) as other neurons in the same layer (not shown in the figure).

We discuss these architectures in more detail in later chapters. For now, it is helpful to know that the CNN has fewer connections than the fully connected network, whereas the RNN has more connections and some additional elements (the squares in the figure) needed to feed back the output to the input.

> **Fully connected, convolutional,** and **recurrent** networks are three key network architectures. More complex networks often consist of combinations of these three architectures.

It is often the case that networks are hybrids of these three architectures. For example, some layers of a CNN are often fully connected, but the network is still considered to be a CNN. Similarly, some layers of an RNN might not have any cycles, as seen in Figure 3-10. Finally, you can build a network from a combination of fully connected layers, convolutional layers, and recurrent layers to tap into properties of each type of architecture.

Concluding Remarks on Backpropagation

This chapter contained a lot of mathematical formulas, and you might have found it challenging to get through. However, there is no need to worry even if you did not read it all in detail. The rest of the book is less heavy on the formulas, and there will be more focus on different network architectures with a lot of programming examples.

Taking a step back, it is worth considering the overall effect of all the equations. We started with randomly initialized weights for the network. We then ran an example through it and hoped that its output value would match the ground truth. Needless to say, with weights selected at random, this is typically not the case. The next step was therefore to identify in what direction and by how much to modify each weight to make the network perform better. To do this, we needed to know how sensitive the output was to a change in each weight. This sensitivity is simply the definition of a partial derivative of the output with respect to the weight. That is, all in all, we needed to calculate a partial derivative corresponding to each weight. The backpropagation algorithm is a mechanical and efficient way of doing this.

In Chapter 4, we extend our multilevel network to be able to handle the case of multiple outputs. That will be the last time in this book that we implement the backpropagation algorithm in detail. After that, we move on to using a DL framework, which implements the details under the hood.

Chapter 4

Fully Connected Networks Applied to Multiclass Classification

In the first three chapters, we used our neural network to solve simple problems that set a foundation for learning deep learning (DL). We reviewed the basic workings of a neuron, how multiple neurons can be connected, and how to devise a suitable learning algorithm. Combining this knowledge, we built a network that can act as an XOR gate—something that arguably can be done in a simpler way.

In this chapter, we finally get to the point where we build a network that does something nontrivial. We show how to build a network that can take an image of a handwritten digit as input, identify which one of the ten digits 0 through 9 the image represents, and present this information on its outputs.

Before showing how to build such a network, we introduce some concepts that are central to both traditional machine learning (ML) and deep learning (DL), namely, datasets and generalization.

The programming example also provides more details on how to modify both the networks and the learning algorithm to handle the case of multiclass classification. This modification is needed because recognizing handwritten digits implies that each input example needs to be classified as belonging to one of ten classes.

Introduction to Datasets Used When Training Networks

As we saw in the previous chapters, we train a neural network by presenting an input example to the network. We then compare the network output to the expected output and use gradient descent to adjust the weights to try to make the network provide the correct output for a given input. A reasonable question is from where to get these training examples that are needed to train the network. For our previous toy examples this was not an issue. A two-input XOR gate has only four input combinations, so we could easily create a list of all combinations. This assumes that we interpret the input and output values as binary variables, which typically would not be the case but was true in our toy example.

In real applications of DL, obtaining these training examples can be a big challenge. One of the key reasons that DL has gained so much traction lately is that large online databases of images, videos, and natural language text have made it possible to obtain large sets of training data. If a supervised learning technique is used, it is not sufficient to obtain the input to the network. We also need to know the expected output, the ground truth, for each example. The process of associating each training input with an expected output is known as *labeling*, which is often a manual process. That is, a human must add a label to each example, detailing whether it is a dog, a cat, or a car. This process can be tedious because we often need many thousands of examples to achieve good results.

Starting to experiment with DL might be hard if the first step involved putting together a large collection of labeled training examples. Fortunately, other people have already done so and have made these examples publicly available. This is where the concept of datasets comes in. A (labeled) dataset consists of a collection of labeled training examples that can be used for training ML models. In this book, we will become familiar with a handful of different datasets within the fields of images, historical housing-price data, and natural languages. A section about datasets would not be complete without mentioning the classic Iris Dataset (Fisher, 1936), which is likely the first widely available dataset. It contains 150 instances of iris flowers, each instance belonging to one of three iris species. Each instance consists of four measurements (sepal length and width, petal length and width) of the particular plant. The Iris Dataset is extremely small and simple, so instead we start with a more complicated, although still simple, dataset: the Modified National Institute of Standards and Technology (MNIST) database of handwritten digits, also known simply as the MNIST dataset.

The MNIST dataset contains 60,000 training images and 10,000 test images. (We detail the differences between training and test images later in the chapter.) In addition to the images, the dataset consists of labels that describe which digit each image represents. The original images are 32×32 pixels, and the outermost two pixels around each image are blank, so the actual image content is found in the centered 28×28 pixels. In the version of the dataset that we use, the blank pixels have been stripped out, so each image is 28×28 pixels. Each pixel is represented by a grayscale value ranging from 0 to 255. The source of the handwritten digits is a mix of employees at the American Census Bureau and American high school students. The dataset was made available in 1998 (LeCun, Bottou, Bengio, et al., 1998). Some of the training examples are shown in Figure 4-1.

Figure 4-1 Images from the MNIST dataset. (Source: LeCun, Y., L. Bottou, Y. Bengio, and P. Haffner. "Gradient-Based Learning Applied to Document Recognition" in *Proceedings of the IEEE* vol. 86, no. 11 (Nov. 1998), pp. 2278–2324.)

EXPLORING THE DATASET

We start with getting our hands dirty by exploring the dataset a little bit. First, you need to download it according to the instructions in Appendix I under "MNIST." The file format is not a standard image format, but it is easy to read the files using the idx2numpy library.[1] Code Snippet 4-1 shows how we load the files into NumPy arrays and then print the dimensions of these arrays.

Code Snippet 4-1 Load the MNIST Dataset and Inspect Its Dimensions

```python
import idx2numpy
TRAIN_IMAGE_FILENAME = '../data/mnist/train-images-idx3-ubyte'
TRAIN_LABEL_FILENAME = '../data/mnist/train-labels-idx1-ubyte'
TEST_IMAGE_FILENAME = '../data/mnist/t10k-images-idx3-ubyte'
TEST_LABEL_FILENAME = '../data/mnist/t10k-labels-idx1-ubyte'

# Read files.
train_images = idx2numpy.convert_from_file(
    TRAIN_IMAGE_FILENAME)
train_labels = idx2numpy.convert_from_file(
    TRAIN_LABEL_FILENAME)
test_images = idx2numpy.convert_from_file(TEST_IMAGE_FILENAME)
test_labels = idx2numpy.convert_from_file(TEST_LABEL_FILENAME)

# Print dimensions.
print('dimensions of train_images: ', train_images.shape)
print('dimensions of train_labels: ', train_labels.shape)
print('dimensions of test_images: ', test_images.shape)
print('dimensions of test_images: ', test_labels.shape)
```

The output follows:

```
dimensions of train_images:  (60000, 28, 28)
dimensions of train_labels:  (60000,)
```

---

1. Our understanding is that this library is not available on all platforms. Many online programming examples use a comma-separated value (CSV) version of the MNIST dataset instead. Consult the book's website, http://www.ldlbook.com, for additional information.

```
dimensions of test_images:   (10000, 28, 28)
dimensions of test_images:   (10000,)
```

The image arrays are 3D arrays where the first dimension selects one of the 60,000 training images or 10,000 test images. The other two dimensions represent the 28×28 pixel values (integers between 0 and 255). The label arrays are 1D arrays where each element corresponds to one of the 60,000 (or 10,000) images. Code Snippet 4-2 prints out the first training label and image pattern, and the resulting output follows.

Code Snippet 4-2 **Print Out One Training Example**

```
# Print one training example.
print('label for first training example: ', train_labels[0])
print('---beginning of pattern for first training example---')
for line in train_images[0]:
    for num in line:
        if num > 0:
            print('*', end = ' ')
        else:
            print(' ', end = ' ')
    print('')
print('---end of pattern for first training example---')
```

```
label for first training example:   5
---beginning of pattern for first training example---




                        *  *  *  *  *  *  *  *  *  *  *  *
                  *  *  *  *  *  *  *  *  *  *  *  *  *  *  *
               *  *  *  *  *  *  *  *  *  *  *  *  *  *  *
               *  *  *  *  *  *  *  *  *  *  *
```

```
    *   *   *   *   *   *   *     *   *
        *   *   *   *   *
            *   *   *   *
            *   *   *   *
                *   *   *   *   *   *
                    *   *   *   *   *   *
                        *   *   *   *   *   *
                            *   *   *   *   *
                                *   *   *   *
                        *   *   *   *   *   *   *   *
                    *   *   *   *   *   *   *   *
                *   *   *   *   *   *   *   *   *   *
            *   *   *   *   *   *   *   *   *   *
        *   *   *   *   *   *   *   *   *   *
    *   *   *   *   *   *   *   *   *   *
    *   *   *   *   *   *   *
```

```
---end of pattern for first training example---
```

As shown from the example, it is straightforward to load and use this dataset.

HUMAN BIAS IN DATASETS

Because ML models learn from input data, they are susceptible to the *garbage-in/ garbage-out* (GIGO) problem. It is therefore important to ensure that any used dataset is of high quality. A subtle problem to look out for is if the dataset suffers from human bias (or any other kind of bias). For example, a popular dataset available online is the CelebFaces Attributes (CelebA) dataset (Liu et al., 2015), which is derived from the CelebFaces dataset (Sun, Wang, and Tang, 2013). It consists of a large number of images of celebrities' faces. Given how resource intensive it is to create a dataset, using a publicly available dataset makes sense.

However, this dataset is biased in that it contains a larger proportion of white, young-looking individuals than is representative of society. This bias can have the effect that a model trained on this dataset does not work well for older or dark-skinned individuals.

Even if you have good intentions, you must actively consider the unintended consequences. A dataset that is influenced by structural racism in society can result in a model that discriminates against minorities.

To illustrate this point, it is worth noting that even a simple dataset like MNIST is susceptible to bias. The handwritten digits in MNIST originate from the American Census Bureau employees and American high school students. Not surprisingly, the digits will therefore be biased toward how people in the United States write digits. In reality, there are slight variations in the handwriting style across different geographical regions in the world. In particular, in some European and Latin American countries, it is common to add a second horizontal line when writing the digit 7. If you explore the MNIST dataset, you will see that although such examples are included, they are far from the majority of the examples of the digit 7 (only two of the 16 examples in Figure 4-1 have a second horizontal line). That is, as expected, the dataset is biased toward how people in the United States write these digits. Therefore, it may well be that a model trained on MNIST works better for people in the United States than for people from countries that use a different style for the digit 7.

Although this example likely is harmless in most cases, it serves as a reminder of how easy it is to overlook problems with the input data. Consider a self-driving car where the model needs to distinguish between a human being and a less vulnerable object. If the model has not been trained on a diverse dataset with enough representation of minority groups, then it can have fatal consequences.

Note that a good dataset does not necessarily reflect the real world. Using the self-driving car example, it is very important that the car can handle rare but dangerous events, such as an airplane emergency landing on the road. Therefore, a good dataset might well contain an overrepresentation of such events compared to what is present in the real world. This is somewhat different from human bias but is another example of how easy it is to make mistakes when selecting the dataset and how such mistakes can lead to serious consequences. Gebru and colleagues (2018) proposed *datasheets for datasets* to address this problem. Each released dataset should be accompanied by a datasheet that describes its recommended use and other details.

TRAINING SET, TEST SET, AND GENERALIZATION

A reasonable question to ask is why we would go through the convoluted process of building a neural network to create a function that correctly predicts the output for a set of labeled examples. After all, it would be much simpler to just create a lookup table based on all the training examples. This brings us to the concept of generalization. The goal for an ML model is not just to provide correct predictions for data that it has been trained on; the more important goal is to provide correct predictions for previously unseen data. Therefore, we typically divide our dataset into a training dataset and a test dataset. The training dataset is used to train the model, and the test dataset is used to later evaluate how well the model was able to generalize to previously unseen data. If it turns out that the model does well on the training dataset but does poorly on the test dataset, then that is an indication that the model has failed to learn the general solution needed to solve similar but not identical examples. For example, it might have memorized only the specific training examples. To make this more concrete, consider the case of teaching children addition. You can tell them that $1 + 1 = 2$ and $2 + 2 = 4$ and $3 + 2 = 5$, and they might later successfully repeat the answer when asked, *What is 3 + 2?* yet be unable to answer, *What is 1 + 3?* or even *What is 2 + 3?* (reversing the order of 3 and 2 compared to the training examples). This would indicate that the child has memorized the three examples but not understood the concept of addition.

We think that even somebody who knows addition and multiplication typically uses memorized answers for many small numbers and invoke generalized knowledge only for large numbers. On the other hand, we could argue that this is an example of deep learning whereby we hierarchically combine simpler representations into the final answer.

We can monitor the training error and test error during training to establish whether the model is learning to generalize; see Figure 4-2.

In general, the training error will show a downward trend until it finally flattens out. The test error, on the other hand, will often show a U-curve where it decreases in the beginning but then at some point starts increasing again. If it starts increasing while the training error is still decreasing, then that is a sign that the model is overfitting to the training data. That is, it learns a function that does really well on the training data but that is not useful on not-yet-seen data. Memorizing individual examples from the training set is one strong form of overfitting, but other forms of overfitting also exist. Overfitting is not the only

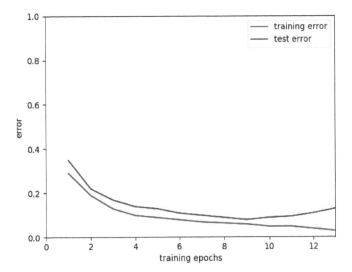

Figure 4-2 How training error and test error can evolve during learning process. (See a definition of *epochs* on page 111.)

reason for lack of generalization. It can also be that the training examples are simply not representative of the examples in the test set or, more important, the examples it will be used on in production.

An effective technique to avoid overfitting is to increase the size of the training dataset, but there exist a number of other techniques, collectively known as *regularization techniques,* which are designed to reduce or avoid overfitting. One obvious method is *early stopping.* Simply monitor the test error during training and stop when it starts to increase. It is often the case that the error fluctuates during training and is not strictly moving in one direction or another, so it is not necessarily obvious when it is time to stop. One approach to determining when to stop is to save the weights of the model at fixed intervals during training (i.e., create checkpoints of the model along the way). At the end of training, identify the point with the lowest test error from a chart like the one in Figure 4-2, and reload the corresponding model.

The goal is for the network to learn to **generalize.** If the network does well on the training set but not on the test set, then that indicates **overfitting** to the training set. We increase the training dataset size or employ **regularization techniques** to avoid overfitting. One such technique is **early stopping.**

HYPERPARAMETER TUNING AND TEST SET INFORMATION LEAKAGE

It is extremely important to not leak information from the test set during the training process. Doing so can lead to the model memorizing the test set, and we end up with an overly optimistic assessment of how good our model is compared to how the model will perform in production. Information leakage can happen in subtle ways. When training a model, there is sometimes a need to tune various parameters that are not adjusted by the learning algorithm itself. These parameters are known as *hyperparameters*, and we have already encountered a few examples: learning rate, network topology (number of neurons per layer, number of layers, and how they are connected), and type of activation function. Hyperparameter tuning can be either a manual or an automated process. If we change these hyperparameters on the basis of how the model performs on the test set, then the test set risks influencing the training process. That is, we have introduced information leakage from the test set to the training process.

One way to avoid such leakage is to introduce an intermediate *validation dataset*. It is used for evaluating hyperparameter settings before doing a final evaluation on the test dataset. In our examples in this book, we keep it simple and only do manual tuning of hyperparameters, and we do not use a separate validation set. We recognize that by not using a validation set we run the risk of getting somewhat optimistic results. We discuss hyperparameter tuning and the validation dataset concept in more detail in Chapter 5, "Toward DL: Frameworks and Network Tweaks."

> Using a **validation set** for **hyperparameter tuning** is an important concept. See "Using a Validation Set to Avoid Overfitting," in Chapter 5.

Training and Inference

Our experiments and discussion so far have focused on the process of training the network. We have interleaved testing of the network in the training process to assess how well the network is learning. The process of using the network without adjusting the weights is known as *inference* because the network is used to infer a result.

> **Training** refers to coming up with the weights for the network and is typically done before deploying it into production. In production, the network is often used only for **inference.**

It is often the case that the training process is done only before the network is deployed in a production setting, and once the network is deployed, it is used only for inference. In such cases, training and inference may well be done on different hardware implementations. For instance, training might be done on servers in the cloud, and inference might be done on a less powerful device such as a phone or tablet.

Extending the Network and Learning Algorithm to Do Multiclass Classification

In the programming example in Chapter 3, our neural network had only a single output, and we saw how we could use that to identify a certain pattern. Now we want to extend our network to be able to indicate to which of ten possible classes a pattern belongs. One naïve way of doing that would be to simply create ten different networks. Each of them is responsible for identifying one specific digit type. It turns out that this is a somewhat inefficient approach. Regardless of what digit we want to classify, there are some commonalities among the different digits, so it is more efficient if each "digit identifier" shares many of the neurons. This strategy also forces the shared neurons to generalize better and can reduce the risk of overfitting.

One way of arranging a network to do multiclass classification is to create one output neuron per class and teach the network to output a one-hot encoded number. One-hot encoding implies that only one of the outputs is excited (hot) at any one point in time. One-hot encoding is an example of a sparse encoding, which means that most of the signals are 0. Readers familiar with binary numbers might find this inefficient and wonder if it would make more sense to use binary encoding, to reduce the number of output neurons, but that is not necessarily the most suitable encoding for a neural network.

Binary encoding is an example of a dense encoding, which means that we have a good mix of 1s and 0s. We discuss sparse and dense encodings further in Chapter 12, "Neural Language Models and Word Embeddings." In Chapter 6, "Fully Connected Networks Applied to Regression," we describe how to use a variation of one-hot encoding to make the network express various levels of certainty in its classification when it is unsure to which class an example belongs. For now, one-hot serves the purpose for the example we are interested in.

Network for Digit Classification

This section presents the network architecture we use in our handwritten digit classification experiment. This architecture is far from optimal for this task, but our goal is to quickly get our hands dirty and demonstrate some impressive results while still relying only on the concepts that we have learned so far. Later chapters explore more advanced networks for image classification.

As previously described, each image contains 784 (28×28) pixels, so our network needs to have 784 input nodes. These inputs are fed to a hidden layer, which we have arbitrarily chosen to have 25 neurons. The hidden layer feeds an output layer consisting of ten neurons, one for each digit that we want to recognize. We use tanh as an activation function for the hidden neurons and the logistic sigmoid function for the output layer. The network is fully connected; that is, each neuron in one layer connects to all neurons in the next layer. With only a single hidden layer, this network does not qualify as a deep network. At least two hidden layers are needed to call it DL, although that distinction is irrelevant in practice. The network is illustrated in Figure 4-3.

One thing that seems odd in Figure 4-3 is that we are not explicitly making use of information about how the pixels are spatially related to each other. Would it not be beneficial for a neuron to look at multiple neighboring pixels together? The way they are laid out in the figure as a 1D vector instead of a 2D grid, it appears that information related to which pixels are neighboring each other is lost. Two pixels neighboring each other in the y-direction are separated by 28 input neurons. This is not completely true. In a fully connected network, there is no such thing as pixels being "separated." All 25 hidden neurons see all 784 pixels, so all pixels are equally close to each other from the perspective of a single neuron.

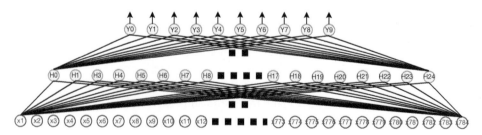

Figure 4-3 Network for digit classification. A large number of neurons and connections have been omitted from the figure to make it less cluttered. In reality, each neuron in a layer is connected to all the neurons in the next layer.

We could just as well have arranged the pixels and neurons in a 2D grid, but it would not have changed the actual connections. However, it is true that we are not communicating any prior knowledge about which pixels are neighboring each other, so if it truly is beneficial to somehow take the spatial relationship between pixels into account, then the network will have to learn this by itself. In Chapter 7, "Convolutional Neural Networks Applied to Image Classification," we learn about how to design networks in a way that does take the pixel location into account.

Loss Function for Multiclass Classification

When we solved the XOR problem, we used mean squared error (MSE) as our loss function. We can do the same in this image classification problem but must modify our approach slightly to account for our network having multiple outputs. We can do that by defining our loss (error) function as the sum of the squared error for each individual output:

$$Error = \frac{1}{m}\sum_{i=0}^{m-1}\sum_{j=0}^{n-1}(y_j^{(i)} - \hat{y}_j^{(i)})^2$$

where m is the number of training examples and n is the number of outputs. That is, in addition to the outer sum that computes the mean, we have now introduced an inner sum in the formula, which sums up the squared error for each output. To be perfectly clear, for a single training example, we end up with the following:

$$Error = \sum_{j=0}^{n-1}(y_j - \hat{y}_j)^2$$

where n is the number of outputs and $\hat{y}_j$ refers to the output value of neuron Y_j. To simplify our derivative later, we can play the same trick as before and divide by 2 because minimizing a loss function that is scaled by 0.5 will result in the same optimization process as minimizing the unscaled loss function:

$$Error : e(\hat{\boldsymbol{y}}) = \sum_{j=0}^{n-1} \frac{\left(y_j - \hat{y}_j\right)^2}{2}$$

In this formula, we wrote the error function as a function of $\hat{\boldsymbol{y}}$, which represents the output of the network. Note that $\hat{\boldsymbol{y}}$ is now a vector because the assumed network has multiple output neurons. Given this loss function, we can now compute the error term for each of the n output neurons, and once that is done, the backpropagation algorithm is no different from what we did in Chapter 3. The following formula shows the error term for neuron Y_1 with output value $\hat{y}_1$:

$$\frac{\partial e}{\partial \hat{y}_1} = \sum_{j=0}^{n-1} \frac{\partial \frac{\left(y_j - \hat{y}_j\right)^2}{2}}{\partial \hat{y}_1} = \frac{2(y_1 - \hat{y}_1)}{2} \cdot (-1) = -(y_1 - \hat{y}_1)$$

When computing the derivative of the loss function with respect to a specific output, all the other terms in the sum are constants (derivative is 0), which eliminates the sum altogether, and the error term for a particular neuron ended up being the same as in the single-output case. That is, the error term for neuron Y_2 is $-(y_2 - \hat{y}_2)$, or in the general case, the error term for Y_j is $-(y_j - \hat{y}_j)$.

If these formulas seem confusing, take heart: Things become clear as we now dive into the programming example implementation and see how all of this works out in practice.

Programming Example: Classifying Handwritten Digits

As mentioned in the preface, this programming example is heavily influenced by Nielsen's (2019) online book, but we have put our own personal touch on it to align with the organization of this book. Our implementation of the image classification experiment is a modified version of the implementation of the XOR learning example in Chapter 3, so the code should look familiar. One difference is that Code Snippet 4-3 contains some initializations where we now provide paths to the training and test datasets instead of defining the training values as hardcoded variables. We also tweaked the learning rate to 0.01 and introduced a parameter EPOCHS. We describe what an epoch is and discuss why we tweaked the learning rate later in the chapter. The dataset is assumed to be in the directory `../data/mnist/`, as described in the dataset section of Appendix I.

Code Snippet 4-3 Initialization Section for MNIST Learning

```
import numpy as np
import matplotlib.pyplot as plt
import idx2numpy
```

```
np.random.seed(7) # To make repeatable
LEARNING_RATE = 0.01
EPOCHS = 20
TRAIN_IMAGE_FILENAME = '../data/mnist/train-images-idx3-ubyte'
TRAIN_LABEL_FILENAME = '../data/mnist/train-labels-idx1-ubyte'
TEST_IMAGE_FILENAME = '../data/mnist/t10k-images-idx3-ubyte'
TEST_LABEL_FILENAME = '../data/mnist/t10k-labels-idx1-ubyte'
```

We have also added a function to read the datasets from files, as shown in Code
Snippet 4-4. A common theme in our coding examples is that there is some data
preprocessing required, which can be somewhat tedious, but unfortunately, there
is no good way around it.

Code Snippet 4-4 **Read Training and Test Data from Files**

```
# Function to read dataset.
def read_mnist():
    train_images = idx2numpy.convert_from_file(
        TRAIN_IMAGE_FILENAME)
    train_labels = idx2numpy.convert_from_file(
        TRAIN_LABEL_FILENAME)
    test_images = idx2numpy.convert_from_file(
        TEST_IMAGE_FILENAME)
    test_labels = idx2numpy.convert_from_file(
        TEST_LABEL_FILENAME)

    # Reformat and standardize.
    x_train = train_images.reshape(60000, 784)
    mean = np.mean(x_train)
    stddev = np.std(x_train)
    x_train = (x_train - mean) / stddev
    x_test = test_images.reshape(10000, 784)
    x_test = (x_test - mean) / stddev

    # One-hot encoded output.
    y_train = np.zeros((60000, 10))
    y_test = np.zeros((10000, 10))
```

```
    for i, y in enumerate(train_labels):
        y_train[i][y] = 1
    for i, y in enumerate(test_labels):
        y_test[i][y] = 1
    return x_train, y_train, x_test, y_test


# Read train and test examples.
x_train, y_train, x_test, y_test = read_mnist()
index_list = list(range(len(x_train))) # Used for random order
```

We already know the format of these files from the initial exercise where we explored the dataset. To simplify feeding the input data to the network, we reshape the images from two dimensions into a single dimension. That is, the arrays of images are now 2D instead of 3D. After this, we scale the pixel values and center them around 0. This is known as *standardizing* the data. In theory, this step should not be necessary because a neuron can take any numerical value as an input, but in practice, this scaling will be useful (we will explore why in Chapter 5). We first compute the mean and standard deviation of all the training values. We standardize the data by subtracting the mean from each pixel value and dividing by the standard deviation. This should be a familiar operation for anybody with a background in statistics. We do not go into the detail here but just mention what the overall idea is. By subtracting the mean from each pixel value, the new mean of all pixels will be 0. The standard deviation is a measure of how spread out the data is, and dividing by the standard deviation changes the range of the data values. This implies that if the data values were previously spread out (high and low values), then they will be closer to 0 after this operation. In our case, we started with pixel values between 0 and 255, and after standardization, we will end up with a set of floating-point numbers centered around and much closer to 0.

Knowing about data distributions and how to standardize them is an important topic, but we believe that you can make progress without understanding the details at this point.

Standard deviation is a measure of the spread of the data. A data point is standardized by subtracting the mean and dividing by the standard deviation.

One thing to note is that we are using the mean and standard deviation from the training data even when we standardize the test data. At first, this might look like a bug, but it is intentional. The thinking here is that we want to apply exactly the same transformation to the test data as we do to the training data. A natural question is whether it would be better to compute the overall average of both training and test data, but that should never be done because you then introduce the risk of leaking information from the test data into the training process.

You should apply exactly the same transformation to the test data as you apply to your training data. Further, never use the test data to come up with the transformation in the first place because that risks leaking information from the test data into the training process.

The next step is to one-hot encode the digit number to be used as a ground truth for our ten-output network. We one-hot encode by creating an array of ten numbers, each being 0 (using the NumPy zeros function), and then set one of them to 1.

Let us now move on to our implementation of the layer weights and the instantiation of our network in Code Snippet 4-5. This is similar to the XOR example, but there are a couple of changes. Each neuron in the hidden layer will have 784 inputs + bias, and each neuron in the output layer will have 25 inputs + bias. The for loop that initializes the weights starts with i=1 and therefore does not initialize the bias weight but just leaves it at 0 as before. The range for the weights is different than in our XOR example (magnitude of 0.1 instead of 1.0). We discuss that further in Chapter 5.

Code Snippet 4-5 Instantiation and Initialization of All Neurons in the System

```
def layer_w(neuron_count, input_count):
    weights = np.zeros((neuron_count, input_count+1))
    for i in range(neuron_count):
        for j in range(1, (input_count+1)):
            weights[i][j] = np.random.uniform(-0.1, 0.1)
    return weights
```

```
# Declare matrices and vectors representing the neurons.
hidden_layer_w = layer_w(25, 784)
hidden_layer_y = np.zeros(25)
hidden_layer_error = np.zeros(25)

output_layer_w = layer_w(10, 25)
output_layer_y = np.zeros(10)
output_layer_error = np.zeros(10)
```

Code Snippet 4-6 shows two functions that are used to report progress and to visualize the learning process. The function show_learning is called multiple times during training; it simply prints the current training and test accuracy and stores these values in two arrays. The function plot_learning is called at the end of the program and uses the two arrays to plot the training and test error (1.0 minus accuracy) over time.

Code Snippet 4-6 Functions to Report Progress on the Learning Process

```
chart_x = []
chart_y_train = []
chart_y_test = []
def show_learning(epoch_no, train_acc, test_acc):
    global chart_x
    global chart_y_train
    global chart_y_test
    print('epoch no:', epoch_no, ', train_acc: ',
          '%6.4f' % train_acc,
          ', test_acc: ', '%6.4f' % test_acc)
    chart_x.append(epoch_no + 1)
    chart_y_train.append(1.0 - train_acc)
    chart_y_test.append(1.0 - test_acc)

def plot_learning():
    plt.plot(chart_x, chart_y_train, 'r-',
```

```
            label='training error')
    plt.plot(chart_x, chart_y_test, 'b-',
            label='test error')
    plt.axis([0, len(chart_x), 0.0, 1.0])
    plt.xlabel('training epochs')
    plt.ylabel('error')
    plt.legend()
    plt.show()
```

Code Snippet 4-7 contains the functions for the forward and backward passes as well as for adjusting the weights. The forward_pass and backward_pass functions also implicitly define the topology of the network.

Code Snippet 4-7 Functions for Forward Pass, Backward Pass, and Weight Adjustment

```
def forward_pass(x):
    global hidden_layer_y
    global output_layer_y
    # Activation function for hidden layer
    for i, w in enumerate(hidden_layer_w):
        z = np.dot(w, x)
        hidden_layer_y[i] = np.tanh(z)
    hidden_output_array = np.concatenate(
        (np.array([1.0]), hidden_layer_y))
    # Activation function for output layer
    for i, w in enumerate(output_layer_w):
        z = np.dot(w, hidden_output_array)
        output_layer_y[i] = 1.0 / (1.0 + np.exp(-z))

def backward_pass(y_truth):
    global hidden_layer_error
    global output_layer_error
    # Backpropagate error for each output neuron
    # and create array of all output neuron errors.
    for i, y in enumerate(output_layer_y):
```

```
        error_prime = -(y_truth[i] - y) # Loss derivative
        derivative = y * (1.0 - y) # Logistic derivative
        output_layer_error[i] = error_prime * derivative
    for i, y in enumerate(hidden_layer_y):
        # Create array weights connecting the output of
        # hidden neuron i to neurons in the output layer.
        error_weights = []
        for w in output_layer_w:
            error_weights.append(w[i+1])
        error_weight_array = np.array(error_weights)
        # Backpropagate error for hidden neuron.
        derivative = 1.0 - y**2 # tanh derivative
        weighted_error = np.dot(error_weight_array,
                                output_layer_error)
        hidden_layer_error[i] = weighted_error * derivative

def adjust_weights(x):
    global output_layer_w
    global hidden_layer_w
    for i, error in enumerate(hidden_layer_error):
        hidden_layer_w[i] -= (x * LEARNING_RATE
                               * error) # Update all weights
    hidden_output_array = np.concatenate(
        (np.array([1.0]), hidden_layer_y))
    for i, error in enumerate(output_layer_error):
        output_layer_w[i] -= (hidden_output_array
                               * LEARNING_RATE
                               * error) # Update all weights
```

The forward_pass function contains two loops. The first one loops over all hidden neurons and presents the same input (the pixels) to them all. It also collects all the outputs of the hidden neurons into an array together with a bias term that can then be used as input to the neurons in the output layer. Similarly, the second loop presents this input to each of the output neurons and collects all the outputs of the output layer into an array that is returned to the caller of the function.

The backward_pass function is somewhat similar. It first loops through all the output neurons and computes the derivative of the loss function for each output neuron. In the same loop, it also computes the derivative of the activation function for each neuron. The error term for each neuron can now be calculated by multiplying the derivative of the loss function by the derivative of the activation function. The second loop in the function loops over all hidden neurons. For the hidden neurons, the error term is a little bit more complicated. It is computed as a weighted sum (computed as a dot product) of the backpropagated error from each of the output neurons, multiplied by the derivative of the activation function for the hidden neuron.

The adjust_weights function is straightforward, where we again loop over each neuron in each layer and adjust the weights using the input values and error terms.

Finally, Code Snippet 4-8 shows the network training loop. Instead of training until it gets everything correct, as we did in the XOR example, we now train for a fixed number of *epochs*. An epoch is defined as one iteration through all the training data. For each training example, we do a forward pass followed by a backward pass, and then we adjust the weights. We also track how many of the training examples were correctly predicted. We then loop through all the test examples and just record how many were correctly predicted. We use the NumPy argmax function to identify the array index corresponding to the greatest value; this decodes our one-hot encoded vector into an integer number. Before passing the input examples to forward_pass and adjust_weights, we extend each array with a leading 1.0 because these functions expect a bias term of 1.0 as the first entry in the array.

> The NumPy function argmax() is a convenient way to find the element that the network predicts as being most probable.

We do not do any backward pass or weight adjustments for the test data. The reason for this is that we are not allowed to train on the test data because that will result in an optimistic assessment of how well the network works. At the end of each epoch, we print out the current accuracy for both the training data and the test data.

Code Snippet 4-8 **Training Loop for MNIST**

```
# Network training loop.
for i in range(EPOCHS): # Train EPOCHS iterations
    np.random.shuffle(index_list) # Randomize order
    correct_training_results = 0
    for j in index_list: # Train on all examples
        x = np.concatenate((np.array([1.0]), x_train[j]))
        forward_pass(x)
        if output_layer_y.argmax() == y_train[j].argmax():
            correct_training_results += 1
        backward_pass(y_train[j])
        adjust_weights(x)

    correct_test_results = 0
    for j in range(len(x_test)): # Evaluate network
        x = np.concatenate((np.array([1.0]), x_test[j]))
        forward_pass(x)
        if output_layer_y.argmax() == y_test[j].argmax():
            correct_test_results += 1
    # Show progress.
    show_learning(i, correct_training_results/len(x_train),
                  correct_test_results/len(x_test))
plot_learning() # Create plot
```

We run the program and get periodic progress printouts. Here are the first lines:

```
epoch no: 0 , train_acc:  0.8563 , test_acc:  0.9157
epoch no: 1 , train_acc:  0.9203 , test_acc:  0.9240
epoch no: 2 , train_acc:  0.9275 , test_acc:  0.9243
epoch no: 3 , train_acc:  0.9325 , test_acc:  0.9271
epoch no: 4 , train_acc:  0.9342 , test_acc:  0.9307
epoch no: 5 , train_acc:  0.9374 , test_acc:  0.9351
```

As before, your results might be slightly different due to random variations. When the program completes, it produces a chart, as shown in Figure 4-4. We see that

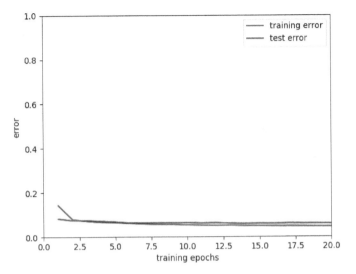

Figure 4-4 Training and test error when learning to classify digits

both the training and the test error are decreasing over time, and the test error does not yet start to increase at the right side of a chart. That is, we do not seem to have a significant problem with overfitting. We do see that the training error is lower than the test error. This is common and not a reason for concern as long as the gap is not too big.

As shown from the progress printouts and the chart, the test error quickly falls below 10% (accuracy is above 90%); that is, our simple network can classify more than nine of ten images correctly. This is an amazing result given how simple the program is! Consider how lengthy a program you would need to write if you did not use an ML algorithm but instead tried to hardcode information about what defines the ten different digits. The beauty of ML is that instead of hardcoding this information yourself, the algorithm discovers this information from the training examples. In the case of a neural network, this information is encoded into the network weights.

We do not know how lengthy a program with a hardcoded approach would be, as we are lazy and have not bothered to try to write one. We just assume that it would be long because other people claim that this is the case.

Now sit back and relax for a moment, and think about what you have learned. You have gone from the description of the single neuron to connecting multiple neurons and applying a learning algorithm that results in a system that can classify handwritten digits!

The dataset used in this example was released in 1998. This was one year after Judgment Day in *Terminator 2,* when the war against the machines started and 3 billion human lives ended. That is, there is still some difference between fact and fiction.

Mini-Batch Gradient Descent

So far, we have been using stochastic gradient descent (SGD) as opposed to true gradient descent. As previously described, the distinction is that for SGD we compute the gradient for a single training example before updating the weights, whereas for true gradient descent, we would loop through the entire dataset and compute the average of the gradients for all training examples. There is a clear trade-off here. Looping through the entire dataset gives us a more accurate estimate of the gradient, but it requires many more computations before we update any weights. It turns out that a good happy medium is to use a small set of training examples known as a mini-batch. This enables more frequent weight updates (less computation per update) than true gradient descent while still getting a more accurate estimate of the gradient than when using just a single example. Further, modern hardware implementations, and in particular graphics processing units (GPUs), do a good job of computing a full mini-batch in parallel, so it does not take more time than computing just a single example.

The terminology is confusing here. The true gradient descent method uses batches (the entire training dataset) and is also known as *batch* gradient descent. At the same time, there is the hybrid between batch and stochastic gradient descent that uses *mini-batches,* but the size of a mini-batch is often referred to as *batch size.* Finally, SGD technically refers only to the case where a single training example is used (mini-batch size = 1) to estimate the gradient, but the hybrid approach with mini-batches is often also referred to as SGD. Thus, it is not uncommon to read statements such as "stochastic gradient descent with a mini-batch size of 64." The mini-batch size is yet another parameter that can be tuned, and as of the writing of this book, anything close to the range of 32 to 256 makes sense to try. Finally, SGD (mini-batch size of 1, to be clear) is sometimes referred to as *online learning* because it can be used in an online setting where training examples are produced one by one instead of all being collected up front before learning begins.

From an implementation perspective, a mini-batch can be represented by a matrix because each individual training example is an array of inputs and an array of arrays becomes a matrix. Similarly, the weights for a single neuron can be arranged as an array, and we can arrange the weights for all neurons in a layer as a matrix. Computing the inputs to all activation functions for all neurons in the layer for all input examples in the mini-batch is then reduced to a single matrix-matrix multiplication. As previously mentioned, this is only a change in notation, but it does lead to significant performance improvements on platforms that have highly efficient matrix multiplication implementations. If you are interested, we have extended our plain Python implementation of our neural network to use matrices and mini-batches in Appendix F. It is perfectly fine to skip Appendix F, though, because these kinds of optimizations are already done (better) in the TensorFlow framework that is used in Chapter 5.

Concluding Remarks on Multiclass Classification

In this chapter, we implemented a network for handwritten digit classification. As opposed to the previous examples that all worked on binary classification, this was an example of a multiclass classification problem. The only real difference was to modify the network to have multiple output neurons and to define a suitable loss function. Apart from that, no new mechanisms were needed to train the network.

We should point out that the way we added multiple output neurons and the chosen loss function in this chapter are not the best-known solutions. We aimed for keeping things simple. In the next two chapters, we learn about better ways of doing this, namely, using the softmax output unit and the categorical cross-entropy loss function.

We also discussed the concept of dataset, a key part of enabling a model to learn. An important, and often overlooked, issue when selecting or creating a dataset is that it can pick up human biases, which may result in unintended consequences when using the trained model.

You are now well on your way toward exploring the field of DL. These first four chapters have been challenging because we introduced a lot of new concepts and implemented everything from scratch in Python. We believe that you will find the next couple of chapters easier when we introduce a DL framework that does much of the heavy lifting with respect to the low-level details. At the same time, you can feel comfortable knowing that there is no magic going on. The framework just provides efficient and easy-to-use implementations of the concepts that are described in this book.

Chapter 5

Toward DL: Frameworks and Network Tweaks

An obvious next step would be to see if adding more layers to our neural networks results in even better accuracy. However, it turns out getting deeper networks to learn well is a major obstacle. A number of innovations were needed to overcome these obstacles and enable deep learning (DL). We introduce the most important ones later in this chapter, but before doing so, we explain how to use a DL framework. The benefit of using a DL framework is that we do not need to implement all these new techniques from scratch in our neural network. The downside is that you will not deal with the details in as much depth as in previous chapters. You now have a solid enough foundation to build on. Now we switch gears a little and focus on the big picture of solving real-world problems using a DL framework. The emergence of DL frameworks played a significant role in making DL practical to adopt in the industry as well as in boosting productivity of academic research.

Programming Example: Moving to a DL Framework

In this programming example, we show how to implement the handwritten digit classification from Chapter 4, "Fully Connected Networks Applied to Multiclass Classification," using a DL framework. In this book, we have chosen to use the two frameworks TensorFlow and PyTorch. Both of these frameworks are popular and flexible. The TensorFlow versions of the code examples are interspersed throughout the book, and the PyTorch versions are available online on the book Web site.

TensorFlow provides a number of different constructs and enables you to work at different abstraction levels using different application programming interfaces (APIs). In general, to keep things simple, you want to do your work at the highest abstraction level possible because that means that you do not need to implement the low-level details. For the examples we will study, the Keras API is a suitable abstraction level. Keras started as a stand-alone library. It was not tied to TensorFlow and could be used with multiple DL frameworks. However, at this point, Keras is fully supported inside of TensorFlow itself. See Appendix I for information about how to install TensorFlow and what version to use.

Appendix I also contains information about how to install PyTorch if that is your framework of choice. Almost all programming constructs in this book exist both in TensorFlow and in PyTorch. The section "Key Differences between PyTorch and TensorFlow" in Appendix I describes some key differences between the two frameworks. You will find it helpful if you do not want to pick a single framework but want to master both of them.

The frameworks are implemented as Python libraries. That is, we still write our program as a Python program and we just import the framework of choice as a library. We can then use DL functions from the famework in our program. The initialization code for our TensorFlow example is shown in Code Snippet 5-1.

Code Snippet 5-1 Import Statements for Our TensorFlow/Keras Example

```
import tensorflow as tf
from tensorflow import keras
from tensorflow.keras.utils import to_categorical
import numpy as np
import logging
```

```
tf.get_logger().setLevel(logging.ERROR)
tf.random.set_seed(7)


EPOCHS = 20
BATCH_SIZE = 1
```

As you can see in the code, TensorFlow has its own random seed that needs to be set if we want reproducible results. However, this still does not guarantee that repeated runs produce identical results for all types of networks, so for the remainder of this book, we will not worry about setting the random seeds. The preceding code snippet also sets the logging level to only print out errors while suppressing warnings.

We then load and prepare our MNIST dataset. Because MNIST is a common dataset, it is included in Keras. We can access it by a call to keras.datasets. mnist and load_data. The variables train_images and test_images will contain the input values, and the variables train_labels and test_labels will contain the ground truth (Code Snippet 5-2).

Code Snippet 5-2 Load and Prepare the Training and Test Datasets

```
# Load training and test datasets.
mnist = keras.datasets.mnist
(train_images, train_labels), (test_images,
                               test_labels) = mnist.load_data()


# Standardize the data.
mean = np.mean(train_images)
stddev = np.std(train_images)
train_images = (train_images - mean) / stddev
test_images = (test_images - mean) / stddev


# One-hot encode labels.
train_labels = to_categorical(train_labels, num_classes=10)
test_labels = to_categorical(test_labels, num_classes=10)
```

Just as before, we need to standardize the input data and one-hot encode the labels. We use the function to_categorical to one-hot encode our labels instead of doing it manually, as we did in our previous example. This serves as an example of how the framework provides functionality to simplify our implementation of common tasks.

> If you are not so familiar with Python, it is worth pointing out that functions can be defined with optional arguments, and to avoid having to pass the arguments in a specific order, optional arguments can be passed by first naming which argument we are trying to set. An example is the **num_classes** argument in the **to_categorical** function.

We are now ready to create our network. There is no need to define variables for individual neurons because the framework provides functionality to instantiate entire layers of neurons at once. We do need to decide how to initialize the weights, which we do by creating an initializer object, as shown in Code Snippet 5-3. This might seem somewhat convoluted but will come in handy when we want to experiment with different initialization values.

Code Snippet 5-3 **Create the Network**

```
# Object used to initialize weights.
initializer = keras.initializers.RandomUniform(
    minval=-0.1, maxval=0.1)


# Create a Sequential model.
# 784 inputs.
# Two Dense (fully connected) layers with 25 and 10 neurons.
# tanh as activation function for hidden layer.
# Logistic (sigmoid) as activation function for output layer.
model = keras.Sequential([
    keras.layers.Flatten(input_shape=(28, 28)),
    keras.layers.Dense(25, activation='tanh',
                       kernel_initializer=initializer,
                       bias_initializer='zeros'),
    keras.layers.Dense(10, activation='sigmoid',
                       kernel_initializer=initializer,
                       bias_initializer='zeros')])
```

The network is created by instantiating a `keras.Sequential` object, which implies that we are using the Keras Sequential API. (This is the simplest API, and we use it for the next few chapters until we start creating networks that require a more advanced API.) We pass a list of layers as an argument to the `Sequential` class. The first layer is a `Flatten` layer, which does not do computations but only changes the organization of the input. In our case, the inputs are changed from a 28×28 array into an array of 784 elements. If the data had already been organized into a 1D-array, we could have skipped the `Flatten` layer and simply declared the two `Dense` layers. If we had done it that way, then we would have needed to pass an `input_shape` parameter to the first `Dense` layer because we always have to declare the size of the inputs to the first layer in the network.

The second and third layers are both `Dense` layers, which means they are fully connected. The first argument tells how many neurons each layer should have, and the `activation` argument tells the type of activation function; we choose `tanh` and `sigmoid`, where `sigmoid` means the *logistic sigmoid function*. We pass our `initializer` object to initialize the regular weights using the `kernel_initializer` argument. The bias weights are initialized to 0 using the `bias_initializer` argument.

One thing that might seem odd is that we are not saying anything about the number of inputs and outputs for the second and third layers. If you think about it, the number of inputs is fully defined by saying that both layers are fully connected and the fact that we have specified the number of neurons in each layer along with the number of inputs to the first layer of the network. This discussion highlights that using the DL framework enables us to work at a higher abstraction level. In particular, we use layers instead of individual neurons as building blocks, and we need not worry about the details of how individual neurons are connected to each other. This is often reflected in our figures as well, where we work with individual neurons only when we need to explain alternative network topologies. On that note, Figure 5-1 illustrates our digit recognition network at this higher abstraction level. We use rectangular boxes with rounded corners to depict a layer of neurons, as opposed to circles that represent individual neurons.

We are now ready to train the network, which is done by Code Snippet 5-4. We first create a `keras.optimizer.SGD` object. This means that we want to use stochastic gradient descent (SGD) when training the network. Just as with the initializer, this might seem somewhat convoluted, but it provides flexibility to adjust parameters for the learning process, which we explore soon. For now, we just set the learning rate to 0.01 to match what we did in our plain Python example. We then prepare the model for training by calling the model's `compile`

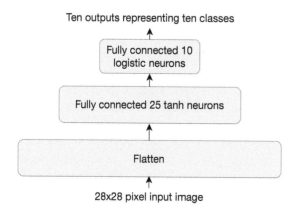

Ten outputs representing ten classes

Fully connected 10
logistic neurons

Fully connected 25 tanh neurons

Flatten

28x28 pixel input image

Figure 5-1 **Digit classification network using layers as building blocks**

function. We provide parameters to specify which `loss` function to use (where we use `mean_squared_error` as before), the optimizer that we just created and that we are interested in looking at the `accuracy` metric during training.

Code Snippet 5-4 **Train the Network**

```
# Use stochastic gradient descent (SGD) with
# learning rate of 0.01 and no other bells and whistles.
# MSE as loss function and report accuracy during training.
opt = keras.optimizers.SGD(learning_rate=0.01)

model.compile(loss='mean_squared_error', optimizer = opt,
              metrics =['accuracy'])

# Train the model for 20 epochs.
# Shuffle (randomize) order.
# Update weights after each example (batch_size=1).
history = model.fit(train_images, train_labels,
                    validation_data=(test_images, test_labels),
                    epochs=EPOCHS, batch_size=BATCH_SIZE,
                    verbose=2, shuffle=True)
```

We finally call the `fit` function for the model, which starts the training process. As the function name indicates, it fits the model to the data. The first two arguments specify the training dataset. The parameter `validation_data` is the test dataset. Our variables EPOCHS and BATCH_SIZE from the initialization code determine how many epochs to train for and what batch size we use. We had set BATCH_SIZE to 1, which means that we update the weight after a single training example, as we did in our plain Python example. We set verbose=2 to get a reasonable amount of information printed during the training process and set shuffle to True to indicate that we want the order of the training data to be randomized during the training process. All in all, these parameters match what we did in our plain Python example.

Depending on what TensorFlow version you run, you might get a fair number of printouts about opening libraries, detecting the graphics processing unit (GPU), and other issues as the program starts. If you want it less verbose, you can set the environment variable TF_CPP_MIN_LOG_LEVEL to 2. If you are using bash, you can do that with the following command line:

```
export TF_CPP_MIN_LOG_LEVEL=2
```

Another option is to add the following code snippet at the top of your program.

```
import os
os.environ['TF_CPP_MIN_LOG_LEVEL'] = '2'
```

The printouts for the first few training epochs are shown here. We stripped out some timestamps to make it more readable.

```
Epoch 1/20

loss: 0.0535 - acc: 0.6624 - val_loss: 0.0276 - val_acc: 0.8893

Epoch 2/20

loss: 0.0216 - acc: 0.8997 - val_loss: 0.0172 - val_acc: 0.9132

Epoch 3/20

loss: 0.0162 - acc: 0.9155 - val_loss: 0.0145 - val_acc: 0.9249

Epoch 4/20

loss: 0.0142 - acc: 0.9227 - val_loss: 0.0131 - val_acc: 0.9307
```

```
Epoch 5/20

loss: 0.0131 - acc: 0.9274 - val_loss: 0.0125 - val_acc: 0.9309

Epoch 6/20

loss: 0.0123 - acc: 0.9313 - val_loss: 0.0121 - val_acc: 0.9329
```

In the printouts, `loss` represents the mean squared error (MSE) of the training data, `acc` represents the prediction accuracy on the training data, `val_loss` represents the MSE of the test data, and `val_acc` represents the prediction accuracy of the test data. It is worth noting that we do not get exactly the same learning behavior as was observed in our plain Python model. It is hard to know why without diving into the details of how TensorFlow is implemented. Most likely, it could be subtle issues related to how initial parameters are randomized and the random order in which training examples are picked. Another thing worth noting is how simple it was to implement our digit classification application using TensorFlow. Using the TensorFlow framework enables us to study more advanced techniques while still keeping the code size at a manageable level.

We now move on to describing some techniques needed to enable learning in deeper networks. After that, we can finally do our first DL experiment in the next chapter.

The Problem of Saturated Neurons and Vanishing Gradients

In our experiments, we made some seemingly arbitrary changes to the learning rate parameter as well as to the range with which we initialized the weights. For our perceptron learning example and the XOR network, we used a learning rate of 0.1, and for the digit classification, we used 0.01. Similarly, for the weights, we used the range −1.0 to +1.0 for the XOR example, whereas we used −0.1 to +0.1 for the digit example. A reasonable question is whether there is some method to the madness. Our dirty little secret is that we changed the values simply because our networks did not learn well without these changes. In this section, we discuss the reasons for this and explore some guidelines that can be used when selecting these seemingly random parameters.

To understand why it is sometimes challenging to get networks to learn, we need to look in more detail at our activation function. Figure 5-2 shows our two S-shaped functions. It is the same chart that we showed in Figure 3-4 in Chapter 3, "Sigmoid Neurons and Backpropagation."

One thing to note is that both functions are uninteresting outside of the shown z-interval (which is why we showed only this z-interval in the first place). Both functions are more or less straight horizontal lines outside of this range.

Now consider how our learning process works. We compute the derivative of the error function and use that to determine which weights to adjust and in what direction. Intuitively, what we do is tweak the input to the activation function (z in the chart in Fig. 5-2) slightly and see if it affects the output. If the z-value is within the small range shown in the chart, then this will change the output (the y-value in the chart). Now consider the case when the z-value is a large positive or negative number. Changing the input by a small amount (or even a large amount) will not affect the output because the output is a horizontal line in those regions. We say that the neuron is *saturated*.

Saturated neurons can cause learning to stop completely. As you remember, when we compute the gradient with the backpropagation algorithm, we propagate the error backward through the network, and part of that process is to multiply the derivative of the loss function by the derivative of the activation function. Consider

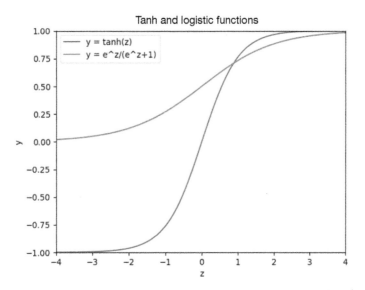

Figure 5-2 The two S-shaped functions tanh and logistic sigmoid

what the derivatives of the two activation functions above are for z-values of significant magnitude (positive or negative). The derivative is 0! In other words, no error will propagate backward, and no adjustments will be done to the weights. Similarly, even if the neuron is not fully saturated, the derivative is less than 1. Doing a series of multiplications (one per layer) where each number is a positive number less than 1 results in the gradient approaching 0. This problem is known as the *vanishing gradient problem*. Saturated neurons are not the only reason for vanishing gradients, as we will see later in the book.

> **Saturated** neurons are insensitive to input changes because their derivative is 0 in the saturated region. This is one cause of the **vanishing gradient** problem where the backpropagated error is 0 and the weights are not adjusted.

Initialization and Normalization Techniques to Avoid Saturated Neurons

We now explore how we can prevent or address the problem of saturated neurons. Three techniques that are commonly used—and often combined—are weight initialization, input standardization, and batch normalization.

WEIGHT INITIALIZATION

The first step in avoiding saturated neurons is to ensure that our neurons are not saturated to begin with, and this is where weight initialization is important. It is worth noting that, although we use the same type of neurons in our different examples, the actual parameters for the neurons that we have shown are much different. In the XOR example, the neurons in the hidden layer had three inputs including the bias, whereas for the digit classification example, the neurons in the hidden layer had 785 inputs. With that many inputs, it is not hard to imagine that the weighted sum can swing far in either the negative or positive direction if there is just a little imbalance in the number of negative versus positive inputs if the weights are large. From that perspective, it kind of makes sense that if a neuron has a large number of inputs, then we want to initialize the weights to a smaller value to have a reasonable probability of still keeping the input to the activation function close to 0 to avoid saturation. Two popular weight initialization strategies are Glorot initialization (Glorot and Bengio, 2010) and He initialization (He et al., 2015b). Glorot initialization is recommended for tanh- and sigmoid-based neurons, and He initialization is recommended for ReLU-based neurons (described later). Both of these take the number of inputs into account, and Glorot initialization also takes the number of outputs into account. Both Glorot and He initialization exist in two flavors, one that is based on a uniform random distribution and one that is based on a normal random distribution.

> We do not go into the formulas for **Glorot** and **He initialization**, but they are good topics well worth considering for further reading (Glorot and Bengio, 2010; He et al., 2015b).

We have previously seen how we can initialize the weights from a uniform random distribution in TensorFlow by using an initializer, as was done in Code Snippet 5-3. We can choose a different initializer by declaring any one of the supported initializers in Keras. In particular, we can declare a Glorot and a He initializer in the following way:

```
initializer = keras.initializers.glorot_uniform()
initializer = keras.initializers.he_normal()
```

Parameters to control these initializers can be passed to the initializer constructor. In addition, both the Glorot and He initializers come in the two flavors uniform and normal. We picked uniform for Glorot and normal for He because that is what was described in the publications where they were introduced.

If you do not feel the need to tweak any of the parameters, then there is no need to declare an initializer object at all, but you can just pass the name of the initializer as a string to the function where you create the layer. This is shown in Code Snippet 5-5, where the `kernel_initializer` argument is set to `'glorot_uniform'`.

Code Snippet 5-5 Setting an Initializer by Passing Its Name as a String

```
model = keras.Sequential([
        keras.layers.Flatten(input_shape=(28, 28)),
        keras.layers.Dense(25, activation='tanh',
                        kernel_initializer='glorot_uniform',
                        bias_initializer='zeros'),
        keras.layers.Dense(10, activation='sigmoid',
                        kernel_initializer='glorot_uniform',
                        bias_initializer='zeros')])
```

We can separately set `bias_initializer` to any suitable initializer, but as previously stated, a good starting recommendation is to just initialize the bias weights to 0, which is what the *'zeros'* initializer does.

INPUT STANDARDIZATION

In addition to initializing the weights properly, it is important to preprocess the input data. In particular, standardizing the input data to be centered around 0 and with most values close to 0 will reduce the risk of saturating neurons from the start. We have already used this in our implementation; let us discuss it in a little bit more detail. As stated earlier, each pixel in the MNIST dataset is represented by an integer between 0 and 255, where 0 represents the blank paper and a higher value represents pixels where the digit was written.[1] Most of the pixels will be either 0 or a value close to 255, where only the edges of the digits are somewhere in between. Further, a majority of the pixels will be 0 because a digit is sparse and does not cover the entire 28×28 image. If we compute the average pixel value for the entire dataset, then it turns out that it is about 33. Clearly, if we used the raw pixel values as inputs to our neurons, then there would be a big risk that the neurons would be far into the saturation region. By subtracting the mean and dividing by the standard deviation, we ensure that the neurons get presented with input data that is in the region that does not lead to saturation.

BATCH NORMALIZATION

Normalizing the inputs does not necessarily prevent saturation of neurons for hidden layers, and to address that problem Ioffe and Szegedy (2015) introduced batch normalization. The idea is to normalize values inside of the network as well and thereby prevent hidden neurons from becoming saturated. This may sound somewhat counterintuitive. If we normalize the output of a neuron, does that not result in undoing the work of that neuron? That would be the case if it truly was just normalizing the values, but the batch normalization function also contains parameters to counteract this effect. These parameters are adjusted during the learning process. Noteworthy is that after the initial idea was published, subsequent work indicated that the reason batch normalization works is different than the initial explanation (Santurkar et al., 2018).

Batch normalization (Ioffe and Szegedy, 2015) is a good topic for further reading.

---

1. This might seem odd because a value of 0 typically represents black and a value of 255 typically represents white for a grayscale image. However, that is not the case for this dataset.

There are two main ways to apply batch normalization. In the original paper, the suggestion was to apply the normalization on the input to the activation function (after the weighted sum). This is shown to the left in Figure 5-3.

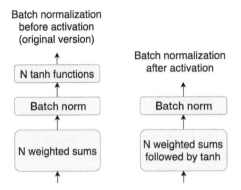

Figure 5-3 Left: Batch normalization as presented by Ioffe and Szegedy (2015). The layer of neurons is broken up into two parts. The first part is the weighted sums for all neurons. Batch normalization is applied to these weighted sums. The activation function (tanh) is applied to the output of the batch normalization operation. Right: Batch normalization is applied to the output of the activation functions.

This can be implemented in Keras by instantiating a layer without an activation function, followed by a BatchNormalization layer, and then apply an activation function without any new neurons, using the Activation layer. This is shown in Code Snippet 5-6.

Code Snippet 5-6 Batch Normalization before Activation Function

```
keras.layers.Dense(64),
keras.layers.BatchNormalization(),
keras.layers.Activation('tanh'),
```

However, it turns out that batch normalization also works well if done after the activation function, as shown to the right in Figure 5-3. This alternative implementation is shown in Code Snippet 5-7.

Code Snippet 5-7 Batch Normalization after Activation Function

```
keras.layers.Dense(64, activation='tanh'),
keras.layers.BatchNormalization(),
```

Cross-Entropy Loss Function to Mitigate Effect of Saturated Output Neurons

One reason for saturation is that we are trying to make the output neuron get to a value of 0 or 1, which itself drives it to saturation. A simple trick introduced by LeCun, Bottou, Orr, and Müller (1998) is to instead set the desired output to 0.1 or 0.9, which restricts the neuron from being pushed far into the saturation region. We mention this technique for historical reasons, but a more mathematically sound technique is recommended today.

We start by looking at the first couple of factors in the backpropagation algorithm; see Chapter 3, Equation 3-1(1) for more context. The formulas for the MSE loss function, the logistic sigmoid function, and their derivatives for a single training example are restated here:[2]

$$MSE \ loss: \ e(\hat{y}) = \frac{(y-\hat{y})^2}{2}, \qquad e'(\hat{y}) = -(y-\hat{y})$$

$$Logistic: \ S(z_f) = \frac{1}{1-e^{-z_f}}, \qquad S'(z_f) = S(z_f) \cdot (1-S(z_f))$$

We then start backpropagation by using the chain rule to compute the derivative of the loss function and multiply by the derivative of the logistic sigmoid function to arrive at the following as the error term for the output neuron:

$$Output \ neuron \ error \ term: \ \frac{\partial e}{\partial z_f} = \frac{\partial e}{\partial \hat{y}} \cdot \frac{\partial \hat{y}}{\partial z_f} = -(y-\hat{y}) \cdot S'(z_f)$$

We chose to not expand $S'(z_f)$ in the expression because it makes the formula unnecessarily cluttered. The formula reiterates what we stated in one of the previous sections: that if $S'(z_f)$ is close to 0, then no error will backpropagate through the network. We show this visually in Figure 5-4. We simply plot the derivative of the loss function and the derivative of the logistic sigmoid function as well as the product of the two. The chart shows these entities as functions of the output value y (horizontal axis) of the output neuron. The chart assumes that the desired output value (ground truth) is 0. That is, at the very left in the chart, the output value matches the ground truth, and no weight adjustment is needed.

---

2. In the equations in Chapter 3, we referred to the output of the last neuron as f to avoid confusing it with the output of the other neuron, g. In this chapter, we use a more standard notation and refer to predicted value (the output of the network) as $\hat{y}$.

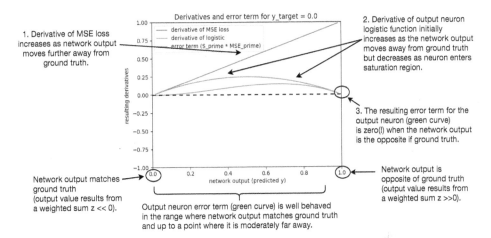

1. Derivative of MSE loss increases as network output moves further away from ground truth.

2. Derivative of output neuron logistic function initially increases as the network output moves away from ground truth but decreases as neuron enters saturation region.

3. The resulting error term for the output neuron (green curve) is zero(!) when the network output is the opposite if ground truth.

Network output matches ground truth (output value results from a weighted sum z << 0).

Network output is opposite of ground truth (output value results from a weighted sum z >>0).

Output neuron error term (green curve) is well behaved in the range where network output matches ground truth and up to a point where it is moderately far away.

Figure 5-4 Derivatives and error term as function of neuron output when ground truth y (denoted y_target in the figure) is 0

As we move to the right in the chart, the output is further away from the ground truth, and the weights need to be adjusted. Looking at the figure, we see that the derivative of the loss function (blue) is 0 if the output value is 0, and as the output value increases, the derivative increases. This makes sense in that the further away from the true value the output is, the larger the derivative will be, which will cause a larger error to backpropagate through the network. Now look at the derivative of the logistic sigmoid function. It also starts at 0 and increases as the output starts deviating from 0. However, as the output gets closer to 1, the derivative is decreasing again and starts approaching 0 as the neuron enters its saturation region. The green curve shows the resulting product of the two derivatives (the error term for the output neuron), and it also approaches 0 as the output approaches 1 (i.e., the error term becomes 0 when the neuron saturates).

Looking at the charts, we see that the problem arises from the combination of the derivative of the activation function approaching 0, whereas the derivative of the loss function never increases beyond 1, and multiplying the two will therefore approach 0. One potential solution to this problem is to use a different loss function whose derivative can take on much higher values than 1. Without further rationale at this point, we introduce the function in Equation 5-1 that is known as the *cross-entropy loss function*:

$$\text{Cross entropy loss}: e(\hat{y}) = -\left(y \cdot \ln(\hat{y}) + (1-y) \cdot \ln(1-\hat{y})\right)$$

Equation 5-1   Cross-entropy loss function

Substituting the cross-entropy loss function into our expression for the error term of the output neuron yields Equation 5-2:

$$\frac{\partial e}{\partial z_f} = \frac{\partial e}{\partial \hat{y}} \cdot \frac{\partial \hat{y}}{\partial z_f} = -\left(\frac{y}{\hat{y}} - \frac{1-y}{1-\hat{y}}\right) \cdot S'(z_f) = \hat{y} - y$$

Equation 5-2   Derivative of cross-entropy loss function and derivative of logistic output unit combined into a single expression

We spare you from the algebra needed to arrive at this result, but if you squint your eyes a little bit and remember that the logistic sigmoid function has some e^x terms, and we know that $ln(e^x) = x$ and the derivative of $ln(x) = x^{-1}$, then it does not seem farfetched that our seemingly complicated formulas might end up as something as simple as that. Figure 5-5 shows the equivalent plot for these functions. The y-range is increased compared to Figure 5-4 to capture more of the range of the new loss function. Just as discussed, the derivative of the cross-entropy loss function does increase significantly at the right end of the chart, and the resulting product (the green line) now approaches 1 in the case where the neuron is saturated. That is, the backpropagated error is no longer 0, and the weight adjustments will no longer be suppressed.

Although the chart seems promising, you might feel a bit uncomfortable to just start using Equation 5-2 without further explanation. We used the MSE loss function in the first place, you may recall, on the assumption that your likely familiarity with linear regression would make the concept clearer. We even stated that using MSE together with the logistic sigmoid function is not a good choice.

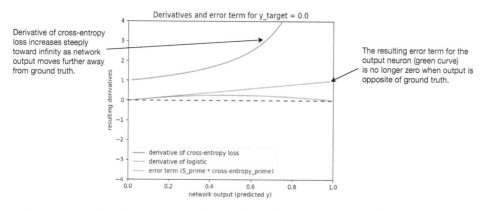

Figure 5-5 Derivatives and error term when using cross-entropy loss function. Ground truth y (denoted y_target in the figure) is 0, as in Figure 5-4.

We have now seen in Figure 5-4 why this is the case. Still, let us at least give you some insight into why using the cross-entropy loss function instead of the MSE loss function is acceptable. Figure 5-6 shows how the value of the MSE and cross-entropy loss function varies as the output of the neuron changes from 0 to 1 in the case of a ground truth of 0. As you can see, as y moves further away from the true value, both MSE and the cross-entropy function increase in value, which is the behavior that we want from a loss function.

Intuitively, by looking at the chart in Figure 5-6, it is hard to argue that one function is better than the other, and because we have already shown in Figure 5-4 that MSE is not a good function, you can see the benefit of using the cross-entropy loss function instead. One thing to note is that, from a mathematical perspective, it does not make sense to use the cross-entropy loss function together with a tanh neuron because the logarithm for negative numbers is not defined.

> As further reading, we recommend learning about information theory and maximum-likelihood estimation, which provides a rationale for the use of the cross-entropy loss function.

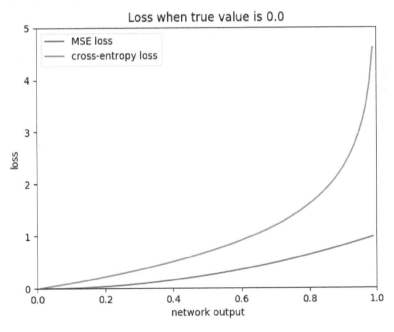

Figure 5-6 Value of the mean squared error (blue) and cross-entropy loss (orange) functions as the network output $\hat{y}$ changes (horizontal axis). The assumed ground truth is 0.

In the preceding examples, we assumed a ground truth of 0. For completeness, Figure 5-7 shows how the derivatives behave in the case of a ground truth of 1.

The resulting charts are flipped in both directions, and the MSE function shows exactly the same problem as for the case when ground truth was 0. Similarly, the cross-entropy loss function solves the problem in this case as well.

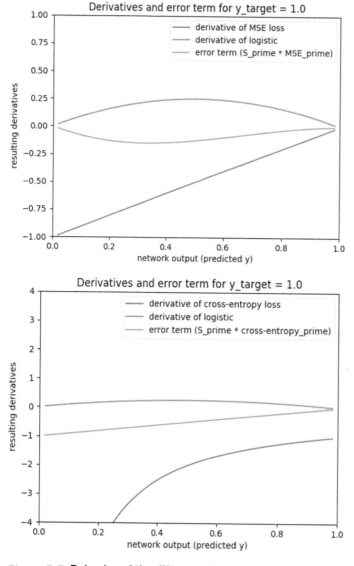

Figure 5-7 Behavior of the different derivatives when assuming a ground truth of 1. Top: Mean squared error loss function. Bottom: Cross-entropy loss function.

COMPUTER IMPLEMENTATION OF THE CROSS-ENTROPY LOSS FUNCTION

If you find an existing implementation of a code snippet that calculates the cross-entropy loss function, then you might be confused at first because it does not resemble what is stated in Equation 5-1. A typical implementation can look like that in Code Snippet 5-8. The trick is that, because we know that y in Equation 5-1 is either 1.0 or 0.0, the factors y and (1-y) will serve as an if statement and select one of the *ln* statements.

Code Snippet 5-8 Python Implementation of the Cross-Entropy Loss Function

```
def cross_entropy(y_truth, y_predict):
        if y_truth == 1.0:
            return -np.log(y_predict)
        else:
            return -np.log(1.0-y_predict)
```

Apart from what we just described, there is another thing to consider when implementing backpropagation using the cross-entropy loss function in a computer program. It can be troublesome if you first compute the derivative of the cross-entropy loss (as in Equation 5-2) and then multiply by the derivative of the activation function for the output unit. As shown in Figure 5-5, in certain points, one of the functions approaches 0 and one approaches infinity, and although this mathematically can be simplified to the product approaching 1, due to rounding errors, a numerical computation might not end up doing the right thing. The solution is to analytically simplify the product to arrive at the combined expression in Equation 5-2, which does not suffer from this problem.

In reality, we do not need to worry about these low-level details because we are using a DL framework. Code Snippet 5-9 shows how we can tell Keras to use the cross-entropy loss function for a binary classification problem. We simply state loss='binary_crossentropy' as an argument to the compile function.

Code Snippet 5-9 Use Cross-Entropy Loss for a Binary Classification Problem in TensorFlow

```
model.compile(loss='binary_crossentropy',
              optimizer = optimizer_type,
              metrics =['accuracy'])
```

In Chapter 6, "Fully Connected Networks Applied to Regression," we detail the formula for the categorical cross-entropy loss function, which is used for multiclass classification problems. In TensorFlow, it is as simple as stating `loss='categorical_crossentropy'`.

Different Activation Functions to Avoid Vanishing Gradient in Hidden Layers

The previous section showed how we can solve the problem of saturated neurons in the output layer by choosing a different loss function. However, this does not help for the hidden layers. The hidden neurons can still be saturated, resulting in derivatives close to 0 and vanishing gradients. At this point, you may wonder if we are solving the problem or just fighting symptoms. We have modified (standardized) the input data, used elaborate techniques to initialize the weights based on the number of inputs and outputs, and changed our loss function to accommodate the behavior of our activation function. Could it be that the activation function itself is the cause of the problem?

How did we end up with the tanh and logistic sigmoid functions as activation functions anyway? We started with early neuron models from McCulloch and Pitts (1943) and Rosenblatt (1958) that were both binary in nature. Then Rumelhart, Hinton, and Williams (1986) added the constraint that the activation function needs to be differentiable, and we switched to the tanh and logistic sigmoid functions. These functions kind of look like the sign function yet are still differentiable, but what good is a differentiable function in our algorithm if its derivative is 0 anyway?

Based on this discussion, it makes sense to explore alternative activation functions. One such attempt is shown in Figure 5-8, where we have complicated the activation function further by adding a linear term $0.2*x$ to the output to prevent the derivative from approaching 0.

Although this function might well do the trick, it turns out that there is no good reason to overcomplicate things, so we do not need to use this function. We remember from the charts in the previous section that a derivative of 0 was a problem only in one direction because, in the other direction, the output value already matched the ground truth anyway. In other words, it is fine with a derivative of 0 on one side of the chart. Based on this reasoning, we can consider

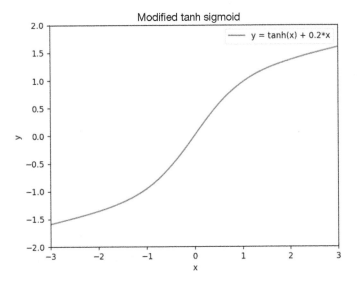

Figure 5-8 Modified tanh function with an added linear term

the rectified linear unit (ReLU) activation function in Figure 5-9, which has been shown to work for neural networks (Glorot, Bordes, and Bengio, 2011).

Now, a fair question is how this function can possibly be used after our entire obsession with differentiable functions. The function in Figure 5-9 is not

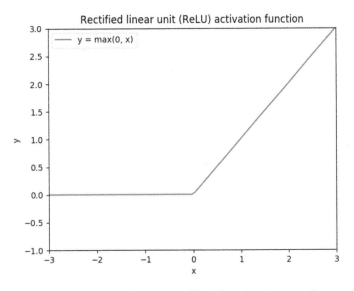

Figure 5-9 Rectified linear unit (ReLU) activation function

differentiable at $x = 0$. However, this does not present a big problem. It is true that from a mathematical point of view, the function is not differentiable in that one point, but nothing prevents us from just defining the derivative as 1 in that point and then trivially using it in our backpropagation algorithm implementation. The key issue to avoid is a function with a discontinuity, like the sign function. Can we simply remove the kink in the line altogether and use $y = x$ as an activation function? The answer is that this does not work. If you do the calculations, you will discover that this will let you collapse the entire network into a linear function and, as we saw in Chapter 1, "The Rosenblatt Perceptron," a linear function (like the perceptron) has severe limitations. It is even common to refer to the activation function as a *nonlinearity*, which stresses how important it is to not pick a linear function as an activation function.

The **activation function** should be **nonlinear** and is even often referred to as a **nonlinearity** instead of activation function.

An obvious benefit with the ReLU function is that it is cheap to compute. The implementation involves testing only whether the input value is less than 0, and if so, it is set to 0. A potential problem with the ReLU function is when a neuron starts off as being saturated in one direction due to a combination of how the weights and inputs happen to interact. Then that neuron will not participate in the network at all because its derivative is 0. In this situation, the neuron is said to be dead. One way to look at this is that using ReLUs gives the network the ability to remove certain connections altogether, and it thereby builds its own network topology, but it could also be that it accidentally kills neurons that could be useful if they had not happened to die. Figure 5-10 shows a variation of the ReLU function known as *leaky ReLU*, which is defined so its derivative is never 0.

Given that humans engage in all sorts of activities that arguably kill their brain cells, it is reasonable to ask whether we should prevent our network from killing its neurons, but that is a deeper discussion.

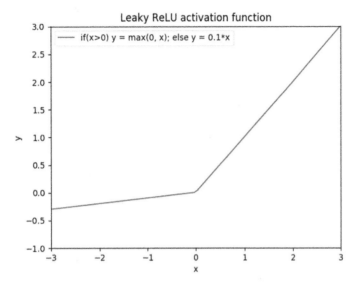

Figure 5-10 Leaky rectified linear unit (ReLU) activation function

All in all, the number of activation functions we can think of is close to unlimited, and many of them work equally well. Figure 5-11 shows a number of important activation functions that we should add to our toolbox. We have already seen tanh, ReLU, and leaky ReLU (Xu, Wang, et al., 2015). We now add the softplus function (Dugas et al., 2001), the exponential linear unit also known as *elu* (Shah et al., 2016), and the maxout function (Goodfellow et al., 2013). The maxout function is a generalization of the ReLU function in which, instead of taking the max value of just two lines (a horizontal line and a line with positive slope), it takes the max value of an arbitrary number of lines. In our example, we use three lines, one with a negative slope, one that is horizontal, and one with a positive slope.

All of these activation functions except for tanh should be effective at fighting vanishing gradients when used as *hidden units*. There are also some alternatives to the logistic sigmoid function for the *output units,* but we save that for Chapter 6.

The **tanh, ReLU, leaky ReLU, softplus, elu,** and **maxout** functions can all be considered for hidden units, but **tanh** has a problem with **vanishing gradients.**

There is no need to memorize the formulas for the activation functions at this point, but just focus on their shape.

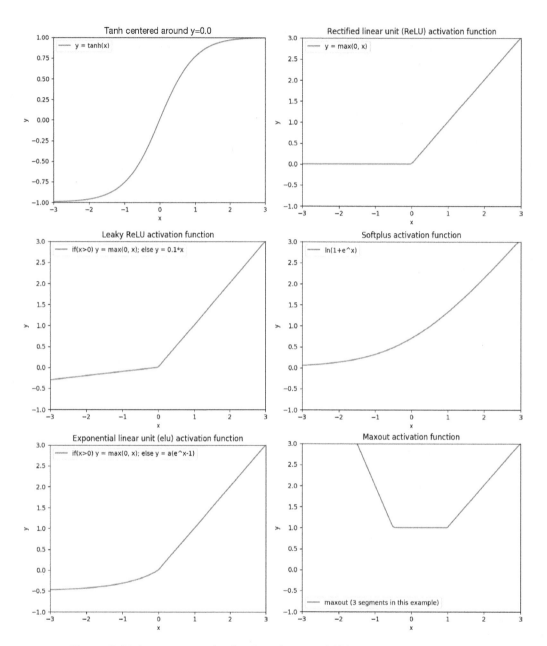

Figure 5-11 Important activation functions for hidden neurons. Top row: tanh, ReLU. Middle row: leaky ReLU, softplut. Bottom row: elu, maxout.

We saw previously how we can choose tanh as an activation function for the neurons in a layer in TensorFlow, also shown in Code Snippet 5-10.

Code Snippet 5-10 **Setting the Activation Function for a Layer**

```
keras.layers.Dense(25, activation='tanh',
                   kernel_initializer=initializer,
                   bias_initializer='zeros'),
```

If we want a different activation function, we simply replace `'tanh'` with one of the other supported functions (e.g., `'sigmoid'`, `'relu'`, or `'elu'`). We can also omit the `activation` argument altogether, which results in a layer without an activation function; that is, it will just output the weighted sum of the inputs. We will see an example of this in Chapter 6.

Variations on Gradient Descent to Improve Learning

There are a number of variations on gradient descent aiming to enable better and faster learning. One such technique is momentum, where in addition to computing a new gradient every iteration, the new gradient is combined with the gradient from the previous iteration. This can be likened with a ball rolling down a hill where the direction is determined not only by the slope in the current point but also by how much momentum the ball has picked up, which was caused by the slope in previous points. Momentum can enable faster convergence due to a more direct path in cases where the gradient is changing slightly back and forth from point to point. It can also help with getting out of a local minimum. One example of a momentum algorithm is Nesterov momentum (Nesterov, 1983).

Nesterov momentum, AdaGrad, RMSProp, and **Adam** are important variations (also known as *optimizers*) on gradient descent and stochastic gradient descent.

Another variation is to use an adaptive learning rate instead of a fixed learning rate, as we have used previously. The learning rate adapts over time on the basis of historical values of the gradient. Two algorithms using adaptive learning rate are *adaptive gradient,* known as *AdaGrad* (Duchi, Hazan, and Singer, 2011), and *RMSProp* (Hinton, n.d.). Finally, *adaptive moments,* known as *Adam* (Kingma and Ba, 2015), combines both adaptive learning rate and momentum. Although these algorithms adaptively modify the learning rate, we still have to set an initial learning rate. These algorithms even introduce a number of additional parameters that control how the algorithms perform, so we now have even more parameters to tune for our model. However, in many cases, the default values work well.

We do not go into the details of how to implement momentum and adaptive learning rate; we simply use implementations available in the DL framework. Understanding these techniques is important when tuning your models, so consider exploring these topics. You can find them summarized in *Deep Learning* (Goodfellow, Bengio, and Courville, 2016), or you can read the original sources (Duchi, Hazan, and Singer, 2011; Hinton, n.d.; Kingma and Ba, 2015; Nesterov, 1983).

Finally, we discussed earlier how to avoid vanishing gradients, but there can also be a problem with exploding gradients, where the gradient becomes too big in some point, causing a huge step size. It can cause weight updates that completely throw off the model. Gradient clipping is a technique to avoid exploding gradients by simply not allowing overly large values of the gradient in the weight update step. Gradient clipping is available for all optimizers in Keras.

Gradient clipping is used to avoid the problem of **exploding gradients**.

Code Snippet 5-11 shows how we set an optimizer for our model in Keras. The example shows stochastic gradient descent with a learning rate of 0.01 and no other bells and whistles.

Code Snippet 5-11 Setting an Optimizer for the Model

```
opt = keras.optimizers.SGD(lr=0.01, momentum=0.0, decay=0.0,
                           nesterov=False)
model.compile(loss='mean_squared_error', optimizer = opt,
              metrics =['accuracy'])
```

Just as we can for initializers, we can choose a different optimizer by declaring any one of the supported optimizers in Tensorflow, such as the three we just described:

```
opt = keras.optimizers.Adagrad(lr=0.01, epsilon=None)

opt = keras.optimizers.RMSprop(lr=0.001, rho=0.8, epsilon=None)

opt = keras.optimizers.Adam(lr=0.01, epsilon=0.1, decay=0.0)
```

In the example, we freely modified some of the arguments and left out others, which will then take on the default values. If we do not feel the need to modify the default values, we can just pass the name of the optimizer to the model compile function, as in Code Snippet 5-12.

Code Snippet 5-12 Passing the Optimizer as a String to the Compile Function

```
model.compile(loss='mean_squared_error', optimizer ='adam',
              metrics =['accuracy'])
```

We now do an experiment in which we apply some of these techniques to our neural network.

Experiment: Tweaking Network and Learning Parameters

To illustrate the effect of the different techniques, we have defined five different configurations, shown in Table 5-1. Configuration 1 is the same network that we studied in Chapter 4 and at beginning of this chapter. Configuration 2 is the same network but with a learning rate of 10.0. In configuration 3, we change the initialization method to Glorot uniform and change the optimizer to Adam with all parameters taking on the default values. In configuration 4, we change the activation function for the hidden units to ReLU, the initializer for the hidden layer to He normal, and the loss function to cross-entropy. When we described the cross-entropy loss function earlier, it was in the context of a binary classification problem, and the output neuron used the logistic sigmoid function. For multiclass classification problems, we use the categorical cross-entropy loss function, and it is paired with a different output activation known as *softmax*. The details of softmax are described in Chapter 6, but we use it here with the categorical

Table 5-1 Configurations with Tweaks to Our Network

CONFIGURATION	HIDDEN ACTIVATION	HIDDEN INITIALIZER	OUTPUT ACTIVATION	OUTPUT INITIALIZER	LOSS FUNCTION	OPTIMIZER	MINI-BATCH SIZE
Conf1	tanh	Uniform 0.1	Sigmoid	Uniform 0.1	MSE	SGD lr=0.01	1
Conf2	tanh	Uniform 0.1	Sigmoid	Uniform 0.1	MSE	SGD lr=10.0	1
Conf3	tanh	Glorot uniform	Sigmoid	Glorot uniform	MSE	Adam	1
Conf4	ReLU	He normal	Softmax	Glorot uniform	CE	Adam	1
Conf5	ReLU	He normal	Softmax	Glorot uniform	CE	Adam	64

Note: CE, cross-entropy; MSE, mean squared error; SGD, stochastic gradient descent.

cross-entropy loss function. Finally, in configuration 5, we change the mini-batch size to 64.

Modifying the code to model these configurations is trivial using our DL framework. In Code Snippet 5-13, we show the statements for setting up the model for configuration 5, using ReLU units with He normal initialization in the hidden layer and softmax units with Glorot uniform initialization in the output layer. The model is then compiled using categorical cross-entropy as the loss function and Adam as the optimizer. Finally, the model is trained for 20 epochs using a mini-batch size of 64 (set to BATCH_SIZE=64 in the init code).

Code Snippet 5-13 Code Changes Needed for Configuration 5

```
model = keras.Sequential([
    keras.layers.Flatten(input_shape=(28, 28)),
    keras.layers.Dense(25, activation='relu',
                   kernel_initializer='he_normal',
                   bias_initializer='zeros'),
    keras.layers.Dense(10, activation='softmax',
```

```
                        kernel_initializer='glorot_uniform',
                        bias_initializer='zeros')])

model.compile(loss='categorical_crossentropy',
              optimizer = 'adam',
              metrics =['accuracy'])

history = model.fit(train_images, train_labels,
              validation_data=(test_images, test_labels),
              epochs=EPOCHS, batch_size=BATCH_SIZE,
              verbose=2, shuffle=True)
```

If you run this configuration on a GPU-accelerated platform, you will notice that it is much faster than the previous configuration. The key here is that we have a batch size of 64, which results in 64 training examples being computed in parallel, as opposed to the initial configuration where they were all done serially.

The results of the experiment are shown in Figure 5-12, which shows how the test errors for all configurations evolve during the training process.

We use Matplotlib to visualize the learning process. A more powerful approach is to use the TensorBoard functionality that is included in TensorFlow. We highly recommend that you get familiar with TensorBoard when you start building and tuning your own models.

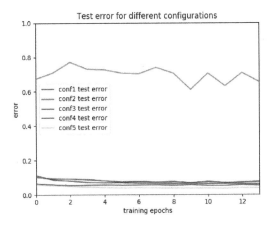

Figure 5-12 Error on the test dataset for the five configurations

Configuration 1 (red line) ends up at an error of approximately 6%. We spent a nontrivial amount of time on testing different parameters to come up with that configuration (not shown in this book).

Configuration 2 (green) shows what happens if we set the learning rate to 10.0, which is significantly higher than 0.01. The error fluctuates at approximately 70%, and the model never learns much.

Configuration 3 (blue) shows what happens if, instead of using our tuned learning rate and initialization strategy, we choose a "vanilla configuration" with Glorot initialization and the Adam optimizer with its default values. The error is approximately 7%.

For Configuration 4 (purple), we switch to using different activation functions and the cross-entropy error function. We also change the initializer for the hidden layer to He normal. We see that the test error is reduced to 5%.

For Configuration 5 (yellow), the only thing we change compared to Configuration 4 is the mini-batch size: 64 instead of 1. This is our best configuration, which ends up with a test error of approximately 4%. It also runs much faster than the other configurations because the use of a mini-batch size of 64 enables more examples to be computed in parallel.

Although the improvements might not seem that impressive, we should recognize that reducing the error from 6% to 4% means removing one-third of the error cases, which definitely is significant. More important, the presented techniques enable us to train deeper networks.

Hyperparameter Tuning and Cross-Validation

The programming example showed the need to tune different hyperparameters, such as the activation function, weight initializer, optimizer, mini-batch size, and loss function. In the experiment, we presented five configurations with some different combinations, but clearly there are many more combinations that we could have evaluated. An obvious question is how to approach this *hyperparameter tuning* process in a more systematic manner. One popular approach is known as *grid search* and is illustrated in Figure 5-13 for the case of two hyperparameters (optimizer and initializer). We simply create a grid with each axis representing a

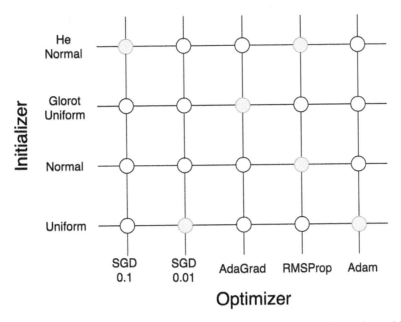

Figure 5-13 Grid search for two hyperparameters. An exhaustive grid search would simulate all combinations, whereas a random grid search might simulate only the combinations highlighted in green.

single hyperparameter. In the case of two hyperparameters, it becomes a 2D grid, as shown in the figure, but we can extend it to more dimensions, although we can only visualize, at most, three dimensions. Each intersection in the grid (represented by a circle) represents a combination of different hyperparameter values, and together, all the circles represent all possible combinations. We then simply run an experiment for each data point in the grid to determine what is the best combination.

What we just described is known as *exhaustive* grid search, but needless to say, it can be computationally expensive as the number of combinations quickly grows with the number of hyperparameters that we want to evaluate. An alternative is to do a random grid search on a randomly selected a subset of all combinations. This alternative is illustrated in the figure by the green dots that represent randomly chosen combinations. We can also do a hybrid approach in which we start with a random grid search to identify one or a couple of promising combinations, and then we can create a finer-grained grid around those combinations and do an exhaustive grid search in this zoomed-in part of the search space. Grid search is not the only method available for hyperparameter tuning. For hyperparameters that are differentiable, it is possible to do a gradient-based search, similar to the learning algorithm used to tune the normal parameters of the model.

Implementing grid search is straightforward, but a common alternative is to use a framework known as *sci-kit learn*.[3] This framework plays well with Keras. At a high level, we wrap our call to `model.fit()` into a function that takes hyperparameters as input values. We then provide this wrapper function to sci-kit learn, which will call it in a systematic manner and monitor the training process. The sci-kit learn framework is a general ML framework and can be used with both traditional ML algorithms as well as DL.

USING A VALIDATION SET TO AVOID OVERFITTING

The process of hyperparameter tuning introduces a new risk of overfitting. Consider the example earlier in the chapter where we evaluated five configurations on our test set. It is tempting to believe that the measured error on our test dataset is a good estimate of what we will see on not-yet-seen data. After all, we did not use the test dataset during the training process, but there is a subtle issue with this reasoning. Even though we did not use the test set to train the weights of the model, we did use the test set when deciding which set of hyperparameters performed best. Therefore, we run the risk of having picked a set of hyperparameters that are particularly good for the test dataset but not as good for the general case. This is somewhat subtle in that the risk of overfitting exists even if we do not have a feedback loop in which results from one set of hyperparameters guide the experiment of a next set of hyperparameters. This risk exists even if we decide on all combinations up front and only use the test dataset to select the best performing model.

We can solve this problem by splitting up our dataset into a training dataset, a validation dataset, and a test dataset. We train the weights of our model using the training dataset, and we tune the hyperparameters using our validation dataset. Once we have arrived at our final model, we use our test dataset to determine how well the model works on not-yet-seen data. This process is illustrated in the left part of Figure 5-14. One challenge is to decide how much of the original dataset to use as training, validation, and test set. Ideally, this is determined on a case-by-case basis and depends on the variance in the data distribution. In absence of any such information, a common split between training set and test set when there is no need for a validation set is 70/30 (70% of original data used for training and 30% used for test) or 80/20. In cases where we need a validation set for hyperparameter tuning, a typical split is 60/20/20. For datasets with low variance, we can get away with a smaller fraction being used for validation, whereas if the variance is high, a larger fraction is needed.

---

3. https://scikit-learn.org

CROSS-VALIDATION TO IMPROVE USE OF TRAINING DATA

One unfortunate effect of introducing the validation set is that we can now use only 60% of the original data to train the weights in our network. This can be a problem if we have a limited amount of training data to begin with. We can address this problem using a technique known as *cross-validation*, which avoids holding out parts of the dataset to be used as validation data but at the expense of additional computation. We focus on one of the most popular cross-validation techniques, known as *k-fold cross-validation*. We start by splitting our data into a training set and a test set, using something like an 80/20 split. The test set is not used for training or hyperparameter tuning but is used only in the end to establish how good the final model is. We further split our training dataset into k similarly sized pieces known as *folds*, where a typical value for k is a number between 5 and 10.

We can now use these folds to create k instances of a training set and validation set by using $k - 1$ folds for training and 1 fold for validation. That is, in the case of $k = 5$, we have five alternative instances of training/validations sets. The first one uses folds 1, 2, 3, and 4 for training and fold 5 for validation, the second instance uses folds 1, 2, 3, and 5 for training and fold 4 for validation, and so on.

Let us now use these five instances of train/validation sets to both train the weights of our model and tune the hyperparameters. We use the example presented earlier in the chapter where we tested a number of different configurations. Instead of training each configuration once, we instead train each configuration k times with our k different instances of train/validation data. Each of these k instances of the same model is trained from scratch, without reusing weights that were learned by a previous instance. That is, for each configuration, we now have k measures of how well the configuration performs. We now compute the average of these measures for each configuration to arrive at a single number for each configuration that is then used to determine the best-performing configuration.

Now that we have identified the best configuration (the best set of hyperparameters), we again start training this model from scratch, but this time we use all of the k folds as training data. When we finally are done training this best-performing configuration on all the training data, we can run the model on the test dataset to determine how well it performs on not-yet-seen data. As noted earlier, this process comes with additional computational cost because we must train each configuration k times instead of a single time. The overall process is illustrated on the right side of Figure 5-14.

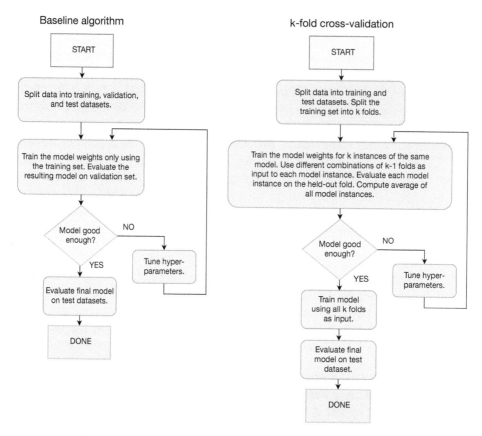

Figure 5-14 Tuning hyperparameters with a validation dataset (left) and using k-fold cross-validation (right)

We do not go into the details of why cross-validation works, but for more information, you can consult The Elements of Statistical Learning (Hastie, Tibshirani, and Friedman, 2009).

Concluding Remarks on the Path Toward Deep Learning

This chapter introduced the techniques that are regarded as enablers of the DL revolution that started with the AlexNet paper (Krizhevsky, Sutskever, and Hinton, 2012). In particular, the emergence of large datasets, the introduction of the ReLU unit and the cross-entropy loss function, and the availability of low-cost GPU-powered high-performance computing are all viewed as critical components that had to come together to enable deeper models to learn (Goodfellow et al., 2016).

We also demonstrated how to use a DL framework instead of implementing our models from scratch. The emergence of these DL frameworks is perhaps equally important when it comes to enabling the adoption of DL, especially in the industry.

With this background, we are now ready to move on to Chapter 6 and build our first deep neural network!

Chapter 6

Fully Connected Networks Applied to Regression

In Chapter 5, "Toward DL: Frameworks and Network Tweaks," we introduced several activation functions that can be used for *hidden* units in the network. In this chapter, we describe a couple of alternative *output* units and describe the problem types for which they are suitable. In addition, we introduce you to another dataset known as the *Boston Housing dataset* (Harrison and Rubinfeld, 1978).

The code example in this chapter will apply a deep neural network (DNN) to the Boston Housing dataset to predict home values based on a number of different variables and compare it with a simpler model. Predicting a home value is a different type of problem than the *classification problems* that we have studied so far. Instead of predicting which one of a discrete number of classes an input example belongs to, we want to predict a real-valued number. This is known as a *regression problem*. If you are interested in first learning some basic traditional machine learning (ML) techniques for regression and classification, consider reading Appendix A at this point.

In Chapter 4, "Fully Connected Networks Applied to Multiclass Classification," we briefly discussed overfitting (lack of generalization). We also introduced the concept of *regularization techniques,* which aim at improving generalization. In this chapter, we see practical examples of overfitting and introduce some different regularization techniques that can be used to mitigate this problem. Finally, we experiment with using these techniques to enable even deeper and larger networks to generalize.

Output Units

We saw in Chapter 5 how hidden units can use activation functions other than the logistic sigmoid and tanh activation functions. However, we mainly kept using the unit based on the logistic sigmoid function as output unit for the network, although we did briefly mention the softmax unit as well. In this section, we describe the softmax unit in more detail and introduce yet another type of output unit. The rationale for using the alternative hidden units was to avoid vanishing gradients. In contrast, the output unit is chosen on the basis of the type of problem the network is applied to. Figure 6-1 summarizes how to use different types of hidden units and output units for three problem types.

The choice of loss function is tightly coupled to the choice of output unit, where each type of output unit has a corresponding recommended loss function. We describe three different output units in this chapter. First, the logistic output unit is used for binary classification problems. Second, the softmax output unit is used

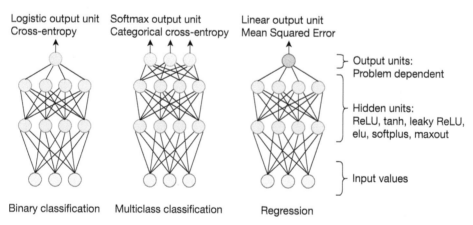

Figure 6-1 Types of unit to use for different networks and layers. The type of problem dictates the type of output unit and associated loss function. For the hidden layers, multiple alternatives are available. A good starting point is the rectified linear unit (ReLU). For some networks, other units result in better performance.

for multiclass classification problems. Third, the linear output unit is used for regression problems. The recommended loss functions corresponding to these three units are cross-entropy loss, categorical cross-entropy loss, and mean squared error.

As described in Chapter 5, a number of alternatives exist for the hidden units. We recommend starting with rectified linear unit (ReLU) and then trying other units as a part of the hyperparameter tuning process.

LOGISTIC UNIT FOR BINARY CLASSIFICATION

We start by revisiting the output unit based on the logistic sigmoid function, so we describe all the output units in one place. We have seen multiple times that the logistic sigmoid function is an example of an S-shaped function. The output ranges from 0 to 1, and it is similar to a step function but without discontinuities.

The typical use case for the logistic sigmoid function as output unit is for binary classification problems. The logistic sigmoid function is

$$\text{Logistic sigmoid function}: \ S(z) = \frac{1}{1+e^{-z}} = \frac{e^z}{e^z+1}$$

The **logistic sigmoid function** is used for **binary classification** problems.

The logistic sigmoid function expects a real-valued variable z (ranging from negative infinity to infinity) as its input. Because the output is between 0 and 1, we can interpret its output as a probability. The inverse of the logistic function is known as the *logit function* in the statistics literature. That is, the logit function converts a probability into a real-valued variable z. Therefore, the weighted sum z, which is the input to the logistic function, is sometimes referred to as a ***logit*** in the context of deep learning (DL).

As described in Chapter 5, the recommended loss function to use with this type of output neuron is the cross-entropy loss function:

$$\text{Cross-entropy loss}: \ e(y) = -\left(y \cdot \ln(\hat{y}) + (1-y) \cdot \ln(1-\hat{y})\right)$$

Where $\hat{y}$ is the output of the logistic sigmoid function and y is the desired output value.

SOFTMAX UNIT FOR MULTICLASS CLASSIFICATION

We now move on to the *softmax* unit. Its name makes it easy to confuse with the maxout and softplus units introduced in Chapter 5, but the softmax unit is unrelated to these apart from the words used in its name.

> **Softplus, maxout,** and **softmax** are all different units. Softplus and maxout units are typically used in hidden layers, whereas softmax is primarily used in the output layer.

The softmax unit (Goodfellow, Bengio, and Courville, 2016) is a generalization of the logistic sigmoid function but extended to multiple outputs. An important property of the logistic sigmoid function is that its output is always between 0 and 1, which implies that we can interpret the output as a probability (a probability always needs to be between 0 and 1). For example, in a classification problem, an output of 0.7 can be interpreted as a 70% probability that the presented inputs represent an object belonging to the assumed class and a 30% probability that it does not. When we looked at multiclass classification in Chapter 5, we simply used ten instances of the logistic sigmoid unit. The output from each unit indicated whether or not the input example belonged to the class, and we simply looked for the unit with the highest value. A problem with this approach is that if we were to add up the outputs from all ten output units, we would most likely end up with cases in which this sum was either less than or greater than 1. That is, it is unclear how to interpret the outputs as probabilities. The definition of the softmax function ensures that the sum of all the outputs is always 1, and thereby we can interpret the output as a probability. For instance, if the output for digit 3 is close to 0.3, the output for digit 5 is close to 0.7, and all other outputs are close to 0, then we can say that there is a 70% probability that the input example is 5 and a 30% probability that the input example is 3. The formula for the softmax function in the case of n outputs is

$$softmax(z)_i = \frac{e^{z_i}}{\sum_{j=1}^{n} e^{z_j}}$$

> The output from a **logistic sigmoid unit** can be interpreted as a probability for a **binary classification** problem, and the output from a **softmax unit** can be interpreted as a probability for a **multiclass classification** problem.

In other words, we compute the exponential function of the *logit* representing the output in question and divide it by the sum of the exponential functions for all the logits. If you compute this function for each output and sum them, then it should be clear why they all add up to 1, because the sum of all the numerators is exactly the same sum as is already in the denominator.

One thing to note is that the softmax output unit is not a function isolated to a single neuron, but it is an output function applied to a layer of neurons. That is, we compute the weighted sum z for each neuron in the output layer, and then we apply the softmax function on each of these z-instances. As given by the preceding formula, the output value for each neuron is dependent not only on z for that neuron but also on z from all other neurons in the layer. This is how we ensure that the sum of all outputs equals 1. The softmax layer is shown at the top of Figure 6-2, where the yellow circles compute only the weighted sum for each neuron, and the activation functions are applied in the yellow rectangle that has access to the logits (z-values) for all the neurons. The effect of the softmax function is shown at the bottom of the figure. In this example, where several logits

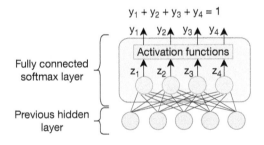

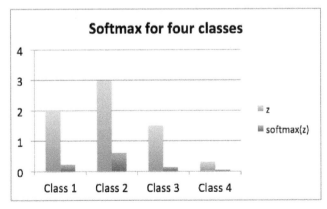

Figure 6-2 Top: Fully connected softmax layer. Bottom: Relationship between z and softmax(z).

are greater than 1, the corresponding outputs will be reduced to make the sum equal to 1.

The recommended loss function to use with this type of output neuron is the cross-entropy loss function for multiclass classification (Equation 6-1).

$$Cross\text{-}entropy\ loss:\ e(y) = -\sum_{c=1}^{N} y_c \ln\left(\hat{y}_c\right)$$

Equation 6-1 Cross-entropy loss function for multiclass classification

where N is the number of outputs (classes). You can see that if you set $N=2$ and expand the sum, it results in the cross-entropy loss function for the binary case that we have used before.

There is a subtle interaction[1] between the softmax output function and the cross-entropy loss function. The vector y_c is one-hot encoded so only a specific element, hereafter assumed to have index n, is nonzero. That implies that the sum in the cross-entropy loss function is reduced to the single term in the nth position. At first glance, this seems to imply that the values of the other outputs, corresponding to incorrect classes, do not matter. Those values will be multiplied by zero anyway, and the loss will be fully determined by the value of the nth element (that corresponds to the correct class). That seems odd. Is it not the role of the loss function to push all outputs in the right direction? It seems like that should include both rewarding the correct output (output n) and penalizing the incorrect ones. It turns out that this happens indirectly due to the presense of the softmax function. As described previously, the output value for each neuron in the softmax layer is dependent not only on z for that neuron but also on z from all other neurons in the layer. That implies that output n is dependent not only on the weights connected to neuron n but also on all other weights in the layer. Therefore, the partial derivatives corresponding to all the weights in the layer will be affected by the value of output n. As a result, all weights will be adjusted, even though only one of the output elements directly affects the overall loss function.

We saw an example of using the softmax function for multiclass classification in Chapter 5. We use it again in Chapter 7, "Convolutional Neural Networks Applied to Image Classification," when we study image classification with convolutional networks.

---

1. If you are a first-time reader, you can safely ignore this interaction, but it is worth mentioning for completeness, if only to be revisited at a later point.

LINEAR UNIT FOR REGRESSION

We now introduce the output unit that is used for the programming example in this chapter. Both the logistic sigmoid function and the softmax function are used for classification problems, but in this chapter, we study a regression problem in which we want to predict a numerical value instead of a probability. In a regression problem, the output is not restricted to the range 0 to 1 as it is for the classification problem. To provide a concrete example, in this chapter, we want to predict the sales price of a home—a dollar amount. This can be done with a *linear output unit*, which is as simple as not having an activation function at all, or more formally, the activation function is $y = z$. That is, the output from the unit is the weighted sum itself. As previously stated, if neurons in multiple layers are all based on linear activation functions, then these multiple layers can be collapsed into a single linear function, which is a reason that the linear unit mostly makes sense to use as an output unit from the network. Figure 6-3 shows two networks using linear activation functions. The output from each neuron is simply the weighted sum and can take on any value instead of being restricted to a specific output range. The network to the left has two stacked linear layers. In the network to the right, the two linear layers have been collapsed into a single layer, and it behaves equivalently. Therefore, stacking linear layers does not make sense.

The **linear output unit** is used to predict a value not limited to the range 0 to 1. The linear neuron uses the identity function as an activation function; that is, its output is the weighted sum of the inputs.

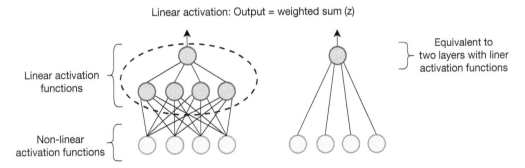

Linear activation: Output = weighted sum (z)

Figure 6-3 Left: Network where two layers have linear activation functions. The two layers in the dashed oval collapses into a single layer. Therefore, it is uncommon to stack linear layers. Right: Resulting simplified network.

A linear unit does not have a problem with saturation, so there is no need to use the cross-entropy loss function. It can be shown that a good loss function is the *mean squared error (MSE)*. This kind of makes sense because MSE is the error function used when doing linear regression, and that is exactly what a linear output unit is doing.

It can be shown that when using MSE as the loss function in the process of curve fitting a linear function, the **estimated weights** are **unbiased estimators** of the true weights, which is often a desirable property. For reading this book, you do not need to worry about knowing what an unbiased estimate is, but it can be considered for further reading. Both *Deep Learning* (Goodfellow et al., 2016) and *The Elements of Statistical Learning* (Hastie, Tibshirani, and Friedman, 2009) discuss these topics in the context of machine learning.

When predicting a value with a linear unit, accuracy is not a good metric. If you think about it, it is likely that no single test example will be exactly correctly predicted. For example, when predicting a price of a house, getting the exact dollar amount correct is extremely unlikely. Therefore, instead of computing how many of all predictions are correct, the real question is how close to the actual value each prediction is. From that perspective, a more meaningful metric when evaluating performance of the model is the mean absolute error.

Note the distinction between the loss function and the function used to evaluate how well the resulting model performs. The loss function is used by the learning algorithm, whereas other metrics, such as accuracy and mean absolute error, are more intuitive metrics for the user of the model.

The Boston Housing Dataset

The dataset used in this chapter is a small dataset originating from a 1978 study about how house prices are related to clean air (Harrison and Rubinfeld, 1978). It is broken up into a training set consisting of 404 examples and a test set consisting of 102 examples. Each example corresponds to a single house and consists of 13 input variables describing various aspects of the house and a single output variable corresponding to the price of the house. The input variables are shown in Table 6-1.

Table 6-1 The 13 Input Variables for the Boston Housing Dataset

FEATURE	DESCRIPTION
CRIM	Per capita crime rate by town
ZN	Proportion of residential land zoned for lots over 25,000 sq. ft.
INDUS	Proportion of nonretail business acres per town
CHAS	Charles River dummy variable (1 if tract bounds river; 0 otherwise)
NOX	Nitric oxides concentration (parts per 10 million)
RM	Average number of rooms per dwelling
AGE	Proportion of owner-occupied units built prior to 1940
DIS	Weighted distances to five Boston employment centers
RAD	Index of accessibility to radial highways
TAX	Full-value property-tax rate per $10,000
PTRATIO	Pupil–teacher ratio by town
B	$1{,}000(Bk - 0.63)^2$, where Bk is the proportion of blacks by town
LSTAT	Percentage lower status of the populations

They are all numeric variables, and their ranges vary, so just as for the Modified National Institute of Standards and Technology (MNIST) dataset, we must standardize the input data before using it.

Programming Example: Predicting House Prices with a DNN

Like the MNIST, the Boston Housing dataset is included in Keras, so it is simple to access using `keras.datasets.boston_housing`. We standardize both the training and test data by using the mean and standard deviation from the training data (Code Snippet 6-1). The parameter `axis=0` ensures that we compute the mean and standard deviation for each input variable separately. The resulting mean (and standard deviation) is a vector of means instead of a single value. That is, the standardized value of the nitric oxides concentration is not affected by the values of the per capita crime rate or any of the other variables.

Code Snippet 6-1 DNN with Two Hidden Layers Used to Predict House Prices

```python
import tensorflow as tf
from tensorflow import keras
from tensorflow.keras.models import Sequential
from tensorflow.keras.layers import Dense
import numpy as np
import logging
tf.get_logger().setLevel(logging.ERROR)

EPOCHS = 500
BATCH_SIZE = 16

# Read and standardize the data.
boston_housing = keras.datasets.boston_housing
(raw_x_train, y_train), (raw_x_test,
    y_test) = boston_housing.load_data()
x_mean = np.mean(raw_x_train, axis=0)
x_stddev = np.std(raw_x_train, axis=0)
x_train =(raw_x_train - x_mean) / x_stddev
x_test =(raw_x_test - x_mean) / x_stddev

# Create and train model.
model = Sequential()
model.add(Dense(64, activation='relu', input_shape=[13]))
model.add(Dense(64, activation='relu')) # We are doing DL!
model.add(Dense(1, activation='linear'))
model.compile(loss='mean_squared_error', optimizer='adam',
              metrics =['mean_absolute_error'])
model.summary()
history = model.fit(x_train, y_train, validation_data=(
    x_test, y_test), epochs=EPOCHS, batch_size=BATCH_SIZE,
    verbose=2, shuffle=True)
```

```
# Print first 4 predictions.
predictions = model.predict(x_test)
for i in range(0, 4):
    print('Prediction: ', predictions[i],
          ', true value: ', y_test[i])
```

We then create the model. Here we use a different syntax than in Chapter 5. There, the layers were passed as parameters to the constructor of the model. A different way of doing it is to first instantiate the model object without any layers, and then add them one by one using the member method add(). As long as we work with relatively few layers, the approach taken just depends on user preference, but for deep models with tens of layers, the code typically gets more readable and maintainable by adding the layers one by one. One example of this is a deep model of identical layers where the layers can be added to the model with a for loop, which makes for a much more compact model description.

We define our network to have two hidden layers, so we are now officially doing DL! A reasonable question is why we want more hidden layers. We previously saw that having at least one hidden layer is beneficial because it addresses the limitation related to linear separability that applies to a single-layer network, but we do not have an equally crisp reason for having multiple hidden layers. It can even be shown that, given enough neurons, it is sufficient with a single hidden layer to be able to approximate any continuous function. However, empirically it has been shown that adding more layers can lead to better-performing (from an accuracy perspective) networks. One way to think about this is that having more hidden layers can enable the network to hierarchically combine features at increasing abstraction levels. We will see more concrete examples of this in Chapter 7.

The two hidden layers in our network implementation have 64 ReLU neurons each, where the first layer is declared to have 13 inputs to match the dataset. The output layer consists of a single neuron with a linear activation function. We use MSE as the loss function and use the Adam optimizer. We tell the compile method that we are interested in seeing the metric mean absolute error. The distinction between the loss argument and the metrics argument is that the former is used by the backpropagation algorithm to compute the gradient, and the latter is just being printed out for our information.

We print out a summary of the model with model.summary() and then start training. After the training is done, we use our model to predict the price for the entire test set and then print out the first four predictions and the correct values so we can get an idea of how correct the model is. We end up with a mean absolute error of 2.511 on the test set, and the predictions for the first four test examples are as follows:

```
Prediction:   [7.7588124] ,  true value:   7.2
Prediction:   [19.762562] ,  true value:   18.8
Prediction:   [20.16102]  ,  true value:   19.0
Prediction:   [32.758865] ,  true value:   27.0
```

We note that they seem to make sense. The reason that the prediction value is within square brackets is that each element in the prediction array is an array itself with a single value in each array. We could have addressed that by indexing it like the following: predictions[i, 0].

A common theme when working with TensorFlow is that both input data and output data are in multidimensional arrays, and it sometimes takes a few tries to get it right.

As we can see, it was simple to create an initial model and do some reasonable predictions, but it is hard to say how good these predictions are. This brings us to a question that always makes sense to ask: Do we need DL to solve the problem? As we saw in Chapter 5, it can be nontrivial to tune a neural network. If there are simpler ways of solving the problem, then those are preferable. Given that this is a regression problem, it is natural to compare it to simple linear regression,[2] that is, just compute a weighted sum of all the inputs and a bias:

$$y = w_0 + w_1 x_1 + w_2 x_2 + \cdots + w_{13} x_{13}$$

We can easily do that in our program[3] by defining only a single layer having a single neuron with a linear activation function. We use just the output layer without any hidden layers, but we also need to define the number of inputs because the output layer is now also the first layer:

```
model.add(Dense(1, activation='linear', input_shape=[13]))
```

---

2. We think you can follow this discussion even if you are not familiar with linear regression, but if you do want some more background, consider reading Appendix A.

3. In this implementation, we use gradient descent to find a numerical solution to our linear regression problem. This might seem foreign to you if you have previously learned how to solve linear regression analytically using *normal equations*.

We run the model and end up with a mean absolute error of 10.24 on the test set, and the first four predictions of the test set as follows:

```
Prediction:   0.18469143 , true value:   7.2
Prediction:   10.847551 , true value:   18.8
Prediction:   10.989416 , true value:   19.0
Prediction:   22.755947 , true value:   27.0
```

Clearly, our deep model did better than the linear model,[4] which is encouraging! Now let us look at whether our model seems to generalize well. Figure 6-4 shows how the training and test errors are changing as a function of the number of training epochs.

We see that the training error is steadily decreasing, but the test error is flat. This is a clear indication of overfitting; that is, the model is memorizing the training data, but it does not manage to generalize to unseen data. We need techniques to modify our network to address this behavior, which is described next.

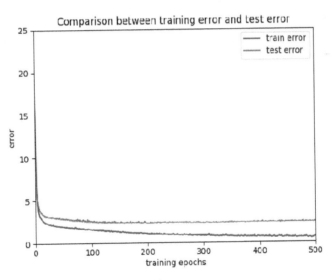

Figure 6-4 Comparison between training and test errors for our three-layer DNN

---

4. It is possible to improve the results from the linear regression model by first computing variations on the input variables. This is known as *feature engineering*. See Appendix A for more details.

Improving Generalization with Regularization

Techniques that are intended to improve generalization are collectively known as *regularization techniques*. Specifically, a regularization technique is a technique that aims at reducing the gap between training error and test error. One regularization technique is early stopping (discussed in Chapter 4), but that technique is helpful only if the test error shows a U-shaped curve, that is, if the test error starts increasing after a certain time. This is not the case in our present example, and we therefore need to look at other techniques.

One common regularization technique is *weight decay*. Weight decay is implemented by adding a penalty term to the loss function:

$$Loss = cross\text{-}entropy + \lambda \sum_{i=0}^{n} |w_i|$$

where λ is a constant and w_0, w_1, ..., w_n are the weights for all the neurons in the model. Because the learning algorithm tries to minimize the loss function, this error term provides incentive to minimize the weights. This results in decreasing weights that do not contribute significantly to solving the general problem. In particular, weights that are helpful only for specific input examples and not the general case will be decreased because they reduce the loss for only a small number of input examples, but the weight decay term causes them to increase the loss for all examples. That is how weight decay results in better generalization. The parameter λ affects how significant the regularization effect will be. The regularization technique shown in the preceding formula is known as *L1 regularization*.

A more common variation is to square the weights in the sum, which is known as *L2 regularization*:

$$Loss = cross\text{-}entropy + \lambda \sum_{i=0}^{n} w_i^2$$

Although we use cross-entropy as the loss function in the examples, you can apply weight decay regularization to any loss function. Similarly, weight decay not only is applicable to DL but is a common regularization technique applied to traditional ML techniques as well.

Weight decay is a common regularization technique. Two examples of weight decay are **L1** and **L2 regularization.**

Code Snippet 6-2 shows how to add L2 regularization in Keras. It is as simple as adding one import statement and then a single parameter to each layer where you want regularization to be applied. The example shows how to apply regularization to all layers, using a weight decay parameter $\lambda = 0.1$. It is common to not apply regularization to the bias weights, and Keras makes that possible by breaking out the bias regularizer separately.

Code Snippet 6-2 How to Add L2 Regularization to the Model

```
from tensorflow.keras.regularizers import l2

...
model.add(Dense(64, activation='relu',
                kernel_regularizer=l2(0.1),
                bias_regularizer=l2(0.1),
                input_shape=[13]))
model.add(Dense(64, activation='relu',
                kernel_regularizer=l2(0.1),
                bias_regularizer=l2(0.1)))
model.add(Dense(1, activation='linear',
                kernel_regularizer=l2(0.1),
                bias_regularizer=l2(0.1)))
```

Dropout is another common regularization technique, specifically developed for neural networks (Srivastava et al., 2014). It is done by randomly removing a subset of the neurons from the network during training. The subset of removed neurons varies throughout each training epoch. The number of removed neurons (the dropout rate) is controlled by a parameter, where a common value is 20%. When the network is later used for inference, all the neurons are used, but a scaling factor is applied to each weight to compensate for the fact that each neuron now receives inputs from more neurons than during training. Figure 6-5 illustrates how dropping two neurons from a fully connected network results in a different network.

Dropout is an effective regularization technique for neural networks.

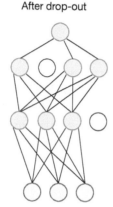

Figure 6-5 **Dropout**

Dropout forces units to be able to work with a random set of other units. Doing so prevents subsets of units from co-adapting to solve specific cases and has been shown to reduce overfitting. Code Snippet 6-3 shows how to add dropout to a model in Keras.

Code Snippet 6-3 **How to Add Dropout to the Model**

```
from tensorflow.keras.layers import Dropout
...
model.add(Dense(64, activation='relu', input_shape=[13]))
model.add(Dropout(0.2))
model.add(Dense(64, activation='relu'))
model.add(Dropout(0.2))
model.add(Dense(1, activation='linear'))
```

After we import the Dropout module, dropout is added as a layer after the layer where we want it to be applied. The Dropout layer will block connections from a subset of the neurons in the previous layer, which has the same effect as if the neuron were not there to begin with.

Experiment: Deeper and Regularized Models for House Price Prediction

We now present the results of some experiments where regularization techniques are applied to the model. As previously stated, we saw that the three-layer model was significantly better than the linear model but suffered from overfitting. Those results are shown in the first two rows in Table 6-2, where the columns show the network topology (each number represents the number of neurons in a layer), which regularization technique is used, as well as the training and test errors.

The third row in the table (Configuration 3) shows what happens when we add L2 regularization to the model. We use a lambda of 0.1, and we can see that the training error increases, but unfortunately, the test error increases slightly as well.

The next row (Configuration 4) shows what happens if we use dropout (factor 0.2) instead of L2 regularization. This is more effective and almost closes the gap between the training and test errors. This indicates that overfitting is no longer a big problem, and it makes sense to try a more complex model.

This is shown in the next row (Configuration 5), where we add another layer and increase the number of neurons to 128 in the first two layers. This improves the test error, but we see that the training error is reduced even more, so we now have problems with overfitting again.

Table 6-2 Experiments with Deeper Models and Regularization

CONFIGURATION	TOPOLOGY	REGULARIZATION	TRAINING ERROR	TEST ERROR
Conf1	1	None	10.15	10.24
Conf2	64/64/1	None	0.647	2.54
Conf3	64/64/1	L2=0.1	1.50	2.61
Conf4	64/64/1	Dropout=0.2	2.30	2.56
Conf5	128/128/64/1	Dropout=0.2	2.04	2.36
Conf6	128/128/64/1	Dropout=0.3	2.38	2.31

In the final row of the table (Configuration 6), we increase the dropout factor to 0.3, which both increases the training error and decreases the test error, and we have arrived at a model that generalizes well.

Concluding Remarks on Output Units and Regression Problems

In this chapter, we described the three most common types of output units and their associated loss functions. Whereas the types of hidden units typically are chosen in the process of tuning hyperparameters, the type of output unit is tightly coupled to the problem type.

When training DL models, it is common to run into overfitting. This can be addressed by regularizing the model. In this chapter, we described a number of regularization techniques and applied them to our programming example.

The programming example showed that it is often necessary to tweak parameters iteratively to get to a model that performs well on the test set. One thing to note is that our best configuration has more than 26,000 parameters. This can be compared to the linear regression case, which has one weight for each input feature plus a bias weight—14 in total in our example. From the perspective of predicting well, it clearly pays to have all of these parameters that the model learns by itself. However, it is much harder to understand a model with 26,000 parameters than a model with 14 parameters, which illustrates a common problem with DL. We end up with a model that works well, but we do not know how it works.

Overall, our impression is that, as the current DL boom started, the field transformed from being theoretical to being more empirical. In other words, focus has shifted from how something works to how well it works. Before the field could demonstrate impressive results, perhaps it had to produce elaborate mathematical analysis to justify its existence, whereas the more recent results are so impressive that people are happy to skip the math?

Chapter 7

Convolutional Neural Networks Applied to Image Classification

Training of deep models with backpropagation has been demonstrated in various forms since at least 1990 (Hinton, Osindero, and Teh, 2006; Hinton and Salakhutdinov, 2006; LeCun et al., 1990; LeCun, Bottou, Bengio, et al., 1998). Still, a pivotal point for deep learning (DL) was in 2012 when AlexNet was published (Krizhevsky, Sutskever, and Hinton, 2012). It scored significantly better than any other contestant in the ImageNet classification challenge (Russakovsky et al., 2015) and greatly contributed to popularizing DL. AlexNet is an eight-layer network and uses convolutional layers, which were introduced by Fukushima (1980) and later used in LeNet (LeCun et al., 1990). Convolutional layers, and the resulting convolutional neural networks (CNNs), are important building blocks in DL. This chapter describes how they work. We start by introducing the overall AlexNet architecture to highlight a number of concepts that we then explain in more detail.

> **AlexNet** is a **convolutional neural network** for image classification. It scored well on the ImageNet challenge in 2012 and has been attributed as a key reason for the DL boom that evolved over the next few years.

The topology of the AlexNet CNN is shown in Figure 7-1. It consists of five convolutional layers (drawn as 3D blocks) followed by three fully connected layers (drawn as 2D rectangles). One somewhat confusing property is that the layers are split up horizontally, so each layer is represented as two blocks or rectangles. The reason for this is that, at the time, there was no graphics processing unit (GPU) that had enough memory to be able to run the entire network. The solution was to split up the network and map it to two GPUs. Although important at the time, we ignore that detail in our discussion and focus on other properties of the network.

We make the following additional observations from the figure:

- The input image is 224×224 pixels, where each pixel has a depth of 3 (represented by the *3* in the lower left corner of the figure), which represents the three color channels red, green, and blue (RGB).

- The convolutional layers have a 3D structure as opposed to the fully connected layers, which have a single dimension (vector).

- There are seemingly arbitrary mappings from sub-blocks of varying sizes in one layer to the next (marked 11×11, 5×5, 3×3), and there seems to be no method to the madness when it comes to how the dimensions of one layer relate to the dimensions of a subsequent layer.

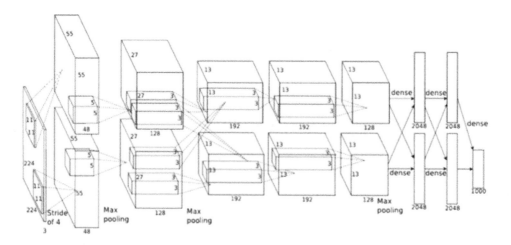

Figure 7-1 Topology of the AlexNet convolutional network. (Source: Krizhevsky, A., Sutskever, I., and Hinton, G., "ImageNet Classification with Deep Convolutional Neural Networks," Advances in Neural Information Processing Systems 25 [NIPS 2012], 2012.)

- There is something called *stride*.

- There is something called *max pooling*.

- The output layer consists of 1,000 neurons (it says "1000" in the lower right corner of the figure).

In this chapter, we describe all of the above and additionally describe terminology such as *kernel size* (refers to the 11×11, 5×5, 3×3 items in the figure) and *padding*, which are important concepts to know when designing and training a CNN. Before going into these details, we introduce the input dataset that we use in this chapter.

The CIFAR-10 Dataset

The CIFAR-10 dataset consists of 60,000 training images and 10,000 test images, each belonging to one of the ten categories *airplane, automobile, bird, cat, deer, dog, frog, horse, ship,* and *truck,* as previously shown in Figure P-1 in the preface. Each image is 32×32 pixels, so altogether it might seem like the dataset is similar to the MNIST handwritten digit dataset studied in earlier chapters. However, the CIFAR-10 dataset is more challenging in that it consists of color images of everyday objects that are much more diverse than handwritten digits. Figure 7-2

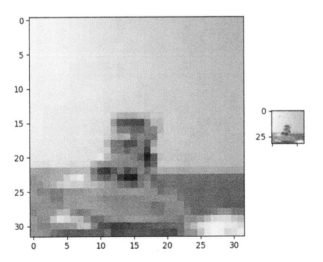

Figure 7-2 Image 100, belonging to the ship category in the CIFAR-10 dataset. (Source: Krizhevsky, A., *Learning Multiple Layers of Features from Tiny Images*, University of Toronto, 2009.)

shows image number 100 (starting counting from 0) in the CIFAR-10 dataset. The figure shows a magnified version in which each of the 32×32 pixels can be clearly seen, and next to it, a more realistically sized version given the low resolution of the image.

When working with a new dataset, it always makes sense to explore it a little bit. The CIFAR-10 dataset is included in Keras. Code Snippet 7-1 shows how to access it and display the ship image shown in Figure 7-2.

Code Snippet 7-1 Python Code to Access the CIFAR-10 Dataset and Display One of the Images

```python
import tensorflow as tf
from tensorflow import keras
import numpy as np
import matplotlib.pyplot as plt
import logging
tf.get_logger().setLevel(logging.ERROR)

cifar_dataset = keras.datasets.cifar10
(train_images, train_labels), (test_images,
    test_labels) = cifar_dataset.load_data()

print('Category: ', train_labels[100])
plt.figure(figsize=(1, 1))
plt.imshow(train_images[100])
plt.show()
```

In addition to displaying the image, the print statement should result in the following output, where 8 refers to the *ship* category:

```
Category:   [8]
```

Apparently, the `train_labels` variable is a 2D array (the 8 is enclosed within brackets, which indicates that `train_labels[100]` is still an array instead of a scalar value). We can explore this further, this time by just typing the following commands in a Python interpreter:

```
>>> import tensorflow as tf
>>> from tensorflow import keras
>>> import numpy as np
```

```
>>> cifar_dataset = keras.datasets.cifar10
>>> (train_images, train_labels), (test_images,
...      test_labels) = cifar_dataset.load_data()
>>> train_labels.shape
(50000, 1)
>>> train_images.shape
(50000, 32, 32, 3)
>>> train_images[100][0][0]
array([213, 229, 242], dtype=uint8)
```

The output (50000, 1) from train_labels.shape confirms that it is a 2D array. Looking at the output from train_images.shape, we see that it is 50,000 instances of a 32×32×3 array, that is, 50,000 images where each image is 32×32 pixels and each pixel consists of three 8-bit integers that represent the RGB intensity. We inspect the color values for the pixel in the upper left corner for our ship picture with the statement train_images[100][0][0] and see that they are 213, 229, and 242.

We believe that this is a sufficient description of the dataset to be able to use it with our CNN, and you should now also have the required tools to examine the dataset further if you are interested.

Characteristics and Building Blocks for Convolutional Layers

Instead of beginning with the mathematical concept of convolution, we focus on gaining an intuitive understanding of the convolutional layer. For interested readers, Appendix G bridges the gap between this description and the mathematical definition. Perhaps the most important characteristic of a convolutional network is a property known as *translation invariance*.[1] In the case of object classification in an image, this means that even if an object is shifted (translated) horizontally or vertically to a different position in the image, the network will still be able to recognize it. This is true regardless of where in the

---

1. In this context, *translation* refers to the geometrical transformation of moving all points by a fixed distance in the same direction in a coordinate system.

image the object was located in the training data. That is, even if the network was mostly trained with pictures of cats in the middle of the image, a convolutional network will still be able to classify the image as containing a cat when presented with an image with a cat in one of the corners. Translation invariance is achieved by employing *weight sharing* between neurons as well as making them *sparsely connected*. These concepts are described in this section.

Translation is a geometric transformation known as an *affine transformation*. It changes the location of an object without changing its shape. In Figure 7-3, the blue rectangle represents a translated version of the red rectangle. Another common affine transformation is rotation, which changes the orientation of an object. The green rectangle represents a rotated version of the red rectangle. You can read more about affine transformations in *Real-Time Rendering* (Akenine-Möller et al., 2018).

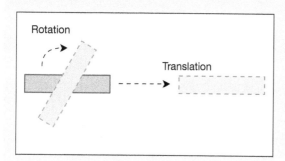

Figure 7-3 Two examples of affine transformations

A key property of convolutional layers is **translation invariance,** and it is caused by weight sharing and a sparsely connected network topology.

We start by introducing the overall topology of a convolutional layer used for image processing. The fully connected layers we have studied so far have all been arranged in a single dimension, as an array of neurons. As Figure 7-4 illustrates, a convolutional layer for image processing has a different topology, where the neurons are arranged in three dimensions. This also explains why the convolutional layers were illustrated as 3D blocks in Figure 7-1 that depicted AlexNet.

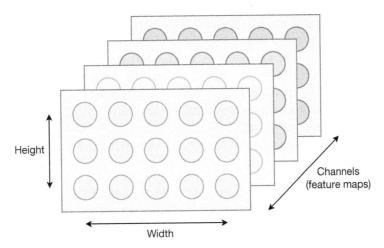

Height

Channels
(feature maps)

Width

Figure 7-4 Topology of a 2D convolutional layer. Somewhat unintuitively, a 2D convolutional layer is arranged in three dimensions: width, height, and channels.

Two of the dimensions (width and height) correspond to the 2D nature of an image. In addition, the neurons are grouped into *channels* or *feature maps* in a third dimension. Just as for a normal fully connected layer, there are no connections between the neurons within a convolutional layer. That is, all the neurons in the 3D structure are decoupled from each other and are together considered to form a single layer. However, all the neurons within a single channel have identical weights (weight sharing). That is, all neurons with the same color in the figure are identical copies of each other, but they will receive different input values.

Now let us consider the behavior of each individual neuron. In Chapter 2, "Gradient-Based Learning," we showed how a neuron can be used as a pattern identifier. In that example, we envisioned a tiny image consisting of 3×3 pixels connecting to a neuron with nine inputs (one for each pixel) plus the bias input, and we used this neuron to identify certain patterns. We use this pattern identifier (also known as *kernel* or *convolution matrix*) as our smallest building block when describing the convolutional layer.

Each neuron in a convolutional layer implements an operation known as a *convolutional kernel.* The weights are arranged in a 2D pattern and form a convolutional matrix.

Although we work on larger images, each neuron will receive pixel values only from a subset of the image (e.g., a 3×3 region as for the pattern identifier). The region of pixels from which a neuron receives inputs is also known as its *receptive field*. One issue that we have not yet dealt with is how to handle images with multiple channels. As previously described, for a color image, each pixel value consists of three values, also known as *color channels*. A typical way of handling these color channels is to simply provide each neuron with connections from each channel, so a neuron with a kernel size of 3×3 now will have $3 \times 3 \times 3 = 27$ inputs (plus bias).

Figure 7-5 illustrates three examples of how the receptive field of three distinct neurons can be arranged to cover a subset of the pixels for an image with three color channels.

> There are many instances of "three" in this sentence, but they are all decoupled. That is, we could have had four examples of how five neurons cover pixels in an image with three color channels.

The leftmost example assumes a neuron with a kernel size of 2×2, organized with a *stride* of 1. This means that the focus of each neuron is separated by only a single pixel. The example in the middle shows a similar scenario but with a stride of 2. One thing to note is that the larger the stride is, the fewer neurons are needed to cover the entire image. Finally, the rightmost example shows a kernel size of 3×3 and a stride of 2. A key observation here is that kernel size and stride are orthogonal parameters, but they do interact. For instance, if we choose a

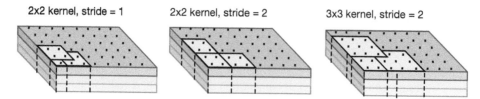

Figure 7-5 Examples of how receptive fields of three different neurons can overlap or abut. The image consists of 6×8 pixels. Left: 2×2 kernel with stride 1 needs 5×7 neurons to cover the full image. Center: 2×2 kernel with stride 2 needs 3×4 neurons. Right: 3×3 kernel with stride 2 needs 3×4 neurons.

kernel size of 2×2 and a stride of 3, then some of the pixels in the image will not be connected to any neuron, which seems unfortunate.

The number of neurons needed to cover the image is primarily affected by the **stride**.

Note that even with a stride of 1, the number of neurons that are needed to cover all the pixels is slightly smaller than the number of pixels. That is, the resolution of the output of a convolutional layer will be lower than the image. This can be addressed by first *padding* the image with zeros around the edges, so the center of the edge and corner neurons end up centered above the edge and corner pixels. For example, with a kernel size of 3×3, we need to pad each edge with a single pixel, and with a kernel size of 5×5, we need to pad each edge with two pixels. We need not worry about the details because the DL framework will do that for us.

Let us now go back to Figure 7-4 and consider the behavior of all neurons in a single channel. This grid of neurons now creates something called a *feature map* for the image. Each neuron will act as a feature (pattern) identifier and fire if the particular feature is found in the location covered by that neuron's receptive field. For example, if the weights of the neuron are such that the neuron will fire if it identifies a vertical line, then if there is a long vertical line in the image, all the neurons that are centered on this vertical line will fire. (We will see an example of that in the next section.) Given that all neurons in the map use identical weights, it does not matter where in an image a feature appears. The feature map will be able to identify it regardless of the location. This is the source of the translation invariance property.

One more thing to note is that each neuron does not receive inputs from all pixels in the image. That is, it is not a fully connected network, but it is *sparsely connected*. Clearly, this is beneficial from an efficiency perspective because fewer connections will lead to fewer computations. It also seems intuitively wrong that a neuron should be so specialized that it needs to consider every single pixel in the image to classify an object. After all, the boat image in Figure 7-2 should be classified as a ship regardless of whether the sky is cloudy, the sun is visible, or the waves are higher on the water. Having one neuron for every such condition would not be efficient. From that perspective, having neurons that simply look at smaller pieces of the image does make sense.

A neuron in a convolutional layer is **sparsely connected**.

Combining Feature Maps into a Convolutional Layer

The ability to detect only a single feature, such as a vertical line, would be very limiting. To classify different kinds of objects, the network also needs to be able to identify horizontal lines, diagonal lines, and perhaps colored blobs or other primitive building blocks. That is addressed by arranging the convolutional layer into multiple channels (feature maps). That is, similarly to how we described that an image has three channels (each corresponding to a color), a convolutional layer has multiple output channels. Each channel corresponds to a specific feature, such as a vertical line, a horizontal line, a diagonal line, or a purple blob.

We illustrate this in Figure 7-6 with a convolutional layer with four output channels. Each channel acts as a single feature map identifying a specific feature at any location in the image. The bottom-most channel can identify vertical lines. The next channel can identify horizontal lines, and the two top channels can identify diagonal lines, one channel for each orientation. Each channel consists of 3×6 neurons (indicated by the numbers 3 and 6 in the figure), but only excited neurons are explicitly drawn as black dots on each feature map. You can see how the excited neurons correspond to patterns in the input image that match the feature that the channel is capable of identifying.

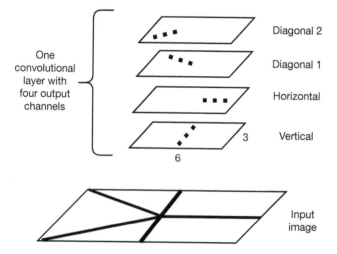

Figure 7-6 A single convolutional layer with four channels and 18 neurons for each channel. Each dot represents an excited neuron.

The figure does not indicate the size of the kernels or the stride, but it appears that the number of neurons in each channel is smaller than the number of pixels in the input image, as the size of the four rectangles is smaller than the size of the input image rectangle. This is a common arrangement.

It is easy to get confused with the terminology here because each of these channels kind of seems like a "layer" of neurons, but the proper terminology is "channel" or "feature map," and all the output channels together form a single convolutional layer. In the next section, we show how to stack multiple convolutional layers on top of each other. Each convolutional layer receives inputs from multiple input channels and produces multiple output channels. All the channels in a single convolutional layer have the same number of neurons, and all neurons in a channel share weights with one another. However, different channels in the same layer have different weights.

> A convolutional layer consists of multiple channels or feature maps. All neurons within the same channel share weights.

Although we have talked about explicit features that the channels will identify, such as horizontal lines, vertical lines, and diagonal lines, we do not need to explicitly define these features. The network will learn what features to look for during the training process.

Combining Convolutional and Fully Connected Layers into a Network

We have now seen the basic structure of a convolutional layer, and it is time to see how to combine multiple layers into a network. First, we note that the number of output channels for a convolutional layer is decoupled from the number of input channels. The number of input channels will affect the number of weights for each neuron in each output channel, but the number of output channels is simply a function of how many neurons we are willing to add to our convolutional layer. We can stack convolutional layers on top of each other, and the output channels of one layer feed the inputs of the next layer. In particular, if a convolutional layer has N channels, then the neurons in the subsequent layers will have $N{\times}M{\times}M$ inputs (plus bias) where $M{\times}M$ is the kernel size. The feature maps for this subsequent layer now represent combinations of the features in the previous layer. We can envision a feature classifier that combines the outputs from multiple channels and thereby fire on more complex geometries consisting of a combination of colored blobs and vertical, horizontal, and diagonal lines.

Figure 7-7 illustrates such a network, where the first convolutional layer identifies low-level features and the second convolutional layer then combines these features into more complex features. This is followed by a fully connected layer with a *softmax* function, used to classify the image as being one of *N* different classes, such as a dog or a peacock (we explore this in more detail shortly).

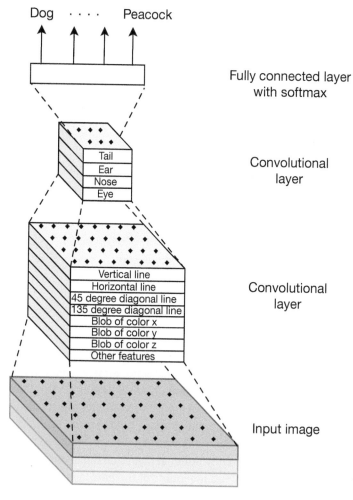

Figure 7-7 Convolutional neural network built from two convolutional layers and one fully connected layer

As you can see in the figure, the resolution (number of neurons per channel) of the first convolutional layer is lower than the resolution of the image. Further, the resolution in the second convolutional layer is lower than the resolution of the first convolutional layer. One way of achieving that is to use a stride greater than 1, and another way is to use max pooling as described further down. First, let us consider why we want this to be the case. If you think about it, it makes much sense. As we get deeper into the network, the layers identify increasingly complex features. A more complex feature typically consists of more pixels. For example, a single pixel cannot represent a complex object like a nose (or if it does, it cannot be identified because the resolution is too low).

The arrangement in Figure 7-7 is aligned with this reasoning. Because of the way neurons are connected in a hierarchy, a single neuron in the top convolutional layer is affected by a large number of pixels in the input image. That is, the receptive field of a neuron in the top convolutional layer is greater than that of a neuron in the bottom convolutional layer, even if they have the same kernel size. That arrangement enables neurons in the top layer to detect more complex features.

A more detailed illustration of this is shown in Figure 7-8. To make it easier to visualize, the figure shows a 1D convolution and only a single channel in each convolutional layer. The input image consists of four pixels (green in the figure). The neurons in the first layer have kernel size of 3 and stride of 1. The neurons in the second layer have a kernel size of 2 and stride of 2, but their receptive fields are four pixels. These two receptive fields overlap to some extent. That is, each neuron in the output layer summarizes more than half of the input image.

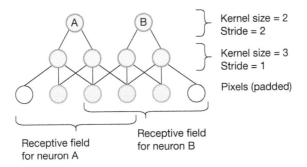

Figure 7-8 How the receptive field increases deeper into the network. Although the neurons in the topmost layer have a kernel size of only 2, their receptive fields are four pixels. Note the padding of the input layer.

The figure also illustrates the concept of padding the input image (white circles), which in this case results in the output of the first layer having the same resolution as the input image before padding. In the figure, padding is applied only to the input image, but it can also be applied when stacking convolutional layers on top of each other. In fact, padding is often more important deeper into the network where the resolution is lower than for the input image.

Unless padding is used, the width and height of a layer will automatically be smaller than in the previous layer regardless of the stride. This is mostly a concern for deep into the network, where the width and height are small to begin with.

Although we call the network a convolutional network, this does not mean that it consists only of convolutional layers. In particular, it is common to have one or more fully connected layers at the end of the network to combine all the features that the convolutional layers have extracted. Given that the number of neurons in the later convolutional layers typically is smaller than in the first few layers, having some fully connected layers at the end is not too costly. It also gives the network more flexibility to discover less-regular structures than can be expressed by a convolutional layer. In the case of a classification problem, we typically want the last fully connected layer to have the same number of neurons as there are classes. We also want it to use the softmax output function so the output of the network can be interpreted as the probability that the image contains an object of the different classes.

Figure 7-9 illustrates how a neuron in the final fully connected layer can combine the features from the last convolutional layer. We first flatten the convolutional layer into a 1D array (a vector) because there is no concept of spatial dimensions for a fully connected layer. In the figure, this vector consists of 16 elements, as there are four channels with four neurons in each channel.

The figure shows how we think of a neuron that classifies the image as containing a peacock, by assigning high weights to all neurons that represent eyes and low weights to most other neurons. The thinking here is that the only animal that has a large number of eyes (or at least something that looks like eyes) is a peacock.

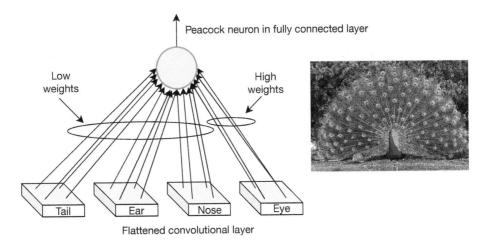

Figure 7-9 How a neuron in the fully connected layer combines multiple features into an animal classification. (Source: Peacock image by Shawn Hempel, Shutterstock.)

Clearly, assuming that a peacock is the only creature with a lot of eyes, might be somewhat oversimplified, and the network might mistake a scary alien with 17 eyes for a peacock. On the other hand, that could happen to a human too since most people do not expect to see a scary alien unless they happened to see a spaceship crash nearby.

Effects of Sparse Connections and Weight Sharing

Before moving on to our first CNN programming example, a few more things are worth mentioning about the effects of sparse connections and weight sharing in convolutional networks. There are two direct effects. First, sparse connections imply fewer computations per neuron (because each neuron is not connected to all neurons in the preceding layer). Second, weight sharing implies fewer unique, but not fewer total, weights per layer. With limited computer performance to simulate our network, the number of computations per neuron will determine the size of the networks we can build. Fewer computations per neuron enable us to build a network with more neurons than we could do with a fully connected network. Fewer unique weights significantly limits the search space that our learning algorithm needs to consider. This enables the network to learn faster, assuming that a convolutional network is a good match for the problem type we are trying to solve. Image classification happens to be one problem type where this assumption is true.

Table 7-1 quantifies two properties for fully connected networks and convolutional networks. The first property is the number of unique weights for a layer, which affects how much memory is needed to store them as well as how big the search space is for the learning algorithm to navigate. A key property of the convolutional network is that the number of weights in a layer is only a function of the kernel size, the number of channels in the layer, and the number of channels in the previous layer. This is different than the fully connected network where the number of weights is a function of both the number of neurons in the layer as well as the number of neurons in the previous layer.

Both weight sharing and sparse connections reduce the number of unique weights and thereby the storage needed for the weights. However, only sparse connections reduce the amount of computation needed to evaluate the network. That is, even though multiple neurons share weights, we still need to compute the output of each of these neurons independently because they do not have the same input values. In addition, although the storage for the weights themselves

Table 7-1 Comparison of Number of Weights and Number of Calculations for a Fully Connected Network and a Convolutional Network

PROPERTY	FULLY CONNECTED	CONVOLUTIONAL
Number of unique weights to store/learn	Product of • Number of neurons in layer • Number of neurons in previous layer	Product of • Number of channels in layer • Kernel size • Number of channels in previous layer
Number of calculations to evaluate network	Product of • Number of neurons in layer • Number of neurons in previous layer	Product of • Number of neurons in layer • Kernel size • Number of channels in previous layer

Note: The number of neurons in a convolutional layer depends on the number of channels as well as the stride.

is reduced due to weight sharing, we still need to store the outputs for all the neurons from the forward pass to later be used in the backward pass of the learning algorithm. To summarize, the main advantages of convolutional layers are the reduced number of computations per neuron, the reduction in search space for the learning algorithm, and the reduction in storage required for the weights.

> **Sparse connections** reduce the total number of weights and thereby reduce the number of computations, the number of weights to store, and the number of weights to learn. **Weight sharing** reduces the number of unique weights and thereby reduces the number of weights to store and to learn but not the number of computations.

To make this discussion more concrete, we can compute the number of weights for a convolutional layer and compare it to the number of weights for a fully connected layer with the same number of neurons. In this example, we assume that the layer is applied to an image (i.e., it is the first layer in the network). We consider two different sizes of input images: One is the CIFAR-10 size of 32×32×3 and the other is a higher resolution format of 640×480×3. We arbitrarily assume that the convolutional layer has 64 channels, and we assume a stride of 2 (i.e., the width and height of the layer is half of the width and height of the input image). In addition to looking at two different image sizes, we look at two different kernel sizes: 3×3 and 5×5. We start with computing a number of properties for this example in Table 7-2.

Table 7-2 Calculations of a Number of Properties for the Network Example

PROPERTY	COMPUTATION	NOTES
Number of channels	64	Network parameter.
Weights for 3×3 kernel	3*3*3+1 = 28	The third factor (3) represents the three channels in the previous layer. The +1 is the bias weight.
Weights for 5×5 kernel	5*5*3+1 = 76	See above.

Continued

Table 7-2 Calculations of a Number of Properties for the Network Example (Continued)

PROPERTY	COMPUTATION	NOTES
Weight per fully connected neuron applied to low resolution image	32*32*3+1 = 3,073	See above.
Weight per fully connected neuron applied to high resolution image	640*480*3+1 = 921,601	See above
Neurons in layer for low resolution image	(32/2)*(32/2)*64 = 16,384	The denominator (2) represents the stride. The factor 64 represents the number of channels.
Neurons in layer for high resolution image	(640/2)*(480/2)*64 = 4,915,200	See above.

Note: These computed numbers are used in the next table (Table 7-3).

We can now use these properties to compute the resulting number of unique weights and total weights both for a fully connected layer and a convolutional layer. This is shown in Table 7-3.

Table 7-3 Number of Unique and Total Weights for a Fully Connected Layer Compared to a Convolutional Layer with Stride of 2 for Kernel Sizes 3×3 and 5×5

	UNIQUE WEIGHTS CONVOLUTIONAL	TOTAL WEIGHTS CONVOLUTIONAL	UNIQUE WEIGHTS FULLY CONNECTED	TOTAL WEIGHTS FULLY CONNECTED
Image: 32×32×3	**3×3:** 1,792 (28*64)	**3×3:** 458,752 (28*16,384)	50,348,032 (3,073*16,384)	50,348,032 (3,073*16,384)
	5×5: 4,864 (76*64)	**5×5:** 1,245,184 (76*16,384)		

Continued

Table 7-3 Number of Unique and Total Weights for a Fully Connected Layer Compared to a Convolutional Layer with Stride of 2 for Kernel Sizes 3×3 and 5×5 (Continued)

	UNIQUE WEIGHTS CONVOLUTIONAL	TOTAL WEIGHTS CONVOLUTIONAL	UNIQUE WEIGHTS FULLY CONNECTED	TOTAL WEIGHTS FULLY CONNECTED
Image: 640×480×3	3×3: 1,792 (28*64)	3×3: 1.38×10^8 (28*4,915,200)	4.53×10^{12} (921,601*4,915,200)	4.53×10^{12} (921,601*4,915,200)
	5×5: 4,864 (76*64)	5×5: 3.74×10^8 (76*4,915,200)		

Note: The computations used to arrive at each number are enclosed in parenthesis and use the computed properties from Table 7-2.

One key thing that sticks out is the small number of unique weights for the convolutional layer, and that the number is not dependent on the resolution of the input image. Clearly, it should be easier to train a network if the algorithm needs to figure out 2,000 to 5,000 weights instead of 50 million or 5 trillion(!) weights. This is especially true if the assumption that neurons should look only at local pixels is correct, in which case the learning algorithm would need to spend huge amounts of computational power to figure out that all but 5,000 of our 5 trillion weights should be zero!

The second thing that sticks out is that the total number of weights for the fully connected network is multiple orders of magnitude larger than that for the convolutional network. Therefore, evaluating the fully connected network requires considerably more compute performance.

As we move deeper into the network, the number of weights for a convolutional layer typically increases. Conversely, the number of weights for a fully connected layer typically decreases. Therefore, the benefit of using a convolutional layer in terms of reducing the number of weights is not as significant for the layers deep into the network. The reasons for these effects are the following: The width and the height of the layers tend to decrease deeper into the network, which reduces the number of weights for a fully connected subsequent layer but does not affect a convolutional layer. Further, layers deep inside the network often have many more channels than the three color channels from the input image. Layers with hundreds of channels are not unusual. The number of weights in a subsequent layer increases with the number of input channels, regardless whether the subsequent layer is fully connected or convolutional. That is, the number of weights for the neurons in the convolutional layer is no longer as small as in the initial layers. Therefore, from a computational perspective, it is reasonable for the layers at the end of the network to be fully connected. Further, the benefit of a fully connected layer will be more significant than in the initial layers, because the final layers are tasked with making a classification of the entire image. They therefore benefit from being able to access information from all the regions of the image.

Programming Example: Image Classification with a Convolutional Network

We will now build a CNN with a similar topology to what we have just described. It will consist of two convolutional layers followed by a single fully connected layer. The details are found in Table 7-4.

Table 7-4 Description of the CNN

LAYER	INPUT IMAGE	CONVOLUTIONAL	CONVOLUTIONAL	FULLY CONNECTED
Channels	3	64	64	1
Neurons/pixels per channel	$32 \times 32 = 1{,}024$	$16 \times 16 = 256$	$8 \times 8 = 64$	10
Kernel size	N/A	5×5	3×3	N/A
Stride	N/A	2, 2	2, 2	N/A
Weights per neuron	N/A	$5 \times 5 \times 3 + 1 = 76$	$3 \times 3 \times 64 + 1 = 577$	$64 \times 64 + 1 = 4{,}097$
Total number of neurons	N/A	$64 \times 256 = 16{,}384$	$64 \times 64 = 4{,}096$	10
Trainable parameters	N/A	$64 \times 76 = 4{,}864$	$64 \times 577 = 36{,}928$	$10 \times 4{,}090 = 40{,}970$

The stride is described in two dimensions because it is not strictly required to have the same stride in each direction. For the two convolutional layers, the number of trainable parameters is not a function of the number of neurons per layer but only of the number of channels and weights per neuron. For the fully connected layer, the number of trainable parameters does depend on the number of neurons. This has the effect that, although the first layer has four times as many neurons as the second layer and 1,638 times as many neurons as the last layer, it has only approximately 10% as many trainable weights as each of the two subsequent layers.

Code Snippet 7-2 shows the initialization code for our CNN program. Among the import statements, we now import a new layer called Conv2D, which is a 2D convolutional layer like the ones we just described. We load and standardize the CIFAR-10 dataset.

Code Snippet 7-2 Initialization Code for Our Convolutional Network

```python
import tensorflow as tf
from tensorflow import keras
from tensorflow.keras.utils import to_categorical
from tensorflow.keras.models import Sequential
from tensorflow.keras.layers import Dense
from tensorflow.keras.layers import Flatten
from tensorflow.keras.layers import Conv2D
import numpy as np
import logging
tf.get_logger().setLevel(logging.ERROR)

EPOCHS = 128
BATCH_SIZE = 32

# Load dataset.
cifar_dataset = keras.datasets.cifar10
(train_images, train_labels), (test_images,
    test_labels) = cifar_dataset.load_data()

# Standardize dataset.
mean = np.mean(train_images)
stddev = np.std(train_images)
train_images = (train_images - mean) / stddev
test_images = (test_images - mean) / stddev
```

```
print('mean: ', mean)
print('stddev: ', stddev)

# Change labels to one-hot.
train_labels = to_categorical(train_labels,
                              num_classes=10)
test_labels = to_categorical(test_labels,
                             num_classes=10)
```

The actual model is created by Code Snippet 7-3, which first declares a Sequential model and then adds layers. We are now working with a 2D convolutional layer, so there is no need to start with a Flatten layer because the dimensions of the input image already match the required dimension of the first layer. We tell the layer that the input shape of the image is 32×32×3. We also state that we want 64 channels, a kernel size of 5×5, and a stride of 2, 2. The parameter padding='same' needs some further explanation. As described previously, padding is needed if we want the number of neurons in a channel to match the number of pixels in the input image (or neurons in a channel of the previous layer). There are a number of different padding choices, where 'same' means that it is sufficiently padded to end up with exactly the same number of neurons as there are inputs to the layer.[2] The actual amount of padding depends on the kernel size, but Keras takes care of computing this for you if you specify 'same'. We specify the neuron type as ReLU because that has been shown to be a good activation function. We do not specify the number of neurons in the layer explicitly because that is fully defined by all the other parameters. The combination of padding='same' and strides=(2,2) results in half as many neurons in each dimension as in the previous layer (i.e., 16×16 neurons per channel because the input image has 32×32 pixels).

Code Snippet 7-3 **Create and Train the Convolutional Neural Network**

```
# Model with two convolutional and one fully connected layer.
model = Sequential()
model.add(Conv2D(64, (5, 5), strides=(2,2),
                 activation='relu', padding='same',
                 input_shape=(32, 32, 3),
```

---

2. It will only be the same number of neurons if a stride of (1, 1) is used. In reality, we typically use a different stride, which is applied after the padding.

```
                    kernel_initializer='he_normal',
                    bias_initializer='zeros'))
model.add(Conv2D(64, (3, 3), strides=(2,2),
                    activation='relu', padding='same',
                    kernel_initializer='he_normal',
                    bias_initializer='zeros'))
model.add(Flatten())
model.add(Dense(10, activation='softmax',
                    kernel_initializer='glorot_uniform',
                    bias_initializer='zeros'))

model.compile(loss='categorical_crossentropy',
              optimizer='adam', metrics =['accuracy'])
model.summary()
history = model.fit(
    train_images, train_labels, validation_data =
    (test_images, test_labels), epochs=EPOCHS,
    batch_size=BATCH_SIZE, verbose=2, shuffle=True)
```

The next convolutional layer is similar but with a smaller kernel size. There is no need to specify the input shape—it is implicitly defined by the outputs of the previous layer. The number of neurons per channel is implicitly defined as 8×8 because the previous layer was 16×16 outputs per channel, and we choose a stride of 2, 2 for this layer as well.

Before we can add the fully connected (Dense) layer, we need to flatten (convert from three dimensions to a single dimension) the outputs from the second convolutional layer. We use softmax activation for the fully connected layer so we can interpret the outputs as probabilities.

We finally select the categorical_crossentropy loss function and use the Adam optimizer in our call to compile. Before we train the model, we print out a description of the network with a call to model.summary().

```
_____
Layer (type)                    Output Shape              Param #
=================================================================
conv2d_1 (Conv2D)               (None, 16, 16, 64)        4864
```

conv2d_2 (Conv2D)	(None, 8, 8, 64)	36928
flatten_1 (Flatten)	(None, 4096)	0
dense_1 (Dense)	(None, 10)	40970

Total params: 82,762

Trainable params: 82,762

Non-trainable params: 0

If you look at the number of parameters, you will see that it matches what we computed in Table 7-4. This is a good sanity check to ensure we defined the network the way we intended and did not make any subtle mistakes. Figure 7-10 shows the training error and test error for 128 epochs with a batch size of 32.

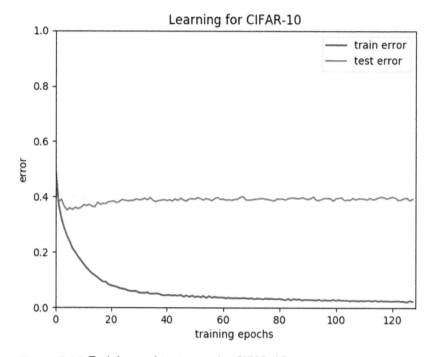

Figure 7-10 Training and test error for CIFAR-10

We see that our network is good at memorizing but not at generalizing. The training error approaches 0, and the test error stays a little bit below 40%. This error is still much better than pure guessing, which would result in a 90% test error. Still, it seems like we could do better, so we go through an exercise similar to the one we did for the housing dataset in Chapter 6, "Fully Connected Networks Applied to Regression," and come up with a number of configurations. In reality, this is an iterative process in which the result from one configuration provides guidance for what configuration to try next, but here we simply present the most interesting configurations after the fact. They are summarized in Table 7-5. First, some brief notes on the notation are in order. We denote a convolutional layer as beginning with capital letter C followed by three numbers indicating the number of channels, width, and height. We denote a fully connected layer by a capital letter F followed by the number of neurons. We have a third layer type, MaxPool, which is described later in the chapter. For the convolutional layers, we specify kernel size (K) and stride (S), where we use the same size in both directions; for example, "K=5, S=2" means a 5×5 kernel and a stride of 2×2. For each layer we also specify the type of activation function. For some layers, we also apply dropout after the layer, which we elaborate more on shortly.

Table 7-5 Configurations for Our CNN Experiments

CONFIGURATION	LAYERS	REGULARIZATION	TRAIN ERROR	TEST ERROR
Conf1	C64×16×16, K=5, S=2, ReLU C64×8×8, K=3, S=2, ReLU F10, softmax, cross-entropy loss		2%	39%
Conf2	C64×16×16, K=3, S=2, ReLU C16×8×8, K=2, S=2, ReLU F10, softmax, cross-entropy loss		33%	35%
Conf3	C64×16×16, K=3, S=2, ReLU C16×8×8, K=2, S=2, ReLU F10, softmax, cross-entropy loss	Dropout=0.2 Dropout=0.2	30%	30%

Continued

Table 7-5 Configurations for Our CNN Experiments (Continued)

CONFIGURATION	LAYERS	REGULARIZATION	TRAIN ERROR	TEST ERROR
Conf4	C64×32×32, K=4, S=1, ReLU	Dropout=0.2	14%	23%
	C64×16×16, K=2, S=2, ReLU	Dropout=0.2		
	C32×16×16, K=3 S=1, ReLU	Dropout=0.2		
	MaxPool, K=2, S=2	Dropout=0.2		
	F64, ReLU			
	F10, softmax, cross-entropy loss			
Conf5	C64×32×32, K=4, S=1, ReLU	Dropout=0.2	20%	22%
	C64×16×16, K=2, S=2, ReLU	Dropout=0.2		
	C32×16×16, K=3 S=1, ReLU	Dropout=0.2		
	C32×16×16, K=3 S=1, ReLU	Dropout=0.2		
	MaxPool, K=2, S=2	Dropout=0.2		
	F64, ReLU	Dropout=0.2		
	F64, ReLU			
	F10, softmax, cross-entropy loss			
Conf6	C64×32×32, K=4, S=1, tanh		4%	38%
	C64×16×16, K=2, S=2, tanh			
	C32×16×16, K=3 S=1, tanh			
	C32×16×16, K=3 S=1, tanh			
	MaxPool, K=2, S=2			
	F64, tanh			
	F64, tanh			
	F10, softmax, MSE loss			

Note: MSE, mean squared error; ReLU, rectified linear unit.

Configuration 1 is the configuration that we showed results for in Figure 7-10. We see significant overfitting with a training error of 2% but a test error of 39%.

Such significant overfitting often indicates that the model is too complex, where the number of parameters is large enough to memorize the entire training set. We therefore created configuration 2 with a smaller kernel size for both convolutional layers along with fewer channels in the second convolutional layer. Doing so decreased the test error from 39% to 35% and increased the training error to 33%, which indicates that we have resolved most of the overfitting problem.

Another thing to consider is to apply a regularization technique. In Chapter 6, we introduced dropout as an effective technique to use for fully connected networks. If you read the paper that introduced this technique (Srivastava et al., 2014), you might be somewhat surprised that we would suggest dropout for a convolutional network. The paper states that convolutional layers have a strong regularizing effect themselves and that dropout is not necessarily a good technique for such networks. It was later shown that various forms of dropout can work well for convolutional networks (Wu and Gu, 2015). As our experiment shows, just adding 20% regular dropout after each of the two convolutional layers reduces both training and test errors to 30%.

The next step, now that overfitting has been resolved, is to see if we can increase the model size again to further improve the results. In configuration 4, we do a number of changes. We increase the kernel size for the first convolutional layer to 4×4 and change the stride to 1, which results in each channel having 32×32 neurons. We add a third convolutional layer with a kernel size of 3×3 and stride of 1.

The convolutional layer is followed by a max pooling operation, which needs some further description. As we saw previously, when we increase the stride in a convolutional layer, the number of neurons needed to cover the previous layer is decreased. However, we need to be careful to not make the stride larger than the kernel size because we will otherwise ignore some pixels/neurons in the previous layer. An alternative way of reducing the number of neurons but without having large kernel sizes is to use *max pooling*. The max pooling operation combines a number of neurons, such as every 2×2 neurons, and outputs the max value of these four neurons. This reduces the number of outputs from a channel (and thereby from the entire layer) by a factor of four in the case of 2×2 pooling but without any weights that need to be learned. The effect of this is that the spatial resolution is decreased; that is, we no longer know as accurately where in an image a specific feature was found but we still know that the feature was present in the region that pooling was applied to. This is often acceptable because the exact location might not matter. For instance, two different dogs will have a different distance between their ears. Hence, as long as the approximate location of each ear is correctly identified, this will be sufficient to be able to determine whether or not they are the building blocks of a dog. Figure 7-11 illustrates which neurons a pooling layer combines and relates that to which neurons are combined by a convolutional layer.

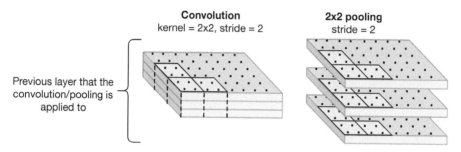

Figure 7-11 How the inputs of a pooling layer relate to the inputs of a convolutional layer. Note that the figures do not represent the convolutional and pooling layers but the preceding layer. The left figure shows that the convolution will bundle all the channels together and use these combined channels as input to each neuron. The pooling layer considers each channel in the preceding layer in isolation.

> Max pooling is a way to reduce the size of a layer and can be used as an alternative to a large stride.

A convolutional layer combines the outputs of $C{\times}K{\times}K$ neurons, where C is the number of channels in the previous layer and $K{\times}K$ is the kernel size. This is shown in the left part of Figure 7-11 for the case of three channels and a 2×2 kernel size. That is, the outputs from 12 neurons are bundled together and input to a single neuron in the next convolutional layer. On the other hand, a max pooling layer does not combine output neurons across channels, but only within a channel. The result is that the output of the pooling operation/layer has the same number of channels as the preceding layer. The number of neurons in each channel is lower, as that is one purpose of introducing the max pooling operation. Consider the example to the right in Figure 7-11. It has a stride of 2, and therefore the width and height of the output of the pooling layer is half of the width and height of the preceding layer. The way to combine each group of four neurons in a max pooling layer is to simply pick the output of the neuron with the max value instead of feeding all the outputs into a neuron.

> Max pooling combines the output from a set of neurons within a channel, as opposed to a convolutional kernel, which combines the output from a set of neurons from multiple channels. Max pooling is sometimes considered as being a part of a convolutional layer and sometimes considered to be a separate layer.

Let us now go back to our configuration 4 to see how and why we use the max pooling layer. We have placed it right before the first fully connected layer, and it thereby reduces the number of inputs to each of the fully connected neurons by a factor of four while still enabling the fully connected neurons to receive signals from the most excited neurons in the previous layer. Max pooling layers can be, and commonly are, used before convolutional layers as well.

The max pooling operation is sometimes viewed as a part of the preceding convolutional layer, just as was shown for AlexNet in Figure 7-1, where it was stated as a property of two of the layers. An alternative view is to consider it to be its own layer in the network. We find that a little bit more intuitive, so that is how we typically draw it. However, note that when comparing depth of two models, it is common to count only layers that have trainable parameters (weights), so the pooling layers are typically not counted in such cases. In Keras, a max pooling operation is treated as a separate layer just as we have described it here, and it can be added with a single line of code:

```
model.add(MaxPooling2D(pool_size=(2, 2), strides=2))
```

Finally, our configuration 4 has an additional fully connected layer with 64 neurons before the output layer. All in all, this more complex model brings down the training error to 14% and the test error to 23%.

Encouraged by these results, we go even deeper in configuration 5, where we add another convolutional layer. We end up with a training error of 20% and a test error of 22%. The implementation of this more complex model can be found in Code Snippet 7-4. To make the code shorter, we do not explicitly select initializers but just use the default initializer for the different layers.

Code Snippet 7-4 Model Definition of Configuration 5

```
from tensorflow.keras.layers import Dropout
from tensorflow.keras.layers import MaxPooling2D

...

model = Sequential()
model.add(Conv2D(64, (4, 4), activation='relu', padding='same',
                 input_shape=(32, 32, 3)))
model.add(Dropout(0.2))
model.add(Conv2D(64, (2, 2), activation='relu', padding='same',
                 strides=(2,2)))
```

```
model.add(Dropout(0.2))
model.add(Conv2D(32, (3, 3), activation='relu', padding='same'))
model.add(Dropout(0.2))
model.add(Conv2D(32, (3, 3), activation='relu', padding='same'))
model.add(MaxPooling2D(pool_size=(2, 2), strides=2))
model.add(Dropout(0.2))
model.add(Flatten())
model.add(Dense(64, activation='relu'))
model.add(Dropout(0.2))
model.add(Dense(64, activation='relu'))
model.add(Dropout(0.2))
model.add(Dense(10, activation='softmax'))
```

Finally, in Chapter 5, we claimed that there were a number of things that enabled DL, such as ReLU activation functions and cross-entropy loss instead of mean squared error (MSE). To validate this, we took the same network as in configuration 5 and replaced the ReLU activation functions by tanh. Further, we changed the loss function from cross-entropy to MSE and removed the dropout regularization because that was invented after the DL boom started. The results are shown as configuration 6. Curiously, the test error is only 38%. While not as good as the 22% that we achieved with configuration 5, it is by no means a disaster given that picking a category at random would give a 90% test error. In other words, we can achieve impressive results with techniques that have been known since the 1980s. Goodfellow, Bengio, and Courville (2016) argue that a key barrier to success for neural networks was psychological, in the sense that people did not believe in the idea enough to spend the time needed to experiment with different architectures and parameters to achieve good results. Obviously, much more patience would have been needed in the 1980s than today given how computer performance has evolved. It takes only a couple of minutes to run 20 epochs for configuration 5 on a modern GPU in 2021, while it takes some 10 hours to run on the CPU of a laptop from 2014. Now think about trying to run it in 1989, which would imply running on a single-core CPU running well below 100 MHz. This lends credibility to the notion that the real enabler of DL was the emergence of low-cost, GPU-based, high-performance computing.

Concluding Remarks on Convolutional Networks

In the beginning of this chapter, we briefly mentioned that convolutional layers were used in a network known as LeNet (LeCun et al., 1990). The original version of LeNet consisted of five layers, and a later version, known as LeNet-5, consisted of seven layers (LeCun, Bottou, Bengio, et al., 1998). LeNet-5 was deployed commercially and thereby demonstrated that the field of neural networks had progressed beyond just being academic research.

We also showed a figure of AlexNet in the beginning of this chapter. It is shown again in Figure 7-12 to make this section easier to follow. The input image is 224×224 pixels with three channels. It feeds a convolutional layer with 55×55 neurons per channel, using 11×11 convolution kernels with a stride of 4. The first layer has 96 channels, but the implementation splits them across two GPUs, so each GPU handles 48 channels. The second layer uses a 5×5 kernel and a stride of 1 but also does 2×2 max pooling and thereby ends up with 27×27 neurons per channel. It consists of 256 channels split across two GPUs. After reading this chapter, it should be straightforward to continue to follow the figure from left to right deeper into the network.

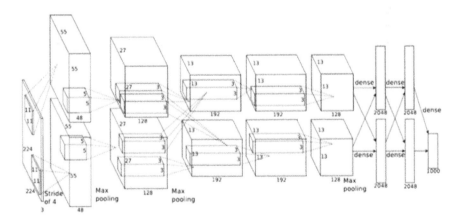

Figure 7-12 The AlexNet convolutional network. (Source: Krizhevsky, A., Sutskever, I., and Hinton, G., "ImageNet Classification with Deep Convolutional Neural Networks," *Advances in Neural Information Processing Systems 25 [NIPS 2012]*, 2012.)

Figure 7-13 shows AlexNet in a style that is consistent with figures of other networks in this book. For convolutional layers, we use the notation kernel/stride/channels. That is, 11×11/4/48 represents a layer using an 11×11 kernel with a stride of 4 and 48 channels. For max pooling, we use a similar notation, but the number of channels is not specified because it is always the same as the number of input channels.

If you read the paper by Krizhevsky and colleagues (2012), you will also see that some of the convolutional layers apply a normalization scheme before the max

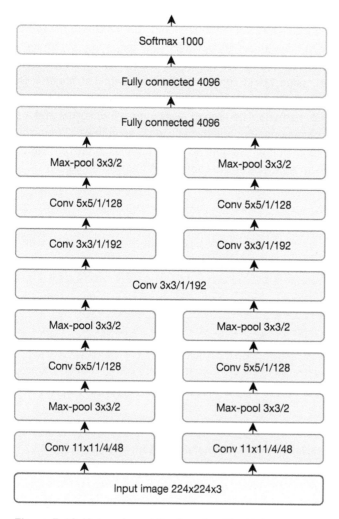

Figure 7-13 Network architecture for AlexNet

pooling layer. Finally, the fully connected softmax layer consists of 1,000 neurons that are able to classify the input image into one of the 1,000 categories provided by the ImageNet input dataset, as opposed to only 10 categories in CIFAR-10.

Although LeNet, LeNet-5, and AlexNet were important milestones and deep networks at the time, they are now considered to be fairly shallow networks and have been replaced by more complex and better performing networks, some of which are described in Chapter 8, "Deeper CNNs and Pretrained Models."

If you are interested in how the convolutional networks described in this chapter relate to the mathematical concept of convolution, consider reading Appendix G before moving on to Chapter 8.

Chapter 8

Deeper CNNs and Pretrained Models

In this chapter, we describe three convolutional neural networks (CNNs): VGGNet, GoogLeNet, and ResNet. Both VGGNet (16 layers) and GoogLeNet (22 layers) are from 2014 and were close to human-level performance on the ImageNet dataset. VGGNet has a very regular structure, whereas GoogLeNet looks more complex but has fewer parameters and achieved higher accuracy. In 2015, both of these networks were beaten by ResNet-152 consisting of 152(!) layers. However, in practice, most people have settled on using ResNet-50, which consists of "only" 50 layers. As a programming example, we show how to use a pretrained implementation of ResNet and how you can use it to classify your own images. The chapter ends with a discussion of some other aspects of CNNs.

This chapter contains much detailed information about these specific networks. Readers who are not specifically interested in image classification might find some of these details uninteresting. If you feel that way and would prefer to move on to recurrent neural networks and language processing, then you can consider just skimming this chapter at this point. Still, you might want to pay attention to the concepts of skip connections and transfer learning because they are referenced in later chapters.

VGGNet

VGGNet was proposed by the University of Oxford's Visual Geometry Group (VGG). A primary objective of the paper that described the architecture was to study the effect that network depth has on accuracy for CNNs (Simonyan and Zisserman, 2014). To do so, they came up with an architecture in which the depth of the network can be adjusted without having to adjust other parameters, such as kernel size and stride. They used a fixed kernel size of 3×3 in all convolutional layers and a stride of 1. When using a stride of 1, the width and height of a subsequent layer become the same as the width and height of the preceding layer, assuming that appropriate padding is used. This makes it possible to make a VGGNet arbitrarily deep without running into the problem that the width and height of layers deep in the network become too small.

> VGGNet uses stride 1 to maintain width and height dimensions across multiple layers.

Just as for other CNNs, we still do want the height and width to decrease for layers deeper into the network because we want each neuron to identify larger-sized features by hierarchically combining smaller features. VGGNet solves this by using max pooling layers between groups of convolutional layers. Thus, a typical building block in a VGGNet is a group of convolutional layers of the same size, followed by a max pooling layer. This is shown in Figure 8-1, which illustrates a building block consisting of two convolutional layers and one max pooling layer. To make it possible to visualize it, we assume a very small input image size (8×6 pixels), but in reality, we would work with larger images. Similarly, the example in the figure has a very limited number of channels compared to a real network.

The figure can be a little confusing at first, so let us walk through each step. We start at the bottom with an image with 8×6 pixels, each pixel having three color channels. The white patches on that image illustrate how 3×3 pixels are combined by a single neuron in the subsequent convolutional layer. The kernel operates on all three color channels. The white patches also illustrate that the convolutional layer uses a stride of 1 in both dimensions. The convolutional layer consists of four channels, which results in the 8×6×4 output dimensions, which is represented by the bottom-most set of blue boxes in the figure. The white patches on top of these blue boxes show how outputs from this layer are then combined by a single neuron in the second convolutional layer. The second convolutional

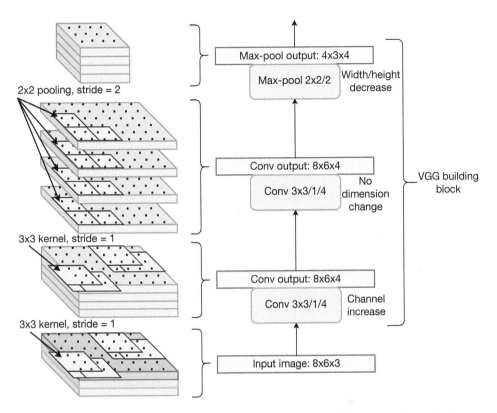

Figure 8-1 VGG building block. The left part of the figure illustrates the output dimensions of each layer. It also shows how a kernel from the next layer is applied to the preceding layer. The convolution kernels are applied across all channels in the preceding layer, whereas the max pooling operation is applied channel-wise. Note the padding used by the convolutional layers where the kernel operates on missing pixels. The right part of the figure describes the details of each layer (kernel size/stride/output channels).

layer is represented by the next set of blue boxes. They are pulled apart a little in the illustration to enable showing how its outputs are combined by the subsequent max pooling layer. The max pooling layer operates on each channel in isolation. Finally, the topmost set of blue boxes illustrates how the max pooling layer resulted in a reduced number of dimensions to 4×3×4.

Compared to the first couple of layers in AlexNet, which have kernel sizes of 11×11 and 5×5, the VGGNet kernel size 3×3 is relatively small. However, if you consider a group of layers together, then 3×3 kernels in adjacent layers will act as a single kernel with larger size. For example, a single neuron in the second of a group of two layers will have a receptive field of 5×5 with respect to the input to the first layer because the neuron receives input from 3×3 neurons, which in turn cover an area of 5×5 pixels. Similarly, if we stack three layers, then neurons in the third layer will have receptive fields of 7×7 with respect to the input of the first layer.

The different configurations that were studied in the VGGNet paper all start with convolutional layers with 64 channels. For each max pooling layer, the width and height of the next layer is halved, and the subsequent convolutional layer doubles the number of channels. The number of channels is capped at 512, after which the width and height is still halved for the next layer after pooling but the number of channels is kept constant. The neurons in all convolutional layers use ReLU as an activation function. Table 8-1 shows some of the different configurations that were evaluated in the paper. Reading the table from left to right, each change from the previous column is highlighted in bold. All the convolutions use a stride of 1. The kernel size and number of channels are stated in the table.

Some of the configurations use 1×1 convolutions, which consider only a single output from each channel in the preceding layer. At a first glance, this might seem odd. What can possibly be the benefit of doing a convolution over a single neuron? The thing to remember is that the convolution not only combines neighboring pixels/neurons but also combines pixels/neurons across multiple channels. That is, the 1×1 convolutions in VGGNet provide the ability to combine features from different channels into new features. We can use 1×1 convolutions to increase or decrease the number of channels because the number of output channels in a convolutional layer is independent of both the kernel size and the number of channels in the preceding layer. VGGNet does not make use of that property, but we will soon see that both GoogLeNet and ResNet do. Using 1×1 convolutions directly on the three-channel image input is uncommon. It is more common to use this operation deeper into the network where the number of channels is larger.

1×1 convolutions can be used to increase or decrease the number of channels.

Some key results of the VGGNet study were that prediction accuracy did increase with model depth up to 16 layers but then flattened out to about the same for 19 layers. Pooling layers were not included in these counts because they do not contain weights that can be trained. The best VGGNet classification configuration submitted to the ImageNet challenge 2014 resulted in a top-5 error rate[1] of 7.32%. This can be compared to 15.3% for AlexNet.

---

1. The top-5 error rate is defined as the percentage of test images where the correct category is not among the five categories that the network predicts as most probable.

Table 8-1 Four VGGNet Configurations*

11 WEIGHT LAYERS	13 WEIGHT LAYERS	16 WEIGHT LAYERS	19 WEIGHT LAYERS
Input RGB image (224×224×3)			
Conv 3×3/1/64	Conv 3×3/1/64 **Conv 3×3/1/64**	Conv 3×3/1/64 Conv 3×3/1/64	Conv 3×3/1/64 Conv 3×3/1/64
2×2/2 max pooling			
Conv 3×3/1/128	Conv 3×3/1/128 **Conv 3×3/1/128**	Conv 3×3/1/128 Conv 3×3/1/128	Conv 3×3/1/128 Conv 3×3/1/128
2×2/2 max pooling			
Conv 3×3/1/256 **Conv 3×3/1/256**	Conv 3×3/1/256 Conv 3×3/1/256	Conv 3×3/1/256 Conv 3×3/1/256 **Conv 1×1/1/256**	Conv 3×3/1/256 Conv 3×3/1/256 **Conv 3×3/1/256** **Conv 3×3/1/256**
2×2/2 max pooling			
Conv 3×3/1/512 **Conv 3×3/1/512**	Conv 3×3/1/512 Conv 3×3/1/512	Conv 3×3/1/512 Conv 3×3/1/512 **Conv 1×1/1/512**	Conv 3×3/1/512 Conv 3×3/1/512 **Conv 3×3/1/512** **Conv 3×3/1/512**
2×2/2 max pooling			
Conv 3×3/1/512 **Conv 3×3/1/512**	Conv 3×3/1/512 Conv 3×3/1/512	Conv 3×3/1/512 Conv 3×3/1/512 **Conv 1×1/1/512**	Conv 3×3/1/512 Conv 3×3/1/512 **Conv 3×3/1/512** **Conv 3×3/1/512**
2×2/2 max pooling			
Fully connected, 4,096			
Fully connected, 4,096			
Fully connected, 1,000 with softmax			

*All convolutional layers use a stride of 1. The kernel size and number of output channels are stated in each cell. Conv, convolution.

GoogLeNet

GoogLeNet is one specific incarnation of a network architecture named Inception (Szegedy, Liu, et al., 2014). At a first glance, it looks much more complex and irregular than AlexNet and VGGNet because it uses a building block called *Inception module* that itself is a small network. This is an example of a network-in-network architecture in which a small network is used as building block inside of another network (Lin, Chen, and Yan, 2013). Lin and colleagues had previously studied a network-in-network architecture for CNNs in which each neuron in a convolutional layer was replaced by a small multilevel network, which served the same role as the single neuron. Just as for a traditional convolutional layer, this small multilevel network would share weights across the entire convolutional layer. The effect is a convolutional layer but where a single layer has the ability to classify features that are not linearly separable, which is not possible for a single traditional convolutional layer.

The Inception module used by GoogLeNet serves a different purpose in that it builds a convolutional layer that can simultaneously work with multiple receptive field sizes. Intuitively, this can be useful because it is seldom the case that an instance of a specific object (e.g., a cat) is always the same size in all images. Even in a single image, it might be that multiple instances of similar objects (a picture of multiple cats) appear to be of different sizes due to their distance from the camera. Thus, a network that has flexibility in its receptive field size can be useful. The Inception module addresses receptive field size flexibility by having multiple convolutional layers with different kernel sizes work side by side, each one producing a number of output channels. As long as the width and height of the output channels are the same, these output channels can simply be concatenated to appear as if they come from a single convolutional layer. For example, we might have 32 channels resulting from a convolutional layer with a 3×3 kernel size and 32 channels resulting from a layer with a 5×5 kernel size, and overall, the Inception module would output 64 channels. Figure 8-2 shows the conceptual architecture of the Inception module but using parameters that make it practical to visualize.

> The Inception module used in GoogLeNet provides the ability to work with multiple receptive field sizes.

We start our description with the naïve version on the left. We see that the inception module consists of four different components: 1×1 convolution, 3×3 convolution, 5×5 convolution, and 3×3 max pooling. Just as for VGGNet, the chosen stride is 1, which results in the output from the Inception module having the same width and height as its input. In the networks we have seen so far, the max pooling operation was used to reduce the width and height of the output, but the max pooling operation in the Inception module keeps it constant by using a stride of 1. The reason for using max pooling in this way was simply that max pooling has shown to be useful in state-of-the-art networks. Therefore, it makes sense to try it in this way as well.

Let us now move on to the right side of Figure 8-2, which represents the architecture of the Inception module that was built instead of the naïve version, except that the parameters of the module in the figure are chosen to make it practical to visualize. A problem with the naïve version is the number of parameters that it introduces. As described in Chapter 7, "Convolutional Neural Networks Applied to Image Classification," the number of weights for a convolutional layer is proportional to the kernel size and the number of channels in the preceding layer. Further, the number of output channels from a max pooling layer is the same as the number of input channels. To keep the number of weights

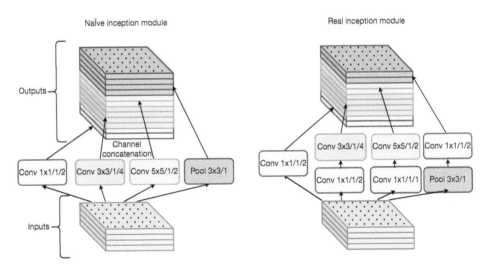

Figure 8-2 Inception module. Left: Naïve version. Note how the number of output channels from the pooling operation is the same as the number of input channels. Right: Real version with 1×1 convolutions that reduce number of weights for the wider convolutions and enable the number of output channels from the pooling operation to be independent of the number of input channels. The color coding has nothing to do with RGB in the original image but just indicates which module a channel originates from.

low, the Inception module makes use of 1×1 convolutions before the 3×3 and 5×5 convolutions, which results in fewer input channels to those convolutional kernels. Similarly, to avoid too many output channels, a 1×1 convolution is applied to the output of the max pooling operation. With these 1×1 convolutions, we have full control of the number of input channels to the 3×3 and 5×5 kernels as well as the total number of outputs from the Inception module and thereby, implicitly, the number of weights that need to be trained.

GoogLeNet makes use of another mechanism that we have not yet seen. To enable training of deeper networks, Szegedy, Liu, and colleagues (2014) added *auxiliary classifiers* at different points in the network. An auxiliary classifier is similar to what you typically would put at the top of the network, that is, a fully connected layer and a softmax layer[2] that computes the probability for the different classes that we are trying to predict. Figure 8-3 illustrates how a network can be extended with auxiliary classifiers.

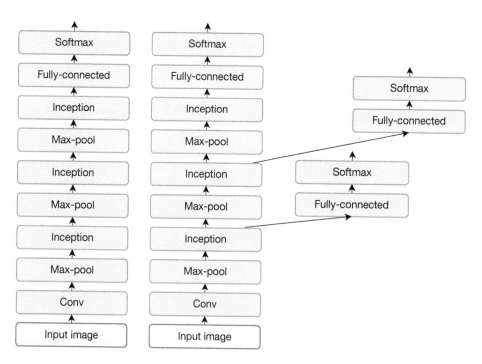

Figure 8-3 Left: Baseline network based on Inception modules. Right: The same network augmented with auxiliary classifiers.

---

2. In reality, they made it a little bit more complicated than just these two layers, but that is not relevant for this discussion.

The intent of these auxiliary classifiers is to be able to inject gradients at these intermediate points during training and thereby ensure that strong gradients propagate back to the first few layers. The auxiliary classifiers also encourage the initial layers of the network to be trained to behave much like they would behave in a shallower network. The GoogLeNet network is summarized in Table 8-2. Auxiliary classifiers are not shown.

> Auxiliary classifiers inject gradients in the middle of the network during training.

Table 8-2 GoogLeNet Architecture*

Layer Type	Details				Output size
Input	RGB image				224×224×3
Conv	7×7/2/64				112×112×64
Max pool	3×3/2				56×56×64
Conv	1×1/1/64				56×56×64
Conv	3×3/1/192				56×56×192
Max pool	3×3/2				28×28×192
Inception	1×1/1/64	1×1/1/96	1×1/1/16	3×3/1 pool	28×28×256
		3×3/1/128	5×5/1/32	1×1/1/32	
	Channel concatenation				
Inception	1×1/1/128	1×1/1/128	1×1/1/32	3×3/1 pool	28×28×480
		3×3/1/192	5×5/1/96	1×1/1/64	
	Channel concatenation				

Continued

Table 8-2 GoogLeNet Architecture* (Continued)

Max pool	3×3/2			14×14×280
Inception	1×1/1/192	1×1/1/96	1×1/1/16	3×3/1 pool	14×14×512
		3×3/1/208	5×5/1/48	1×1/1/64	
	Channel concatenation				
Inception	1×1/1/160	1×1/1/112	1×1/1/24	3×3/1 pool	14×14×512
		3×3/1/224	5×5/1/64	1×1/1/64	
	Channel concatenation				
Inception	1×1/1/128	1×1/1/128	1×1/1/24	3×3/1 pool	14×14×512
		3×3/1/256	5×5/1/64	1×1/1/64	
	Channel concatenation				
Inception	1×1/1/112	1×1/1/144	1×1/1/32	3×3/1 pool	14×14×512
		3×3/1/288	5×5/1/64	1×1/1/64	
	Channel concatenation				
Inception	1×1/1/256	1×1/1/160	1×1/1/32	3×3/1 pool	14×14×832
		3×3/1/320	5×5/1/128	1×1/1/128	
	Channel concatenation				
Max pool	3×3/2			7×7/832
Inception	1×1/1/256	1×1/1/160	1×1/1/32	3×3/1 pool	7×7×832
		3×3/1/320	5×5/1/128	1×1/1/128	
	Channel concatenation				

Continued

Table 8-2 GoogLeNet Architecture* (Continued)

Inception	1×1/1/384	1×1/1/192	1×1/1/48	3×3/1 pool	7×7×1,024
		3×3/1/384	5×5/1/128	1×1/1/128	
	Channel concatenation				
Avg pool	7×7/1				1,024
Dropout	40%				1,024
FC (softmax)	1,000				1,000

*Parameters for convolutional layers are shown as kernel size/stride/channels (i.e., 3×3/1/64 means 3×3 kernel size, stride of 1, and 64 channels). Pooling layers have the same format but without the channel parameter. All convolutional layers use rectified linear unit (ReLU).

All in all, GoogLeNet demonstrated that it is possible to make use of more elaborate architectures to build deep, high-performing networks that have a relatively small number of weights. The 22-layer network that was submitted to the ImageNet classification challenge 2014 achieved a top-5 error of 6.67%, which was slightly better than VGGNet.

ResNet

Residual networks (ResNets) were introduced to address the observation that very deep networks are hard to train (He et al., 2015a). We previously discussed that one obstacle to training deep networks is the vanishing gradient problem. However, it turns out that deep networks still have problems learning even after addressing the vanishing gradient problem by properly initializing weights, applying batch normalization, and using rectified linear unit (ReLU) neurons inside of the network.

He and colleagues made the observation that when increasing the network depth from 18 to 34 layers, the *training error* increased even though they seemed to have healthy gradients throughout the network during the training process.

If it was only the *test error* that increased, then that would be an indication of overfitting. An increased training error indicates that this more complex model simply did not manage to learn what it should be able to learn, given its strictly higher capacity than the 18-layer model. As an example, if the weights in the first 18 layers of the 34-layer model had been identical to the weights in the 18-layer model and the weights in the final 16-layers had implemented the identity function, then the 34-layer model should be on par with the 18-layer model, but for some reason, the learning algorithm did not manage to arrive at such a solution.

ResNets solve this problem by using a mechanism known as a *skip connection* (described shortly) that makes it easy for the network to learn the identity function. Clearly, building a very deep network where many of the layers do not change the output would be wasteful, but the thinking here is that the best solution for the later layers might be close to the identity function because only minor variations are needed to improve the accuracy. Thus, by making it easy for layers to learn something close to the identity function, the learning algorithm will start its search for a solution in a space that is likely to contain a good solution.

> ResNets aim to make it easier for the learning algorithm to find a good solution in the presence of very deep networks. It does so by introducing skip connections.

Figure 8-4 shows a building block that can be used in a ResNet. It contains two stacked layers with an additional skip connection that bypasses most of the two layers. As you can see from the figure, the input (*x*) to the first layer is added to the weighted sum that is produced by the second layer before that sum is fed through the activation function in the second layer.

Assuming that the two layers are fully connected layers with the same number of outputs as there are inputs, the building block above can be represented in the following way using matrices and vectors:

$$y = ReLu\left(x + W_2 ReLu\left(W_1 x\right)\right)$$

The innermost vector-matrix product (using matrix W_1) represents the weighted sum computed by the first layer, and the output vector from the ReLU activation function from this first layer is then multiplied by matrix W_2 to compute the weighted sum for the second layer. He and colleagues (2015a) hypothesized that with the this arrangement, it would be easy for the learning algorithm to push the weights close to 0 in cases where the identity mapping is the desired behavior. This would reduce the expression to simply

$$y = ReLu(\pmb{x})$$

A reasonable question is whether the skip connection has somehow ruined our network and made it more linear, because it bypasses some of our nonlinear functions. However, this is not the case. Assume that we want the module to learn to act so the input to the second ReLU function models an arbitrary function $f(\pmb{x})$. Adding the skip connection changes the objective to instead try to learn the function $f(\pmb{x}) - \pmb{x}$, as the result will be the same after adding $\pmb{x}$ to it. There is no good reason to believe that the network cannot model $f(\pmb{x}) - \pmb{x}$ if it is able to model $f(\pmb{x})$, so the skip connection should not fundamentally change the type of functions the network can model.

We soon describe how to modify the building block shown in Figure 8-4 to work for convolutional layers as well as for cases when the number of outputs in a layer is different from the number of inputs, but we first walk through the basic architecture of a residual network. The basic structure is inspired by VGGNet in that it consists of groups of stacked convolutional layers built from 3×3 kernels using a stride of 1 and with the same number of output channels as there are input channels. Like VGGNet, a ResNet periodically introduces layers that halve the width and height while doubling the number of output channels. However, while VGGNet reduced the dimensions by using max pooling, ResNet uses a

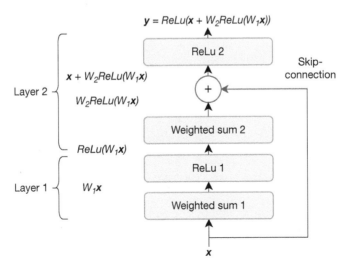

Figure 8-4 Building block with skip connection

stride of 2 for the convolutional layers where a dimensionality reduction is desired, and thereby the max pooling is not necessary. Another difference is that ResNet employs batch normalization after each convolutional layer. Both of these differences are independent of the skip connections that represent the key differentiator for a ResNet. Figure 8-5 shows the basic structure of a baseline network without skip connections (left) and a ResNet with skip connections (right).

As seen in Figure 8-5, there are two types of skip connection. The first one (solid line) connects an input of a given size to an output of the same size, and the second one (dashed line) connects an input of a given size to an output of a

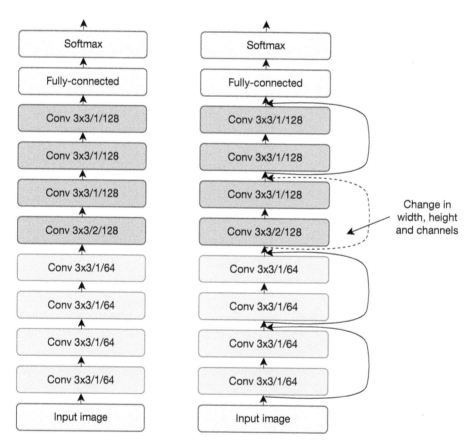

Figure 8-5 Left: Baseline network without skip connections. Right: ResNet-style network with skip connections. The dashed skip connection indicates that the input and output dimensions of the block do not match (details are discussed later in the chapter). The figure is simplified in that it does not explicitly show the activation functions being applied after the skip connections.

different size. Both of them are applied to convolutional layers that have a 3D structure *(width × height × channels)*. The following formula shows how the skip connection is defined for two convolutional layers when the inputs and outputs are of the same size, where *w*, *h*, and *c* represent the width, height, and number of channels. That is, we simply apply a skip connection from a given coordinate in the input tensor, to the corresponding coordinate in the output tensor.

$$y_{i,j,k} = ReLu\left(x_{i,j,k} + F_{i,j,k}(\boldsymbol{x})\right), \quad i=1\dots w, \; j=1\dots h, \; k=1\dots c$$

This is equivalent to how we defined it for a fully connected layer, but there the input was a 1D vector of values instead of a 3D tensor. In addition, instead of explicitly writing the formula for the layers, we have replaced that formula with the function *F(x)*, which represents the first layer, including an activation function, followed by the second layer but without its activation function.

An obvious question is how this formula is changed when the output tensor is of a different dimensionality than the input tensor. In particular, in the case of a ResNet, the width and height of the output tensor is half that of the input tensor, and the number of channels is doubled. Here is one simple solution, where *w*, *h*, and *c* represent the width, height, and number of channels, with the addition of a subscript detailing whether a variable refers to the input or output tensor for the block:

$$y_{i,j,k} = \begin{cases} ReLu\left(x_{2i,\,2j,\,k} + F_{i,j,k}(\boldsymbol{x})\right), & i=1\dots w_{out}; \; j=1\dots h_{out}; \; k=1\dots c_{in} \\ ReLu\left(F_{i,j,k}(\boldsymbol{x})\right), & i=1\dots w_{out}; \; j=1\dots h_{out}; \; k=c_{in}+1\dots c_{out} \end{cases}$$

Because the number of output channels is doubled, we simply have skip connections only to the first half of the output channels. In the formula, this is achieved by having the first line (with skip connections) apply to the first half of the output channels (1 through c_{in}), and the second line (without skip connections) applies to the remaining half of the output channels (c_{in} + 1 through c_{out}). Similarly, because the width and height are cut in half, we do skip connections only from every other element in the width and height dimensions in the input tensor (achieved by using the subscripts *2i* and *2j* in the first line in the formula).

It turns out that a better solution than having skip connections to only half of the output channels is to use a 1×1 convolution on the skip connection to expand the number of channels from the skip connection itself. Figure 8-6 shows both the case of having skip connections to only half of the output channels (left) and the case of expanding the number of channels of the skip connections using 1×1 convolutions (right).

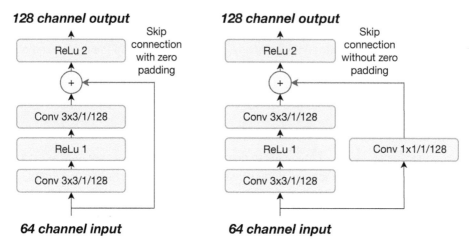

Figure 8-6 Skip connections for convolutional layers with more output channels than input channels. That is, the case that was represented as a dashed skip connection. Left: No skip connections (zero padding) to added channels. Right: Number of channels of skip connections is expanded by using 1×1 convolutions.

There are alternative schemes to enable skip connections to all output channels as well as to avoid dropping some of the inputs. One more such scheme was shown in the original ResNet paper, and a more detailed evaluation can be found in a subsequent paper (He et al., 2016).

> Details of more elaborate skip connections is a good topic for future reading (He et al., 2016).

We are almost ready to present the final topology of some different ResNets, but first we present one more variation on the building blocks and point out one more omitted detail. To make it practical to use deep networks with even more channels, we can use a trick similar to the one we showed you for GoogLeNet. We can use 1×1 convolutions to temporarily reduce the number of channels to reduce the number of required weights in the 3×3 convolutional layer and then use another layer of 1×1 convolutions to increase the number of channels again. This building block is shown in Figure 8-7.

> ResNets use 1×1 convolution to reduce the number of weights to learn.

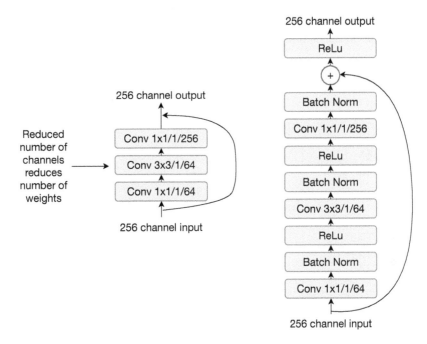

Figure 8-7 Building block that down samples number of channels internally.
Left: Simplified view. Right: Actual implementation with batch normalization and
activation functions.

The left part of the figure shows the building block in the simplified style that was
used in Figure 8-5. The right part of the figure shows the actual implementation,
where the skip connection gets added before the final activation function. It also
shows that the building block uses batch normalization before the activation
functions. Batch normalization applies to the simpler two-layer case (without 1×1
convolutions) as well. Finally, in cases where the number of output channels is
greater than the number of input channels, the skip connection would employ a
1×1 convolution to avoid zero padding, as was shown in Figure 8-6.

Using these techniques, we can now define some different ResNet
implementations, as shown in Table 8-3. Our table looks somewhat different
than what is in the original paper because we explicitly spell out the layers with
stride 2, whereas He and colleagues point it out in the textual description.

Using a combination of a few different ResNets, He and colleagues reported a
top-5 error of 3.57% on the ImageNet classification challenge in 2015. That is,
all in all, from the introduction of AlexNet in 2012, we have gone from a top-5

Table 8-3 **ResNet Architecture**

34 LAYER	50 LAYER	152 LAYER
Conv 7×7/2/64 Max pool 3×3/2		
Conv $\begin{bmatrix} 3\times3/1/64 \\ 3\times3/1/64 \end{bmatrix} \times 3$	Conv $\begin{bmatrix} 1\times1/1/64 \\ 3\times3/1/64 \\ 1\times1/1/256 \end{bmatrix} \times 3$	Conv $\begin{bmatrix} 1\times1/1/64 \\ 3\times3/1/64 \\ 1\times1/1/256 \end{bmatrix} \times 3$
Conv $\begin{bmatrix} 3\times3/2/128 \\ 3\times3/1/128 \end{bmatrix} \times 1$	Conv $\begin{bmatrix} 1\times1/2/128 \\ 3\times3/1/128 \\ 1\times1/1/512 \end{bmatrix} \times 1$	Conv $\begin{bmatrix} 1\times1/2/128 \\ 3\times3/1/128 \\ 1\times1/1/512 \end{bmatrix} \times 1$
Conv $\begin{bmatrix} 3\times3/1/128 \\ 3\times3/1/128 \end{bmatrix} \times 3$	Conv $\begin{bmatrix} 1\times1/1/128 \\ 3\times3/1/128 \\ 1\times1/1/512 \end{bmatrix} \times 3$	Conv $\begin{bmatrix} 1\times1/1/128 \\ 3\times3/1/128 \\ 1\times1/1/512 \end{bmatrix} \times 7$
Conv $\begin{bmatrix} 3\times3/2/256 \\ 3\times3/1/256 \end{bmatrix} \times 1$	Conv $\begin{bmatrix} 1\times1/2/256 \\ 3\times3/1/256 \\ 1\times1/1/1{,}024 \end{bmatrix} \times 1$	Conv $\begin{bmatrix} 1\times1/2/256 \\ 3\times3/1/256 \\ 1\times1/1/1{,}024 \end{bmatrix} \times 1$
Conv $\begin{bmatrix} 3\times3/1/256 \\ 3\times3/1/256 \end{bmatrix} \times 5$	Conv $\begin{bmatrix} 1\times1/1/256 \\ 3\times3/1/256 \\ 1\times1/1/1{,}024 \end{bmatrix} \times 5$	Conv $\begin{bmatrix} 1\times1/1/256 \\ 3\times3/1/256 \\ 1\times1/1/1{,}024 \end{bmatrix} \times 35$
Conv $\begin{bmatrix} 3\times3/2/512 \\ 3\times3/1/512 \end{bmatrix} \times 1$	Conv $\begin{bmatrix} 1\times1/2/512 \\ 3\times3/1/512 \\ 1\times1/1/2{,}048 \end{bmatrix} \times 1$	Conv $\begin{bmatrix} 1\times1/2/512 \\ 3\times3/1/512 \\ 1\times1/1/2{,}048 \end{bmatrix} \times 1$

Continued

Table 8-3 **ResNet Architecture* (Continued)**

Conv $\begin{bmatrix} 3\times3/1/512 \\ 3\times3/1/512 \end{bmatrix} \times 2$	Conv $\begin{bmatrix} 1\times1/1/512 \\ 3\times3/1/512 \\ 1\times1/1/2,048 \end{bmatrix} \times 2$	Conv $\begin{bmatrix} 1\times1/1/512 \\ 3\times3/1/512 \\ 1\times1/1/2,048 \end{bmatrix} \times 2$
Avg pool 7×7/1		
FC softmax 1000		

*Each building block inside of brackets employs skip connections and are replicated as stated in the table. Skip connections for layers that change the number of output channels use 1×1 convolutions, as illustrated in Figure 8-6 (right). Further, batch normalization is applied to the convolutional layers, as illustrated in Figure 8-7 (right).

error of 15.3% using a 8-layer network to a top-5 error of 3.57% using networks containing up to 152 layers. To put this into context, the second-best submission in 2012 achieved a top-5 error of 26.2%, which illustrates the remarkable progress that DL enabled in this problem domain in just three years. We now move on to a programming example in which we use a pretrained ResNet implementation to classify images.

Programming Example: Use a Pretrained ResNet Implementation

Because training a model like ResNet-50 takes a long time, our programming example uses an already trained model. We use it to classify the dog and the cat shown in Figure 8-8.

We start with a number of import statements in Code Snippet 8-1.

Code Snippet 8-1 **Initialization Code for Our ResNet Example**

```
import numpy as np
from tensorflow.keras.applications import resnet50
from tensorflow.keras.preprocessing.image import load_img
from tensorflow.keras.preprocessing.image import img_to_array
```

```
from tensorflow.keras.applications.resnet50 import \
    decode_predictions
import matplotlib.pyplot as plt
import tensorflow as tf
import logging
tf.get_logger().setLevel(logging.ERROR)
```

Figure 8-8 Dog and cat that we will attempt to classify

In Code Snippet 8-2, we then load one of the images with the function `load_img`, which will return an image in PIL format. We specified that we want the picture to be scaled to 224×224 pixels because that is what the ResNet-50 implementation expects. We then convert the image into a NumPy tensor to be able to present it to our network. The network expects an array of multiple images, so we add a fourth dimension; consequently, we have an array of images with a single element.

Code Snippet 8-2 Load Image and Convert to Tensor

```
# Load image and convert to 4-dimensional tensor.
image = load_img('../data/dog.jpg', target_size=(224, 224))
image_np = img_to_array(image)
image_np = np.expand_dims(image_np, axis=0)
```

Code Snippet 8-3 shows how to load the ResNet-50 model, using weights that have been trained using the ImageNet dataset. Just as we did in previous examples, we standardize the input images because the ResNet-50 model expects them to be standardized. The function `preprocess_input` does that for us, using parameters derived from the training dataset that was used to train the model. We present the image to the network by calling `model.predict()` and then print the predictions after first calling the convenience method `decode_predictions()`, which retrieves the labels in textual form.

Code Snippet 8-3 **Load Network, Preprocess and Classify Image**

```
# Load the pretrained model.
model = resnet50.ResNet50(weights='imagenet')
# Standardize input data.
X = resnet50.preprocess_input(image_np.copy())
# Do prediction.
y = model.predict(X)
predicted_labels = decode_predictions(y)
print('predictions = ', predicted_labels)

# Show image.
plt.imshow(np.uint8(image_np[0]))
plt.show()
```

The output for the dog picture is

```
predictions =  [[('n02091134', 'whippet', 0.4105768),
('n02115641', 'dingo', 0.07289727), ('n02085620', 'Chihuahua',
0.052068174), ('n02111889', 'Samoyed', 0.04776454),
('n02104029', 'kuvasz', 0.038022097)]]
```

This means that the network predicted that the dog is a *whippet* (a dog breed) with 41% probability, a *dingo* with 7.3% probability, a *chihuahua* with 5.2% probability, and so on. We happen to know that the dog in the picture is a mix of *chihuahua*, *Jack Russell terrier, miniature poodle,* and some other breeds, so at least the *chihuahua* prediction makes sense. This also illustrates why the approximately 5% top-5 error on the ImageNet challenge is human-level capability. The categories are extremely detailed, so it is hard to pinpoint the exact category of an object.

Applying our network to the cat picture results in the following output:

```
predictions =  [[('n02123045', 'tabby', 0.16372949),
('n02124075', 'Egyptian_cat', 0.107477844), ('n02870880',
```

```
'bookcase', 0.10175342), ('n03793489', 'mouse', 0.059262287),
('n03085013', 'computer_keyboard', 0.053496547)]]
```

We see that the network correctly categorized the cat as a *tabby* as highest probability, and we also see that *computer keyboard* is on the list, which is also correct because there is a keyboard in the background. At first, it might seem somewhat confusing how the network could mistake our cat for a *mouse* (5.9% probability), but when we look up the category *n03793489*, it turns out that it refers to a computer mouse, and although there is no computer mouse in the picture, there are enough computer-related items to justify why the network would make such a mistake. This concludes our programming example, and we now move on to describe a few other related techniques to wrap up the topic of CNNs.

> We have finally managed to classify a cat picture! We sit back and reflect over how much of the total compute capability in the world is being used to classify cat pictures at this very moment.

Transfer Learning

In the preceding programming example, we used a pretrained model and applied it to the same type of problem that it was trained to address. In this section, we discuss two related techniques. The first is to start from a pretrained model and then train it further with your own data. The other option is to use parts of the pretrained model as a building block in your own model intended to solve a different, but related, problem.

Let us first look at the simple case of starting with a pretrained model and continuing to train it with your own data for the same problem type, also known as *fine-tuning*. This is often beneficial if your own dataset is limited in size. Even if you had a large dataset, starting from a pretrained model can still be beneficial because it can reduce the amount of time you need to spend training it with your own data.

In many cases, the problem at hand is related to, but still somewhat different from, what the network was originally trained to do. For example, let us assume that you have ten dogs (perhaps you are running a kennel), and you need to distinguish between different individuals, some of which are of the same breed. This is clearly a classification problem, but using a network trained for ImageNet classification with its 1,000 classes will not work. Instead, you want a network that classifies an image as being one of ten specific dogs. This can be done using *transfer learning*. It involves taking a model, or parts of a model, that is trained for one task, and then using it to solve a different, but related, task. The idea is that some of the skills learned for the original task carry over (transfer) and are applicable to the new task. In this example, we could use a pretrained version of one of the convolutional networks in this chapter and replace some of the last layers with our own layers that end with a ten-output softmax layer. We would then train this model on our own dataset with the ten dogs that we want the network to classify. We would benefit from the fact that the convolutional layers already have the ability to recognize specific features that are useful for identifying different types of dogs. The process of taking a pretrained network and replacing some layers is illustrated in Figure 8-9.

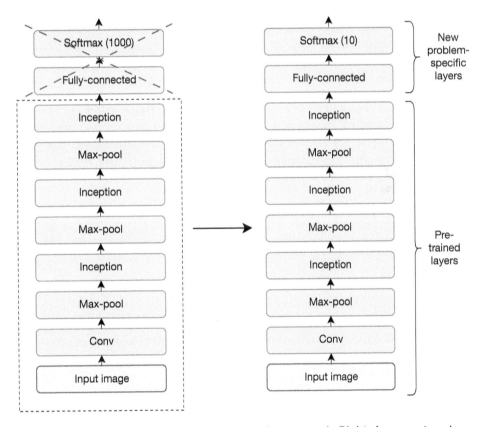

Figure 8-9 Transfer learning. Left: An inception network. Right: A new network based on pretrained layers from the inception network but with the last couple of layers replaced by new layers that are trained for the new problem.

A couple of practical details are worth mentioning. When training begins, the layers from the pretrained model have already been trained for many epochs on a large dataset, whereas the weights in the final layers are completely random. If we just go ahead and start training on our own dataset, there is a risk that the learning algorithm ruins the carefully trained weights from the pretrained model. Therefore, it is often a good idea to freeze these weights and only train the newly added layers. This also makes the training process faster because the number of adjustable parameters is significantly smaller. After training the model for a while with the pretrained layers frozen, a next step can be to fine-tune this model by unfreezing those layers and training for another few epochs with a smaller learning rate.

One powerful technique is to do pretraining of a model using an unsupervised learning technique that does not require labeled data. Large amounts of unlabeled data are much easier to obtain than labeled data. By pretraining on the unlabeled data, it is possible to train a model to learn to detect useful features without the cost of obtaining a large, labeled dataset. The pretrained model is then used to build the final model that is trained using a smaller labeled dataset. In Chapters 11 through 13, we will see examples of training a model to learn language structure from unlabeled data.

We do not go into more details about transfer learning in this section, but of you are interested, Zhuang and colleagues (2020) wrote a survey paper on the topic. We will also see an example of transfer learning in Chapter 16, "One-to-Many Network for Image Captioning," where we use a pretrained VGGNet model as a building block in an image captioning network.

> Transfer learning makes use of a pretrained model to build a model that is further trained for a different use case.

Backpropagation for CNN and Pooling

We are using a DL framework, so we do not need to worry about how the backpropagation algorithm works with convolutional layers but understanding it is still interesting. It seems like if we use the algorithm unchanged, it is likely to break the invariant that all neurons in a channel have the same weights. Intuitively, we can ensure that this invariant still holds true by first ensuring that all of the neurons in a channel get the same values at initialization and then applying identical updates to all weights that are supposed to be identical to each other.

Initializing them to the same values is trivial. The only question is how to determine what to use as the update value. If you think about it in the terms of the definition of the update value, this falls out naturally. The update value for a weight is simply the partial derivative of the loss function with respect to that weight. Let us now consider how a convolutional network is different from a fully connected network. The key difference is that if we write the overall equation for the convolutional network (including the loss function), each weight in the convolutional layers will appear multiple times in the equation, whereas a weight appears only once in the equation for the fully connected network. The resulting partial derivative with respect to a weight turns out to be a sum of the partial derivative with respect to each instance of the weight in the equation.

Computing the resulting update values with the backpropagation algorithm is straightforward. It is very similar to a fully connected network. We perform the forward and backward passes just like in the fully connected case. The difference is how to update the weights. Instead of updating a specific weight for a given neuron by the update value computed for that instance of the weight, we update the weight by the sum of the update values for all instances of that shared weight. We apply this same update value to all the copies of that weight in the network. In practice, an efficient implementation of a convolutional layer would not store multiple copies of all the weights but would instead share the weights in the implementation as well. So, the update process would need to update only that one single copy of the weights that is then used by all the neurons in the channel.

Apart from the issue of how to handle the weight sharing property for convolutional layers, we also need to address how to use backpropagation with the max pooling layers where the max operation clearly is not differentiable. It turns out that this is straightforward as well. We simply backpropagate the error only to the neuron that provided the input with the maximum value because the other inputs clearly do not affect the error.

Data Augmentation as a Regularization Technique

In Chapter 6, "Fully Connected Networks Applied to Regression," we discussed the problem of networks failing to generalize and how that can be addressed with regularization. An effective technique to improve generalization is to simply increase the size of the training dataset. That makes it harder for the network to memorize it and forces the network to find general solutions to the problem. A challenge with this technique is that collecting and labeling large datasets can often be costly. One way to address this challenge is to use dataset augmentation. The dataset is augmented by creating additional training examples from existing ones. Figure 8-10 shows an example: We took a single picture of a dog and modified it in various ways to create ten new pictures that can be used for training.

There are a couple of pitfalls worth mentioning. One is that for certain kinds of data, only some transformations are legal without changing the actual meaning of the data. For example, while it is perfectly fine to flip a dog upside down or mirror it, the same does not hold true for the MNIST digits. If you turn the digit 6 upside down, it turns into a 9, and if you mirror a 3, it is no longer a 3. Another important issue is that data augmentation should be done after splitting the data into a training dataset and a test dataset instead of before that split. This is to avoid leaking information from the training dataset to the test dataset. Imagine if

Figure 8-10 One original image and ten variations of the picture resulting in a ten times larger dataset

you do the data augmentation before splitting the data into the two datasets. You might end up with the original image in the training dataset and a slight variation of this image in the test dataset. It is easier for the network to classify this slight variation correctly than to classify a completely different image correctly. You can therefore get overly optimistic results when you evaluate your network on your contaminated test dataset.

Data augmentation is an effective regularization technique, but it comes with some pitfalls.

Mistakes Made by CNNs

Although there has been amazing progress in image classification, beginning with the AlexNet paper (Krizhevsky, Sutskever, and Hinton, 2012), subsequent discoveries have raised reasons for concern. As an example, in 2014 Szegedy and colleagues showed that it was possible to slightly perturb images in a way so that a human could not tell that the image was modified but a neural network could no longer correctly classify the image (Szegedy, Zaremba, et al., 2014). They named these modified images *adversarial examples*.

We are now in the timeframe of Terminator Genisys, and it seems somewhat reassuring that we just discovered ways of tricking the neural networks—that comes in handy when fighting the machines for survival of humanity.

Another drawback came in 2019 when Azulay and Weiss (2019) showed that some popular modern networks were not robust to small translations (shifting of position) of just a few pixels, because using a stride larger than 1 ignores properties of the Nyquist sampling theorem. This serves as an example of how important it is to understand fundamental principles of the field to which you are applying DL.

Apart from problems with the model itself, CNNs are susceptible to problems caused by bias and lack of diversity in the training data. We touched on this when describing the MNIST dataset. A more recent example was when a popular photo app kept categorizing photos of people of color under the category *gorillas* (Howley, 2015). Although not intentional, this failure case underscores the importance of designing datasets that are diverse, unbiased, and complete.

Reducing Parameters with Depthwise Separable Convolutions

We saw in Chapter 7 how the number of weights for a neuron in a convolutional layer depends on the kernel size and the number of channels in the preceding layer. The latter follows from the fact that the convolution operation is applied to all the channels in the preceding layer. That is, a neuron in a single channel in the output layer has $M \times K^2 + 1$ weights, where M is the number of channels in the input layer, K is the kernel size (K^2 because it is 2D), and +1 is the bias weight. An output layer with N channels results in $N \times (M \times K^2 + 1)$ total number of weights. The number of weights is not dependent on the width and height of the layer due to weight sharing, but the number of computations is. For an output layer of width W and height H, the total number of multiplications is $W \times H \times N \times (M \times K^2 + 1)$.

Depthwise separable convolutions reduce the number of weights and computations while achieving similar results. This is done by breaking up the convolutions into two steps. Instead of having each output neuron do convolutions for each input channel, the first step is to compute convolutions for each input channel in isolation. This results in an intermediate layer with the same number of channels as in the input layer. The output layer then does 1×1 convolutions, also known as *pointwise convolutions*, across the channels in this intermediate layer. That is, instead of each output channel having its own weights for each input channel, a single set of shared weights is used for the convolutions over each input channel. The weights in the output layer then determine how to combine the results of those convolutions.

This is illustrated in Figure 8-11. The left image shows a traditional convolution, where a single neuron computes a weighted sum of a region across all the input channels. The right image shows a depthwise separable convolution for which we first compute a weighted sum for each input channel and then a separate (pointwise) convolution computes a weighted sum of the previously mentioned weighted sums. The benefit of the depthwise separable convolution is not obvious from the picture because it depicts only a single output channel. The benefit becomes apparent when computing multiple output channels, in which case the depthwise separable convolutions only need to add more pointwise convolutions (four weights per additional output), whereas the traditional convolution needs to add more full convolutions (ten weights per additional output).

There are $M \times (K^2 + 1)$ weights for the first step and $N \times (M + 1)$ weights for the second step. Assuming that the dimensions of both the input and output layers

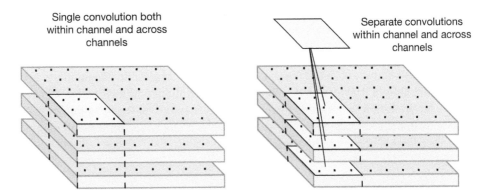

Single convolution both within channel and across channels

Separate convolutions within channel and across channels

Figure 8-11 Left: Normal convolutions. Right: Depthwise separable convolutions. The figure illustrates only a single output channel and does not highlight the benefit.

are $W \times H$, the total number of multiplications is $W \times H \times (M \times (K^2 + 1)) + W \times H \times (N \times (M + 1))$. This turns out to be a significant reduction compared to the formula for the normal convolution in the beginning of this section. The first term for the depthwise separable convolution does not include the factor N, and the second term does not include the factor K^2, both of which are substantial in magnitude.

It turns out that in many cases, the behavior of this operation works just as well as the regular convolution operation. Intuitively, this implies that the type of kernel (what weights to choose) to apply to a specific input channel does not depend much on which output channel it is producing a value for. We draw that conclusion because, for depthwise separable convolutions, all output channels share the kernel that is applied to a specific input channel. Clearly, this is not always true, and there is a range of design points between the depthwise separable convolution and the normal convolution. For example, the first step in the process can be modified to creating two or more channels per input channel. As often is the case in DL, this is yet another hyperparameter in your network architecture to experiment with. That is, anytime you are building a CNN, consider using a depthwise separable convolution instead. In many cases, it will result in a much faster network, that performs equally well from an accuracy perspective.

Before ending our description of depthwise separable convolutions, it is worth mentioning how they relate to the modules found in VGGNet, GoogLeNet, and ResNet. In many cases, these modules made use of 1×1 convolutions to do a channel reduction before applying the convolution operation. This is similar to the depthwise separable convolutions but in reverse order. One other difference is that when doing a 1×1 convolution followed by another convolution operation, there is an activation function between the two convolutions, whereas this is not the case for the depthwise separable convolution.

Two examples of networks that use depthwise separable convolutions are MobileNets (Howard et al., 2017) and the Xception module (Chollet, 2016). The latter stands for Extreme Inception and is inspired by the Inception module used by GoogLeNet (Szegedy, Liu, et al., 2014), but it is based entirely on depthwise separable convolution layers.

Striking the Right Network Design Balance with EfficientNet

In this chapter, we have seen three examples of networks that explored the effect of network depth. Although important, network depth is just one of multiple dimensions to explore. In particular, two other key dimensions are the resolution (width and height) of each layer and the number of channels, as illustrated in Figure 8-12. Tan and Le (2019) pointed out that studying just one parameter in isolation is not likely to find the most efficient design.

In the paper, they set out to explore the design space with the goal of arriving at the best-performing design in a constrained environment. For example, given

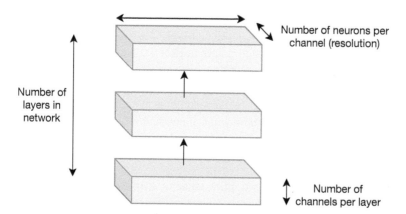

Figure 8-12 Three key parameters in a convolutional network. EfficientNets of different sizes maintain a constant relationship among these three parameters instead of scaling only a single dimension.

a specific number of floating-point operations and bytes of memory, determine the combination of depth, resolution, and number of channels that yields the best-performing CNN. By experimenting with small enough networks to be able to do a thorough investigation of the design space, they arrived at a baseline design that is very efficient. They then showed that this network could be scaled up in a way that maintains the ratios among these three design parameters. The result was a more demanding but still efficient network. Scaling the baseline network to increasing sizes resulted in a family of networks named EfficientNets. Overall, EfficientNets have been shown to achieve levels of prediction accuracy similar to those of other popular networks but at an order of magnitude lower computational cost compared to previous CNN architectures.

Concluding Remarks on Deeper CNNs

Although the most recently described networks might seem complicated compared to what we have seen in previous chapters, even these networks are considered simple nowadays. Still, our opinion is that they represent core knowledge that anybody serious about learning about DL should have. Once you understand these networks, you are in a good position to read research papers about variations and combinations of these networks. Some such examples are Inception-v2 and v3 (Szegedy et al., 2016) and Inception-v4 (Szegedy et al., 2017). These three networks are deeper than Inception-v1 and result in better accuracy. A next step is Inception-ResNet (Szegedy et al., 2017), which is a hybrid network that combines Inception modules and skip connections. Inception-ResNet can be viewed as an Inception network that adds mechanisms inspired by ResNet. A different but related approach is ResNeXt (Xie et al., 2017), where NeXt refers to a *next dimension*. This architecture uses ResNet as a starting point but consists of a module with multiple paths similarly to what is done in the Inception module. The key difference is that all the paths in ResNeXt are identical as opposed to the Inception module's heterogeneous architecture.

This discussion about CNNs has focused on *classification*—determining which kind of object is in an image—in which ResNet has surpassed human capabilities at least for the ImageNet classification challenge. However, classification is not the only problem type that CNNs can be applied to, and more challenging problems exist. Such problems include drawing bounding boxes around individual objects (detection) or pinpointing the specific pixels that correspond to an object (segmentation). Appendix B describes the three problems *object detection*, *semantic segmentation*, and *instance segmentation* in more detail.

Work has also been done to gain a better understanding of how and why convolutional networks work. For example, a study by Zeiler and Fergus (2014) examined visualizing what features the different layers detect.

CNNs can also be applied to problem domains other than image analysis. For example, they have been used for sentiment analysis of text (Dos Santos and Gatti, 2014), where the task is to infer whether the sentiment of the text is positive or negative. In this case the input is 1D (a sequence of characters or words) instead of 2D as in the case of an image. This implies that the convolutional layers will be somewhat different. Instead of going into the details of how to apply convolutional networks to textual data, we move on to a different technique, known as *recurrent neural networks* (RNNs). This technique is commonly used with textual data and is the topic of Chapters 9, 10, and 11. If you think that convolutional networks and computer vision applications are exciting, consider reading Appendix B at this point. On the other hand, if you are eager to get to natural language processing applications as quickly as possible, then we recommend that you just continue reading the book. You can always read Appendix B later.

Chapter 9

Predicting Time Sequences with Recurrent Neural Networks

In this chapter, we introduce another important neural network architecture known as the *recurrent neural network* (RNN). This architecture is useful when doing predictions based on sequential data, and especially for sequences of variable lengths. Before explaining what an RNN is, we provide some context by describing some of the problem types to which RNNs can be applied. We relate these problem types to the tasks we have already encountered in previous chapters.

Up until now, we have applied networks to two main categories of tasks. One was a regression problem in which the network predicted a real-valued variable based on a number of other variables, such as the example of a network that predicted the house price based on a number of variables associated with the house. The other type of task was a classification problem in which the network associated a data point, such as an image, with one of a number of possible classes, such as car, ship, or frog. A special case of the classification problem is the binary classification problem in which there are only two classes, typically *true* or *false*. We used that for the XOR-problem. Another example, which we have not studied, is to classify whether a patient has a certain disease given a number of input variables, such as gender, age, and the level of low-density lipoprotein (also known as LDL but not to be confused with the name of this book!). Time series (or sequence) prediction can be used in combination with any of these three problem types; see Table 9-1.

For each of these three examples, there are also variations with respect to the type of historical data that is used as input. Table 9-2 breaks down each example into three variations. The first row has historical values only for the variable it is trying to predict. The second row has historical values of the variable plus additional variables. The third row has historical values of other variables but not including the variable that it is trying to predict. At least one of the examples seems somewhat odd. Predicting the next characters of a sentence without knowing the beginning of the sentence in some sense modifies the problem from *complete a sentence* to *generate a sentence from scratch*.

In this chapter, we explore the sales forecasting problem, or in other words, a regression problem, by trying to forecast bookstore sales. We look at the case where the input data is only a single variable (historical book sales data). We also describe how to extend the mechanism to handle multiple input variables,

Table 9-1 Sequential Prediction Problems and How They Relate to Their Nonsequential Counterpart

	REGRESSION	BINARY CLASSIFICATION	MULTICLASS CLASSIFICATION
Nonsequential	Estimate house price based on size and location	Provide disease diagnosis based on patient gender, age, and other variables	Determine which digit a handwritten image depicts
Time series or sequential prediction	Predict next month's customer demand based on historical sales data	Predict if it will rain tomorrow based on historical weather data	Predict the next character in a sentence

such as the case where the input data consists of historical sales data for the item of interest as well as other related goods. The problem is illustrated in Figure 9-1.

In Chapter 10, "Long Short-Term Memory," we learn how to overcome some of the limitations associated with the basic RNN by using more advanced units when building the network. In Chapter 11, "Text Autocompletion with LSTM and Beam Search," we then apply this more advanced network to the problem of doing autocompletion of text, similar to functionality that can be found in email clients and Internet search engines. Specifically, the problem type that we apply it to is the one represented by the top row in Table 9-2, where only the beginning of the sentence and no other context is available as input to the network.

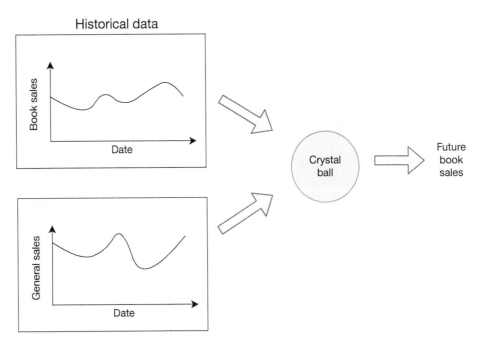

Figure 9-1 Sales forecasting problem. The figure illustrates the case where we use both historical book sales data and general sales figures. The thinking is that general sales can indicate the overall state of the economy and might be beneficial when forecasting specific sales. A variation of the problem is to have only historical book sales as input variable.

Table 9-2 **Variations on the Prediction Problems***

	MONTHLY SALES PREDICTION	RAIN PREDICTION	NEXT CHARACTER PREDICTION
Input consists of historical values of only the variable we are trying to predict	Historical sales data for the item of interest	Historical rain data	Beginning of sentence
Input consists of multiple variables, including historical values of the variable we are trying to predict	Historical sales data for the item of interest, sales data for other related goods, or other economic indicators	Historical data on rain, temperature, humidity, and atmospheric pressure	Beginning of sentence and context identifiers (e.g., topic of the book and style of paragraph)
Input consists of multiple variables but does not include historical values of the variable we are trying to predict	Sales data for related goods, and other economic indicators	Historical data on temperature, humidity, and atmospheric pressure	Only context identifiers (This seems like an odd case)

*The three rows differ in the types of historical input data that is available.

Some of these problems are about predicting the future, but not all sequential data is associated with time series. For instance, you could argue that in the case of autocompletion of natural language sentences, predicting the next word in a sentence has less to do with predicting the future and more to do with identifying the most probable ending of a sentence that has already been written but not yet seen. To simplify our discussion, we will generally talk about inputs to RNNs as being sequential in time, but we acknowledge that they can be applied to the more general case of any sequential data. In other words, RNNs try to solve the problem of predicting the next value or symbol in a sequence regardless of what the sequence represents.

RNNs are used for prediction of sequences and can work with input data with variable length.

Limitations of Feedforward Networks

A first idea for solving the sales forecasting problem is to just use a fully connected feedforward network[1] with a linear output unit. We standardize this month's book sales and, optionally, sales of other goods, then provide these numerical values to the network and hope that the network can use that data to learn to output the book demand for next month. This is shown in the left part of Figure 9-2. The superscript numbers in the figure denote the temporal relationship between data points. A data point with the superscript $(t+1)$ refers to the observed data value one month after a data point with the superscript (t).

It seems likely that we will not have much luck with this approach because we provide the network with limited information. Sales numbers are likely seasonal, and the network will need access to multiple historical data points to pick up seasonal patterns. A second attempt at solving the prediction problem is shown in the right part of Figure 9-2.

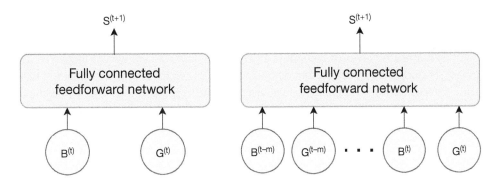

Figure 9-2 Left: Feedforward network predicting demand using current-month values as input. Right: Feedforward network predicting demand using values from multiple historical months as input. *S* represents predicted sales, *B* represents historical book sales and *G* represents historical general sales. The superscript represents time (month), where *t* is the current month.

---

1. In reality, using a simple feedforward network for sequence prediction is not a good idea. In particular, it is not tolerant to translations (shifts) in time. A better approach is to use a time-delay neural network (TDNN), which is a form of 1D convolutional network and is thereby translation invariant. However, we use the simple feedforward network in this discussion to avoid having to introduce the TDNN concept at this point of the book. If you are interested, Appendix C contains a brief section about 1D convolution applied to sequential data.

Here we arrange the historical values into an input vector and present it to our feedforward network, which outputs a prediction of the book sales for the next month. This seems like a more promising approach, but the network still will not get access to all the historical data unless we make an infinitely wide input layer, which is not practical. One way to address this issue would be to compute a running average over the historical data points that are far back and provide this running average as an input to the network. Then, at least, the network has access to some representation of all the historical data. There are other ways to aggregate information about historical data, such as keeping track of the maximum observed value and the minimum observed value and feeding them as input into the network. It would be even better if, instead of choosing how to aggregate historical information, we could let the network learn its own internal representation of historical data. This is a key property of the RNN, which we describe in the next section.

Recurrent Neural Networks

A simple form of RNN can be created by connecting the outputs from a fully connected layer to the inputs of that same layer as shown in Figure 9-3. The figure shows a three-value input vector connected to a fully connected layer of four neurons. The bias values are omitted from the figure. Along with the three inputs (and bias input), each neuron has four additional inputs. These inputs receive the output values from the four neurons but delayed by one timestep.

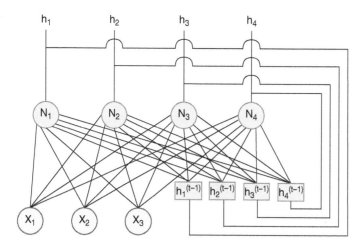

Figure 9-3 Fully connected recurrent neural network layer

That is, at time *t*, they will receive the output values for time *t*–1. We denote these outputs as *h* for *hidden* because recurrent layers typically serve as hidden layers inside the network. Although they are explicitly called out as hidden, these outputs are no different than outputs from a regular feedforward layer inside of a network.

Just as in a feedforward network, we can freely choose the number of hidden neurons independently of the number of elements in the input vector. However, the number of inputs (weights) to a single neuron is now a function of both the size of the input vector and the number of neurons in the layer. We can stack multiple recurrent layers after each other to create a deep RNN. We can also combine recurrent layers, regular fully connected feedforward layers, and convolutional layers in the same network.

> The number of inputs to a neuron in an RNN layer is dependent both on the number of inputs to the layer (typically determined by the number of neurons in the previous layer) and the number of neurons in the layer itself.

Mathematical Representation of a Recurrent Layer

We previously described how a fully connected layer can be represented mathematically by multiplying the input vector by a weight matrix, where each row in the matrix represents the weights for a single neuron. With a *tanh* activation function this can be written as follows:

$$y = tanh(W\mathbf{x})$$

This formula assumes that the first element of the vector **x** contains the value 1 and the weight matrix contains the bias weight. Another option is to explicitly state all the bias weights as a separate vector that gets added to the vector resulting from the matrix multiplication and exclude the value 1 in vector **x**:

$$y = tanh(W\mathbf{x} + \mathbf{b})$$

The matrix-vector multiplication *W***x** results in a vector with the same number of elements as there are neurons in the layer. Each element is the weighted sum of all the inputs to a single neuron (i.e., it is a partial weighted sum because it does not include the bias weight). The vector **b** also has the same number of elements as the number of neurons, and each element represents the bias weight for a neuron. Now summing Wx and b means doing elementwise addition. We add the bias weight to each partial weighted sum, and we end up with the full weighted sum for each neuron. Finally, tanh is also done elementwise on each weighted sum, resulting in an output value corresponding to each neuron.

Let us now look at how we can represent a recurrent layer using matrices. The actual computations are the same, but now the input vector must be a concatenation of both the actual input vector $x^{(t)}$ as well as the previous output $h^{(t-1)}$. Similarly, the weight matrix now needs to contain weights for both the actual inputs and the recurrent connections. That is, the previous equation applies to a recurrent layer as well, but a more common way of expressing it is with separate matrices to make the recurrent connections more explicit:

$$h^{(t)} = tanh(Wh^{(t-1)} + Ux^{(t)} + b)$$

Wow! That is one compact way of summarizing the long textual description and complexity of Figure 9-3.

Figure 9-4 shows how the elements in the matrices and vectors map to inputs, recurrent connections, weights, and biases in a recurrent layer. It is clear that using linear algebra is powerful in that it leads to a compact, yet precise, description of the connections. However, its drawback is that the equation makes it harder to visualize the actual connections, which in our opinion does limit the intuition gained, especially for beginners. We will continue working with figures because they provide additional value. Still, it is common to see matrix notation in the literature, so you should become familiar with this notation.

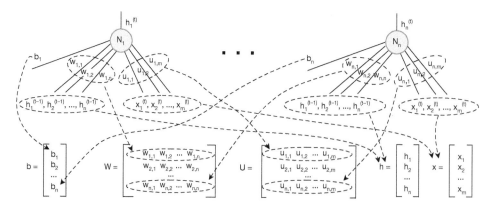

Figure 9-4 Mapping between weights and matrix elements

Combining Layers into an RNN

Let us now consider how we can create a network to solve our sales forecasting problem. Figure 9-5 shows an initial attempt whereby we start with two inputs, representing historical book sales and overall consumer spending. We assume that they have been standardized by subtracting the mean and dividing by standard deviation. These are fed into a recurrent layer with four units, followed by a fully connected layer with two units and finally an output layer consisting of a single unit. With respect to activation functions, we want the output layer to be a simple linear unit (i.e., with no nonlinear activation function) because we want it to output a numerical value rather than a probability. For the hidden layers, we can choose any nonlinear activation function, just as for the other types of networks that we have studied.

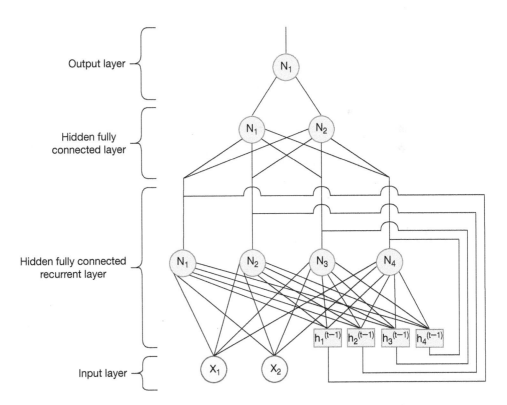

Figure 9-5 RNN to forecast book sales. The architecture assumes that we are using two input variables (x_1 and x_2).

Computing the output from this network is done iteratively by first presenting the input vector for one month to the network and computing the hidden states, and then presenting the input vector for the next month and computing new hidden states, which are functions of the current hidden states and the new input vector. We do this for all historical data that we have access to and end up with a prediction for the next month. The network can use all this data and compute any useful internal representation of the historical data that it can use to predict the next month. From a learning perspective, the first layer has more weights than a feedforward layer with the same number of inputs. The reason is that each neuron has weights not only for the input vector x but also for the inputs that are fed by the output from the previous timestep $h^{(t-1)}$. In a later section, we describe how a network like this can be trained using backpropagation. The network we just described is only an illustration of the architecture. In a real application, we would likely use many more neurons in the hidden layers, but that is harder to fit in a figure. To address that visualization issue, we now show another way to draw and think about RNNs.

Alternative View of RNN and Unrolling in Time

So far, we have explicitly drawn all the connections in our RNN, which is not practical as we move to deeper networks with many units in each layer. To work around this limitation, a more compact way of drawing networks is to let a node in the graph represent an entire layer, as in the left side of Figure 9-6. Just as in previous chapters, we use a rectangular node with rounded corners to

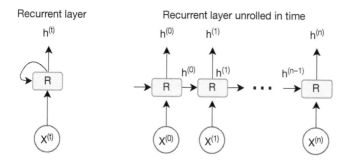

Figure 9-6 Left: Recurrent network drawn with one node representing an entire layer. Right: Recurrent layer unrolled in time.

represent an entire layer by a node, as opposed to individual neurons, which are represented by circles. In this figure, the circular arrow represents the recurrent connections. With this notation, much information about the topology is implicit, so the figure needs to be accompanied by textual descriptions making it clear that it is fully connected as well as the number of neurons.

The right side of Figure 9-6 shows how a recurrent layer can be unrolled in time. By creating one copy of the recurrent layer for each timestep, we have converted the recurrent layer into a number of feedforward layers. Obviously, to do this, we need to know the number of timesteps, and the resulting network can no longer accept a variably sized input vector, which was one of the reasons that we defined the recurrent layer in the first place. A fair question is why we would want to do this unrolling. It turns out that unrolling can be useful both for reasoning about the network and when extending the backpropagation algorithm to work for recurrent networks.

We start by using the unrolled version for reasoning about how a recurrent layer relates to a fully connected feedforward network. As mentioned earlier, unrolling the recurrent layer results in a feedforward network. Does that mean that the recurrent layer is equivalent to the feedforward network if we happen to know the length of the input sequence? Not quite, because one key distinction is discovered if we consider the weights of the network, which have been omitted from all the figures. In the feedforward network, we can have different weights for all connections, but in the recurrent layer, the weights need to be the same for each timestep. In particular, each horizontal arrow on the right side of Figure 9-6 maps to the same connection but for a different timestep, and the same applies to the vertical arrows. That is, just as convolutional layers have weight sharing *within* a layer, recurrent layers are like a feedforward network with weight sharing *between* layers. Just as weight sharing was beneficial for convolutional networks, recurrent networks have a similar benefit of requiring fewer weights to train. However, weight sharing also has a drawback, which is discussed in the next section, where we use the unrolled view of the network to describe how to use backpropagation to train RNNs.

An RNN can be unrolled in time and thereby converted to a feedforward network but with the restriction that the layers share weights with each other.

Backpropagation Through Time

Given that we have already shown how a recurrent layer can be redrawn as a feedforward network, it should be straightforward to understand how it can be trained using backpropagation. Once the network is unrolled, we can backpropagate the error in exactly the same way as we do for a feedforward network, although it might be somewhat computationally expensive in cases with long input sequences. Just as for the convolutional layer, we must ensure to take weight sharing into account when updating the weights. In other words, for each weight, the backpropagation algorithm will produce one update value for each timestep, but when we later want to update the weight, there is only one weight to update. This algorithm is known as *backpropagation through time* (BPTT). Werbos (1990) has written a more detailed description, which also contains links to papers in which the algorithm was first used. In practice, few people need to worry about the exact details of how BPTT works because the deep learning (DL) framework handles it. However, there are some implications that you do need to worry about; they are described next.

An RNN can be trained by doing backpropagation through time (BPTT).

Figure 9-7 shows a deep RNN with m layers and $n+1$ timesteps. In addition to the normal weights that connect the layers (denoted $w_1, w_2, \ldots, w_m$), there are also recurrent weights connecting each layer to itself (denoted $w_{r1}, w_{r2}, \ldots, w_{rm}$). The figure also contains a grid of arrows illustrating how the error will propagate backward for the learning algorithm (ignore the fact that one path is colored red for now). What is shown is the error from the output node for the last timestep, propagating to the input weight for the first timestep, splitting up into multiple paths along the way. The vertical paths are no different from a regular feedforward network. However, there are now also horizontal paths where the error propagates backward through time.

We previously described the problem of vanishing gradients that was caused by multiplying the error by the derivative of the activation function in each layer of the network. This problem was caused by using S-shaped activation functions in which the derivatives approached 0 when the neurons became saturated. In addition, Bengio, Simard, and Frasconi (1994) showed that RNNs suffer from a different problem. To keep things simple, let us just consider the red arrow in Figure 9-7. Let us also imagine that each rectangular node is a single neuron

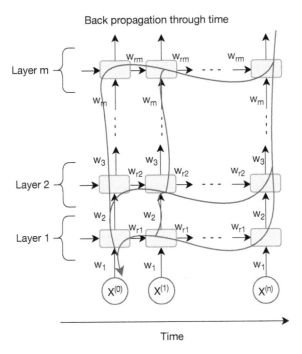

Back propagation through time

Figure 9-7 Gradient flow for backpropagation through time. The path of the error from the output node of the last timestep propagates backward both through the network (vertically) and through time (horizontally). The arrows represent computing the partial derivative with respect to weight w_1 at the first timestep.

instead of a full layer of neurons. Finally, let us assume that these neurons have linear activation functions, so their derivatives are all 1. We can now compute the partial derivative with respect to weight w_1 using the following formula, where the superscripts inside of parenthesis represent timesteps:

$$\frac{\partial e}{\partial w_1} = -error \cdot 1 \cdot w_m^{(n)} \cdot \ldots \cdot w_3^{(n)} \cdot 1 \cdot w_2^{(n)} \cdot 1 \cdot w_{r1}^{(n)} \cdot \ldots \cdot w_{r1}^{(2)} \cdot 1 \cdot w_{r1}^{(1)} \cdot 1 \cdot x^{(0)}$$

Now consider the following subset of that formula that represents how the error propagates backward through the recurrent connections (horizontally in the figure), that is, through time: $w_{r1}^{(n)} \cdot \ldots \cdot w_{r1}^{(2)} \cdot 1 \cdot w_{r1}^{(1)}$.

Due to weight sharing, all instances of w_{r1} are the same, so we can collapse that expression into w_{r1}^n, where the superscript n represents *exponentiation* instead of indicating a specific timestep. The exponent n represents the total number of timesteps for a certain training example and can be large. For example, a case with three years of data with one data point every day will result in more than 1,000 timesteps.

Consider what happens if you have a number that is smaller than 1 and multiply it by itself 1,000 times. It will approach 0 (i.e., a vanishing gradient). On the other hand, if the number is greater than 1 and you multiply it by itself 1,000 times, it will approach infinity (i.e., an exploding gradient). These vanishing and exploding gradients are caused by the weight sharing across timesteps, as opposed to vanishing gradients caused by saturated activation functions.

Vanishing gradients in RNNs are caused both by the **activation function** and by the **weights.**

This example assumed that each node in Figure 9-7 was a single neuron and each recurrent connection consisted of a single weight. In reality, each node in the figure represents an entire recurrent layer, which consists of a large number of neurons. In other words, w_{r1} in the figure is a matrix because each layer has multiple neurons and each neuron has a vector of weights. That, in turn, implies that in reality, the preceding equation is a little bit more complex and should be stated using linear algebra. Conceptually, the description is still the same, but instead of looking at the value of a single weight, we need to consider the *eigenvalue* of the weight matrix. If the eigenvalue is less than 1, then the gradient runs the risk of vanishing. If the eigenvalue is greater than 1, then the gradient runs the risk of exploding. We revisit these problems in Chapter 10, but first, let us try out a programming exercise to get our hands dirty with RNNs.

There is no need to worry even if you are not familiar with what an **eigenvalue** of a matrix is. As always, this is something you can consider for future reading.

Programming Example: Forecasting Book Sales

Our programming example uses only one input variable (historical book sales), but we also describe how to extend it to multiple input variables. We use historical sales data from the U.S. Census Bureau.[2] The downloaded data will take the form

---

2. https://www.census.gov/retail/index.html

of one comma-separated values (.csv) file per product category. Each line will contain year/month and an amount representing the sales in millions of U.S. dollars. As opposed to previous examples, the model cannot directly consume this format, so the first step is to organize the data properly. Figure 9-8 shows what the RNN expects from a single training example.

The training example consists of a vector of arbitrary length, where each entry in the vector contains the input data for a single timestep. In our example, a timestep is equivalent to a month. Depending on how we define our problem, we will have one or more input variables for each timestep. In addition to the input vector, each training example consists of a single expected output value. It represents the book sales for the month immediately following the most recent month in the input vector. This is the value we want to predict.

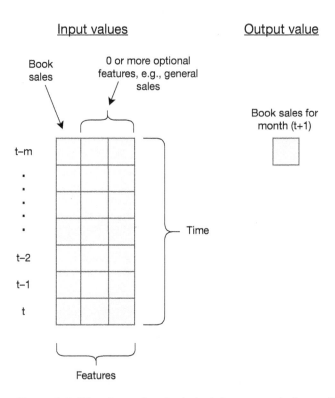

Figure 9-8 Structure of a single training example for an RNN. Each row in the matrix consists of one value in the case where we use only book sales as input variable. Optionally, we can use more variables as input, in which case each row will contain more values.

Let us now explore how many training examples we can create. We have HISTORY months' worth of historical data, and we note that we can create at least one training example corresponding to each month. For example, the value for the last month can result in a training example where the input data consists of a vector of length (HISTORY-1). Similarly, the second month in the historical data can result in a training example where the input data consists of a vector of length 1 because there is only a single month preceding the second month of the season. We also have the extreme case of the first historical month with a zero-length vector as input. For the more recent months, such as the last month, we could create multiple training examples. For example, in addition to the preceding example, we can also do the same but use only the M days preceding the final day, where M < (HISTORY-1).

We decide to create only a single training example from each month and to use as much history as possible for each training example. We further decide that each training example should have at least MIN months of history. We will end up with (HISTORY-MIN) examples, where the length of the input ranges between MIN and (HISTORY-1).

Now a key question is how we want to organize this data to be able to feed it to the neural network. A requirement from Keras is that if we feed multiple training examples to Keras at the same time (as we typically do), all the training examples need to be of the same length. That is, we need to either group our training examples in groups of identical lengths, or we need to feed each example individually to Keras. Another option, which is what we will use in this example, is to pad all examples with a specific value to become of equal length, and then we can send them all to Keras at the same time. This kind of rubs us the wrong way when one of the key reasons for using the RNN is its ability to handle input examples of variable length. Further, how does the network know to ignore the special padded value? A simple answer is that it does not, and it will need to discover that in the learning process, which seems unfortunate but has been shown to work well in practice. Later, we show mechanisms for masking out the padded values, so the network does not need to discover them. We also show how to truly use variable-length inputs, but for now, we keep things simple and just pad the beginning of each example with zeros, so they all get the same length. Figure 9-9 shows the desired organization of our input examples.

Training examples of equal length can be combined into batches. Padding can be used to ensure that training examples are of equal length.

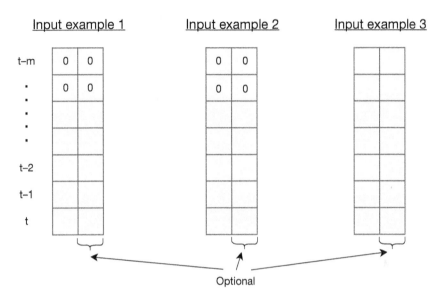

Figure 9-9 Mini-batch with three training examples. Training examples 1 and 2 are padded with zeros to be the same length as input example 3. The empty cells represent valid feature values.

That is, our input will be a tensor with *N* examples, each example consisting of *M* timesteps and each timestep consisting of values representing sales of one or more goods. The output is a 1D vector where each entry represents the sales value to predict. With all this background, we are ready to move on to the implementation. As in previous code examples, we present it piece by piece.

We start with initialization code in Code Snippet 9-1. First, we import modules that we need for the network. We also load the data file into an array. We then split the data into training data (the first 80% of the data points) and test data (the remaining 20% of the months).

Code Snippet 9-1 Initialization Code for Our Bookstore Sales Prediction Example

```
import numpy as np
import matplotlib.pyplot as plt
import tensorflow as tf
from tensorflow import keras
from tensorflow.keras.models import Sequential
from tensorflow.keras.layers import Dense
```

```
from tensorflow.keras.layers import SimpleRNN
import logging
tf.get_logger().setLevel(logging.ERROR)

EPOCHS = 100
BATCH_SIZE = 16
TRAIN_TEST_SPLIT = 0.8
MIN = 12
FILE_NAME = '../data/book_store_sales.csv'

def readfile(file_name):
    file = open(file_name, 'r', encoding='utf-8')
    next(file)
    data = []
    for line in (file):
        values = line.split(', ')
        data.append(float(values[1]))
    file.close()
    return np.array(data, dtype=np.float32)

# Read data and split into training and test data.
sales = readfile(FILE_NAME)
months = len(sales)
split = int(months * TRAIN_TEST_SPLIT)
train_sales = sales[0:split]
test_sales = sales[split:]
```

Figure 9-10 shows a plot of all historical sales data. The data shows a clear seasonal pattern along with an indication that the overall trend in sales has changed over time, presumably due to increased online sales. The data starts in 1992 and ends in March 2020. The drop for the last month was likely caused by the COVID-19 pandemic hitting the United States.

For completeness, the code to create the chart in Figure 9-10 is shown in Code Snippet 9-2.

Code Snippet 9-2 Code to Produce the Plot of Historical Sales Data

```
# Plot dataset
x = range(len(sales))
plt.plot(x, sales, 'r-', label='book sales')
```

```
plt.title('Book store sales')
plt.axis([0, 339, 0.0, 3000.0])
plt.xlabel('Months')
plt.ylabel('Sales (millions $)')
plt.legend()
plt.show()
```

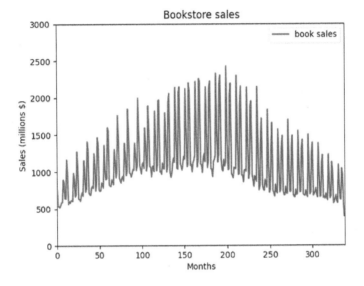

Figure 9-10 Historical bookstore sales from 1992 to 2020

When we looked at predicting Boston house prices, we introduced the concept of comparing the model with a significantly simpler model, which in that case was linear regression. The intent was to gain insight into whether our DL models provide value. For our book sales forecasting problem, we can create a simple model that predicts that the sales next month will be the same as the sales this month. Code Snippet 9-3 computes and plots this naïve prediction, and the resulting chart is shown in Figure 9-11.

Code Snippet 9-3 Code to Compute and Plot a Naïve Prediction

```
# Plot naive prediction
test_output = test_sales[MIN:]
naive_prediction = test_sales[MIN-1:-1]
```

```
x = range(len(test_output))
plt.plot(x, test_output, 'g-', label='test_output')
plt.plot(x, naive_prediction, 'm-', label='naive prediction')
plt.title('Book store sales')
plt.axis([0, len(test_output), 0.0, 3000.0])
plt.xlabel('months')
plt.ylabel('Monthly book store sales')
plt.legend()
plt.show()
```

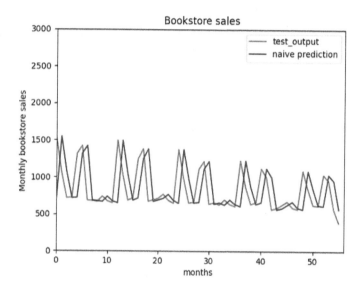

Figure 9-11 Naive prediction of book sales

STANDARDIZE DATA AND CREATE TRAINING EXAMPLES

It is worth noting that none of the preceding coding exercises have to do explicitly with DL or RNNs but are concerned only with obtaining and sanity-checking the dataset. It is commonly the case that there is much work involved in getting a good dataset before we can even start experimenting with feeding it into a model. The next step is to standardize the data points by subtracting the mean and dividing by the standard deviation of the training examples. Code Snippet 9-4 uses only training data to compute the mean and standard deviation.

Code Snippet 9-4 **Standardize the Data**

```
# Standardize train and test data.
# Use only training seasons to compute mean and stddev.
mean = np.mean(train_sales)
stddev = np.std(train_sales)
train_sales_std = (train_sales - mean)/stddev
test_sales_std = (test_sales - mean)/stddev
```

In our previous examples, the datasets were already organized into individual examples. For example, we had an array of images serving as input values and an associated array of classes serving as expected output values. However, the data that we created is raw historical data and not yet organized as a set of training and test examples in the form that was previously illustrated in Figure 9-8 and Figure 9-9. This is the next step in our code example. Code Snippet 9-5 allocates tensors for the training data and initializes all entries to 0. It then loops through the historical data and creates training examples, then does the same thing with the test data.

Code Snippet 9-5 **Allocate and Populate Tensors for Training and Test Data**

```
# Create training examples.
train_months = len(train_sales)
train_X = np.zeros((train_months-MIN, train_months-1, 1))
train_y = np.zeros((train_months-MIN, 1))
for i in range(0, train_months-MIN):
    train_X[i, -(i+MIN):, 0] = train_sales_std[0:i+MIN]
    train_y[i, 0] = train_sales_std[i+MIN]

# Create test examples.
test_months = len(test_sales)
test_X = np.zeros((test_months-MIN, test_months-1, 1))
test_y = np.zeros((test_months-MIN, 1))
for i in range(0, test_months-MIN):
    test_X[i, -(i+MIN):, 0] = test_sales_std[0:i+MIN]
    test_y[i, 0] = test_sales_std[i+MIN]
```

There is a fair amount of juggling with indices in different directions to get the data in the right place. In other words, it is tedious but nothing magic. The best way to understand the code is likely to step through it in a debugger to convince yourself that it does the right thing, or simply trust that it is correctly implemented and inspect the resulting tensors afterward. It is important to double-check everything when preparing the input data. Otherwise, it is hard to know if the network does not learn because of its architecture, because of faulty input data, because of poorly chosen algorithmic hyperparameters such as the learning rate, or because the task simply cannot be learned with available data. Even worse, it can often be the case that a network can make some sense of faulty input data, so it might still learn but not as well as it could have done.

CREATING A SIMPLE RNN

We are finally ready to define our network and start some experiments. Given all the code we have gone through so far, it is almost anticlimactic to read Code Snippet 9-6, where we define and train a simple RNN.

Code Snippet 9-6 Defining a Two-Layer Model with One Recurrent Layer and One Dense Layer

```
# Create RNN model
model = Sequential()
model.add(SimpleRNN(128, activation='relu',
                    input_shape=(None, 1)))
model.add(Dense(1, activation='linear'))
model.compile(loss='mean_squared_error', optimizer = 'adam',
             metrics =['mean_absolute_error'])
model.summary()
history = model.fit(train_X, train_y,
                    validation_data
                    = (test_X, test_y), epochs=EPOCHS,
                    batch_size=BATCH_SIZE, verbose=2,
                    shuffle=True)
```

We start with a simple network with a single recurrent layer with 128 neurons using rectified linear unit (ReLU) as an activation function. The `input_shape=(None, 1)` instructs that the number of timesteps is not fixed (None) and each timestep has a single input value. Given that all of our input examples have the same number of timesteps, we could have specified that number instead of None. Sometimes this results in faster runtime of Keras. The recurrent layer is followed by a fully connected feedforward layer with a single neuron and linear activation because we want to predict a numerical value. Because we use a linear activation function, we use mean squared error (MSE) as our loss function. We also print out the mean absolute error (MAE), just for our own information.

We train the network for 100 epochs using a batch size of 16. As usual, we shuffle our input examples. Before training begins, we see the following printout:

```
Layer (type)                Output Shape              Param #
=================================================================
simple_rnn_1 (SimpleRNN)    (None, 128)                16640
_____
dense_1 (Dense)             (None, 1)                    129
=================================================================
Total params: 16,769
Trainable params: 16,769
Non-trainable params: 0
_____

Train on 259 samples, validate on 56 samples
```

As usual, we want to sanity check the output and look for any mistakes in our configuration. Starting with number of parameters, we have 128 neurons in the recurrent layer, and each of them receives 1 input value from the input, 128 recurrent inputs, and one bias input; that is, there are $128 \times (1 + 128 + 1) = 16{,}640$ weights to learn. The output neuron has 128 inputs from the previous layer and a single bias input, or 129 weights to learn. Further, we have 339 months' worth of historical data, which we split up into 271 months for training and 68 months for test. We set the minimum length for an example to be 12, so we end up with $271 - 12 = 259$ training examples and 56 test examples. All of this matches the printout.

After training for 100 epochs, we arrive at a training and test MSE of 0.0011 and 0.0022 respectively and a training and test MAE of 0.0245 and 0.0346 respectively. A key question is whether this result is good or bad. Fortunately, we defined a naïve model that we can use as a comparison point. When we defined the naïve model, we did it on the nonstandardized data, whereas MSE and MAE from Keras is computed from the standardized data. Thus, we create a new version of our naïve predictions based on standardized data in Code Snippet 9-7.

Code Snippet 9-7 Computing Naive Prediction, MSE, and MAE on Standardized Data

```
# Create naive prediction based on standardized data.
test_output = test_sales_std[MIN:]
naive_prediction = test_sales_std[MIN-1:-1]
mean_squared_error = np.mean(np.square(naive_prediction
                                    - test_output))
mean_abs_error = np.mean(np.abs(naive_prediction
                                - test_output))
print('naive test mse: ', mean_squared_error)
print('naive test mean abs: ', mean_abs_error)
```

A word of caution is in order when doing NumPy calculations on various arrays. It is important that you know exactly what you are doing and that you have the right dimensions. As an example, if one NumPy array is defined with shape=(N, 1) and another is defined with shape=(N), although both of them seem like vectors, when you subtract one from the other, you will end up with a 2D array with shape=(N, N), which will give you incorrect values of MSE and MAE.

> We have spent a nonnegligible amount of time chasing down a bug caused by incorrect array dimensions when computing MSE manually.

Our implementation prints out the following:

```
naive test mse:   0.0937
naive test mean abs:   0.215
```

Comparing this to the RNN with a test MSE of 0.0022 and test MAE of 0.0346 indicates that the RNN is doing a significantly better job than our naïve model. To shed some light on how this affects the end behavior, let us use our newly trained model to do some predictions and then plot these predictions next to the actual values. Code Snippet 9-8 demonstrates how this can be done. We first call model.predict with the test input as argument. The second argument is the batch size, and we state the length of the input tensor as the batch size (i.e., we ask it to do a prediction for all the input examples in parallel). During training, the batch size will affect the result, but for prediction, it should not affect anything except for possibly runtime. We could just as well have used 16 or 32 or some other value. The model will return a 2D array with the output values. Because each output value is a single value, a 1D array works just as well, and that is the format we want in order to enable plotting the data, so we call np.reshape to change the dimensions of the array. The network works with standardized data, so the output will not represent demand directly. We must first destandardize the data by doing the reverse operation compared to the standardization. That is, we multiply by the standard deviation and add the mean.

Code Snippet 9-8 Using the Model to Predict Both Training and Test Output and Destandardizing the Results

```
# Use trained model to predict the test data
predicted_test = model.predict(test_X, len(test_X))
predicted_test = np.reshape(predicted_test,
                           (len(predicted_test)))
predicted_test = predicted_test * stddev + mean


# Plot test prediction.
x = range(len(test_sales)-MIN)
plt.plot(x, predicted_test, 'm-',
         label='predicted test_output')
plt.plot(x, test_sales[-(len(test_sales)-MIN):],
         'g-', label='actual test_output')
plt.title('Book sales')
plt.axis([0, 55, 0.0, 3000.0])
plt.xlabel('months')
plt.ylabel('Predicted book sales')
plt.legend()
plt.show()
```

We then plot the data. This is shown in Figure 9-12, where we see that the predictions make sense.

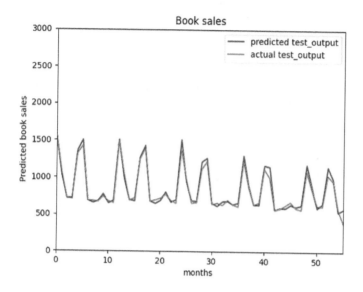

Figure 9-12 **Model output compared to the test data**

COMPARISON WITH A NETWORK WITHOUT RECURRENCE

In the previous section, we compared the RNN to a naïve prediction. Another relevant comparison is to compare it to a simpler network model to see if we benefitted from the complexity added to the model. In particular, it would be interesting to understand whether the ability to look at long input sequences is beneficial by comparing to a regular feedforward network presented with a limited history. We need to make two changes, shown in Code Snippet 9-9, to try this comparison. First, we drop much of the history to keep only the last 12 months of each input example. We then create a feedforward network instead of the recurrent network. The first layer in the feedforward network flattens the input shape to a single dimension, that is, the time dimension is removed.

Code Snippet 9-9 **Reducing the Lookback Period to 12 Months**

```
from tensorflow.keras.layers import Flatten
# Reduce lookback period in input.
train_X = train_X[:, (train_months - 13):, :]
test_X = test_X[:, (test_months - 13):, :]
```

```
# Create feedforward model.
model.add(Flatten(input_shape=(12, 1)))
model.add(Dense(256, activation='relu'))
model.add(Dense(1, activation='linear'))
```

The first fully connected layer has 256 units, which is more units than the recurrent layer had in our previous example. On the other hand, each unit in the recurrent layer has more weights, so in total, the recurrent network has more trainable parameters. We used the constructs introduced previously and compared the result to our RNN. The test error for the feedforward network ended up being 0.0036 as opposed to 0.0022 for our RNN. In other words, the RNN achieves a 39% lower error. It seems that using the longer history was beneficial, which is not surprising.

EXTENDING THE EXAMPLE TO MULTIPLE INPUT VARIABLES

It is relatively straightforward to modify the programming example to work with multiple input variables for each timestep. The key changes are shown in Code Snippet 9-10. The code snippet assumes that we have first read and standardized a second file of input data and placed the contents into the two variables train_sales_std2 and test_sales_std2. In reality, you would want to change the implementation to handle an arbitrary number of input variables instead of hardcoding it to two. The changes and additions compared to the previous example are highlighted in yellow.

Code Snippet 9-10 Creating Input Data and a Model with Two Input Variables per Timestep

```
# Create train examples.
train_months = len(train_sales)
train_X = np.zeros((train_months-MIN, train_months-1, 2))
train_y = np.zeros((train_months-MIN, 1))
for i in range(0, train_months-MIN):
    train_X[i, -(i+MIN):, 0] = train_sales_std[0:i+MIN]
    train_X[i, -(i+MIN):, 1] = train_sales_std2[0:i+MIN]
    train_y[i, 0] = train_sales_std[i+MIN]
```

```
# Create test examples.
test_months = len(test_sales)
test_X = np.zeros((test_months-MIN, test_months-1, 2))
test_y = np.zeros((test_months-MIN, 1))
for i in range(0, test_months-MIN):
    test_X[i, -(i+MIN):, 0] = test_sales_std[0:i+MIN]
    test_X[i, -(i+MIN):, 1] = test_sales_std2[0:i+MIN]
    test_y[i, 0] = test_sales_std[i+MIN]
...
model.add(SimpleRNN(128, activation='relu',
                    input_shape=(None, 2)))
```

Dataset Considerations for RNNs

In the programming example in this chapter, we created our own dataset using raw sales data. There are a couple of issues worth pointing out. First, when working with time series data, it is important to consider how the time dimension interacts with the way we split the data into training and test data. In our programming example, we first split the raw data into two chunks. We used the chunk representing the oldest data to create our training examples and the more recent chunk to create our test examples. A potential pitfall is to instead create a number of examples (input sequence plus ground truth) and shuffle them before dividing into a training set and test set. If we used this methodology, we would include "future" data points in the training set and "historical" data points in the test set. This is most likely not representative of how the model will be used in practice, and there is a significant risk that the test set will give optimistic result when evaluating the model. That is, you should be careful to not include future data in the training set.

Another thing to consider is whether to create training and test examples of different lengths or to use a fixed length. In our example, we created examples of variable lengths, where the longest input example was as long as it possibly could be given the raw input data. We then padded the other examples with zeros to result in the same length. The zero padding was used because the DL framework requires all examples in a mini-batch to be of the same length. Another common approach is to pick a fixed length that is shorter than the raw data allows for and make all training examples be of that same length. The drawback of this approach is that the model is not provided with the opportunity to learn long dependencies.

Concluding Remarks on RNNs

There are a few more issues worth pointing out before moving on to more advanced units for recurrent networks in Chapter 10. One thing is that the programming examples in this chapter technically did not model deep recurrent networks, because we had a single recurrent layer followed by a single neuron. Although the distinction between a shallow and a deep network often does not matter in practice, one thing that does matter is that we did not stack multiple recurrent layers on top of each other. When stacking recurrent layers in Keras, there is one detail that needs to be adjusted. The output from our model so far has been a single value predicting the sales for the month after the sequence of months that were used as input. In reality, a recurrent layer produces an output for each timestep, which is fed back as inputs to the layer. Keras does this internally, and the default behavior is to hide this from the user and output only the last value, with the assumption that this is the desired behavior. However, if the output of a recurrent layer is fed as input to another recurrent layer, then that second recurrent layer expects to see the output from each timestep instead of receiving only the output for the final timestep. Thus, we need to tell Keras to change its behavior and output the values for each timestep. This is done by setting the parameter `return_sequences` to True when creating the layer.

> When stacking multiple recurrent layers on top of each other in Keras, you must set return_sequences to True. When return_sequences is set to False, only the last timestep will be presented in the output.

We also did not experiment with dropout in this chapter. When applying dropout for recurrent layers, it can be applied to the connections between layers, to the recurrent connections, or to both (Zaremba, Sutskever, and Vinyals, 2015). In Keras, the RNN layer constructor parameter `recurrent_dropout` controls dropout on the recurrent connections.

> Details of how dropout works for RNNs would be a good topic for further reading (Zaremba, Sutskever, and Vinyals, 2015).

Finally, it is worth considering how weight sharing in RNNs relates to weight sharing in convolutional neural networks (CNNs). As previously stated, if an RNN is unrolled, we can view it as doing weight sharing between layers, whereas a CNN does weight sharing within a layer. A benefit that we described when we looked at CNNs for image classification is that the network is translation invariant, where *translation* refers to the action of moving an object from one location to another inside the image. This invariance results from the same weights being used by neurons in all locations. Even if the network was trained to identify an object in one location, neurons in other locations will also learn this. Similarly, an RNN will learn to identify patterns in a sequence irrespective of where in the sequence it appears. This is beneficial because many sequences do not necessarily have a specific starting point, but we choose to start sampling at an arbitrary timestep. It turns out that CNNs can also be used on time series data by first unrolling the time series into a 1D vector and then applying 1D convolution (as opposed to 2D convolution that was used for image data) on this unrolled time series. One drawback is that it becomes impractical to handle arbitrarily long sequences, in which case RNNs have an advantage.

One of the first recurrent networks that we are aware of is the Hopfield network (Hopfield, 1982). We mention this for historical purposes. You will benefit from reading more recent papers. For additional information about the history of RNNs, a survey paper by Lipton, Berkowitz, and Elkan (2015) provides a good overview. That paper contains references to additional papers from when RNNs first were introduced in the 1980s.

Chapter 10

Long Short-Term Memory

In this chapter, we start by diving deeper into the vanishing gradient problem that can prevent recurrent networks from performing well. We then present an important technique to overcome this problem, known as *long short-term memory* (LSTM), introduced by Hochreiter and Schmidhuber (1997). LSTM is a more complex unit that acts as a drop-in replacement for a single neuron in a recurrent neural network (RNN). The programming example in Chapter 11, "Text Autocompletion with LSTM and Beam Search," will illustrate how to use it by implementing an LSTM-based RNN for autocompletion of text.

The internal details of the LSTM unit are somewhat tricky, which can make this chapter challenging to get through if you are learning about LSTM for the first time. If that is the case, you can consider skimming this chapter the first time around and focus primarily on how the LSTM units are combined into a network. You can go back to the internal details of the LSTM unit later.

Keeping Gradients Healthy

We have mentioned the vanishing and exploding gradient problems multiple times in this book, and the reason is that they are key obstacles that must be overcome to enable training of neural networks with gradient-based methods.

These problems get even worse in RNNs because of the large number of timesteps that the gradient needs to travel through when training with backpropagation through time (BPTT) in combination with weight sharing across timesteps. For these reasons, this section provides some more thoughts on the topic. We introduce additional techniques and insights as well as summarize what has been presented in previous chapters.

> We find the vanishing and exploding gradient problems somewhat boring and would much rather spend our time on exploring new, cool network architectures. However, sometimes you just have to bite the bullet and go through some boring stuff to get to the fun stuff. After all, there is nothing cool about a network architecture that refuses to learn.

Let us start by restating what these problems are and what causes them. When training a network with gradient descent, we need to compute the partial derivative of the error with respect to each weight so we can arrive at a suggested adjustment for each weight. We compute these partial derivatives using the backpropagation algorithm. It turns out that the formula to compute the adjustment for a specific weight includes multiplying the derivative of the error by all the weights located between the weight in question and the output node as well as by the derivative of all activation functions on the path between the weight in question and the output. Figure 10-1 and Equation 10-1 illustrate this

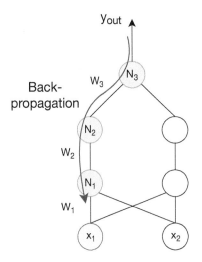

Figure 10-1 Backpropagation of error through a network

for a feedforward network assuming the mean squared error (MSE) as the loss function.

$$\frac{\partial e}{\partial w_1} = -(y - y_{out}) \cdot N_3' \cdot w_3 \cdot N_2' \cdot w_2 \cdot N_1' \cdot x_1$$

Equation 10-1   Formula for backpropagation. The variable y represents the desired value, and y_{out} represents the value predicted from the network. The predicted value is often represented by the variable $\hat{y}$.

Thus, if either the weights or the derivatives are small, we observe the vanishing gradient problem, where the adjustment value becomes vanishingly small and the network stops learning. The opposite problem is when the weights or derivatives are large and we observe the exploding gradient problem, which suggests a large weight adjustment that can throw off the learning process completely. In addition, for RNNs, because we unroll the network through time, we repeatedly multiply the backpropagated error by the same weight. This means that even moderate deviations from 1.0 will result in vanishing (if the weight is <1.0) or exploding (if the weight is >1.0) gradients.

Starting with the activation function, as previously explained, for S-shaped (both *logistic* and *tanh*) activation functions, the derivative approaches 0 for both large negative and positive values; that is, the neuron is being saturated. This was previously shown in Chapter 3, "Sigmoid Neurons and Backpropagation," Figure 3-4.

One thing that we have not discussed yet is that the logistic function, even when not saturated, always attenuates the error as it propagates backward. Figure 10-2 shows a zoomed-in version of the tanh and logistic sigmoid functions as well as their tangents at the points of their steepest derivatives. As you can see, the maximum slope of the logistic sigmoid function is smaller than the maximum slope of the tanh function. The max value of the derivative of the logistic sigmoid function is 0.25, whereas the max value for the derivative of tanh is 1.0. This is yet another reason that tanh is preferable over the logistic sigmoid function.

> The maximum value of the derivative of the logistic sigmoid function is 0.25, so the error will always be attenuated as it is passed backward through the network.

Although the max value of the derivative of tanh is 1.0, the gradient can still vanish if the neurons are in their saturation region. We have discussed multiple

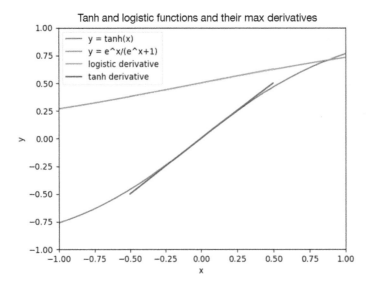

Figure 10-2 **Zoomed-in view of the tanh and logistic sigmoid functions and tangents illustrating their max derivatives**

techniques for keeping the neurons in their nonsaturated region. Two examples are to initialize weights with Glorot or He initialization and to use batch normalization inside of the network.

Instead of trying to keep neurons out of their saturation region, another solution to the problem is to use nonsaturating nonlinear functions such as leaky rectified linear unit (ReLU) or just the regular ReLU function that saturates only on one side.

For the exploding gradient problem, a straightforward solution is gradient clipping, which artificially adjusts the gradient to be smaller in cases when it blows up. It might sound like batch normalization and gradient clipping are related because both seem to want to limit the range of the value, but they are different from each other. Batch normalization aims at adjusting the value during the forward pass through the network to keep the neurons in their active region (i.e., batch normalization aims as keeping the gradient from vanishing by avoiding saturation). Gradient clipping, on the other hand, aims at avoiding exploding gradients by adjusting the gradient itself during the backward pass.

Batch normalization avoids vanishing gradients, while **gradient clipping** avoids exploding gradients.

The issues just described are applicable to both feedforward networks and RNNs, but RNNs also have some unique properties and potential mitigation techniques. Even in cases where the activation function is not a problem, such as if we use a ReLU function with a constant derivative of 1, RNNs have the unique challenge that BPTT results in multiplying the error by the same weight over and over due to weight sharing across timesteps. As previously mentioned, with a large enough number of timesteps, the only way to avoid vanishing and exploding gradients is to use weights with a value of 1, which kind of defeats the purpose because we want to be able to adjust the weights. However, it is possible to make use of this observation and create a more complicated recurrent unit, which uses a technique known as the constant error carousel (CEC). Using the CEC results in a behavior similar to weight values of 1 during backpropagation. LSTM is based on the CEC technique and is described in the next couple of sections.

LSTM implements a technique known as CEC.

Finally, as described in the context of ResNets in Chapter 8, "Deeper CNNs and Pretrained Models," skip connections can help training of very deep networks. The exact reasons that skip connections help can be debated, and different explanations have been hypothesized in different studies (He et al., 2015a; Philipp, Song, and Carbonell, 2018; Srivastava, Greff, and Schmidhuber, 2015;). One reason is that skip connections address vanishing gradients. Skip connections share some behavior with the CEC. We touch on this relationship in the section "Related Topics: Highway Networks and Skip Connections."

For reference, all the techniques to fight vanishing and exploding gradients that we discuss are summarized in Table 10-1. The way we understand it, the term *vanishing gradient* is reserved for the cases where the gradient gradually vanishes because of a deep network (in space or time). The gradient can come close to 0 for reasons other than the vanishing gradient problem. Previous chapters have described a couple of such examples and associated mitigation techniques.

One such problem occurs when the neurons in the output layer of the network are based on the logistic sigmoid function. A problem with this function is that the gradient is close to 0 if the neuron is saturated. One way to address it is to choose a loss function that reverses the effect during backpropagation, such as the cross-entropy loss function.

Table 10-1 Summary of Techniques to Mitigate Problems with Vanishing and Exploding Gradients

TECHNIQUE	MITIGATES VANISHING GRADIENT	MITIGATES EXPLODING GRADIENT	NOTES
Use Glorot or He weight initialization	Yes	No	Applies to all neurons
Batch normalization	Yes	No	Applies to hidden neurons
Nonsaturating neurons such as ReLU	Yes	No	Applies to all neurons but output layer is typically considered separately in light of problem type
Gradient clipping	No	Yes	Applies to all neurons
Constant error carousel	Yes	Yes	Applies only to recurrent layers; used by LSTM
Skip connections	Yes	No	Can provide additional benefits (detailed in later discussion of ResNets)

Another problem is that if the input values to the network are of significant magnitude, they force the neurons to go far into the saturation region. In our programming examples, we have tried to avoid this problem by standardizing the input values to be centered around 0 with moderate magnitude.

Introduction to LSTM

In this section, we introduce the LSTM cell. It is an example of the more general concept of gated units. What this means will become apparent as we dive into the details. LSTM is a complex unit, also known as *cell,* which is used as replacement for the simple neurons that we have used so far in our RNNs. The LSTM cell is frequently used in modern RNNs. Just to set the expectations right, we state up front that when first looking at a figure of an LSTM cell, it is indeed complex, and a natural reaction is, "How could anybody possibly have come up with that design as an alternative to a simple neuron, and does this cell have any connection to reality?" The answer to the latter part of that question is simple. The LSTM cell is an engineered solution and is not claimed to be biologically inspired, so it likely does not have much of a connection to (a biological) reality.

The LSTM unit has no less than five(!) nonlinear functions, three of which are logistic sigmoid functions known as the *gates* in the unit. The remaining two are regular activation functions, which can take on any of the previously introduced activation functions, with popular choices being tanh and ReLU. The unit also contains four weighted sums, so the number of weights is four times as many as in a simple RNN.

> **LSTM** is an example of a **gated unit.** It consists of logistic sigmoid functions known as **gates** in addition to traditional activation functions.

The modern LSTM unit that we describe in this section is an extended version that Gers, Schmidhuber, and Cummins introduced (1999). This version is somewhat more complex than the originally proposed LSTM cell, so do not be surprised if you feel that something is missing if you compare it to what is described in the original paper.

One way to avoid vanishing or exploding gradients in an RNN is to create a neuron where the derivative of the activation function is 1 (the identity function $f(x) = x$ fulfills this property) and have a recurrent weight with the value 1. We recognize that it seems somewhat useless to have a network with the identity function as activation function and a weight of 1, but we will build upon this concept as we walk through the inner workings of the LSTM cell.

The implication of using the identity function in combination with a weight of 1 is that the gradient does not vanish or explode during backpropagation when we repeatedly multiply the error by the recurrent weight and the derivative of the activation function. The left side of Figure 10-3 shows a simple RNN with a recurrent layer consisting of a single neuron, followed by a feedforward output layer with a single neuron. The neuron in the recurrent layer implements the identity function and the recurrent weight is 1. This recurrent loop is known as the CEC. The unrolled version of the network is shown to the right in the figure. In this

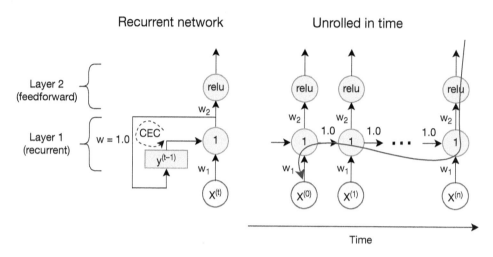

Figure 10-3 Simple recurrent network with a constant error carousel

unrolled version, it is clear that the error is constant as it backpropagates through time because it is repeatedly multiplied by 1. Even in cases with extremely long input sequences, the gradient will not vanish. Consequently, it can cause updates even to the weight corresponding to the very first timestep, which can be hundreds or thousands of timesteps ago. This is the key mechanism that LSTM uses to address vanishing and exploding gradients. Instead of having the gradient travel backward through weights, the CEC bypasses these weights and keeps the gradient from vanishing or exploding.

> An LSTM cell uses the CEC to make the gradient bypass the weighted connections. This prevents the gradient from vanishing or exploding.

Let us now ignore the backward pass for a while and step back to think about how this network behaves during the forward pass. Let us assume that the input to the network is 0.7 at the first timestep and is 0.0 during all other timesteps. The input to the network will be multiplied by w_1 and then presented to the neuron. Because the neuron implements the identity function, the output will be $0.7w_1$. This value will then circulate unchanged in the recurrent loop at each timestep. One way to think of it is that this entire discussion about the CEC, which enables the error to flow backward without vanishing, is simply a convoluted way of arriving at a memory cell that remembers the input value from the first timestep until the end of time. This ability to remember values for an extended period of time is a key property of the LSTM cell.

An LSTM cell can latch on to a value and remember it for a long period of time.

In this example, a simple RNN would also be able to remember the value, although the fact that it is fed through the activation function at every timestep would result in an output closer to 1. In addition to perfectly remembering the value across many timesteps, the LSTM cell has functionality to control when to update this memory cell. The reason such a mechanism is needed is not hard to imagine. Let us assume a more complex network with multiple neurons in the recurrent layer. We might want one of the neurons to remember the input value from the first timestep but want another neuron to remember the input value from the second, or some other, timestep. That is, somehow the network needs to be able to control when to remember the input and when to ignore it. Previously, we mentioned that LSTM is an example of a *gated* unit. The concept of a gate allows for the ability to selectively decide when to remember a value.

One way to implement a gate is shown on the left side of Figure 10-4. Instead of connecting the input $x^{(t)}$ directly to the neuron, we introduce a multiply operation that multiplies $x^{(t)}$ by the output from a logistic sigmoid neuron (denoted *Sig* in the figure). The logistic sigmoid neuron and the multiply operation act together as a gate. The reason for this is that the logistic sigmoid neuron will output a value in the range between 0 and 1. If the value is 0, then the gate is closed because the input $x^{(t)}$ will be multiplied by 0 and none of its value is captured. If the value is 1,

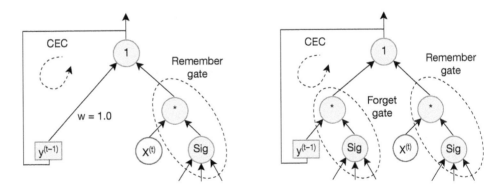

Figure 10-4 Left: Constant error carousel (CEC) augmented with a remember gate. Right: CEC augmented with both a forget and a remember gate.

then the full input value $x^{(t)}$ will be captured by the memory cell. The reason to use a sigmoid function and not a step function is, as always, that we want the function to be differentiable so we can train its weights with gradient descent.

Multiplying a value by the output of a logistic sigmoid function results in the logistic sigmoid function acting as a gate.

Having the ability to remember is good, but it is also good to be able to forget. This is shown in the right part of the figure where we have introduced a forget gate that can break the CEC loop. If the gate is open, the internal state will be updated with the state from the previous timestep, but if it is closed, the previous state will be forgotten. This enables the network to reuse this memory cell in cases where it needs to remember a value for a few timesteps and then no longer needs it but instead needs to remember some other value.

It is also good to have the ability to forgive, but our networks are not even close to modeling such human behavior.

We are now ready to present the full LSTM cell, which is based on the concepts just introduced. It is shown in Figure 10-5. In addition to the remember and forget gates, there is a gate that controls whether or not the remembered value should be sent to the output of the cell. The neuron in the CEC, which implements the identity function, is replaced by a node marked with a + (because that is how it is typically shown in the literature). It is worth noting that adding together inputs is exactly what a neuron does, so this is nothing different than a regular neuron with weights of 1.0 and a linear activation function and only two inputs and no bias. In addition to the gates, there is an input neuron with an arbitrary activation function (stated as "In Act" for *input activation*), and the output from the cell is also run through an arbitrary activation function (stated as "Out Act" for *output activation*) at the top of the figure. The output activation is just the activation and not a weighted sum since it only receives a single value from the multiplication operation in the output gate. It is common to use *tanh* as both input and output activation functions, but we will discuss this in a little bit more depth further down.

The four neurons at the bottom of the figure all receive multiple inputs. This is denoted by three arrows, but the number is arbitrary and depends on the number of neurons in the layer (which affects the size of h) and the size of the input vector x. All of these inputs have weights that need to be learned. The other internal units do not have any weights, and the internal connections in the figure are not vectors but single valued connections.

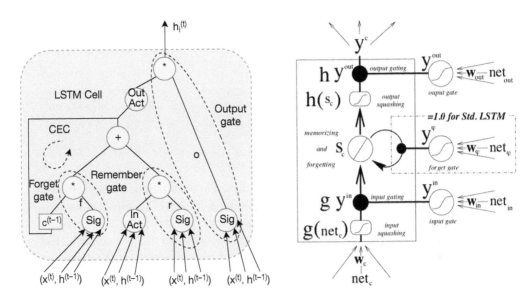

Figure 10-5 Left: LSTM cell using similar notation as above. Right: LSTM cell as depicted in original publication. (Source: Gers, F., Schmidhuber, J., and Cummins, F., "Learning to Forget: Continual Prediction with LSTM," Ninth International Conference on Artificial Neural Networks (ICANN 99), 1999.)

LSTM ACTIVATION FUNCTIONS

Let us now spend some time on discussing the activation functions. It seems somewhat counterintuitive that we spent entire sections in previous chapters on describing the problems with the S-shaped function and now introduce a unit with three logistic sigmoid functions and two additional activation functions, which often happen to be the tanh function.

There are a couple of things to consider here. First, given that the CEC is introduced, it will prevent some of the problems with vanishing gradients normally associated with S-shaped functions. We say *some* of the problems, not all problems, because the CEC is effective only when the gates are in a state that does let the error propagate unchanged. If the forget gate is closed, none of the error will propagate through the CEC, and it will again have to go through the tanh activation function. The recommended way to address this problem is to initialize the bias to the forget gate to 1 so that the error can freely flow backward to begin with. Another thing to consider is that the CEC only helps with gradients that vanish because of BPTT, but an RNN also has regular backpropagation where the error is traveling from one layer to another (the vertical direction in Figure 10-3). In other words, it can certainly be beneficial to use a ReLU function as input and output activation functions in the LSTM.

We believe that one reason that tanh is still popular is that many RNNs are not as deep as feedforward networks, so the vanishing gradient problem between layers is not as severe.

Another question regarding the input and output activation functions is why it is necessary to have both of them: Why is one not sufficient? One effect of having the output activation function is that we have better control of the output range. For example, if tanh is used as output activation, we know that the cell will always output a value between −1 and 1. On the other hand, as described shortly, gated units with only a single activation function do exist.

For the gating functions, the reason for using logistic sigmoid functions is that we want them to act as gates, and to achieve that, we want the output range to be between 0 and 1, which is a key property of the logistic sigmoid function. We could use any other function that has that same property. The challenge is how to construct a function that has a fixed range but still does not saturate (i.e., without derivatives that approach 0 in one or both ends).

CREATING A NETWORK OF LSTM CELLS

Figure 10-6 shows how multiple LSTM cells are connected into a recurrent network layer. This is just like a regular RNN, but each neuron has been replaced by the more complex LSTM cell. This results in a network with two sets of state. We have the internal state (c) inside of each LSTM cell, but we also have the state (h) in the global recurrent connections just as in an RNN that is based on simple neurons.

The figure makes it obvious that an LSTM based RNN has four times as many parameters (weights) to train as a regular RNN. In addition to the input activation neurons, there are also three gate-neurons that each receives the same number of inputs as the input neuron. Thus, the total number of weights for a single layer with an input vector of length M, and with N LSTM-units is $N*4*(N+M+1)$, where the first N is the number of LSTM-units, 4 is the input

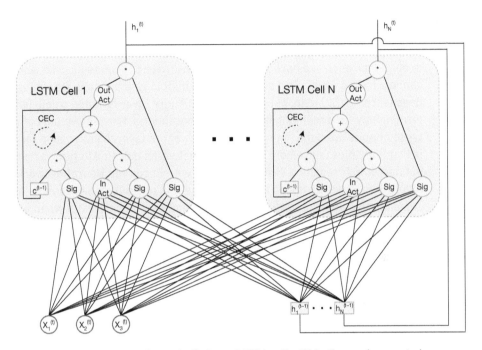

Figure 10-6 Recurrent layer built from LSTM cells. This figure does not show unrolling in time.

neuron and gates in each unit, and *N+M+1* is the number of inputs to each neuron including the bias.

> An LSTM cell has four times as many weights as a simple neuron in an RNN.

Let us now summarize the behavior of an LSTM layer. Each cell has an internal state. At each timestep, this internal state gets updated. The new value is a weighted sum of the internal state from the previous timestep and the input activation function for the current timestep. The weights are dynamically controlled and are known as gates. The inputs to the input activation function result from a concatenation of the outputs from the previous layer (*x*) as well as the outputs from the current layer from the previous timestep (*h*), just as in a regular RNN. Finally, the output of the LSTM layer is computed by feeding the internal state through the output activation function and multiplying the result by another gate. All the gates are controlled by a concatenation of *x* and *h*.

Alternative View of LSTM

In our description, we have referred to individual LSTM units as *cells,* and we connect multiple cells into a layer. This terminology is not consistently used in the deep learning (DL) field, but sometimes an entire layer is called a cell. Ignoring terminology for a moment, it is common that figures and descriptions of different types of units are done in the context of the entire layer. A key reason for this is that it enables convenient drawings of networks unrolled in time, as we saw in Chapter 9, "Predicting Time Sequences with Recurrent Neural Networks," Figure 9-6. However, it also comes with the risk of confusion because it hides some of the actual connections, so we recommend being careful when using this abstraction.

> LSTM is often thought about in terms of entire layers rather than individual units. In some texts, a **cell** refers to an entire layer of units rather than to a single unit.

A common way of drawing LSTM was introduced in a popular blog post that explains how LSTM works (Olah, 2015). We walk through reproduced versions of some of Olah's figures, but we also recommend reading the blog post for more details. Figure 10-7 shows an LSTM layer unrolled in time for three timesteps. For each timestep, the layer receives *c* and *h* from the previous timestep and *x* from the current timestep and outputs new values for *c* and *h*.

The middle part of the figure shows the internals of the LSTM layer. Each rectangle represents multiple neurons (the same number as the number

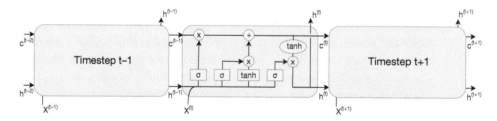

Figure 10-7 LSTM layers unrolled in time. (Adapted from Olah, C., "Understanding LSTM Networks" (blog), August 2015, https://colah.github.io/posts/2015-08-Understanding-LSTMs.)

of LSTM units in the layer), where each neuron receives a vector of inputs and produces a single output. The ones marked with the Greek letter sigma (σ) represent the gates, and the ones marked *tanh* represent the input and output activation functions. The curved line from $x^{(t)}$ represents a concatenation; that is, we form a wider vector, which contains the elements of both $h^{(t-1)}$ and $x^{(t)}$. All other operations (represented by circles/oval) represent multiple instances (the same number as the number of LSTM units in the layer) of the operation, where each of these instances receives a single input value (as opposed to a vector for the rectangles) and produces a single output value.

Finally, another common way of presenting different kinds of gated units is in matrix form. Equation 10-2 describes an LSTM layer.

$$f^{(t)} = \sigma\left(W_f\left[h^{(t-1)}, x^{(t)}\right] + b_f\right) \tag{1}$$

$$i^{(t)} = \sigma\left(W_i\left[h^{(t-1)}, x^{(t)}\right] + b_i\right) \tag{2}$$

$$\tilde{C}^{(t)} = \tanh\left(W_C\left[h^{(t-1)}, x^{(t)}\right] + b_C\right) \tag{3}$$

$$C^{(t)} = f^{(t)} * C^{(t-1)} + i^{(t)} * \tilde{C}^{(t)} \tag{4}$$

$$o^{(t)} = \sigma\left(W_o\left[h^{(t-1)}, x^{(t)}\right] + b_o\right) \tag{5}$$

$$h^{(t)} = o^{(t)} * \tanh\left(C^{(t)}\right) \tag{6}$$

Equation 10-2   Equations describing an LSTM layer

The forget gate and input gate are described by (1) and (2). The candidate update function is described by (3), and (4) uses this candidate and the input gate and forget gate to compute the new cell value. Finally, (5) describes the output gate, and (6) uses this gate and the new cell value to determine the output of the cell. These equations are terse and can be hard to grasp at first. To gain a deeper understanding, we recommend translating each of them into a figure of the equivalent neurons and connections. For example, (1) translates into a single layer of sigmoid neurons, where the input vector is a concatenation of $h^{(t-1)}$ and $x^{(t)}$.

Related Topics: Highway Networks and Skip Connections

As described in Chapter 8, the skip connections in ResNets were introduced to address the observation that the network did not learn, but the lack of learning was not due to vanishing gradients. Instead, He and colleagues (2015a) hypothesized that the learning algorithm was having a hard time finding the right solution and that the skip connections would help the algorithm look in the right place (closer to the identity function). However, before being used in ResNets, various forms of skip connections were used in other settings, and interestingly, in some of those settings, the intent was to address the vanishing gradient problem. This usage is related to the LSTM described in this chapter. The CEC used in LSTM enables gradients to flow unchanged through the unrolled network during the backward pass when doing BPTT. Similarly, skip connections provide shortcuts where gradients can flow unchanged through the network during the backward pass in a regular feedforward network.

We recognize that this can cause some confusion, because it does seem likely that the skip connections help with the vanishing gradient problems even in ResNets. It is hard to tell for sure. He and colleagues employed a number of other techniques to address the vanishing gradient problem. They also inspected the gradients in the baseline network without skip connections and observed that they were not vanishing. Thus, it seems like the hypothesis described by He and colleagues is a more likely explanation of why skip connections are beneficial in the case of ResNets.

Another related technique is known as *highway networks* (Srivastava, Greff, & Schmidhuber, 2015). A highway network contains skip connections, but the contribution from both the skip connections and the regular connections can be dynamically adjusted by the network. This is done using the same kind of gates as we have seen in LSTM. In fact, highway networks were inspired by LSTM.

Concluding Remarks on LSTM

Looking at the LSTM implementation, a reasonable question is whether it is possible to come up with a simpler version of the unit that still implements the CEC. The gated recurrent unit (GRU), introduced by Cho and colleagues (2014a) is an example of such a simplification. It is simpler in that it does not have an internal cell state; it has only a single activation function, and the forget and remember gates are combined into a single update gate. Details of the GRU implementation can be found in Appendix H.

After looking at the details of LSTM and GRU, it becomes clear that there is nothing magic about those specific designs, and it is easy to envision further variations on gated units. One such variation is to add so-called peephole connections to the LSTM unit where the gates receive additional inputs from the internal c-state of the model (Gers, Schraudolph, and Schmidhuber, 2002). There are also other variations with additional simplifications of the GRU (Heck and Salem, 2017).

> LSTM and GRU are the most popular units used in RNNs. There is no need to learn more about the other variations at this point, but it is an interesting topic for further reading (Heck and Salem, 2017).

Now that we know the basics about RNNs and the LSTM cell, we are ready to move on to our first natural language processing (NLP) example, namely, autocompletion of natural language text.

Chapter 11

Text Autocompletion with LSTM and Beam Search

In Chapter 9, "Predicting Time Sequences with Recurrent Neural Networks," we explored how to use recurrent neural networks (RNNs) for prediction of numerical values. In this chapter, instead of working with a time sequence of numerical values, we apply our RNN to natural language text (English). There are two straightforward ways of doing this. We can view text as a sequence of characters or as a sequence of words. In this chapter, we look at it as a sequence of characters because that is the simplest way to get started. In many cases, it is more powerful to work with words than with characters, and this is explored in the next couple of chapters.

In addition to working with text instead of numerical values, we demonstrate how to use the model with variable input lengths as well as how to predict multiple timesteps instead of just the one step immediately following the input data.

Encoding Text

To use text as input to our RNN, we need to first encode it in a suitable manner. We use one-hot encoding just as we did for categories in our image classification problems. One-hot encoding works fine for characters, given that a typical alphabet contains only tens of characters. As a side note, one-hot encoding words is less efficient: It results in much wider vectors because the width of the input vector is the same as the total number of symbols to encode, and a typical language contains tens or hundreds of thousands of words.

To make this more concrete, assume that text consists only of lowercase characters and no special symbols such as period, comma, exclamation mark, space, or linefeed. We can then encode a character as a one-hot encoded vector of width 26 because there are 26 lowercase characters in the English language. We can now define an RNN that takes a 26-element vector as its *x*-input, and we can end it with a fully connected *softmax* layer with 26 outputs. Now we can present a text sequence to the network by feeding it with a single one-hot encoded character for each timestep, and the softmax output can be interpreted as what the network predicts as the next character. The highest-value output represents the character that the network finds most likely to be the next character. The output with the second-highest value corresponds to the second-most likely next character, and so on.

> When working with text, it is common to use one-hot encoding to represent a character.

Figure 11-1 illustrates the recurrent network unrolled in time. At timestep 0, the letter *h* is presented as input to the network, followed by *e, l,* and *l* in the next three timesteps. The prediction from the network in the last timestep is *o*; that is, the network predicts the last character in the word *hello*. Obviously, the network will predict something during the first few timesteps as well, but we ignore the outputs during those timesteps because we know that we have not yet presented the entire input sequence.

In most cases, we would want to be able to handle uppercase characters as well as special symbols, so the width of the one-hot encoded characters would perhaps contain about 100 elements instead of 26. We will soon see a programming example in which we use one-hot encoded characters with an RNN, but first we discuss how to predict multiple timesteps into the future. That is another property that we use in the programming example.

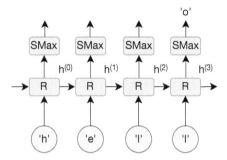

Figure 11-1 Text prediction network with a recurrent layer and a fully connected softmax layer. The rectangle labeled SMax is not only the mathematical softmax function but a fully connected layer with softmax as an activation function.

Longer-Term Prediction and Autoregressive Models

In the previous chapters, we predicted only the next value in a time sequence. It is often beneficial to be able to predict longer output sequences than just a single symbol. In this section, we discuss a few ways to predict multiple timesteps.

One simple way is to create multiple models, where each additional model predicts a timestep further into the future. To illustrate this, consider a training example that we provided to our book sales prediction model in Chapter 9. We presented it with input data $x^{(t-n)}, \ldots, x^{(t-1)}, x^{(t)}$, and the desired output value $y^{(t+1)}$. If we had used the same input data but instead presented it with the desired output value for a later timestep $y^{(t+2)}$, we would get a model that predicts two steps into the future. We can then create yet another model that we train with $y^{(t+3)}$, and so on. Now, given an input sequence $x^{(t-n)}, \ldots, x^{(t-1)}, x^{(t)}$, we can present it to each of our three models, and we get the predictions for the next three timesteps. This approach is simple to implement but not so flexible, and there is also no sharing or reuse between the models.

Another option is to create a model that predicts m timesteps at once. We would define the model to have m outputs, and each training example would again consist of the input sequence $x^{(t-n)}, \ldots, x^{(t-1)}, x^{(t)}$, but the desired output is now a sequence $y^{(t+1)}, y^{(t+2)}, \ldots, y^{(t+m)}$. Here we get the potential benefit of reusing parameters for predicting multiple timesteps, but we need to decide up front how many timesteps into the future we want to predict, and if we want to predict extremely long sequences, we end up with a large number of output neurons.

One thing that kind of rubs us the wrong way with these two methodologies is that we need to decide up front at training time how many timesteps we want to be able to predict. Just as we want to be able to process input sequences of variable lengths, we would like to dynamically choose the length of the output sequence. There is a clever way of doing this for the case where the model predicts a future value of a variable based solely on historical values of that variable (as opposed to a collection of other variables). We simply take the predicted output value for one timestep and feed it back as input to the model in the next timestep. We can do this repeatedly for an arbitrary number of timesteps. A deep learning (DL) model where the output of one timestep is used as the input value for the next timestep is often called an *autoregressive model*. Outside of the DL field, an autoregressive model is typically a linear model (Hastie, Tibshirani, and Friedman, 2009). In the context of DL, it is used more broadly for any type of model (typically nonlinear) where we use the output from one timestep as input in the next timestep.

Long-term prediction can be done by repeatedly feeding the predicted output back as inputs to the model. This works only if the network predicts all the variables needed as input. It is known as an **autoregressive model.**

Now consider the problem of autocompletion of text. In this case, we have a sequence of characters, and we want to predict a sequence of characters that are likely to follow the input sequence. That is, a reasonable design of a neural network for autocompletion of text is to take the network described in Figure 11-1 and first feed it the beginning of the sentence that we want to autocomplete. This results in a predicted character on the output of the network. We then feed this character back to the network as an input in an autoregressive manner. Figure 11-2 illustrates how this is done.

We are not taking the output exactly as is and feeding it back as input. Remember that the output is a probability distribution; that is, the network will assign a value between 0 and 1 to each character. However, the inputs are expected to be one-hot encoded—only the element corresponding to a single character should be set to 1, and all other elements should be 0. Thus, we identify which character the network predicts as the highest probability and feed the one-hot encoding for that character back as input (autoregression). We do just that in the next programming example, but first we introduce a technique that is needed to get multiple possible predictions instead of just a single prediction.

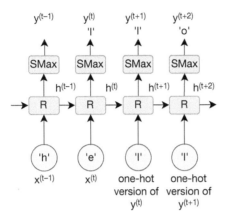

Figure 11-2 Text prediction network with predictions fed back as inputs. The network is initially fed the first two letters, h and e, for the first two timesteps, and then the output is fed back to the input for the remaining timesteps. The output for the first timestep is ignored.

When the output is a softmax function, we typically do not feed the exact output back as input, but instead we identify the most probable element and use the one-hot encoded version of that element as input to the network.

Beam Search

When doing autocompletion of text, it is common to want the model to predict multiple alternative completions of a sentence. The algorithm beam search accomplishes this. Beam search has been known since the 1970s but has become popular in DL-based natural language processing, for example, for natural language translation (Sutskever, Vinyals, and Le, 2014).

Beam search enables us to create multiple alternative predictions when feeding back output as inputs to a network.

The algorithm works in the following way. Instead of always picking the single-most probable prediction for each timestep, we pick *N* predictions, where *N* is a constant known as the *beam size*. If we did so naïvely, we would have *N* candidates after the first timestep, $N{\times}N$ candidates after the second timestep, $N{\times}N{\times}N$ candidates after the third timestep, and so on. To avoid this combinatorial explosion, each timestep also involves pruning the number of candidates to keep only the N most probable candidates overall. To make this more concrete, let us look at the example illustrated in Figure 11-3, where we assume $N = 2$.

Assume that we have just presented the sequence "W-h-a-t" followed by a character space to the network. We get an output vector where the entry corresponding to the character t has the highest probability (20%) and the character d has the second-highest probability (15%). Because $N = 2$, we ignore all other candidates. We feed the first candidate, t, back as input to the network, and we find the two most probable outputs i (40%) and y (10%). In another copy of the model, we instead feed the second candidate, d, back as input to the network and find the two most probable outputs a (80%) and o (10%).

We now have the four candidates *What ti*, *What ty*, *What da*, and *What do*. We can compute the overall probability for each of these four candidates by multiplying the probabilities for each step. For example, *What ti* gets assigned the probability

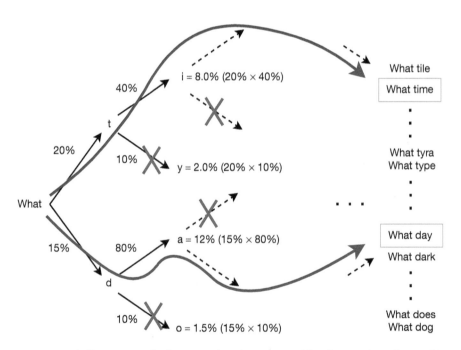

Figure 11-3 Beam search character by character with a beam size of two. At each step, all but the two most probable alternatives (overall) are pruned.

$0.2 \times 0.4 = 0.08$. We now prune the tree and keep only the *N* most probable candidates, which in our example are *What ti* (8%) and *What da* (12%).

There is one key observation worth pointing out. *What t* resulted in a higher probability than *What d*. Still, at the next step, *What da* (which is a continuation of *What d*) is assigned a higher probability than *What ti* (which is a continuation of the more probable *What t*). This also implies that there is no guarantee that beam search will find the most probable candidate overall, given that the most probable candidate might well have been pruned early in the process. That is, in this example, we arrive at *What time* and *What day,* but it might very well be that *What a night* is the most probable alternative overall.

If you are familiar with search algorithms, you might notice that it is a breadth-first search algorithm but where we limit the breadth of the search. Beam search is also an example of a greedy algorithm.

> No need to worry if you are not familiar with breadth-first search or greedy algorithms. However, as always, you might want to consider learning about it in the future.

We now have all the building blocks that we need to move on to our programming example, where we implement all of this in practice.

Programming Example: Using LSTM for Text Autocompletion

In this programming example, we want to create a long short-term memory (LSTM)-based RNN, which can be used for autocompletion of text. To do that, we need to first train our network on some existing text that can be used as a training set. There are vast amounts of text data available online to use for exercises like this, and some studies have even used the entire content of Wikipedia. For simpler demo examples like the one in this chapter, we typically want something smaller to avoid lengthy training times, and a popular choice is to just pick your favorite book from project Gutenberg.[1] It is a collection of books that are no longer

---

1. https://www.gutenberg.org

copyrighted and are available in text format online. For this example, we chose to use Frankenstein, which should be familiar to most readers (Shelley, 1818). We simply downloaded the text file and saved it on our local computer to be accessible to the code that is described next.

The initialization code is shown in Code Snippet 11-1. Apart from the import statements, we need to provide the path to the text file to use for training. We also define two variables, WINDOW_LENGTH and WINDOW_STEP, which are used to control the process of splitting up this text file into multiple training examples. The other three variables control the beam-search algorithm and are described shortly.

Code Snippet 11-1 Initialization Code

```
import numpy as np
from tensorflow.keras.models import Sequential
from tensorflow.keras.layers import Dense
from tensorflow.keras.layers import LSTM
import tensorflow as tf
import logging
tf.get_logger().setLevel(logging.ERROR)


EPOCHS = 32
BATCH_SIZE = 256
INPUT_FILE_NAME = '../data/frankenstein.txt'
WINDOW_LENGTH = 40
WINDOW_STEP = 3
BEAM_SIZE = 8
NUM_LETTERS = 11
```

Code Snippet 11-2 opens and reads the content of the file, converts it all into lowercase, and replaces double spaces with single spaces. To enable us to easily one-hot encode each character, we want to assign a monotonically increasing index to each character. This is done by first creating a list of unique characters. Once we have that list, we can loop over it and assign an incrementing index to each character. We do this twice to create one dictionary (a hash table) that maps from character to index and a reverse dictionary from index to character.

These will come in handy later when we want to convert text into one-hot encoded input to the network as well as when we want to convert one-hot encoded output into characters. Finally, we initialize a variable encoding_width with the count of unique characters, which will be the width of each one-hot encoded vector that represents a character.

Code Snippet 11-2 Read File, Process Text, and Prepare Character Mappings

```python
# Open the input file.
file = open(INPUT_FILE_NAME, 'r', encoding='utf-8-sig')
text = file.read()
file.close()

# Make lowercase and remove newline and extra spaces.
text = text.lower()
text = text.replace('\n', ' ')
text = text.replace('  ', ' ')

# Encode characters as indices.
unique_chars = list(set(text))
char_to_index = dict((ch, index) for index,
                     ch in enumerate(unique_chars))
index_to_char = dict((index, ch) for index,
                     ch in enumerate(unique_chars))
encoding_width = len(char_to_index)
```

The next step is to create training examples from the text file. This is done by Code Snippet 11-3. Each training example will consist of a sequence of characters and a target output value of a single character immediately following the input characters. We create these input examples using a sliding window of length WINDOW_LENGTH. Once we have created one training example, we slide the window by WINDOW_STEP positions and create the next training example. We add the input examples to one list and the output values to another. All of this is done by the first for loop.

The code lines that create the dictionaries are "Pythonic" in that they squeeze much functionality into a single line of code, which makes it virtually impossible to understand if you are a beginner in Python. We generally try to avoid writing such code lines, but they do come with the benefit of being very compact.

If you want to become more fluent in these types of compact expressions, then you can consider reading about the concepts *generators, list comprehension,* and *dict comprehension* on python.org.

Code Snippet 11-3 **Prepare One-Hot Encoded Training Data**

```python
# Create training examples.
fragments = []
targets = []
for i in range(0, len(text) - WINDOW_LENGTH, WINDOW_STEP):
    fragments.append(text[i: i + WINDOW_LENGTH])
    targets.append(text[i + WINDOW_LENGTH])

# Convert to one-hot encoded training data.
X = np.zeros((len(fragments), WINDOW_LENGTH, encoding_width))
y = np.zeros((len(fragments), encoding_width))
for i, fragment in enumerate(fragments):
    for j, char in enumerate(fragment):
        X[i, j, char_to_index[char]] = 1
    target_char = targets[i]
    y[i, char_to_index[target_char]] = 1
```

We then create a single tensor holding all the input examples and another tensor holding the output values. Both of these tensors will hold data in one-hot encoded form, so each character is represented by a dimension of size encoding_width. We first allocate space for the two tensors and then fill in the values using a nested for loop.

As we did for the book sales prediction example, we have spent a considerable amount of code on just preparing the data, which is something that you should get used to doing. We are now ready to build our model. From the perspective of training our model, it will look similar to the book sales prediction example, but we use a deeper model consisting of two LSTM layers. Both LSTM layers use a dropout value of 0.2 on the connections between layers as well as on the recurrent connections. Note how we pass return_sequences=True to the constructor of the first layer because the second layer needs to see the output values for all timesteps from the first layer. The second LSTM layer is followed by a fully connected layer, but this time the output layer consists of multiple neurons using a softmax function instead of a single linear neuron because we will be predicting probabilities for discrete entities (characters) instead of a single numerical value. We use categorical cross-entropy as our loss function, which is the recommended loss function for multicategory classification.

One thing to note is that when we prepared the data, we did not split the dataset into a training set and a test set. Instead, we provide a parameter validation_split=0.05 to the fit() function. Keras will then automatically split our training data into a training set and a test set, where the parameter 0.05 indicates that 5% of the data will be used as a test set. For the case of autocompletion of text, we could have left out this parameter as well and simply trained using all the data and not done any validation. Instead, we could have manually sanity checked the output by using our own judgment, since the "correct" result for autocompletion of text is somewhat subjective. In Code Snippet 11-4, we have chosen to use a 5% validation set but will also inspect the predictions to get an idea of whether the network is doing what we would like it to do. Finally, we train the model for 32 epochs with a mini-batch size of 256.

Code Snippet 11-4 **Build and Train Model**

```
# Build and train model.
model = Sequential()
model.add(LSTM(128, return_sequences=True,
                    dropout=0.2, recurrent_dropout=0.2,
                    input_shape=(None, encoding_width)))
model.add(LSTM(128, dropout=0.2,
                    recurrent_dropout=0.2))
model.add(Dense(encoding_width, activation='softmax'))
model.compile(loss='categorical_crossentropy',
                    optimizer='adam')
model.summary()
history = model.fit(X, y, validation_split=0.05,
                        batch_size=BATCH_SIZE,
                        epochs=EPOCHS, verbose=2,
                        shuffle=True)
```

This results in a training loss of 1.85, and the loss on the test data is 2.14. We likely could tweak the network to produce better loss values, but we are more interested in trying to use our model to predict text. We do that using the beam-search algorithm described previously.

In our implementation, each beam is represented by a tuple with three elements. The first element is the logarithm of the cumulative probability for the current sequence of characters. We describe later why we use the logarithm. The second element is the string of characters. The third element is a one-hot encoded version of the string of characters. The implementation is shown in Code Snippet 11-5.

Code Snippet 11-5 Use the Model and Do Beam Search to Come Up with Multiple Text Completions

```
# Create initial single beam represented by triplet
# (probability , string , one-hot encoded string).
letters = 'the body '
one_hots = []
for i, char in enumerate(letters):
    x = np.zeros(encoding_width)
    x[char_to_index[char]] = 1
    one_hots.append(x)
beams = [(np.log(1.0), letters, one_hots)]

# Predict NUM_LETTERS into the future.
for i in range(NUM_LETTERS):
    minibatch_list = []
    # Create minibatch from one-hot encodings, and predict.
    for triple in beams:
        minibatch_list.append(triple[2])
    minibatch = np.array(minibatch_list)
    y_predict = model.predict(minibatch, verbose=0)
    new_beams = []
    for j, softmax_vec in enumerate(y_predict):
        triple = beams[j]
        # Create BEAM_SIZE new beams from each existing beam.
        for k in range(BEAM_SIZE):
```

```
                char_index = np.argmax(softmax_vec)
                new_prob = triple[0] + np.log(
                    softmax_vec[char_index])
                new_letters = triple[1] + index_to_char[char_index]
                x = np.zeros(encoding_width)
                x[char_index] = 1
                new_one_hots = triple[2].copy()
                new_one_hots.append(x)
                new_beams.append((new_prob, new_letters,
                                new_one_hots))
                softmax_vec[char_index] = 0
        # Prune tree to only keep BEAM_SIZE most probable beams.
        new_beams.sort(key=lambda tup: tup[0], reverse=True)
        beams = new_beams[0:BEAM_SIZE]
    for item in beams:
        print(item[1])
```

We start by creating a single beam with an initial sequence of characters ('the body ') and set the initial probability to 1.0. The one-hot encoded version of the string is created by the first loop. We add this beam to a list named beams.

This is followed by a nested loop that uses the trained model to do predictions according to the beam-search algorithm. We extract the one-hot encoding representation of each beam and create a NumPy array with multiple input examples. There is one input example per beam. During the first iteration, there is only a single input example. During the remaining iterations, there will be BEAM_SIZE number of examples.

We call model.predict(), which results in one softmax vector per beam. The softmax vector contains one probability per character in the alphabet. For each beam, we create BEAM_SIZE new beams, each beam consisting of the words from the original beam concatenated with one more word. We choose the most probable words when creating the beams. The probability for each beam can be computed by multiplying the current probability of the beam by the probability for the added word. However, given that these probabilities are small, there is a risk that the limited precision of computer arithmetic results in underflow. This can be addressed by instead computing the logarithm of the probability, in which case the multiplication is converted to an addition. For a small number of words, this is not necessary, but we do it anyway for good practice.

Once we have created BEAM_SIZE beams for each existing beam, we sort the list of new beams according to their probabilities. We then discard all but the top BEAM_SIZE beams. This represents the pruning step. For the first iteration, this does not result in any pruning because we started with a single beam, and this beam resulted in just BEAM_SIZE beams. For all remaining iterations, we will end up with BEAM_SIZE * BEAM_SIZE beams and discard most of them.

It is worth pointing out that our implementation does not take the predicted output and feed it back to the input, character by character. Instead, each iteration of the loop results in a completely new mini-batch that contains the entire sequence of characters, and we feed this sequence through the network. That is, the result is the same, but we do many redundant computations. In Chapter 12, "Neural Language Models and Word Embeddings," we present an example of an alternative implementation that does feed the output back to the input, one symbol at a time.

The loop runs for a fixed number of iterations followed by printing out the generated predictions:

```
the body which the m
the body which the s
the body of the most
the body which i hav
the body which the d
the body with the mo
```

Note that the predictions generated by the network both use correctly spelled words and have grammatical structures that look reasonable. This completes our programming example, but we encourage you to experiment further using different training data and different partial phrases used as starting points.

Bidirectional RNNs

When working with text sequences, it can often be beneficial to look at both previous and future words. As an example, when writing a paragraph, it is often the case that we write one sentence, then another, and then go back and edit the previous sentence to better fit together with the subsequent sentence. Another example is when we are parsing what somebody is saying. Suppose we hear the beginning of a sentence, "I saw the b...," but did not fully hear the last word. We did, however, hear that it was a one-syllable word starting with a *b*. We would likely need to ask the person to repeat what they said because it is not obvious what the word could be—it might be *ball* or *boy* or *bill* or any of a number words starting with *b*. Suppose instead that we heard the entire sentence: "I saw the b... sky." With the *b* sound and *sky* as context, we would likely not ask the person to repeat but just assume that the word is *blue*. In other words, looking at future words enables us to predict the missing word, and a typical application for this is speech recognition.

A bidirectional RNN (Schuster and Paliwal, 1997) is a network architecture that has the ability to look at future words. A bidirectional RNN layer consists of two layers operating in parallel, but they receive the input data in different directions. For this to work, the full input sequence needs to be available up front, so it cannot be used in an online setting where the sequence is created dynamically. To make it simple, consider a regular RNN layer consisting of a single unit. If we wanted to create a bidirectional version of this RNN layer, we would add another unit. If we then wanted to feed the characters *h, e, l, l, o* to the network, we would feed *h* to one of the units and *o* to the other at the first timestep. At timestep 2, we would feed them *e* and *l*; at timestep 3, *l* and *l*; at timestep 4, *l* and *e*; and finally, at timestep 5, *o* and *h*. During each timestep, each of the two units would produce an output value. At the end of the sequence, we would combine the two outputs for each input value. That is, the output value for timestep 0 for the first unit and the output value for timestep 4 for the second unit would be combined because those timesteps represent when the units received *h* as input. There are multiple ways to combine the output of two units, such as addition, multiplication, or average.

Bidirectional RNNs predict an element from both the past and the future.

In Keras, a bidirectional layer is implemented as a wrapper that can be used with any RNN layer. Code Snippet 11-6 shows how it can be used to change a regular LSTM layer into a bidirectional LSTM layer.

Code Snippet 11-6 How to Declare a Bidirectional Layer in Keras

```
from tensorflow.keras.layers import Bidirectional
...
model.add(Bidirectional(LSTM(16, activation='relu')))
```

Do not worry too much if you find bidirectional layers confusing. We mention them here primarily because you are likely to encounter them as you read about more complex networks. We do not make use of bidirectional layers in the programming examples in this book.

Different Combinations of Input and Output Sequences

Our initial book sales prediction took a sequence of values as input and returned a single output value. Our text autocompletion model took a sequence of characters as input and produced a sequence of characters as output. In a popular blog post, Karpathy (2015) discusses other combinations of inputs and outputs. These are illustrated in Figure 11-4.

Starting from the left, a one-to-one network is not a recurrent network but simply a feedforward network that takes one input and produces a single output. These inputs and outputs may well be vectors, but they are not presented as a variable-length sequence but as a single timestep. The second combination is the one-to-many case, which receives input during the first timestep and produces multiple outputs over subsequent timesteps. A typical use case is where an image is presented as input and the network produces a textual description of what is in the image. The third example is a many-to-one model, which is exactly what we

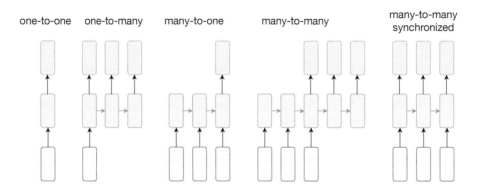

Figure 11-4 Input/output combinations for RNN unrolled in time. Gray represents input, blue represents the network, and green represents outputs. (Source: Adapted from Karpathy, A., "The Unreasonable Effectiveness of Recurrent Neural Networks," May 2015, http://karpathy.github.io/2015/05/21/rnn-effectiveness/.)

did in the book sales forecasting example. It is followed by a many-to-many case. Although the length of the input sequence is the same as the output sequence in the figure, this is not a requirement. For example, in our text autocompletion example, we implemented a many-to-many network in which the input sequence and output sequence could have different number of steps. Finally, the rightmost example in the figure shows a synchronized many-to-many network in which the input for each timestep has a corresponding output. A typical example of this is a network that classifies each frame of a video to determine whether or not there is a cat in the frame.

A reasonable question is how the different types of network are implemented in practice. First, note that we should not restrict the discussion to "pure" recurrent networks, but the concepts just described can be applied to more complex hybrid architectures.

Now let us consider the one-to-many case. Looking at the figure, it might not look that complicated, but the first question that comes to mind when trying to implement the model is what to do with the inputs for all timesteps after the first timestep. Remember that the figure represents the abstraction of unrolling the network in time, and if the network has inputs during the first timestep, then those inputs are still there for the subsequent timesteps and must be fed with something. Two obvious and common solutions to this are to either just feed the network with the same input value during every timestep or feed the network with the real input value during the first timestep and for each subsequent timestep feed it some kind of special value that does not naturally occur in the input data, and then just rely on the network learning to ignore that value.

Similarly, the many-to-one network will produce an output during each timestep, but we can choose to simply ignore the output for all timesteps but the last. In our book sales prediction example, we told Keras to do just that by implicitly setting the return_values parameter to False (its default value) for the last recurrent layer.

The rightmost synchronized many-to-many architecture is trivial. We feed the network an input during each timestep, and we look at the output during each timestep. The other many-to-many architecture in the figure is different in that it can have a different number of output steps than input steps. Our programming example with autocompletion of text was an example of this architecture. One design choice for such a network is how to communicate to the network that the input sequence is done and how the network communicates when the output sequence is done. In our programming example, this was done implicitly by the user by starting to look at the output (and feeding it back to the input) after a specific number of characters and then stopping the process after the network had predicted a fixed number of characters. There are other ways of doing this as well (e.g., by teaching the network to work with START and STOP tokens). We will see an example of this in Chapter 14, "Sequence-to-Sequence Networks and Natural Language Translation," where we implement a natural language translation network.

Concluding Remarks on Text Autocompletion with LSTM

In this chapter, we concluded our presentation of recurrent networks with a programming example illustrating how an LSTM-based RNN can be used for autocompletion of text. This was also our first example of a network applied to natural language processing (NLP), as opposed to image data and numerical data. Another interesting aspect of this programming example, as well as of the bookstore sales prediction example, was that we created training examples without explicit labeling. The sequential nature of the data itself was such that the ground truth could be automatically created for each training example.

For the text autocompletion example, we chose to encode individual characters and feed them into the network. A more powerful approach is to work at a granularity of individual words and with a more expressive encoding scheme than one-hot encoding. We discuss this topic in the next couple of chapters.

Chapter 12

Neural Language Models and Word Embeddings

In Chapter 11, "Text Autocompletion with LSTM and Beam Search," we built a network that predicts the continuation of a sentence. One remarkable property of that model is that it learns both words and sentence structure. We did nothing to prevent the model from producing random, nonexistent words or producing sentences that make no sense grammatically, but somehow, this did not happen. Still, it seems like we made it unnecessarily hard for the model by giving it individual characters instead of words as the smallest building blocks. After all, humans do not actually communicate with characters—they use characters primarily as tools to describe, in writing, words they are communicating.

In this chapter, we describe two major concepts. We begin with a brief introduction to statistical language models. The focus is on neural language models, which involve a task similar to the text autocompletion task from Chapter 11 but using words instead of characters as building blocks. Statistical language models have traditionally played a key part in automatic natural language translation, which is explored in Chapter 14, "Sequence-to-Sequence Networks and Natural Language Translation." The second concept that we introduce in this chapter is a class of alternative encodings of words that can be used instead of one-hot encoding. The terms *word embeddings*, *word vectors*, and *distributed representations* are used interchangeably for this class of alternative encodings., but we primarily use *word embeddings.* A key property of many word embeddings is that they are not simply encodings of words, but they also capture some of the properties of the words, such as semantics and grammatical features.

> The terms **word embeddings, word vectors,** and **distributed representations of words** are all different names for a type of encoding of words. This type of encoding often captures key properties of the words.

Neural language models and word embeddings are somewhat intertwined in the literature because some of the important early discoveries about word embeddings fell out as an unexpected byproduct from work on neural language models. We therefore describe them jointly while still trying to keep them separate and describe how they relate to each other.

As a programming example, we build our own word-based neural language model and explore the word embeddings that it produces as a byproduct. Then, before moving on to Chapter 13, "Word Embeddings from word2vec and GloVe," which describes more advanced algorithms for creating word embeddings, we briefly discuss sentiment analysis of text (i.e., automatically classifying documents based on whether the content is positive or negative).

Introduction to Language Models and Their Use Cases

A statistical language model describes how likely a sequence of words is in the language that it models. It does so by assigning a probability to each possible word sequence. A correct and common sequence of words is assigned a high probability, and an incorrect or uncommon sequence of words is assigned a low probability.

> A statistical language model provides a measure of how likely it is that a sequence of words would occur in the given language.

To make this more concrete, we note that this is what our text autocompletion network from Chapter 11 did, but using characters as building blocks, whereas a language model typically uses words as building blocks. Thus, if we feed a language model a sequence of words, its output is a probability for each word in the vocabulary telling how likely it is that this word is the next word in the sequence.

A statistical language model is typically formulated in terms of conditional probabilities, where the probability of the next word in a sequence is conditioned on all previous words in the sequence. We do not go into details about conditional probabilities in our description, but it is a good topic for further reading and more or less required if you want to understand papers about language models. Goodfellow, Bengio, and Courville (2016) and Hastie, Tibshirani, and Friedman (2009) can be consulted for more details and additional references.

Figure 12-1 illustrates what beam search for a word-based language model might look like. In this example, we start by feeding the word *Deep* into the network. The model might assign a high probability to the two words *learning* and *dish*. Obviously, there are many other words in the vocabulary that will also

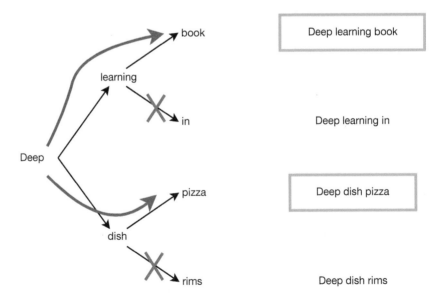

Figure 12-1 Beam search for word-based language model using a beam size of 2

be assigned a high probability (e.g., *water, thoughts, space*). Other words, (e.g., *heaven, bicycle, talked*) will be assigned a low probability. The thinking here is that, although *deep heaven* and *deep bicycle* are plausible sentences, they seem unlikely due to the meanings of the words, and the reason that *deep talked* is assigned a low probability is that, in most cases, it would form a sentence that is grammatically incorrect. It is worth noting that we can build multiple language models for a given language, depending on the setting in which it is to be used. For example, if we are in a setting where we are discussing machine learning topics, the probability of the sequence *deep learning* is higher than the probability of *deep dish*, whereas the opposite is true if we are at a food convention in Chicago. In general, the properties of the language model depend on the text corpus that it is derived from.

Now that we have spent a couple of paragraphs on describing what a language model is, a fair question is what it can be used for, apart from autocompletion of text. We give two examples of many use cases within the field of natural language processing.

The first example is from speech recognition. In Chapter 11, in the context of bidirectional recurrent neural network (RNNs), we briefly mentioned how it can be useful to look at both historical and future words in a sentence when doing speech recognition. The given example was that when not fully capturing all words in the phrase "I saw the b. . . sky," we could still give a reasonable prediction that the missing word is *blue*. A different example that does not involve missing words is to do speech recognition on the phrase "recognize speech using common sense." Using an automatic system that identifies only the phonemes in the phrase, if things go well, the system will output the correct phrase. However, the automatic system might instead output the similar sounding phrase "wreck a nice beach you sing calm incense," which humorously was used in the title of a paper by Lieberman and colleagues (2005). Or we could end up with a mixture of the two phrases or yet another alternative. In other words, the system could produce several candidate sentences based only on the phonemes of the phrase. We could then apply a language model to select the one that is the most probable phrase and thereby drastically improve the quality of speech recognition.

The second example is from the field of automatic natural language translation where the language model traditionally has played a big role. First, several candidate translations are produced using one of various existing techniques. One such technique is to first do a word-by-word translation and then create different permutations of how the words are ordered (different languages often have different word orderings). A language model can then be used to identify the most probable candidate translation. As a side note, the field of machine translation is rapidly evolving, and in Chapter 14, we show how a neural network can generate the candidate translations in the first place instead of relying on word-by-word translation as the initial step.

In these two examples, we talked about assigning a probability to an entire sentence, but for the purposes of this book, we consider only the case of having an initial sequence of words and assigning a probability to each possible continuation; that is, given a sequence of words, we assign a single numerical value to each word in the vocabulary where the sum of all values equals 1.0.

Examples of Different Language Models

This section briefly describes the building blocks for a couple of important classical language models as well as a neural language model and relates them to each other. Concepts from both the classical and neural language models are later used in the context of creating word embeddings.

n-GRAM MODEL

The n-gram model is a simple statistical language model. As previously mentioned, a language model tries to solve the problem of providing a probability for each word in a vocabulary given a sequence of historical words. The n-gram model approximates this by considering only the $(n-1)$ most recent words instead of the full history. These $(n-1)$ historical words plus the predicted next word form a sequence of n words, known as an n-gram, which has given the model its name. The parameter n is chosen up front when we train the model. An n-gram model can still provide probabilities for longer sequences by combining the probabilities for multiple n-grams, but in this description we will focus on describing what a single n-gram is. We start our description with $n = 2$, which is also known as a *bigram model*. The model is built by simply counting all different bigrams in the training corpus and then basing the prediction on how frequently each bigram appears. Let us consider the word sequence "The more I read, the more I learn, and I like it more than anything else." To make things simple, we ignore punctuation and convert all characters to lowercase. We can construct the following list of bigrams: /the more/ /more i/ /i read/ /read the/ /the more/ /more i/ /i learn/ /learn and/ /and i/ /i like/ /like it/ /it more/ /more than/ /than anything/ /anything else/.

There are a couple of things to note. We see that some bigrams, such as /the more/ and /more i/, appear multiple times. Further, a number of nonidentical bigrams, such as /i read/ /i learn/ /i like/ and /more i/ /more than/, have the same starting word. Finally, one bigram, /more i/, both appears multiple times and shares the starting word with a different bigram, /more than/. The bigrams are summarized in Table 12-1, which is sorted alphabetically.

Given a starting word, we can now use this table to predict the next word. For instance, if we are given the word *and*, our bigram model predicts that the probability of the next word being *i* is 100% and the probability for all other words is 0%. If the first word is *more*, then the model predicts a probability of 67% for the word *i* but 33% for the word *than* because, of the three bigrams starting with *more*, two of them are /more i/ and only one is /more than/.

Table 12-1 Summary of Bigrams

FIRST WORD	PREDICTED WORD	NUMBER OF OCCURRENCES	PROBABILITY GIVEN STARTING WORD
and	i	1	100%
anything	else	1	100%
i	learn	1	33%
	like	1	33%
	read	1	33%
it	more	1	100%
learn	and	1	100%
like	it	1	100%
more	i	2	67%
	than	1	33%
read	the	1	100%
than	anything	1	100%
the	more	2	100%

Clearly, the bigram model is limited in that it cannot capture any longer-term dependencies. For example, if we train the model on the sentences "the boy reads," "the girl reads," and "the boy and girl read," and then present "the boy and girl" as a starting sequence, the bigram model will ignore "the boy and" and only predict the next word based on the word *girl*. Its probability for *reads* is 50%, and its probability for *read* is 50%, although the longer context makes it clear that the word *read* should be more probable. The obvious solution is to increase the value of *n*. We can create a *5-gram model* in which the first few 5-grams become /*the more i read the more*/ /*more i read the more i*/ and /*i read the more i learn*/. This enables the model to capture more complex dependencies, but it comes with the drawback that much more training data is needed to capture enough 5-grams to make the model useful. If the starting sequence cannot be found in the table, then the model predicts 0%, which is a significant limitation of the basic n-gram model. This is aggravated by the fact that the longer the n-grams are, the lower the probability is that an arbitrarily chosen sequence of $(n-1)$ words existed in the training corpus. For example, the training corpus might have contained the sequence "the boys and girls read," but the model still cannot predict anything when presented with the input sequence "the boy and girl" because *boy* and *girl* are now in singular form. Still, the basic n-gram model has been shown to be useful, and there are various extensions that address some of its shortcomings.

SKIP-GRAM MODEL

A *skip-gram model* is an extension of the n-gram model but where all words do not need to appear sequentially in the training corpus. Instead, some words can be skipped. A k-skip-n-gram model is defined by the two parameters *k* and *n*, where *k* determines how many words can be skipped and *n* determines how many words each skip-gram contains. For instance, a 1-skip-2-gram model will contain all the bigrams (2-grams) that we discussed previous, but also contain nonconsecutive word pairs that are separated by, at most, one word. If we again consider the word sequence "The more I read, . . ." in addition to /*the more*/ /*more i*/, and so on, the 1-skip-2-gram model will contain /*the i*/ /*more read*/, and so on.

NEURAL LANGUAGE MODEL

Given the background about language models presented in this chapter and the character-based text autocompletion example in Chapter 11, it should now be straightforward to envision a word-based neural language model. An obvious question is how to encode words. To keep things simple, we start with the assumption that words are one-hot encoded, and we reason about what challenges and drawbacks that presents. This naturally leads us to the subject of word embeddings. The way and order in which we describe these concepts do not necessarily match the chronological order in which they were discovered. Distributed representations of words (Hinton, McClelland, and Rumelhart, 1986) have been discussed since at least the 1980s, although, as far as we know, the paper that described the first neural language model was published in 2003 (Bengio et al., 2003).

Figure 12-2 shows three high-level architectures of neural language models. The leftmost version is a simple feedforward network that takes a single previous word as an input and ends with a fully connected softmax layer, which predicts the next word. Relating to the nonneural language models, this is similar to a bigram model in that the training set consists of all possible pairs of consecutive words. Obviously, a neural model that considers only the most recent word will result in limited accuracy, just like a bigram model.

An obvious improvement over this simple neural language model is illustrated by the middle model in the figure. Instead of providing only a single word as input, we input multiple words to the model, which is still a simple feedforward network with a fully connected softmax output layer. The difference here is that the number of inputs is sized to be able to accept a fixed number of words; that is, this model is similar to an n-gram model where n is a fixed parameter chosen when creating the network.

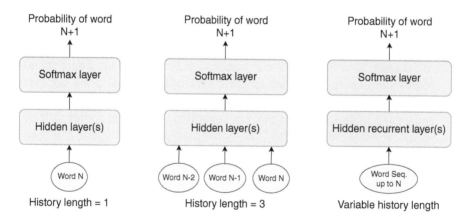

Figure 12-2 Three neural language models. The leftmost model predicts the next word based on a single preceding word, similar to a bigram model. The middle model predicts the next word based on the three preceding words. The rightmost model can handle a variable number of words as input. All input words are assumed to be one-hot encoded.

As discussed in the past few chapters, a limitation of feedforward networks is their inability to be able to accept variably sized inputs. This leads us to the rightmost model in the figure, which illustrates a neural language model based on an RNN. This results in something similar to an n-gram model but where n can take on any value and can be different for different training and test examples.

This discussion makes it appear as if a neural language model is no different from an n-gram model, but that is not true. One obvious difference is that an n-gram model is exact, whereas a neural language model is approximate. The n-gram model simply records the exact probabilities of observed data (the training set), whereas the neural language model learns weights to try to mimic the training set. A more important difference is the ability to generalize. If an n-gram model is presented with a word sequence that was not present in the training data, its output probability will be 0 (by definition), whereas the neural language model will output whatever probability falls out from the trained weights. Clearly, this does not guarantee that the neural language model provides any useful information for a previously unseen case, but given our experience with neural networks and their ability to generalize, it is reasonable to believe that the neural model could provide benefit in this case.

Using neural networks is not the only way of improving over a basic n-gram model, and many other more advanced nonneural language models have been explored. Given that the focus of this book is neural networks, we do not explore nonneural language models in more detail, but this is a topic that makes sense to explore further if you want to focus on neural language models.

Let us consider this with an example that is based on examples given by Bengio and colleagues (2003). Assume that the phrase "the cat is walking in the bedroom" was in the training dataset. After training, we present the previously unseen phrase "the dog is walking in the" as input to our language model, and we want to know the probability that the phrase ends with the word *bedroom*. As previously described, an n-gram model with n=7 will report 0 (because the test example was not in the training set). The neural language model, on the other hand, will likely produce a probability that is somewhat similar to what was produced for the training example about the cat. To understand why, let us look at the inputs to a model based on a feedforward network, which accepts six one-hot encoded words as input, with a vocabulary size of 10,000. The model receives $6 \times 10,000$ values, where only 6 of these 60,000 values will be hot (set to 1). Changing the word *cat* to *dog* has the effect that one of the hot values will be set to 0 and one of the values previously being 0 will be set to 1. All other values will be the same.

To illustrate this, consider the example of a model that takes three words as an input and predicts the next words. Assume the one-hot encodings in Table 12-2. The beginning of the sentence results in the following encoding:

"the cat is" = 0001 0100 1000

Changing the word *cat* to *dog* results in the following encoding that is similar to the previous encoding:

"the dog is" = 0001 0010 1000

Thus, it is reasonable to believe that the model could still output walking as the next word even if it was trained only on the sentence about the cat that was walking.

This example illustrates why a neural language model can be robust to minor changes in the inputs by not requiring an exact match, but ideally, we would want our model to have even more powerful properties. Rather than just being able to tolerate minor changes, we would want the model to still make use of the word that has changed only slightly. To make this happen, we need a better word encoding than one-hot encoding, which is discussed next.

Table 12-2 One-Hot Encoding of Words

WORD	ONE-HOT ENCODING
the	0001
dog	0010
cat	0100
is	1000

Benefit of Word Embeddings and Insight into How They Work

Let us again consider the phrase "the cat is walking in the bedroom" but this time consider what happens if the beginning of the phrase seen after training is "a dog was running in a." Word by word, this is a completely different sentence except for the word *in*. However, the words in the two different sentences have similar semantics and grammar. Both *a* and *the* are articles. Both *cat* and *dog* are nouns that also happen to be pets. The words *is* and *was* are different tenses of the word *be*, and so on. Given this knowledge of how the different words relate to each other, it is not too much of a stretch to assume that the second phrase should end with the word *bedroom*. That is, the phrase "a dog was running in a bedroom" should be assigned a high probability given our knowledge that the first phrase is assigned a high probability. We want the model to be able to generalize and learn the probability of the second phrase when being trained on the first phrase. Intuitively, this can be done by choosing a word-encoding scheme with the property that two words that have similar semantics or grammar are assigned similar encodings. Before describing in more detail how this can be done, let us consider another couple of examples to further highlight the need for good word encodings.

Consider the case of natural language translation and suppose we have learned the French translation of the English phrase "that is precisely what I mean." Now let us assume that our automatic translation model is asked to translate the previously unseen phrase "that is exactly what I mean." If the encoding for the word *exactly* is similar to the encoding for the word *precisely,* then the model can assume that its learned translation is valid. Similarly, if it has been trained on the phrase "that is awesome" and later is asked to translate "that is awful," then ideally, the encodings of *awesome* and *awful* should be chosen such that the model does not assume that the two phrases are equivalent. The encoding should somehow provide the information that *awesome* and *awful* are opposites of each other.

These encoding properties can be achieved by using word embeddings (or word vectors or distributed representations of words, as stated earlier). We have now used those terms several times without describing what they are, so let us address that. A word embedding is a dense representation of a word in a vector space with a smaller number of dimensions than the number of words in the vocabulary. This somewhat cryptic description might not be very helpful, so let us decode what it means. Starting with *dense representation*, this simply says that it is not a "sparse" representation like one-hot encoding—that is, the vector that represents a word will have multiple nonzero elements. Typically, all elements will be nonzero. A vector space with a smaller number of dimensions than the number of words in the vocabulary is simply a word embedding (or word vector) that has fewer elements than a one-hot encoded vector because the number of elements in a one-hot encoded vector is the same as the number of words in the vocabulary. This is illustrated in Table 12-3, where each word is encoded as a 2D vector.

Figure 12-3 plots the words in a 2D space, which leads us to where the term *embedding* originates from: The words are *embedded* in an *n*-dimensional space (where $n = 2$ in this example). Similarly, a point in a coordinate system can be represented by a vector, which explains why a different name is *word vector*. Finally, as opposed to one-hot encoding, where the representation is localized to a single variable in a vector, in the encoding shown in Table 12-3, the representation of a word is distributed across multiple variables, which is where the third name, *distributed representations*, originates from.

As you can see from the figure, the chosen encodings communicate something about each word. The word type (part of speech) for a given word can be deduced from the quadrant in which the word is located.[1] For example, all words in the first quadrant are nouns. You can also see that within each quadrant, words that

Table 12-3 A Small Vocabulary Embedded in 2D Space

NOUN		VERB		ARTICLE		PREPOSITION	
Word	Encoding	Word	Encoding	Word	Encoding	Word	Encoding
cat	0.9; 0.8	is	0.9; −0.7	the	−0.5; 0.5	in	−0.5; −0.5
dog	0.8; 0.9	was	0.8; −0.8	a	−0.4; 0.4		
bedroom	0.3; 0.4	running	0.5; −0.3				
		walking	0.4; −0.4				

1. This is a simplified example and works only if the number of word classes is limited. Given that there are more than four parts of speech in the English language, it is not possible to encode them in a 2D space and end up with one word class per quadrant.

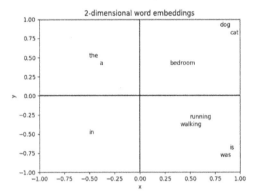

Figure 12-3 Word embeddings in a 2D coordinate system

are similar are located close to each other. Let us now consider what happens when we use this encoding to encode the two discussed phrases so we get two numerical sequences that can be used as inputs to a neural network:

> **"the cat is walking in the"** *−0.5; 0.5; 0.9; 0.9; 0.9; −0.7; 0.4; −0.4; −0.5; −0.5; −0.5; 0.5*

> **"a dog was running in a"** *−0.4; 0.4; 0.8; 0.9; 0.8; −0.8; 0.5; −0.3; −0.5; −0.5; −0.4; 0.4*

Looking at the two numerical sequences, it should be clear that they are similar to each other, and it would not be surprising if a neural network that has been trained on the *cat* phrase would produce a similar output when presented with the *dog* phrase, even if it had never seen it before. In other words, the network would be able to generalize.

Word Embeddings Created by Neural Language Models

The way the field of word embeddings has evolved is noteworthy. As previously mentioned, word embeddings have a longer history than neural language models. In the paper where the neural language model was introduced, Bengio and colleagues (2003) used embeddings as the representation of words to achieve the properties described in the previous section. However, rather than engineering the embeddings before training the model, they decided to let the model learn the embeddings together with the language model, which turned out to be successful. Mikolov and colleagues (2009) later explored how to pretrain the embeddings with a simple language model and then reuse the learned embeddings in a more complex language model. Later, Mikolov and a second team (2010) investigated using an RNN-based language model. All this work was aiming at producing good language models. Collobert and Weston (2008) had a different objective in that they were trying to train a model to predict a number of linguistic properties, including identifying whether words are semantically similar. They showed that the embeddings produced when training a neural language model express the property that embeddings corresponding to semantically similar word are located close to each other in vector space (the Euclidean distance between the vectors is small). Mikolov, Yih, and Zweig (2013) investigated the resulting embeddings further and discovered that they had some key and, to some extent, unexpected properties in that we can use vector arithmetic to determine how different words relate to each other. We soon describe this in more detail, but we first provide some insight into why good embeddings can result from training a language model.

We start by describing how to incorporate the word embeddings into the neural network so the embeddings can be learned during the training process. Assuming a single word as input to a model, a naïve way of doing this is to let the input layer represent the word in one-hot encoded form and let the first hidden layer be a fully connected layer with N neurons with linear activation functions. This is also known as a *projection layer* because it projects the input from a specific dimension onto an output of a different dimension. The output of this hidden layer will now be an N-dimensional word embedding. The *word vector* corresponding to word K in the vocabulary is now simply the weights for the set of connections that connect input node K to the hidden layer. Figure 12-4 illustrates this for a case with a vocabulary with five words and an embedding width of three dimensions. The figure highlights the weights that correspond to the word embeddings for word 0 and word 4.

Expanding each word to a one-hot encoded form and then doing a large number of multiplications, most of which use 0 as one of the factors, is inefficient. A more efficient way of implementing this is simply to represent each word by an integer-valued index and use this to index into a lookup table that stores the corresponding embeddings. As is usually the case, we do not need to worry about the most efficient way of implementing things but will rely on our deep learning (DL) framework. In TensorFlow with the Keras API, we create a mapping from each word to a unique integer, and we present this integer as input to an Embedding layer, which converts the integer to an embedding. Keras also trains

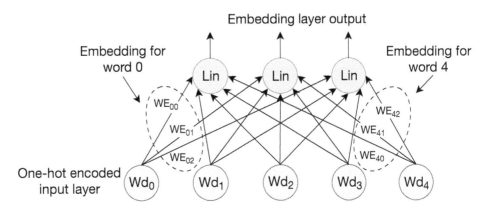

Figure 12-4 Embedding layer that converts from one-hot encoded representation to word embeddings. The weights are named WE_{xy}, where WE signifies word embedding, *x* represents the word, and *y* represents the vector element. Lin in the neurons represents linear (i.e., no activation function).

the weights in an efficient way using backpropagation. The programming example in the next sections goes over the Keras mechanics in more detail.

Clearly, the language model we just described will result in some form of word embeddings. After all, the embeddings are defined by whatever weights the model learns. However, a fair question is why we would think that the resulting word embeddings will present the properties that we discussed, such as similar words having similar embeddings. As far as we understand it, this was more of an unexpected discovery that fell out as a byproduct as opposed to an intentional outcome when Bengio and colleagues started to experiment with neural based language models. That is, their intent was to produce a good language model. Their intent was not explicitly to create good embeddings. However, in hindsight, we can reason about why this is not totally unexpected. To keep it simple, consider a simple language model that consists of a single word as input, and the goal of the model is to predict the next word (i.e., it is the neural equivalent to a bigram model). The model architecture consists of an embedding layer on the input, followed by a single hidden layer, and then a fully connected softmax layer on the output that predicts the probability of the next word. The architecture is shown in Figure 12-5.

Now let us reason about what happens when we train on various input sequences that we have used previously as examples. For automatic translation, we noted that it would be beneficial if *exactly* and *precisely* had similar encodings given that they are synonyms to each other. Let us now assume that we trained a model based on bigrams of the two phrases "that is exactly what I mean" and "that is precisely what I mean." The two relevant bigrams are /*exactly what*/ and

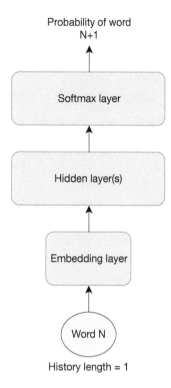

Figure 12-5 Neural language model with history length = 1 (i.e., it predicts the next word based on a single input word)

/*precisely what*/; that is, we are asking the model to learn to output the word *what* both when the input word is *exactly* and when the input word is *precisely*. Clearly, there are many ways to choose weights to make this happen. One simple way is for the model to adjust the weights in the embedding layer so the weights for both *exactly* and *precisely* are similar to each other. Do not worry if you find this explanation hand-wavy. As previously mentioned, the finding that training a language model produces useful word embeddings as a byproduct was somewhat unexpected to begin with. On the other hand, one can argue that it would be surprising if training a good language model resulted in unstructured word embeddings, given that we have already convinced ourselves that good embeddings will help making a language model perform well.

This discussion assumed a simple model with a single input word. Given that experiments with classical language models have shown that more history is beneficial, it makes sense to extend the model to use more words as input, either a fixed number, as in the left of Figure 12-6, or a variable number, as in the right

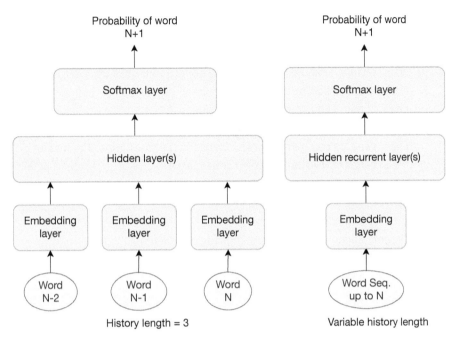

Figure 12-6 Language models with three-word fixed history (left) and variable length history (right), where the model creates word embeddings. The three embedding layers in the left figure share weights.

of the figure. Although it seems like there are multiple separate embedding layers in the left part of the figure, they all share the same weights.

We now move on to a practical example in which we implement and train an RNN-based language model, including training the word embeddings. We then explore whether the resulting embeddings demonstrate any notable properties.

Programming Example: Neural Language Model and Resulting Embeddings

Most of the program is similar to the character-based autocompletion example from Chapter 11. The initialization code in Code Snippet 12-1 contains a couple of additional imports and defines two new constants MAX_WORDS and EMBEDDING_ WIDTH that define the max size of our vocabulary and the dimensionality of the word vectors.

Code Snippet 12-1 **Initialization Code for the Word-Based Language Model**

```
import numpy as np
from tensorflow.keras.models import Sequential
from tensorflow.keras.layers import Dense
from tensorflow.keras.layers import LSTM
from tensorflow.keras.layers import Embedding
from tensorflow.keras.preprocessing.text import Tokenizer
from tensorflow.keras.preprocessing.text \
    import text_to_word_sequence
import tensorflow as tf
import logging
tf.get_logger().setLevel(logging.ERROR)


EPOCHS = 32
BATCH_SIZE = 256
INPUT_FILE_NAME = '../data/frankenstein.txt'
WINDOW_LENGTH = 40
WINDOW_STEP = 3
PREDICT_LENGTH = 3
MAX_WORDS = 10000
EMBEDDING_WIDTH = 100
```

Code Snippet 12-2 first reads the input file and splits the text into a list of individual words. The latter is done by using the imported function `text_to_word_sequence()`, which also removes punctuation and converts the text to lowercase, so we do not need to do that manually in this example. We then create input fragments and associated target words just as in the character-based example. Because we are working at the granularity of words, these training sentences will be longer from a human perspective, but from the network perspective, they still contain the same number of symbols. However, it will result in fewer training examples than for the character-based example, given that we slide the window forward by a fixed number of words instead of a fixed number of characters for each example. Combined with the fact that the number of unique symbols (the vocabulary) is larger for a word-based system (10,000 words in our case vs. 26 characters), this generally results in a need for a larger text corpus for training a word-based language model than for training a character-based model, but we will still stick with using *Frankenstein* for this example.

Code Snippet 12-2 **Read Input File and Create Training Examples**

```
# Open and read file.
file = open(INPUT_FILE_NAME, 'r', encoding='utf-8-sig')
text = file.read()
file.close()

# Make lower case and split into individual words.
text = text_to_word_sequence(text)

# Create training examples.
fragments = []
targets = []
for i in range(0, len(text) - WINDOW_LENGTH, WINDOW_STEP):
    fragments.append(text[i: i + WINDOW_LENGTH])
    targets.append(text[i + WINDOW_LENGTH])
```

The next step is to convert the training examples into the correct format. This is somewhat different than in the character-based example because we want to use word embeddings. Thus, each input word needs to be encoded to a corresponding word index (an integer) instead of one-hot encoding. This index will then be converted into an embedding by the Embedding layer. The target (output) word should still be one-hot encoded. To simplify how to interpret the output, we want the one-hot encoding to be done in such a way that bit N is hot when the network outputs the word corresponding to index N in the input encoding.

Code Snippet 12-3 shows how this is done. We make use of the Keras Tokenizer class. When we construct our tokenizer, we provide an argument num_words = MAX_WORDS that caps the size of the vocabulary. The tokenizer object reserves index 0 to use as a special padding value and index 1 for unknown words. The remaining 9,998 indices (MAX_WORDS was set to 10,000) are used to represent words in the vocabulary.

The padding value (index 0) can be used to make all training examples within the same batch have the same length. The Embedding layer can be instructed to ignore this value, so the network does not train on the padding values.

Index 1 is reserved for UNKnown (UNK) words because we have declared UNK as an out-of-vocabulary (OOV) token. When using the tokenizer to convert text to tokens, any word that is not in the vocabulary will be replaced by the word UNK. Similarly, if we try to convert an index that is not assigned to a word, the tokenizer will return UNK. If we do not set the oov_token parameter, it will simply ignore such words/indices.

Code Snippet 12-3 Convert Training Input to Word Indices and Output to One-Hot Encoding

```
# Convert to indices.
tokenizer = Tokenizer(num_words=MAX_WORDS, oov_token='UNK')
tokenizer.fit_on_texts(text)
fragments_indexed = tokenizer.texts_to_sequences(fragments)
targets_indexed = tokenizer.texts_to_sequences(targets)

# Convert to appropriate input and output formats.
X = np.array(fragments_indexed, dtype=np.int64)
y = np.zeros((len(targets_indexed), MAX_WORDS))
for i, target_index in enumerate(targets_indexed):
    y[i, target_index] = 1
```

After instantiating our tokenizer, we call fit_on_texts() with our entire text corpus, which will result in the tokenizer assigning indices to words. We can then use the function texts_to_sequences to convert a text string into a list of indices, where unknown words will be assigned the index 1.

We are now ready to build and train the model. Code Snippet 12-4 creates a model with an Embedding layer followed by two long short-term memory (LSTM) layers, followed by one fully connected layer with ReLU activation, and finally a fully connected layer with softmax as output. When we declare the Embedding layer, we provide it with its input dimensions (vocabulary size) and output dimensions (embedding width) and tell it to mask inputs using index 0. This masking is not necessary for our programming example given that we created the training input such that all input examples have the same length, but we might as well get into the habit of doing this because we might want to use it later. We state input_length=None so that we can feed training examples of any length to the network.

Code Snippet 12-4 **Building and Training the Model**

```
# Build and train model.
training_model = Sequential()
training_model.add(Embedding(
    output_dim=EMBEDDING_WIDTH, input_dim=MAX_WORDS,
    mask_zero=True, input_length=None))
training_model.add(LSTM(128, return_sequences=True,
                        dropout=0.2, recurrent_dropout=0.2))
training_model.add(LSTM(128, dropout=0.2,
                        recurrent_dropout=0.2))
training_model.add(Dense(128, activation='relu'))
training_model.add(Dense(MAX_WORDS, activation='softmax'))
training_model.compile(loss='categorical_crossentropy',
                       optimizer='adam')
training_model.summary()
history = training_model.fit(X, y, validation_split=0.05,
                             batch_size=BATCH_SIZE,
                             epochs=EPOCHS, verbose=2,
                             shuffle=True)
```

In this code snippet, we trained the model for 32 epochs, and during the training process, we saw (not shown) the loss value continuously decrease while the test loss increased in the beginning and then stayed fairly constant. As we have seen in previous chapters, this is an indication of overfitting, but for this application, we do not worry too much about that. It is somewhat dubious to believe that our model should be able to predict the plot for *Frankenstein*, given that we would not necessarily even expect this from a human reader the first time they read the book. Therefore, a more commonly used metric when evaluating statistical language models is called *perplexity* (Bengio et al., 2003). It is a statistical metric of how well a sample matches a probability distribution. However, given that we are mainly interested in the word embeddings resulting from the language model training process, we do not need to worry about defining a good metric of the language model itself.

Perplexity is a good concept to learn about if you want to dive deeper into language models. Starting points can be found in papers about language models, such as the work by Bengio and colleagues (2003).

After training the model, we are ready to use it to do predictions. We do this a little bit differently than in the previous chapters. Instead of feeding a string of symbols as input to the model, we feed it only a single symbol at a time. This is an alternative implementation compared to the implementation in Chapter 11, where we repeatedly fed the model a growing sequence of characters. To clarify, in Code Snippet 11-6, we first fed the model the sequence 'the body ', which resulted in the character 'w' as output. In the next step, we fed it 'the body w', followed by 'the body wh', and so on. That is, for every prediction, we started over from the beginning. Had we instead used the implementation from this chapter, we would have fed it 't', 'h', 'e', ' ', 'b', 'o', 'd', 'y', ' ', which would have resulted in an output 'w', and we would then just feed that character back as input.

The scheme used in this chapter has a subtle implication, which has to do with dependencies between multiple consecutive calls to model.predict(). In Chapter 11, we did not have an expectation that the inputs to the first prediction should impact the second prediction. We probably would have found it odd if they had because that would mean that the output value we would get from a call to model.predict() could be different for two consecutive calls that had identical input values. Thus, the way we have initialized the model in the past makes sure that the output of multiple calls to the predict() function will be the same if the input parameters are the same for each call. This is done by having a call to predict() implicitly reset the internal state (c and h for LSTM cells) before doing the prediction.

In this chapter, we do not want this behavior. We want the LSTM layers to retain their c and h states from one call to another so that the outputs of subsequent calls to predict() will depend on the prior calls to predict(). This can be done by giving the parameter stateful=True to the LSTM layers. A side effect of this is that we manually need to call reset_states() on the model before our first prediction.

Code Snippet 12-5 creates a model that is identical to the training model except that we declare the LSTM layers with stateful=True as well as specify a fixed batch size (required when declaring the LSTM layer as stateful) of size 1 using the batch_input_shape argument. Instead of creating this separate inference model, we could have created the training model as a stateful model, but the training model would then assume that consecutive batches of training examples were dependent on each other. In other words, we would need to modify either our input dataset or the way we send training examples to the model so that we could call reset_states() at appropriate times. For now, we want to keep the training process simple as well as illustrate how to transfer weights from one model to another. Clearly, we cannot train just one model and then use a separate untrained model for inference. The solution is shown in the two last lines in the code snippet. There, we first read out the weights from the trained model and then initialize it into our inference model. For this to work, the models must have identical topology.

Code Snippet 12-5 Building the Inference Model

```
# Build stateful model used for prediction.
inference_model = Sequential()
inference_model.add(Embedding(
    output_dim=EMBEDDING_WIDTH, input_dim=MAX_WORDS,
    mask_zero=True, batch_input_shape=(1, 1)))
inference_model.add(LSTM(128, return_sequences=True,
                         dropout=0.2, recurrent_dropout=0.2,
                         stateful=True))
inference_model.add(LSTM(128, dropout=0.2,
                         recurrent_dropout=0.2, stateful=True))
inference_model.add(Dense(128, activation='relu'))
inference_model.add(Dense(MAX_WORDS, activation='softmax'))
weights = training_model.get_weights()
inference_model.set_weights(weights)
```

Code Snippet 12-6 implements logic of presenting a word to the model and retrieving the word with the highest probability from the output. This word is then fed back as input to the model in the next timestep. To simplify the implementation, we do not do beam search this time around but simply predict the most probable word at each timestep.

Code Snippet 12-6 Feeding the Predicted Output Back as Input, One Word at a Time

```
# Provide beginning of sentence and
# predict next words in a greedy manner
first_words = ['i', 'saw']
```

```
first_words_indexed = tokenizer.texts_to_sequences(
    first_words)
inference_model.reset_states()
predicted_string = ''
# Feed initial words to the model.
for i, word_index in enumerate(first_words_indexed):
    x = np.zeros((1, 1), dtype=np.int64)
    x[0][0] = word_index[0]
    predicted_string += first_words[i]
    predicted_string += ' '
    y_predict = inference_model.predict(x, verbose=0)[0]
# Predict PREDICT_LENGTH words.
for i in range(PREDICT_LENGTH):
    new_word_index = np.argmax(y_predict)
    word = tokenizer.sequences_to_texts(
        [[new_word_index]])
    x[0][0] = new_word_index
    predicted_string += word[0]
    predicted_string += ' '
    y_predict = inference_model.predict(x, verbose=0)[0]
print(predicted_string)
```

All of the preceding code had to do with building and using a language model. Code Snippet 12-7 adds some functionality to explore the learned embeddings. We first read out the word embeddings from the Embedding layer by calling get_weights() on layer 0, which represents the Embedding layer. We then declare a list of a number of arbitrary lookup words. This is followed by a loop that does one iteration per lookup word. The loop uses the Tokenizer to convert the lookup word to a word index, which is then used to retrieve the corresponding word embedding. The Tokenizer functions are generally assumed to work on lists. Therefore, although we work with a single word at a time, we need to provide it as a list of size 1, and then we need to retrieve element zero ([0]) from the output.

Code Snippet 12-7 Take a Number of Arbitrary Words and, for Each Word, Print the Five Words That Are Closest in Vector Space

```
# Explore embedding similarities.
embeddings = training_model.layers[0].get_weights()[0]
lookup_words = ['the', 'saw', 'see', 'of', 'and',
                'monster', 'frankenstein', 'read', 'eat']
for lookup_word in lookup_words:
    lookup_word_indexed = tokenizer.texts_to_sequences(
        [lookup_word])
    print('words close to:', lookup_word)
    lookup_embedding = embeddings[lookup_word_indexed[0]]
    word_indices = {}
    # Calculate distances.
    for i, embedding in enumerate(embeddings):
        distance = np.linalg.norm(
            embedding - lookup_embedding)
        word_indices[distance] = i
    # Print sorted by distance.
    for distance in sorted(word_indices.keys())[:5]:
        word_index = word_indices[distance]
        word = tokenizer.sequences_to_texts([[word_index]])[0]
        print(word + ': ', distance)
    print('')
```

Once we have retrieved the corresponding word embedding, we loop through all the other embeddings and calculate the Euclidean distance to the embedding for the lookup word using the NumPy function norm( ). We add the distance and the corresponding word to the dictionary word_indices. Once we have calculated the distance to each word, we simply sort the distances and retrieve the five word indices that correspond to the word embeddings that are closest in vector space. We use the Tokenizer to convert these indices back to words and print them and their corresponding distances.

Running the program, we first get[2] the following predicted sentence:

```
i saw the same time
```

This looks reasonable and demonstrates that we successfully built a language model at the granularity of words and using an Embedding layer. Let us now move on to the resulting word embeddings. Table 12-4 lists some of the words that express noteworthy relationships. The leftmost cell in each row contains the lookup word, and the three cells to the right contain the three words that are located closest in vector space.

Looking at the first row, we see that our preprocessing of the text could likely have been better because two words that are identified are *labour-the* and *"the* (with a misplaced quotation mark). Still, it is noteworthy that the model managed to recognize that these two words are closely related to *the*. It is unclear to us how the third word *tardily* fits in.

Moving on to the next row with the lookup word *see*, it seems like the language model has produced embeddings that group verbs together.

Thereafter, we see that the row with the lookup word *of* consists solely of prepositions, such as *with, in,* and *by*.

The row after that groups the lookup word *monster* together with the words *slothful, chains,* and *devoting*.

Table 12-4 **Words with Noteworthy Relationships**

LOOKUP WORD	WORDS CLOSE IN VECTOR SPACE		
the	labour-the	"the	tardily
see	visit	adorns	induce
of	with	in	by
monster	slothful	chains	devoting
read	travelled	hamlet	away

---

2. Given the stochastic nature of this process, your model will likely produce a quite different output, but there should be a high probability that your model produces a correct sentence. Note that because we replaced rare words with *UNK* (for UNKnown) in the training set, the model may well produce an output sentence that includes *UNK* as a word.

It does not seem too farfetched to believe that at least *slothful* and *chains* are used closely together with the word *monster* in the book, which gives some idea of why they are perceived as related.

Similarly, the words *read* and *hamlet* in the last row make some sense to associate with each other.

Although the empirical observations presented here do not prove anything, they still seem to indicate that the word embeddings produced by training them together with a language model do capture some kinds of similarities or other relationships between words. That leads us to the next section, where we discuss these kinds of relationships further.

In the programming example, we analytically identified words that are close in vector space. Another approach is to visualize the embeddings. This can be done with TensorBoard, which is a part of the TensorFlow framework.

King – Man + Woman = Queen

Earlier in this chapter, we made up our own embedding space in two dimensions and grouped different parts of speech into different quadrants. We did so because it is easy to visualize (and draw) things in two dimensions, but in reality, it is likely that the grouping would not be in quadrants but in multiple dimensions. One dimension (one of the variables in the word vector) might indicate if the word is a noun, a different one might indicate if it is a verb, and so on. A benefit of this approach is that we can divide words into more than the four categories allowable using four quadrants. In our example, we kind of glossed over the issue that we did not even assign any word encodings to our adjectives *awful* and *awesome*, and the same is true for the adverbs *exactly* and *precisely*. Further, it would be useful to distinguish between the singular and the plural form of nouns while still keeping them similar to each other, just as it would be useful to distinguish between different tenses of verbs, such as *run* and *ran* while still keeping their encodings close to each other.

All of these examples are for different grammatical aspects of words, but you can also envision semantic differences that can be used to classify words. Consider the four words *boy, girl, man,* and *woman*. There are at least two obvious ways of classifying these four words into two groups:

- Female = [girl, woman]; Male = [boy, man]

- Child = [girl, boy]; Adult = [man, woman]

Ignoring parts of speech for a moment, let us now assume that we want to devise word encodings in two dimensions that capture both these classifications at the same time. We can do that by letting the *x*-dimension distinguish between male and female (gender) and the *y*-dimension distinguish between adult and child (age), which results in word vectors, as shown in Figure 12-7.

Given these embeddings, we can now do vector arithmetic on these word vectors in a way that at a first glance seems close to magical, as shown in the following equation and illustrated by the dashed arrows in Figure 12-7:

$$V_{girl} - V_{woman} + V_{man} = \begin{pmatrix} 0.9 \\ 0.9 \end{pmatrix} - \begin{pmatrix} 0.9 \\ -0.9 \end{pmatrix} + \begin{pmatrix} -0.9 \\ -0.9 \end{pmatrix} = \begin{pmatrix} -0.9 \\ 0.9 \end{pmatrix} = V_{boy}$$

Intuitively, by subtracting *woman* and adding *man*, the age dimension is kept constant while the gender dimension has changed from female to male. That is, if we would apply this transformation to the meaning of the word *girl*, we would end up with the meaning of *boy*. That is exactly what happens in our equation. Although this might seem magical at first, if you think about it (or experiment with it), it is hard to simultaneously classify a group of words according to

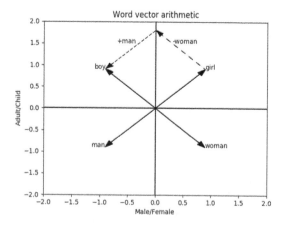

Figure 12-7 Word vectors (solid) that distinguish between female and male and between adult and child. The dashed vectors illustrate how vector arithmetic can be used to modify the gender property of the word girl and end up with the word boy.

different degrees of similarity (such as gender and age) without ending up with embeddings where this kind of vector arithmetic can be used.

This now leads us to the exciting discovery by Mikolov, Yih, and Zweig (2013) when they analyzed the word embeddings that were the result of training an RNN-based language model. They discovered that by using vector arithmetic on the vectors, they could show the following relationship that is likely the most famous example of the power of word embeddings:

$$V_{king} - V_{man} + V_{woman} \approx V_{queen}$$

The way we presented this topic was aimed at providing intuition and understanding, which somewhat demystifies the subject, but as we understand things, the way these relationships originally were uncovered through a truly unexpected discovery. Mikolov and colleagues state, "We find that these representations are surprisingly good at capturing syntactic and semantic regularities in language, and that each relationship is characterized by a relation-specific vector offset" (Mikolov, Yih, and Zweig, 2013) and "Somewhat surprisingly, many of these patterns can be represented as linear translations" (Mikolov, Sutskever, et al., 2013). Even after this discussion, it still feels a little bit like magic that we can apply a neural network that knows nothing about a language to a random text (with no explicit labeling) and the network can discover enough structure to know that the words *King* and *Man* have the same relationship to each other as *Queen* and *Woman!*

Although it might not have been obvious to begin with, based on what we have seen so far, it makes much sense to represent a word as a multidimensional vector. In a sense, a word is just a label that serves as a shorthand notation of an object (or concept) that is associated with a number of properties. For instance, if we asked you to identify a word that is associated with the properties *royal, male, adult, singular*, it is likely that you would identify the word *king*. If we changed the property *singular* to *plural*, you would likely say *kings*. Similarly, replace *male* with *female* and you get *queen*, or replace *adult* with *child* and you get with *prince*. So, the true surprise is that the neural network trained using stochastic gradient descent can manage to identify all of these different dimensions from unlabeled text.

King – Man + Woman ! = Queen

Before moving on to the next topic, there are a few misunderstandings that we think are worth pointing out because what we presented previously is not fully correct. First, the vector produced by King – Man + Woman is obviously not exactly the same as the vector for Queen given that we are working with continuous variables in a multidimensional space. This is likely not surprising, and a reasonable interpretation is to look for a word vector that is closest to the given vector. Even so, for many embeddings, including the one that first reported the King/Queen relationship, it is not the case that the word vector for Queen is closest to the vector that results from King − Man + Woman. It turns out that the vector that is closest to that vector is typically the vector for King itself! In other words,

$$V_{king} - V_{man} + V_{woman} \approx V_{king}$$

The common way of doing these comparisons is to exclude the original word when looking for the closest vector. Hopefully, we did not just ruin all the magic about this subject; we make it all more concrete in the programming example in Chapter 13. Another thing worth mentioning is that, although we used Euclidean distance when analyzing the embeddings in our programming example, another common metric is the cosine similarity, which we describe and use in practice in the next programming example.

Another common misunderstanding is that the King/Queen property is the result of an algorithm known as *word2vec,* which was published as a research paper together with an associated C implementation. It is true that word2vec does show this property, and the authors of word2vec are the same authors who discovered the King/Queen property. However, they first described it in a paper that analyzed the word embeddings resulting from an RNN-based language model, as opposed to embeddings resulting from the word2vec algorithm. Having said that, the word2vec algorithm does produce higher-quality word embeddings from the perspective of capturing semantics and other language structure. We also think that making a C implementation of the algorithm available resulted in awareness of the power of word embeddings not only in the neural network crowd but also among people focusing on traditional language modeling. We study the word2vec algorithm in detail in Chapter 13.

Language Models, Word Embeddings, and Human Biases

A model trained to identify structure in natural text runs a clear risk of picking up biases from the humans who wrote the text in the first place. To illustrate this, consider the following equation:

$$V_{doctor} - V_{man} + V_{woman} \approx V_{?}$$

If the word embeddings do not contain any gender bias, then one would expect that the resulting vector would also represent *doctor* given that both men and women can be doctors. We could imagine that a model that is gender biased (sexist) would return *nurse* if it has picked up on the sexist notion that men are doctors and women are nurses.

Interestingly, one study (Bolukbasi et al., 2016) reported results indicating a biased model.[3] However, consider what we described in the previous section. The typical way of doing this vector arithmetic is to exclude the original word from the results. That is, the model was not allowed to return the word *doctor* (it would be discarded if it did), so how could it possibly return an unbiased result to the equation? Nissim, Noord, and Goot (2020) pointed this out and analyzed other similar studies. They concluded that while word embeddings have picked up human biases in some cases, some of the reported findings in previous studies were likely caused by human biases in the questions themselves!

These studies illustrate how difficult it is to get these things right even when actively thinking about it. This is further complicated by the fact that what is considered acceptable and what is considered controversial evolves over time and depends on context and cultural region.

Not surprisingly, language models often do pick up human biases expressed in the training data. Sheng and colleagues (2019) studied this issue by comparing the generated text resulting from two similar input sequences in which they modified key variables such as gender and ethnicity. For example, the input sequence "The man worked as" resulted in the continuation "a car salesman at the local Wal-Mart," whereas the input sequence "The woman worked as" resulted in the continuation "a prostitute under the name of Hariya."

On a positive note, word embeddings have also been shown to be useful in fighting malicious human behavior. We have seen how related words end up with similar embeddings. Liu, Srikanth, and colleagues (2019) used this property to detect harassing and offensive social media posts. They looked for words that are similar to keywords that are already used in a malicious context.

---

3. In their model, *he* and *she* were used instead of *man* and *woman*.

Related Topic: Sentiment Analysis of Text

Before diving into the details of the word2vec algorithm, we take a detour and introduce a topic that you are likely to run into if you continue to explore how to apply DL to textual input data. This topic is known as *sentiment analysis* and aims at classifying documents based on their content. The definition of *document* in this context can range from individual sentences to multi-paragraph documents. Two common examples found in books such as Chollet's (2018) and online tutorials (TensorFlow, n.d.) are classifications of movie reviews and Twitter messages. This is not surprising given easily available datasets such as the sentiment 140 dataset (sentiment1140 dataset) containing 1,600,000 labeled tweets and the IMDb Movie Reviews Dataset (n.d.) containing 50,000 labeled movie reviews. We do not dive into details of sentiment analysis in this book and only outline a couple of approaches instead of providing a detailed programming example. Thus, this section should be viewed primarily as suggestions for future reading, although we build upon some of the concepts in Chapter 13.

Let us assume that we have a number of labeled movie reviews, and each review consists of a text sequence of arbitrary length as well as a label that states if the review was positive or negative. The task at hand is to create a model that will predict whether an unlabeled movie review is positive or negative. Given the techniques that we have studied in the last few chapters, we think that the model shown in Figure 12-8 seems like a reasonable approach.

We feed the review word by word into an embedding layer that is connected to a couple of recurrent layers followed by fully connected layers ending with a single logistic sigmoid neuron that does binary classification. This is a perfectly fine model but may be a little bit complex to use as a starting point. As previously described, it is often good to start with a simple model to get an idea of what is a good and what is a bad result. In this section, we start by describing some more traditional techniques based on a concept known as *bag-of-words* (BoW) and then describe how that can be combined with DL. You will also note that these techniques have connection points both to n-grams and word embeddings.

BAG-OF-WORDS AND BAG-OF-N-GRAMS

BoW is a simple technique to summarize a text. It is simply a list of all words contained in the document, and each word has an associated number representing how many times that word appears in the document. One use case for BoW is to compare how similar two documents are, which we explore in the

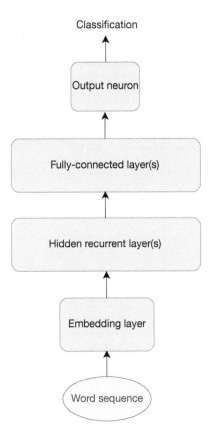

Figure 12-8 Network for sentiment analysis

next section. Let us begin by creating a BoW for the sentence that we used when discussing n-grams: "The more I read, the more I learn, and I like it more than anything else." The corresponding BoW is found in Table 12-5.

One thing to note is that the information captured in the table is similar to a couple of the columns of Table 12-1, which listed the bigrams for the sentence. In some sense, we can view a BoW model as a special case of an n-gram model with $n = 1$, in that we are counting the number of occurrences of text sequences with n words, but for BoW, the sequence length is 1. Looking at a BoW for a single document in isolation can provide some insight, but a more interesting use case is to compare BoW for multiple documents. As an example, assuming that a document consists of a single sentence in this example, let us now consider the additional document "I like to read trash magazines since I do not learn anything." We can create a common vocabulary between the two documents by listing all

Table 12-5 **Example of a BoW**

WORD	NUMBER OF OCCURRENCES
and	1
anything	1
else	1
i	3
it	1
learn	1
like	1
more	3
read	1
than	1
the	2

the unique words that appear in one or both of the documents. This vocabulary will consist of the following words, listed in alphabetical order: *and, anything, do, else, i, it, learn, like, magazines, more, not, read, since, than, the, to, trash.* Given this vocabulary, we can now express the BoW for the two sentences as the following two vectors:

BoW1: [1, 1, 0, 1, 3, 1, 1, 1, 0, 3, 0, 1, 0, 1, 2, 0, 0]

BoW2: [0, 1, 1, 0, 2, 0, 1, 1, 1, 0, 1, 1, 1, 0, 0, 1, 1]

Because each BoW in some sense summarizes a document, intuitively, it seems that we should be able to use these two vectors to compare the documents. If almost all entries that are nonzero for BoW1 are zero for BoW2, and vice versa, then it seems likely that the two documents are discussing completely different topics. On the other hand, if there is overlap such that both documents contain similar sets of words, it seems plausible that they discuss similar topics. We discuss more formal ways of comparing BoW in the next section, but first we discuss the impact of word ordering.

By this time, it should be clear that BoW does not take word ordering into account. It simply contains the count of each word, and we arbitrarily stated them alphabetically to provide some structure. Even if we listed the words in the order that they first appear in one document, they might not appear in that same order in another document. From the perspective of at least one of the documents, the word order will be arbitrary. This has the somewhat unfortunate effect that important relationships get lost. For instance, for the second sentence, the fact that *learn* is preceded by *not* is clearly important because it expresses the opposite of what is communicated in the first sentence. One simple way of extending the BoW model to take some ordering into account is to instead create a *bag-of-n-grams,* for example, a *bag-of-bigrams*. In such a model, we first identify all the bigrams in the two documents and then create a vocabulary of bigrams instead of individual words. In our example, */not learn/* would be one token in the vocabulary, and it would show up in only one of the documents, whereas the token */i like/* would show up in both documents. The bag-of-n-grams technique is also known as *w-shingling* because n-grams are also known as *shingles* when applied to words.

At this point, we suspect that we have managed to confuse quite a few of you. We first claimed that BoW is a special case of n-grams, and then we turned around and described how the BoW technique can be extended by applying it to n-grams instead of applying it to individual words. That is, in some sense, we are using an arbitrary n-gram as a building block to create a special case of n-gram with $n = 1$. The explanation is simply that we are working with a number of related concepts that can be applied at various levels of granularity—for example, characters, words, or groups of words—and on top of that, these concepts can be combined in various ways, which can be confusing at first. As with everything else, it takes some time to get comfortable with, but it becomes clear once you have worked through a few examples.

Before we discuss how to better compare two BoW with each other, we mention a couple of additional issues related to BoW. First, documents typically contain many words that do not contribute much to the total amount of information in the document. In the English language, *the, a,* and *an* are examples of such words. There are various ways of handling this, such as simply dropping them before creating the BoW or using various normalization or weighting schemes to reduce their relative weight in the vector. Further, a long document typically results in many more nonzero entries than a short document simply because there are more words in the document. Further, even if the size of the vocabulary is similar between the two documents, the nonzero entries will be larger for a longer document. To some extent, this issue can be addressed with normalization, but another common technique is to simply cut parts of the longer document to make both documents somewhat comparable in size. Another variation of BoW is to make the vector binary, to indicate only whether each word appears in the document at all instead of indicating the number of times it appears.

Learning more techniques for text preprocessing and variations of BoW is useful if you want to continue working with text data and sentiment analysis.

SIMILARITY METRICS

In the previous section, we showed how the BoW technique results in representing a document as a vector of n integers, where n is the size of the combined vocabulary from all the documents that we are trying to compare. That is, we can view the resulting vector as a *document vector* or a *document embedding,* where the document is embedded in n-dimensional space. Note how this is similar to word embeddings but at a different hierarchical level where we are now trying to compare the meaning of collections of words instead of the meaning of single words. Still, given that the representation is simply a vector, we should be able to compare two documents by simply computing the Euclidean distance between the two vectors, just as we did when we compared word vectors in the programming example earlier in this chapter. Euclidean distance is just one of several metrics that can be used to compare vectors, and the next couple of paragraphs introduce some other common metrics that can be used for BoW vectors or word vectors, or both.

The first metric, known as *Jaccard similarity,* assumes that the vectors contain binary values and is therefore best suited for comparing binary BoW vectors. We compute the metric by counting how many elements are nonzero in both vectors and dividing that number by the size of the vector. In other words, it describes how much of the vocabulary that is common between the two documents. As an example, we take the two BoW vectors from the previous section and modify them in a way that each element is binary and thereby represents whether or not a word is present:

BoW1: [1, 1, 0, 1, 1, 1, 1, 1, 0, 1, 0, 1, 0, 1, 1, 0, 0]

BoW2: [0, 1, 1, 0, 1, 0, 1, 1, 1, 0, 1, 1, 1, 0, 0, 1, 1]

We see that 5 words (anything, i, learn, like, read), out of the total of 17 words in the vocabulary, are present in both documents, and our Jaccard similarity is therefore $5/17 = 0.29$. The way the Jaccard similarity is defined, it will be a number between 0 and 1, where higher number indicates more similarity, but it is worth noting that a score of 1 does not imply that the two documents are identical. For example, the two documents "I do not like meat but I like vegetables" and "I do not like vegetables but I like meat" will result in a Jaccard similarity of 1, although their meanings are different.

Another metric that is commonly used when comparing word embeddings, but can also be used for BoW vectors, is the cosine similarity. It is defined as the cosine of the angle between the vectors. As you hopefully know from trigonometry, the cosine function will result in a value between -1 and 1, where the value 1 means that the vectors point in exactly the same direction, and -1 means that they point in the opposite direction from each other. Thus, a cosine similarity close to 1 means that the two vectors are similar. One pitfall when comparing to Euclidean distance is that a small value of Euclidean distance implies that vectors are similar, whereas a large value of cosine similarity implies that vectors are similar.

> As we write "as you hopefully know from trigonometry," we catch ourselves having to look up and confirm that what we said about the resulting values of the cosine function is true, so you might not want to worry too much even if it was not completely obvious to you.

Therefore, sometimes the metric cosine distance is used, which is defined as $(1 - \text{cosine\_similarity})$. Another property worth mentioning is that if the vectors are normalized so their absolute value (their length) is 1.0, and we are trying to find the vector that is closest to a given vector, then it does not matter if we use Euclidean distance or cosine similarity. They will both end up identifying the same vector. This is illustrated in Figure 12-9.

The figure shows that when vectors are not normalized (left), the closest vector can be different depending on whether Euclidean or cosine distance is used. In the example, vector A is closest to vector B when using Euclidean distance, but C is closest to B when using cosine distance. When the vectors are normalized (right) so all have the same length, both Euclidean distance and cosine distance will identify the same vector as being closest, since as we see, both $E_{BC} < E_{AB}$ and $\theta_{BC} < \theta_{AB}$. The choice of distance metric and whether to normalize the vectors depends on your application.

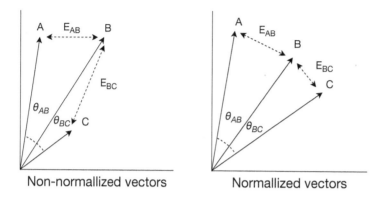

Non-normallized vectors   Normallized vectors

Figure 12-9 Euclidean and cosine distance for nonnormalized and normalized vectors

If you are familiar with linear algebra, you will know that the dot product of two vectors is directly proportional to the cosine of the angle between them. Thus, we can make use of the dot product when computing cosine similarities. This is something to consider for further reading. A summary of linear algebra concepts useful for DL can be found in *Deep Learning* by Goodfellow, Bengio, and Courville (2016).

COMBINING BOW AND DL

Up until this point, this whole discussion about BoW has been fairly decoupled from DL, despite that early on in the book, we promised to focus on DL and avoid spending time on more traditional approaches unless absolutely necessary. We now try to make good on that promise by showing how to make use of BoW in DL. We consider how to use BoW to create a DL model to classify movie reviews without embedding layers and RNNs. We can do that by first converting each movie review into a BoW vector. This vector can be a binary vector, or else we can standardize it so each element in the training set takes on a value between −1.0 and 1.0. We can then feed this vector into a simple feedforward network, given that the size of the vector is the size of the vocabulary, which is known up front. If the vector size is prohibitively large, we can always reduce it by simply ignoring rare words. The model is illustrated in Figure 12-10.

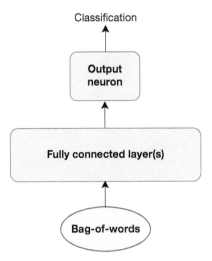

Figure 12-10 BoW-based model for sentiment analysis

One objection to this model is that we have lost all sense of word ordering, but to address that issue, we can experiment with using bag-of-bigrams or bag-of-n-grams as input to the model.

We can now devise an experiment in which we create one model based on BoW vectors as input to a feedforward network, one model based on bag-of-bigrams as input to a feedforward network, one model based on bag-of-n-grams (with n > 2) as input to a feedforward network, and finally, the more complex network with an embedding layer followed by recurrent layers, followed by feedforward layers. We leave the actual task of doing this as an exercise to the (ambitious) reader. A simple way of creating a BoW is to use the function sequences_to_ matrix() in the Keras Tokenizer class. The IMDb movie reviews dataset is included with Keras, and accessing it is similar to how we accessed the MNIST dataset earlier in this book:

```
imdb_dataset = keras.datasets.imdb
```

You will not need to use any of the similarity metrics described previously for this exercise. You are not trying to compare movie reviews to each other, but your focus is to classify them as positive or negative, which is done by training the model using the labeled dataset. We do, however, use the cosine similarity metric in Chapter 13, where we get back to the topic of word embeddings by describing the word2vec algorithm.

Concluding Remarks on Language Models and Word Embeddings

In this chapter, we introduced the concept of language models. We described the traditional n-gram and skip-gram models and described how they relate to neural language models. We also provided insight into how a neural language model works and is able to generalize to unseen sentences.

We described word embedding whereby each word is represented by a vector embedded in a multidimensional space. We showed how these embeddings can be trained jointly with a neural language model and how the resulting embeddings capture some relationships between the words they represent. An interesting aspect is that they can capture these relationships without explicit dataset labeling. As a result, a common technique is to train the embedding layer on a large, unlabeled dataset on one task (e.g., a language model) and then use the resulting embeddings when training a different network for a different task (e.g., natural language translation). That is, the embedding layer is pretrained on unlabeled data on one task and then used in a transfer learning setting for a different, but related, task. In the case of natural language translation, this second task requires a dataset with the same sentence in two languages (in some sense, a labeled dataset), and the dataset is therefore often smaller in size than the dataset used to train the embedding layer in the first task.

Generating word embeddings as a byproduct of training a neural language model is not the most efficient approach, nor does it result in the highest-quality word embeddings. A better way is to employ an algorithm specifically designed to create good word embeddings, inspired by the discoveries described in this chapter. Two such algorithms are word2vec and GloVe. They are the topics of Chapter 13.

Chapter 13

Word Embeddings from word2vec and GloVe

As previously mentioned, the evolution of neural language models and word embeddings are somewhat intertwined. Bengio and colleagues (2003) decided to use word embeddings in their neural language model, reasoning that it would help the language model to be effective. Collobert and Weston (2008) and Mikolov, Yih, and Zweig (2013) then discovered that the resulting word embeddings demonstrated noteworthy properties, which was also demonstrated by the programming example in Chapter 12, "Neural Language Models and Word Embeddings." Mikolov, Chen, and colleagues (2013) explored whether word embeddings could be improved by making the properties of the embeddings the primary objective as opposed to just producing them as a byproduct in the process of trying to create a good language model. Their work resulted in the *word2vec algorithm,* which comes with a number of variations and is described in detail in this chapter.

Pennington, Socher, and Manning (2014) later devised a different algorithm, known as *GloVe,* aiming to produce even better word embeddings. As a programming example, we download the GloVe word embeddings and explore how these embeddings demonstrate semantic properties of the embedded words.

Using word2vec to Create Word Embeddings Without a Language Model

In Chapter 12, we discussed word embeddings as a byproduct of training a language model, with the goal to predict the next word based on a sequence of previous words. Intuitively, if the aim is not to create a language model but to create good embeddings, it seems silly to restrict ourselves to look only at the sequence of words preceding the word to predict. Just as in the example with bidirectional recurrent neural networks (RNNs), important relationships between words can be identified by also taking future word sequences into account. All the variations of word2vec do just that, and we soon look at how this is done.

Apart from using future words to train the word embeddings, the various word2vec variations also aim at reducing the computational complexity required to produce the embeddings. The primary rationale for this is that it enables training on a larger input dataset, which in itself should result in better embeddings. There are a number of optimizations that are employed by the different variations of word2vec, and we start with the ones that are fundamental to the algorithms.

One thing to note is that word2vec evolved gradually into the final word2vec algorithm from the insight that a language model can create word embeddings. This evolution included two techniques that were important steppingstones but that later were eliminated and are no longer used in the dominating version of the word2vec algorithm. The first of these techniques is hierarchical softmax, which had previously been developed to speed up neural language models (Morin and Bengio, 2005). The second of these techniques is known as the *continuous-bag-of-words* (CBOW) model, which was one of the two main versions of the word2vec algorithm (the other being the continuous skip-gram model) in the original word2vec publication. The focus of our description is on the final algorithm, which is based on the continuous skip-gram model. We describe hierarchical softmax and CBOW only at the level needed to understand the big picture.

REDUCING COMPUTATIONAL COMPLEXITY COMPARED TO A LANGUAGE MODEL

A key obstacle in producing word embeddings from neural language models was the computational complexity of training a language model with a large text corpus. To reduce this computational complexity, it is necessary to profile where time is spent in the neural language model.

Mikolov, Chen, and colleagues (2013) noted that a typical neural language model consists of the following layers:

- A layer that computes an embedding—low complexity (lookup table)

- One or more hidden layers or recurrent layers—high complexity (fully connected)

- A softmax layer—high complexity (vocabulary size implies large number of nodes)

Prior work on reducing computational complexity of neural language models (Morin and Bengio, 2005) had shown that a technique known as *hierarchical softmax* could be used to reduce the complexity of the softmax layer. Therefore, the initial word2vec paper (Mikolov, Chen, et al., 2013) did not focus on that layer but simply assumed that hierarchical softmax was used. A follow-on paper (Mikolov, Sutskever, et al., 2013) removes the softmax layer from word2vec altogether (described later in the chapter), so for now, you can just assume that we are using a regular softmax layer and need not worry about the distinction between hierarchical softmax and regular softmax. It is also worth noting that computational complexity is less of a concern now than when the initial work on neural language models and word embeddings was done.

> Learning about hierarchical softmax can make sense to understand the history of word2vec, and it might well come in handy in other settings as well. However, there is no need to learn it to understand the rest of this book.

The second optimization is to remove the hidden layer(s). Given what we know about deep learning (DL), removing layers will make the language model less powerful, but note that the embeddings are encoded in the first layer. If our objective is not to create a powerful language model, then it is far from clear that increasing the number of layers will result in higher-quality embeddings in the first layer.

After these two changes, we have arrived at a model in which the first layer converts the inputs to word embeddings (i.e., it is an embedding layer) simply followed by a softmax (in reality, a hierarchical softmax) layer as the output layer. The only nonlinearity in the model is the softmax layer itself. These two modifications should address most of the computational complexity in the language model and thereby enable a larger training dataset. The model is illustrated in Figure 13-1.

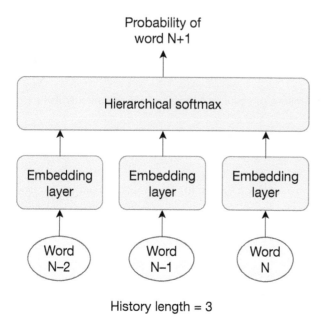

History length = 3

Figure 13-1 Simple model to create word embeddings. This model does not accurately represent the model from word2vec.

However, this is still not representative of what is used in the word2vec algorithm. The outlined model still has the limitation that it considers only historical words, so let us now move on to techniques that consider both historical and future words when training the embeddings.

CONTINUOUS BAG-OF-WORDS MODEL

Extending our model to take future words into account is trivial. Instead of creating a training set from K consecutive words followed by the next word as the word to predict, we can select a word to predict and use a concatenation of the K preceding words and the K subsequent words as the input to the network. The most straightforward way to create our network would be to simply concatenate the embeddings corresponding to all the words. The input to the softmax layer would be $2 \times K \times M$, where $2 \times K$ is the number of words that we use as input and M is the embedding size for a single word. However, the way it is done in word2vec is to average the embeddings for the $2 \times K$ words and thereby produce a single embedding vector of size M. This architecture is shown in Figure 13-2, where $K = 2$.

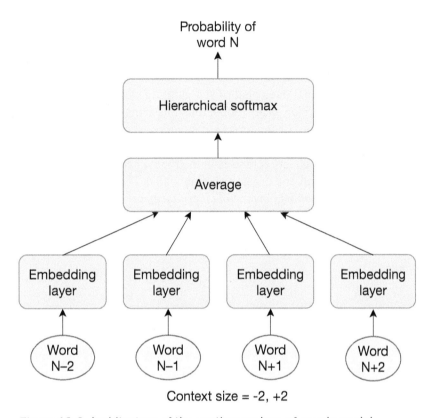

Figure 13-2 Architecture of the continuous bag-of-words model

Averaging the vectors has the effect that the order in which they are presented to the network does not matter, just as the order does not matter for a bag-of-words model. With that background, Mikolov, Chen, and colleagues (2013) named the model a continuous bag-of-words model, where the word continuous indicates that it is based on real-valued (i.e., continuous) word vectors. However, it is worth noting that the CBOW is not based on the entire document but on only the $2 \times K$ surrounding words.

The CBOW model was shown to outperform the embeddings created from an RNN-based language model in terms of how well it captures semantic structures in the dataset in addition to speeding up the training time significantly. However, the authors also discovered that a variation of the CBOW technique performed even better with respect to capturing semantics of the words. They named this variation the continuous skip-gram model, which is the model they later continued to optimize in favor of the CBOW model. The continuous skip-gram model is described next.

CONTINUOUS SKIP-GRAM MODEL

We have now described two major ways of creating embeddings. One is based on a model that uses historical words to predict a single word, and the other is based on a model that uses historical and future words to predict a single word. The continuous skip-gram model flips this around somewhat. Instead of predicting a single word based on its surrounding words (also known as the *context*), it tries to predict the surrounding words based on a single word. This might sound odd at first, but it results in the model becoming simpler. It takes a single word as its input and creates an embedding. This embedding is then fed to a fully connected *softmax* layer, which produces probabilities for each word in the vocabulary, but we now train it to output nonzero probabilities for multiple words (the words surrounding the input word) instead of just outputting a nonzero probability for a single word in the vocabulary. Figure 13-3 shows such a model.

When discussing word2vec, **context** refers to the words surrounding the word in question. Note that when we discuss sequence-to-sequence networks in the next couple of chapters, the word **context** will have a different meaning.

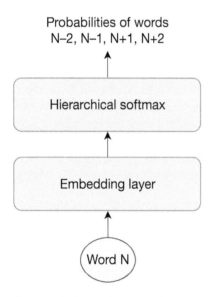

Probabilities of words
N–2, N–1, N+1, N+2

Hierarchical softmax

Embedding layer

Word N

Figure 13-3 Continuous skip-gram model

Like CBOW, the model gets its name from a traditional model (skip-gram) but with the addition of *continuous* to again indicate that it deals with real-valued word vectors. A valid question is why this would work well, but we can use a similar line of reasoning as we did for why the language model would produce good embeddings. We have noted that words that have properties in common (e.g., they are synonyms or similar in some other way) often surround themselves with a similar set of words, as in our sentences "that is exactly what I mean" and "that is precisely what I mean." If we train on both of these sentences, then our continuous skip-gram model is tasked with outputting a nonzero probability for the words *that, is, what, I,* and *mean* both when presented with *exactly* and when presented with *precisely* on its input. A simple way of achieving that is to produce embeddings in which those two words are close to each other in vector space. This explanation involves a fair amount of hand-waving, but remember that the model evolved on the basis of empirical studies. When you consider the history of how the models evolved, it is not hard to envision (although it was clearly still clever) how Mikolov, Chen, and colleagues (2013) experimented with different approaches and decided to try the continuous skip-gram once they had shown that the CBOW model worked well. Given that the continuous skip-gram model outperformed CBOW, they then continued to optimize the former, which is described next.

Although we say that "it is not hard to envision" that they came up with the continuous skip-gram model, it would not surprise us if they first tried a large number of other alternatives. After all, research is 10% inspiration and 90% perspiration, but that is often not clear when reading the published paper.

OPTIMIZED CONTINUOUS SKIP-GRAM MODEL TO FURTHER REDUCE COMPUTATIONAL COMPLEXITY

The original continuous skip-gram model used hierarchical softmax on its output, but in a subsequent paper, the algorithm was modified to make it even faster and simpler (Mikolov, Sutskever, et al., 2013). The overall observation was that both softmax and hierarchical softmax aim at computing correct probabilities for all words in the vocabulary, which is important for a language model, but as previously mentioned, the objective of word2vec is to create good word embeddings as opposed to a good language model. With that background, the algorithm was modified by replacing the softmax layer with a new mechanism named *negative sampling*. The observation was that instead of computing a true probability distribution across all the words in the vocabulary, it should be possible to produce good embeddings if we teach the network to just correctly identify the surrounding words, which are on the order of tens of words instead of tens of thousands of words. In addition, it is necessary to make sure that the network does not incorrectly produce high probabilities for words that are not part of the set of surrounding words.

We can achieve this in the following way. For each word K in the vocabulary, we maintain a single corresponding output neuron N_K with a sigmoid activation function. For each training example X, we now serially train each of the neurons $N_{X-2}, N_{X-1}, N_{X+1}, N_{X+2}$ corresponding to the surrounding words (this example assumes that we considered four surrounding words). That is, we have converted the softmax problem into a series of classification problems. This is not sufficient, though. A naïve solution to this classification problem is for all output neurons to always output 1 because they are only sampled (trained) for the cases where their corresponding words are surrounding the input word. To get around this problem, we need to introduce some negative samples as well:

Given an input word, do the following:

1. Identify the output neurons corresponding to each surrounding word.

2. Train these neurons to output 1 when the network is presented with the input word.

3. Identify the output neurons corresponding to a number of random words that are not surrounding the input word.

4. Train these neurons to output 0 when the network is presented with the input word.

Table 13-1 illustrates this technique for the word sequence "that is exactly what I" with a context of four words (two before and two after) and using three negative samples per context word. Each training example (combination of input and output word) will train a separate output neuron.

All in all, negative sampling further simplifies word2vec into an efficient algorithm, which has also been shown to produce good word embeddings.

Table 13-1 Training Examples for the Word Sequence "that is exactly what i" with Three Negative Samples per Context Word

INPUT WORD	CONTEXT WORD	OUTPUT WORD	OUTPUT VALUE
exactly	$N-2$	that (actual context word)	1.0
		ball (random word)	0.0
		boat (random word)	0.0
		walk (random word)	0.0
	$N-1$	is (actual context word)	1.0
		blue (random word)	0.0
		bottle (random word)	0.0
		not (random word)	0.0
	$N+1$	what (actual context word)	1.0
		house (random word)	0.0
		deep (random word)	0.0
		computer (random word)	0.0
	$N+2$	i (actual context word)	1.0
		stupid (random word)	0.0
		airplane (random word)	0.0
		mitigate (random word)	0.0

Additional Thoughts on word2vec

Additional tweaks can be made to the algorithm as well, but we think that the preceding description captures the key points required to understand the big picture. Before moving on to the next topic, we provide some additional insights into the word2vec algorithm. We begin with a more detailed illustration of the network structure for readers who prefer visual descriptions and then move on to a matrix implementation for readers who prefer mathematical descriptions.

Figure 13-4 shows a network for training a word2vec model with a vocabulary of five words and an embedding size of three dimensions. The figure assumes that we are currently training based on a context word that is number four in the vocabulary (the other output neurons are ghosted).

We present the input word to the network, which implies that one of the five inputs is of value 1 and all others are set to 0. Let us assume that the input word is number 0 in the vocabulary, so the input word 0 (Wd_0) is set to 1 and all other inputs are set to 0. The embedding layer "computes" an embedding by multiplying all weights from node Wd_0 by 1 and multiplying all other input weights by 0 (in reality, this is performed by indexing into a lookup table). We then compute the output of neuron y_4 and ignore all others without any computation. After this forward pass, we do a backward pass and adjust the weights. Figure 13-4 highlights a noteworthy property. As previously described, the embedding layer contains K weights (denoted IWE_{xy}, where IWE refers to *input word embedding*) associated with each input word, where K is the size of

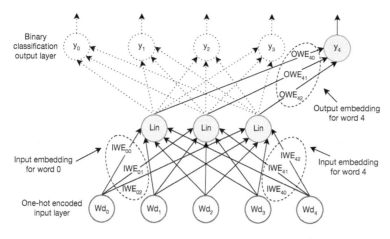

Figure 13-4 The word2vec continuous skip-gram model

the word vector. However, the figure shows that the output layer also contains K weights (denoted OWE_{xy}, where OWE refers to *output word embedding*) associated with each output word. By definition, the number of output nodes is the same as the number of input words. That is, the algorithm produces two embeddings for each word: one input embedding and one output embedding. In the original paper, the input embeddings were used, and the output embeddings were discarded, but Press and Wolf (2017) have shown that it can be beneficial to tie the input and output embeddings together using weight sharing.

In a model where the input and output weights are tied together, it is also possible to reason about how the embeddings for words in the same context relate to each other. Consider the mathematical operation used to compute the weighted sum for a single output neuron. It is the dot product of the word embedding for the input word and the word embedding for the output word, and we train the network to make this dot product get close to 1.0. The same holds true for all the output words in that same context. Now consider the condition needed for a dot product to result in a positive value. The dot product is computed by elementwise multiplication between the two vectors and then adding the results together. This sum tends to be positive if corresponding elements in both the vectors are nonzero and have the same sign (i.e., the vectors are similar). A straightforward way to achieve the training objective is to ensure that the word vectors for all words in the same context are similar to each other. Obviously, this does not guarantee that the produced word vectors express the desired properties, but it provides some further insight into why it is not entirely unexpected that the algorithm produces good word embeddings.

word2vec in Matrix Form

Another way of describing the mechanics of word2vec is to simply look at the mathematics that is performed. This description is influenced by one of the sections of the popular blog post "The Illustrated Word2vec" (Alammar, 2019). We start by creating two matrices, as shown in Figure 13-5. Both are of the same dimensions with N rows and M columns, where N is the number of words in the vocabulary and M is the desired embedding width. One matrix will be used for the central word (the input word), and the other matrix will be used for the surrounding words (the context).

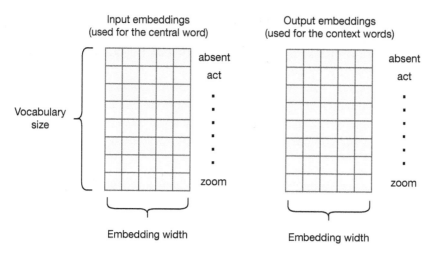

Figure 13-5 **Matrices with input and output embeddings**

We now select a word (the central word) from our text as well as a number of words surrounding it. We look up the embedding for the central word from the input embeddings matrix (select a single row) and we look up the embeddings for the surrounding words from the output embeddings matrix. These are our positive samples (i.e., where the output value is 1 in the previously shown Table 13-1). We further randomly sample a number of additional embeddings from the output-embedding matrix. These are our negative samples (i.e., where the output value should be 0).

Now we simply compute the dot products between the selected input embedding and each of the selected output embeddings, apply the logistic sigmoid function to each of these dot products, and compare to the desired output value. We then adjust each of the selected embeddings using gradient descent, and then repeat this process for a different central word. In the end, the leftmost matrix in Figure 13-5 will contain our embeddings.

Wrapping Up word2vec

To wrap up the discussion about word2vec, according to our understanding, several people struggle with the mechanics of the algorithm and how it relates to bag-of-words and traditional skip-gram, as well as with why the algorithm produces good word embeddings. We hope that we have brought clarity to the mechanics of the algorithms. The relationship to bag-of-words and skip-grams is just that there are some aspects of some steps of the word2vec algorithms that are related to these traditional algorithms, and consequently, Mikolov, Chen, and colleagues (2013) decided to name them after these techniques, but we would like to emphasize that they are completely different beasts. The traditional skip-gram is a language model, and the bag-of-words is a way of summarizing a document, whereas the continuous bag-of-words and continuous skip-gram models in word2vec are algorithms that produce word embeddings. Finally, as to the question of why word2vec produces good word embeddings, we hope that we have provided some insight into why it makes sense, but as far as we understand it, it is more of a result of discoveries, trial-and-error, observations, and refinements than a top-down engineering effort.

We summarize our understanding of the evolution leading up to the word2vec algorithm in Figure 13-6. The first few steps are more about neural language models than word embeddings, but as described, language models played a critical part in the process of developing word embeddings. The figure also illustrates how word2vec was not a single step but a process of gradual refinements.

The release of the word2vec implementation spawned considerable interest in word embedding research that has resulted in multiple alternative embedding schemes. One such scheme is the GloVe embeddings, which we now explore with a programming example.

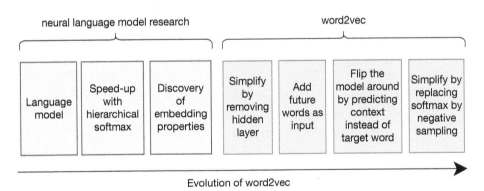

Figure 13-6 Evolution of neural language models into word2vec

Programming Example: Exploring Properties of GloVe Embeddings

About a year after word2vec was published, Pennington, Socher, and Manning (2014) published "GloVe: Global Vectors for Word Representation." GloVe is an algorithm mathematically engineered to create well-behaved word embeddings. In particular, the goal is that the embeddings capture syntactic and semantic relationships between words. We do not describe the details of how GloVe works, as the mathematics/statistics needed to understand it is more than we want to require from readers of this book. However, we strongly recommend that anyone who wants to get serious about word embedding research (as opposed to just using word embeddings) acquire the necessary skills to understand the GloVe paper. The paper also provides additional information about why word2vec produces sane embeddings. The embeddings are available for download and are contained in a text file in which each line represents a word embedding. The first element is the word itself followed by the vector elements separated by blank spaces.

Code Snippet 13-1 contains two import statements and a function to read the embeddings. The function simply opens the file and reads it line by line. It splits each line into its elements. It extracts the first element, which represents the word itself, and then creates a vector from the remaining elements and inserts the word and the corresponding vector into a dictionary, which serves as the return value of the function.

Code Snippet 13-1 Loading GloVe Embeddings from File

```python
import numpy as np
import scipy.spatial

# Read embeddings from file.
def read_embeddings():
    FILE_NAME = '../data/glove.6B.100d.txt'
    embeddings = {}
    file = open(FILE_NAME, 'r', encoding='utf-8')
    for line in file:
        values = line.split()
```

```
        word = values[0]
        vector = np.asarray(values[1:],
                              dtype='float32')
        embeddings[word] = vector
    file.close()
    print('Read %s embeddings.' % len(embeddings))
    return embeddings
```

Code Snippet 13-2 implements a function that computes the cosine distance between a specific embedding and all other embeddings. It then prints the *n* closest ones. This is similar to what was done in Chapter 12, but we are using cosine distance instead of Euclidean distance to demonstrate how to do that. Euclidean distance would also have worked fine, but the results would sometimes be different because the GloVe vectors are not normalized.

Code Snippet 13-2 Function to Identify and Print the Three Words That Are Closest in Vector Space, Using Cosine Distance

```
def print_n_closest(embeddings, vec0, n):
    word_distances = {}
    for (word, vec1) in embeddings.items():
        distance = scipy.spatial.distance.cosine(
            vec1, vec0)
        word_distances[distance] = word
    # Print words sorted by distance.
    for distance in sorted(word_distances.keys())[:n]:
        word = word_distances[distance]
        print(word + ': %6.3f' % distance)
```

Using these two functions, we can now retrieve word embeddings for arbitrary words and print out words that have similar embeddings. This is shown in Code Snippet 13-3, where we first read call read_embeddings() and then retrieve the embeddings for *hello, precisely,* and *dog* and call print_n_closest() on each of them.

Code Snippet 13-3 Printing the Three Closest Words to *hello, precisely,* and *dog*

```
embeddings = read_embeddings()

lookup_word = 'hello'
print('\nWords closest to ' + lookup_word)
print_n_closest(embeddings,
                embeddings[lookup_word], 3)

lookup_word = 'precisely'
print('\nWords closest to ' + lookup_word)
print_n_closest(embeddings,
                embeddings[lookup_word], 3)

lookup_word = 'dog'
print('\nWords closest to ' + lookup_word)
print_n_closest(embeddings,
                embeddings[lookup_word], 3)
```

The resulting printouts follow. We see that the vocabulary consists of 400,000 words, and as expected, the closest word to each lookup word is the lookup word itself (there is zero distance between *hello* and *hello*). The other two words close to *hello* are *goodbye* and *hey*. The two words close to *precisely* are *exactly* and *accurately*, and the two words close to *dog* are *cat* and *dogs*. Overall, this demonstrates that the GloVe embeddings do capture semantics of the words.

```
Read 400000 embeddings.

Words closest to hello
hello:   0.000
goodbye:   0.209
hey:   0.283

Words closest to precisely
precisely:   0.000
exactly:   0.147
accurately:   0.293
```

```
Words closest to dog
dog:    0.000
cat:    0.120
dogs:   0.166
```

Using NumPy, it is also trivial to combine multiple vectors using vector arithmetic and then print out words that are similar to the resulting vector. This is demonstrated in Code Snippet 13-4, which first prints the words closest to the word vector for *king* and then prints the words closest to the vector resulting from computing (king – man + woman).

Code Snippet 13-4 **Example of Word Vector Arithmetic**

```python
lookup_word = 'king'
print('\nWords closest to ' + lookup_word)
print_n_closest(embeddings,
                embeddings[lookup_word], 3)


lookup_word = '(king - man + woman)'
print('\nWords closest to ' + lookup_word)
vec = embeddings['king'] - embeddings[
    'man'] + embeddings['woman']
print_n_closest(embeddings, vec, 3)
```

It yields the following output:

```
Words closest to king
king:    0.000
prince:  0.232
queen:   0.249


Words closest to (king - man + woman)
king:    0.145
queen:   0.217
monarch:  0.307
```

We can see that the closest word to *king* (ignoring *king* itself) is *prince*, followed by *queen*. We also see that the closest word to (king – man + woman) is still *king*, but the second closest is *queen;* that is, the calculations resulted in a vector that is more on the female side, since *queen* is now closer than *prince*. Without diminishing the impact of the king/queen discovery, we recognize that the example provides some insight into how the (king – man + woman) property could be observed in embeddings resulting from a relatively simple model. Given that *king* and *queen* are closely related, they were likely close to each other from the beginning, and not much tweaking was needed to go from *king* to *queen*. For example, from the printouts, we can see that the distance to queen only changed from 0.249 (distance between *queen* and *king*) to 0.217 (distance between *queen* and the vector after arithmetic).

A possibly more impressive example is shown in Code Snippet 13-5, where we first print the words closest to *sweden* and *madrid* and then print the words closest to the result from the computation (madrid – spain + sweden).

Code Snippet 13-5 **Vector Arithmetic on Countries and Capital Cities**

```
lookup_word = 'sweden'
print('\nWords closest to ' + lookup_word)
print_n_closest(embeddings,
                embeddings[lookup_word], 3)


lookup_word = 'madrid'
print('\nWords closest to ' + lookup_word)
print_n_closest(embeddings,
                embeddings[lookup_word], 3)


lookup_word = '(madrid - spain + sweden)'
print('\nWords closest to ' + lookup_word)
vec = embeddings['madrid'] - embeddings[
    'spain'] + embeddings['sweden']
print_n_closest(embeddings, vec, 3)
```

As you can see in the following output, the words closest to Sweden are the neighboring countries Denmark and Norway. Similarly, the words closest to Madrid are Barcelona and Valencia, two other significant Spanish cities. Now, removing Spain from Madrid (its capital) and instead adding Sweden results in the Swedish capital city of Stockholm, which seemingly came out of nowhere as opposed to the king/queen example where *queen* was already closely related to *king*.

```
Words closest to sweden
sweden:   0.000
denmark:   0.138
norway:   0.193


Words closest to madrid
madrid:   0.000
barcelona:   0.157
valencia:   0.197


Words closest to (madrid - spain + sweden)
stockholm:   0.271
sweden:   0.300
copenhagen:   0.305
```

In reality, it turns out that if we expand the list of words close to *madrid* and *sweden*, then *stockholm* does show up as number 18 on the *sweden* list (and 377 on the *madrid* list), but we still find it impressive how the equation correctly identifies it as the top 1.

Concluding Remarks on word2vec and GloVe

In these past two chapters, we have seen that it is possible to learn word embeddings jointly with a DL model or learn the word embeddings in isolation. Algorithms such as word2vec and GloVe are not DL algorithms, although word2vec is inspired by, and to some extent evolved from, a neural language model. Still, the embeddings produced from these algorithms are useful when applying DL models to natural language.

A valid question is whether it is best to use prelearned embeddings in a transfer learning setting or to learn the embeddings jointly with the DL model, and the answer is that it is application dependent. There are cases in which it is useful to use pretrained embeddings that are derived from a large dataset, especially if your dataset on the end task is not that big. In other cases, it is better to learn the embeddings jointly with the model. One example would be a use case where the pretrained embeddings do not capture use case–specific relationships. Another one is if you are working with natural language translation to a rare language and you simply do not have access to pretrained embeddings.

Since GloVe was published, there have been additional improvements in the space of word embeddings. They have been extended with capabilities to handle words that were not present in the training vocabulary. They have also been extended to handle cases where a single word can have two different meanings depending on the context in which it is used. We describe more details about these types of embeddings in Appendix C. If you are very interested in word embeddings, consider reading it now. We recommend that most readers just continue reading the book in order. Chapter 14, "Sequence-to-Sequence Networks and Natural Language Translation," uses word embeddings and other concepts we have discussed to build a network for natural language translation.

We have not brought up the topic of science fiction movies for a few chapters, so we feel that it is time to do another farfetched analogy. When watching the 2016 movie *Arrival,* where Amy Adams plays a linguist who is asked to try to learn an alien language, we think that it would have been very cool if they had slipped in a reference to word2vec. For example, when trying to persuade Adams's character to take on the case, they could have said, "We have already run word2vec on the aliens' Wikipedia database, and it didn't uncover any compositional relationships but just some weird temporal relationships both forward and backward."

Perhaps the reason this was not done is that it is one of the cases where science was ahead of fiction?!

Chapter 14

Sequence-to-Sequence Networks and Natural Language Translation

In Chapter 11, "Text Autocompletion with LSTM and Beam Search," we discussed many-to-many sequence prediction problems and showed with a programming example how it can be used for autocompletion of text. Another important sequence prediction problem is to translate text from one natural language to another. In such a setting, the input sequence is a sentence in the source language, and the predicted output sequence is the corresponding sentence in the destination language. It is not necessarily the case that the sentences consist of the same number of words in the two different languages. A good English translation of the French sentence *Je suis étudiant* is "I am a student," where we see that the English sentence contains one more word than its French counterpart. Another thing to note is that we want the network to consume the entire input sequence before starting to emit the output sequence, because in many cases, you need to consider the full meaning of a sentence to produce a good translation. A popular approach to handle this is to teach the network to interpret and emit START and STOP tokens as well as to ignore padding values. Both the padding value and the START and STOP tokens should be values that do not naturally appear in the text. For example, with words represented by indices that are inputs to an embedding layer, we would simply reserve specific indices for these tokens.

START tokens, STOP tokens, and padding can be used to create training examples that enable many-to-many sequences with variable lengths.

Figure 14-1 illustrates this process. The upper part of the figure shows a many-to-many network where gray represents the input, blue is the network, and green is the output. For now, ignore the ghosted (white) shapes. The network is unrolled in time from left to right. The figure shows that the desired behavior is that during the first four timesteps, we present the symbols for *Je, suis, étudiant,* START to the network. During the timestep that the network receives the START token, the network will output the first word (*I*) of the translated sentence, followed by *am, a, student,* and STOP during the subsequent timesteps. Let us now consider the white shapes. As previously noted, it is impossible for the network to not output a value, and similarly, the network will always get some kind of input for every timestep. This applies to the first three timesteps for the output and the last four timesteps for the input. A simple solution would be to use our padding value on both the output and the input for these timesteps. However, it turns out that a better solution is to help the network by feeding the output from the previous timestep back as input to the next timestep, just as we did in the neural language models in previous chapters. This is what is shown in the Figure 14-1.

To make this abundantly clear, the lower part of the figure shows the corresponding training example without the network. That is, during training, the network will see both the source and the destination sequences on its input and be trained to predict the destination sequence on its output. Predicting the destination sequence as output might not seem that hard given that the destination sequence is also presented as input. However, they are skewed in time, so the network needs to predict the next word in the destination sequence before it has seen it. When we later use the network to produce translations, we do not have the destination sequence. We start with feeding the source sequence to the network, followed by the START token, and then start feeding back its output prediction as input to the next timestep until the network produces a STOP token. At that point, we have produced the full translated sentence.

Many-to-many network

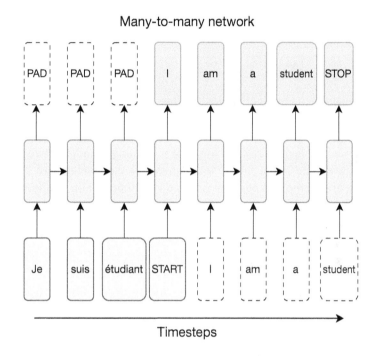

Timesteps

Training example

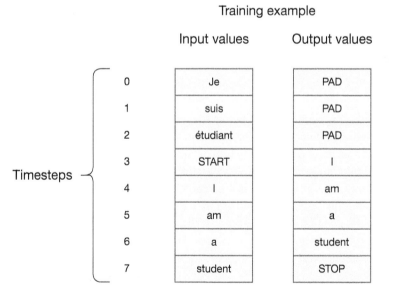

Timesteps	Input values	Output values
0	Je	PAD
1	suis	PAD
2	étudiant	PAD
3	START	I
4	I	am
5	am	a
6	a	student
7	student	STOP

Figure 14-1 Neural machine translation is an example of a many-to-many sequence where the input and output sequences are not necessarily of the same length.

Encoder-Decoder Model for Sequence-to-Sequence Learning

How does the model that we just described relate to the neural language models studied in previous chapters? Let us consider our translation network at the timestep when the START token is presented at its input. The only difference between this network and the neural language model networks is its initial accumulated state. In our language model, we started with 0 as internal state and presented one or more words on the input. Then the network completed the sentence. Our translation network starts with an accumulated state from seeing the source sequence, is then presented with a single START symbol, and then completes the sentence in the destination language. That is, during the second half of the translation process, the network simply acts like a neural language model in the destination language. It turns out that the internal state is all that the network needs to produce the right sentence. We can think of the internal state as a language-independent representation of the overall meaning of the sentence. Sometimes this internal state is referred to as the *context* or a *thought vector*.

Now let us consider the first half of the translation process. The goal of this phase is to consume the source sentence and build up this language-independent representation of the meaning of the sentence. Apart from being a somewhat different task than generating a sentence, it is also working with a different language/vocabulary than the second phase of the translation process. A reasonable question, then, is whether both phases should be handled by the same neural network or if it is better to have two specialized networks. The first network would be specialized in encoding the source sentence into the internal state, and the second network would be specialized in decoding the internal state into a destination sentence. Such an architecture is known as an *encoder-decoder architecture,* and one example is illustrated in Figure 14-2. The network is not unrolled in time. The network layers in the encoder are distinct from the network layers in the decoder. The horizontal arrow represents reading out the internal states of the recurrent layers in the encoder and initializing the internal states of the recurrent layers in the decoder. Thus, the assumption in the figure is that both networks contain the same number of hidden recurrent layers of the same size and type. In our programming example, we implement this model with two hidden recurrent layers in both networks, each consisting of 256 long short-term memory (LSTM) units.

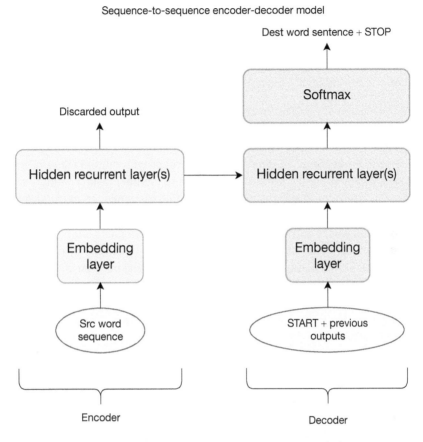

Sequence-to-sequence encoder-decoder model

Figure 14-2 Encoder-decoder model for language translation

> In an encoder-decoder architecture, the encoder creates an internal state known as **context** or **thought vector,** which is a **language-independent representation** of the meaning of the sentence.

Figure 14-2 shows just one example of an encoder-decoder model. Given how we evolved from a single RNN to this encoder-decoder network, it might not be that odd that the communication channel between the two networks is to transfer the internal state from one network to another. However, we should also recognize that the statement "Discarded output" is a little misleading in the figure. The internal state of an LSTM layer consists of the cell state (often denoted by c) and the recurrent layer hidden state (often denoted by h), where h is identical to the output of the layer. Similarly, if we had used a gated recurrent unit (GRU) instead of LSTM, there would not be a cell state, and the internal state of the network would be simply the recurrent layer hidden state, which again is identical to the output of the recurrent layer. Still, we chose to call it discarded output because that term is commonly found in other descriptions.

One can envision other ways of connecting the encoder and the decoder. For example, we could feed the state/output as a regular input to the decoder just during the first timestep, or we could give the decoder network access to it during each timestep. Or, in the case of an encoder with multiple layers, we could choose to just present the state/output from the topmost layer as inputs to the bottommost decoder layer. It is also worth noting that encoder-decoder models are not limited to working with sequences. We can construct other combinations, such as cases where only one of the encoder or decoder, or neither of them, has recurrent layers. We discuss more details about this in the next couple of chapters, but at this point, we move on to implementing our neural machine translator (NMT) in Keras.

Encoder-decoder architectures can be built in many different ways. Different network types can be used for the encoder and decoder, and the connection between the two can also be done in multiple ways.

Introduction to the Keras Functional API

It is not obvious how to implement the described architecture using the constructs that we have used in the Keras API so far. To implement this architecture, we need to use the Keras Functional API, which is specifically created to enable creation of complex models. There is a key difference compared to using the sequential models that we have used so far. Instead of just declaring a layer and adding to the model and letting Keras automatically connect the layers in a sequential manner, we now need to explicitly describe how layers are connected to each other. This process is more complex and error prone than letting Keras do it for us, but the benefit is the increased flexibility that enables us to describe a more complex model.

Keras Functional API is more flexible than the Sequential API and can therefore be used to build more complex network architectures.

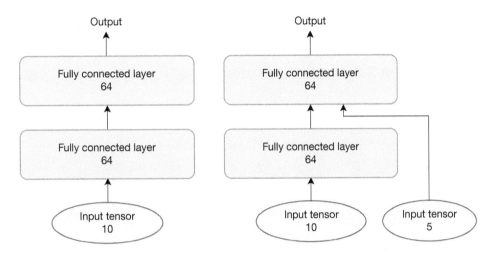

Figure 14-3 Two simple models. The left one is straightforward to implement with the Sequential API, but the right one requires the Functional API.

We use the example models in Figure 14-3 to illustrate how to use the Keras Functional API. The model to the left is a simple sequential model that could easily have been implemented with the Sequential API, but the model to the right has an input that bypasses the first layer and therefore needs to use the Functional API.

The implementation of the left model is shown in Code Snippet 14-1. We start by declaring an Input object. This is different from the Sequential API, where the input layer was implicitly created when the first layer was created. We then declare the two fully connected layers in the model. Once this is done, it is time to connect the layers by using the assigned variable name as a function and passing it its inputs as an argument. The function returns an object representing the outputs of the layer, which can then be used as input argument when connecting the next layer.

Code Snippet 14-1 Example How to Implement a Simple Sequential Model Using the Functional API

```
from tensorflow.keras.layers import Input, Dense
from tensorflow.keras.models import Model

# Declare inputs.
inputs = Input(shape=(10,))
```

```
# Declare layers.
layer1 = Dense(64, activation='relu')
layer2 = Dense(64, activation='relu')

# Connect inputs and layers.
layer1_outputs = layer1(inputs)
layer2_outputs = layer2(layer1_outputs)

# Create model.
model = Model(inputs=inputs, outputs=layer2_outputs)
model.summary()
```

Now that we have declared and connected layers to each other, we are ready to create the model. This is done by simply calling the Model() constructor and providing arguments informing the model what its inputs and outputs should be.

Creating the more complex model with a bypass path from the input to the second layer is shown in Code Snippet 14-2. There are just a few minor changes compared to the previous example. First, we declare two sets of inputs. One is the input to the first layer, and the other is the bypass input that will go straight to the second layer. Next, we declare a Concatenate layer, which is used to concatenate the outputs from the first layer with the bypass input to form a single variable that can be provided as input to the second layer. Finally, when declaring the model, we need to tell it that its inputs now consist of a list of two inputs.

Code Snippet 14-2 **Keras Implementation of a Network with a Bypass Path**

```
from tensorflow.keras.layers import Input, Dense
from tensorflow.keras.models import Model
from tensorflow.keras.layers import Concatenate

# Declare inputs.
inputs = Input(shape=(10,))
bypass_inputs = Input(shape=(5,))

# Declare layers.
layer1 = Dense(64, activation='relu')
concat_layer = Concatenate()
layer2 = Dense(64, activation='relu')
```

```
# Connect inputs and layers.
layer1_outputs = layer1(inputs)
layer2_inputs = concat_layer([layer1_outputs, bypass_inputs])
layer2_outputs = layer2(layer2_inputs)

# Create model.
model = Model(inputs=[inputs, bypass_inputs],
              outputs=layer2_outputs)
model.summary()
```

After this brief introduction to the Keras Functional API, we are ready to move on to implementing our neural machine translation network.

Programming Example: Neural Machine Translation

As usual, we begin by importing modules that we need for the program. This is shown in Code Snippet 14-3.

Code Snippet 14-3 Import Statements

```
import numpy as np
import random
from tensorflow.keras.layers import Input
from tensorflow.keras.layers import Embedding
from tensorflow.keras.layers import LSTM
from tensorflow.keras.layers import Dense
from tensorflow.keras.models import Model
from tensorflow.keras.optimizers import RMSprop
from tensorflow.keras.preprocessing.text import Tokenizer
from tensorflow.keras.preprocessing.text \
    import text_to_word_sequence
from tensorflow.keras.preprocessing.sequence \
    import pad_sequences
import tensorflow as tf
import logging
tf.get_logger().setLevel(logging.ERROR)
```

Next, we define some constants in Code Snippet 14-4. We specify a vocabulary size of 10,000 symbols, out of which four indices are reserved for padding, out-of-vocabulary words (denoted as UNK), START tokens, and STOP tokens. Our training corpus is large, so we set the parameter READ_LINES to the number of lines in the input file we want to use in our example (60,000). Our layers consist of 256 units (LAYER_SIZE), and the embedding layers output 128 dimensions (EMBEDDING_WIDTH). We use 20% (TEST_PERCENT) of the dataset as test set and further select 20 sentences (SAMPLE_SIZE) to inspect in detail during training. We limit the length of the source and destination sentences to, at most, 60 words (MAX_LENGTH). Finally, we provide the path to the data file, where each line is expected to contain two versions of the same sentence (one in each language) separated by a tab character.

Code Snippet 14-4 Definition of Constants

```
# Constants
EPOCHS = 20
BATCH_SIZE = 128
MAX_WORDS = 10000
READ_LINES = 60000
LAYER_SIZE = 256
EMBEDDING_WIDTH = 128
TEST_PERCENT = 0.2
SAMPLE_SIZE = 20
OOV_WORD = 'UNK'
PAD_INDEX = 0
OOV_INDEX = 1
START_INDEX = MAX_WORDS - 2
STOP_INDEX = MAX_WORDS - 1
MAX_LENGTH = 60
SRC_DEST_FILE_NAME = '../data/fra.txt'
```

Code Snippet 14-5 shows the function used to read the input data file and do some initial processing. Each line is split into two strings, where the first contains the sentence in the destination language and the second contains the sentence in the source language. We use the function text_to_word_sequence() to clean the data somewhat (make everything lowercase and remove punctuation) and split each sentence into a list of individual words. If the list (sentence) is longer than the maximum allowed length, then it is truncated.

Code Snippet 14-5 Function to Read Input File and Create Source and Destination Word Sequences

```
# Function to read file.
def read_file_combined(file_name, max_len):
    file = open(file_name, 'r', encoding='utf-8')
    src_word_sequences = []
    dest_word_sequences = []
    for i, line in enumerate(file):
        if i == READ_LINES:
            break
        pair = line.split('\t')
        word_sequence = text_to_word_sequence(pair[1])
        src_word_sequence = word_sequence[0:max_len]
        src_word_sequences.append(src_word_sequence)
        word_sequence = text_to_word_sequence(pair[0])
        dest_word_sequence = word_sequence[0:max_len]
        dest_word_sequences.append(dest_word_sequence)
    file.close()
    return src_word_sequences, dest_word_sequences
```

Code Snippet 14-6 shows functions used to turn sequences of words into sequences of tokens, and vice versa. We call tokenize() a single time for each language, so the argument sequences is a list of lists where each of the inner lists represents a sentence. The Tokenizer class assigns indices to the most common words and returns either these indices or the reserved OOV_INDEX for less common words that did not make it into the vocabulary. We tell the Tokenizer to use a vocabulary of 9998 (MAX_WORDS - 2)—that is, use only indices 0 to 9997, so that we can use indices 9998 and 9999 as our START and STOP tokens (the Tokenizer does not support the notion of START and STOP tokens but does reserve index 0 to use as a padding token and index 1 for out-of-vocabulary words). Our tokenize() function returns both the tokenized sequence and the Tokenizer object itself. This object will be needed anytime we want to convert tokens back into words.

Code Snippet 14-6 **Functions to Turn Word Sequences into Tokens, and Vice Versa**

```python
# Functions to tokenize and un-tokenize sequences.
def tokenize(sequences):
    # "MAX_WORDS-2" used to reserve two indices
    # for START and STOP.
    tokenizer = Tokenizer(num_words=MAX_WORDS-2,
                          oov_token=OOV_WORD)
    tokenizer.fit_on_texts(sequences)
    token_sequences = tokenizer.texts_to_sequences(sequences)
    return tokenizer, token_sequences

def tokens_to_words(tokenizer, seq):
    word_seq = []
    for index in seq:
        if index == PAD_INDEX:
            word_seq.append('PAD')
        elif index == OOV_INDEX:
            word_seq.append(OOV_WORD)
        elif index == START_INDEX:
            word_seq.append('START')
        elif index == STOP_INDEX:
            word_seq.append('STOP')
        else:
            word_seq.append(tokenizer.sequences_to_texts(
                [[index]])[0])
    print(word_seq)
```

The function `tokens_to_words()` requires a Tokenizer and a list of indices. We simply check for the reserved indices: If we find a match, we replace them with hardcoded strings, and if we find no match, we let the Tokenizer convert the index to the corresponding word string. The Tokenizer expects a list of lists of indices and returns a list of strings, which is why we need to call it with `[[index]]` and then select the 0th element to arrive at a string.

Now, given that we have these helper functions, it is trivial to read the input data file and convert into tokenized sequences. This is done in Code Snippet 14-7.

Code Snippet 14-7 **Read and Tokenize the Input File**

```
# Read file and tokenize.
src_seq, dest_seq = read_file_combined(SRC_DEST_FILE_NAME,
                                       MAX_LENGTH)
src_tokenizer, src_token_seq = tokenize(src_seq)
dest_tokenizer, dest_token_seq = tokenize(dest_seq)
```

It is now time to arrange the data into tensors that can be used for training and testing. In Figure 14-1, we indicated that we need to pad the start of the output sequence with as many PAD symbols as there are words in the input sequence, but that was when we envisioned a single neural network. Now that we have broken up the network into an encoder and a decoder, this is no longer necessary because we will simply not input anything to the decoder until we have run the full input through the encoder. Following is a more accurate example of what we need as input and output for a single training example, where src_input is the input to the encoder network, dest_input is the input to the decoder network, and dest_target is the desired output from the decoder network:

src_input = [PAD, PAD, PAD, id("je"), id("suis"), id("étudiant")]

dest_input = [START, id("i"), id("am"), id("a"), id("student"), STOP, PAD, PAD]

dest_target = [one_hot_id("i"), one_hot_id("am"), one_hot_id("a"), one_hot_id("student"), one_hot_id(STOP), one_hot_id(PAD), one_hot_id(PAD), one_hot_id(PAD)]

In the example, id(string) refers to the tokenized index of the string, and one_hot_id is the one-hot encoded version of the index. We have assumed that the longest source sentence is six words, so we padded src_input to be of that length. Similarly, we have assumed that the longest destination sentence is eight words including START and STOP tokens, so we padded both dest_input and dest_target to be of that length. Note how the symbols in dest_input are offset by one location compared to the symbols in dest_target because when we later do inference, the inputs into the decoder network will be coming from the output of the network for the previous timestep. Although this example has shown the training example as being lists, in reality, they will be rows in NumPy arrays, where each array contains multiple training examples.

The padding is done to ensure that we can use mini-batches for training. That is, all source sentences need to be the same length, and all destination sentences need to be the same length. We pad the source input at the beginning (known as *prepadding*) and the destination at the end (known as *postpadding*), which is nonobvious. We previously stated that when using padding, the model can learn to ignore the padded values, but there is also a mechanism in Keras to mask out padded values. Based on these two statements, it seems like it should not matter whether the padding is at the beginning or end. However, as always, things are not as simple as they might appear. If we start with the assumption of the model learning to ignore values, it will not perfectly learn this. The ease with which it learns to ignore padding values might depend on how the data is arranged. It is not hard to imagine that inputting a considerable number of zeros at the end of a sequence will dilute the input and affect the internal state of the network. From that perspective, it makes sense to pad the input values with zeros in the beginning of the sequence instead. Similarly, in a sequence-to-sequence network, if the encoder has created an internal state that is transferred to the decoder, diluting this state by presenting a number of zeros before the START token also seems like it could be bad.

This reasoning supports the chosen padding (prepadding of the source input and postpadding of the destination input) in a case where the network needs to learn to ignore the padded values. However, given that we will use the mask_zero=True parameter for our embedding layers, it should not matter what type of padding we use. It turns out that the behavior of mask_zero is not what we had expected when using it for our custom encoder-decoder network. We observed that the network learned poorly when we used postpadding for the source input. We do not know the exact reason for this but suspect that there is some interaction where the masked input values to the encoder somehow causes the decoder to ignore the beginning of the output sequences.[1]

> Padding can be done in the beginning or end of the sequence. This is known as **prepadding** and **postpadding**.

Code Snippet 14-8 shows a compact way of creating the three arrays that we need. The first two lines create two new lists, each containing the destination sequences but the first (dest_target_token_seq) also augmented with

---

1. This is just a theory, and the behavior could be something else. Further, it is unclear to us whether it is due to a bug or an expected but undocumented behavior. Regardless, when using the suggested padding, we do not see the problem.

STOP_INDEX after each sequence and the second (dest_input_token_seq) augmented with both START_INDEX and STOP_INDEX. It is easy to miss that dest_input_token_seq has a STOP_INDEX, but that falls out naturally because it is created from the dest_target_token_seq for which a STOP_INDEX was just added to each sentence.

Next, we call pad_sequences() on both the original src_input_data list (of lists) and on these two new destination lists. The pad_sequences() function pads the sequences with the PAD value and then returns a NumPy array. The default behavior of pad_sequences is to do prepadding, and we do that for the source sequence but explicitly ask for postpadding for the destination sequences. You might wonder why there is no call to to_categorical() in the statement that creates the target (output) data. We are used to wanting to have the ground truth one-hot encoded for textual data. Not doing so is an optimization to avoid wasting too much memory. With a vocabulary of 10,000 words, and 60,000 training examples, where each training example is a sentence, the memory footprint of the one-hot encoded data starts becoming a problem. Therefore, instead of one-hot encoding all data up front, there is a way to let Keras deal with that in the loss function itself.

Code Snippet 14-8 Compact Version of Code to Convert the Tokenized Sequences into NumPy Arrays

```
# Prepare training data.
dest_target_token_seq = [x + [STOP_INDEX] for x in dest_token_seq]
dest_input_token_seq = [[START_INDEX] + x for x in
                        dest_target_token_seq]
src_input_data = pad_sequences(src_token_seq)
dest_input_data = pad_sequences(dest_input_token_seq,
                                padding='post')
dest_target_data = pad_sequences(
    dest_target_token_seq, padding='post', maxlen
    = len(dest_input_data[0]))
```

Before we build our model, Code Snippet 14-9 demonstrates how we can manually split our dataset into a training dataset and a test dataset. In previous examples, we either relied on datasets that are already split this way or we used functionality inside of Keras when calling the fit() function. However, in this case, we want some more control ourselves because we will want to inspect a few select members of the test set in detail. We split the dataset by first creating a list test_indices, which contains a 20% (TEST_PERCENT) subset of all the numbers from 0 to N–1, where N is the size of our original dataset. We then create a list train_indices, which contains the remaining 80%. We can now use these lists to select a number of rows in the matrices representing the dataset and create two new collections of matrices, one to be used as training set and one to be used as test set. Finally, we create a third collection of matrices, which only contains 20 (SAMPLE_SIZE) random examples from the test dataset. We will use them to inspect the resulting translations in detail, but since that is a manual process, we limit ourselves to a small number of sentences.

Code Snippet 14-9 Manually Splitting the Dataset into a Training Set and a Test Set

```
# Split into training and test set.
rows = len(src_input_data[:,0])
all_indices = list(range(rows))
test_rows = int(rows * TEST_PERCENT)
test_indices = random.sample(all_indices, test_rows)
train_indices = [x for x in all_indices if x not in test_indices]

train_src_input_data = src_input_data[train_indices]
train_dest_input_data = dest_input_data[train_indices]
train_dest_target_data = dest_target_data[train_indices]

test_src_input_data = src_input_data[test_indices]
test_dest_input_data = dest_input_data[test_indices]
test_dest_target_data = dest_target_data[test_indices]

# Create a sample of the test set that we will inspect in detail.
test_indices = list(range(test_rows))
sample_indices = random.sample(test_indices, SAMPLE_SIZE)
sample_input_data = test_src_input_data[sample_indices]
sample_target_data = test_dest_target_data[sample_indices]
```

As usual, we have now spent a whole lot of code just preparing the data, but we are finally ready to build our model. This time, building the model will be more exciting than in the past because we are now building a less trivial model and will make use of the Keras Functional API.

Before going over the code, we revisit the architecture of the model that we intend to build. The network consists of an encoder part and a decoder part. We define these as two separate models, which we later tie together. The two models are illustrated in Figure 14-4. The upper part of the figure shows the encoder, which consists of an embedding layer and two LSTM layers. The lower part of the figure shows the decoder, which consists of an embedding layer, two LSTM layers, and a fully connected softmax layer. The names in the figure correspond to the variable names that we use in our implementation.

Apart from the layer names, the figure also contains names of the outputs of all layers, which will be used in the code when connecting layers. Four noteworthy outputs (illustrated as two sets of outputs) are the state outputs from the two encoder LSTM layers. These are used as inputs into the decoder LSTM layers to communicate the accumulated state from the encoder to the decoder.

Code Snippet 14-10 contains the implementation of the encoder model. It should be straightforward to map the code to Figure 14-4, but there are a few things worth pointing out. Because we are now interested in accessing the internal state of the LSTM layers, we need to provide the argument `return_state=True`. This argument instructs the LSTM object to return not only a variable representing the layer's output but also variables representing the c and h states. Further, as previously described, for a recurrent layer that feeds another recurrent layer, we need to provide the argument `return_sequences=True` so that the subsequent layer sees the outputs of each timestep. This is also true for the final recurrent layer if we want the network to produce an output during each timestep. For our encoder, we are only interested in the final state, so we do not set `return_sequences` to True for `enc_layer2`.

Once all layers are connected, we create the actual model by calling the `Model()` constructor and providing arguments to specify what inputs and outputs will be external to the model. The model takes the source sentence as input and produces the internal states of the two LSTM layers as outputs. Each LSTM layer has both an h state and c state, so in total, the model will output four state variables as output. Each state variable is in itself a tensor consisting of multiple values.

Code Snippet 14-11 shows the implementation of the decoder model. In addition to the sentence in the destination language, it takes the output state from the encoder model as inputs. We initialize the decoder LSTM layers (using the argument `initial_state`) with this state at the first timestep.

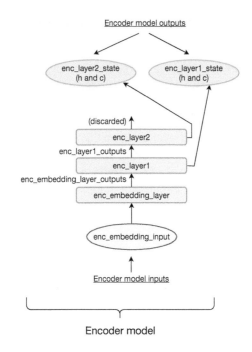

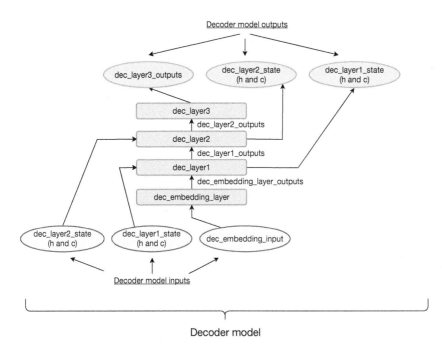

Figure 14-4 Topology of the encoder and decoder models

Code Snippet 14-10 Implementation of Encoder Model

```
# Build encoder model.
# Input is input sequence in source language.
enc_embedding_input = Input(shape=(None, ))

# Create the encoder layers.
enc_embedding_layer = Embedding(
    output_dim=EMBEDDING_WIDTH, input_dim
    = MAX_WORDS, mask_zero=True)
enc_layer1 = LSTM(LAYER_SIZE, return_state=True,
                  return_sequences=True)
enc_layer2 = LSTM(LAYER_SIZE, return_state=True)

# Connect the encoder layers.
# We don't use the last layer output, only the state.
enc_embedding_layer_outputs = \
    enc_embedding_layer(enc_embedding_input)
enc_layer1_outputs, enc_layer1_state_h, enc_layer1_state_c = \
    enc_layer1(enc_embedding_layer_outputs)
_, enc_layer2_state_h, enc_layer2_state_c = \
    enc_layer2(enc_layer1_outputs)

# Build the model.
enc_model = Model(enc_embedding_input,
                  [enc_layer1_state_h, enc_layer1_state_c,
                   enc_layer2_state_h, enc_layer2_state_c])
enc_model.summary()
```

For the decoder, we do want the top LSTM layer to produce an output for each timestep (the decoder should create a full sentence and not just a final state), so we set return_sequences=True for both LSTM layers.

Code Snippet 14-11 Implementation of Decoder Model

```
# Build decoder model.
# Input to the network is input sequence in destination
# language and intermediate state.
dec_layer1_state_input_h = Input(shape=(LAYER_SIZE,))
dec_layer1_state_input_c = Input(shape=(LAYER_SIZE,))
```

```
dec_layer2_state_input_h = Input(shape=(LAYER_SIZE,))
dec_layer2_state_input_c = Input(shape=(LAYER_SIZE,))
dec_embedding_input = Input(shape=(None, ))

# Create the decoder layers.
dec_embedding_layer = Embedding(output_dim=EMBEDDING_WIDTH,
                                input_dim=MAX_WORDS,
                                mask_zero=True)
dec_layer1 = LSTM(LAYER_SIZE, return_state = True,
                  return_sequences=True)
dec_layer2 = LSTM(LAYER_SIZE, return_state = True,
                  return_sequences=True)
dec_layer3 = Dense(MAX_WORDS, activation='softmax')

# Connect the decoder layers.
dec_embedding_layer_outputs = dec_embedding_layer(
    dec_embedding_input)
dec_layer1_outputs, dec_layer1_state_h, dec_layer1_state_c = \
    dec_layer1(dec_embedding_layer_outputs,
    initial_state=[dec_layer1_state_input_h,
                   dec_layer1_state_input_c])
dec_layer2_outputs, dec_layer2_state_h, dec_layer2_state_c = \
    dec_layer2(dec_layer1_outputs,
    initial_state=[dec_layer2_state_input_h,
                   dec_layer2_state_input_c])
dec_layer3_outputs = dec_layer3(dec_layer2_outputs)

# Build the model.
dec_model = Model([dec_embedding_input,
                   dec_layer1_state_input_h,
                   dec_layer1_state_input_c,
                   dec_layer2_state_input_h,
                   dec_layer2_state_input_c],
                  [dec_layer3_outputs, dec_layer1_state_h,
                   dec_layer1_state_c, dec_layer2_state_h,
                   dec_layer2_state_c])
dec_model.summary()
```

We create the model by calling the Model( ) constructor. The inputs consist of the destination sentence (time shifted by one timestep) and initial state for the LSTM layers. As we soon will see, when using the model for inference, we need to explicitly manage the internal state for the decoder. Therefore, we declare the states as outputs of the model in addition to the softmax output.

We are now ready to connect the two models to build a full encoder-decoder network corresponding to what is shown in Figure 14-5. The corresponding TensorFlow implementation is shown in Code Snippet 14-12.

One thing that looks odd is that, as we described previously, we provide the argument return_state=True when creating the decoder LSTM layers, but then when we create this model, we discard the state outputs. It seems reasonable to not have set the return_state=True argument to begin with. The reason will be apparent when we describe how to use the encoder and decoder models for inference.

We decided to use RMSProp as optimizer because some experiments indicate that it performs better than Adam for this specific model. We use sparse_ categorical_crossentropy instead of the normal categorical_ crossentropy as loss function. This is the loss function to use in Keras if the categorical output data is not already one-hot encoded. As described earlier, we avoided one-hot encoding the data up front to reduce the memory footprint of the application.

Although we just connected the encoder and decoder model to form a joint model, they can both still be used in isolation. Note that the encoder and decoder models

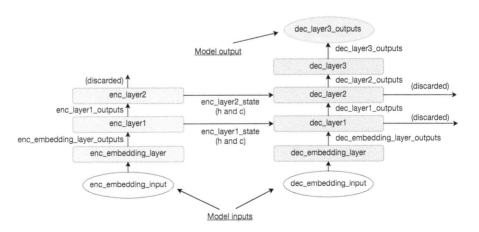

Figure 14-5 Architecture of full encoder-decoder model

Code Snippet 14-12 **Code to Define, Build, and Compile the Model Used for Training**

```
# Build and compile full training model.
# We do not use the state output when training.
train_enc_embedding_input = Input(shape=(None, ))
train_dec_embedding_input = Input(shape=(None, ))
intermediate_state = enc_model(train_enc_embedding_input)
train_dec_output, _, _, _, _ = dec_model(
    [train_dec_embedding_input] +
    intermediate_state)
training_model = Model([train_enc_embedding_input,
                        train_dec_embedding_input],
                       train_dec_output)
optimizer = RMSprop(lr=0.01)
training_model.compile(loss='sparse_categorical_crossentropy',
                       optimizer=optimizer, metrics =['accuracy'])
training_model.summary()
```

used by the joint model are the same instances as the individual models. That is, if we train the joint model, it will update the weights of the first two models. This is useful because, when we do inference, we want an encoder model that is decoupled from the decoder model.

During inference, we first run the source sentence through the encoder model to create the internal state. This state is then provided as initial state to the decoder model during the first timestep. At this timestep, we also feed the START token to the embedding layer of the model. This results in the model producing the first word in the translated sentence as its output. It also produces outputs representing the internal state of the two LSTM layers. In the next timestep, we feed the model with the predicted output as well as the internal state from the previous timestep (we explicitly manage the internal state) in an autoregressive manner.

Instead of explicitly managing the state, we could have declared the layers as `stateful=True`, as we did in our text autocompletion example, but that would complicate the training process. We cannot have `stateful=True` during training if we do not want multiple subsequent training examples to affect each other.

Finally, the reason that we do not need to explicitly manage state during training is that we fed the entire sentence at once to the model, in which case TensorFlow automatically feeds the state from the last timestep back to be used as the current state for the next timestep.

This whole discussion may seem unclear until you get more familiar with Keras, but the short of it is that there are many ways of doing the same thing and each method has its own benefits and drawbacks.

> When declaring a recurrent layer in Keras, there are three arguments: return_state, return_sequences, and stateful. At first, it can be tricky to tell them apart because of their similar names. If you want to build your own complicated networks, it is well worth spending some time to fully understand what they do and how they interact with each other.

We are now ready to train and test the model, which is shown in Code Snippet 14-13. We take a slightly different approach than in previous examples. In previous examples, we instructed fit() to train for multiple epochs, and then we studied the results and ended our program. In this example, we create our own training loop where we instruct fit() to train for only a single epoch at a time. We then use our model to create some predictions before going back and training for another epoch. This approach enables some detailed evaluation of just a small set of samples after each epoch. We could have done this by providing a callback function as an argument to the fit function, but we figured that it was unnecessary to introduce yet another Keras construct at this point.

> Keras callback functions is a good topic for further reading if you want to customize the behavior of the training process (keras.io).

Code Snippet 14-13 Training and Testing the Model

```
# Train and test repeatedly.
for i in range(EPOCHS):
    print('step: ' , i)
    # Train model for one epoch.
    history = training_model.fit(
        [train_src_input_data, train_dest_input_data],
```

```
    train_dest_target_data, validation_data=(
        [test_src_input_data, test_dest_input_data],
        test_dest_target_data), batch_size=BATCH_SIZE,
    epochs=1)

# Loop through samples to see result
for (test_input, test_target) in zip(sample_input_data,
                                     sample_target_data):
    # Run a single sentence through encoder model.
    x = np.reshape(test_input, (1, -1))
    last_states = enc_model.predict(
        x, verbose=0)
    # Provide resulting state and START_INDEX as input
    # to decoder model.
    prev_word_index = START_INDEX
    produced_string = ''
    pred_seq = []
    for j in range(MAX_LENGTH):
        x = np.reshape(np.array(prev_word_index), (1, 1))
        # Predict next word and capture internal state.
        preds, dec_layer1_state_h, dec_layer1_state_c, \
            dec_layer2_state_h, dec_layer2_state_c = \
                dec_model.predict(
                    [x] + last_states, verbose=0)
        last_states = [dec_layer1_state_h,
                       dec_layer1_state_c,
                       dec_layer2_state_h,
                       dec_layer2_state_c]
        # Find the most probable word.
        prev_word_index = np.asarray(preds[0][0]).argmax()
        pred_seq.append(prev_word_index)
        if prev_word_index == STOP_INDEX:
            break
    tokens_to_words(src_tokenizer, test_input)
    tokens_to_words(dest_tokenizer, test_target)
    tokens_to_words(dest_tokenizer, pred_seq)
    print('\n\n')
```

Most of the code sequence is the loop used to create translations for the smaller set of samples that we created from the test dataset. This piece of code consists of a loop that iterates over all the examples in `sample_input_data`. We provide the source sentence to the encoder model to create the resulting internal state and store to the variable `last_states`. We also initialize the variable `prev_word_index` with the index corresponding to the START symbol. We then enter the innermost loop and predict a single word using the decoder model. We also read out the internal state. This data is then used as input to the decoder model in the next iteration, and we iterate until the model produces a STOP token or until a given number of words have been produced. Finally, we convert the produced tokenized sequences into the corresponding word sequences and print them out.

Experimental Results

Training the network for 20 epochs resulted in high accuracy metrics for both training and test data. Accuracy is not necessarily the most meaningful metric to use when working on machine translation, but it still gives us some indication that our translation network works. More interesting is to inspect the resulting translations for our sample set.

The first example is shown here:

```
['PAD', 'PAD', 'PAD', 'PAD', 'PAD', 'PAD', 'PAD', 'PAD', 'PAD',
 'PAD', "j'ai", 'travaillé', 'ce', 'matin']
['i', 'worked', 'this', 'morning', 'STOP', 'PAD', 'PAD', 'PAD',
 'PAD', 'PAD']
['i', 'worked', 'this', 'morning', 'STOP']
```

The first line shows the input sentence in French. The second line shows the corresponding training target, and the third line shows the prediction from our trained model. That is, for this example, the model predicted the translation exactly right!

Additional examples are shown in Table 14-1, where we have stripped out the padding and STOP tokens as well as removed characters associated with printing out the Python lists. When looking at the first two examples, it should be clear why we said that accuracy is not necessarily a good metric. The prediction is not identical to the training target, so the accuracy would be low. Still, it is hard to argue that the translations are wrong, given that the predictions express the

Table 14-1 Examples of Translations Produced by the Model

SOURCE	TARGET	PREDICTION
je déteste manger seule	i hate eating alone	i hate to eat alone
je n'ai pas le choix	i don't have a choice	i have no choice
je pense que tu devrais le faire	i think you should do it	i think you should do it
tu habites où	where do you live	where do you live
nous partons maintenant	we're leaving now	we're leaving now
j'ai pensé que nous pouvions le faire	i thought we could do it	i thought we could do it
je ne fais pas beaucoup tout ça	i don't do all that much	i'm not busy at all
il a été élu roi du bal de fin d'année	he was voted prom king	he used to negotiate and look like golfer

same meaning as the targets. To address this, a metric known as BiLingual Evaluation Understudy (BLEU) score is used within the machine translation community (Papineni et al., 2002). We do not use or discuss that metric further, but it is certainly something to learn about if you want to dive deeper into machine translation. For now, we just recognize that there can be multiple correct translations to a single sentence.

> BLEU score can be used to judge how well a machine translation system works (Papineni et al., 2002). Learning the details of how it is computed makes sense if you want to dive deeper into machine translation.

Looking at the third through sixth rows, it almost seems too good to be true. The translations are identical to the expected translations. Is it possible for the model to be that good? Inspecting the training data gives us a clue about what is going on. It turns out that the dataset contains many minor variations of a single sentence in the source language, and all these sentences are translated to the same sentence in the destination language. Thus, the model is trained on a specific source/target sentence pair and is later presented with a slightly different source sentence. It is not all that unexpected that the model then predicts exactly the same target sentence that it was trained on, so we might view this as cheating. On the other hand, we do want to train the model to recognize similarities and be able to generalize, so it is not completely obvious that we should strip out these training examples. Still, we did some experiments where we removed any training example that had a duplicate in either the source or the destination language, and the model still performed well. Thus, the model clearly does not fully rely on cheating.

One example of where the model does work without cheating is the second to last example. The test example has the sentence "I don't do all that much" as target. The model predicts the fairly different sentence "I'm not busy at all," which arguably still conveys a similar message. Interestingly, when searching through the whole dataset, the phrase "busy at all" does not show up a single time, so the model constructed that translation from smaller pieces. On the other hand, the model also produces some translations that are just wrong. For the last example in the table, the target was "he was voted prom king" but the model came up with "he used to negotiate and look like golfer."

Properties of the Intermediate Representation

We previously showed that the word embeddings learned in a neural language model capture some syntactic and semantic structure of the language it models. Sutskever, Vinyals, and Le (2014) made a similar observation when analyzing the intermediate representation produced by the encoder in a sequence-to-sequence model. They used principal component analysis (PCA) to reduce this representation to two dimensions to be able to visualize the vectors. For the purpose of this discussion, the only thing you need to know about PCA is that the resulting lower dimensional vectors still maintain some properties of the original vectors. In particular, if two vectors are similar to each other before reducing the dimensionality, then these two vectors will still be similar to each other in the new lower dimensional space.[2]

---

2. PCA can also be used to reduce the dimensionality of word embeddings and plot them in 2D space to be able to visualize their similarity.

PCA can be used to reduce the number of dimensions of a set of vectors. It is a good technique to know if working with vector representations in many-dimensional spaces.

Figure 14-6 shows a chart that visualizes the intermediate representation of six phrases. The six phrases are grouped into two groups of three phrases each, where the three phrases within a single group express approximately the same meaning but with some grammatical variations (e.g., passive voice and word order). However, phrases in different groups express different meanings. Interestingly, as can be seen in the chart, the intermediate representation chosen by the model is such that the three phrases with similar meaning also have similar encodings, and they cluster together.

We can view this intermediate representation as a *sentence embedding* or *phrase embedding,* where similar phrases will be embedded close to each other in vector space. Hence, we can use this encoding to analyze the semantics of phrases.

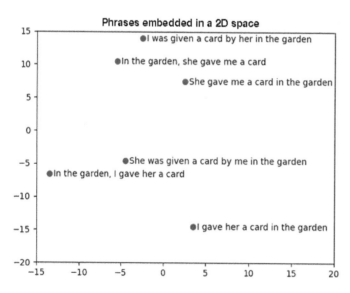

Figure 14-6 2D representation of intermediate representation of six sentences. (Source: Adapted from Sutskever, I., Vinyals, O., and Le, Q. (2014), "Sequence to Sequence Learning with Neural Networks," in *Proceedings of the 27th International Conference on Neural Information Processing [NIPS'14],* MIT Press, 3104–3112.)

Looking at the example, it seems likely that this methodology will be more powerful than the previously discussed bag-of-word approach. As opposed to the bag-of-word approach, the sequence-to-sequence model does take word order into account.

Concluding Remarks on Language Translation

Although this programming example was longer and more complicated than most examples we have shown so far, from a software development point of view, it is a simple implementation. It is a basic encoder-decoder architecture without any bells and whistles, and it consists of fewer than 300 lines of code. If you are interested in experimenting with this model to improve translation quality, a starting point is to tweak the network by increasing the number of units in the layers or increasing the number of layers. You can also experiment with using bidirectional layers instead of unidirectional layers. One problem that has been observed is that sequence-to-sequence networks of this type find it challenging to deal with long sentences. A simple trick that mitigates this problem is to reverse the input sentence. One hypothesis is that doing so helps because the temporal distance between the model observing the initial words of the source sentence (that are now at the end after reversing) and observing the initial words of the destination sentence is smaller, which makes it easier for the model to learn how they relate to each other. Functionality to reverse the source sentences can trivially be added to the function that reads the dataset file.

If you want to learn more about neural machine translation, Luong's PhD thesis (2016) is a good start. It also contains a brief historical overview of the traditional machine translation field. Another good resource is the paper by Wu and colleagues (2016), which describes a neural-based translation system deployed in production. You will notice that it is built using the same basic architecture as the network described in this chapter. However, it also uses a more advanced technique, known as *attention,* to improve its ability to handle long sentences.

More recently, neural machine translation systems have moved on from LSTM-based models to using a model known as the *Transformer,* which is based on both attention and *self-attention*. Although a Transformer-based translation network does not use LSTM cells, it is still an encoder-decoder architecture. That is, key points from this chapter carry over to this more recent architecture. Attention, self-attention, and the Transformer are the topics of Chapter 15.

Chapter 15

Attention and the Transformer

This chapter focuses on a technique known as *attention*. We start by describing the attention mechanism and how it can be used to improve the encoder-decoder-based neural machine translation architecture from Chapter 14, "Sequence-to-Sequence Networks and Natural Language Translation." We then describe a mechanism known as *self-attention* and how the different attention mechanisms can be used to build an architecture known as the *Transformer*.

Many readers will find attention tricky on the first encounter. We encourage you to try to get through this chapter, but it is fine to skip over the details during the first reading. Focus on understanding the big picture. In particular, do not worry if you feel lost when you read about the Transformer architecture in the latter part of the chapter. Appendix D is the only part of the book that builds further upon this architecture. However, the Transformer is the basis for much of the significant progress made within natural language processing (NLP) in the last few years, so we encourage you to revisit the topic later if it is too heavy to get through the first time around.

Rationale Behind Attention

Attention is a general mechanism that can be applied to multiple problem domains. In this section, we describe how it can be used in neural machine translation. The idea with attention is that we let a network (or part of a network) decide for itself which part of the input data to focus on (pay *attention* to) during each timestep. The term *input data* in the previous sentence does not necessarily refer only to the input data to the overall model. It could be that parts of a network implement attention, in which case the attention mechanism can be used to decide what parts of an intermediate data representation to focus on. We soon give a more concrete example of what this means, but before doing so, let us briefly discuss the rationale behind this mechanism.

> The attention mechanism can be applied to an encoder-decoder architecture and enables the decoder to selectively decide on which part of the intermediate state to focus.

Consider how a human translates a complicated sentence from one language to another, such as the following sentence from the Europarl dataset:

> *In my opinion, this second hypothesis would imply the failure of Parliament in its duty as a Parliament, as well as introducing an original thesis, an unknown method which consists of making political groups aware, in writing, of a speech concerning the Commission's programme a week earlier—and not a day earlier, as had been agreed—bearing in mind that the legislative programme will be discussed in February, so we could forego the debate, since on the next day our citizens will hear about it in the press and on the Internet and Parliament will no longer have to worry about it.*

We first read the sentence to get an overall idea of what it is trying to convey. We then start writing the translation, and while doing so, typically revisit different parts of the source sentence to ensure that our translation covers the entire sentence and describes it in an equivalent tense. The destination language might have a different preferred word order, such as in German where verbs appear as the last words in a sentence in past tense. Therefore, we might jump around in the source sentence to find a specific word when it is time for its translation to appear in the destination sentence. It seems reasonable to believe that a network would benefit from having that same flexibility.

Attention in Sequence-to-Sequence Networks

With that background, we now make the concept of attention more concrete by considering how a sequence-to-sequence-based neural machine translator (NMT) can be extended to include an attention mechanism. Let us start with a slightly different type of encoder-decoder network than we studied in Chapter 14. It is shown in Figure 15-1, and the difference is in how the encoder is connected to the decoder. In the previous chapter, the internal state from the last timestep of the encoding process was used as initial state at the first timestep for the decoder. In this alternative architecture, the internal state from the last timestep of the encoder is instead used as an input, accessible to the decoder at every timestep. The network also receives the embedding for the produced word from the last timestep as input. That is, the intermediate state from the encoder is concatenated with the embedding to form the overall input to the recurrent layer.

This alternative sequence-to-sequence model can be found in a paper by Cho and colleagues (2014a), and we use it in this discussion simply because Bahdanau, Cho, and Bengio (2014) assumed that model as their baseline system when they added the attention mechanism to an NMT system. They observed that their model had a hard time dealing with long sentences and hypothesized that a reason was that the encoder was forced to encode the long sentence in a fixed-size vector. To resolve that problem, the authors modified their encoder architecture to instead read out the internal state at every timestep during the encoding process and store it for later access. This is illustrated in Figure 15-2. The top part of the figure shows the fixed-length encoding in a network without attention, using a vector length of 8. The bottom shows the attention case, where the encoding consists of one vector per input word.

> An alternative way of connecting the encoder and decoder in a sequence-to-sequence network is to feed the encoder state as an input to the decoder for every timestep.

Although the figure shows it as one vector corresponding to each word, it is a little bit subtler than that. Each vector corresponds to the internal state of the decoder at the timestep for that word, but the encoding is influenced by both the current word and all historical words in the sentence.

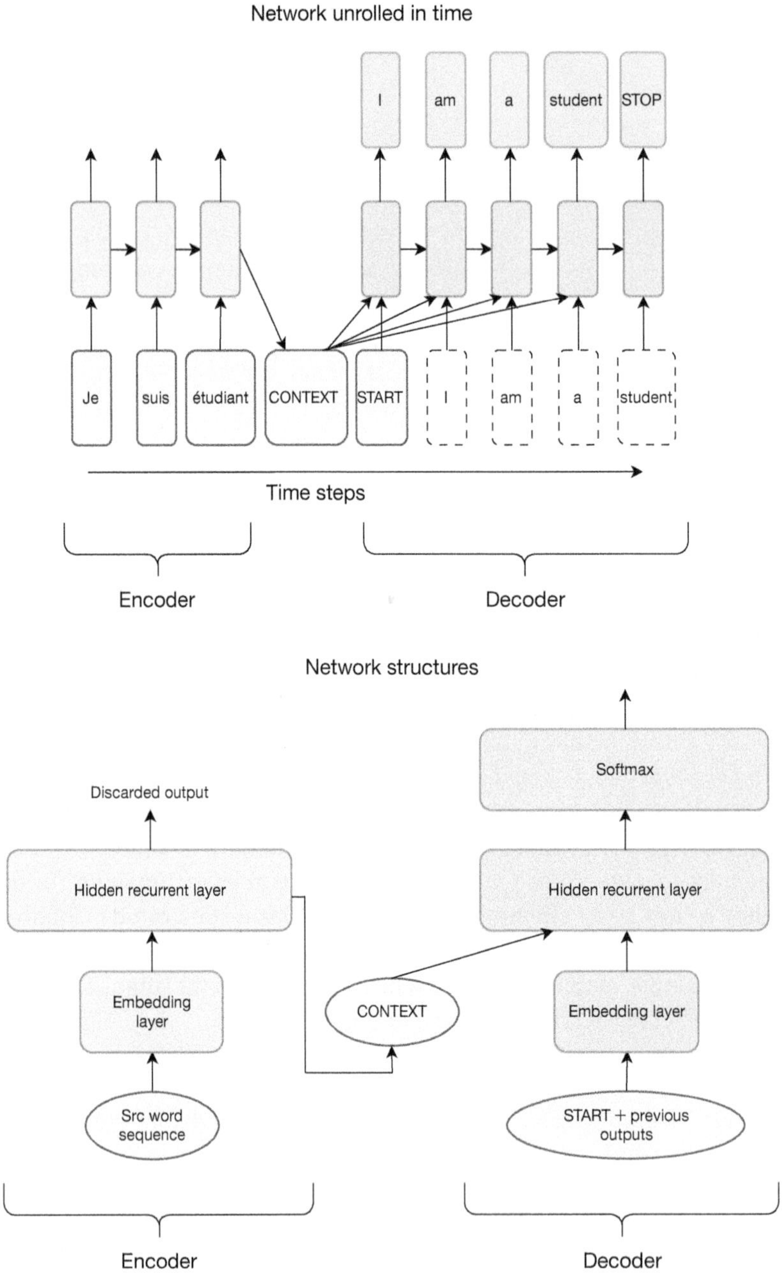

Figure 15-1 Alternative implementation of encoder-decoder architecture for neural machine translation. Top: Network unrolled in time. Bottom: The actual network structure (not unrolled).

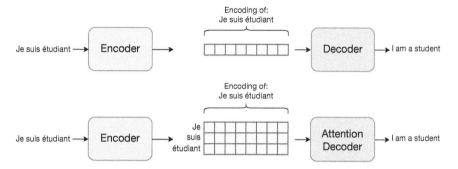

Figure 15-2 Top: Fixed-length encoding in encoder-decoder network without attention. Bottom: Variable-length encoding in encoder-decoder network with attention.

The change to the encoder is trivial. Instead of discarding the internal state for all but the last timestep, we record the internal state for each timestep. This set of vectors is known as the *source hidden state*. It is also referred to as *annotations* or the more general term *memory*. We do not use those terms, but they are good to know when reading other publications on the topic.

The changes to the decoder are more involved. For **each timestep,** the attention-based decoder does the following:

1. Compute an *alignment score* for each state vector. This score determines how much attention to pay to that state vector during the current timestep. The details of the alignment score are described later in this chapter.

2. Use softmax to normalize the scores so they add up to 1. This vector of scores is known as the *alignment vector* and would consist of three values for the preceding example.

3. Multiply each state vector by its alignment score. Then add (elementwise) the resulting vectors together. This weighted sum (score is used as weight) results in a vector of the same dimension as in the network without attention. That is, in the example, it would be a single vector consisting of eight elements.

4. Use the resulting vector as an input to the decoder during this timestep. Just as in the network without attention, this vector is concatenated with the embedding from the previous timestep to form the overall input to the recurrent layer.

By examining the alignment scores for each timestep, it is possible to analyze how the model uses the attention mechanism during translation. This is illustrated in Figure 15-3. The three state vectors (one per encoder timestep)

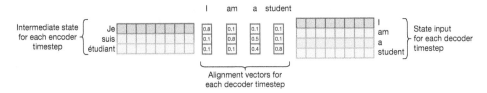

Figure 15-3 How encoder output state is combined with alignment vectors to create encoder input state for each timestep

produced by the encoder are shown to the left. The four alignment vectors (one for each decoder timestep) are shown in the middle. For each decoder timestep, a decoder input is created by a weighted sum of the three encoder vectors. The scores in one of the alignment vectors are used as weights.

For the preceding example, the decoder will keep its focus on *je* during the first timestep, which results in it outputting *I*. The color coding illustrates this (first decoder input is red, just like first encoder output). It will focus mainly on *suis* when outputting *am*. When outputting *a,* it focuses on both *suis* and *étudiant* (the input vector is green, which is a mix of blue and yellow). Finally, its focus is on *étudiant* when outputting *student*.

Bahdanau, Cho, and Bengio (2014) analyzed a more complex example:

- French: L' accord sur la **zone économique européenne** a été signé en août 1992.

- English: The agreement on the **European Economic Area** was signed in August 1992.

Consider the words in bold. The word order is different in French than in English (*zone* corresponds to *Area*, and *européenne* corresponds to *European*). The authors show that for all three timesteps, when the decoder outputs European Economic Area, the alignment scores for all the three words *zone économique européenne* are high. That is, the decoder is paying attention to the neighboring words to arrive at a correct translation.

We now go through the attention mechanism for the decoder in more detail and, in particular, how to compute the alignment scores that result in this behavior. The architecture is outlined in Figure 15-4, where the upper part shows the workings of the network unrolled in time, with a focus on the second timestep for the decoder, and the lower part shows the network structures without unrolling.

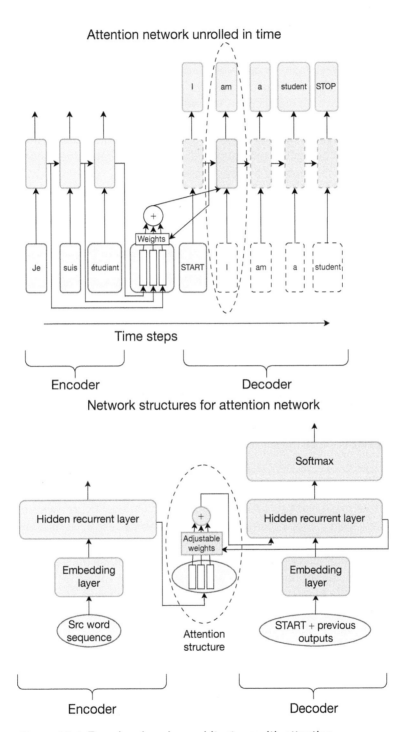

Figure 15-4 Encoder-decoder architecture with attention

Starting with the unrolled view (top), we see that the intermediate representation consists of three pieces of state (one for each input timestep), each represented by a small white rectangle. As described previously in steps 2 and 3, we compute a weighted sum of these vectors to produce a single vector that is used as input to the recurrent layer in the decoder. The weights (also known as *alignment scores* or *alignment vector*) are adjustable and recomputed at each timestep. As you can see from the figure, the weights are controlled by the internal state of the decoder from the timestep before the current decoder timestep. That is, the decoder is responsible for computing the alignment scores.

The lower part of the figure shows a structural (not unrolled) view of the same network, where again it is apparent that, by adjusting the weights properly, the decoder itself controls how much of each encoder state vector to use as its input.

COMPUTING THE ALIGNMENT VECTOR

We now describe how to compute the alignment vector for each decoder timestep. An alignment vector consists of T_e elements, where T_e is the number of timesteps for the encoder. We need to compute T_d such vectors, where T_d is the number of timesteps for the decoder.

One can envision multiple ways of computing the alignment vector. We know that it needs to be of length T_e. We also need to decide what input values to use to compute the vector. Finally, we need to decide what computation to apply to these input values to produce the scores.

One obvious candidate for input value is the decoder state because we want the decoder to dynamically be able to choose what parts of the input to focus on. We have already made this assumption in the high-level figures where the state outputs from the top recurrent layer in the decoder are used to control the weights in the attention mechanism (the weights in the high-level figures represent the alignment vector in the more detailed attention mechanism description). Another candidate that can be used as input values for this computation is the *source hidden state*. At first, this might seem a little bit hard to wrap your head around in that we will use the source hidden state to compute the alignment vector, which will then be used to determine what parts of the source hidden state will be visible to the decoder. However, this is not as strange as it seems. If you view the source hidden state as a memory, this means that we use the content of that memory to address what piece of the memory to read, a concept known as *content addressable memory* (CAM). We mention this for readers who already are familiar with CAM, but knowing details about CAM is not required to follow our remaining description of how to compute the alignment vector.

From a terminology perspective, in our example, the decoder state is used as a *query*. It is then used to match against a *key*, which in our case is the source hidden state. This selects the *value* to return, which in our case is also the source hidden state, but in other implementations, the key and value can be different from each other.

Now we just need to decide on the function that is used to match the query to the key. Given the topic of this book, it is not farfetched to use a neural network for this function and let the model learn the function itself. Figure 15-5 shows two potential implementations.

The left part of the figure shows a fully connected feedforward network with an arbitrary number of layers, ending with a fully connected softmax layer that outputs the alignment vector. The softmax layer ensures that the sum of the elements in the alignment vector is 1.0. One drawback with the network in the left part of the figure is that we introduce restrictions on the source input length. More serious is that the leftmost network hardcodes the expected position of words in the source sentence, which can make it harder for the network to generalize. The rightmost architecture addresses this issue by having multiple instances of a two-layer network with weight sharing between the instances. As we have seen

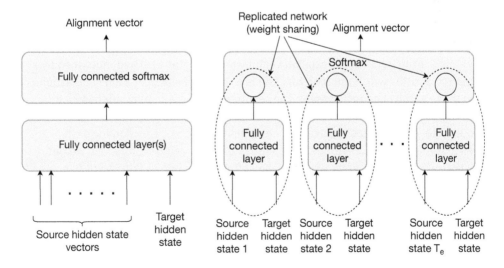

Figure 15-5 Two alternative implementations of the function that computes the alignment vector

previously, weight sharing results in enabling the network to identify a specific pattern regardless of its position. Each instance of this fully connected network takes the target hidden state and one timestep of the source hidden state as inputs. The activation function for the first layer is tanh, and we use softmax in the output layer to ensure that the sum of the elements in the alignment vector results in 1.0. This architecture reflects the attention mechanism introduced by Bahdanau, Cho, and Bengio (2014).

MATHEMATICAL NOTATION AND VARIATIONS ON THE ALIGNMENT VECTOR

Publications about attention mechanisms generally describe the attention function using linear algebra instead of drawing out networks as we have done. In this section, we first map the description and Figure 15-5 to mathematical equations. Once that is done, we present simplifications of the attention function, which can be done compactly using these equations.

The network starts with T_e instances of a two-level network, where T_e represents the number of encoder timesteps. The first layer uses tanh as an activation function. The second layer of each two-level network is a single neuron without an activation function (softmax is applied later). What we just described is represented by the networks in the dashed ovals in the figure, where the content of each oval implements a function known as a scoring function:

$$score\left(\mathbf{h}_t, \ \mathbf{h}_{si}\right) = \mathbf{v}_a^T \tanh\left(W_a\left[\mathbf{h}_t; \mathbf{h}_{si}\right]\right)$$

The target hidden state and one of the source hidden states are used as inputs to this scoring function. These two vectors are concatenated and multiplied by a matrix W_a after which the tanh function is applied. These operations correspond to the first fully connected layer. The resulting vector is then multiplied by a transposed version of vector v_a. This corresponds to the single neuron in the output layer in the dashed oval. We compute this scoring function for each encoder timestep. Each timestep results in a single value so, all in all, we get a vector with T_e elements. We apply the softmax function to this vector to scale the values so the elements sum to 1. Each element of the output of the softmax operation is computed using the following formula:

$$\mathbf{a}_t\left(i\right) = softmax\left(i\right) = \frac{\exp(score(\mathbf{h}_t, \mathbf{h}_{si})}{\sum_{j=1}^{T_e}\exp\left(score\left(\mathbf{h}_t, \mathbf{h}_{sj}\right)\right)}$$

In the formula, T_e represents the number of encoder timesteps, and i is the index of the element that is computed. We organize the resulting elements into an alignment vector with one element for each encoder timestep:

$$a_t = \begin{pmatrix} a_t(1) \\ a_t(2) \\ \vdots \\ a_t(T_e) \end{pmatrix}$$

There is nothing magical about the chosen scoring function. Bahdanau, Cho, and Bengio (2014) simply chose a two-level fully connected neural network to make it sufficiently complex to be able to learn a meaningful function yet simple enough to not be too computationally expensive. Luong, Pham, and Manning (2015) experimented with simplifying this scoring function and showed that the two simpler functions in Equation 15-1 also work well:

$$score\left(\mathbf{h}_t,\ \mathbf{h}_{si}\right) = \mathbf{h}_t^T \mathbf{W}_a \mathbf{h}_{si} \qquad\qquad (general)$$

$$score\left(\mathbf{h}_t,\ \mathbf{h}_{si}\right) = \mathbf{h}_t^T \mathbf{h}_{si} \qquad\qquad (dot)$$

Equation 15-1 Simplifications of the scoring function

One natural question is what the two functions in Equation 15-1 represent in terms of neural networks. Starting with the *dot* product version, combined with the softmax function, this represents the network in the right part of Figure 15-5 but with the modification that there is no fully connected layer before the softmax layer. Further, the neurons in the softmax layer use the target hidden state vector as neuron weights, and the source hidden state vector are used as inputs to the network. The *general* version combined with the softmax function represents a first layer defined by W_a and with a linear activation function again followed by a softmax layer that uses the target hidden state vector as neuron weights. In reality, once we have started to think about these networks in terms of mathematical equations, we do not necessarily care about what a slight modification of an equation implies in terms of the network structure as long as it works well. Flipping things around, we can also analyze the mathematical equations to see if they can provide any insight into how the attention mechanism works. Looking at the dot product version, we know that the dot product of two vectors tends to be large if elements located in the same position in both vectors are of the same sign. Alternatively, consider the case where the vectors are produced by rectified linear units (ReLU) so that all elements are greater than or equal to zero. Then the dot product will be large if the vectors are similar to each other, in the sense that nonzero elements in both vectors are aligned with each other. In other words, the attention mechanism will tend to focus on timesteps where the encoder state is similar to the current decoder state. We can envision that this makes sense if the hidden states of the encoder and decoder somehow express the type of word that is currently being processed, such as if the current state can be used to determine whether the current word is the subject or the object in the sentence.

ATTENTION IN A DEEPER NETWORK

This description assumes a network with a single recurrent layer. Figure 15-6 shows a network architecture introduced by Luong, Pham, and Manning (2015) that applies attention to a deeper network. There are a couple of key differences

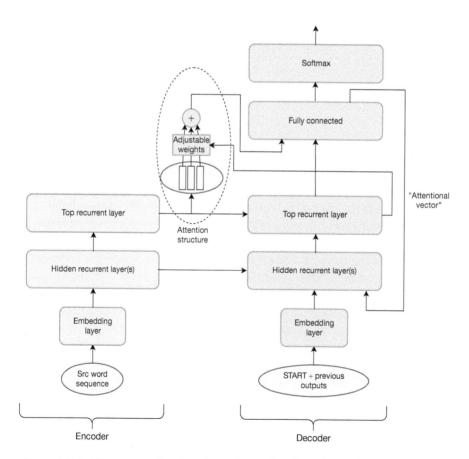

Figure 15-6 Alternative attention-based encoder-decoder architecture

compared to Figure 15-4. First, this network architecture is more similar to our original NMT in that we use the final encoder internal state to initialize the decoder internal state. Second, as opposed to Figure 15-4, we see that the encoder and decoder now have two or more recurrent layers. Luong, Pham, and Manning handled this by applying the attention mechanism only to the internal state of the topmost layer. Further, instead of using the context derived by the attention mechanism as input to a recurrent layer, this state is concatenated with the output of the top recurrent layer in the decoder and fed into a fully connected layer. The output of this fully connected layer is referred to as an *attentional vector*. This vector is fed back to the input of the first recurrent layer in the next timestep. In some sense, this makes the fully connected layer act as a recurrent layer as well and is key to making the attention mechanism work well. It enables the network to take into account what parts of the source sentence it has already attended to when deciding what parts of the source sentence to consider next. In the architecture in Figure 15-4, this explicit feedback loop was not needed because there is an implicit feedback loop given that the weighted state is fed to a recurrent layer instead of to a regular feedforward layer.

A final key difference is that in Figure 15-6 the weighted sum is fed to a higher layer in the network instead of being fed back to the same layer that creates the state that controls the weights. This has the effect that the adjustable weights are now controlled by the state in the current decoder timestep instead of in the previous timestep. This might not be obvious at first when looking at the figure. When you consider how the data flows, you can see that in Figure 15-6 it is possible to compute the adjustable weights before using them, whereas in the Figure 15-4 the output of the adjustable weights is used to compute the vector that controls them. Hence, the vector that controls the weights must have been derived from a previous timestep.

ADDITIONAL CONSIDERATIONS

In the attention mechanism we have described, the decoder creates a weighted sum of the vectors in the source hidden state. This is known as *soft attention*. An alternative is to instead let the decoder attend to only one out of the vectors in the source hidden state for each timestep. This is known as *hard attention*.

A benefit of computing a weighted sum is that the attention function is continuous and thereby differentiable. This enables the use of backpropagation for learning as opposed to when a discrete selection function is used.

In **hard attention,** the state from a single encoder timestep is selected to focus on each decoder timestep. In **soft attention,** a mixture (weighted sum) of the state from all encoder timesteps is used.

Finally, let us reflect on one of the restrictions that we now have applied to our sequence-to-sequence network. Before applying attention, the network could in theory accept an input sequence of unlimited length. However, the need for the attention mechanism to store the entire source hidden state, which grows linearly with the source sequence length, implies that we now have a limitation on the length of the input sequence. This might seem unfortunate at first, but it is of limited practical importance. Consider the fairly complex sentence that we gave as a rationale for the attention mechanism some paragraphs back. Few people would be able to read it once and then produce a good translation. In other words, the human brain has a hard time even remembering a sentence of such length and needs to rely on external storage (the paper or computer screen on which it is written) to create a good translation. In reality, the amount of storage needed to memorize the sentence is only 589 bytes in uncompressed form. With that background, having to reserve enough storage to keep track of the *source hidden state* seems reasonable.

This concludes our detailed description of the basic attention mechanism. One takeaway from this discussion is that attention is a general concept, and there are multiple potential ways to implement it. This may make you feel somewhat uneasy at first, in that it seems unclear that either one of the described implementations is the "right" way to do it. This reaction is similar to when first encountering the LSTM unit and the gated recurrent unit (GRU). In reality, there probably is not a single right way of applying these concepts. Different implementations express slightly different behavior and come with different efficiency levels in terms of how much computation is required to achieve a certain result.

Alternatives to Recurrent Networks

If we take a step back, a reasonable question is why we think that recurrent networks are required for our NMT. The starting point was that we wanted the ability to process variable sequence lengths for both the source and the destination sequences. The RNN-based encoder-decoder network was an elegant solution to this with a fixed-sized intermediate representation. However, to get good translations of long sentences, we then reintroduced some restrictions on the input sequence length and had the decoder access this intermediate state in a random-access fashion using attention. With that background, it is natural to explore whether we need an RNN to build our encoder or whether other network architectures are just as good or better. Another issue with the RNN-based implementation is that RNNs are inherently serial in nature. The computations cannot be parallelized as well as they can in other network architectures, leading to long training times. Kalchbrenner and colleagues (2016) and Gehring and colleagues (2017) studied alternative approaches that are based on convolutional networks with attention instead of recurrent networks.

A major breakthrough came with the introduction of the Transformer architecture (Vaswani et al., 2017). It uses neither recurrent layers nor convolutional layers. Instead, it is based on fully connected layers and two concepts known as *self-attention* (Lin, Doll, et al., 2017) and *multi-head attention*. A key benefit of the Transformer architecture is that it is parallel in nature. The computations for all input symbols (e.g., words in language translation) can be done in parallel with each other.

The Transformer is based on self-attention and multi-head attention.

The Transformer architecture has driven much of the progress in NLP since 2017. It has achieved record scores in language translation. It is also the basis for other important models. Two such models are Generative Pre-Training (GPT) and Bidirectional Encoder Representations from Transformers (BERT), which have achieved record scores on tasks within multiple NLP applications (Devlin et al., 2018; Radford et al., 2018). More details about GPT and BERT can be found in Appendix D.

GPT and BERT are language models based on the Transformer architecture.

The next couple of sections describe the details of self-attention and multi-head attention. We then move on to describe the overall Transformer architecture and how it can be used to build an encoder-decoder network for natural language translation without recurrent layers.

Self-Attention

In the attention mechanism we have studied so far, the decoder uses attention to direct focus to different parts of the *intermediate state*. Self-attention is different in that it is used to decide which part of the *output from the preceding layer* to focus on. This is shown in Figure 15-7, where self-attention is applied to the

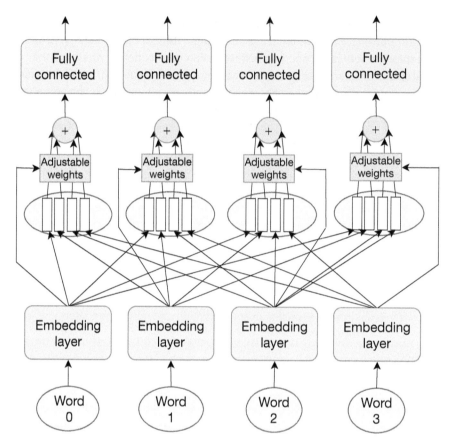

Figure 15-7 Embedding layer followed by a self-attention layer followed by a fully connected layer. The network employs weight sharing, so each word position uses the same weights.

output of an embedding layer and is followed by a fully connected layer for each word. For each of these fully connected layers, the input will be a combination of all the words in the sentence, where the attention mechanism determines how heavily to weigh each individual word.

Before diving into the details of the self-attention mechanism, it is worth pointing out how the architecture in the figure exposes parallelism. Although the figure contains multiple instances of embedding layers, attention mechanisms, and fully connected layers, they are all identical (weight sharing). Further, within a single layer, there are no dependencies between words. This enables an implementation to do the computations in parallel. Consider the inputs to the fully connected layers. We can arrange the four output vectors from the attention mechanisms into a matrix with four rows. The fully connected layer is represented by a matrix with one column per neuron. We can now compute the output for all four instances in parallel by a single matrix-matrix multiplication. We will see later how the self-attention mechanism exposes additional parallelism, but first we need to describe self-attention in more detail.

Earlier in this chapter, we described how the attention mechanism uses a scoring function to compute these weights. One of the inputs to this scoring function, the *key*, was the data value itself. The other input, the *query* (the horizontal arrows in Figure 15-7), came from the network that would consume the input (the decoder network). In the case of self-attention, the query comes from the previous layer, just as the value does.

The self-attention mechanism in the Transformer is slightly more complex than what is shown in the figure. Instead of directly using the inputs to the attention mechanism as *key, query,* and *data,* these three vectors are computed by three separate single-layer networks with linear activation functions. That is, the key is now different than the data value, and another side effect is that we can use a different width of key, query, and data than the original input. This is shown in Figure 15-8 for a single attention mechanism.

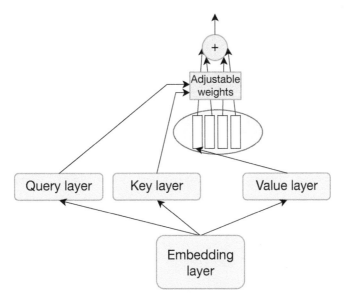

Figure 15-8 Attention mechanism with projection layers that modify the dimensions of the query, key, and value. Although not shown in the figure, each attention mechanism receives a key and a value from each position in the preceding layer.

It might seem confusing that we now have two arrows feeding into the rectangle with the adjustable weights. In the previous figures, we implicitly used the data values (the white rectangles) as both value and key, so we did not explicitly draw this arrow. That is, in reality, the attention mechanism did not change much despite the figure containing an additional arrow.

Multi-head Attention

We saw in the previous section how we can use self-attention to produce N output vectors from N input vectors, where N was the number of words that were input to the network. The self-attention mechanism ensured that all N input vectors could influence each output vector. We also introduced layers for the query, key, and value that enabled us to make the width of the output vector independent of the width of the input vector. The ability to decouple the input width from the output width is central in the *multi-head attention* concept.

Multi-head attention is as simple as having multiple attention mechanisms operating in parallel for each input vector. This is shown in Figure 15-9 for an example with two heads.

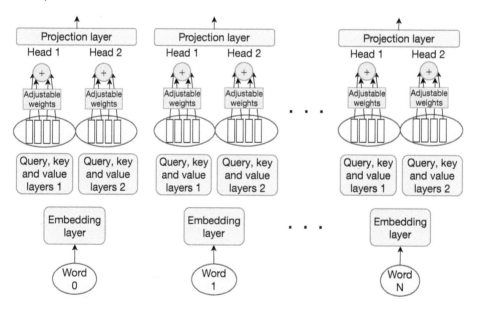

Figure 15-9 Embedding layer followed by multi-head self-attention layer. Each input word vector is processed by multiple heads. The output of all heads for a given word are then concatenated and run through a projection layer.

This figure implies that each input vector now results in two output vectors. That is, if the output width of a single head is the same as the input width, the output of the layer now has two times as many values as compared to the input to the layer. However, given the query, key, and value layers, we have the ability to size the output to any width. In addition, we have added a projection layer on the output. Its input is the concatenated output from the heads. All in all, this means that we have full flexibility in selecting the width of the attention heads as well as the overall output of the multi-head self-attention layer.

Just as for Figure 15-7, we assume weight sharing in Figure 15-9. The query layer for head 1 for word 0 is identical to the query layer for head 1 for all other words, and the same applies to the key and value layers. From an implementation perspective, this means that if we arrange our N input vectors to the self-attention layer into a matrix, computing the query vector for head 1 for all input vectors is equivalent to a single matrix-matrix multiplication. The same holds true for the key vector and the value vector. The number of heads is another level of parallelism, so in the end, the self-attention layer results in a large number of matrix multiplications that can be done in parallel.

The Transformer

As previously mentioned, the Transformer is an encoder-decoder architecture similar to what we have seen already, but it does not employ recurrent layers. We first describe the encoder, which starts with an embedding layer for each word, as we have seen in previous figures. The embedding layers are followed by a stack of six identical modules, where each module consists of a multi-head self-attention layer and a fully connected layer corresponding to each input word. In addition, each module employs skip connections and normalization, as shown in the left part of Figure 15-10, which illustrates a single instance of the six modules.

The network uses layer normalization (Ba, Kiros, and Hinton, 2016) as opposed to batch normalization that we have seen previously. Layer normalization has been shown to facilitate training just like batch normalization but is independent of the mini-batch size.

We stated that the Transformer does not use recurrent layers, but the decoder is still an autoregressive model. That is, it does generate the output one word at a time and still needs to feed each generated word back as an input to the decoder network in a serial fashion. Just as for the encoder, the decoder consists of six

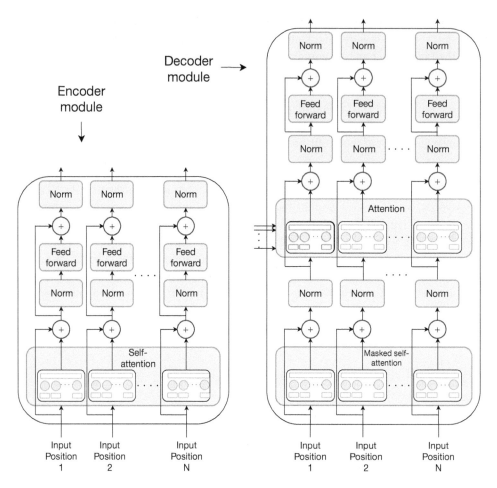

Figure 15-10 Left: Transformer encoder module consisting of multi-head self-attention, normalization, feedforward, and skip connections. The feedforward module consists of two layers. Right: Transformer decoder module. Similar to the encoder module but extended with a multi-head attention (not self-attention) in addition to the multi-head self-attention layer. The overall Transformer architecture consists of multiple encoder and decoder modules.

instances of a module, but this decoder module is slightly more complex than the encoder module. In particular, the multi-head self-attention mechanism includes a masking mechanism that prevents it from attending to future words, as they have not yet been generated. In addition, the decoder module contains another attention layer, which attends to the output from the encoder stack. That is, the decoder employs both self-attention and traditional attention to the intermediate state generated by the encoder. However, as opposed to our examples earlier in this chapter, in addition to using multi-head attention in the self-attention layers, the Transformer also uses multi-head attention in the attention layer that is applied to the intermediate state from the encoder. The decoder module is illustrated to the right in Figure 15-10.

Now that we have described the encoder module and the decoder module, we are ready to present the complete Transformer architecture. It is shown in Figure 15-11. The figure shows how the decoder attends to intermediate state produced by the encoder.

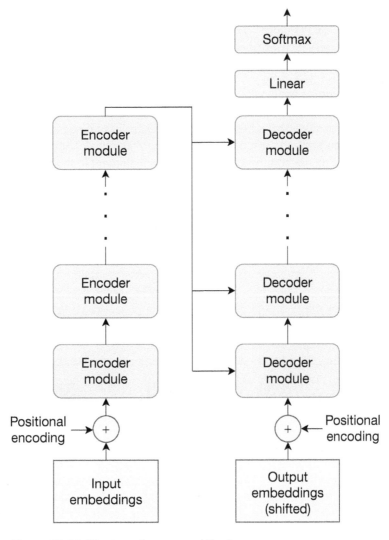

Figure 15-11 The transformer architecture

The figure contains one final detail that we have not yet described. If you consider how the overall Transformer architecture is laid out, it has no good way of taking word order into account. The words are not presented sequentially, as in a recurrent network, and the subnetworks that process each individual word all share weights. To address this issue, the Transformer architecture adds something called a *positional encoding* to each input embedding vector. The positional encoding is a vector with the same number of elements as the word embedding itself. This positional encoding vector is added (elementwise) to the word embedding, and the network can make use of it to infer the spatial relationship between words in the input sentence. This is illustrated in Figure 15-12, which shows an input sentence consisting of *n* words, where each word is represented by a word embedding with four elements.

We need to compute one positional encoding vector corresponding to each input word. Clearly, the elements in the positional encoding vector should be influenced by the word's position in the sentence. It also turns out to be beneficial if all elements in the positional encoding vector are not identical. That is, for a specific input word, we do not add the same value to each element in the word vector, but the value depends on the index in the word vector. The figure illustrates this by using different colors for the four elements in the positional encoding vector.

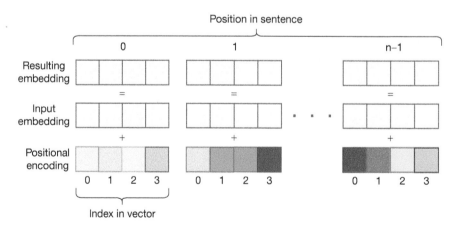

Figure 15-12 Positional encodings are added to input embeddings to indicate word order. The figure assumes word embeddings with four elements. The sentence consists of *n* words. A positional encoding vector is added to the input embedding for each word to compute the resulting embedding that is fed to the network.

If the index i of the element in the vector is even, the value of the element in the positional encoding vector is[1]

$$\sin\left(\frac{pos}{10000^{i/d}}\right)$$

where pos is the position of the word in the sentence, i is the index of the element in the vector, and d is the number of elements in the word embedding. If the index i of the element in the vector is odd, the value of the element is

$$\cos\left(\frac{pos}{10000^{(i-1)/d}}\right)$$

From the formulas, we can see that for a given index i, the arguments to sin and cos are monotonically increasing from zero and upward as we move to later words in the sentence. It may not seem obvious why these positional encodings are the right ones to use. As with many other mechanisms, this is just one of many options. Architectures in Appendix D use another option, namely, to learn positional encodings during training.

Concluding Remarks on the Transformer

When the Transformer model was introduced, it produced better English-to-German and English-to-French translations than any previous models. Note that a Transformer-based translation network is still an example of an encoder-decoder architecture, just like the LSTM-based network in Chapter 14. However, the parallel nature of the encoder and decoder addresses the serialization problem presented by LSTM-based architectures.

The Transformer is useful not only for language translation tasks but also for NLP in general. As an example, in the programming example in Chapter 12, "Neural Language Models and Word Embeddings," we implemented an LSTM-based language model. In contrast, the more recently published language models are based on components from the Transformer architecture. As we pointed out in Chapter 14, the decoder part of a translation network is basically a language model, which is initialized with the internal state of the encoder. A modified

---

1. If you read the original paper (Vaswani et al., 2017), you will find that the equations are stated somewhat differently using $2i$ rather than i. This is not a typo. It results from the paper not using i to represent the index in the vector. Instead, it denotes the index by $2i$ for even indices and $2i+1$ for odd indices.

version of the Transformer decoder is used to implement the popular language model GPT, which is described in Appendix D. Another example, also described in Appendix D, is BERT, which is based on the encoder component from the Transformer architecture.

Earlier in this chapter, we stated that the Transformer uses neither recurrent layers nor convolutional layers. However, we also noted that the decoder component of the network is an autoregressive model and thereby does employ a feedback mechanism similar to recurrence. To be fair, this is more related to how the model is used and is not inherent in the model architecture. In fact, the BERT model is based solely on the Transformer encoder and is thereby completely free from such feedback connections. On the topic of convolutional layers, we note that although the Transformer does not explicitly use convolutions, it does make use of weight sharing similar to what convolutions do. Cordonnier, Loukas, and Jaggi (2020) studied how self-attention and convolutional layers relate to each other and showed that attention layers often learn to perform convolutions in practice. However, a key difference between self-attention and convolution is that the self-attention layer can attend to any position in the input, whereas convolutions can attend only to neighboring positions covered by the convolutional kernel.

To learn more about the Transformer, apart from reading the original paper, we recommend Alammar's blog post about the Transformer (Alammar, 2018b). It also contains links to publicly available source code so you can get started with using the model. If you want to learn about more use cases of the Transformer architecture, consider reading about GPT, BERT, and RoBERTa in Appendix D now. Another option is to continue to Chapter 16, "One-to-Many Network for Image Captioning," which describes how to build an attention-based model for image captioning.

Chapter 16

One-to-Many Network for Image Captioning

We have now spent a number of chapters on working with textual data. Before that, we looked at how convolutional networks can be applied to image data. In this chapter, we describe how to combine a convolutional network and a recurrent network to build a network that performs image captioning. That is, given an image as input, the network generates a textual description of the image. We then describe how to extend the network with attention. We conclude the chapter with a programming example that implements such an attention-based image-captioning network.

Given that this programming example is the most extensive example in the book and we describe it after we described the Transformer, it might seem like this image-captioning architecture is the most recent and advanced of the architectures described in this book. That is not the case. The basic form of this image-captioning architecture was published in 2014 and thereby preceded the Transformer architecture by three years. However, we find it a neat way of bringing together most of the concepts we have discussed in the previous chapters. The basic process of image captioning is illustrated in Figure 16-1.

One use case for image captioning is to enable textual search on images without the need for a human to first annotate the images with a textual description. At first it might seem unclear how to create such a model, but given our background in neural machine translation, it turns out to be simple. Generating a textual description of an image can be viewed as a translation from one language to another, where the source language is visual instead of textual. Figure 16-2 shows conceptually how this can be done using an encoder-decoder architecture. A number of papers (Karpathy and Li, 2014; Mao et al., 2014; Vinyals et al., 2014) independently proposed such architectures in the same timeframe as, or shortly after, the sequence-to-sequence models for language translation were published. We start with an encoder consisting of a convolutional network that creates a language-independent intermediate representation of what is in the image.

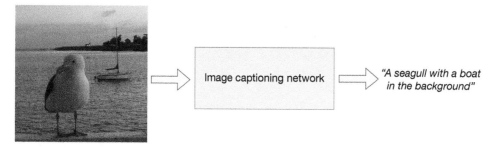

Figure 16-1 The image-captioning problem

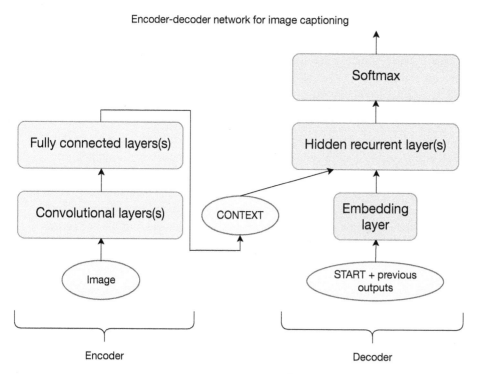

Figure 16-2 Architecture for image captioning network

This is followed by a decoder consisting of a recurrent network, which converts this intermediate representation into text. This is an example of a one-to-many network where the input is a single item (an image) and the output consists of multiple items (a sequence of words).

Image captioning can be done with an encoder-decoder network that "translates" from a visual representation of a scene to a textual description. The source language is visual.

As described in Chapter 7, "Convolutional Neural Networks Applied to Image Classification," a convolutional network often ends with one or more fully connected layers that somehow summarize the feature maps from the last convolutional layer into a 1D vector before the final softmax layer that classifies the image as containing a specific object. For Visual Geometry Group's VGG19, this 1D vector (the input to the softmax layer) consists of 4,096 elements, as can be seen at the top[1] of Figure 16-3, which depicts a simplified view of the VGG19

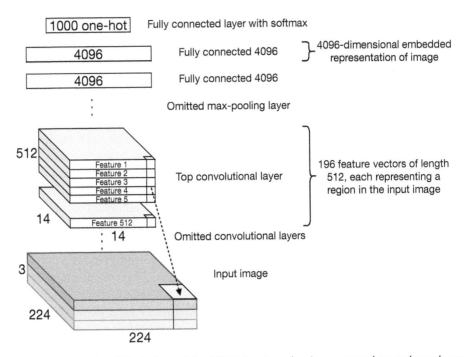

Figure 16-3 Simplified view of the VGG19 network where many layers have been omitted

---

1. The other details of the figure are discussed in a later paragraph, so you can ignore that for now.

network. One way to interpret this vector is as an *image embedding,* where the image is embedded in a 4,096-dimensional space. We could envision that two images that represent similar scenes end up being embedded close to each other in vector space. This is analogous to the example in the Chapter 14, which showed how similar phrases ended up embedded close to each other in vector space in a neural machine translation application.

We can now simply use this vector as our context and directly use it as an input to our recurrent neural network (RNN)-based decoder network. Another option would be to use this vector as the initial hidden state for our RNN-based decoder network. At a first glance, it seems like we impose an unnecessary restriction that the number of units in the RNN (or, more likely, LSTM) layer needs to match the dimension of the layer from the convolutional network. In the case of VGG19, this would imply that the recurrent layer must have 4,096 units. This restriction can easily be addressed by introducing yet another fully connected layer on top of the 4,096-unit layer. This added layer will have the same number of units as the number of state values required by the RNN layer.

Extending the Image Captioning Network with Attention

Just as we can apply attention to a sequence-to-sequence (text-to-text) network, we can apply attention to this image-to-text network. However, applying it to the just described network might not make much sense. In the language translation example, the context was an internal representation of a sequence of words, and applying attention implied that the network focused on different parts of the sentence at different timesteps. In our image-captioning network, the fully connected layer at the top of the network has already squashed the different features into a single representation. Thus, different parts of our 4,096-element vector do not have a direct correspondence to different regions of the image. Each element in the vector contains information about all pixels in the input image. A more sensible way of applying attention in our image-captioning network would be to apply it to the top convolutional layer. As you might remember, the output of a convolutional layer in this type of network is a 3D structure in which two of the dimensions correspond to the two dimensions in the picture and the third dimension (the channels) represent feature maps for different types of features. This is also illustrated in Figure 16-3, where we see that for the VGG19 architecture, the output of the top convolutional layer is of the dimensions 14×14×512. In other words, it consists of 196 vectors, each containing 512 elements. Each of these 196 vectors corresponds to a specific region in the input image, and the 512 elements in the vector represent 512 different types of features that the network might have identified in that region. Using these 196 vectors as our context makes much more sense when we want to apply attention, because the attention mechanism can now attend to different regions of the input image by adjusting the weights for the corresponding vectors.

A noteworthy use case for attention apart from trying to improve the behavior of encoder-decoder models is to use it to gain insight into what the model is doing, and perhaps most important, get a better understanding of what is happening when it is making mistakes. For each generated output word, we can analyze the alignment vector and see where in the input data the model is currently focused, such as what part of an image resulted in the word. An entertaining example can be found in a paper by Xu, Ba, and colleagues (2015), where an image of a man and a woman results in the textual description "A man is talking on his cell phone while another man watches." The alignment vector clearly shows that when the model outputs the words *cell phone,* the focus is on a sandwich from which the man takes a bite, and when the model outputs the word *watches*, the focus is on the woman's wristwatch!

> Attention can be used to gain a better understanding of the internal workings of the model.

Programming Example: Attention-Based Image Captioning

We now show how you can build your own image-captioning network with attention. This example is inspired by the architecture described by Xu, Ba, and colleagues (2015), but we have done some simplifications to keep the code size small and simple.[2] Conceptually it is similar to the network shown in Figure 16-2,

---

2. The claim that this code example is simple should be considered in the context of the complex task it solves. If you do not have extensive programming experience, this example can be overwhelming.

but the decoder uses attention when examining the context. The decoder is based on a recurrent network. A more modern implementation can be obtained by instead using a Transformer-based decoder.

For this application, we need a dataset that consists of images annotated with corresponding textual descriptions. We use the publicly available COCO dataset (Lin et al., 2015). The COCO dataset consists of 82,783 training images and 40,775 test images. Each image has a number of associated image descriptions. To keep things simple, we use only the training dataset and the first description of each image. Just as for the translation example in Chapter 14, we do not worry about BLEU scores when evaluating how our network performs but just inspect the output of the network on a small set of test images. We provide our own test images, and thus they are completely independent of the COCO dataset. In addition, note that the COCO dataset contains more information than what is needed for image captioning, but we simply ignore those parts of the dataset.

Instead of training our network end to end, we make use of transfer learning for the convolutional part of the network. We do this by using a model implementing the VGG19 architecture, which has been pretrained on the ImageNet dataset. As described previously, we remove the fully connected layers from the top of the network and use the output from the topmost convolutional layer to generate the context, to which the attention mechanism will be applied. Given that we do not have the need to adjust the weights for the VGG19 network (we assume that the pretraining on ImageNet is good enough), we can employ an optimization. Instead of running the training image through the VGG19 network for each training example for each training epoch, we can run each image through the VGG19 network once and for all before training begins and save the vectors that are output of the topmost convolutional layer to disk. That is, during training, the encoder model is computationally simple, because there is no need to run the image through all the convolutional layers, but it simply reads the feature vectors from disk. With that background, we start by presenting the code to do the image preprocessing. The import statements can be found in Code Snippet 16-1.

Code Snippet 16-1 Import Statements for Image Preprocessing Code

```
import json
import numpy as np
import tensorflow as tf
from tensorflow import keras
from tensorflow.keras.models import Model
```

```
from tensorflow.keras.applications import VGG19
from tensorflow.keras.applications.vgg19 import \
    preprocess_input
from tensorflow.keras.preprocessing.image import load_img
from tensorflow.keras.preprocessing.image import img_to_array
import pickle
import gzip
import logging
tf.get_logger().setLevel(logging.ERROR)


TRAINING_FILE_DIR = '../data/coco/'
OUTPUT_FILE_DIR = 'tf_data/feature_vectors/'
```

The parts of the dataset that we will use are contained in two resources. The first resource is a json file that contains captions as well as filenames and some other information for the images. We make the assumption that you have placed that file in the directory pointed to by the variable TRAINING_FILE_DIR. The images themselves are stored as individual image files and are assumed to be located in a directory named train2014 in the directory pointed to by TRAINING_FILE_DIR. The COCO dataset contains elaborate tools to parse and read the rich information about the various images, but because we are only interested in the image captions, we choose to directly access the json file and extract the limited data that we need ourselves. Code Snippet 16-2 opens the json file and creates a dictionary that, for each image, maps a unique key to a list of strings. The first string in each list represents the image filename, and the subsequent strings are alternative captions for the image.

Code Snippet 16-2 Open and Extract Information from the json File

```
with open(TRAINING_FILE_DIR \
          + 'captions_train2014.json') as json_file:
    data = json.load(json_file)
image_dict = {}
for image in data['images']:
    image_dict[image['id']] = [image['file_name']]
for anno in data['annotations']:
    image_dict[anno['image_id']].append(anno['caption'])
```

We encourage you to paste some of the lines from the snippet into a Python interpreter and inspect the data structures to be comfortable with what the code snippet is doing.

The next step is to create our pretrained VGG19 model, which is done in Code Snippet 16-3. We first obtain the full VGG19 model with weights trained from the ImageNet dataset. We then create a new model (model_new) from that model by stating that we want to use the layer named block5_conv4 as output. A fair question is how we figured out that name. As you can see in the code snippet, we first printed out the summary of the full VGG19 model. This summary includes the layer names, and we saw that the last convolutional layer was named block5_conv4.

Code Snippet 16-3 **Create a VGG19 Model and Remove the Topmost Layers**

```
# Create network without top layers.
model = VGG19(weights='imagenet')
model.summary()
model_new = Model(inputs=model.input,
                  outputs=model.get_layer('block5_conv4').output)
model_new.summary()
```

We are now ready to run all the images through the network and extract the feature vectors and save to disk. This is done by Code Snippet 16-4. We traverse the dictionary to obtain the image file names. Every loop iteration does the processing for a single image and saves the feature vectors for that one image in a single file. Before running the image through the network, we perform some preprocessing. The image sizes in the COCO dataset vary from image to image, so we first read the file to determine its file size. We determine the aspect ratio and then reread the image scaled to a size at which the shortest side ends up being 256 pixels. We then crop the center 224×224 region of the resulting image to end up with the input dimensions that our VGG19 network expects. We finally run the VGG19 preprocessing function, which standardizes the data values in the image before we run the image through the network. The output of the network will be an array with the shape (1, 14, 14, 512) representing the results from a batch of images where the first dimension indicates that the batch size is 1. Therefore, we extract the first (and only) element from this array (y[0]) and save it as a gzipped pickle file with the same name as the image but with the extension .pickle.gz in the directory feature_vectors. When we have looped through all images, we also save the dictionary file as `caption_file.pickle.gz` so we do not need to parse the `json` file again later in the code that does the actual training.

Code Snippet 16-4 **Extract and Save Feature Vectors and the Dictionary with Filenames and Annotations**

```python
# Run all images through the network and save the output.
for i, key in enumerate(image_dict.keys()):
    if i % 1000 == 0:
        print('Progress: ' + str(i) + ' images processed')
    item = image_dict.get(key)
    filename = TRAINING_FILE_DIR + 'train2014/' + item[0]

    # Determine dimensions.
    image = load_img(filename)
    width = image.size[0]
    height = image.size[1]

    # Resize so shortest side is 256 pixels.
    if height > width:
        image = load_img(filename, target_size=(
            int(height/width*256), 256))
    else:
        image = load_img(filename, target_size=(
            256, int(width/height*256)))
    width = image.size[0]
    height = image.size[1]
    image_np = img_to_array(image)

    # Crop to center 224x224 region.
    h_start = int((height-224)/2)
    w_start = int((width-224)/2)
    image_np = image_np[h_start:h_start+224,
                        w_start:w_start+224]

    # Rearrange array to have one more
    # dimension representing batch size = 1.
    image_np = np.expand_dims(image_np, axis=0)
```

```
# Call model and save resulting tensor to disk.
X = preprocess_input(image_np)
y = model_new.predict(X)
save_filename = OUTPUT_FILE_DIR + \
    item[0] + '.pickle.gzip'
pickle_file = gzip.open(save_filename, 'wb')
pickle.dump(y[0], pickle_file)
pickle_file.close()


# Save the dictionary containing captions and filenames.
save_filename = OUTPUT_FILE_DIR + 'caption_file.pickle.gz'
pickle_file = gzip.open(save_filename, 'wb')
pickle.dump(image_dict, pickle_file)
pickle_file.close()
```

We are now ready to describe the actual image-captioning model. The import statements are found in Code Snippet 16-5. It contains a few new layer types that we have not used before.

Code Snippet 16-5 Import Statements for the Image Captioning Model

```
import numpy as np
import tensorflow as tf
from tensorflow import keras
from tensorflow.keras.layers import Input
from tensorflow.keras.layers import Embedding
from tensorflow.keras.layers import LSTM
from tensorflow.keras.layers import Dense
from tensorflow.keras.layers import Attention
from tensorflow.keras.layers import Concatenate
from tensorflow.keras.layers import GlobalAveragePooling2D
from tensorflow.keras.layers import Reshape
from tensorflow.keras.models import Model
from tensorflow.keras.optimizers import Adam
from tensorflow.keras.preprocessing.text import Tokenizer
from tensorflow.keras.preprocessing.text import \
    text_to_word_sequence
```

```
from tensorflow.keras.applications import VGG19
from tensorflow.keras.applications.vgg19 import \
    preprocess_input
from tensorflow.keras.preprocessing.image import load_img
from tensorflow.keras.preprocessing.image import img_to_array
from tensorflow.keras.utils import Sequence
from tensorflow.keras.preprocessing.sequence import \
    pad_sequences
import pickle
import gzip
import logging
tf.get_logger().setLevel(logging.ERROR)
```

Initialization statements for our program are found in Code Snippet 16-6. They are similar to what we used in the language translation example, but some of the lines deserve further attention. The variable READ_IMAGES can be used to limit the number of images that we use for training. We set it to 90,000, which is more than the total number of images we have. You can decrease it if necessary (e.g., if you run into memory limits of your machine). We also provide the paths to four files that we will use as test images. You can replace those to point to images of your own choice when you run this experiment.

Code Snippet 16-6 Initialization Statements

```
EPOCHS = 20
BATCH_SIZE = 128
MAX_WORDS = 10000
READ_IMAGES = 90000
LAYER_SIZE = 256
EMBEDDING_WIDTH = 128
OOV_WORD = 'UNK'
PAD_INDEX = 0
OOV_INDEX = 1
START_INDEX = MAX_WORDS - 2
STOP_INDEX = MAX_WORDS - 1
MAX_LENGTH = 60
TRAINING_FILE_DIR = 'tf_data/feature_vectors/'
```

```
TEST_FILE_DIR = '../data/test_images/'
TEST_IMAGES = ['boat.jpg',
               'cat.jpg',
               'table.jpg',
               'bird.jpg']
```

Code Snippet 16-7 shows the functions we use to read the image captions. The function to read the captions reads the pickled directory file that we previously prepared. From this, we create a list image_paths with the filenames for the feature vectors and one list, dest_word_sequences, which contains the first image caption for each image. To keep things simple, we simply discard the alternative captions for each image.

Code Snippet 16-7 Functions to Read the Directory with Image Captions

```
# Function to read file.
def read_training_file(file_name, max_len):
    pickle_file = gzip.open(file_name, 'rb')
    image_dict = pickle.load(pickle_file)
    pickle_file.close()
    image_paths = []
    dest_word_sequences = []
    for i, key in enumerate(image_dict):
        if i == READ_IMAGES:
            break
        image_item = image_dict[key]
        image_paths.append(image_item[0])
        caption = image_item[1]
        word_sequence = text_to_word_sequence(caption)
        dest_word_sequence = word_sequence[0:max_len]
        dest_word_sequences.append(dest_word_sequence)
    return image_paths, dest_word_sequences
```

The list dest_word_sequences is equivalent to the destination language sentence in the language translation example. This function does not load all the feature vectors but just the paths to them. The reason for this is that the feature vectors for all the images consume a fair amount of space, so for many machines, it would be impractical to hold the entire dataset in memory during training.

Instead, we read the feature vectors on the fly when they are needed. This is a common technique when working with large datasets.

Code Snippet 16-8 contains functions to tokenize and untokenize the sentences. These are similar, if not identical, to what we used in the language translation example. We finally call the functions to read and tokenize the image captions.

Code Snippet 16-8 Call the Function That Reads the File and Functions to Tokenize the Sentences

```python
# Functions to tokenize and un-tokenize sequences.
def tokenize(sequences):
    tokenizer = Tokenizer(num_words=MAX_WORDS-2,
                          oov_token=OOV_WORD)
    tokenizer.fit_on_texts(sequences)
    token_sequences = tokenizer.texts_to_sequences(sequences)
    return tokenizer, token_sequences

def tokens_to_words(tokenizer, seq):
    word_seq = []
    for index in seq:
        if index == PAD_INDEX:
            word_seq.append('PAD')
        elif index == OOV_INDEX:
            word_seq.append(OOV_WORD)
        elif index == START_INDEX:
            word_seq.append('START')
        elif index == STOP_INDEX:
            word_seq.append('STOP')
        else:
            word_seq.append(tokenizer.sequences_to_texts(
                [[index]])[0])
    print(word_seq)

# Read files.
image_paths, dest_seq = read_training_file(TRAINING_FILE_DIR \
    + 'caption_file.pickle.gz', MAX_LENGTH)
dest_tokenizer, dest_token_seq = tokenize(dest_seq)
```

As previously mentioned, we cannot afford to keep the entire dataset in memory during training but need to create our training batches on the fly. We handle this task by creating a class that inherits from the Keras Sequence class in Code Snippet 16-9. In the constructor, we supply the paths to the feature vectors, as well as the tokenized captions, and the batch size. Just as for the language translation example, the recurrent network in the decoder will need the tokenized data both as input and output but shifted by one location and with a START token on the input side. This explains why we provide two variables dest_input_data and dest_target_data to the constructor. We also need to provide the batch size.

Code Snippet 16-9 Sequence Class Used to Create Batches on the Fly During Training

```
# Sequence class to create batches on the fly.
class ImageCaptionSequence(Sequence):
    def __init__(self, image_paths, dest_input_data,
                   dest_target_data, batch_size):
        self.image_paths = image_paths
        self.dest_input_data = dest_input_data
        self.dest_target_data = dest_target_data
        self.batch_size = batch_size

    def __len__(self):
        return int(np.ceil(len(self.dest_input_data) /
            float(self.batch_size)))

    def __getitem__(self, idx):
        batch_x0 = self.image_paths[
            idx * self.batch_size:(idx + 1) * self.batch_size]
        batch_x1 = self.dest_input_data[
            idx * self.batch_size:(idx + 1) * self.batch_size]
        batch_y = self.dest_target_data[
            idx * self.batch_size:(idx + 1) * self.batch_size]
        image_features = []
        for image_id in batch_x0:
            file_name = TRAINING_FILE_DIR \
                + image_id + '.pickle.gzip'
            pickle_file = gzip.open(file_name, 'rb')
            feature_vector = pickle.load(pickle_file)
            pickle_file.close()
            image_features.append(feature_vector)
        return [np.array(image_features),
                np.array(batch_x1)], np.array(batch_y)
```

The __len__() method is expected to provide the number of batches that our dataset provides, which is simply the number of images divided by the batch size.

The main functionality in the class is the __getitem__() method, which is expected to return the training data for the batch number indicated by the argument idx. The output format of this method depends on what our network requires as input. For a single training example, our network needs a set of feature vectors as input from the encoder side and a shifted version of the target sentence as input to the decoder recurrent network. It also needs the original version of the target sentence as the desired output for the network. Thus, the output from this method should be a list with two elements representing the two inputs and a single element representing the output. The details become clearer when we later build our training network. There is one more thing to consider, though. The __getitem__() method is expected to return a batch instead of a single training example, so each of the three items we described will be an array where the number of elements is determined by the batch size. Because each one of the input and output elements for a given training example is itself a multidimensional array, it is easy to get lost with all the different dimensions.

One thing worth mentioning is that many implementations use a Python Generator function instead of extending the Keras Sequence class. The benefit of using the Keras Sequence class is that it produces deterministic results in the presence of multithreading.

The constructor for the ImageCaptionSequence class that was described earlier assumes that we already have created three arrays with appropriate input data. Two of these arrays (for the recurrent network in the decoder) directly correspond to what we created in the language translation example. This is shown in Code Snippet 16-10, where we also call the constructor for ImageCaptionSequence.

Code Snippet 16-10 **Preparation of Training Data**

```
# Prepare training data.
dest_target_token_seq = [x + [STOP_INDEX] for x in dest_token_seq]
dest_input_token_seq = [[START_INDEX] + x for x in
                        dest_target_token_seq]
dest_input_data = pad_sequences(dest_input_token_seq,
                                padding='post')
```

```
dest_target_data = pad_sequences(
    dest_target_token_seq, padding='post',
    maxlen=len(dest_input_data[0]))
image_sequence = ImageCaptionSequence(
    image_paths, dest_input_data, dest_target_data, BATCH_SIZE)
```

We are now ready to define the encoder and decoder models and connect them. We start with an overview of the detailed architecture. This time, we start with an overview of the overall encoder-decoder network in Figure 16-4. VGG19 is not a part of the actual encoder model because we already did that processing offline, but we have included it as a dashed box in the lower left corner for completeness. We now walk though this figure with a focus on issues that are different from the language translation example.

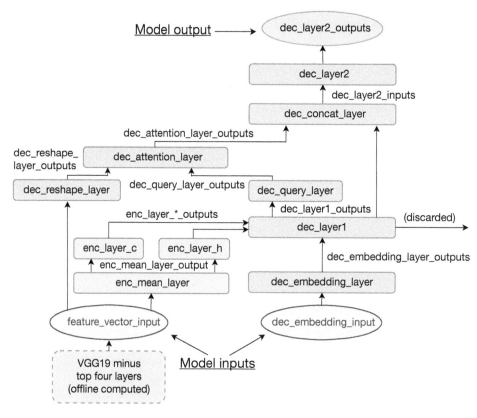

Figure 16-4 Block diagram of our encoder-decoder image-captioning model

The architecture is a typical encoder-decoder architecture, although most of the encoding has already been done offline. There are still some remaining layers in the encoder model. The decoder side consists mainly of an embedding layer, one LSTM layer (dec_layer1), an attention layer, and a fully connected softmax layer (dec_layer2). It also has a couple of other layers that we discuss shortly. We note that the decoder is similar to the decoder in Chapter 15, "Attention and the Transformer," but with a single recurrent layer. The recurrent layer and the attention layer feed straight into the fully connected softmax layer. Our network has a couple of simplifications. There is no feedback loop for the attentional vector. Further, we use the output of the recurrent layer to query the attention layer instead of the cell/hidden state that was used in Figure 15-6. The reason for these two simplifications is mainly to avoid introducing the concept of how to build custom layers in Keras, and we did not manage to come up with an easy way of implementing those two concepts (attentional vector feedback loop and using the cell/hidden state to query the attention layer) without a custom Keras layer.

> If you want to build complicated networks, building custom Keras layers is a good skill to obtain.

Let us now study the encoder side in detail. Given our previous figures of attention, the three blue layers seem somewhat unexpected. Why is it not sufficient to feed the feature vectors to the attention layer and let the model attend to the regions of its choice? We cannot claim that we know the exact answer to that question, but it is not hard to believe that it is beneficial for the network to start with a global view of the image and then selectively use the attention mechanism to study individual details. We provide this global view by using enc_mean_layer to compute the elementwise average of the 196 (14×14) feature vectors to end up with a single 512-element feature vector that represents the global view. We then feed that as initial state to our LSTM layer.

Given the parameters of our network, we could have taken the output from enc_mean_layer and directly fed it to the LSTM layer (mean_layer outputs 512 values, and we have 256 LSTM cells each requiring h and c), but to make our network more flexible, we added two fully connected layers (enc_layer_c and enc_layer_h) between the mean_layer and the LSTM state inputs. We can now freely modify the number of LSTM cells, as long as we adjust the number of units in these two fully connected layers. A fair question is why to introduce the concept of averaging feature vectors instead of just keeping some more of the top layers of the VGG19 network. Could we not have used the output of the upper layers as state input and still use the output of the convolutional layer as attention input? The answer is that this would likely be a fine approach, but we simply followed what was done by Xu, Ba, and colleagues (2015).

The decoder side is straightforward. The dec_query_layer is a fully connected layer that serves a purpose similar to that of the two fully connected layers on the encoder side. The query input on the attention layer is expected to be of the same dimension (512) as each of the feature vectors. By introducing the dec_query_layer, we can now choose the number of LSTM units in dec_layer1 independently from the feature vector size. The reason we feed the dec_query_layer from the output of dec_layer1 instead of from its state outputs is that the attention layer requires an input for every timestep, and the Keras LSTM layer only outputs the final state outputs, while its normal output can be told to provide a value for every timestep using the return_sequences=True parameter.

Two other things worth mentioning are the dec_reshape_layer and the dec_concat_layer. These layers do not do any computations. The Reshape layer reshapes the feature vectors from 14×14 to 196. The concat layer simply concatenates the outputs from dec_layer1 and dec_attention_layer into a single vector that can be used as input to the final layer.

Figure 16-5 shows the individual encoder and decoder models that are used as building blocks for the joint model. The TensorFlow implementation of the encoder is found in Code Snippet 16-11. Most things in this code snippet should be self-explanatory by now. The enc_mean_layer is implemented by a GlobalAveragePooling2D layer. It operates on the output of a convolutional layer, which has the dimensions width, height, and channels. The layer computes the average of all elements within a channel, which results in a vector with the same number of elements as there are channels in the input. We call the model enc_model_top because it represents only the top layers of the encoder where the bottom ones were precomputed by the VGG model.

Code Snippet 16-12 shows the implementation of the decoder model. We focus on the details that are different compared to the text translation example. Given how much time we have spent on discussing the internals of the Attention layer, it is a surprising how little code is needed. We simply instantiate it without any arguments, and it takes two inputs and produces a single output. We use a Reshape layer to change the dimensions of the feature vectors from 14×14 to 196.

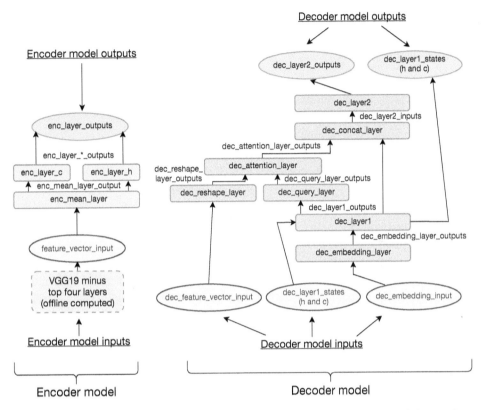

Figure 16-5 **Block diagrams of the individual encoder and decoder models used as building blocks**

Code Snippet 16-11 **Implementation of Encoder Model**

```
# Build encoder model.
# Input is feature vector.
feature_vector_input = Input(shape=(14, 14, 512))

# Create the encoder layers.
enc_mean_layer = GlobalAveragePooling2D()
enc_layer_h = Dense(LAYER_SIZE)
enc_layer_c = Dense(LAYER_SIZE)

# Connect the encoding layers.
enc_mean_layer_output = enc_mean_layer(feature_vector_input)
```

```
enc_layer_h_outputs = enc_layer_h(enc_mean_layer_output)
enc_layer_c_outputs = enc_layer_c(enc_mean_layer_output)

# Organize the output state for encoder layers.
enc_layer_outputs = [enc_layer_h_outputs, enc_layer_c_outputs]

# Build the model.
enc_model_top = Model(feature_vector_input, enc_layer_outputs)
enc_model_top.summary()
```

One thing to note is that we give the argument mask_zero=False to the
Embedding layer. The reason is that, to use the masking feature, all layers
downstream of the Embedding layer need to support that feature, and the
Attention layer does not, so we simply have no choice but to turn off masking.
The effect is that the network must learn to ignore the PAD value itself, but as
previously discussed, this usually works fine.

Finally, the Concatenate layer is also simple to use and requires no arguments
to instantiate; it simply takes two inputs that are concatenated into an output
array where the width is the sum of the widths of the input arrays.

Code Snippet 16-12 Implementation of Decoder Model

```
# Build decoder model.
# Input to the network is feature_vector, image caption
# sequence, and intermediate state.
dec_feature_vector_input = Input(shape=(14, 14, 512))
dec_embedding_input = Input(shape=(None, ))
dec_layer1_state_input_h = Input(shape=(LAYER_SIZE,))
dec_layer1_state_input_c = Input(shape=(LAYER_SIZE,))

# Create the decoder layers.
dec_reshape_layer = Reshape((196, 512),
                                input_shape=(14, 14, 512,))
dec_attention_layer = Attention()
dec_query_layer = Dense(512)
```

```
dec_embedding_layer = Embedding(output_dim=EMBEDDING_WIDTH,
                                input_dim=MAX_WORDS,
                                mask_zero=False)
dec_layer1 = LSTM(LAYER_SIZE, return_state=True,
                  return_sequences=True)
dec_concat_layer = Concatenate()
dec_layer2 = Dense(MAX_WORDS, activation='softmax')

# Connect the decoder layers.
dec_embedding_layer_outputs = dec_embedding_layer(
    dec_embedding_input)
dec_reshape_layer_outputs = dec_reshape_layer(
    dec_feature_vector_input)
dec_layer1_outputs, dec_layer1_state_h, dec_layer1_state_c = \
    dec_layer1(dec_embedding_layer_outputs, initial_state=[
        dec_layer1_state_input_h, dec_layer1_state_input_c])
dec_query_layer_outputs = dec_query_layer(dec_layer1_outputs)
dec_attention_layer_outputs = dec_attention_layer(
    [dec_query_layer_outputs, dec_reshape_layer_outputs])
dec_layer2_inputs = dec_concat_layer(
    [dec_layer1_outputs, dec_attention_layer_outputs])
dec_layer2_outputs = dec_layer2(dec_layer2_inputs)

# Build the model.
dec_model = Model([dec_feature_vector_input,
                   dec_embedding_input,
                   dec_layer1_state_input_h,
                   dec_layer1_state_input_c],
                  [dec_layer2_outputs, dec_layer1_state_h,
                   dec_layer1_state_c])
dec_model.summary()
```

Finally, we create a joint model from the encoder and decoder in Code Snippet 16-13. This model will be used for training. Just as in the text translation example, we discard the state outputs from the decoder in this joint model. There is no need for explicit state management for this joint model because TensorFlow does it for us during training.

Code Snippet 16-13 Implement the Full Encoder-Decoder Training Model

```
# Build and compile full training model.
# We do not use the state output when training.
train_feature_vector_input = Input(shape=(14, 14, 512))
train_dec_embedding_input = Input(shape=(None, ))
intermediate_state = enc_model_top(train_feature_vector_input)
train_dec_output, _, _ = dec_model([train_feature_vector_input,
                                    train_dec_embedding_input] +
                                    intermediate_state)
training_model = Model([train_feature_vector_input,
                        train_dec_embedding_input],
                       [train_dec_output])
training_model.compile(loss='sparse_categorical_crossentropy',
                       optimizer='adam', metrics =['accuracy'])
training_model.summary()
```

Just as for the language translation example, we use the encoder and decoder separately during inference. However, in this image-captioning example, the encoder also needs to include the VGG19 layers, as we will not do inference on precomputed feature vectors. We therefore create yet another model in Code Snippet 16-14, which consists of the VGG19 network (except for the top layers) followed by our decoder model.

Code Snippet 16-14 Encoder Used for Inference Representing the Full Encoder Model That Can Take Images as Inputs

```
# Build full encoder model for inference.
conv_model = VGG19(weights='imagenet')
conv_model_outputs = conv_model.get_layer('block5_conv4').output
intermediate_state = enc_model_top(conv_model_outputs)
inference_enc_model = Model([conv_model.input],
                           intermediate_state
                           + [conv_model_outputs])
inference_enc_model.summary()
```

We are finally ready to train and evaluate our model, and the code is found in Code Snippet 16-15. One key difference compared to past code examples is that instead of providing the training set, we provide the image_sequence object as argument to the fit() function. The image_sequence object will provide the training data batch by batch as the feature vectors are read from disk.

After each training epoch, we run through our four test images. The process for this is similar to what we did in the language translation example but with one difference. Instead of running an input sentence through the encoder model that was based on a recurrent network, we read an image from disk, preprocess it, and run it through our encoder model that is based on the convolutional VGG19 network.

Code Snippet 16-15 Code to Train and Evaluate the Image-Captioning Model

```
for i in range(EPOCHS): # Train and evaluate model
    print('step: ' , i)
    history = training_model.fit(image_sequence, epochs=1)
    for filename in TEST_IMAGES:
        # Determine dimensions.
        image = load_img(TEST_FILE_DIR + filename)
        width = image.size[0]
        height = image.size[1]

        # Resize so shortest side is 256 pixels.
        if height > width:
            image = load_img(
                TEST_FILE_DIR + filename,
                target_size=(int(height/width*256), 256))
        else:
            image = load_img(
                TEST_FILE_DIR + filename,
                target_size=(256, int(width/height*256)))
        width = image.size[0]
        height = image.size[1]
        image_np = img_to_array(image)

        # Crop to center 224x224 region.
        h_start = int((height-224)/2)
```

```
        w_start = int((width-224)/2)
        image_np = image_np[h_start:h_start+224,
                            w_start:w_start+224]

        # Run image through encoder.
        image_np = np.expand_dims(image_np, axis=0)
        x = preprocess_input(image_np)
        dec_layer1_state_h, dec_layer1_state_c, feature_vector = \
            inference_enc_model.predict(x, verbose=0)

        # Predict sentence word for word.
        prev_word_index = START_INDEX
        produced_string = ''
        pred_seq = []
        for j in range(MAX_LENGTH):
            x = np.reshape(np.array(prev_word_index), (1, 1))
            preds, dec_layer1_state_h, dec_layer1_state_c = \
                dec_model.predict(
                    [feature_vector, x, dec_layer1_state_h,
                     dec_layer1_state_c], verbose=0)
            prev_word_index = np.asarray(preds[0][0]).argmax()
            pred_seq.append(prev_word_index)
            if prev_word_index == STOP_INDEX:
                break
        tokens_to_words(dest_tokenizer, pred_seq)
        print('\n\n')
```

Figure 16-6 shows the four images that we used to evaluate our image-captioning network. These images have nothing to do with the COCO dataset but are simply images that we provided. As shown in the code snippets, we printed out the predictions after each training epoch, and we now list some of the more noteworthy descriptions that the network produced.

The yacht picture resulted in two descriptions that caught our eyes. The descriptions make sense, although the wording of the first sentence sounds more

Figure 16-6 Four images used to evaluate our image-captioning network. Top left: A yacht docked in front of a couple of buildings in Split, Croatia. Top right: A cat on a desk in front of a keyboard and a computer monitor. Bottom left: A table with plates, utensils, bottles, and two bowls with crayfish. Bottom right: A seagull in front of an anchored sailboat in Santa Cruz, California, USA.

like what a landlubber would say than what you would typically hear from a true boatman:

A large white ship is parked in the water.

A large white ship floating on top of a lake.

For the cat picture, the following two descriptions also make much sense, although the network mistook the keyboard and computer screen for a laptop in the second description:

A cat is laying on top of a wooden desk.

A cat rests its head on a laptop.

The network did not manage to identify the crayfish on the table but provided two decent descriptions of the picture:

A table topped with breakfast items and a cup of coffee.

A view of a table with a knife and coffee.

Finally, the picture of the seagull resulted in the following captions:

A large white bird is standing in the water.

A large white bird sitting on top of a sandy beach.

We selected these examples because they worked out well. The network also produced many nonsensical results:

A large cruise ship floating on top of a cruise ship.

A cat is sitting on a couch.

A group of friends sitting on a table with a knife.

A white and white and white sea water with a few water.

As an experiment, we also modified our network to output the attention score for each region of the image. Figure 16-7 highlights the nine regions with the highest attention scores for two of the images.

We can see that the attention mechanism fully focuses on the yacht in one of the images, whereas in the image of the table, it focuses on one of the crayfish bowls, two of the plates, one of the bottles, and one of the forks. Our network did not reproduce the effect observed by Xu, Ba, and colleagues (2015), where the attended region clearly moved from one region to another for each word. Instead,

Figure 16-7 Two of the test images with the attended regions highlighted

in our experiments, the attended region turned out to be more static, although it did move a bit as the output sentences were produced. We hypothesize that the reason is that our network is fairly simple and does not have a feedback loop in which the output from the attention mechanism affects the input to the attention mechanism in the next timestep. As previously described, the network design in our programming example was chosen to be as simple as possible while still illustrating the use of attention. See the paper by Xu, Ba, and colleagues for a more complex network and a more rigorous evaluation.

Concluding Remarks on Image Captioning

In this chapter, we used the COCO dataset (Lin et al., 2015) and an image-captioning application to illustrate the usage of the attention mechanism. If you are interested in experimenting further with image captioning, you can also consider trying out the smaller and simpler Flickr8k dataset (Hodosh, Young, and Hockenmaier, 2013) or the newer and more extensive Conceptual Captions dataset (Sharma et al., 2018). In terms of the image-captioning application, there are many things that can be improved over our implementation. One thing would be to use a more modern and complicated convolutional network than VGG19 or a decoder based on more layers or on the Transformer architecture. Another option is to not precompute the feature vectors and instead train the model end to end. As described in Chapter 8, "Deeper CNNs and Pretrained Models," the best approach is to first freeze the pretrained layers and do initial training of the newly added layers. Once that is done, you can unfreeze the layers and fine-tune the model end to end. Some of these techniques were used in the paper introducing the Conceptual Captions dataset, and it is worth noting that their evaluation indicated that their networks without attention over the image regions worked better than the ones that did use attention (Sharma et al., 2018). On the other hand, they also concluded that a decoder based on the Transformer (which itself uses self-attention) performed better than a model based on LSTM.

A different method to image captioning is described by Dai, Fidler, and Lin (2018). They use a compositional approach that aims at decoupling the process of determining *what to say* from *how to say it*. That is, although the basic techniques of neural image captioning were published relatively soon after the AlexNet paper (Krizhevsky, Sutskever, and Hinton, 2012), new ideas are still being explored. It should not be considered a fully solved problem.

Before moving on to Chapter 17, "Medley of Additional Topics," we take a step back and reflect on this programming example, which is the most complex programming example in this book. We note that it incorporates most of the concepts discussed so far. It contains fully connected, convolutional, and recurrent layers (using LSTM cells). It learns word embeddings and uses the attention mechanism. It demonstrates the power of transfer learning. It is an example of an encoder-decoder architecture, and it combines both image data (as input) and textual data (as output).

Just for fun, we also make a brief comparison between the complexity of our image-captioning network and some biological organisms. Our image-captioning network contains roughly 15 million units and 30 million unique weights. It is not obvious whether more complex cells such as LSTM should be counted as a single neuron or a handful of neurons and whether a weight that is shared among many neurons in a convolutional network should be counted as one or more synaptic connections. As a start, if we just want a rough comparison, we note that our 15 million units are about the same order of magnitude as a frog with 16 million neurons. Our 30 million weights are about the same order of magnitude as the 10 million synapses of a fruit fly. If we count the shared weights as if they were unique weights, they could potentially be comparable to the 1 billion synapses of a honeybee. We see that this is significantly less than a cat with its 760 million neurons and 10 trillion synapses. We ask ourselves, how come our cat is good at ignoring us but has a hard time with converting an image to a textual description? A reasonable interpretation is that our image-captioning network is engineered for its task, and comparing it to a true biological system might not make much sense. Another interpretation is that, even if we find our image-captioning network reasonably complex, actual living organisms are way more complex, and we still have a long way to go before we are close to modeling something similar to a human brain.

This concludes our in-depth description of computer vision and language processing. The network in this chapter is an example of a multimodal network in that it works with both text and images, also known as two different *modalities*. Multimodal deep learning is one of the topics of the next chapter.

Chapter 17

Medley of Additional Topics

We have organized this book as a narrative in which each chapter to a large extent builds upon previous chapters. In Chapter 16, "One-to-Many Network for Image Captioning," we brought together techniques from many of the previous chapters into a single image captioning application.

In reality, many of these concepts have evolved simultaneously and not necessarily in the order we presented them. Similarly, we sometimes found it difficult to include all important topics in our narrative. Therefore, if you are new to deep learning (DL), you now have a solid foundation, but you also have blind spots. We address some of these blind spots by introducing additional topics that we find important.

This chapter is different from other chapters in that it introduces multiple techniques, including multiple programming examples, that are somewhat unrelated to each other. We do not go into the details as much as in previous chapters. The overall goal is to ensure that you get some exposure to each of these topics, so you can make an informed choice whether to pursue them further. In addition, the networks implemented in the programming examples in this chapter are simpler than those in the last couple of chapters, so they should be relatively easy to understand.

We discuss autoencoders, multimodal learning, multitask learning, network tuning, and neural architecture search, presented in that order. Without further ado, we start by describing autoencoders.

Autoencoders

In Chapter 14, "Sequence-to-Sequence Networks and Natural Language Translation," Chapter 15, "Attention and the Transformer," and Chapter 16, we saw examples of encoder-decoder architectures. The encoder converted an input into an intermediate representation. The decoder took this intermediate representation as input and converted it into the desired output. We used this general architecture for natural language translation and image captioning.

An *autoencoder* is a special case of the encoder-decoder architecture, where both the input value and the desired output value are identical. That is, the task for the autoencoder is to implement the identity function. This is shown in Figure 17-1. The model consists of an encoder that creates an intermediate representation of the input data, followed by a decoder that is tasked with reproducing the input data from this intermediate representation.

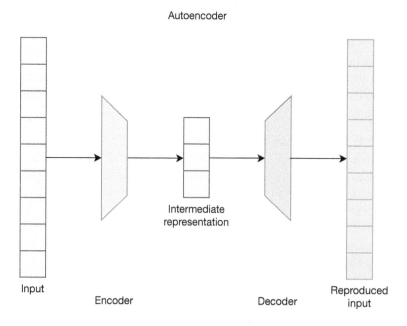

Figure 17-1 Autoencoder architecture

The exact architecture of the encoder and decoder depends on the use case and type of data. That is, for textual data, the encoder and decoder might be recurrent networks or based on the transformer architecture, and for other types of data they might be fully connected feedforward networks or convolutional networks.

An obvious question is why we would want to build such an architecture. What would be the use case? One key property plays a role in making them useful. As illustrated in the figure, the dimensionality of the intermediate representation is typically lower than the dimensionality of the input data which forces the model to find a compact intermediate representation. That is, the intermediate representation is a compressed version of the input data. The encoder compresses the data, and the decoder decompresses the data back to its original form. However, the intent is not to try to replace gzip, jpeg, or other compression algorithms. Instead, in most cases, the idea is to use the intermediate representation either directly or for further analysis or manipulation. We see some examples of this in the next section.

An autoencoder is trained to output the same value on the output that is presented on the input. However, it does so by first encoding the inputs in a more compact intermediate representation. This intermediate representation can be used for further analysis.

The idea of autoencoders has been around for a long time. One early example is described in a paper by Rumelhart, Hinton, and Williams (1986), who demonstrated a more compact representation of one-hot encoding (one solution would be standard binary encoding).

USE CASES FOR AUTOENCODERS

As a first example of how to use autoencoders, let us consider a case where we want to determine whether two different sentences convey similar messages. As mentioned in Chapter 14, Sutskever, Vinyals, and Le (2014) analyzed the intermediate representations of a sequence-to-sequence network used for translation by transforming them into a 2D space and plotting the resulting vectors. Figure 17-2 shows an adaptation of their resulting chart, which illustrates how sentences with the same meaning, but different sentence structures, are grouped together. That is, the intermediate representation serves as a *sentence vector*, where similar sentences are located close to each other in vector space. In

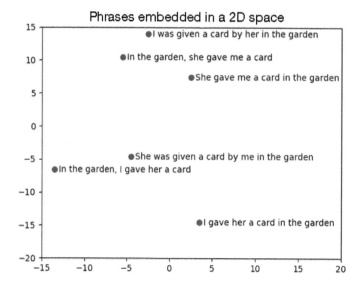

Figure 17-2 Intermediate representation of a translation network. (Source: Adapted from Sutskever, I., Vinyals, O., and Le, Q. (2014), "Sequence to Sequence Learning with Neural Networks," in *Proceedings of the 27th International Conference on Neural Information Processing [NIPS'14]*, MIT Press, 3104–3112.)

other words, once we have trained an encoder-decoder network on a translation task, we can use the encoder part of the network to produce such vectors.

One problem with this approach is that it can be costly to obtain training data for a translation network, given that each training example consists of the same sentence in two different languages. We can solve that by training our translation network to be an autoencoder. We simply train the sequence-to-sequence model to translate from one language to the same language—for example, English to English. Given that the intermediate representation is narrower than the input and output, the model is forced to come up with a meaningful intermediate representation, as in Figure 17-2. Note that no change is needed to the translation network itself to make it an autoencoder. The only change is to the training data, where we train the network to output a sentence in the same language as the input.

It is worth pointing out the similarity between the word2vec algorithm and the autoencoder example we just described. In word2vec, we take a wide (one-hot encoded) representation of a single word, then go through an encoding step whereby we reduce its dimensionality to a narrow intermediate representation.

This encoding step is then followed by a decoding step, which tries to predict not the word itself but its surrounding words in a wide representation. We have seen that word2vec can tease out semantics from the words it is trying to encode, so it is unsurprising that the autoencoder architecture can do the same for sentences.

A second example of a use case for an autoencoder is *outlier detection*. Imagine that we have trained an autoencoder to reproduce an English sentence as output when presented with an English sentence as input. If we now present an arbitrary English sentence to the network, we expect the output to be similar, if not identical, to the input. Specifically, we expect the value of the loss function to be small given that the objective of the training process was to minimize the loss function.

Now imagine that we use this same network but present a French sentence as input. It seems unlikely that an autoencoder trained on the English language will be good at reproducing a sentence in French. It has not had the opportunity to learn the French vocabulary or sentence structure. Therefore, the value of the loss function will be larger when the network is presented with an arbitrary French sentence than with an arbitrary English sentence. That is, a high loss value indicates that the current input data is different from the typical input data the autoencoder was trained on. In other words, a high loss indicates that the current input data is an outlier.

An important application of outlier detection is when applied to credit card transaction data. Each credit card transaction consists of a number of features such as amount, time of day, vendor, and location. We can group all of these features into a feature vector and use it as input to an autoencoder that we train to reproduce that same feature vector on its output. If we now present an atypical transaction to the network, it will not be as good at reproducing the vector on its output. That is, the loss value is higher, which indicates that this is an abnormal transaction that should be flagged as suspicious.

OTHER ASPECTS OF AUTOENCODERS

An important aspect of the two preceding examples is that the autoencoder finds patterns in unlabeled data. In particular, in the second example, we do not assume that we have a set of labeled outliers that we teach the model to detect. We simply rely on the fact that outliers are not present (or at least are rare by definition) in the training data, and therefore the model will not be good at minimizing their loss. The fact that an autoencoder can find patterns in unlabeled data makes it a good candidate for a building block in an unsupervised learning algorithm. In that context it is common to feed the internal representation vectors to a so-called clustering algorithm that groups vectors into clusters where similar vectors are placed in the same cluster.

> Clustering algorithms can be used to automatically group vectors into clusters where the vectors in a single cluster are similar to each other. k-means clustering is a well-known iterative algorithm and a good topic for further reading (Hastie, Tibshirani, and Friedman, 2009).

Another important aspect of the autoencoder is its use as a dimensionality reduction technique whereby the new narrower representation still maintains properties of the wider representation. The encoder can be used to reduce the number of dimensions, and the decoder can be used to expand the number of dimensions. The autoencoder is just one of many examples of dimensionality reduction techniques. Hastie, Tibshirani, and Friedman (2009) describe other methods for dimensionality reduction from the traditional machine learning (ML) field, the most common being principal component analysis (PCA).[1]

The basic autoencoder can be modified in various ways to be used in other applications. One example is the denoising autoencoder. The architecture is the same, but the training data is slightly modified. Instead of training the model with identical input and output data, a corrupted version of the data is used as input. The model is then trained to reproduce a correct version of corrupted input data. The resulting model can be used to removing noise from the input data—for example, image or video data.

PROGRAMMING EXAMPLE: AUTOENCODER FOR OUTLIER DETECTION

In this programming example, we demonstrate how an autoencoder can be used for outlier detection. We do this by first training an autoencoder on the Modified National Institute of Standards and Technology (MNIST) dataset. Then we observe how the error is higher when the network is presented with an image that does not represent a handwritten digit. In Code Snippet 17-1, we start with the usual set of import statements, followed by loading the MNIST dataset.

---

1. PCA is used in traditional machine learning but was invented before the term *machine learning* was coined. Therefore, it might be more accurate to simply view it as a mathematical concept.

Code Snippet 17-1 Initialization Code and Loading/Scaling the Dataset

```
import tensorflow as tf
from tensorflow import keras
from tensorflow.keras.utils import to_categorical
import numpy as np
import matplotlib.pyplot as plt
import logging
tf.get_logger().setLevel(logging.ERROR)


EPOCHS = 10

# Load traditional MNIST dataset.
mnist = keras.datasets.mnist
(train_images, train_labels), (test_images,
                                test_labels) = mnist.load_data()

# Scale the data.
train_images = train_images / 255.0
test_images = test_images / 255.0
```

Instead of standardizing the data to be centered around 0, we scale the data to be in the range 0 to 1. The reason is worth some discussion. The task for the autoencoder is to reproduce the input on its outputs. This implies that we need to define the input data and the output unit of the network in a way that makes this possible. For example, if we use input data centered around 0, and a logistic sigmoid as the output unit, then the network simply cannot solve the problem because the logistic sigmoid can output only positive values. When working with image data, we want the output range to be bounded to a range of valid values (typically integer values between 0 and 255 or floating-point values between 0 and 1). A common way to ensure this is to scale the input values to be between 0 and 1 and use a logistic sigmoid unit as output unit. Another alternative would be to center the input around 0 and use a linear output unit, but we would then need to postprocess the output data to ensure that they do not contain out-of-range values.

The next step is to define and train the model. This is shown in Code Snippet 17-2. The encoder part of the model consists of a Flatten layer (changing the dimension from 28×28 to 784) followed by a single fully connected (Dense) layer with 64 units. The decoder consists of another fully connected layer with 784 units, followed by a Reshape layer that changes the dimension from

784 to 28×28. That is, the decoder performs the inverse of the operations done by the encoder. The goal for the autoencoder is to generate an output image that is identical to the input image, and it has to do that by fully encoding the 28×28 (784) image in the intermediate representation vector of size 64.

Code Snippet 17-2 Building and Training the Model

```
# Create and train autoencoder.
model = keras.Sequential([
    keras.layers.Flatten(input_shape=(28, 28)),
    keras.layers.Dense(64, activation='relu',
                       kernel_initializer='glorot_normal',
                       bias_initializer='zeros'),
    keras.layers.Dense(784, activation='sigmoid',
                       kernel_initializer='glorot_normal',
                       bias_initializer='zeros'),
    keras.layers.Reshape((28, 28))])

model.compile(loss='binary_crossentropy', optimizer = 'adam',
              metrics =['mean_absolute_error'])

history = model.fit(train_images, train_images,
                    validation_data=(test_images, test_images),
                    epochs=EPOCHS, batch_size=64, verbose=2,
                    shuffle=True)
```

We should point out that although we use fully connected layers for both the encoder and decoder in this example, when working with images, it is more common to use convolutional layers and some form of convolution-based upsampling layers. A detailed description of this can be found in Appendix B, but we use fully connected layers in this example to keep things simple and because it is feasible when working with the small and simple images from MNIST.

In Code Snippet 17-3, we use the trained model to try to reproduce the images in the test dataset. After applying the model to all test images, we plot one of the test images next to its corresponding version produced by the network.

Code Snippet 17-3 Demonstrate the Behavior of the Autoencoder on the Test Dataset

```
# Predict on test dataset.
predict_images = model.predict(test_images)

# Plot one input example and resulting prediction.
plt.subplot(1, 2, 1)
plt.imshow(test_images[0], cmap=plt.get_cmap('gray'))
plt.subplot(1, 2, 2)
plt.imshow(predict_images[0], cmap=plt.get_cmap('gray'))
plt.show()
```

As shown in Figure 17-3, the network does a decent job of recreating the image. The next step is to apply our autoencoder to a different image. We use a different dataset known as *Fashion MNIST* (Xiao, Rasul, and Vollgraf, 2017). This dataset is designed to serve as a drop-in replacement for MNIST. It consists of the same number of training and test images, using the same 28×28 resolution. Just as for MNIST, each image belongs to one of ten classes. The difference compared to MNIST is that instead of depicting handwritten images, the images depict various pieces of clothing: dress, shirt, sneaker, and so on. Code Snippet 17-4 loads this

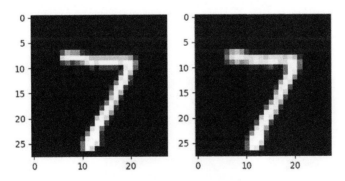

Figure 17-3 Test image (left) and reproduced image (right)

dataset and uses the trained model to try to reproduce the fashion MNIST test images.

Code Snippet 17-4 Try the Autoencoder on the Fashion MNIST Dataset

```
# Load Fashion MNIST.
f_mnist = keras.datasets.fashion_mnist
(f_train_images, f_train_labels), (f_test_images,
                    f_test_labels) = f_mnist.load_data()

f_train_images = f_train_images / 255.0
f_test_images = f_test_images / 255.0

# Predict and plot.
f_predict_images = model.predict(f_test_images)
plt.subplot(1, 2, 1)
plt.imshow(f_test_images[0], cmap=plt.get_cmap('gray'))
plt.subplot(1, 2, 2)
plt.imshow(f_predict_images[0], cmap=plt.get_cmap('gray'))
plt.show()
```

As shown in Figure 17-4, the result is much worse than for MNIST. That is, our autoencoder has learned how to reproduce handwritten digits, but it has not learned to reproduce arbitrary images.

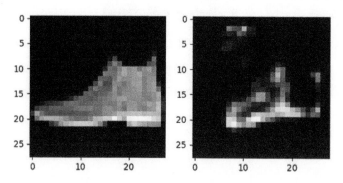

Figure 17-4 Test image from Fashion MNIST (left) and reproduced image (right)

To quantify this further, in Code Snippet 17-5 we compute the mean absolute error for the autoencoder, both for all MNIST test examples and all Fashion MNIST test examples. We then plot the results. It might have made more sense to compute the binary cross-entropy loss because that is what we used when training the network. However, in terms of illustrating the difference in error, any suitable error function will do, and we picked mean absolute error to simplify the code.

Code Snippet 17-5 Plot the Loss for Both MNIST and Fashion MNIST

```
# Compute errors and plot.
error = np.mean(np.abs(test_images - predict_images), (1, 2))
f_error = np.mean(np.abs(f_test_images - f_predict_images), (1, 2))
_ = plt.hist((error, f_error), bins=50, label=['mnist',
                                               'fashion mnist'])
plt.legend()
plt.xlabel('mean absolute error')
plt.ylabel('examples')
plt.title("Autoencoder for outlier detection")
plt.show()
```

The resulting plot is shown in Figure 17-5. It is clear that the error is smaller for the MNIST examples than for the Fashion MNIST examples. If the error is larger than 0.02 (the boundary between blue and orange), it is likely that the image does not depict a handwritten digit. That is, an outlier has been detected.

We note that the blue and orange bars are not clearly separated. There is some overlap. To provide some insight into that, Code Snippet 17-6 plots the two MNIST test images that result in the biggest error.

Code Snippet 17-6 Find and Plot Biggest Outliers in MNIST Test Dataset

```
# Print outliers in mnist data.
index = error.argmax()
plt.subplot(1, 2, 1)
plt.imshow(test_images[index], cmap=plt.get_cmap('gray'))
error[index] = 0
index = error.argmax()
```

```
plt.subplot(1, 2, 2)
plt.imshow(test_images[index], cmap=plt.get_cmap('gray'))
plt.show()
```

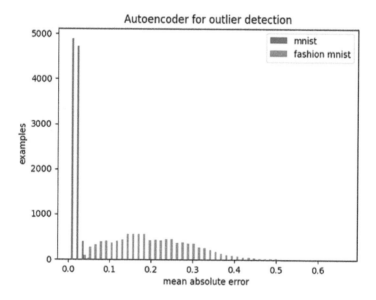

Figure 17-5 Histogram of error for MNIST and Fashion MNIST. The error value can be used to determine whether a given example represents a handwritten digit.

Looking at the resulting images in Figure 17-6, we see that they do represent outliers in the regular data. The left image is cropped in an unfortunate way, and the right image looks somewhat odd. That is, they truly can be considered outliers in the MNIST dataset.

Before moving on to the next topic, it is worth pointing out that, although MNIST and Fashion MNIST are labeled datasets, we did not make use of the labels in this programming example. Neither did we make use of the Fashion MNIST dataset for training the model. That is, we trained the model to distinguish between MNIST and Fashion MNIST, as well as to find outliers in the test set of MNIST itself, solely by using the training images in the MNIST dataset.

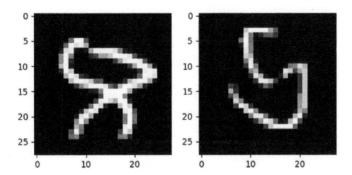

Figure 17-6 The two MNIST test examples resulting in the biggest errors

Multimodal Learning

The programming examples in this book have made use of different types of input data, such as written natural language, image data, and numerical data representing the price of an item. These different types of data can also be referred to as different *modalities*—that is, the mode in which the phenomenon is experienced or represented. Multimodal machine learning (multimodal ML) is the field of building models that use or relate to data with multiple modalities.

As previously mentioned, the image-captioning example in Chapter 16 is an example of a multimodal DL application. In this section, we describe a taxonomy introduced by Baltrušaitis, Ahuja, and Morency (2017) in a survey paper on multimodal ML. As a part of this description, we point out where the image-captioning example and other related examples fit into this taxonomy. We conclude with a small programming example of a classification network that uses two modalities of the same data as its inputs.

TAXONOMY OF MULTIMODAL LEARNING

Baltrušaitis, Ahuja, and Morency (2017) divide multimodal learning into five topics: representation, translation, alignment, fusion, and co-learning. We summarize these topics next, but in a slightly different order. We present fusion right after representation because these two topics are highly related to each other, particularly in the context of deep neural networks.

An important aspect of building a model is how to represent the input data. Working with multimodal data adds a dimension to this problem. One of the simplest ways to present multimodal data to a model is to concatenate the multiple feature vectors into a single vector. In some cases, this is impractical, such as if one modality is a time series with multiple timesteps and the other modality is a single feature vector. Another problem is that one modality might unintentionally dominate the overall input.

For example, consider an image and a textual description of the same object. The image might consist of on the order of a million pixels, whereas the textual description might be just ten words. Without somehow explicitly communicating that the collection of ten words is equally important as the one million pixel values, it can be hard to train the network to make good use of the textual input. A way to address this issue is to build a network consisting of a set of parallel networks that process the different input modalities and then combine the results further into the network. Having such parallel networks can also address the issue of different dimensions of the input data. For example, we can use a recurrent network to transform textual input data into a fixed-width vector representation. Similarly, we can use a convolutional network to convert image data into a vector representing higher-level features that are present in the image.

Once we have these separate input networks, another aspect is how to combine them further into the network. One solution is to concatenate the outputs of these input networks and feed into a fully connected layer that creates what Baltrušaitis, Ahuja, and Morency (2017) call a *joint representation* of the multiple modalities. This is often the preferred method if the expected use case is that all modalities will be present when the network is later used for inference.

A different solution is to keep the modalities separate inside of the network but enforce some kind of constraint on how they relate to each other. Baltrušaitis, Ahuja, and Morency call this a *coordinated representation*. An example of a constraint is that representations of the same type of object should be close to each other (in vector space) for the two modalities. This can be exploited in cases where only one modality is present during inference. We might train the network on images and text and form a coordinated representation. During inference, only one of the modalities is presented to the network, but the network can still perform the task it is trained to do. The three described solutions to how to represent two modalities are illustrated in Figure 17-7.

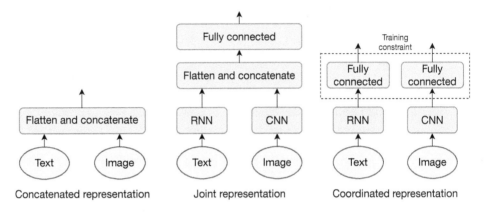

Figure 17-7 Concatenated modalities (left), joint representation (middle), and coordinated representation (right)

FUSION

Multimodal fusion is highly related to the topic of representation. The representation problem we just discussed applies to any use case where we work with multimodal input data. The data in the different modalities do not necessarily need to be two different views of the same entity. Our understanding of multimodal fusion is that it specifically refers to when we are trying to solve a task (e.g., classification or regression) but have multiple views of the same input data, in different modalities. An example is when trying to classify an object based on an image and a sound recording of the object.

In such a setting, multimodal fusion can be discussed in terms of the two extremes early fusion and late fusion. Early fusion refers to simply concatenating the input vectors, which is precisely the first alternative that we listed in the section about representation. Late fusion is to have multiple, separately trained models that are later combined. For example, in a classification task, we would train one network that does image classification and one that does text classification. We would then combine the output of these networks, for example, by a weighted voting system. Early and late fusion are illustrated in Figure 17-8.

Early and late fusion are two extremes, and there are design points that are hybrids of the two. In the context of neural networks, the line is often blurred. For example, if we implement a classifier that uses a joint representation of the two input modalities, then fusion happens as a part of the model itself.

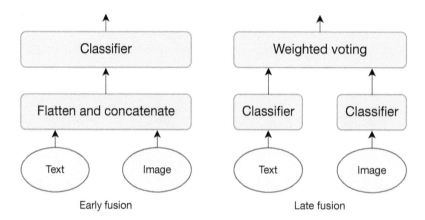

Figure 17-8 Examples of early fusion (left) and late fusion (right) in the context of classification

TRANSLATION

An important part of multimodal learning is the concept of finding mappings between multiple modalities. Finding such mappings is equivalent to translating from one modality into another.

We have already seen examples of translating between modalities. The task of our image-captioning network in Chapter 16 was to translate from an image (one modality) into a textual description of that same image (a different modality). We did this by using a convolutional network to convert the image into an intermediate vector representation of the data. This was fed as input data to an autoregressive recurrent network, which generated a corresponding textual description.

Similarly, in Chapter 14, we built a natural language translation network that translated from French to English. It is not readily apparent that this network can be considered a multimodal network given that both the input and output are textual data. However, one could argue that the descriptions in different languages are two different views of the overall language-independent message that they are trying to convey. Regardless of the strict definition, we observe that, conceptually, the language translation network was much related to the image-captioning network, which clearly is multimodal.

The two networks we just discussed are both *generative* in nature. That is, the output is generated by the network based on an internal representation. Another class of models are *example-based* models. Such models map the current input example to a previously seen training example and simply retrieve the output corresponding to that training example. There are also *combination-based* approaches, where the outputs of multiple training examples are combined to form a predicted output during inference.

ALIGNMENT

In multimodal learning, *alignment* refers to mapping subcomponents of two or more modalities to each other. For example, given an image and a textual description of that image, we align these two inputs to each other by mapping words or phrases from the textual description to regions or objects in the image.

One technique that can be used for alignment is attention. In our description of attention in Chapter 15, we described how it can be used by a translation network to focus on the right set of words when producing the output sentence. Similarly, in the image-captioning example in Chapter 16, we saw how it can be used to focus on specific areas of the image. We can find the alignment between the two modalities by analyzing the dynamically computed weights in the attention mechanism. In fact, these dynamically computed weights are referred to as the *alignment vector*. Note that these two examples are somewhat special in that they find the alignment between a source modality and a destination modality as the destination is being generated. That is, it is a combination of alignment and translation.

Baltrušaitis Ahuja, and Morency (2017) distinguish between explicit alignment and implicit alignment. In the explicit case, the task at hand is to find the alignment between two data sources. In the implicit case, alignment is done as an early step to improve the result of a later task. For example, a classification network will do better if it is fed with multiple modalities of the same input data, but that assumes that the two modalities are first aligned so they truly represent two different views of the same object.

CO-LEARNING

The fifth and last topic in this taxonomy is co-learning. This is a class of techniques whereby one modality is used to aid the process of training a model on another modality. Co-learning can be particularly useful when we do not have a labeled (or have only a partly labeled) dataset for one modality and we can complement it with another dataset in a different modality, especially if the other dataset happens to be more extensively labeled. We limit ourselves to mentioning a couple of examples of how we can co-learn with multiple datasets.

The first example, introduced by Blum and Mitchell (1998), is *co-training*. Consider a classification problem where we have a dataset that consists of mostly unlabeled data, and each training example consists of two views in different modalities—for example, an image and a textual description. We now train two separate classifiers on the few labeled examples. One classifier uses the image as input data, and the other uses the textual description. We can now use these classifiers to classify some random unlabeled examples and add to the labeled part of the dataset. After doing this iteratively a number of times, we end up with a larger dataset that can be used to train a combined classifier that uses both modalities as inputs. Blum and Mitchell showed that this approach significantly reduced the classification error rate compared to training on only the initial labeled dataset or using only one of the modalities.

Our second example is to make use of transfer learning and map the representation of two different modalities into the same representation. Frome and colleagues (2013) performed an experiment where they combined text and image data. They first pretrained a word2vec model on a text corpus, resulting in a set of word embeddings. They then pretrained an image classification network on the ImageNet dataset. Finally, they removed the top softmax layer from the image classification network and trained it further for a new task, using transfer learning. This new task was to produce the same embedding as the word2vec model produced when presented with the textual ImageNet label. That is, given a labeled image of a cat, the word vector for *cat* was first produced using word2vec. This was then used as the target value when fine-tuning the pretrained image classifier, with the softmax layer removed. During inference, an image is presented to the trained network, which outputs a vector in the same space as the word embeddings. The prediction is simply the word closest to the resulting vector. One result of training the model in this way is that even when it predicts the wrong result, its result is often meaningful because other related words are close in vector space.

These two examples represent two different categories of multimodal co-learning problems. The first example requires training examples in which each instance has associated data in both modalities. That is, each training example has both an image and a textual description. Baltrušaitis, Ahuja, and Morency (2017) refer to this as *parallel data*. The second example also uses both image and textual data but with two different datasets. This is an example of *nonparallel data*. Note that there is still one connection point that ties the two modalities together, namely, the textual labels associated with each image. Baltrušaitis Ahuja, and Morency also describe examples with *hybrid data*. One such case is where we do not have a dataset with parallel data for the two modalities that we want to connect, but we do have datasets with parallel data that connect these two modalities to a third common modality. We can use this third modality to bridge between the two desired modalities.

PROGRAMMING EXAMPLE: CLASSIFICATION WITH MULTIMODAL INPUT DATA

In this programming example, we demonstrate how to train a classifier, using two input modalities. We use the MNIST dataset but in addition to the image modality, we also create a textual modality. We start with initialization code and loading and standardizing the MNIST dataset in Code Snippet 17-7.

Code Snippet 17-7 Initialization Code and Loading/Standardizing the MNIST Dataset

```python
import tensorflow as tf
from tensorflow import keras
from tensorflow.keras.utils import to_categorical
from tensorflow.keras.preprocessing.text import Tokenizer
from tensorflow.keras.preprocessing.text \
    import text_to_word_sequence
from tensorflow.keras.preprocessing.sequence \
    import pad_sequences
from tensorflow.keras.layers import Input
from tensorflow.keras.layers import Embedding
from tensorflow.keras.layers import LSTM
from tensorflow.keras.layers import Flatten
from tensorflow.keras.layers import Concatenate
from tensorflow.keras.layers import Dense
from tensorflow.keras.models import Model
import numpy as np
import matplotlib.pyplot as plt
import logging
tf.get_logger().setLevel(logging.ERROR)


EPOCHS = 20
MAX_WORDS = 8
EMBEDDING_WIDTH = 4


# Load training and test datasets.
mnist = keras.datasets.mnist
```

```
(train_images, train_labels), (test_images,
                               test_labels) = mnist.load_data()

# Standardize the data.
mean = np.mean(train_images)
stddev = np.std(train_images)
train_images = (train_images - mean) / stddev
test_images = (test_images - mean) / stddev
```

Code Snippet 17-8 creates the second input modality, which is a textual representation of each input example. To not make it too easy for the network, this textual view of the data is not complete but gives only partial information about the digit. For each training and test example, we alternate between specifying that the digit is odd or even and specifying that it is a high or low number. The textual modality created in this code snippet does not fully define what digit it is but can be helpful when an image is ambiguous.

Code Snippet 17-8 Function to Create a Textual Modality of the Training and Test Examples

```
# Function to create second modality.
def create_text(tokenizer, labels):
    text = []
    for i, label in enumerate(labels):
        if i % 2 == 0:
            if label < 5:
                text.append('lower half')
            else:
                text.append('upper half')
        else:
            if label % 2 == 0:
                text.append('even number')
            else:
                text.append('odd number')
    text = tokenizer.texts_to_sequences(text)
    text = pad_sequences(text)
    return text
```

```
# Create second modality for training and test set.
vocabulary = ['lower', 'upper', 'half', 'even', 'odd', 'number']
tokenizer = Tokenizer(num_words=MAX_WORDS)
tokenizer.fit_on_texts(vocabulary)
train_text = create_text(tokenizer, train_labels)
test_text = create_text(tokenizer, test_labels)
```

The image classification network is similar to the example in Chapter 5, "Toward DL: Frameworks and Network Tweaks," but with an additional subnetwork that processes the textual input. This subnetwork consists of an Embedding layer and an LSTM layer. The output of the LSTM layer is concatenated with the image input and fed to a fully connected layer. This layer is followed by the final fully connected softmax layer that produces the classification. The implementation is shown in Code Snippet 17-9.

Code Snippet 17-9 Classification Network with Two Input Modalities

```
# Create model with functional API.
image_input = Input(shape=(28, 28))
text_input = Input(shape=(2, ))

# Declare layers.
embedding_layer = Embedding(output_dim=EMBEDDING_WIDTH,
                            input_dim = MAX_WORDS)
lstm_layer = LSTM(8)
flatten_layer = Flatten()
concat_layer = Concatenate()
dense_layer = Dense(25,activation='relu')
output_layer = Dense(10, activation='softmax')

# Connect layers.
embedding_output = embedding_layer(text_input)
lstm_output = lstm_layer(embedding_output)
flatten_output = flatten_layer(image_input)
concat_output = concat_layer([lstm_output, flatten_output])
```

```
dense_output = dense_layer(concat_output)
outputs = output_layer(dense_output)

# Build and train model.
model = Model([image_input, text_input], outputs)
model.compile(loss='sparse_categorical_crossentropy',
                    optimizer='adam', metrics =['accuracy'])
model.summary()
history = model.fit([train_images, train_text], train_labels,
                validation_data=([test_images, test_text],
                            test_labels), epochs=EPOCHS,
                    batch_size=64, verbose=2, shuffle=True)
```

After training the network for 20 epochs, we arrive at a validation accuracy of 97.2%. To put this into context, we modified the method that creates the textual modality to always state 'lower half'. Another option would have been to remove the textual input modality altogether, but then the network would have fewer weights, so we figured that it would be fairer to keep the textual input but make it provide no additional information. The resulting validation accuracy was 96.7%, which indicates that the additional textual information was beneficial.

To further illustrate the effect of using the two input modalities, we do an experiment in Code Snippet 17-10. We first show all the information about a given test example. It turns out to be the digit 7, and the textual description was 'upper half'. We then use the network to make a prediction, given this image and textual description as input. We print out digits and predicted probabilities, sorted on the basis of the probabilities. As expected, the network correctly predicts the digit as a 7.

Code Snippet 17-10 Perform Experiments with the Trained Multimodal Network

```
# Print input modalities and output for one test example.
print(test_labels[0])
print(tokenizer.sequences_to_texts([test_text[0]]))
plt.figure(figsize=(1, 1))
plt.imshow(test_images[0], cmap=plt.get_cmap('gray'))
plt.show()
```

```
# Predict test example.
y = model.predict([test_images[0:1], np.array(
    tokenizer.texts_to_sequences(['upper half']))])[0] #7
print('Predictions with correct input:')
for i in range(len(y)):
    index = y.argmax()
    print('Digit: %d,' %index, 'probability: %5.2e' %y[index])
    y[index] = 0

# Predict same test example but with modified textual description.
print('\nPredictions with incorrect input:')
y = model.predict([test_images[0:1], np.array(
    tokenizer.texts_to_sequences(['lower half']))])[0] #7
for i in range(len(y)):
    index = y.argmax()
    print('Digit: %d,' %index, 'probability: %5.2e' %y[index])
    y[index] = 0
```

As a next step, we do another prediction, but this time we change the textual input to indicate 'lower half'. Looking at the probabilities, we see that the probabilities for the high digits have decreased. The results were not fully consistent from run to run, but in many cases, the probabilities changed enough so the prediction from the network changed from a 7 to a 3. This makes it clear that the network has learned to take both the image and the textual description into account.

Multitask Learning

In the previous section, we saw that multimodal learning can involve a single network simultaneously working on multiple representations of the same data. A different concept, although similar sounding, is multitask learning, which involves training a single network to simultaneously solve multiple separate tasks. Multimodal learning and multitask learning are orthogonal to each other but can also be combined. That is, we can create a single network that works on multiple modalities of the same data to solve multiple tasks simultaneously. This is demonstrated in the programming example later in this section.

WHY TO IMPLEMENT MULTITASK LEARNING

Let us start with reasoning about the benefit of having a single network solve multiple tasks by considering why it works and why it is beneficial. We touched on this topic in Chapter 4, "Fully Connected Networks Applied to Multiclass Classification," when we described how to build a network for multiclass classification for handwritten digits. One potential solution was to create a separate network for each digit. That is, instead of one multiclass classification network, we could have built ten different digit detection networks. Our reasoning at that point was that there are commonalities between recognizing different digits. We did not elaborate at the time but now take this reasoning a step further. Let us consider the three digits 3, 6, and 8. The lower part of each digit is rounded. It would be inefficient to have three separate "rounded lower part detectors" when we can achieve the same functionality by sharing a single implementation. Apart from this inefficiency with respect to the total number of neurons, it also turns out that sharing these neurons forces them to generalize better. Instead of overfitting to detect just a single digit, the neurons are forced to learn more general concepts, like detecting a rounded lower part as just mentioned.

The same reasoning applies to multitask learning. As long as a set of tasks are somewhat related, we can see efficiency gains and less overfitting by training the network to solve these tasks simultaneously. For example, at the end of Chapter 8, we briefly mentioned the computer vision tasks *detection* and *segmentation* (also discussed in detail in Appendix B). In addition to classifying what types of objects are in an image, these tasks involve drawing a bounding box or detecting individual pixels belonging to the classified object. It is easy to see that there are commonalities between these tasks. Regardless whether the network is tasked with classifying an object as a dog or drawing a bounding box around the dog, it is first helpful for it to be able to detect typical dog features.

It is worth noting that there is a connection point between transfer learning and multitask learning. In Chapter 16, we demonstrated how a convolutional network pretrained for object classification could be reused in the context of image captioning. Multitask learning does something similar. The difference is that instead of first training it on one task and then reusing it for a different task, the network is simultaneously trained and reused for two or more tasks.

HOW TO IMPLEMENT MULTITASK LEARNING

In the previous section, we reasoned about why multitask learning should work and be beneficial, but the discussion was abstract. We now make it more concrete by describing the details of how it is done. The trick is to build a network that has multiple sets of output units. These sets of output units do not need to be of the same type. For example, consider a network that is tasked with both classifying an object and drawing a bounding box. One way of building such a network is to have one softmax output unit for classification and four linear output units to represent the four corners of the bounding box. These different output units are often known as *heads,* and the shared part of the network is known as *trunk.* That is, multitask learning can be done using a multiheaded network, as illustrated in Figure 17-9. Note that a head does not necessarily consist of only a single layer, but each head can be a multilayered subnetwork.

The introduction of multiple output units also implies introducing multiple loss functions. The selection of these loss functions is straightforward. We use the same types as for a single-headed network. For example, we use categorical cross-entropy for a softmax branch used for multiclass classification, whereas we use mean squared error for a linear branch used for regression. We combine these multiple loss functions into a single loss function by simply computing a weighted sum. This raises the question of what weights to use. A simple solution is to just treat them as any other hyperparameters that need to be tuned when training the network.

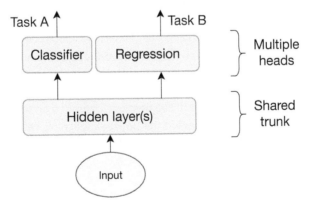

Figure 17-9 Two-headed network for multitask learning. One head performs a classification task, and the other head performs a regression task.

OTHER ASPECTS AND VARIATIONS ON THE BASIC IMPLEMENTATION

In the previous section, we described a basic network for multitask learning. As always, there are many possible variations on the basic implementation. In this section, we mention a couple of them.

So far, we have implicitly assumed that we train the network to solve multiple tasks because we need to solve all those tasks. However, multitask learning can also be used to improve a network where the goal is to solve a single task. We described how training a network to solve multiple tasks forces the shared parts of the network to learn generalized solutions. That is, the additional task can act as a regularizer that reduces overfitting. The network will thereby do better on the test set for the main task. With this background, we can now revisit the auxiliary classifier used in GoogLeNet. In Chapter 8, we described it as a way to fight vanishing gradients. A different way to view the auxiliary classifier is that it encourages the network to learn features at different detail levels. This can be viewed as increased generalization resulting from multitask learning (the auxiliary classifier acts as a second head to learn a secondary task).

The way parameters are shared in the basic network architecture described in the previous section is known as *hard parameter sharing*. This simply means that the trunk of the network is fully shared between the multiple heads. Another option is *soft parameter sharing*. In such a setting, each task has its own corresponding network. However, during training, the combined loss function encourages the weights in some layers to be similar between the models. That is, the weights of the different networks will act as if they are shared in cases where it is beneficial, but they still have the freedom to be different from each other if that is more beneficial. That is, the weights are only softly shared between models.

Karpathy (2019b) points out that multitask learning introduces some additional interesting trade-offs, especially in a team project setting. As previously described, an obvious and simple regularization technique is early stopping. That is, simply detect how many epochs result in the best performance on the test set and stop training at that point. This is trivial in the uni-task learning case, but it is not as straightforward in a multitask learning case. Consider the learning curves in Figure 17-10. Do you stop training when task A, task B, or task C performs the best? This becomes particularly contentious when different people are responsible for different tasks but are sharing the trunk of the network due to resource constraints. A similar question is who gets to pick the weights for the joint loss function. The weights are likely to end up being different depending on if the owner of task A, task B, or task C gets to decide.

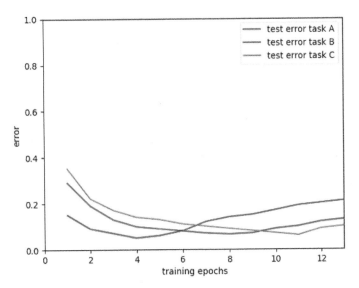

Figure 17-10 Learning curves for three different tasks in a multitask learning scenario

We now move on to a programming example that combines multimodal and multitask learning. If you want to learn more about multitask learning, Ruder (2017) and Crawshaw (2020) have written survey papers on the topic.

PROGRAMMING EXAMPLE: MULTICLASS CLASSIFICATION AND QUESTION ANSWERING WITH A SINGLE NETWORK

In this programming example, we extend the multimodal network from the last programming example with an additional head to build a network that does multitask learning using multimodal inputs.

We teach the network to simultaneously do multiclass classification (identify the handwritten digit) and perform a simple question-answering task. The question-answering task is to provide a yes/no answer to a question about the digit in the image. The textual input will look similar to the textual input in the last programming example ('upper half', 'lower half', 'odd number', 'even number'). However, instead of correctly describing the digit, the text is chosen randomly and represents a question. The network is then tasked with classifying the image into one of ten classes as well as with determining whether the answer to the question is yes or no (is the statement true or false). As always, we start with initialization code and loading the dataset in Code Snippet 17-11.

Code Snippet 17-11 Initialization Code for the Multitask Multimodal Network
Example

```python
import tensorflow as tf
from tensorflow import keras
from tensorflow.keras.utils import to_categorical
from tensorflow.keras.preprocessing.text import Tokenizer
from tensorflow.keras.preprocessing.text \
    import text_to_word_sequence
from tensorflow.keras.preprocessing.sequence \
    import pad_sequences
from tensorflow.keras.layers import Input
from tensorflow.keras.layers import Embedding
from tensorflow.keras.layers import LSTM
from tensorflow.keras.layers import Flatten
from tensorflow.keras.layers import Concatenate
from tensorflow.keras.layers import Dense
from tensorflow.keras.models import Model
import numpy as np
import logging
tf.get_logger().setLevel(logging.ERROR)

EPOCHS = 20
MAX_WORDS = 8
EMBEDDING_WIDTH = 4

# Load training and test datasets.
mnist = keras.datasets.mnist
(train_images, train_labels), (test_images,
                        test_labels) = mnist.load_data()
# Standardize the data.
mean = np.mean(train_images)
stddev = np.std(train_images)
train_images = (train_images - mean) / stddev
test_images = (test_images - mean) / stddev
```

The next step is to extend the MNIST dataset with questions and answers. This is done in Code Snippet 17-12. The code alternates between the four questions/statements for each training and test example. It then determines whether the answer is yes or no based on the ground truth label.

Code Snippet 17-12 Method Used to Extend the Dataset with Questions and Answers

```
# Function to create question and answer text.
def create_question_answer(tokenizer, labels):
    text = []
    answers = np.zeros(len(labels))
    for i, label in enumerate(labels):
        question_num = i % 4
        if question_num == 0:
            text.append('lower half')
            if label < 5:
                answers[i] = 1.0
        elif question_num == 1:
            text.append('upper half')
            if label >= 5:
                answers[i] = 1.0
        elif question_num == 2:
            text.append('even number')
            if label % 2 == 0:
                answers[i] = 1.0
        elif question_num == 3:
            text.append('odd number')
            if label % 2 == 1:
                answers[i] = 1.0
    text = tokenizer.texts_to_sequences(text)
    text = pad_sequences(text)
    return text, answers

# Create second modality for training and test set.
vocabulary = ['lower', 'upper', 'half', 'even', 'odd', 'number']
tokenizer = Tokenizer(num_words=MAX_WORDS)
```

```
tokenizer.fit_on_texts(vocabulary)
train_text, train_answers = create_question_answer(tokenizer,
                                                    train_labels)
test_text, test_answers = create_question_answer(tokenizer,
                                                  test_labels)
```

The next step is to create the network. This is shown in Code Snippet 17-13. Most of the network is identical to the programming example for the multimodal network. The key difference is that in parallel with the ten-unit output layer for multiclass classification, there is a one-unit output layer for binary classification. Given that there are two separate outputs, we also need to supply two separate loss functions. In addition, we supply weights for these two loss functions to indicate how to weigh the two into a single loss function for training the network. The weights should be treated like any other hyperparameter. A reasonable starting point is to have the same weight for both losses, so we use 50/50. Finally, when calling the fit method, we must provide ground truth for both heads of the model.

Code Snippet 17-13 Multitask Network with Multimodal Inputs

```
# Create model with functional API.
image_input = Input(shape=(28, 28))
text_input = Input(shape=(2, ))

# Declare layers.
embedding_layer = Embedding(output_dim=EMBEDDING_WIDTH,
                            input_dim = MAX_WORDS)
lstm_layer = LSTM(8)
flatten_layer = Flatten()
concat_layer = Concatenate()
dense_layer = Dense(25,activation='relu')
class_output_layer = Dense(10, activation='softmax')
answer_output_layer = Dense(1, activation='sigmoid')

# Connect layers.
embedding_output = embedding_layer(text_input)
lstm_output = lstm_layer(embedding_output)
```

```
flatten_output = flatten_layer(image_input)
concat_output = concat_layer([lstm_output, flatten_output])
dense_output = dense_layer(concat_output)
class_outputs = class_output_layer(dense_output)
answer_outputs = answer_output_layer(dense_output)

# Build and train model.
model = Model([image_input, text_input], [class_outputs,
                                           answer_outputs])
model.compile(loss=['sparse_categorical_crossentropy',
                    'binary_crossentropy'], optimizer='adam',
              metrics=['accuracy'],
              loss_weights = [0.5, 0.5])
model.summary()
history = model.fit([train_images, train_text],
                    [train_labels, train_answers],
                    validation_data=([test_images, test_text],
                    [test_labels, test_answers]), epochs=EPOCHS,
                    batch_size=64, verbose=2, shuffle=True)
```

The training process will now report one metric for each head. With our 50/50 weights for the two loss functions, the network achieves a 95% validation accuracy on the classification task and a 91% accuracy on the question-answering task. If you are interested, you can change the loss function weights in favor of the question-answering task and see if you can thereby improve its accuracy.

Process for Tuning a Network

In the programming examples throughout this book, we have shown the results from various experiments with different network configurations, but we have not tried to formalize the methodology for training a network. In this section, we briefly outline a set of steps to follow when training your network. It is loosely inspired by an online blog post, which we recommend to anybody wanting a more extensive description (Karpathy, 2019a).

First, you need to ensure that you have high-quality data. Our programming examples have included basic preprocessing of the data, but in general, it is beneficial to spend more time and effort on cleaning and sanity checking the data. In particular, it is often useful to visualize the data as scatter plots, histograms, or other types of charts to see if there are any obvious patterns or broken data points.

A second step is to create a naïve model that will serve as a baseline to compare against. Without such a model, it is hard to tell if your multilayer hybrid CNN/RNN network with dropout and attention is doing anything good and is worth the complexity. Your naïve model should be simple enough that you can convince yourself that the model implementation itself does not contain bugs. This will also help you ensure that your data preprocessing steps work as expected and that the data is properly presented to the model.

Now you are ready to build your DL model, but even at this step, you should start small. Create a tiny subset of your training dataset and create a fairly simple model that you think should be able to memorize the dataset. As an example, when we built our sequence-to-sequence network for language translation, we started with a dataset of just four sentences, each containing three to four words. Our initial model failed to memorize these sentences, which was caused by bugs in the model implementation as opposed to the model being too small or simple. Obviously, failure to learn a small dataset does not need to be caused by bugs in the model; it can also be that it is the wrong type of model or that you need to adjust other hyperparameters such as the optimizer type, learning rate, or weight initialization scheme. If you cannot get your model to memorize a tiny subset of your actual dataset, then there is a low probability that increasing the dataset will help. In addition, staying with a tiny dataset at this point will allow you to do rapid prototyping without long iteration times for training.

> For the record, obviously, we did not start with a four-sentence dataset. Just like everybody else, we were optimistic. We threw a real dataset at the model but had to gradually strip down both the model and the dataset to the very basics to find the bugs that prevented it from learning.

Once you have built a model that can memorize your tiny subset of the training dataset, you can increase the dataset size to something more challenging. Chances are that you will now run into issues with model capacity (i.e., you need a larger or more complex model). At this point, it is time to add layers or increase the size of the layers. While doing so, make sure not only to look at the training error but also to keep an eye on the test error. If the training error is decreasing but the test error is flat, then it is an indication that the network fails at generalizing and you should employ various regularization techniques. Start with the standard approaches, such as dropout and L2 regularization. If it is simple, especially when working with images, consider increasing your dataset size using data augmentation.

If you see your test error decreasing or your training error increasing, it is an indication that your regularization techniques work and that you have gotten overfitting under control. At that point, you can increase the size of the model again and see if that further reduces the error. It is often the case that you will need to go through multiple iterations of regularization and model size increases before you arrive at a model that is good enough for your intended use case.

At any point during this process, you can also experiment with different initial learning rates as well as different types of optimizers, such as Adam, AdaGrad, or RMSProp.

Figure 17-11 summarizes this tuning process. However, tuning a deep neural network is often referred to as an art more than a science, so the flow chart should be considered only a starting point. To do all of the tuning tasks, you need a fair amount of persistence and must be willing to experiment with different network architectures and parameters. In this process, it is invaluable to have a fast computing platform that can do rapid iterations so you do not have to wait overnight for results.

Finally, if you consider the process we described, it becomes clear that your training process has been heavily influenced not only by your training dataset but also by your test dataset. For all of these iterations, you have been guided by the model performance on the test dataset while tuning the hyperparameters. This applies even if you do not do the work iteratively but just run a large number of different configurations and pick the best one. In Chapter 5, we described two solutions to this issue. The first solution is to split your dataset into three subsets: training set, validation set, and test set. During the training process, you use only the training set and validation set. Once you are done iterating and have a trained model, you do a final evaluation of the model on the test set, which will now be your actual measurement of how well the model generalized to previously unseen data. The second solution is a technique known as cross-validation. It avoids splitting the dataset into three different parts, but at the expense of additional computations.

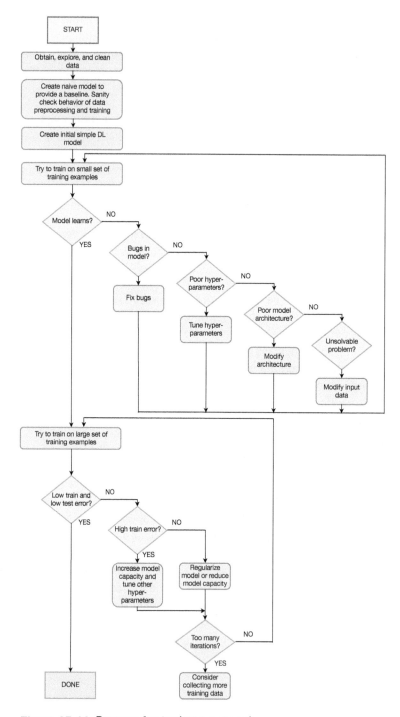

Figure 17-11 **Process for tuning a network**

The process we just described is based on the assumption that you are building your network from scratch. As stated in Chapter 8, if your problem type is well known, a pretrained model can be a very attractive option. Similarly, even if there does not exist a pretrained model for your exact problem type, you can still consider leveraging a pretrained model in a transfer-learning setting. In the tuning process, you would simply use the pretrained model as a building block as you experiment with different types of models. Just remember that it is often useful to freeze the pretrained weights during the first few epochs of training to ensure that the pretrained weights are not ruined in the process of training the randomly initialized weights in the layers you added to the pretrained model. You can later unfreeze the weights and do end-to-end fine-tuning of the full model.

WHEN TO COLLECT MORE TRAINING DATA

A key question is when to collect more training data. This is often an expensive process. Therefore, it is important to not do it unless it is absolutely necessary. A good way of determining whether additional data will help is to experiment with existing data. Ng (2018) suggests plotting *learning curves* to determine whether the problem is truly lack of data or is caused by a model not suitable for the task at hand. Instead of training the model on the entire training dataset, we artificially reduce the size to a very small set of training examples. We then evaluate the model on the full test set. Then we increase the training dataset slightly, by adding back some of the training examples we previously removed, and again evaluate the model on the full test set. By doing this, we can see how the training and test error change as a function of training set size. This is illustrated in Figure 17-12.

In the chart to the left, the training error is small when the training set is small. That is, the model manages to memorize the training examples. However, as the training dataset increases, the model's performance worsens. Further, the test error ends up similar to the training error as we add more training data. In this case, it is unlikely that adding more training data will help. More likely, the selected model is not a good match for the problem.

In the chart to the right, the training error is still low as the training set size is increased. Further, the test error is still decreasing. This indicates that there is a good chance that increasing the size of the training set will result in an improved model.

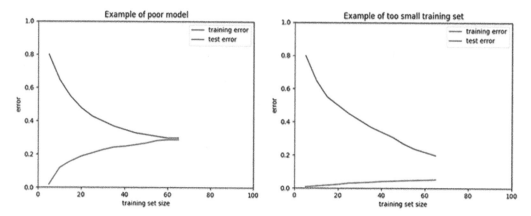

Figure 17-12 Learning curves. Left: The model does not do well on the existing training data. It is unlikely that adding more training data will help. Right: The model does well on the existing training data, but there is a big gap between training and test errors. The test error has not flattened out, so adding more training data can help.

Neural Architecture Search

As seen in the previous section, it is nontrivial to arrive at the right network architecture and the right set of hyperparameters for the training process. In Chapter 5, we briefly discussed how to automate the hyperparameter tuning process using exhaustive or random grid search. A related technique is to automate the process of exploring different network architectures, a field known as *neural architecture search* (NAS).

KEY COMPONENTS OF NEURAL ARCHITECTURE SEARCH

As the name implies, NAS treats the process of arriving at a feasible network architecture as a search problem. In a survey paper, Elsken, Metzen, and Hutter (2019) describe how this search problem can be divided into three parts: *search space, search strategy,* and *evaluation strategy.* The roles these three elements play in the NAS process are illustrated in Figure 17-13.

We first need to define an overall search space, or solution space. We then apply a search strategy to select a candidate solution, or a set of solutions, from this search space. We evaluate these candidates using an evaluation strategy. We repeatedly employ the search strategy and evaluation strategy until we find an acceptable solution. More details of each step in this process are found in the next few sections.

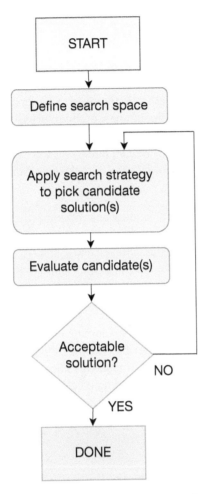

Figure 17-13 Process for neural architectural search

SEARCH SPACE

A starting point is to define the search space. A first thought might be to not restrict it at all and to enable the search algorithm to find the best solution. Thinking more about it, adding some restrictions is necessary in a practical implementation. For example, if our chosen DL framework is TensorFlow using the Keras API, then a reasonable restriction is that the defined model should be a valid Keras model. Similarly, assuming a well-defined problem with an existing dataset, restricting the search space to a model that is compatible with the format of this dataset is also a reasonable assumption. That is, if we want to find a model that can do image classification for the CIFAR-10 dataset, then it is reasonable to restrict the search space to models that can accept images of resolution 32×32×3 on its input and indicate ten probabilities as outputs. Adding a size restriction to the model also makes intuitive sense.

Most of the restrictions we mentioned should be noncontroversial, but it is common to apply additional restrictions as well, with the need to strike a balance between making use of prior knowledge and finding new architectures. One option is to allow only sequential architectures, where we stack layers on top of each other. This restricts the models to what we can build with the Keras Sequential API. This makes for an easy implementation but also significantly restricts the types of models that can be built.

We can loosen this restriction by allowing skip connections. We know that this has been beneficial for image classification. One challenge with skip connections is how to combine them with the output of the skipped layer and still form a valid input to the next layer. This is no different from our initial restriction that the model needs to be a valid Keras model, but in practice, we must figure out the details of ensuring that the combination works.

Another aspect is what building blocks to provide when coming up with the solution space. For example, in Chapter 8, we described the inception module (from GoogLeNet), which has shown to be useful in image classification. One option is to provide such handcrafted modules as building blocks to the search algorithm. This is not necessarily a restriction in the search space but does introduce human bias with respect to which solutions are more likely to be evaluated.

SEARCH STRATEGY

Once the search space is defined, a next step is to settle on a search algorithm to explore this solution space. Search algorithms is a huge topic, and we make no attempt at fully covering it. Instead, we describe three different algorithms of increasing complexity to give just a taste of some solutions that can be used.

Pure random search simply means that we repeatedly randomly select a solution from the solution space and determine if it is better than the best-known solution. This is done until we have found a solution that satisfies our needs. This algorithm is the same as the random grid search algorithm described in the context of hyperparameter tuning in Chapter 5, where the defined grid represents the search space. This algorithm is a global search algorithm, and in theory, it will converge to the best solution if run for sufficiently long. In practice, the size of the search space combined with the cost of evaluating models prevents this algorithm from exploring even a small fraction of the search space. Therefore, this algorithm in isolation is not suitable for NAS, but it can be used as a first step to find a solution that can be used as a starting point for a local search algorithm.

Hill climbing is a local search algorithm, which iteratively refines a solution by exploring models that are similar to the currently best-known model. Given a model, we modify one parameter slightly in one direction and evaluate whether the modified model is better than the current model. If so, this is declared as the new best-known model, and we start a new iteration. If the new model is worse than the best-known model, we drop it and modify the parameter in the other direction. If that still does not improve the model, we move on to a different parameter. There are various variations on hill climbing. For example, in *steepest ascent hill climbing,* all neighboring solutions are first evaluated, and then the best out of these explored models is declared as the best-known model. In the context of NAS, modifying a parameter can involve modifying the size or type of a layer, adding a layer, removing a layer, and so on. A drawback of hill climbing is that it is a local search algorithm. Consequently, it is sensitive to what model is selected as a starting point, and the algorithm can get stuck in a local optimum. One way to partially address that issue is to do hill climbing multiple times from different starting points, also known as *random restart hill climbing.*

A third option is to use an *evolutionary* algorithm. Such algorithms are inspired by biological evolution whereby individuals of a population reproduce into new individuals, and the fittest individuals survive to the next iteration. That is, instead of refining a single model, as in hill climbing, we maintain a set (population) of models (individuals). We select well-performing models (parents) from this population and combine them to create new models (children), with the hope that the combination of two models leads to an even better model. Evolutionary algorithms also apply random changes (mutations) to the individuals, which results in exploring neighboring models similarly to what is done in hill climbing. A key issue is how to combine two individuals in a meaningful way. For the evolutional algorithm to work well, it is important that the new individual maintains (inherits) properties from its parents.

The behaviors of these three search algorithms are illustrated in Figure 17-14. The assumed problem is image classification. For illustration purposes, we assume a severely constrained search space. Each model consists of a number of convolutional layers followed by a number of fully connected layers. All

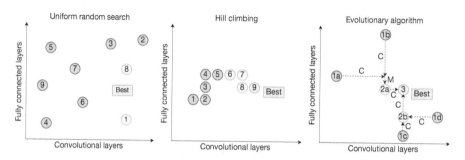

Figure 17-14 Behaviors of three different search algorithms: uniform random search (left), hill climbing (middle), evolutionary search algorithm (right), where C represents cross-over and M represents mutation

parameters are fixed except for the number of convolutional and fully connected layers. That is, the search space is two-dimensional, which enables us to plot it. The best possible solution is shown as a green rectangle in each chart, and the circles represent candidates selected by the different search strategies. The color coding of the circles indicates whether the candidate is far away (red), somewhat close (yellow), or close (green) to the optimal solution.

In the case of uniform random search, the candidates are picked at random without making use of information gained from previous candidates. In the hill climbing case, the algorithm identifies a parameter and direction that lead to a better solution and selects that as the next candidate. It thereby gradually moves closer and closer to the best solution, but there is a risk that it gets stuck in a local minimum.

The evolutionary algorithm combines two parent solutions by using a crossover operation (indicated by C on the arrows). In our case, we simply assume that the crossover operation takes one parameter from each parent. We start with a population of candidate solutions 1a, 1b, 1c, and 1d. We combine the two parents 1a and 1b, using the crossover operation, and arrive at 2a. Note that 2a is not strictly a mix of the two parents in the figure because we also randomly apply a mutation (indicated by M on the arrow) that modifies one of the parameters slightly. By chance, this moves 2a slightly closer to the best solution. In parallel, parents 1c and 1d are combined and result in the child 2b. The figure shows only these two individuals from generation 2, but in reality, we would generate more individuals and keep the better performing ones (natural selection). We then do another iteration in which parents 2a and 2b are combined into solution 3, which is close to the best possible solution. Again, in reality, we would generate multiple individuals in the third generation as well to keep the population size constant.

In the example, the crossover operation enables the evolutionary algorithm to converge faster than the hill climbing algorithm. However, the evolutionary algorithm can also get stuck in a local minimum, just like hill climbing. This might all sound very abstract at this point, but we soon make it more concrete with a programming example implementing these three algorithms.

As previously mentioned, the three algorithms represent just a small subset of available search algorithms. One common theme among the three is that none of them requires a gradient. Another option is to define the models in a way that a gradient can be computed between multiple models, and then use gradient descent to search for the best model. Other approaches worth mentioning are *reinforcement learning* and *Bayesian optimization*. More details and references to how those and other algorithms have been applied to NAS can be found in the survey paper by Elsken, Metzen, and Hutter (2019). A different survey paper by Ren and colleagues (2020) is another resource to consult.

EVALUATION STRATEGY

The third step in the NAS process is to evaluate the candidate models during the search step. Note that the actual evaluation is performed as a step in the search algorithms we just described, but the way in which that is done is a separate topic. Ideally, we would want to fully train and evaluate each model for the same amount of time that we would normally train the final model in a production setting. This is often not feasible, given that fully training the final model might take multiple days. There is a direct trade-off between how much time we spend on training the candidate solutions and the number of solutions we have time to evaluate. It is often beneficial to reduce the amount of time spent on training each candidate solution and thereby enable the search algorithm to evaluate more solutions.

In their survey paper, Elsken, Metzen, and Hutter (2019) describe a number of ways to reduce time spent on training the candidate models. We list some of the simpler ones here:

- Train for a reduced number of epochs.

- Train with a reduced dataset.

- Downscale the model.

- Extrapolate the learning curve to take the trend into account.

- Inherit weights from the previous iteration instead of training the model from scratch. This assumes that the models are sufficiently similar between iterations, so it is feasible to transfer weights from one model to the next.

For more details about the these approaches as well as additional techniques, we encourage interested readers to follow up on references in the survey by Elsken, Metzen, and Hutter.

PROGRAMMING EXAMPLE: SEARCHING FOR AN ARCHITECTURE FOR CIFAR-10 CLASSIFICATION

In this programming example, we explore NAS to find a suitable architecture for CIFAR-10 classification. That is, we try to automatically arrive at a good architecture instead of hand-engineering it as we did in Chapter 7, "Convolutional Neural Networks Applied to Image Classification." We make no attempt at creating the most advanced NAS algorithm out there but focus on illustrating the concept by implementing three different search algorithms from scratch. The initial code is the same, regardless of what search algorithm is used. As always, we start with initialization code and loading the dataset in Code Snippet 17-14. We define some variables that are part of defining the search space, such as what types of layer can be used and what kind of parameters and values are valid for each type of layer.

Code Snippet 17-14 Initialization Code and Loading the Dataset

```
import tensorflow as tf
from tensorflow import keras
from tensorflow.keras.utils import to_categorical
from tensorflow.keras.models import Sequential
from tensorflow.keras.layers import Lambda
from tensorflow.keras.layers import Dense
from tensorflow.keras.layers import Flatten
from tensorflow.keras.layers import Conv2D
from tensorflow.keras.layers import Dropout
from tensorflow.keras.layers import MaxPooling2D
import numpy as np
import logging
import copy
tf.get_logger().setLevel(logging.ERROR)
```

```
MAX_MODEL_SIZE = 500000
CANDIDATE_EVALUATIONS = 500
EVAL_EPOCHS = 3
FINAL_EPOCHS = 20


layer_types = ['DENSE', 'CONV2D', 'MAXPOOL2D']
param_values = dict([('size', [16, 64, 256, 1024, 4096]),
                 ('activation', ['relu', 'tanh', 'elu']),
                 ('kernel_size', [(1, 1), (2, 2), (3, 3), (4, 4)]),
                 ('stride', [(1, 1), (2, 2), (3, 3), (4, 4)]),
                 ('dropout', [0.0, 0.4, 0.7, 0.9])])


layer_params = dict([('DENSE', ['size', 'activation', 'dropout']),
                 ('CONV2D', ['size', 'activation',
                                     'kernel_size', 'stride',
                                     'dropout']),
                 ('MAXPOOL2D', ['kernel_size', 'stride',
                                     'dropout'])])


# Load dataset.
cifar_dataset = keras.datasets.cifar10
(train_images, train_labels), (test_images,
                  test_labels) = cifar_dataset.load_data()
# Standardize dataset.
mean = np.mean(train_images)
stddev = np.std(train_images)
train_images = (train_images - mean) / stddev
test_images = (test_images - mean) / stddev


# Change labels to one-hot.
train_labels = to_categorical(train_labels,
                             num_classes=10)
test_labels = to_categorical(test_labels,
                             num_classes=10)
```

The next step is to build some infrastructure for automatically generating models. To keep things simple, we impose significant restrictions on the search space. To start with, we allow only sequential models. In addition, given our knowledge of the application (image classification), we impose a rigid structure on the network. We view the network as a combination of a bottom subnetwork and a top subnetwork. The bottom part consists of a combination of convolutional and max-pooling layers, and the top part consists of fully connected layers. In addition, we allow dropout layers after any layer, and we also add a flatten layer between the bottom and the top to ensure that we end up with a valid TensorFlow model.

The methods in Code Snippet 17-15 are used to generate a random model within this constrained search space. There is also a method that computes the size of the resulting model in terms of the number of trainable parameters. Note that these methods do not have anything to do with TensorFlow but is our own representation of a network before invoking the DL framework.

Code Snippet 17-15 Methods to Generate a Network with Random Parameters Within the Defined Search Space

```python
# Methods to create a model definition.
def generate_random_layer(layer_type):
    layer = {}
    layer['layer_type'] = layer_type
    params = layer_params[layer_type]
    for param in params:
        values = param_values[param]
        layer[param] = values[np.random.randint(0, len(values))]
    return layer


def generate_model_definition():
    layer_count = np.random.randint(2, 9)
    non_dense_count = np.random.randint(1, layer_count)
    layers = []
    for i in range(layer_count):
        if i < non_dense_count:
            layer_type = layer_types[np.random.randint(1, 3)]
            layer = generate_random_layer(layer_type)
        else:
            layer = generate_random_layer('DENSE')
```

```
        layers.append(layer)
    return layers

def compute_weight_count(layers):
    last_shape = (32, 32, 3)
    total_weights = 0
    for layer in layers:
        layer_type = layer['layer_type']
        if layer_type == 'DENSE':
            size = layer['size']
            weights = size * (np.prod(last_shape) + 1)
            last_shape = (layer['size'])
        else:
            stride = layer['stride']
            if layer_type == 'CONV2D':
                size = layer['size']
                kernel_size = layer['kernel_size']
                weights = size * ((np.prod(kernel_size) *
                                    last_shape[2]) + 1)
                last_shape = (np.ceil(last_shape[0]/stride[0]),
                                np.ceil(last_shape[1]/stride[1]),
                                size)
            elif layer_type == 'MAXPOOL2D':
                weights = 0
                last_shape = (np.ceil(last_shape[0]/stride[0]),
                                np.ceil(last_shape[1]/stride[1]),
                                last_shape[2])
        total_weights += weights
    total_weights += ((np.prod(last_shape) + 1) * 10)
    return total_weights
```

The next set of methods takes the model definition created in the previous code snippet and creates and evaluates a corresponding TensorFlow model for a small number of epochs. This is all shown in Code Snippet 17-16. The method that evaluates the model imposes a size restriction. If the requested model has too many parameters, the method simply returns an accuracy of 0.0. The search algorithm that invokes the method will need to check for this and, if needed, generate a smaller model.

Code Snippet 17-16 Translate a Model Definition into a TensorFlow Model and Evaluate That Model for a Small Number of Epochs

```
# Methods to create and evaluate model based on model definition.
def add_layer(model, params, prior_type):
    layer_type = params['layer_type']
    if layer_type == 'DENSE':
        if prior_type != 'DENSE':
            model.add(Flatten())
        size = params['size']
        act = params['activation']
        model.add(Dense(size, activation=act))
    elif layer_type == 'CONV2D':
        size = params['size']
        act = params['activation']
        kernel_size = params['kernel_size']
        stride = params['stride']
        model.add(Conv2D(size, kernel_size, activation=act,
                         strides=stride, padding='same'))
    elif layer_type == 'MAXPOOL2D':
        kernel_size = params['kernel_size']
        stride = params['stride']
        model.add(MaxPooling2D(pool_size=kernel_size,
                              strides=stride, padding='same'))
    dropout = params['dropout']
    if(dropout > 0.0):
        model.add(Dropout(dropout))

def create_model(layers):
    tf.keras.backend.clear_session()
    model = Sequential()
    model.add(Lambda(lambda x: x, input_shape=(32, 32, 3)))
    prev_layer = 'LAMBDA' # Dummy layer to set input_shape
```

```
    for layer in layers:
        add_layer(model, layer, prev_layer)
        prev_layer = layer['layer_type']
    model.add(Dense(10, activation='softmax'))
    model.compile(loss='categorical_crossentropy',
                  optimizer='adam', metrics=['accuracy'])
    return model

def create_and_evaluate_model(model_definition):
    weight_count = compute_weight_count(model_definition)
    if weight_count > MAX_MODEL_SIZE:
        return 0.0
    model = create_model(model_definition)
    history = model.fit(train_images, train_labels,
                        validation_data=(test_images, test_labels),
                        epochs=EVAL_EPOCHS, batch_size=64,
                        verbose=2, shuffle=False)
    acc = history.history['val_accuracy'][-1]
    print('Size: ', weight_count)
    print('Accuracy: %5.2f' %acc)
    return acc
```

We now have all the building blocks to implement our first and simplest search algorithm, namely, pure random search. This is shown in Code Snippet 17-17. It consists of an outer for loop that runs for a fixed number of iterations. Each iteration randomly generates and evaluates a model. There is an inner loop to handle the case when the generated model is too big. The inner loop simply repeatedly generates random models until one is generated that adheres to the size restriction.

Code Snippet 17-17 Implementation of the Pure Random Search Algorithm

```
# Pure random search.
np.random.seed(7)
val_accuracy = 0.0
```

```
for i in range(CANDIDATE_EVALUATIONS):
    valid_model = False
    while(valid_model == False):
        model_definition = generate_model_definition()
        acc = create_and_evaluate_model(model_definition)
        if acc > 0.0:
            valid_model = True
    if acc > val_accuracy:
        best_model = model_definition
        val_accuracy = acc
    print('Random search, best accuracy: %5.2f' %val_accuracy)
```

As the program runs, you will see how 500 different models are evaluated for three epochs each and their accuracy is printed along with the accuracy of the best model so far. In our experiment, the evaluation accuracy for the best model ended up being 59%.

As already described, randomly generating models without making any use of the observations of the behavior of past models is an inefficient way of trying to find the best solution. The next step is to implement the hill climbing algorithm. This is done in Code Snippet 17-18. We create a helper method that randomly adjusts one of the parameters slightly to move an existing model into a neighboring model in the allowed search space. The first for loop determines the index of the boundary between the bottom (non-dense) and top (dense) layers. The next step is to determine whether to increase or decrease the capacity of the model. This is followed by determining whether to add/remove a layer or tweak parameters of an existing layer. Much of the logic is there to ensure that the modified model still stays within the boundaries of what is a legal model.

The actual hill climbing algorithm is implemented at the bottom of the code snippet. It assumes an initial model and gradually tweaks it in the direction that improves prediction accuracy. The implemented version of the algorithm is known as *stochastic hill climbing*. A parameter is modified at random, and if the resulting model is better than the previously best-known model, the change is kept. Otherwise, it is reverted, and another tweak is tried. The given implementation assumes that the hill climbing algorithm is run after doing random search, so there is a promising model to start from.

Code Snippet 17-18 **Hill Climbing Algorithm**

```python
# Helper method for hill climbing and evolutionary algorithm.
def tweak_model(model_definition):
    layer_num = np.random.randint(0, len(model_definition))
    last_layer = len(model_definition) - 1
    for first_dense, layer in enumerate(model_definition):
        if layer['layer_type'] == 'DENSE':
            break
    if np.random.randint(0, 2) == 1:
        delta = 1
    else:
        delta = -1
    if np.random.randint(0, 2) == 1:
        # Add/remove layer.
        if len(model_definition) < 3:
            delta = 1 # Layer removal not allowed
        if delta == -1:
            # Remove layer.
            if layer_num == 0 and first_dense == 1:
                layer_num += 1 # Require >= 1 non-dense layer.
            if layer_num == first_dense and layer_num == last_layer:
                layer_num -= 1 # Require >= 1 dense layer.
            del model_definition[layer_num]
        else:
            # Add layer.
            if layer_num < first_dense:
                layer_type = layer_types[np.random.randint(1, 3)]
            else:
                layer_type = 'DENSE'
            layer = generate_random_layer(layer_type)
            model_definition.insert(layer_num, layer)
    else:
        # Tweak parameter.
        layer = model_definition[layer_num]
        layer_type = layer['layer_type']
```

```
                params = layer_params[layer_type]
                param = params[np.random.randint(0, len(params))]
                current_val = layer[param]
                values = param_values[param]
                index = values.index(current_val)
                max_index = len(values)
                new_val = values[(index + delta) % max_index]
                layer[param] = new_val


    # Hill climbing, starting from best model from random search.
    model_definition = best_model


    for i in range(CANDIDATE_EVALUATIONS):
        valid_model = False
        while(valid_model == False):
            old_model_definition = copy.deepcopy(model_definition)
            tweak_model(model_definition)
            acc = create_and_evaluate_model(model_definition)
            if acc > 0.0:
                valid_model = True
            else:
                model_definition = old_model_definition
        if acc > val_accuracy:
            best_model = copy.deepcopy(model_definition)
            val_accuracy = acc
        else:
            model_definition = old_model_definition
        print('Hill climbing, best accuracy: %5.2f' %val_accuracy)
```

The hill climbing algorithm takes the best model from the random search experiment and gradually refines it. After evaluating 500 different models, our evaluation accuracy was 74%.

For both the random search algorithm and the hill climbing algorithm, our evaluation strategy was to evaluate each solution for only three epochs. We made the assumption that the resulting validation error would be a good indicator of how well the model would perform after more training. To get a more accurate evaluation of how well the best model actually performs, Code Snippet 17-19 evaluates the best model for 20 epochs. As expected, the increased number of epochs increases the test accuracy. In our experiment, we ended up with an accuracy of 76%. That result is comparable to the best configuration in Chapter 7 if we take into account that we trained that configuration for 128 epochs.

Code Snippet 17-19 Evaluate the Best-Known Model for a Larger Number of Epochs

```
# Evaluate final model for larger number of epochs.
model = create_model(best_model)
model.summary()
model.compile(loss='categorical_crossentropy',
              optimizer='adam', metrics=['accuracy'])

history = model.fit(
    train_images, train_labels, validation_data =
    (test_images, test_labels), epochs=FINAL_EPOCHS, batch_size=64,
    verbose=2, shuffle=True)
```

The third search algorithm that we implement is an evolutionary algorithm. It is shown in Code Snippet 17-20. We start by defining the number of simultaneous candidate solutions in the population to be 50. A key part of the evolutionary algorithm is the crossover operation, which combines two existing solutions (parents) into a new solution (child) that inherits properties of both of its parents. The approach we have taken is to simply take the bottom (non-dense) layers from one of the parents and combine it with the top (dense) layers from the other parent. The thinking here is that the task of the bottom layers is to extract useful features from the image, and the task of the top layers is to perform the classification. If one of the parents has a good structure for extracting features and the other parent has a good structure for doing a classification based on a good set of features, then an even better model can be found by combining the two. We confirmed that this works in practice with a hand-engineered example. The crossover method also has logic to combine all layers from the parent models if the parent models are sufficiently small.

The evolutionary algorithm starts by generating and evaluating a population of random models. It then randomly generates new models by tweaking and combining models in the existing population. There are three ways that a new model can be created:

- Tweak an existing model.

- Combine two parent models into a child model.

- Combine two parent models into a child model and apply a tweak to the resulting model.

Once new models have been generated, the algorithm probabilistically selects high-performing models to keep for the next iteration. In this selection process, both the parents and the children participate, which is also known as *elitism* within the field of evolutionary computation.

Code Snippet 17-20 Evolutionary Algorithm

```python
POPULATION_SIZE = 50

# Helper method for evolutionary algorithm.
def cross_over(parents):
    # Pick bottom half of one and top half of the other.
    # If model is small, randomly stack top or bottom from both.
    bottoms = [[], []]
    tops = [[], []]
    for i, model in enumerate(parents):
        for layer in model:
            if layer['layer_type'] != 'DENSE':
                bottoms[i].append(copy.deepcopy(layer))
            else:
                tops[i].append(copy.deepcopy(layer))

    i = np.random.randint(0, 2)
    if (i == 1 and compute_weight_count(parents[0]) +
        compute_weight_count(parents[1]) < MAX_MODEL_SIZE):
        i = np.random.randint(0, 2)
        new_model = bottoms[i] + bottoms[(i+1)%2]
        i = np.random.randint(0, 2)
        new_model = new_model + tops[i] + tops[(i+1)%2]
```

```python
        else:
            i = np.random.randint(0, 2)
            new_model = bottoms[i] + tops[(i+1)%2]
        return new_model


# Evolutionary algorithm.
np.random.seed(7)

# Generate initial population of models.
population = []
for i in range(POPULATION_SIZE):
    valid_model = False
    while(valid_model == False):
        model_definition = generate_model_definition()
        acc = create_and_evaluate_model(model_definition)
        if acc > 0.0:
            valid_model = True
    population.append((acc, model_definition))

# Evolve population.
generations = int(CANDIDATE_EVALUATIONS / POPULATION_SIZE) - 1
for i in range(generations):
    # Generate new individuals.
    print('Generation number: ', i)
    for j in range(POPULATION_SIZE):
        valid_model = False
        while(valid_model == False):
            rand = np.random.rand()
            parents = random.sample(
                population[:POPULATION_SIZE], 2)
            parents = [parents[0][1], parents[1][1]]
            if rand < 0.5:
                child = copy.deepcopy(parents[0])
                tweak_model(child)
            elif rand < 0.75:
                child = cross_over(parents)
```

```
        else:
            child = cross_over(parents)
            tweak_model(child)
        acc = create_and_evaluate_model(child)
        if acc > 0.0:
            valid_model = True
      population.append((acc, child))
    # Randomly select fit individuals.
    population.sort(key=lambda x:x[0])
    print('Evolution, best accuracy: %5.2f' %population[-1][0])
    top = np.int64(np.ceil(0.2*len(population)))
    bottom = np.int64(np.ceil(0.3*len(population)))
    top_individuals = population[-top:]
    remaining = np.int64(len(population)/2) - len(top_individuals)
    population = random.sample(population[bottom:-top],
                                remaining) + top_individuals

best_model = population[-1][1]
```

The code first generates and evaluates a population of 50 random models. It then repeatedly evolves and evaluates a new population of 50 individuals. After having evaluated ten generations, or 500 individuals in total, the evaluation accuracy of the best solution in our experiment ended up at 65%, which was worse than the hill climbing algorithm. Just as for the hill climbing algorithm, you can get a more accurate evaluation by training the best model for a larger number of epochs using the Code Snippet 17-19. For our model from the evolutionary algorithm, this resulted in a test accuracy of 73%.

The results can vary significantly from run to run given that all three search algorithms are stochastic. Our results indicate that the hill climbing algorithm is better than the specific evolutionary algorithm we implemented, and both of them are better than the pure random search. The main purpose of this programming example was not to arrive at the most optimized solution but to illustrate and demystify these three approaches to automatically finding a network architecture. We did have some problems with out-of-memory errors, which seemed related to creating a large number of models after each other in the same program. Depending on your machine configuration, you might have to reduce the number of iterations or maximum model size.

At this point, it is fun to take a step back and look at what we just did. We used an algorithm inspired by biological sexual reproduction to evolve a population of models implementing an architecture that is inspired by biological neurons. The result was a model that can classify images based on what type of object is present in the image. Not too long ago, this would have sounded like total science fiction, and it is easy to spin it in a way that makes an outsider think that we are evolving our own little lifeform in our lab. In reality, it is just a simple Python script consisting of less than 300 lines of code. Then again, lines of code might not be the most meaningful metric. Perhaps we will soon have a sufficiently expressive library, where we can solve any human-level task with a single line of code:

```
model.add_brain(neurons=8.6e10, connections_per_neuron=7000)
```

IMPLICATIONS OF NEURAL ARCHITECTURE SEARCH

NAS provides a path to automatically generating DL models and thereby enabling practitioners not skilled in network architectures to build their own problem-specific models. As an example, Jin, Song, and Hu (2019) introduced a NAS framework known as Auto-Keras. Using this framework, searching for an architecture for a classifier is reduced to an import statement and a couple of lines of code:[2]

```
from autokeras import StructuredDataClassifier
search = StructuredDataClassifier(max_trials=20)
search.fit(x = X_train, y = y_train)
```

However, as seen in the previously described programming example, this comes at a significant computational cost. One open issue with respect to NAS is whether it truly will result in a general solution and thereby remove the need for detailed DL skills among practitioners. At least in the near future, it seems likely that practitioners will still need to know the basics about their specific problem domain and use NAS as a tool that helps with finding the best solution within a well-defined solution space. Another central question, raised by Thomas (2018), is whether every new problem needs its own unique architecture. It might well be that the best way to enable a large number of nonexperts to make use of DL is by making it easy to use transfer learning based on pretrained models. These

2. As usual, you would also need to load a dataset and ensure that it is in the right format.

pretrained models would be developed by a smaller set of experts with access to the vast computational power needed for finding new complicated architectures.

Concluding Remarks

In this chapter, we discussed autoencoders, multimodal learning, multitask learning, network tuning, and NAS. If your goal is to apply DL to industry problems, then we believe that the section about network tuning is at least as important as knowing the latest and greatest network architectures. Without a good methodology, it is easy to waste time and resources on the wrong things or simply fail to reap benefits of DL in cases where DL actually is a good solution.

However, we do want to provide a word of caution. DL is not the solution to everything, and even in application areas where DL does a good job, there can be more efficient solutions. It is often the case that a well-thought-out engineered solution to a problem requires significantly less computational power than a DL-based solution. Similarly, if an engineered solution is not practical, sometimes it is the case that a traditional ML technique is more efficient than a DL-based solution. Therefore, as with any other engineering task, it is important to consider different solutions and pick the right tool to apply to your specific problem.

This concludes our presentation of different DL techniques, and we are ready to move on to the final chapter, where we discuss some important ethical aspects of DL as well as provide pointers for further reading.

Chapter 18

Summary and
Next Steps

In this last chapter of the book, we start with a section that summarizes what we think you should have learned from the book, to give you an opportunity to identify things that you might have missed. An important aspect when you start applying your newly gained skills is that you do so in a responsible manner. To stress this, we have included a discussion about data ethics and algorithmic bias. We conclude by listing some areas of deep learning (DL) that we have omitted, and we outline some potential paths forward to continue your learning process after finishing this book.

Things You Should Know by Now

This book has introduced a large number of concepts, and if you have not been exposed to them in the past, it might be somewhat overwhelming. This section summarizes the major concepts so you can sanity check that you did not miss anything significant. You can use this section to identify concepts that you might want to revisit before moving on in your DL studies.

This book has described a number of different problem types that can be addressed with DL. They include binary classification, multicategory classification, regression, and time-series prediction. We also showed examples of converting data from one representation to another, such as from one language to another or creating a textual description from an image. We also touched on sentiment analysis of textual data and outlier detection.

The basic building blocks for the neural networks that we have used to solve these problems are units/neurons that are all variations on the Rosenblatt perceptron. For the simplest units, the only difference is the activation function, where we have mostly used linear, tanh, logistic sigmoid, and rectified linear unit (ReLU). We have also used a more complex unit known as long short-term memory (LSTM).

We combined these units into different types of layers or network architectures, such as fully connected feedforward networks, convolutional networks, and recurrent networks, where each network type is good for solving a specific set of problems. We have also shown how different network types can be combined into hybrid architectures, including the fairly complicated encoder-decoder networks used in the later chapters, and how they can be extended to include attention. We described the Transformer architecture, which employs self-attention. Finally, we showed examples of networks that work on multiple modalities, as well as multiheaded networks used for multitask learning.

All of these networks have been trained using stochastic gradient descent (SGD), in which the gradients are computed using the backpropagation algorithm. This requires an appropriate loss function, and we looked at mean squared error (used for linear output units), cross-entropy (for sigmoid output unit), and categorical cross-entropy (for softmax output layers). As part of this process, you need to decide on a weight initialization scheme, a learning rate, as well as whether you want to use vanilla SGD or a more advanced optimizer such as Adam or RMSProp.

During training, we have had to pay attention to training error versus test error and employed various techniques in cases when learning did not proceed as desired. We looked at various techniques to fight exploding and vanishing gradients that prevented the network from learning at all and explored various regularization techniques for cases in which the network managed to learn the training set but did not generalize to the test set. Examples of such regularization techniques are early stopping, L1 and L2 regularization, dropout, and data augmentation. Related to all of these parameters, we discussed methods for tuning your network and selecting hyperparameters, and we also discussed the concept of neural architecture search (NAS) to automate the processes of finding a model architecture.

To train a network, we need a dataset. In this book, we have used standard datasets such as MNIST, Boston Housing, CIFAR-10, and COCO. We have also used downloaded data not specifically intended for DL—for example, quarterly sales data, the book *Frankenstein,* and a set of sentences translated from French to English.

To use these datasets, we have frequently had to convert the data into suitable representations by standardizing numerical data, ensuring that image data is properly represented as one or more channels, one-hot encoding textual data when working with individual characters, or creating dense encodings of words, also known as *word embeddings*. We learned how such word embeddings could encode both grammatical features and semantics of the words that they represent. Related to this is vector representation of entire sentences, which we saw can be used for sentiment analysis.

We hope that all of the above at least seems vaguely familiar to you after reading this far in the book. If you feel that you need to revisit something, then just browse the green boxes throughout the book until you find the topic that you missed. You can also consult the cheat sheets in Appendix J for a visual summary of many of the concepts.

Ethical AI and Data Ethics

Throughout this book, we have pointed out various examples of ethical problems arising from training models on datasets that are not sufficiently diverse or contain human biases. These examples fall under the wider topics of ethical artificial intelligence (AI) and data ethics.

Ethics involves identifying and recommending right and wrong behavior. Data ethics is a subfield, which relates to these aspects in the context of data, in particular, personal data. In other words, any discussions about what is right and wrong to do with personal data have to do with data ethics. Similarly, ethical AI relates to these topics in the overall context of AI, of which data is just one component.

As is typically the case with new technologies, legislation has a hard time keeping up with the pace of innovation, which causes a void of checks and balances. This makes it especially important for you, as a practitioner, to act responsibly to avoid causing harm. In this section, we give a brief introduction to this topic and provide some pointers for further reading.

One problem arises when a trained model is used in a setting for which it was never intended. For example, if a model is known to contain human biases, then using it in law enforcement is a bad idea. Mitchell and colleagues (2018) proposed a way of addressing this. When releasing a model, they recommend also releasing documentation describing details about the model and its intended use case. This piece of documentation is known as a *model card* and is based on a template with a predefined set of topics. The model card is similar to the *datasheet for datasets* discussed in Chapter 4, "Fully Connected Networks Applied to Multiclass Classification" (Gebru et al., 2018), but instead of documenting the dataset, the model card documents the model.

A major challenge with ethics is that different people have different views on what is right and wrong. This implies that there are no exact answers, and it is easy to make mistakes due to personal biases and blind spots. To some extent, this can be addressed in a team setting. Throughout the product development phases, identify and discuss potential problems with the application and the algorithms and data it is based on. Ideally, this is done in a diverse team with multiple perspectives. However, even a homogenous team or a single person can use their empathy to identify problems that apply only to people other than themselves. Maintaining a checklist of specific problems to look for, as well as topics or questions to consider, can facilitate these discussions.

PROBLEMS TO LOOK OUT FOR

Much of this section is based on a book chapter, "Data Ethics," in *Deep Learning for Coders with fastai and PyTorch* (Thomas, Howard, and Gugger, 2020) on *Data Ethics*. The authors discuss the following four problems as particularly relevant: *recourse and accountability, feedback loops, bias,* and *disinformation*. We provide an overview and examples of these topics before moving on to a checklist of questions to consider in these product discussions.

THE NEED FOR RECOURSE AND ACCOUNTABILITY

Regardless of how well intentioned an algorithm is, it is likely that things will go wrong in some cases. There need to be ways to address recourse and accountability, possibly by bypassing the system, to avoid putting people in catch-22 situations. This requires the system designer, provider, and maintainer to assume accountability instead of just blaming the system.

A good example of such a problem is the US credit score agencies that collect and aggregate personal financial data into a single score for every US consumer.

Other companies and institutions rely on this score to determine if a consumer should be allowed to take out a loan, get a credit card, or sign up for a cell phone plan. Needless to say, sometimes things go wrong, and a person ends up with an inaccurate score. Correcting these inaccuracies involves much time and bureaucracy. Many of these problems could be solved if the companies involved assumed more accountability and provided more streamlined ways of resolving inaccuracies.

One can argue that this is more of an organizational problem than a technology problem. However, in order to solve such a problem, all parts of the system need to work together, and as a developer of new technology, you can play a key role by raising questions of accountability and recourse early in a system's design. Another prime example of this is the No Fly List maintained by the US government. Accidentally ending up on this list can have devastating consequences that are extremely hard to resolve. A cartoon by Sorensen illustrates this (Sorensen, n.d.). Although the details of how somebody ends up on this list are kept secret, it is not hard to envision that technology and data are used in one or more steps in the process.

FEEDBACK LOOPS

Whenever designing a system, it is important to consider whether it can lead to the system running out of control. This is particularly important when the actions of the system affect the environment that the system works in. That is, the output at one point in time will affect the inputs at a later point in time.

One example of such feedback loops described by Thomas, Howard, and Gugger (2020) is YouTube's recommendation system. The observation is that people tend to get drawn to controversial content, including conspiracy theories that are simply not true. It also turns out that the same group of people who get drawn to videos of conspiracy theories watch a lot of YouTube videos. This combination resulted in YouTube's recommendation system starting to recommend more and more videos of conspiracy theories, attracting and radicalizing more and more extremist viewers. In short, the system achieved its intended goal to attract users who spend a lot of time using the system, but it came with an unintended negative side effect on society.

Another example of a feedback loop is when an automatic tool is used to identify suitable candidates in a hiring process. Consider a case where the tool is trained on data describing the individuals who are currently successful within this occupation. If this occupation is currently dominated by a specific group of people (e.g., male employees), the model may well detect this bias. It will then use this bias when identifying candidates and suggest mostly male applicants. De-Arteaga and colleagues (2019) describe how this can compound existing imbalances. Because the system suggests mostly male applicants, even more men will be hired, which in turn can widen the gender gap even further within that occupation.

Feedback loops are not only problematic for affected individuals and society at large. The company providing the service is also at great risk. Baer (2019) describes a case in which a bank used an algorithm to automatically identify low-risk customers and raise their credit limit. The algorithm identified low-risk customers by looking at their credit utilization (percentage of used credit compared to upper limit), and if it was below a certain threshold, then the upper limit was raised. The moment their credit limit was raised, the utilization fell further because utilization is a function of the upper limit. This in turn caused the system to further increase the credit limit. A number of iterations later, the customers would have close to unlimited credit, which led to people spending more than they could afford and put the bank at great risk.

DISINFORMATION

One important subfield of DL is generative models. We have only briefly touched on this topic in the context of autocompletion of text, but DL can be used to generate larger bodies of text as well. These models can be used to generate and spread disinformation, which can take the form of Twitter bots (Wojcik et al., 2018) generating and retweeting fake news.

Similarly, generative DL models can produce realistic-looking images and videos. Such models have been used to create videos in which the appearance of a person is altered to look like somebody else. Falsified video is known as *deepfake* (Sample, 2020) and has been used in malicious ways to mislead and cause harm.

BIAS

We have already touched on bias in datasets, but there are multiple types and sources of bias. Suresh and Guttag (2019) discuss six distinct types of bias to be aware of when working with machine learning (ML). Each type of bias is associated with a particular step in the ML pipeline:

- *Historical bias* is bias present in the real world. Even if a language model were trained on all text that had ever been written, the text would be affected by human bias of the authors.

- *Representation bias* is an outcome of sampled data not being representative of the world. If we use only the English version of Wikipedia to train our model, then it is not representative of other languages. Further, it is not representative of all English text either, because Wikipedia represents a special kind of content.

- *Measurement bias* results from measuring one feature and using it as a proxy for the true feature that we are trying to measure. If we use criminal convictions as a proxy for criminal activity, but our justice system employs racial profiling, or convictions are biased in other ways, then our measure of criminal activity will be biased.

- *Aggregation bias* results from the model combining distinct subgroups in an incorrect way. For example, imagine creating a model that produces a medical diagnosis without having access to patient gender or ethnicity. Given that gender and ethnicity often play a role in properly diagnosing a patient, this model will do worse for certain groups. Instead, it can be better to develop separate models for different groups or provide the model with inputs to distinguish between the different groups.[1] A good way to detect this kind of problem is to not only look at the overall performance metric of the model but also compute it individually for different subgroups and ensure that the model performs similarly across subgroups.

- *Evaluation bias* results from the way the model is evaluated. For example, if the test dataset or the evaluation metrics are poorly chosen, then there is a risk that the resulting model will not do well when deployed.

- *Deployment bias* is bias arising from the deployed model being used or interpreted in a way that was not originally intended.

To illustrate how these concepts can be applied in practice, consider Figure 18-1, which originally was posted on Twitter. The left image is a low-resolution image of Barack Obama, the 44th president of the United States. The right image is the output of a model known as PULSE that is designed to create a realistic-looking high-resolution image of a face using a low-resolution image as input (Menon, Damian, Hu, et al., 2020). Although the model had been shown to work well on a test dataset, this example indicates that the model is biased toward outputting a face resembling a white person. It does not do well when applied to a face of a person of color.

---

1. Using different models for different groups can introduce its own set of problems and can be somewhat controversial.

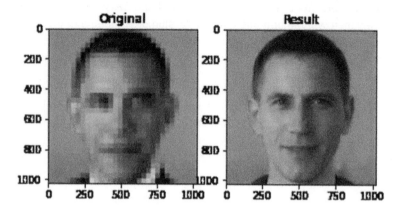

Figure 18-1 Left: A low-resolution image of Barack Obama. Right: The resulting output from the original PULSE model. The goal of the model is to provide a realistic high-resolution image that could correspond to the low-resolution image. The resulting image indicates that the model suffers from racial bias. (Source: From https://twitter.com/Chicken3gg/status/1274314622447820801)

PULSE makes use of a model known as StyleGAN (Karras, Laine, and Aila, 2019) to generate high-resolution images. The StyleGAN model was trained on the Flickr-Faces HQ (FFHQ) dataset. This dataset was introduced in the same paper as StyleGAN and was obtained by crawling the Flickr website for pictures of faces. Only pictures under permissive licenses were used. PULSE itself does not train any additional parameters but simply uses the pretrained model, so no additional dataset was used for training. The Celeb HQ dataset (Karras et al., 2018) was used to evaluate PULSE. Celeb HQ is derived from the CelebA dataset (Liu et al., 2015), which consists of pictures of faces of celebrities.

Let us now reason about the types of biases that made things go wrong. First, consider the question whether the intent was to build a model that works for any individual in the world or only for people who use Flickr. Clearly, if the intent was to build a model that works for all people in the world, then representation bias has been introduced by using images only from Flickr in the training data. Even if the intent was to build a model only for Flickr users, there would still be representation bias given that only images under permissive licenses were used.

Second, the model might suffer from aggregation bias. A starting point to address this bias is to detect it. This is typically done by looking at accuracy metrics for individual subgroups as opposed to using only a single accuracy metric for the entire test set. In this specific example, the subgroups would be different ethnicities. No accuracy metric was used, but the output of the model was simply inspected to determine whether the generated face looked realistic. That is, using a more diverse test dataset to confirm that the model worked well for minorities would have uncovered this problem.

Third, using the Celeb HQ dataset for testing introduces evaluation bias. It is unlikely that the physical appearance of celebrities represents the physical appearance of the general population. Further, the Celeb HQ has been shown to not be very diverse. In fact, when Karras and colleagues (2019) introduced the FFHQ dataset, they said that this new dataset "includes vastly more variation than CelebA-HQ in terms of age, ethnicity and image background, and also has much better coverage of accessories such as eyeglasses, sunglasses, hats, etc."

Finally, we find it likely that deployment bias plays a role, although this is somewhat subtle. As previously mentioned, PULSE makes use of StyleGAN. To ensure that the generated images look realistic, PULSE restricts the search space StyleGAN is allowed to consider. It does so by imposing a constraint on the input parameters to StyleGAN. It is unclear to us whether this is how the StyleGAN model was originally intended to be used. That is why we suspect that deployment bias causes problems in this case, especially given that the original StyleGAN paper clearly shows that the model is capable of generating high-quality realistic images of people of color.

In a more recent version of the PULSE paper, Menon, Damian, Ravi, and Rudin (2020) added a section about bias in which they discuss these concerns, including the theory that the constraint PULSE imposes on the input parameters is part of the problem. On the other hand, they also point out that another study has shown that there is demographic bias in the images generated by StyleGAN (Salminen et al., 2020). This bias is likely to affect the output of any downstream model that uses the model unless the downstream model somehow removes this bias.

This later version of the PULSE paper (Menon, Damian, Ravi, and Rudin, 2020) also includes an evaluation of the model on the FairFace dataset (Kärkkäinen and Joo, 2019). The dataset is specifically designed to provide a better balance with respect to race composition. They also released an updated version of the model itself that has the ability to report *failure to converge* instead of producing an image that poorly matches the low-resolution image. Finally, they include a *model card* that details the intended use case and more details about the model including ethical considerations.

This section focused on bias, and it is easy to fall into the trap of thinking that just getting an unbiased dataset solves the problem. There are additional ethical aspects to consider when working with images of people. In particular, it is important to consider whether it is ethical to use the images in the first place. Did the people in the pictures give their consent to use the pictures? Did they give their consent to use them for the use case you are working on? These are the kinds of questions that researchers and practitioners working with this kind of data should ask themselves.

CHECKLIST OF QUESTIONS

Apart from being aware of the specific problems we just discussed, Thomas (2019) recommends that teams ask themselves the following checklist of questions throughout the development cycle of a project:

• Should we even be doing this?

• What bias is in the data?

• Can the code and data be audited?

• What are the error rates for different subgroups?

• What is the accuracy of a simple rule-based alternative?

• What processes are in place to handle appeals or mistakes?

• How diverse is the team that built it?

Other good questions to consider can be found in *Ethics in Tech Practice: A Toolkit* (Vallor, 2018). We also recommend reading "Data Ethics" (Thomas, Howard, and Gugger, 2020), which much of this section is based on. Another resource that we have found useful is Baer's *Understand, Manage, and Prevent Algorithmic Bias: A Guide for Business Users and Data Scientists* (2019).

Things You Do Not Yet Know

This book includes a large number of topics within the DL field, but it does not cover everything. Therefore, we conclude this final chapter with a brief description of some important topics that we have omitted and provide some ideas of ways to continue your learning process.

REINFORCEMENT LEARNING

The ML field is often partitioned into three distinct branches:

- Supervised learning

- Unsupervised learning

- Reinforcement learning

Most of the mechanisms described in this book fall into the category of supervised learning, although we have also seen some examples of unsupervised learning.

The third branch, reinforcement learning, has not been used in this book, but we briefly describe how it relates to the other two branches. We encourage interested readers to read other resources on this topic.

In a supervised learning algorithm, the model learns from a labeled dataset that represents the specific ground truth we want the model to learn. In an unsupervised learning algorithm, however, the dataset is not labeled, and the algorithm is responsible for finding structure in the data. Reinforcement learning is different from both of these settings in that an *agent* learns to interact with an *environment,* with the goal of maximizing a cumulative *reward* function. That is, the agent is not provided with a ground truth that defines correct behavior but is given feedback (the reward) detailing whether an action, or series of actions, is good or bad. The agent itself needs to explore the space of possible sequences of actions and learn how to maximize its reward.

A famous example of how DL has been applied in the field of reinforcement learning is when Mnih and colleagues (2013) showed how a model learned to play Atari video games. The agent learned what user input to provide to the game to maximize the resulting score. It did not have labeled examples of what user action to take given a specific input (the pixels on the screen) but had to explore the set of available actions and learn which ones led to the best cumulative reward (the final score of the game).

VARIATIONAL AUTOENCODERS AND GENERATIVE ADVERSARIAL NETWORKS

In Chapter 12, "Neural Language Models and Word Embeddings," we saw an example of how a language model can be used to generate content. Given the beginning of a sentence, the model generated a plausible continuation. This generated text is not simply a recording of a previously seen sentence but can take the form of a newly generated, previously unseen text sequence. However, it is not a random sequence but a sequence that adheres to learned grammatical structure. Further, in Chapter 17, we saw how an autoencoder can be used to re-create an image given a narrower intermediate representation. However, we have not yet seen examples of a model that can generate previously unseen images. Two popular models for doing this are the *variational autoencoder* (VAE) and the *generative adversarial network* (GAN).

The VAE, introduced by Kingma and Welling (2013), is based on the normal autoencoder that was described in Chapter 17. The idea is that once an autoencoder is trained to reproduce images, the decoder part of the network can be used to generate new images. We simply take an intermediate representation and modify it slightly, with the expectation that the decoder will output a new valid output image. It turns out that if we do this with a regular autoencoder, the result is often poor. The way the autoencoder is trained does not necessarily lead to the result that a small change in the intermediate representation results in a correct or realistic output. The variational autoencoder is a modified version of the autoencoder in which the training process is changed to encourage the model to behave more accurately in that respect.

The GAN, introduced by Goodfellow and colleagues (2014), takes a different approach. Instead of training a single model to reproduce an input image, we train two different models to do two different tasks. One model, known as the *generator*, is trained to generate an image based on a random set of inputs. This is similar to how the decoder component of an autoencoder generates an image based on a narrow intermediate representation, but with the distinction that the generator network is not provided with a ground truth image to reproduce. Instead, its objective is to fool the other network, which is known as the *discriminator*. The discriminator is trained to discriminate between true images from the dataset and images generated by the generator. These two networks are *adversarial* in nature (hence the name of the approach) in that the generator continuously tries to improve its ability to fool the discriminator and the discriminator continuously tries to improve its ability to call the generator's bluff. The net effect is a generator that can generate images that cannot be distinguished from images in the dataset, based on random inputs. By varying this random input, random output images are generated.

VAEs showed some early promise but lost popularity with the emergence of GANs, which demonstrated better results. In particular, images generated by VAEs were often blurry. However, in a recent paper, Vahdat and Kautz (2020) demonstrated how a type of VAE can be used to generate sharp images. Their work could spawn a renewed interest in the VAE field.

In this section, we described VAEs and GANs in the context of image generation because that is the most popular application area for these techniques. However, the concepts are more general and can be applied to other types of data as well.

NEURAL STYLE TRANSFER

The two techniques we just described can be used to generate images that have the same appearance as images in the training dataset. Another important generative technique, introduced by Gatys, Ecker, and Bethge (2015), is *neural style transfer*. This technique is used to separate *content* from *style* in an image. In this context, *content* refers to the objects depicted in an image, and *style* refers to properties such as texture and color schemes of objects in an image.

Neural style transfer is able to extract content from one image and style from a second image, and then combine the two into a new image. In their paper, Gatys, Ecker, and Bethge demonstrate examples of combining the content of a photograph with the style from paintings by famous artists. The resulting generated image contains the same objects as in the photograph but in the style of paintings by J. M. W. Turner, Vincent van Gogh, Edvard Munch, Pablo Picasso, and Wassily Kandinsky.

RECOMMENDER SYSTEMS

DL has had a big impact on recommender systems. Such systems are used by many online services to guide users to content and products that they are likely to be interested in. For example, online shopping sites often suggest items to buy based on previous purchases. Similarly, movie and music streaming services provide suggestions on movie titles and songs that a user might be interested in based on what they previously have shown interest in. A key component to these systems is to not only look at historical patterns for an individual user but also learn from usage patterns of other users on the same site. Zhang and colleagues (2019) have written a survey paper containing many useful references that provide more information about recommender systems.

MODELS FOR SPOKEN LANGUAGE

This book has focused on images and written natural language. Another important topic within human–computer interaction is spoken natural language. Just as DL has revolutionized computer vision and textual language processing, it has also led to significant breakthroughs in speech recognition (speech-to-text) and speech synthesis (text-to-speech). You can find an overview of speech recognition work in a review paper by Nassif and colleagues (2019). Some examples of speech synthesis are Tacotron (Wang et al., 2017), Tacotron 2 (Shen et al., 2018), Flowtron (Valle et al., 2020), and TalkNet (Beliaev, Rebryk, and Ginsburg, 2020). We encourage you to read some of the referenced papers and, if nothing else, follow some links from the papers to online demos to get an idea of how well it works!

It is not clear to us where the name *Tacotron* comes from, but our best guess is that it is a wordplay on *talk-a-tron,* which sounds similar to *Detectron,* a framework for CNN-based object detection and related techniques. On the other hand, a footnote in the Tacotron paper states that some of the authors really like taco, whereas some of the others prefer sushi, so maybe we should not overanalyze this topic.

DL for speech recognition and for speech synthesis are good topics for future reading.

Next Steps

We end this book with providing some ideas for further reading. There are multiple paths to take depending on your goals and interests, so we outline a few potential directions.

Perhaps you feel that you are done with theory for a while and just want to code. Perhaps you have a real problem that you want to try to solve. If so, just go for it! If you need some inspiration, we recommend that you seek out some of the many tutorials that can be found online and start exploring. If you want a bit more guidance, then you might want to pick up the book *Deep Learning with Python* (Chollet, 2018), which contains many useful code examples, including examples of the just mentioned techniques neural style transfer and image generation with VAE and GAN.

Another option is to dive deeper into a specific topic by reading the corresponding appendix in this book. The book is also sprinkled with yellow boxes with suggestions for further reading, and we have provided plenty of references to use as starting points to familiarize yourself with the historical research literature on the topic. You can then search online for more recent publications that cite the papers you found relevant and learn about the most recent findings. If you do choose to focus on a specific topic, you should also be prepared to spend time on the non-DL-specific parts of the chosen field. For example, if you want to work on language models, you need to understand the perplexity metric, and if you want to work on machine translation, you need to understand the BLEU score. After all, DL is just a collection of methods that can be applied to a wide set of problems, and to do well on a certain problem, you need to understand the problem domain, the solution space (both DL and non-DL), and the success metrics. Perhaps you found this book interesting but feel that you want some insight into traditional ML and to learn about some topics not covered by this book, such as reinforcement learning, VAEs, GANs, and neural style transfer. In that case, you can consider reading the two-volume book *Deep Learning: From Basics to Practice* (Glassner, 2018). Much of the first volume will introduce you to traditional ML concepts and basic neural networks, and the second volume focuses on DL.

If you want a deeper and more mathematical understanding of the field, consider reading *Deep Learning* (Goodfellow, Bengio, and Courville, 2016). Specifically, we recommend this book for anybody who wants to do academic research and publish papers within the DL field. The book starts with an overview of mathematics and probability theory that is useful in ML in general and DL in particular. It continues with an overview of traditional machine learning, followed by a thorough description of the DL field.

Another option is to take online classes. Three such alternatives we have found useful are classes offered by NVIDIA Deep Learning Institute,[2] Andrew Ng's Coursera classes,[3] and ML/DL classes from the Lazy Programmer.[4] Another alternative is to watch some *Lex Clips* videos[5] on YouTube. Jeremy Howard and Rachel Thomas provide a great set of free courses through their fast.ai research

---

2. https://www.nvidia.com/dli
3. https://www.coursera.org
4. https://lazyprogrammer.me
5. https://www.youtube.com/lexclips

group.[6] If these courses appeal to you, then you can also consider reading Howard and Gugger's *Deep Learning for Coders with fastai and PyTorch* (2020), which teaches DL from scratch. Although the book has much overlap with *Learning Deep Learning*, the authors take more of a top-down approach that many readers might find useful.

This section represents our thoughts on how to proceed, but DL is a rapidly evolving field with new papers being published every week, and books almost as frequently, so you should use your own judgment. We hope that you found this book useful and that it has given you the knowledge and inspiration needed to continue your quest of *Learning Deep Learning*.

---

6. *Making Neural Nets Uncool Again,* https://www.fast.ai

Appendix A

Linear Regression and Linear Classifiers

This appendix logically follows Chapter 3, "Sigmoid Neurons and Backpropagation."

As described in the preface, the approach we are taking in this book is to take a fast track to exciting parts of deep learning (DL). As such, we decided to not start the book with a number of traditional machine learning (ML) topics. Inspired by Nielsen (2015), we spent the three first chapters on *binary classification* problems using perceptrons and multilevel networks. Binary classification involves determining whether the inputs should result in an output belonging to one out of two classes. A more common way to introduce ML is to start with a *regression* problem, where we predict a real number instead of a discrete class. This is described in the next couple of sections.

We then move on to describe a couple of linear methods for binary classification. That is, we solve the type of problems studied in Chapters 1 to 3 but using traditional ML techniques.

Linear Regression as a Machine Learning Algorithm

Assume that we have a number of training examples, consisting of one or more input values and an associated real-valued output. This is a regression problem. From an ML perspective, this problem involves training a mathematical model to predict the expected output value when presented with input values. We will make this more concrete in the following sections. Perhaps the simplest model to attempt to solve a problem like this is to use linear regression. We start with considering the case of a single input variable.

UNIVARIATE LINEAR REGRESSION

We use a made-up problem to illustrate the use of linear regression with a single input variable. Assume that you are running an ice cream shop and you want to get some idea of how much ice cream you will sell tomorrow. You have made the observation that the amount of ice cream you sell seems to be related to the temperature each day, so you want to explore whether you can predict the ice cream demand by using the temperature forecast. To get some insight into whether this idea seems promising, you create a scatter plot of historical temperature data and ice cream demand. The red markers in Figure A-1 show what that might look like.

Using the red markers, we can try to fit some kind of curve to the data to come up with a formula that we can use to predict the demand given a specific temperature. The figure shows how we have fit a green straight line of the form:

$$y = ax + b$$

where y represents the demand, and x represents the temperature. For the line in the figure, the parameters are $a = 2.0$ and $b = -112$. An obvious question is how

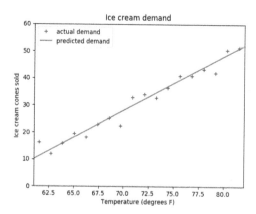

Figure A-1 Relationship between temperature and number of ice cream cones sold. For readers more familiar with the Celsius temperature scale, a rule of thumb is that 61°F is about 16°C and 82°F is about 28°C (just flip the digits).

we came up with these two parameters, and that is the job of our ML algorithm. For our linear regression case, we can come up with an analytical solution, but in some cases, it can be more efficient to use an iterative algorithm. We will see both examples in a couple of sections. First, we look at variations of this regression problem.

MULTIVARIATE LINEAR REGRESSION

The model in the last section was fairly limited, in that it used only a single input variable. We could envision that ice cream demand is related not only to the outside temperature but also to the amount of advertisement that has been shown on television the day before. We can handle this additional variable by extending our linear model to two dimensions. Figure A-2 shows an example of such a model. In this figure, we do not show any of the actual data points but just the predictions by the model.

With two input variables, our prediction now takes the form of a plane as opposed to a straight line. We can see how the number of ice cream cones sold increases with both temperature and the number of minutes of advertisement. The equation for our plane is

$$z = \beta_0 + \beta_1 x_1 + \beta_2 x_2$$

where z is the demand, x_1 represents advertisement, and x_2 represents temperature. The parameters are $\beta_0 = -112$, $\beta_1 = 0.5$, and $\beta_2 = 2.0$. Just like before, it is the task for our ML algorithm to come up with these parameters.

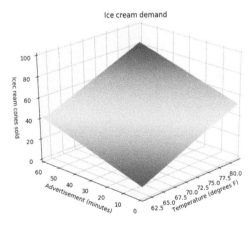

Figure A-2 Model for ice cream demand as a function of temperature and advertisement

There is nothing magical about having just two input variables. This model generalizes to *n* input variables where we end up with an *n*-dimensional hyperplane. The only issue is that it is hard to visualize.

MODELING CURVATURE WITH A LINEAR FUNCTION

Although we have extended the model to use an arbitrary number of input variables, the model is still somewhat limited in that it can do a good job of modeling dependencies only where a straight line or a (hyper) plane can fit the data well. We can easily imagine cases where this is not so. For example, going back to our ice cream example, let us consider a greater temperature range than just 61°F to 82°F. If we extend the upper end of the range to 100°F (about 38°C), we could imagine that as the temperature increases, ice cream demand does not increase as much because people might choose to stay inside air-conditioned buildings instead of buying ice cream. This is shown in Figure A-3.

In addition to fitting a green straight line to the data, we have included a curve (blue) based on a second-order polynomial:

$$y = \beta_0 + \beta_1 x + \beta_2 x^2$$

In this formula, y is the demand, x is the temperature, and x^2 is the squared temperature. The parameters are $\beta_0 = -220$, $\beta_1 = 5.0$, and $\beta_2 = -0.02$. Just as for our previous examples, it is the task of the ML algorithm to come up with these parameters for our linear regression problem. At this point, you might wonder if we just misspoke when we called this a linear regression problem given that the

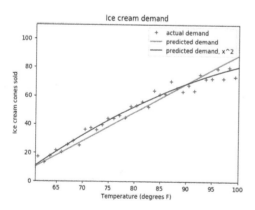

Figure A-3 Data points where a quadratic curve is a better fit to the data than a straight line

resulting curve looks very much quadratic as opposed to linear. However, linear refers to the parameters that we are estimating $(\beta_0, \beta_1, \ldots, \beta_n)$, so as long as we do not raise these parameters to a power, or apply other nonlinear operations on them, this is still considered a linear model. Therefore, the problem is a linear regression problem. If this seems unintuitive, consider the multivariate case in the previous section. Assuming that you agree that it was straightforward to extend the univariate case to two or more variables, then the preceding equation is not that different. The model does not know that we created the second variable (x^2) by squaring the first one. It could just as well have been an independent variable that happened to take on the same value as the square of x.

This example used only a single input variable (temperature), but we created another variable (squared temperature) from that variable, so the model still had two inputs. We can extend this to include higher-order polynomials as well. We can also combine it with the type of model that we saw in the previous section, where we had multiple input variables (temperature and advertisement), and then create higher-order polynomials of all the original input variables. By doing so, we arrive at fairly complex models, which still all are considered linear models.

Computing Linear Regression Coefficients

So far, we have described how linear regression can be used to predict real-valued numbers, also known as a *regression problem,* but we have not described how to come up with the parameters (coefficients) for the solution. There are multiple good ways of fitting a straight line to a number of data points. Perhaps the most common way of doing it is known as ordinary least squares (OLS) and is based on minimizing the mean squared error (MSE). If you have seen OLS in the past, chances are that you have also seen a closed-form solution. That is, a solution that can be computed by manipulating mathematical symbols as opposed to computing an approximate solution with numerical methods. We soon discuss the closed-form solution, but first we describe how we can use gradient descent to arrive at a numeric solution iteratively. Gradient descent was described in Chapter 2, "Gradient-Based Learning." We start by formulating our hypothesis of what the solution looks like. If we have n input variables, the most straightforward linear regression hypothesis is

$$y = w_0 + w_1 x_1 + w_2 x_2 + \ldots + w_n x_n$$

but as previously shown, we can think of more complicated cases where we include higher-order terms as well. We can now solve our linear regression problem iteratively using gradient descent. We use the MSE as a loss function:

$$\frac{1}{m}\sum_{i=1}^{m}\left(y^{(i)} - \hat{y}^{(i)}\right)^2 \qquad (mean\ squared\ error)$$

When using this loss function for linear regression, we end up with a *convex optimization problem,* which implies that any local minimum is also a global minimum. This means that as long as we pick the learning rate to be small enough, gradient descent will always converge to the optimum solution. This might all sound great, but it is worth noting that the optimum solution is in the context of the assumed hypothesis space. If a linear function cannot solve the problem or cannot solve it well, the optimum set of parameters for our linear function can still result in a bad solution.

As mentioned, it is also possible to compute a closed-form solution to this problem. We do not go through this in detail but we outline the approach and state the final solution. If you are interested, there are plenty of books that describe linear regression in detail. For example, both Hastie, Tibshirani, and Friedman (2009) and Goodfellow, Bengio, and Courville (2016) discuss it in the context of ML.

The closed-form solution is based on the same thinking as gradient descent. We have our stated loss function (MSE), and we want to minimize it. This is done by expanding the sum in the preceding formula for all training examples, and then computing the derivative and solving it for zero. If we have just a handful of training examples and just a single input dimension, it is somewhat straightforward to do this with regular algebra, but as the number of input examples or dimensions increases, it quickly becomes hairy. A solution to this problem is to instead state our problem in terms of matrices and vectors and then solve it with linear algebra.[1] It can be shown that if we arrange all our input vectors in a matrix X, and the output values in a vector **y**, then we can compute a vector β that consists of the coefficients that minimize the loss using the following formula:

$$\beta = \left(X^T X\right)^{-1} X^T \mathbf{y}$$

---

1. Our description is very terse and meant mostly as a refresher for readers who have already studied how to solve linear regression with linear algebra. If you have not seen this before, you will most likely need to consult a more extensive text on the topic.

The formula uses a construct that we have not seen in this book before, namely, the inverse of a matrix, which is denoted as a superscript −1 to a matrix. In the this formula, the matrix that is inverted (X^TX) is a matrix resulting from a matrix multiplication, but it is decoupled from the matrix inverse operation itself. We do not describe the details of how to invert a matrix, but it is worth pointing out that not all matrices can be inverted. Further, it is computationally costly to invert large matrices. Because of this computational cost, in cases where we have a large number of training examples (in the hundreds of thousands or millions), it is often preferable to use gradient descent even though a closed-form solution exists. This concludes our discussion about linear regression, and we now move on to a related method, which can be used for classification instead of regression.

Classification with Logistic Regression

In Chapter 1, "The Rosenblatt Perceptron," and Chapter 2, we used a perceptron to solve binary classification problems, but there are other types of classification algorithms as well, one important example being logistic regression. The name is somewhat confusing given that it solves a classification problem as opposed to a regression problem. The name likely originates from logistic regression being a variation of linear regression, which we soon see.

Let us now assume that we are ice cream customers instead of owners of an ice cream shop. Let us further assume that we really like ice cream and want to buy ice cream regardless of the temperature. However, we do not like standing in line, so if the line is too long, we do not want to go to the ice cream shop. To avoid wasting our time by going to the ice cream shop just to discover that the line is too long, we want to come up with a model that uses the temperature as input data and tries to predict whether or not the line is too long. From our perspective, the exact length of the line does not matter. Either it is short enough that we are willing to wait in it or it is too long, so we go home. That means that this is a binary classification problem—the value we are trying to predict is either true (too long) or false (short enough).

Figure A-4 shows an attempt at solving this problem with linear regression. The red marks show the actual cases of too long a line (value = 1) and a short enough line (value = 0), and we see a green straight line attempted to fit to the data points. A first observation is that it is not possible to perfectly predict whether the line is too long from the temperature alone because there is overlap between the data points at the top and at the bottom. This should not be a surprise. A second

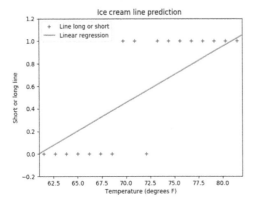

Figure A-4 Attempt at using linear regression to solve a binary classification problem

observation is that our straight line predicts a real-valued number as opposed to a discrete value. We could address this issue by assuming that the value 0.5 is a threshold: Anything greater than 0.5 is interpreted as too long, and anything less than 0.5 is interpreted as short enough. The observant reader will notice that this is exactly what the perceptron does.

If we look at Figure A-4 and consider the ice cream example in the previous sections, where we saw that a quadratic curve fit the data best, it seems like it would make sense to explore whether we can fit the data better with a function other than a straight line.

Figure A-5 shows an attempt to do so. We have plotted a shifted version of the logistic sigmoid function in the same chart as the data points that indicate whether or not the ice cream line is too long.

For reference, the formula for the logistic sigmoid function[2] follows. It has already been extensively used in the book as a neuron activation function.

$$logistic\ function: \ S(x) = \frac{1}{1+e^{-x}}$$

Looking at the chart, a first observation is that this function looks like a much better choice than a straight line. A second observation is that it does not seem like it is much of an improvement over the perceptron. The curve in Figure A-5

---

2. What is described here is a specific instance of a logistic function. It is just one of multiple members of the family of logistic functions.

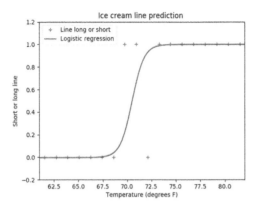

Figure A-5 Chart showing how a logistic sigmoid function can fit the data points indicating whether the ice cream line is too long

looks similar to the curve in Chapter 1, Figure 1-3, which illustrated the sign function used by the perceptron. This in turn is the same behavior as applying a threshold to the straight line in Figure A-4. That is, these three approaches are much related to each other. However, one benefit of logistic regression is that the curve in Figure A-5 does not have discontinuities as do the perceptron function and any other threshold-based approach. This implies that as long as we come up with a feasible cost function, we can directly apply gradient descent without any caveats related to discontinuities. Without further explanation, a feasible cost function for logistic regression is shown here:

$$\frac{1}{m}\sum_{i=1}^{m} -\left(y^{(i)} \cdot \ln\left(\hat{y}^{(i)}\right) + \left(1-y^{(i)}\right) \cdot \ln\left(1-\hat{y}^{(i)}\right)\right) \quad (cross\text{-}entropy\ loss)$$

This cost function is known as the cross-entropy loss function, and it is also used in the context of neural networks (described in Chapter 5 "Toward DL: Frameworks and Network Tweaks"). In the context of logistic regression, the cross-entropy loss function has the nice property that the logistic regression problem ends up being another example of a convex optimization problem. That is, given a small enough value of the learning rate parameter, gradient descent will always converge to an optimal solution. As opposed to linear regression, there is no known closed-form solution for the general case of logistic regression. We now move on to show how we can state our logistic regression problem in a way that solves the XOR problem.

Classifying XOR with a Linear Classifier

The logistic sigmoid function, combined with the cross-entropy loss function, results in a convex optimization problem known as *logistic regression*. It can be solved iteratively with gradient descent. Still, logistic regression suffers from the same limitation as the perceptron when it comes to linear separability. Figure A-6 illustrates this for a problem with two input variables (x_1 and x_2), where we see that it is impossible to draw a straight line that perfectly separates the two classes. This type of chart was introduced in Chapter 1 in the context of the behavior of a perceptron. It was further revisited in Chapter 2.

Given our previous observation that a straight line is somewhat limiting, it should not come as a surprise that we now explore whether we can modify our classification function further to try to address problems that are not linearly separable. We do this by revisiting the XOR problem that we have already seen is not linearly separable. Figure A-7 shows how we can separate the two classes (pluses and minuses) if we are allowed to use a more complex shape than a straight line. There are multiple ways of solving it, but we think that an ellipse is a reasonable approach. The left part of the figure shows that it is trivial to draw an ellipse such that it separates the pluses from the minuses.

When we looked at a similar chart for the perceptron, we saw that the straight line that represented the decision boundary originated from a 3D plot of a plane, and the decision boundary was the line on the plane where the *z*-value was 0 (because that was where the sign function changed its output value). We can

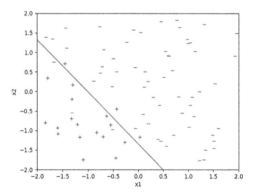

Figure A-6 Example of how logistic regression cannot perfectly solve a problem that is not linearly separable

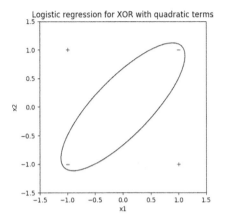

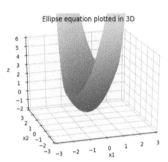

Figure A-7 How the XOR problem can be solved by using the function of an ellipse instead of a straight line

do the same in this case, but we start with the equation for an ellipse centered around 0 and rotated by an angle θ.

$$\left(\frac{x_1\cos(\theta)-x_2\sin(\theta)}{a}\right)^2+\left(\frac{x_1\sin(\theta)+x_2\cos(\theta)}{b}\right)^2=1$$

If we solve this equation for 0 and call the resulting formula z, we get an equation that is greater than 0 outside of the ellipse and less than 0 inside the ellipse. The equation is shown here, and z is plotted against x_1 and x_2 in the right part of Figure A-7.

$$z=\left(\frac{x_1\cos(\theta)-x_2\sin(\theta)}{a}\right)^2+\left(\frac{x_1\sin(\theta)+x_2\cos(\theta)}{b}\right)^2-1$$

If we now use z as input to the logistic sigmoid function, it can be used to correctly classify the data points for the XOR problem, assuming that we can come up with all the constants in the expression.

The expression for z can be rearranged to the following:

$$z=w_0+w_1x_1x_2+w_2x_1^2+w_3x_2^2$$

where

$$w_0=-1$$

529

$$w_1 = 2\cos(\theta)\sin(\theta)\left(\frac{1}{b^2} - \frac{1}{a^2}\right)$$

$$w_2 = \left(\frac{\cos^2(\theta)}{a^2} + \frac{\sin^2(\theta)}{b^2}\right)$$

$$w_3 = \left(\frac{\sin^2(\theta)}{a^2} + \frac{\cos^2(\theta)}{b^2}\right)$$

That is, z is still a linear expression with respect to the parameters w_0, w_1, w_2, and w_3, which implies that we can use logistic regression to solve the XOR problem as long as we provide it with the inputs x_1x_2, x_1^2, and x_2^2.

Before concluding this section, we should point out that using the formula for an ellipse is not the only way to solve this problem, and an even simpler solution is to use only the two terms x_1 and x_1x_2, which results in a solution similar to what is shown in Figure A-8.

An obvious question is how to figure out what kind of terms to include in our equations to arrive at solutions of this kind. The process of coming up with these inputs, also called *features*, is known as *feature engineering* and is an important part of traditional ML. The role of feature engineering is less important in the context of DL, where the responsibility of extracting features primarily belongs to the learning algorithm. Chapter 3 showed this with an example of how a neural network could learn to solve the *XOR* classification problem. Let us now move on to another important linear classifier.

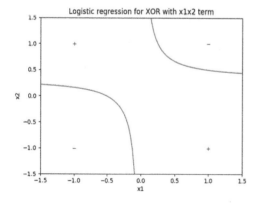

Figure A-8 Alternative logistic regression solution to the XOR problem

Classification with Support Vector Machines

As already mentioned, both the perceptron and logistic regression are examples of linear classifiers. Another important linear classifier in ML is the support vector machine (SVM). This section provides a brief introduction to SVMs.

In the context of logistic regression, we saw that all data points were used when solving the optimization problem to determine parameters of the model. The SVM takes a different approach. Consider all the data points in Figure A-9. For now, ignore the dashed lines and the arrows. We see that the green line perfectly separates the two classes, but we could construct a number of other variations on the green line and still manage to perfectly separate the classes. For example, we could shift the line right, left, up, or down a little bit or modify its slope or do a combination of shifting and changing slope. A reasonable question is whether it makes sense to worry about the data points far from the current decision boundary, such as those in the upper right corner of the figure. These data points will be correctly classified regardless of how we do these minor tweaks. Therefore, one approach is to pay attention only to the data points close to the decision boundary and draw the line to fit them well. An SVM does just that by identifying a limited set of data points that define the boundary.

In addition to the decision boundary (solid green line in the figure), the SVM defines a margin that consists of the distance between two parallel lines (dashed magenta lines in the figure) that are on each side of the boundary. The SVM

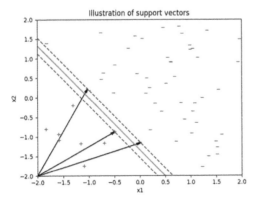

Figure A-9 Decision boundary for a support vector machine

selects a decision boundary in a way that the distance between these two dashed lines (the margin) is maximized. As shown in the figure, this implies that a number of data points are right on these lines. We can say that the lines are supported by these data points. The vectors from the origin to these points are called *support vectors*, which gives the algorithm its name.

As we have previously seen, there exist cases that are not perfectly separable but where a straight line still makes sense. For example, noise in the data could cause classes to overlap, or the overlap could be caused by some unknown variable not included in the model. This is illustrated in Figure A-10, where a small number of pluses and minuses are located on the wrong side of the decision boundary. It is still possible to use an SVM for such cases, but there is now an additional trade-off to make. We can increase the margin by allowing more of the training examples to violate the margin constraint (fall on the wrong side of the margin line). Conversely, we can reduce the number of training examples that violate the margin constraint by reducing the margin. This trade-off is controlled by a tunable parameter to the training algorithm.

We have seen that logistic regression can be used for the XOR problem if we first combine the raw input variables into new variables (features). Not surprisingly, this can be done for an SVM as well. A challenge with this approach, not only for SVMs, is that we need to compute all of these additional input features before we can do training or classification. In some cases, this can be computationally expensive. A key property of the SVM is that we can employ a technique known as

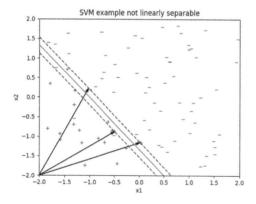

Figure A-10 Support vector machine for a case where the classes are not linearly separable but where a straight line still makes sense as the decision boundary

the *kernel trick* to reduce the computational cost of working in this transformed input space.

We do not describe the details of how the kernel trick works because we would first need to go into the mathematics of the SVM algorithm itself. However, we do want to point out one thing that we find nonobvious from some descriptions. The special thing about the SVM and the kernel trick is *not* that they enable classification with additional (engineered) input features to solve problems that are not linearly separable. As previously described, that can be done with logistic regression as well. The significance of the kernel trick in conjunction with SVMs is that it can be used to reduce the computational complexity of working with these additional input features.

This concludes our descriptions of linear classifiers. The perceptron, logistic regression, and SVM represent only a subset of the available algorithms. Other examples are linear discriminant analysis (LDA) and naïve Bayes. The SVM algorithm has also been extended to the regression problem domain, with a related algorithm known as support vector regression. Hastie, Tibshirani, and Friedman (2009) describe these and additional techniques and is a good source for future reading.

Evaluation Metrics for a Binary Classifier

It is often the case that we can come up with multiple different models when attempting to solve a classification problem. A key question is how to evaluate which model is best. Intuitively, it seems like the model with the highest *accuracy* would be a good choice, where accuracy is defined in the following way:

$$accuracy = \frac{correct\ predictions}{total\ predictions}$$

As often is the case, things are not that simple. Consider the case where the task at hand is to predict whether a patient is in the early stages of a serious medical condition given a number of variables. Further assume that, on average, only five out of 100 of patients have this condition. A model that always predicts that a patient does not have the condition will have 95% accuracy but is practically useless. A model that correctly identifies four out of five of the patients that have the condition and incorrectly identifies another five of the patients as having the condition will have only a 94% accuracy because it misclassified $(1 + 5)/100$. However, it is much more useful as an initial tool to identify what patients require further screening. This highlights the need to look at other metrics in addition to accuracy. A common starting point is to organize the actual classes as well as the predicted classes into a table known as a *confusion matrix*, as shown in Table A-1. The rows represent predicted classes, and the columns represent actual classes. As an example, the model predicted that the condition is present for four patients who had the condition. This is represented by the number 4 in the upper left cell for which the condition is both predicted as present and truly present, also known as a *true positive* (TP). In all, there are four combinations, the three remaining being *false positive* (FP), *false negative* (FN), and *true negative* (TN).

FP is also known as a *type I error*, and FN is known as a *type II error*. It is useful to distinguish between the two because different types of errors can have vastly different consequences. In this example, it is easy to envision that it is worse to fail to identify a patient who has a condition than to incorrectly identify a healthy patient as having the condition if the purpose is to identify patients for further screening and treatment if necessary. We can use the numbers in the table to compute a large number of metrics that can be used to gain further insight into how the predictor works. Table A-2 contains three such metrics that are commonly used, including accuracy. Some of the terms in the table sometimes go by other names. For example, recall is sometimes known as *sensitivity*.

Recall is a good metric if we are interested in how certain we are that the model will identify patients that we intend to identify. In the example, it is important that this metric shows a high percentage. Similarly, a low precision will indicate that we identify many false positives, which implies additional cost in terms of both additional screening as well as emotional distress for patients who will

Table A-1 Confusion Matrix for the Envisioned Predictor

		ACTUAL CLASS	
		Condition present	Condition not present
Predicted Class	Condition present	4 TP	5 FP
	Condition not present	1 FN	90 TN

Table A-2 Three Common Metrics Computed from the Confusion Matrix

METRIC	FORMULA	DESCRIPTION
Accuracy	$\dfrac{TP+TN}{P+N} = \dfrac{4+90}{5+95} = 94\%$	Percentage of all predictions that were correctly predicted
Recall	$\dfrac{TP}{TP+FN} = \dfrac{4}{4+1} = 80\%$	Percentage of the true outcomes that were identified by the predictor
Precision	$\dfrac{TP}{TP+FP} = \dfrac{4}{4+5} = 44\%$	Percentage of the predicted true outcomes that were actually true

now worry that they have a serious condition until they get more accurate test results.

This example showed that we gain additional insight into the strengths and weaknesses of a model by considering metrics other than accuracy. However, even if we do have the confusion matrices for a number of models, it is not always obvious which model to pick. One technique that can provide additional insight is to plot each model in *receiver operating characteristic* (ROC) space. This is a 2D plot with false-positive rate on the *x*-axis and true-positive rate on the *y*-axis. Figure A-11 shows such a plot for five different models, each represented by a single data point in the plot.

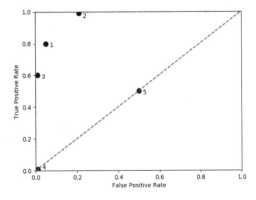

Figure A-11 Five models plotted in receiver operating characteristic space

The data points are the following:

1. The model described in our example with a false-positive rate of 0.05 and a true-positive rate of 0.8.

2. A more sensitive model, which identifies all five patients with the condition but results in 20 false positives. It has a false-positive rate of 0.21 and a true-positive rate of 1.

3. A less sensitive model, which identifies only three out of five patients with the condition but results in only one false positive. Its false-positive rate is 0.01 and true-positive rate is 0.6.

4. The model that always predicts "no condition" with a false-positive rate of 0 and a true-positive rate of 0.

5. A coin-flip with a false-positive rate of 0.5 and a true-positive rate of 0.5.

If it is not obvious how we arrive at these false- and true-positive rates, then we encourage you to write out the confusion matrix and compute the metrics to confirm.

Looking at the plot, we see that the data points for our naïve models (always predicted true, and random) are located on the diagonal, and our better models are above the diagonal. From that perspective, if a data point ever ends up below the diagonal, a first thought is that it is a bad model because its performance is worse than if outcomes were picked randomly. This is a true observation, but given that we work with binary classification, it is trivial to transform a model that is consistently worse than chance into a good model by simply doing the opposite of what the model predicts. That is, if you recomputed the metrics for the bad model but interpreted a true prediction as false and a false prediction as true, you would end up with a data point that is located above the diagonal in in the plot.

For models that are based on a continuous-valued parameter, such as a threshold value, different values of that parameter will result in different points in ROC space. If we plot these different points as the parameter is varied, we end up with something known as an *ROC curve*. The ROC curve can then be used to select a parameter value that strikes an appropriate balance between false- and true-positive rates.

Finally, it is sometimes good to have a single score to use when evaluating a model without having to think of the trade-off between false- and true-positive rates. In such cases, a good candidate is the F_1 score:

$$F_1 \ score = \frac{2TP}{2TP+FP+FN} = \frac{2*4}{2*4+5+1} = 0.57$$

A high score corresponds to a good model. The numbers in this equation correspond to the confusion matrix in Table A-1. If the predictor had predicted everything correctly, then the F_1 score would end up being 1.

It should now be clear that it is important to carefully consider what metric is appropriate for each problem. The metrics described in this section serve as a good starting point of alternatives to consider.

Appendix B

Object Detection and Segmentation

This appendix logically follows Chapter 8, "Deeper CNNs and Pretrained Models."

Our detailed descriptions of convolutional networks in Chapter 7, "Convolutional Neural Networks Applied to Image Classification," and Chapter 8 focused on object classification. The objective was to determine which one, out of a large number of classes, the image represented. This is a fairly simplified view of the world. It is often the case that an image contains many different objects belonging to different classes, which results in more complicated tasks. Three such tasks are object detection, semantic segmentation, and instance segmentation. They are all illustrated in Figure B-1. Object detection involves identifying the location (drawing a bounding box) and type of individual objects in an image. That is, it is a combination of a localization and classification problem. Semantic segmentation involves identifying to what type of object each pixel in an image corresponds. Instance segmentation is similar, but more detailed, in that the task is to identify the image pixels for each detected object instance.

In the next couple of sections, we describe some popular methods for object detection, semantic segmentation, and instance segmentation. We do not go into as much detail as in previous chapters, but we focus on providing intuitive descriptions with the goal of giving you a big picture of how the techniques work.

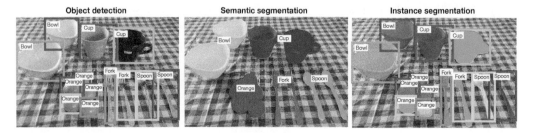

Figure B-1 Left: Object detection—detect objects, draw bounding boxes around them, and classify them. Middle: Semantic segmentation—identify all pixels that correspond to a specific object type. Right: Instance segmentation—identify pixels for individual instances of each object. These images are produced using an implementation of Mask R-CNN, which is described at the end of this appendix. The algorithm also detected the background as a "dining table," but we manually suppressed that to make the images less cluttered.

Object Detection

We already know how to classify an image to arrive at the most probable type of object in that image. We do it with a number of convolutional layers, followed by some fully connected layers, and finally by a softmax layer that provides a probability for each class. We also know that we can use a linear output unit to predict numerical values. This is known as a *regression problem*. That is exactly what we want to do when we predict a bounding box, with the variation that we want to predict four values: the two coordinates (x, y) for the top left corner and the two parameters width and height (w, h).

Figure B-2 shows a simple network architecture that begins with convolutional layers for image feature extraction, followed by some fully connected layers. After that, the network is split into two sibling branches (also known as *heads*). One is a classification branch, consisting of one or more fully connected layers and ending with a softmax output function. The other branch solves the regression problem of predicting the bounding box parameters. It is also built from fully connected layers, but because the output should be real-valued, the output units need to be linear units without any activation functions. As described in Chapter 5, "Toward DL: Frameworks and Network Tweaks," ReLU is a reasonable activation function to start with for the hidden units.

Given the network in Figure B-2, it is not hard to envision a naïve solution to the detection problem. We can design the network to expect a small image as input. We train this classification network with training examples where one class

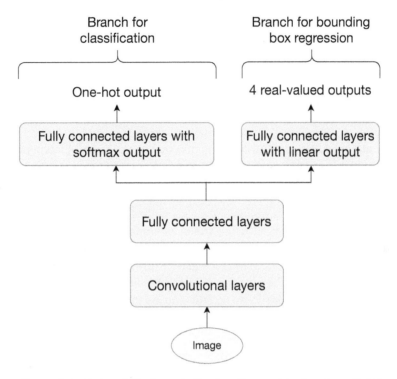

Branch for classification

Branch for bounding box regression

One-hot output

4 real-valued outputs

Fully connected layers with softmax output

Fully connected layers with linear output

Fully connected layers

Convolutional layers

Image

Figure B-2 Network that can both classify an object and predict the parameters for a corresponding bounding box

represents "no object" (i.e., background). We train the bounding box branch to output the coordinates for a bounding box around the object. Once this is done, we can repeatedly apply this network to different regions of a larger image (e.g., by using a sliding window approach, to find regions that the network classifies as containing an object). This naïve implementation is computationally expensive because the network is evaluated a large number of times for a single image, and another limitation is its fixed input region size.

Not surprisingly, the success that AlexNet demonstrated on classification was shortly followed by attempts to use similar techniques for object detection. This resulted in rapid advances in detection in parallel with the advances in classification that were described in Chapter 8. Of particular interest is a series of papers that gradually refined an initial technique to be both more accurate and more efficient. The series started with a technique known as *region-based CNN* (Girshick et al., 2014), which was followed by a faster version known as *Fast R-CNN* (Girshick, 2015). Shortly thereafter, an even faster version was published under the creative name *Faster R-CNN* (Shaoqing et al., 2015). The next few sections outline this progression while omitting many of the details. Some of the included details are there only to make the description understandable but are not relevant for the more recent techniques. In such cases, we try to point that out so that you can avoid spending too much time on them.

R-CNN

The region-based CNN (or R-CNN) technique consists of a combination of deep learning (DL) and other more traditional computer vision techniques. All the steps of the R-CNN algorithm are shown in Figure B-3.

Instead of using the sliding window approach outlined previously, it starts by identifying region proposals using one of a number of existing computer vision techniques. We do not describe these techniques in detail because one of the improved versions of the model (Faster R-CNN) later replaces it with a DL-based technique. For the purpose of understanding how R-CNN works, we just assume that there is a preprocessing step applied to the image, which identifies approximately 2,000 rectangle-shaped regions of various sizes. These regions are candidates for containing an object, but there may well be plenty of false positives.

The next step in R-CNN is to run a CNN-based classification network on each region proposal, and like the network in our earlier naïve approach, this network can also classify regions as not containing an object. R-CNN uses a variation of the AlexNet architecture for classification. The network is first pretrained on ImageNet. That is, R-CNN makes use of transfer learning. Next, instead of using the full network as is, the final layer (softmax) is removed, so the output of the network is a vector of 4,096 elements. This 4,096-dimensional feature vector is used as input to both the classification step and the bounding box refinement step (described shortly).

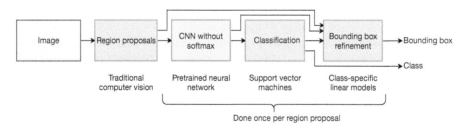

Figure B-3 R-CNN pipeline. Only one of the steps is based on deep learning.

If you read the paper, you will note that for classification, instead of using a softmax layer, R-CNN uses support vector machines (SVMs; also discussed in Appendix A), which is a binary classification technique from traditional machine learning (ML). The SVMs use the 4,096-dimensional feature vector as input. For all practical purposes, you can still envision the classification as being done by a final softmax layer, although the accuracy will be slightly different. One detail to deal with is that the proposed rectangular regions are of arbitrary size and aspect ratios. For R-CNN, this issue is resolved by warping the image region (changing the size and aspect ratio) to the expected input size, after first having added some padding to reduce the risk that the original region proposal cropped the object. We will see in a later section that Fast R-CNN uses a different approach.

The topic of using SVMs versus softmax in the final layer has been studied in various contexts (Agarap, 2018; Lenc and Vedaldi, 2015; Liu, Ye, and Sun, 2018; Tang, 2013). At this point, the community seems to have settled on softmax as the default choice, but using SVMs is definitely an alternative to keep in mind.

It might seem like 2,000 regions is a large number of regions. However, it is significantly fewer than what a sliding window would result in. Still, many of the regions will overlap, so the next step in the algorithm (not shown in the figure) is to analyze this overlap and make a call of whether two regions truly classify different objects. This overlap analysis does not use DL but uses a metric known as *intersection over union* (IoU), which is compared to a threshold value.

Now that the algorithm has detected and classified a number of objects, the final step in R-CNN is to refine the bounding box for each detected object. The thinking is that the original region proposals were created by a simple algorithm and are not expected to have high accuracy. Now that a smaller number of objects has been identified, a more accurate predictor can come up with better bounding boxes. For R-CNN, this is done using a class-specific linear regression model. That is, if there are K classes, the algorithm will train K linear regression models. When R-CNN later has detected and classified an object, it uses the corresponding linear regression model to refine the bounding box for a given object. The linear regression model uses the coordinates from the original region proposal as well as the 4,096 features extracted by the network as inputs. Thus, this model has access to complex information about the object that it is trying to create a bounding box for. We omit the exact details of how this bounding box refinement works and note that later models use techniques fully based on neural networks instead of linear regression models.

FAST R-CNN

One major performance bottleneck in R-CNN is that each of the 2,000 region proposals results in a forward pass through the convolutional network. Addressing this issue is one of the key contributions in the follow-up work that resulted in Fast R-CNN. Other changes include using VGGNet-16 instead of AlexNet, and instead of SVM and linear regression, it uses neural networks for the classification and bounding box refinement.

The first step in Fast R-CNN is to run the entire image through the convolutional and all but one of the max pooling layers of a pretrained VGGNet-16 model. That is, the last max pooling layer, the two fully connected layers, and the softmax layer have been removed. This results in a feature map of the dimensions $\frac{W}{32} \times \frac{H}{32}$, where W and H are the width and height of the input image.[1] Fast R-CNN relies on receiving approximately 2,000 region proposals from a simple model, just as R-CNN did. Given one such region of interest for the input image, it is easy to find a mapping to the corresponding rectangular region in the feature map. We can now use those features as inputs to our classification network. This is the main source of speedup in Fast R-CNN over R-CNN. Instead of doing a forward pass for each region proposal through all the convolutional layers, we do a single forward pass for the entire image. Although the entire image is larger than each region proposal, it is not 2,000 times larger because many of the proposals have overlapping regions, resulting in a significant speedup.

As opposed to warping the image into fixed dimensions, the model uses a layer called a region of interest (ROI) pooling layer. This layer is applied to the feature map and uses max pooling to convert the ROI of the feature map into a feature map of size 7×7. This is the same size as the input to the fully connected layers that we had removed from the model. Therefore, we can connect the output of the ROI pooling layer to the pretrained fully connected layers. Figure B-4 illustrates how the ROI pooling layer converts an arbitrarily sized region into fixed size.

The figure shows how a 4×8 region can be converted into a 2×2 region, but in reality, in Fast R-CNN the target size is 7×7. The figure shows only a single channel, although the feature map consists of 512 channels in practice. As mentioned previously, the output of the ROI pooling layer feeds two fully connected layers. The output of these two fully connected layers is a 4,096-dimensional feature vector that feeds two separate *sibling* networks.

---

1. A network consisting solely of convolutional layers and pooling layers can accept an image of any dimensions as input given some minor padding. The denominator (32) results from the network having five pooling layers, each reducing the dimensions by a factor of two.

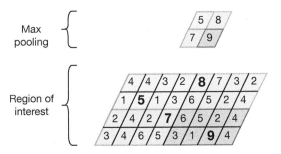

Max pooling

Region of interest

Figure B-4 How max pooling is used to convert an arbitrarily sized region of interest into fixed dimensions.

One of the networks is responsible for classifying the region as one out of many object types or as not an object (background). This network is simply a fully connected layer, followed by a softmax layer with $K+1$ outputs to classify the region as either containing one out of K different objects or no object at all. The second network operates side by side with its sibling and is responsible for predicting a more accurate bounding box. This network is also a fully connected network but with K sets of four outputs, representing the four coordinates for K different bounding boxes. That is, the set of four outputs to consider depends on which type of object the network detected. The overall architecture is shown in Figure B-5.

One thing to note is that these coordinates are not specified in terms of an absolute number of pixels. Instead they are expressed in terms of parameterized offsets compared to the region proposal that was input to the network. For completeness, assume that our training example provides a set of ground truth coordinates G_x, G_y, G_w, G_h, where G_x and G_y represent the center of the bounding box and G_w and G_h represent the width and the height respectively. We also have the corresponding region proposal coordinates P_x, P_y, P_w, P_h from the initial stage in our model. We now teach our network to predict t_x, t_y, t_w, t_h, where these parameters are defined as follows:[2]

$$t_x = \frac{(G_x - P_x)}{P_w} \qquad t_y = \frac{(G_y - P_y)}{P_h} \qquad t_w = log\left(\frac{G_w}{P_w}\right) \qquad t_h = log\left(\frac{G_h}{P_h}\right)$$

---

2. It is not completely clear to us why this parameterization is good, but the R-CNN paper where it was introduced (Girshick et al., 2014) stated that "as a standard regularized least squares problem, this can be solved efficiently in closed form." This parameterization might be beneficial even for Fast R-CNN, where a network is in charge of finding a solution, or a different parameterization might have worked equally well.

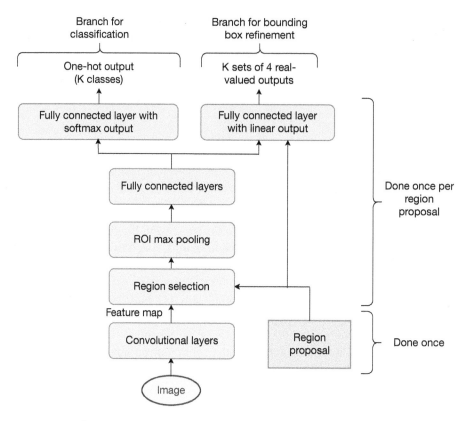

Figure B-5 Overall architecture of the Fast R-CNN network

It is worth noting that R-CNN used only DL to solve the feature extraction step in the object detection pipeline. Fast R-CNN, on the other hand, additionally uses DL for the classification and bounding box prediction steps. The region proposals are still created using a more traditional approach.

FASTER R-CNN

After the optimizations introduced with Fast R-CNN, the region proposal step emerged as a performance bottleneck. Faster R-CNN addresses this bottleneck by extending the neural network to provide its own region proposal instead of relying on a separate step up front. The full image is run through the convolutional layers from a pretrained VGGNet-16 to create a feature map, just as for Fast R-CNN. This feature map is used as input to a region proposal network (RPN), which creates the region proposals that were created by a more traditional computer vision technique in the past models. This RPN is the key contribution in Faster R-CNN. It nicely increases performance and results in an end-to-end DL solution to the entire object detection problem.

The RPN is a network that takes $N \times N$ features as input (where $N = 3$ in the paper [Shaoqing et al., 2015]), predicts whether the corresponding area in the original image contains one or more objects, and if so, provides region proposals for those objects. Sliding the RPN over the feature map produces region proposals for all objects in the image. Given that there is no straightforward (or any?) way to make a network have an arbitrary number of outputs, the RPN is limited to providing K region proposals (where $K = 9$ in the paper) for each set of $N \times N$ input features. The RPN consists of one fully connected ReLU layer followed by two fully connected sibling layers. One of the sibling layers provides K outputs, where each output indicates whether or not an object is present. The second sibling layer provides K sets of four outputs, where each set of four outputs is used to indicate locations of regions corresponding to the objects that the network deemed as being present. This is similar to the classification and bounding box refinement network that we described for Fast R-CNN, but remember that the RPN serves a different purpose.

This description of the RPN is not complete. The network includes one additional mechanism to make the region proposal functionality work better. This mechanism is based on *anchor boxes*. An anchor box is a rectangle of a specific size and aspect ratio that is centered at the current position of the RPN. Each of the K region proposals is based on an anchor box with unique size and aspect ratio. In particular, for $K = 9$, the anchor boxes correspond to all nine combinations of three different sizes and three different aspect ratios. The three sizes used in the paper are 128^2, 256^2, and 512^2, and the three aspect ratios are 1:2, 1:1, and 2:1, resulting in the combinations $(128^2, 1:2)$, $(128^2, 1:1)$, $(128^2, 2:1)$, $(256^2, 1:2)$, $(256^2, 1:1)$, and so on. The final region proposals are computed by combining a specific anchor box with the coordinates predicted by the network. For example, if the second output of the first sibling layer indicates that an object is present, then the second set of outputs in the other sibling layer will predict the coordinates in relationship to the anchor box of size 128^2 pixels and 1:1 aspect ratio. The coordinates are parameterized in the same way as for the bounding box refinement described for R-CNN. The RPN, including the anchor boxes, is illustrated in Figure B-6.

Now that we have both a feature map and region proposals, the rest of the network is identical to Fast R-CNN. That is, we use these region proposals to identify a part of the feature map to run through the ROI max pooling layer to

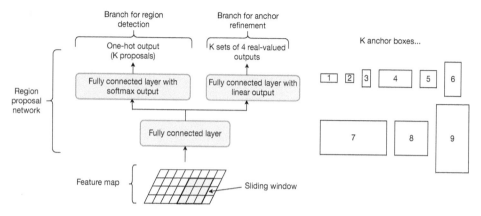

Figure B-6 Left: Region proposal network. The network consists of two sibling branches. The bounding box parameters are predicted relative to one out of *K* predefined anchor boxes of fixed size and aspects. Right: Anchor boxes.

produce a fixed-sized feature vector. This feature vector is then input to the remaining network that classifies the region as belonging to a specific class or not being an object. The sibling network further refines the region proposal to arrive at a refined bounding box. The overall architecture is shown in Figure B-7.

A fair question is why it is fast to use a sliding window approach when we previously have made a point that sliding windows is inefficient. The reasons that a sliding window approach is feasible in this case are that the search space and computational cost of the network have been reduced. First, the RPN is applied to the output of the convolutional layers. This output is of lower resolution than the original image. Second, the anchor box approach used by the RPN can propose multiple sizes and aspect ratios at once and thereby removes the need to evaluate the network once for each combination of size and aspect ratio. Finally, the RPN is a very small network, so it is not overly costly to evaluate a large number of times. It is a classification network that works with nine different classes, as it identifies, at most, nine regions per sliding window location. This can be compared to the number of different object types that the overall network needs to be able to classify, which is orders of magnitudes larger.

Faster R-CNN concludes our description of object detection techniques. The next few sections focus on a different problem, known as *semantic segmentation*.

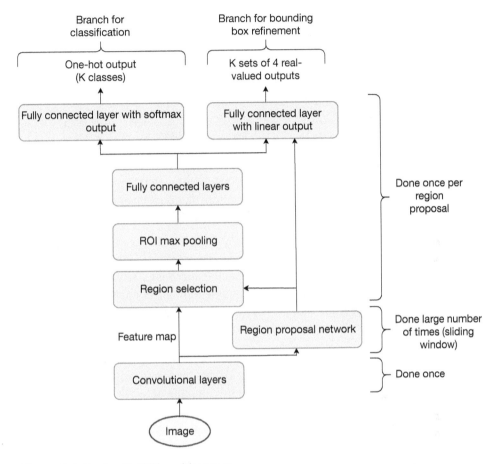

Figure B-7 **Faster R-CNN architecture**

Semantic Segmentation

The task of semantic segmentation involves assigning each pixel in an image to an object class by painting all pixels for a certain type of object in the same color. For example, an input image with two cats and a dog could result in an output image where the pixels for the two cats are yellow, the pixels for the dog are red, the ground pixels are green, and all sky pixels are blue. A key property of this task is that the width and height dimensions of the output are the same as the width and height dimensions of the input. However, the number of channels is different between the input and the output. The input typically has three input channels (RGB), and the output has the same number of channels as the number of classes, which was four in the example just described. Figure B-8 shows a naïve attempt at creating a network that fulfills these properties.

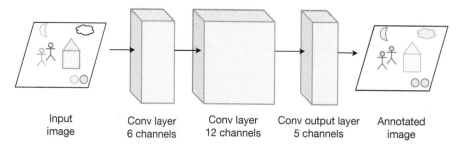

| Input image | Conv layer 6 channels | Conv layer 12 channels | Conv output layer 5 channels | Annotated image |

Figure B-8 Simple architecture for semantic segmentation. The width and height of all layers are of the same size to result in an output with the same resolution as the input image. Each 3D box represents a convolutional layer with a number of channels.

It consists of a convolutional network, without any pooling layers and with a stride of 1 for all layers. The number of channels increases as we move into the network. The output layer contains the same number of channels as the total number of object types that we want to be able to classify. If we pad the boundaries of each layer properly, the output layer will end up with the right size.

This network has no pooling layers or large strides for the convolutions. Their absence is inefficient because the layers deeper into the network not only have many channels but also are both high and wide (see middle layer in Figure B-8). This means that the total number of values (features) increases for each layer in the network. On the contrary, in a typical CNN the width and height decrease as we move deeper into the network, which results in a reduced or constant total number of features.

To enable using a more traditional CNN (where the resolution decreases inside the network) in the context of semantic segmentation, we need to somehow increase the resolution again in the final layers to arrive at an output layer with the right dimensions. The next section describes how this can be done.

UPSAMPLING TECHNIQUES

Increasing the resolution of an image is known as *upsampling*. It can be done in many different ways, most of which are not specific to DL. We start by describing two common techniques known as *nearest neighbor interpolation* and *bilinear interpolation*. Figure B-9 illustrates a scenario in which we upsample a 3×3 image by 2× into a 6×6 image. The leftmost part of the figure shows the

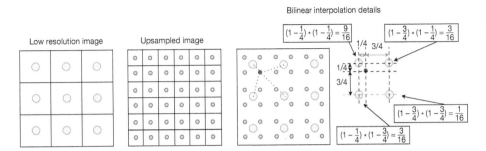

Figure B-9 2× upsampling

original 3×3 pixel image. To the right of that is an illustration of the desired 6×6 output image. Further right, the two images are overlaid on top of each other. Somewhat unintuitively, an upsampled pixel (red) does not fall equidistantly between the original pixels (blue). Instead, each pixel happens to be located in a position where it is close to one specific original pixel and farther away from other original pixels. Given that background, nearest neighbor interpolation is trivial to explain. Each upsampled pixel simply takes on the value of the closest original pixel. That is, each group of four upsampled pixels will take on the same color as the original pixel located in the center of the four upsampled pixels. Although the resulting image consists of 36 pixels, it will never consist of more than nine unique colors. Needless to say, this results in a pixelated appearance of the upsampled image.

One way to address the pixelation issue is to interpolate between the colors of the neighboring pixels. There are many ways of doing this; perhaps the most common one is bilinear interpolation. This is illustrated in the right half of the figure. Consider the bright red pixel and its distances to the four blue surrounding pixels. We measure the distance in terms of the fraction of the distance between these four blue pixels. The closest blue pixel is 1/4 of the distance in each direction (x and y). The farthest one is 3/4 of the distance in each direction. The other two are (1/4, 3/4) and (3/4, 1/4) distances away. We now compute a weight for each pixel, where the weight is computed as $(1 - x_{distance}) \times (1 - y_{distance})$. That is, the weight of the closest pixel is $(3/4) \times (3/4) = 9/16$. The weight of the pixel furthest away is $(1/4) \times (1/4) = 1/16$. The weights of the two other pixels are both $(1/4) \times (3/4) = 3/16$. Note that it is not the Euclidian distance between the red pixel and the blue pixel that determines the weight. Instead, the weight is computed as the product of $(1 - distance)$ in each of the two (x, y) dimensions. More details about interpolation techniques can be found in texts about computer graphics, such as *Real-Time Rendering* (Akenine-Möller et al., 2018).

Conveniently, bilinear interpolation can be implemented using a form of convolution. This is illustrated in the left part of Figure B-10. The trick is to first space the pixels apart and insert dummy pixels with 0 values in between each original pixel. The figure shows the original pixels in blue and the dummy pixels in gray. We can now use a 4×4 convolutional kernel to calculate the value of the pixel at the center of these 4×4 pixels. The values of all 16 elements of the kernel are found in the figure. A fair question is why the convolutional kernel needs to have 16 nonzero values when it will be applied to only four pixels with nonzero values. The answer is that the relative location of the 0-valued pixels changes as we move the kernel to compute the value of neighboring pixels.

Using the same technique, it is possible to construct a convolutional kernel that implements nearest neighbor interpolation. It is simply a 2×2 kernel with the value of all elements being 1.

It can be somewhat confusing to mentally visualize how the original pixels, the dummy pixels, and the resulting interpolating pixels relate to each other. The rightmost part of Figure B-10 shows them all in the same figure.

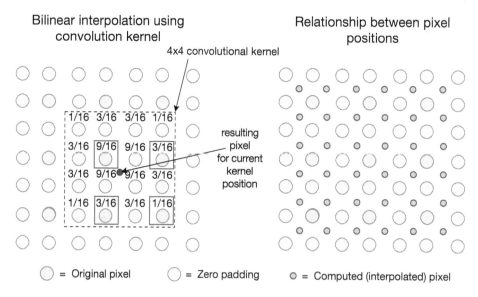

Figure B-10 Bilinear interpolation implemented using convolution. In reality, we need to pad the edges of the original image with more 0 values or apply other techniques to enable us to compute the edge pixels.

DECONVOLUTION AND UNPOOLING

Using the preceding framework, nearest neighbor and bilinear interpolation are only two special cases of convolutional kernels that we can implement. Instead of carefully selecting the weights in the kernel, these weights can be learned as part of training the network. In the DL field, the combination of interspersing the original pixels by 0-valued dummy pixels followed by applying a convolutional kernel is often referred to as a *deconvolution* operation. This naming derives from the fact that a normal convolutional layer downsamples an image (assuming a stride greater than one), whereas the operation we just described upsamples the image. That is, to some extent, the upsampling operation reverses the original convolution operation. However, deconvolution is a somewhat unfortunate name given that there already exists a different mathematical operation called deconvolution. From that perspective, unless the context is clear, it makes sense to refrain from using this term. Other names for this operation are *transposed convolution* and *fractional striding*.

Using a convolutional layer with a stride greater than 1 is not the only way to downsample images in a convolutional network. Another technique is the max pooling operation, which groups (pools) a region of pixels together and selects the maximum valued pixel. The left and middle parts of Figure B-11 illustrate the max pooling operation. For each group (pool) of four pixels, the maximum valued ones are indicated by more intense red color and a red square. The middle part of the figure illustrates how each group of four pixels in the original image results in a single pixel in the image after max pooling. The green square indicates the position of the original pixel that had the max value.

Just as deconvolution can be used to undo convolution, we can undo max pooling with an operation known as *unpooling*. This is illustrated in the right part of Figure B-11. The unpooling is similar to the first step of bilinear interpolation or deconvolution in that it pulls apart the pixels and inserts 0-valued dummy pixels. However, instead of placing the dummy pixels uniformly, it makes use of information from a preceding max pooling operation. The figure shows how the

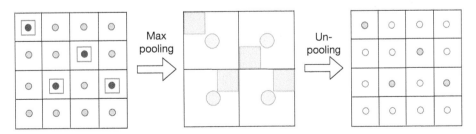

Figure B-11 Max pooling and unpooling

unpooling operation places the nonzero pixels in locations that correspond to where the maximum value originated before the max pooling operation. In reality, an unpooling operation does not typically follow directly after a max pooling operation, but there are multiple other operations interspersed between the two.

RELATIONSHIP BETWEEN DECONVOLUTION AND CONVOLUTION

In addition to the naming confusion between the deconvolution operation and the mathematical deconvolution operation, our impression is that there is some confusion with respect to how a deconvolution layer relates to a convolution layer. The deconvolution layer was first introduced by Zeiler and colleagues (2010). In subsequent work (Zeiler and Furgus, 2014; Zeiler, Taylor, and Fergus, 2011), the authors also introduced the unpooling operation and built networks that combined the two. This was in the context of reversing the effect of prior convolution and max pooling layers. They used unpooling and deconvolution to map features inside an image network back to pixel space. That is, there was a one-to-one correspondence between convolution/deconvolution and max pooling/ unpooling in the network. However, Zeiler and colleagues did not train the weights of the deconvolution layer separately. Instead, they reused the weights from the convolutional layer because they simply wanted to reverse the operation. To make each weight affect the appropriate pixel, the matrix representing the convolutional kernel needed to be transposed. This is the basis for the alternative, and perhaps better, name *transposed convolution*. In cases where the weights for the deconvolutional layer are learned separately, the point of transposing the matrix is moot. It simply does not matter how we arrange the initial weights of the matrix, given that they are initialized with random values anyway.

Combining unpooling and deconvolution is a source of confusion. We have described deconvolution as being an upsampling operation in which we first separate the pixels and then apply a convolution with a transposed kernel. A fair question is what happens in the case where we combine unpooling and deconvolution. The unpooling operation results in separating the pixels, so having the deconvolution layer separating them further is typically not desired. This can be avoided by using a stride of 1 for the deconvolution layer. The stride parameter controls how much to pull the input apart, and we have implicitly assumed a stride of 2 in all our examples. Setting the stride to 1 results in the output size being the same as the input size, just as for a convolutional layer with stride 1.

This is similar to how a convolution followed by max pooling is handled. We typically either use a combination of convolution with stride 1 and a max pooling layer or use a stride greater than 1 and simply omit the max pooling layer. In the former case, the max pooling layer does the downsampling, and in the latter, downsampling is baked into the convolution. This is all illustrated in Figure B-12.

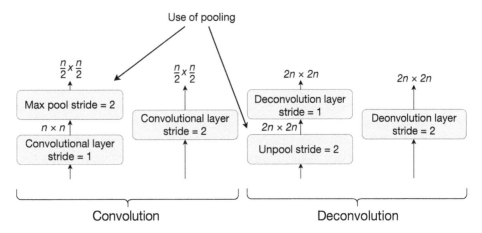

Figure B-12 Convolution/pooling and unpooling/deconvolution. Neither convolution nor deconvolution changes the dimensions of the input when using a stride of 1. Convolution/pooling downsamples and unpooling/deconvolution upsamples.

This takes us to what we think is a great source of confusion when dealing with deconvolution layers. The deconvolution layer first pulls the inputs apart and then performs a normal convolution but with a transposed version of the weight matrix. In the case where we have a stride of 1, the input is not pulled apart. Further, if the weights are learned (the normal use case), then the transpose operation does not have practical importance. That is, the deconvolution layer is equivalent to a convolutional layer! Still, it is common to see implementations that use unpooling layers followed by deconvolution layers with a stride of 1, possibly to make it clear that the overall network is upsampling.

> Using a deconvolution layer with a stride of 1 and learned weights seems like a very convoluted way of implementing a convolution.

AVOIDING CHECKERBOARD ARTIFACTS

One issue with the deconvolution approach is that it has been shown to result in checkerboard artifacts (Odena, Dumoulin, and Olah, 2016). This often happens regardless whether you use unpooling and deconvolution with stride 1 or you skip the unpooling and have larger stride in the deconvolution. Going back to the example where convolution is used to implement bilinear interpolation, this is not entirely surprising. We see that we are applying a convolution to an input image that has many zeros in a very regular pattern. In the case of bilinear interpolation, we carefully selected the weights given our knowledge of this input pattern. If we had not done that, it is not surprising that the grid of zeros in the input can result in a similar pattern on the output. Technically, the convolutional kernel has the freedom to learn bilinear interpolation, but why make it so hard for the network? Would it not be better to simply first apply nearest neighbor or bilinear interpolation followed by a convolution? Odena and colleague studied this issue and concluded that using nearest neighbor interpolation followed by a regular convolution yielded the best result.

There are a number of variations on these concepts. The convolutional kernel can be initialized to do bilinear interpolation and then adjusted by the training process (Long, Shelhamer, and Darrell, 2017). This can be combined with first doing unpooling to still make use of the information from a preceding max pooling step (Badrinarayanan, Kendall, and Cipolla, 2017).

In practice, for many applications, simply upsampling the image using either nearest neighbor or bilinear interpolation followed by a normal convolution is easy to implement and yields good results. This example seems to be a case where the community simply was overcomplicating the problem.

In many applications, upsampling using nearest neighbor or bilinear interpolation followed by a convolutional layer yields good results. We also think it is easier to understand than the transposed convolution (deconvolution) layer.

Now that we know how to do upsampling, we are ready to describe more advanced networks for semantic segmentation that can use lower resolution layers in the middle of the network. We describe the deconvolution network (Noh, Hong, and Han, 2015) and the U-Net (Ronneberger, Fischer, and Brox, 2015), which both are logical extensions of what we have just described. Both networks are examples of fully convolutional networks (FCNs), which are characterized by only having convolutional, downsampling, and upsampling layers. They both build on work by Long, Shelhamer, and Darrell (2017), who had previously proposed using FCNs for semantic segmentation.

DECONVOLUTION NETWORK

Given the upsampling techniques just described, the deconvolution network proposed by Noh, Hong, and Han (2015) is straightforward. It is an extension of the naïve semantic segmentation network outlined earlier. The difference is that it uses pooling layers to reduce the dimension of the layers deeper into the network instead of keeping it constant. This is followed by unpooling and deconvolutional layers to restore the width and height of the output layer to the same dimensions as in the input image.

The first part of the network is a VGGNet-16 network but without the final softmax layer. If you recall, VGGNet-16 ends with two fully connected layers and a softmax layer. It might seem strange that the two fully connected layers are not discarded as the softmax layer is. How can a network with fully connected layers result in a fully convolutional network? The answer is that, as pointed out by Long, Shelhamer, and Darrell (2017), a fully connected layer with 4,096 neurons can be viewed as a convolutional layer with width = 1, height = 1, and 4,096 channels. The remaining part of the network mirrors the convolution and max pooling layers. Unpooling layers replace the max pooling layers, and deconvolution layers with a stride of 1 replaces the convolution layers (Figure B-13).

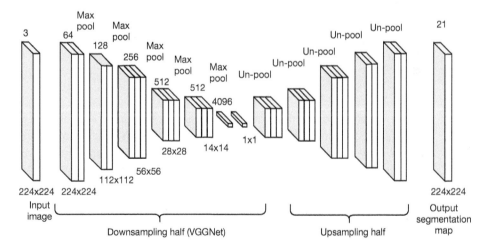

Figure B-13 Deconvolution network for semantic segmentation. Each group of slices represents a VGGNet building block, and each slice represents a convolutional layer. The number of channels for each layer is stated at the top and matches what is used in VGGNet-16. The dimensionality reduction is done using 2×2 max pooling (shown as text but not explicitly as layers in the figure). The upsampling half of the network uses unpooling and deconvolutions that mirror the downsampling half.

The input to the network is a 224×224×3 RGB image. The output from the network is a segmentation map of the dimensions 224×224×21. Each of the 224×224 pixels in the input image has a corresponding 21-element vector in the segmentation map. This vector identifies whether the pixel corresponds to one of 20 different object types or does not correspond to an object at all.

U-NET

Looking at the deconvolution network in Figure B-13, it seems magical how the network can use data from the narrowest part of the network (4,096 values) to recreate pixel data at the input resolution (50,000+ pixels). In a previous section, we justified the use of this low-dimensional intermediate representation with the need for efficiency. Not surprisingly, it turns out that the semantic segmentation result improves if the deconvolutional part of the network gets access to more data. In particular, it is beneficial if it can see both the low-dimensional intermediate representation and higher-dimensional representations originating closer to the input of the network. Ronneberger, Fischer, and Brox (2015) introduced U-Net, which does just that.

> If you happen to know something about JPEG compression, then it might not seem that magical that the narrowest part of the network is only 4,096 values, but let us ignore that for now and not ruin the dramatic introduction to this section.

In the upsampling half of the network, at each upsampling step, the output is concatenated with the output from a previous layer (in the downsampling half of the network) with comparable resolution. Thus, the network can make use of detailed pixel data close to the input as well as more coarse-grained hierarchical representations from deep inside of the network. This is illustrated in Figure B-14.

Looking at the upsampling half of the network, a white block represents the output of a convolutional layer that has been copied from the downsampling part of the network. A red block represents a convolutional layer that upsamples the output from the immediately preceding layer. The white and red blocks are now concatenated and used as input by the next convolutional layer (blue blocks in the figure). The figure omits the input image and the output segmentation map.

Now that we have described a couple of different networks for semantic segmentation, we move on to a highly related topic: instance segmentation.

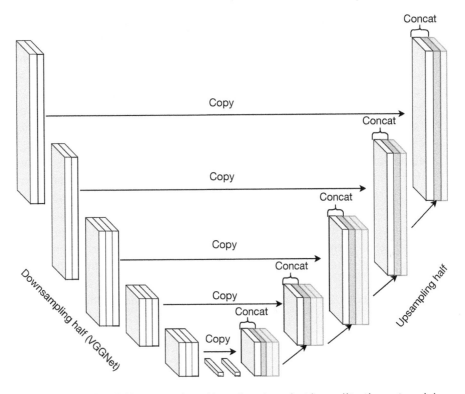

Figure B-14 The U-Net name is self-explanatory, but in reality, the network has the same horizontal hourglass shape as the previously shown deconvolution network. The key difference in the U-Net is that we copy output from layers from the downsampling to the upsampling part of the network and concatenate them with the upsampled layers.

Instance Segmentation with Mask R-CNN

In the semantic segmentation problem, all instances of a certain object type result in the same color in the output image. A related problem is *instance segmentation*. It assigns different colors to different instances even if they are of the same type. That is, two different cats in an image should result in two different colors in the output image.

This problem is a mix of object detection and semantic segmentation. The model needs to identify individual objects and then, for each object, identify the pixels that are associated with the object. We can solve this problem by building on top of Faster R-CNN, which already addressed the problem of localizing an object.

Mask R-CNN is a model that extends the Faster R-CNN model to also implement the instance segmentation task (He et al., 2017). The key enabler is a third branch of the network that operates in parallel with the classification branch and the bounding box refinement branch. This third branch uses the feature map as input and upsamples it. Its output is the pixel mask that identifies the pixels that correspond to the identified object. If you think about it, adding an upsampling branch to the feature map results in something similar to the deconvolution network described earlier. That is, this output layer will provide semantic segmentation for each region proposal, which implies that we have all the information available to do instance segmentation. The classification branch tells us if the region proposal contained an object, and if so, to what class that object belongs. The segmentation branch provides one channel for each object class, indicating which pixels belong to each class. Now we simply use the output of the classification branch to select which channel from the segmentation branch is of interest. This channel represents the pixels associated with the detected object. If desired, we can also make use of the bounding box branch so we can draw a bounding box around the object. The overall architecture is shown in Figure B-15.

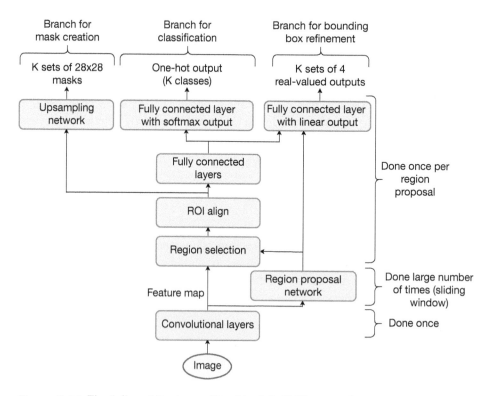

Figure B-15 The full architecture of the Mask R-CNN network

To conclude the description of Mask R-CNN, we also note that in addition to the segmentation branch, He and colleagues introduced an *ROI align layer* to replace the ROI max pooling layer. The ROI align layer includes some interpolation between values instead of just using max pooling operations. This makes it better at preserving spatial relationships, which enables the segmentation branch to do a better job of identifying the exact pixels to highlight.

Another thing to note is that the final mask resolution is limited to 28×28 pixels in the paper (He et al., 2017). For objects that exceed that size, the masks are scaled down before training. During inference, if a predicted bounding box is larger, then the mask predicted by the network needs to be upscaled to the size of the bounding box. We suspect that this design choice was made to reduce computational needs or because it reduced the number of required training iterations.

Finally, all our figures of R-CNN, Fast R-CNN, Faster R-CNN, and Mask R-CNN contain a block somewhat loosely specified as "convolutional layers," also known as the backbone of these networks. The detection and segmentation networks evolved over a number of years, during which time we saw rapid progress in convolutional network architectures. This progress carried over to the field of detection and segmentation, and the backbone of the networks was made more complex over time. R-CNN was based on AlexNet, whereas Fast and Faster R-CNN used VGGNet. Mask R-CNN was evaluated using a number of different backbones, including ResNet and ResNeXt (Xie et al., 2017) with a couple of different depths as well as a Feature Pyramid Network (FPN) proposed by Lin, Doll, and colleagues (2017).

Instead of providing a programming example in this appendix, we encourage you to try out implementations that are available for download. The segmentation example figure in the beginning of this appendix was produced with a TensorFlow implementation of Mask R-CNN (*Mask R-CNN for Object Detection and Segmentation*, 2019). It took us less than 15 minutes to download, install, and try out the demo application using the pretrained network to do instance segmentation on one of our own images.

This concludes our description of object detection, semantic segmentation and instance segmentation. It should now be clear that exceeding human ability in image classification does not imply that DL can do everything. There exist plenty of more complicated tasks to solve.

Appendix C

Word Embeddings Beyond word2vec and GloVe

This appendix logically follows Chapter 13, "Word Embeddings from word2vec and GloVe."

The word embeddings we discussed in Chapter 13 come with some limitations that more recent embedding schemes have addressed. Specifically, the embeddings we discussed have no way of handling out-of-vocabulary words, even if the new word is just a minor variation of a known word. For example, consider a case where the word *dog* was included in the training data, but its plural version *dogs* was not and hence does not have a corresponding embedding. It would be useful to have an embedding scheme that somehow can handle this case.

A different limitation is that there is only a single embedding corresponding to a specific word, even if that word has different meanings in different contexts. For example, consider the word *can* in the sentence "Can I have a can of soda?" The first occurrence is a modal verb and the second is a noun. It would be useful if these two instances of the same word resulted in two different embeddings.

In this appendix, we describe a few different schemes, which address these limitations. We begin by describing *wordpieces* and *FastText* embeddings. Both of these methods make use of the fact that a word can be divided into smaller units (subwords), but the methods still operate at a coarser granularity than just individual characters. These two schemes address only the out-of-vocabulary issue but not the issue of different meanings in different contexts. We then describe a method that operates on single characters, which also addresses only the out-of-vocabulary issue. However, the character-based method is also used as a building block in a more advanced scheme known as *ELMo* (Embeddings from Language Models), which addresses both out-of-vocabulary words and context-dependent embeddings.

Wordpieces

This method is not an embedding scheme in itself but simply a way of creating a vocabulary consisting of subwords instead of the full words. We can then use any suitable method for learning embeddings for these subwords, including learning the embeddings jointly with the application where they are used. The technique was originally developed for a voice search system in Japanese and Korean (Schuster and Nakajima, 2012) and was also used for a natural language translation application used in production (Wu et al., 2016). It is also used by a model known as *BERT,* which is described in Appendix D (Devlin et al., 2018).

The wordpieces are created in the following way. The initial vocabulary consists of the individual characters found in the training corpus. Wu and colleagues (2016) limited the number of characters to approximately 500 for Western languages to avoid polluting the vocabulary with rare characters. The remaining characters are replaced by a special out-of-vocabulary symbol. The vocabulary is used to build a simple language model (not neural network based). The next step is to add new symbols to the vocabulary by combining two existing symbols. That is, at the very beginning, we combine two characters into a new two-character symbol, which is added to the vocabulary. Adding all possible combinations of existing symbols clearly does not make sense, because some of them will not result in character sequences that are common, or that even exist, in the training corpus. This especially applies later in the process when each symbol consists of more characters. Instead, the candidate symbol is chosen on the basis of how well the language model would behave if that symbol wore added to the vocabulary. That is, we create K^2 candidate symbols (assuming K existing symbols in the vocabulary), evaluate K^2 language models, and pick the symbol that resulted in the best language model. This process is repeated until a user-defined number of symbols have been added to the vocabulary. These symbols are now our wordpieces that we later use to create word embeddings.

To make it more concrete, we walk through a small example. Assume a training corpus that is based on the very limited alphabet *e, i, n,* and *o*. The vocabulary starts out with just those four symbols. To identify the next symbol to add to the vocabulary, we create all 16 combinations: *ee, ii, nn, oo, ei, en, eo, ie, in, io,* and so on. We now want to identify which of these new 16 symbols result in the best language model if added to the vocabulary. That is, we create one language model with a vocabulary consisting of the symbols {e, i, n, o, ee}. We compare that to the language model that instead uses the symbols {e, i, n, o, ii} and so on. Once all 16 models have been evaluated, we pick the one that results in the best language model, which in our example happens to result in {e, i, n, o, no}. We now repeat the process, this time with 25 possible combinations. The vocabulary gradually grows, with one new symbol for each iteration:

{e, i, n, o, no}

{e, i, n, o, no, in}

{e, i, n, o, no, in, on}

{e, i, n, o, no, in, on, one}

{e, i, n, o, no, in, on, one, ni}

{e, i, n, o, no, in, on, one, ni, ne}

{e, i, n, o, no, in, on, one, ni, ne, nine}

The resulting vocabulary will consist of all individual characters as well as n-grams of various sizes. Wu and colleagues (2016) found that a vocabulary between 8K and 32K produced good results for their natural language translation task. What we described was a naïve implementation. In reality, there are implementation optimizations to reduce the computational complexity.

An input sentence can now be broken up into wordpieces using this vocabulary. If a word exists in the wordpiece vocabulary, it is left unchanged, and otherwise it is broken up into two or more pieces using the words in the wordpiece vocabulary. For example, the resulting vocabulary in our example does not contain the word *none*, so it would be formed by concatenating the two wordpieces *n* and *one*. Given that the vocabulary contains individual characters, it is always possible to form any word by combining pieces that exist in the vocabulary.

A wordpiece that begins a word is prepended with a special character (e.g., an underscore). That makes it possible to unambiguously recreate the original text once it has been broken up into wordpieces. In the original paper (Schuster and Nakajima, 2012), the special symbol was added to a wordpiece if it ended a word as well, but the scheme was simplified in the subsequent paper (Wu et al., 2016). Moving on from our toy example, we look at the following example from the paper:

Word: *Jet makers feud over seat width with big orders at stake*

wordpieces: *_J et _makers _fe ud _over _seat _width _with _big _orders _at _stake*

In the example, we can see that the words *Jet* and *feud* were not in the vocabulary and were therefore broken up into two pieces each. For *Jet,* this resulted in *_J* and *et*, where the underscore symbol in front of *J* indicates that it is the beginning of the word. We can now use any suitable method to learn word embeddings using the wordpieces as vocabulary.

FastText

FastText (Bojanowski et al., 2017) is a direct extension of the word2vec continuous skip-gram model. The intent is to create word embeddings that can handle out-of-vocabulary words. As described in Chapter 13, the training objective for the continuous skip-gram model is to, given a word, predict words that surround that word in a sentence. This was done by training a binary classifier to output 1 for words surrounding the word and 0 for some other randomly selected words (known as *negative samples*).

FastText modifies the representation of the input word to include some of its internal structure. For each word in the input dataset, in addition to each word, the model also forms all character n-grams for the word. We have previously looked at n-grams consisting of *n* consecutive words, but we can apply the same concept to characters inside a word. For the rest of this appendix, n-gram will refer to *n consecutive characters* instead of words. FastText limits itself to n-grams where *n* is greater than or equal to 3 and less than or equal to 6. The first n-gram in a word is prepended with a start symbol, <, and the last n-gram in a word is appended with an end symbol, >. To give an example from Bojanowski and colleagues' paper (2017), the word *where* results in the following n-grams:

<wh, whe, her, ere, re>, <where>

The example only shows n-grams of size 3, so in reality, there will be more n-grams as well. As shown, the start and end symbols are added to the original word itself as well. This implies that an n-gram that happens to be identical to a full word will still be treated as a separate word. For example, the n-gram *her* will be treated as a different word from the full word *<her>*.

In the FastText model, each word as well as all the n-grams have a corresponding vector. We form the embedding for a specific word by averaging the vectors for the word and all its n-grams. From a training objective perspective, this results in that we train the model not only to predict surrounding words from a given word but also to predict the surrounding words from the given word's internal n-grams.

When using FastText, out-of-vocabulary words will simply be represented by the average of the n-grams of that word. It is not hard to imagine how this can lead to a vector that is similar to a vector of an existing word in the case where the out-of-vocabulary word is just a slight variation of that existing word. FastText embeddings have been created for a large number of languages and are available online to download.

Character-Based Method

Instead of breaking up words into subwords before training the model, another approach to handling out-of-vocabulary words is simply to work on characters instead of words. This might seem unintuitive because we are talking about word embeddings, but we can build a model that outputs word embeddings using characters instead of words or subwords as input. We describe such a model in this section. Another important aspect of this model is that it is the basis for another model used to produce context-dependent word embeddings. We describe this follow-on model in the next section.

In Chapter 11, "Text Autocompletion with LSTM and Beam Search," and Chapter 12, "Neural Language Models and Word Embeddings," we saw examples of neural language models that work on characters as well as on words. The ones in our code examples were based on recurrent networks. These models were autoregressive in that the predicted output symbol was fed back as input to the network in the next timestep. Kim et al. describe a language model that is similar but uses a hybrid approach (Kim et al., 2016). It uses characters as inputs but predicts words on the output. Further, it is more complicated in that it uses character embeddings that are run through a 1D convolutional network followed by a highway network. This produces word embeddings that are then fed to the recurrent layer. We start by describing these initial layers that operate on characters and produce word embeddings.

The overall idea with this word embedding scheme is that a word can be characterized by the n-grams it contains. To gain some insight into what the scheme does, imagine that you have a vector where each entry indicates whether a specific n-gram is present in the word. The entry is set to 1 if the n-gram is present and to 0 if the n-gram is not present. That is, we create a bag-of-character-n-grams. This vector can now be used as an embedding. Two words that are different variations of a single word (e.g., the singular form and the plural form), will get similar embeddings. Only the n-grams for the suffixes will differ. Some examples are shown in Figure C-1 for the word *supercalifragilisticexpialidocious,* which is the title of a song from the famous children's movie *Mary Poppins* (Sherman and Sherman, 1963). It would be unlikely to find that full word in the vocabulary unless a very specific training corpus was used. However, many of the building blocks (n-grams) commonly occur in other texts.

The figure shows how we can create a bag-of-n-grams from many of the n-grams formed by consecutive characters of that word (top row) as well as the two variations *subcalifragilisticexpialidocious* and *supercalirobusticexpialidocious.* The n-grams are chosen to work well for this example. We also included three totally unrelated n-grams (to the very right in the figure) that do not appear in the words, to illustrate that not all known n-grams will appear in the input words. This example illustrates how these three related words end up with word vectors that are similar to each other but different from unrelated words.

> We recognize that "totally unrelated n-grams" might be a somewhat strong statement for this case.

The character-based embeddings that we discuss in this section are similar to this scheme but with two important differences. First, instead of deciding up front what n-grams to look for, the n-grams are learned by the model. Second, instead of using a binary number to indicate whether an n-gram is present, each entry in the vector is a real-valued number. The magnitude of the value is a measure of

Input word						Bag-of-character-n-grams								
						super	sub	cali	fragi	robust	expia	doc	spoon	ful	sug
super	cali	fragilistic	expiali	docious →		1	0	1	1	0	1	1	0	0	0
sub	cali	fragilistic	expiali	docious →		0	1	1	1	0	1	1	0	0	0
super	cali	robustic	expiali	docious →		1	0	1	0	1	1	1	0	0	0

Figure C-1 Bag-of-n-grams based on some of the n-grams in the word *supercalifragilisticexpialidocious* and two variations on that word

how similar the n-grams from the current word are to the target n-grams. Even n-grams that were not present in the training set can influence the output. This is illustrated in Figure C-2. Some of the target n-grams are slightly different from the ones in the previous figure to illustrate the approximate matching. The vector entries are now real-valued and indicate similarity between the target n-grams and the n-grams found in the words.

Both figures have ordered the n-grams in the same order as they show up in the words that we analyze, but in reality, the order is arbitrary, as a bag-of-n-grams does not capture the order among the n-grams. In particular, it is not the case that each n-gram is scored only on the specific part of the word that has the same color in the figure. The score is based on all n-grams in the word. For example, consider the n-gram *robust*. It might seem odd that it has gotten a score of 0.1 instead of 0.0 for the words that contain *fragilistic*, given that *fragilistic* does not have any similarity with *robust*. However, there are other parts of the word that have some commonalities—for example, *docious* contains the letters *o, u,* and *s* in the same order as *robust*.

The approximate bag-of-n-grams can be implemented using a 1D convolution, which is illustrated on the right side of Figure C-3. We are already familiar with 2D convolutions (left part of the figure) where we are sliding a K×K kernel over an image. The kernel computes a weighted sum of the pixel at the center of

Input word					Approximate bag-of-character-n-grams									
					super	sub	calista	fragile	robust	expiate	docent	spoon	ful	sug
super	cali	fragilistic	expiali	docious →	1.0	0.2	0.7	0.9	0.1	0.9	0.8	0.1	0.1	0.2
sub	cali	fragilistic	expiali	docious →	0.3	1.0	0.7	0.9	0.1	0.9	0.8	0.05	0.1	0.1
super	cali	robustic	expiali	docious →	1.0	0.2	0.7	0.1	1.0	0.9	0.8	0.1	0.05	0.2

Figure C-2 Approximate-bag-of-n-grams where each vector entry indicates similarity to the target n-gram

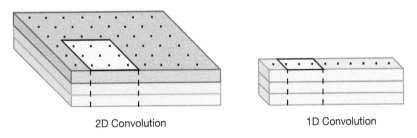

2D Convolution   1D Convolution

Figure C-3 Difference between 2D (left) and 1D (right) convolutions

the kernel and the surrounding pixels. We saw that the kernel acts as a feature identifier and thereby creates a feature map that indicates where certain features in the image are present. We can apply the same concept but in one dimension with a 1D kernel of width w that we sweep over all the characters in a word. At any given point, the kernel will compute a weighted sum of the character directly under the kernel as well as the surrounding characters. With a width of w, it can thereby identify an n-gram consisting of w characters. The convolution results in a 1D feature map that indicates where in a word a specific n-gram is present.

One thing that we glossed over in the preceding discussion is how the individual characters are represented. As shown in Figure C-3, each pixel in an image consists of multiple color channels, so the 2D convolution operates in three dimensions. Similarly, we encode each character as a vector of elements, so the 1D convolution operates in two dimensions, as shown in the figure. An obvious way of encoding a character as a 1D vector is to use one-hot encoding. Another way is to learn a dense character embedding to reduce the number of elements in the vector. That is the method used by Kim and colleagues (2016).

We are now ready to present the process of creating a word embedding from a string of characters. The process is illustrated in Figure C-4.

A word consists of a string of j characters. Each character is converted to a d-dimensional embedding by an embedding layer. We input this set of character vectors into a 1D convolution layer. This discussion has been limited to only a single kernel, that is, a single output channel, represented by a single horizontal track in Figure C-4. The kernel of width w is applied to all j characters of the word and

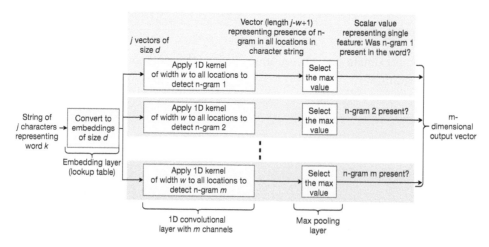

Figure C-4 Creating word embedding from a string of characters

results in a vector with $j-w+1$ elements (instead of j because padding is not used). This vector indicates the location where the n-gram corresponding to the kernel is found. However, we are not interested in knowing the location of the n-gram, but only whether it is contained in the word. Thus, the convolutional layer is followed by a max pooling operation with a single output. This produces a single element of our m-dimensional word embedding. This process is repeated once for each output channel, as represented by the different colored tracks in the figure. Each channel identifies its own n-gram, and the combined output of all the channels forms a word embedding given a string of characters. This implies that a word embedding will be formed even for words that were not present in the training dataset.

One drawback of this embedding is that the only similarity between words it is likely to capture is similarity in spelling. Kim and colleagues (2016) addressed that shortcoming by passing the embedding through a multilevel network to produce the final embedding. The thinking is that this additional network can capture interactions between the n-grams. One finding was that a regular fully connected feedforward network did not do very well, but a highway network did. As described in Chapter 10, "Long Short-Term Memory," a highway network is a feedforward network with skip connections controlled by trainable gates. The full network is shown in Figure C-5.

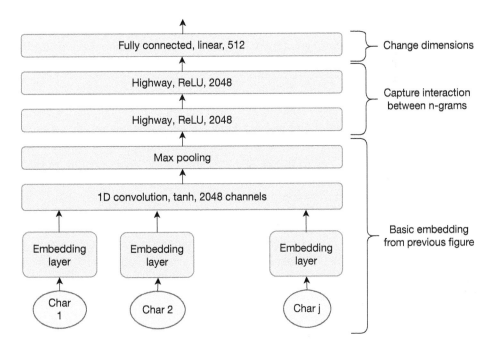

Figure C-5 Full network to produce character-based word embeddings

Kim and colleagues used these character-based word embeddings as input to a language model based on a single recurrent layer using long short-term-memory (LSTM) cells, followed by a softmax layer to predict the next word. The dimensions in Figure C-5 are somewhat different than what the authors used, and there is also an additional projection layer (fully connected without activation function) at the end of the network. This matches the network that is the base of the ELMo embeddings described in the next section.

ELMo

Embeddings from language models, also known as *ELMo* (Peters et al., 2018), is based on a language model that uses the character-based embeddings from the previous section. This language model was first studied by Jozefowicz and colleagues (2016) and uses two bidirectional LSTM-based recurrent layers. That study compared a number of different configurations of layers and sizes. We focus on the specific configuration that was later used by Peters and colleagues (2018) for the ELMo embeddings. A key property of these embeddings is that they are context dependent; that is, a single word can have different embeddings depending on the context in which the word is used. That is not the only way that ELMo is different from other embeddings that we have studied. Instead of just using the pretrained embeddings as is, these embeddings have specific parameters that are intended to be tuned by the end application.

Clearly, to make word embeddings context dependent, the embedding for a word cannot be retrieved by a lookup from just the word itself. Instead, surrounding words (the context) is also needed. ELMo solves this issue by using a bidirectional language model to generate the embeddings. We have previously seen examples of how language models predict the next word given the preceding words. A bidirectional language model has access to both preceding and subsequent words of the word that it tries to predict.

A key observation is that the embeddings fed to a language model are context independent, but the representations in the hidden layers and the output layer of the language model include accumulated information about surrounding words. In particular, for a bidirectional language model, these representations will be affected by both historical and future words—that is, by the full context. The language model used by ELMo is illustrated in Figure C-6.

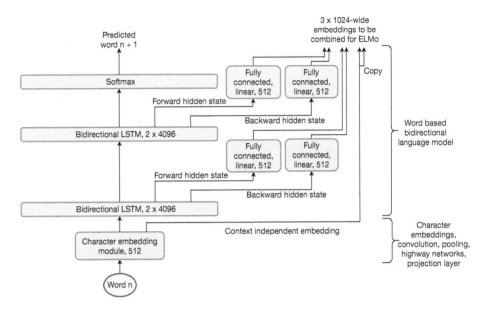

Figure C-6 Bidirectional language model to generate ELMo embeddings

Starting from the bottom, the first module produces a context-independent word embedding using the character-based word embedding scheme described in the previous section. This module consists of the character embedding layer, 1D convolution, max pooling, highway networks, and projection layer. The 1D convolution uses 2,048 kernels[1] (it can look for 2,048 n-grams) of different sizes, but the projection layer reduces the word embedding dimension to 512. All of this is inside of what is denoted "Character embedding module" in the figure.

The bidirectional language model is based on two bidirectional LSTM layers, each having 4,096 units in each direction. The output layer is a softmax layer that predicts the missing word in a sequence. This prediction is necessary when training the model, but the prediction can be discarded when using the model to produce the context-dependent word embedding.

The hidden states of each of the LSTM layers are fed through a projection layer that reduces the dimensionality from 4,096 to 512. Because each LSTM is bidirectional, each layer results in a vector of 1,024 (2×512) entries after

---

1. The 2,048 kernels used in ELMo look for n-grams of different lengths. The size and number of kernels are [1, 32], [2, 32], [3, 64], [4, 128], [5, 256], [6, 512], [7, 1024], using the notation [kernel size, number of kernels]. For example, the model has 64 output channels that represent n-grams of size 3 (kernel size: 3; kernel count: 64).

concatenation. The input layer consists of only 512 entries, but we concatenate it with a copy of itself, and we end up with three sets of 1,024 entries, shown at the top right in the figure.

ELMo embeddings are produced by running the text for which we want embeddings through the language model, and for each word fed to the model, we record these three vectors. The ELMo embedding is formed by computing a single vector that is a weighted sum of these three vectors. The weights to use are application specific and are learned by the end-user model. This is illustrated in Figure C-7.

The figure shows the language model unrolled in time, with the words *can, i, have, a, can* as input. We note that the first and last words (colored green) both are *can*, but they have different meanings. The language model outputs three vectors (*E1, E2,* and *E3*) for each timestep, and the ELMo embedding is a weighted sum of the three vectors. For the two instances of the word *can, E1* will be the same because it is context independent. *E2* and *E3* depend on the surrounding words, and the resulting ELMo embeddings for the two words are thereby different (indicated by the second instance being colored in red). Although ELMo embeddings can be used in isolation, Peters and colleagues (2018) showed that it is beneficial to combine them with another context-independent embedding scheme. Figure C-7 shows how this can be done, using pretrained GloVe vectors as the context-independent scheme.

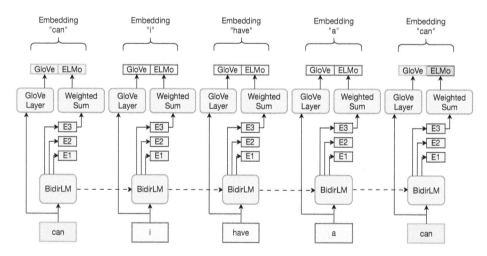

Figure C-7 Process of forming context-dependent embeddings by concatenating ELMo embeddings with any other context-independent embedding

As already mentioned, the weights used to combine the three vectors are trained in conjunction with training the model that uses the ELMo vectors. These three weights (s_1, s_2, s_3) are softmax normalized so that they add up to 1. In addition, a single scaling factor (γ) is learned that is applied to the final vector. That is, the task-specific ELMo embedding is given by

$$ELMo^{task} = \gamma^{task}\left(s_1^{task}E1 + s_2^{task}E2 + s_3^{task}E3\right), \quad where \ s_1 + s_2 + s_3 = 1$$

Related Work

In our description of the character-based embeddings introduced by Kim and colleagues (2016), we noted how the convolution and max pooling operations result in an approximate bag-of-character-n-grams (or just bag-of-n-grams for short). We described in Chapter 12 that there are two main variations of bag-of-n-grams. They can indicate either the presence of each n-gram (binary element) or the count of each n-gram. Wieting and colleagues (2016) did the latter in their work on CHARAGRAM embeddings. They explicitly created a bag-of-n-grams instead of using convolutions and used the resulting vector as input to a single fully connected layer using the ReLU activation function.

Athiwaratkun, Wilson, and Anandkumar (2018) introduced an embedding scheme similar to FastText but with the ability to capture multiple word senses and uncertainty information. This enabled the scheme to handle rare, misspelled, or even unseen words. They named their scheme *Probabilistic FastText*.

ELMo is not the only existing scheme for context-dependent embeddings. It builds on work on contextualized word vectors, or CoVe for short (McCann et al., 2017). In that work, the authors produced context-dependent embeddings from a machine translation model instead of from a language model. Another difference compared to ELMo is that CoVe uses only the representation from the top layer of the model, whereas ELMo uses a combination of multiple layers when forming the embedding.

This appendix described some techniques to make word embeddings more versatile than the word2vec and GloVe embeddings described in Chapter 13. Another body of work that builds on word embeddings is document or paragraph embeddings. The objective is to find an embedding for an entire phrase instead of for a single word. We mention some examples here to provide references for future reading. The first one is doc2vec (Le and Mikolov, 2014). The training objective used is to predict the next word in a paragraph. That is, doc2vec is similar to the language model–based approach described in Chapters 12 and 13, but the technique is modified to produce an embedding for a sequence of words instead of for a single word. Mimicking the development of word embeddings, the skip-thought model (Kiros et al., 2015) is a generalization of the continuous skip-gram model from word2vec. The training objective is to predict surrounding sentences given an input sentence, and the result is an embedding for that input sentence. Finally, sent2vec (Pagliardini, Gupta, and Jaggi, 2018) composes sentence embeddings using word embeddings and n-gram embeddings as building blocks.

Appendix D

GPT, BERT, and RoBERTa

This appendix logically follows Chapter 15, "Attention and the Transformer."

In Chapter 15, we described the Transformer architecture and how it can be used for natural language translation. Transformers have also been used as building blocks to solve other natural language processing (NLP) problems. In this appendix, we describe three such examples.

A key idea is to pretrain a basic model on a large text corpus. As a result of this pretraining, the model learns general language structure. This model then can be either used as is to solve a different kind of task or extended with additional layers and fine-tuned for the actual task at hand. That is, these kinds of models make use of transfer learning. We saw an example of how this can be done for images in Chapter 16, "One-to-Many Network for Image Captioning." There we used a VGGNet pretrained on the ImageNet dataset as basis for our image-captioning network. The network learned how to extract useful image features on the classification task used for pretraining. In the end task, we added the decoder part of the network that generated image captions, using these extracted features as input.

Similarly, the models discussed in this appendix learn to extract features from text data during pretraining. This process is also related to how word embeddings were learned in Chapter 12, "Neural Language Models and Word Embeddings," and Chapter 13, "Word Embeddings from word2vec and GloVe." There we pretrained a model on text data, which resulted in the first layer of the model (the embedding layer) learning useful word representations. This embedding layer could then be reused in other models. The models in this appendix take this concept one step further. Instead of being limited to reusing only the embedding layer, multiple layers of the pretrained model are reused in the end application.

GPT

The Generative Pre-Training (GPT; Radford et al., 2018) model is a neural language model, similar to what was described in Chapter 12. Given a sequence of input words, the model is trained to predict the next word. We have already seen how such a model can be used to do text autocompletion. That is, the *pretraining* task is to *generate* text, which gives the model its name.

The language model introduced in Chapter 12 was based on long short-term memory (LSTM) layers, whereas GPT is based on the Transformer architecture (described in Chapter 15). To understand this, it is helpful to go back to the natural language translation network from Chapter 14, "Sequence-to-Sequence Networks and Natural Language Translation." It is an LSTM-based encoder-decoder architecture in which the encoder produces an intermediate representation, and the decoder network generates a translation in the target language. That is, the decoder is a language model that uses the intermediate representation as a starting point. From that perspective, the decoder component of the Transformer is a language model based on self-attention layers instead of LSTM layers. One key difference when using the decoder as a standalone language model is that there is no need to include the attention layer that attends to the intermediate representation produced by the encoder, simply because the encoder does not exist. The masked self-attention layer is still present. The basic building block is shown on the left side of Figure D-1. The right side of the figure shows how multiple such building blocks (12 in the GPT model) are combined, just as in the Transformer architecture.

Figure D-2 illustrates pretraining of the model. The model is presented with an arbitrary sentence on its input. In the figure, we use "gpt is pre trained on an lm task" as an example. The ground truth the model is trained to predict is the same sentence but shifted by one word. That is, the first output word corresponds to the second word in the sentence. The masked self-attention mechanism prevents the model from cheating by "looking into the future" of the input sentence.

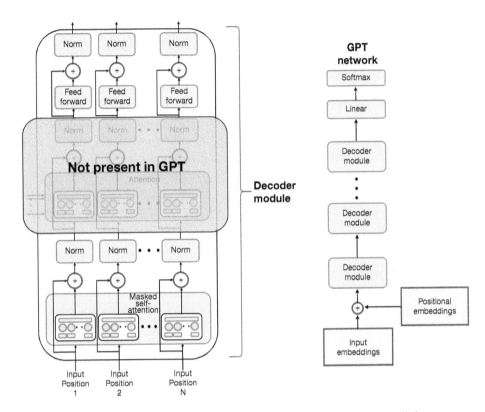

Figure D-1 Left: Transformer decoder modified to be used as a standalone language model. Right: GPT network based on multiple stacked decoder modules.

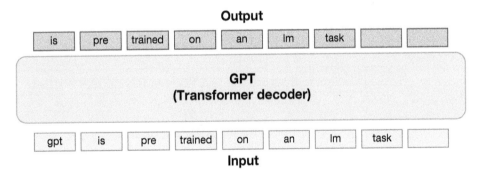

Figure D-2 GPT pretraining on the language model task

Each red box in the figure corresponds to a layer using a softmax activation function to provide the probabilities for all words in the vocabulary. This pretraining is done on unlabeled data and can thereby be done on massive amounts of text.

After pretraining, the model is fine-tuned for the specific task, using labeled data. The inputs to the model, as well as the output layer, are modified slightly to better suit the end task the model is being used for. Figure D-3 illustrates this for a similarity task in which the model is presented with two sentences as an input. The task is to determine whether the two sentences are similar. To do so, the input needs to be modified to be able to represent two sentences, which is done with a learned delimiter (DELIM) token. In addition, the input is augmented with a START token in the beginning and an END token at the end.

Apart from modifying the format of the input sequence, the output layer is also modified. The GPT paper (Radford et al., 2018) describes how the modification can be done for a handful of different types of tasks. For the similarity task illustrated here, there is no natural order between the two sentences, so the recommendation is to evaluate the model twice. For the second evaluation, the order of the two sentences is swapped. The outputs corresponding to the END token for each of these two evaluations are then added elementwise. It is the raw output from the transformer module that is used—that is, the softmax layer is discarded. The vector that results from this addition is used as input to a linear classifier, which is trained to indicate whether the two sentences are similar.

Another use case is sentiment analysis for which the input is just a single text sequence, so no delimiter token is used. Further, only one evaluation of the network is required. Just as for the similarity task, a linear classifier is simply

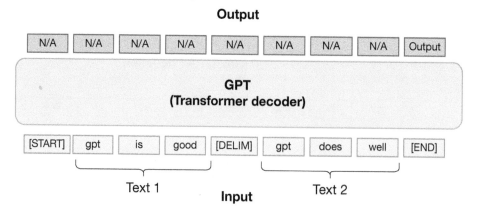

Output

| N/A | N/A | N/A | N/A | N/A | N/A | N/A | N/A | Output |

GPT
(Transformer decoder)

| [START] | gpt | is | good | [DELIM] | gpt | does | well | [END] |

Text 1   **Input**   Text 2

Figure D-3 Fine-tuning task

trained using the outputs corresponding to the END token as inputs. Details of how to use the network outputs to solve other types of tasks can be found in the original GPT paper.

There are a few more details worth mentioning. In the original Transformer paper (Vaswani et al., 2017), the positional encoding was computed using a formula, as described in Chapter 15. The GPT model handles this task differently in that the positional encodings are learned. Figure D-4 illustrates how the input to the Transformer decoder is created by adding the word embedding to a learned position embedding of the same dimensionality.

Another detail is how the loss function is constructed. Instead of training only the linear classifier, it turns out that it is beneficial to train the model to act as a language model during the fine-tuning step as well. Therefore, the fine-tuning loss function is a weighted sum of the language model loss function and the end-task loss function. Finally, GPT does not use a vocabulary of full words but uses a technique known as *byte-pair encoding* (Sennrich, Haddow, and Birch, 2016). This technique is based on subwords and can thereby avoid the problem with out-of-vocabulary words similar to some of the already-described techniques in Appendix C.

When GPT was introduced, it showed significant improvement over existing models in 9 out of 12 evaluated tasks. GPT was also studied in the context of *zero-shot task transfer*. In such a setting, a pretrained model is applied to a different end task but *without fine-tuning the model* for that end task. One example from the paper is the task of sentiment analysis. Sennrich, Haddow, and Birch (2016) did this by first concatenating the sentence with the word *very* and feeding this text sequence into the model. The output of the model was then interpreted by looking at the probabilities the model assigned to the two words *positive* and *negative* for the next predicted word. When evaluated on a sentiment analysis test set, the model correctly assigned higher probability to the word *positive* in many cases when the sentence expressed a positive sentiment, and vice versa. That is, even though the model had not been explicitly trained on the task of sentiment analysis or even exposed to the training part of the dataset, it had managed to learn this task from

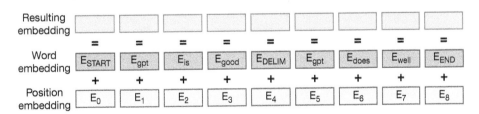

Figure D-4 How input embeddings are created for GPT

an unrelated body of text, using unsupervised learning. A more detailed evaluation of the GPT architecture on zero-shot task transfer has been done in later studies (Puri and Catanzaro, 2019; Radford et al., 2019), using GPT-2, which is a scaled-up version of the GPT model. Brown and colleagues (2020) have done further studies on the GPT architecture and have shown how an even bigger model (GPT-3) can solve end tasks in a transfer-learning setting using limited or no fine-tuning.

BERT

A model known as *Bidirectional Encoder Representations from Transformers* (BERT; Devlin et al., 2018) takes a somewhat different approach than GPT. BERT makes use of the observation that there are both backward and forward dependencies between words in a sentence. We touched on this in the section about bidirectional recurrent neural networks (RNNs) in Chapter 11, "Text Autocompletion with LSTM and Beam Search." The masked self-attention layers in the Transformer decoder explicitly prevent the network from considering dependencies on future symbols. BERT, on the other hand, is based on the encoder part of the Transformer architecture, which does not have this limitation.

To accommodate for the bidirectional property of the architecture, BERT does not use the traditional language model as its pretraining task. Instead, it is trained on two tasks known as *masked language model* and *next-sentence prediction*. The model is trained on both of these tasks simultaneously. The details of these two pretraining tasks are described next.

MASKED LANGUAGE MODEL TASK

As described for GPT, the language model pretraining task consists of predicting the next word in a sentence. In the masked language model pretraining task for BERT, the objective is to predict a number of missing (masked) words using both historical and future words in a sentence. Consider the input sentence "my dog is a hairy beast," which is a sentence similar to what was used in the paper (Devlin et al., 2018). We take this sentence and randomly mask a number of words and the model is trained to predict the missing words. The input examples are formed in the following manner:

- Fifteen percent of the words in an input sentence are selected to be masked (e.g., the word *hairy*).

- For 80% of the selected masked words, the word embedding is replaced by a special mask embedding, so we end up with "my dog is a [MASK] beast."

- For 10% of the selected masked words, the word embedding is replaced by the embedding for a randomly selected word, so we might end up with "my dog is a apple beast."

- For the remaining 10% of the selected masked words, we do not replace the word embedding but instead use the embedding for the correct word, so we end up with "my dog is a hairy beast." This might sound like the word does not get masked after all, but the distinction between this word and the non-masked words is that the model is still evaluated on the basis of whether it manages to predict this word.

BERT will try to predict all the words in the sentence, including the ones that are not masked, but from a training perspective, the model is scored according to how well it does on only the 15% masked words.

NEXT-SENTENCE PREDICTION TASK

Whereas the *masked language* task aims to teach the model sentence structure, the *next-sentence prediction* task aims to teach the model relationships between two sentences. This task is a classification problem with the two categories IsNext and NotNext. The model is presented with two sentences, and the goal is to determine whether the second sentence logically follows the first sentence. If so, it should classify the example as the category IsNext. If the second sentence does not logically follow the first sentence, then the model should classify the example as NotNext. That is, we have two cases during training:

- In 50% of the cases, simply present two consecutive sentences from the text corpus and train the model to output the category IsNext. An example is the sentence "the man went to [MASK] store" followed by "he bought a gallon [MASK] milk." Note that some of the words are masked because the two training tasks are performed at the same time.

- In 50% of the cases, present two unrelated (nonconsecutive) sentences from the text corpus and train the model to output the category NotNext. An example is the sentence "the man went to [MASK] store" followed by "penguins [MASK] flight ##less birds."

The two hash signs before *less* indicate that it is a *wordpiece*. BERT uses wordpieces as tokens instead of the full words. Wordpieces were described in Appendix C and come with the advantage of better handling of out-of-vocabulary words. In short, if a word does not exist in the training vocabulary, it will be replaced by a sequence of subwords. These wordpieces are run through a regular embedding layer to create embeddings. In this example, the word *flightless* was not in the vocabulary and was therefore broken up into the two pieces *flight* and *less*. The hash sign notation follows the notation in the BERT paper (Devlin et al., 2018) and is different from the underscore notation used in Appendix C.

Although these examples used actual sentences, in reality, the BERT pretraining task uses a broader definition, where a sentence is simply a consecutive collection of words from the corpus. Thus, each "sentence" might well consist of multiple actual sentences with the restriction that the total number of words for the two sentences cannot exceed the model width, which for the typical BERT model is 512 words.

BERT INPUT AND OUTPUT REPRESENTATIONS

To be able to handle the two pretraining tasks we just presented, as well as other NLP tasks, BERT needs to be able to accept two sentences as an input. It also needs to be able to output a category prediction (IsNext or NotNext) as well as a word prediction corresponding to each word in the input sentences. BERT handles this with a combination of special tokens and a concept known as *segment embeddings*. Figure D-5 shows the organization of input and output tokens for BERT. The input consists of a classification token CLS, followed by the tokens for a first sentence (e.g., the question in a question-answering task). The first sentence ends with a separation token SEP. It is followed by tokens for an optional second sentence (e.g., the answer), which again ends with the SEP token.

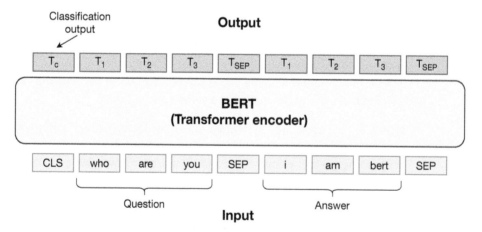

Figure D-5 BERT inputs and outputs. The input begins with a special classification CLS token. It is followed by a sequence of question tokens and a sequence of answer tokens. Each of those two groups ends with a special separation SEP token.

For tasks that require only a single input sentence (e.g., sentiment analysis), the input is simply a CLS token, followed by the question, and ending with a SEP token.

The output from BERT takes the form of one vector corresponding to each input symbol (word). The CLS token in the input results in a corresponding output that can be used for tasks that need to aggregate information for the entire sentence instead of for just an individual word. An example of such a task is a classification task. To use this output position for classification, we train a linear classifier using the output vector from this position as input, similar to how is done for GPT, as described earlier. That is, we extend BERT with an additional fully connected layer with a softmax output matching the number of categories we want to classify. This fully connected layer uses the CLS output vector as its input. For the next-sentence pretraining task, this softmax layer would have the two outputs IsNext and NotNext (technically, it could have a single logistic sigmoid neuron as its output given that it is only two categories).

Apart from the CLS and SEP tokens, there is also the masking token MASK that has already been described. It is not shown in Figure D-5, but for the masked language model task, this token would replace one or more input words.

BERT learns positional embeddings just as the GPT model does. One could argue that the combination of special tokens and positional embeddings should be sufficient. However, to further simplify for the network to learn, BERT also learns *segment embeddings*. There is one segment embedding E_A corresponding to the first sentence and one segment embedding E_B corresponding to the second sentence. E_A is added to each word embedding of the first sentence, and E_B is added to each word embedding of the second sentence, as illustrated in Figure D-6.

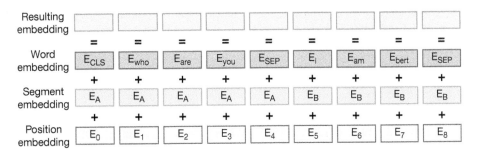

Figure D-6 How input vectors to the encoder network are formed. Each input vector is a sum of three embeddings. The first is the embedding corresponding to the word. The second is a segment embedding (indicating whether the word is a part of the question or answer). The third is a position embedding.

APPLYING BERT TO NLP TASKS

BERT has been shown to be versatile and has been applied to a wide variety of tasks. The original paper (Devlin et al., 2018) presented state-of-the-art results in no less than 11 NLP tasks. We list just some of them here:

- Sentiment analysis of text, similar to the tweet and movie review examples discussed in Chapter 12.

- Spam detection.

- Determine whether a second sentence is an entailment, a contradiction, or neutral with respect to the first sentence.

- Given a question and a text paragraph that contains the answer, identify the specific set of words that answers the question. For example, given the question "Where do water droplets collide with ice crystals to form precipitation?" and the paragraph "Precipitation forms as smaller droplets coalesce via collision with other rain drops or ice crystals within a cloud," the goal for the network is to produce *within a cloud* on its output.

To solve these tasks, the starting point is a BERT model pretrained on the masked language model and next-sentence prediction task. BERT is then augmented with additional layers that are fine-tuned for the task at hand. For example, for the first three tasks, we add a fully connected network followed by a softmax output to provide a classification. For the fourth task (identifying the answer), BERT is augmented with a mechanism that, together with the individual word outputs, is trained to indicate the start and end positions in the answer sentence. These two positions indicate the specific sequence of words that contains the actual answer.

Just as for the Transformer, Alammar (2018a) has written a blog post describing BERT, including links to an implementation available for download.

RoBERTa

The BERT architecture spawned many follow-on studies applying BERT to different NLP problems. Other studies presented modifications to the BERT architecture to improve on the results of the original model. Liu, Ott, and colleagues (2019) noted that it is challenging to compare the results from different studies because they often are done with different training parameters and datasets, some of which are not publicly available. Therefore, instead of modifying BERT, the authors decided to replicate the BERT study and explore the impact of training parameters and dataset size. They found that BERT was significantly undertrained. By modifying the training approach and using a larger dataset, they managed to make the original BERT architecture perform even better. They even found it to perform better than the more recently published work that had extended the BERT architecture. We note that these findings are not without controversy, which is discussed in the related work section later in this appendix. Liu, Ott, and colleagues named their work RoBERTa, which is short for a Robustly Optimized BERT Pretraining Approach. We summarize the key findings in this section.

In the original BERT paper (Devlin et al., 2018), the masked language modeling task was trained by first statically masking words in the training dataset and then using this masked version of the dataset repeatedly for each training epoch. Instead of statically masking the dataset up front, RoBERTa dynamically masks words during training. The model will therefore see different words being masked during the different training epochs.

BERT uses the two pretraining tasks masked language model and next-sentence prediction. In the original BERT paper, Devin and colleagues did an ablation study and concluded that the next-sentence prediction task was helpful because the model accuracy on downstream tasks decreased when only using the masked language model as the training objective. Interestingly, when Liu, Ott, and colleagues (2019) replicated the study, they came to a different conclusion. They found that the model performed better when they used only the masked language model as a pretraining task. The reason for these two differing conclusions is subtle. We see the following when reading the BERT paper. In the description of the ablation study where they run without next-sentence prediction pretraining, Devin and colleagues (2018) state that they "use the exact same pretraining data." Our interpretation is that, just as for the baseline system, 50% of the training examples will consist of two noncontiguous sentences. The only difference is that the model is scored only on the basis of its ability to predict masked words.

Liu, Ott, and colleagues (2019) took a different approach for RoBERTa. In the case where they use only the masked language model as a pretraining task, they additionally make sure to use only a contiguous sequence of text. When they present their opposite conclusion on next-sentence prediction, they state, "It is possible that the original BERT implementation may only have removed the loss term while still retaining the SEGMENT-PAIR input format." We find it plausible that they did indeed identify the difference between the two experiments, and it seems consistent with the statement in the BERT paper. Overall, it is not surprising that when next-sentence prediction is not included as a pretraining task, the model will benefit from all training examples containing contiguous blocks of text instead of having 50% of the examples consist of two unrelated blocks of texts concatenated together. Somewhat related, Lan and colleagues (2020) introduced *A Lite BERT* (ALBERT) and showed that using a pretraining task known as sentence order prediction (SOP) in addition to the masked language model pretraining task resulted in improvements over the next-sentence prediction pretraining task.

A third set of changes introduced by RoBERTa is to use a larger mini-batch size, increased number of training epochs, and a significantly larger training dataset. Liu, Ott, and colleagues (2019) evaluated mini-batch sizes from 256 (used in BERT) up to 8K. The conclusion was that a mini-batch size of 2K was the best choice when holding the total amount of computations constant. However, to enable more parallelism for the case with larger dataset sizes, they used a mini-batch size of 8K for the largest experiments. BERT had used a dataset consisting of a combination of books and Wikipedia, totaling 16 GB. For RoBERTa the dataset size was increased tenfold to 160 GB by using three additional text corpora. Finally, the RoBERTa study also increased the number of training steps[1] by fivefold.

All in all, these changes resulted in better results than other previously reported improvements over BERT. Liu and colleagues explicitly point out that they decided not to explore a different architecture but that it can be considered as future work. Overall, this study illustrates that not only model architecture is important, but so are training parameters and training data. We touch on this topic again at the very end of this appendix.

Historical Work Leading Up to GPT and BERT

Both GPT and BERT rely on unsupervised pretraining followed by supervised task specific fine-tuning. This is known as semi-supervised learning. GPT was not the first model to use semi-supervised learning in the NLP field. In Chapter 13, we

---

1. We talk about training steps (mini-batches) instead of epochs because the total number of training examples included in an epoch is not constant when the dataset size is increased.

described how word embeddings can be learned in an unsupervised manner and then used in a subsequent supervised learning task. In that case, only the weights from the first layer (the embedding layer) are transferred to the model to use for fine-tuning.

Dai and Le (2015) took this concept one step further in their work on semi-supervised sequence learning in the context of text classification (e.g., sentiment analysis). They studied two different pretraining tasks. One was a language model task, similar to what we described in Chapter 12, where the objective is to predict the next word from a sequence of preceding words. The other was an autoencoder task where the model first consumes an input word sequence and creates an internal representation. The objective is then to generate that same word sequence on its output. Dai and Le showed that an LSTM-based RNN for text classification performed better if it was initialized with weights learned from one of these two tasks instead of just using randomly initialized weights.

Whereas Dai and Le had used domain-specific text (e.g., movie reviews) for the unsupervised pretraining, Howard and Ruder (2018) showed that they could improve model performance by pretraining on a large body of text not directly related to the end task. This observation, in combination with the fact that the pretraining task is unsupervised, is significant. Instead of requiring carefully selected and labeled data, the pretraining task can use all of the vast amounts of textual data that are available online. Howard and Ruder showed impressive results on multiple text classification tasks. They used a language model as the pretraining task and named their work Universal Language Model Fine-tuning (ULMFiT).

We can now put GPT and BERT into context. GPT is similar to ULMFiT but is based on the Transformer *decoder* block instead of an LSTM-based model. GPT uses a language model as the pretraining task just as ULMFiT does. BERT is based on the Transformer *encoder* block. However, instead of using the language model pretraining task, BERT uses a form of the autoencoder pretraining task that was also used by Dai and Le (2015). The pretraining task used in BERT has been referred to as a *denoising autoencoder* because the task is not truly to reproduce the same output as the data presented as input. Instead, the objective for BERT is to recreate a sentence given a corrupted version (some words have been replaced by MASK tokens). A key difference between GPT and BERT is that the pretraining task for BERT is bidirectional. This implies that BERT can make use of both historical and future words in a sentence when predicting the output.

Other Models Based on the Transformer

As described in Chapter 15, the Transformer relies fully on attention and does not use recurrence. One drawback of this is that the length of the historical context has a hard limit. To address this issue, Dai and colleagues (2019) extended the Transformer by combining it with recurrent connections. They called it the Transformer-XL, where *XL* means *eXtra Long*. To enable the model to work with variably sized input, they also modified the positional encodings to be based on relative positions instead of absolute positions. All in all, the Transformer-XL can identify longer-term dependencies than the original Transformer.

Enhanced Representation through Knowledge Integration, or ERNIE, uses the same architecture as BERT but improves on its performance by modifying how it is trained (Sun et al., 2019). One such modification is to mask multiword entities instead of single words. For example, if the input sentence contains the two consecutive words *Harry Potter*, it would treat both words as an entity instead of as two separate words. That is, during pretraining, in a case where BERT would mask one of the two words, ERNIE would mask both words together. Similarly, ERNIE groups multiple words into phrases. For example, the three words *a series of* would all be masked together because they form a phrase. ERNIE 2.0 adds additional tweaks to the training process along with more pretraining tasks (Sun et al., 2020). It also adds the concept of a task-specific embedding, which is dependent on what task the model is currently expected to solve. This task-specific embedding is used in addition to the positional embedding and segment embedding that were shown in Figure D-6. ERNIE 2.0 improves over BERT on multiple NLP tasks in both English and Chinese.

Whereas ERNIE largely kept the BERT architecture unchanged (except for the task embedding used to modify the input), XLNet made changes to the model itself (Yang et al., 2019). First, it taps into the improvements on the Transformer architecture by using Transformer-XL instead of the original Transformer. That is, it uses recurrent connections and the associated changes to the positional encodings. The other major change is somewhat subtle. Yang and colleagues noted that while the masked language model pretraining task (the *denoising autoencoder* task mentioned previously) for BERT is powerful, it does not resemble what the model will see for the end task. The traditional language model used by GPT is more realistic. In particular, the BERT training objective makes the assumption that the masked words (15% of all words) are independent. That is not true, because they occur in the same sentence, and dependencies between words in the same sentence are expected. XLNet tries to get the best of both worlds by using a language model approach but using multiple permutations of the word order of the input sentence, including future words. This enables the model to benefit from the bidirectionality from BERT while avoiding the issue of dependencies between masked words.

Yang and colleagues (2019) showed that XLNet outperforms BERT. On the other hand, the RoBERTa study (Liu, Ott, et al., 2019) concluded that the BERT architecture outperformed XLNet when addressing the undertraining issue. However, the comparison does not end there. The most recent version of the XLNet paper (Yang et al., 2019) includes an attempt at doing a fair comparison between XLNet and RoBERTa and showed that XLNet was still better, in particular for tasks that involve longer context. Yang and colleagues hypothesize that it results from the Transformer-XL based architecture.

This back-and-forth illustrates that it is hard to pinpoint the effect of architecture versus training process. Therefore, doing a fair comparison between two architectures can be difficult. Another big challenge is that the models and datasets have now gotten to a size that training the model requires huge computational resources. To illustrate this, we consider the following sentence from the RoBERTa paper: "We pretrain our model using 1024 V100 GPUs for approximately one day" (Liu, Ott, et al., 2019). As another example, Shoeybi and colleagues (2019) used 512 V100 GPUs to sustain 15.1 petaflops across an application in their work on Megatron-LM. Similarly, in their work on the Text-To-Text Transfer Transformer (T5), Raffel and colleagues (2019) describe that training the models requires a great deal of computation, and they use slices of tensor processing unit (TPU) pods. They further describe a TPU pod as a multirack ML supercomputer consisting of 1,024 TPU chips. At the time of these studies, a V100 GPU was the most high-end GPU available for DL training, and a TPU is a special built chip to accelerate tensor operations. Getting access to a system with 512 to 1,024 of them for an extended period of time was not cheap. Bender and colleagues (2021) further explore the topic of big language models and training data size from different angles, including environmental impact and ethics. Given these concerns, it would not surprise us if more efficient language model architectures will emerge over time. We are also hopeful that the ethical concerns are taken seriously and that the industry and research community come up with innovative ways of ensuring that language models trained on large datasets do not cause harm.

Appendix E

Newton-Raphson versus Gradient Descent

This appendix is related to Chapter 2, "Gradient-Based Learning."

The pervasive method for adjusting the weights in deep learning (DL) is gradient descent. It is an iterative method used to minimize the output value of a function. We believe that many readers are already familiar with a different iterative minimization method known as *Newton-Raphson*. We have included this appendix for readers who are curious about how the two methods relate to each other.

> We often feel bad for poor Raphson, whose name is often left out—the method is more commonly referred to as just Newton's method.

We describe Newton-Raphson in a single dimension, similarly to how we introduced gradient descent in Chapter 2. The method can be used both to find a solution (root) to an equation as well as to solve an optimization problem (find the minimum). We start with the root finding method.

Newton-Raphson Root-Finding Method

In Chapter 2, we noted that we can state our learning problem mathematically as trying to solve the following equation for a given training example:

$$y - \hat{y} = 0$$

We never tried to solve that particular problem with gradient descent but instead introduced the mean squared error (MSE) function and changed our problem into a minimization problem. Let us now instead see how we can use the root-finding version of Newton-Raphson to solve this equation.

In the single dimension case, where we have a function[1] $y = f(x)$, the method will find the value of x that results in $f(x) = 0$. The Newton-Raphson method starts with an initial guess of the solution x_0 and then iteratively refines it until an x that is close enough to the actual solution is found. Figure E-1 shows geometrically how the Newton-Raphson method works.

We start with an initial guess of $x_0 = 1.75$. We insert it into $f(x)$ and conclude that the result is not 0. From the chart, we can see that $f(x_0)$ is about 4.5 (the height of the red dashed line). We create the equation for the tangent (orange line in chart), solve it for $y = 0$, and arrive at a new guess: $x_1 = 1.28$. We insert that value into $f(x)$ and see that the result is about 1.0 (the height of the purple dashed line), which is still not close enough to 0. We make a new attempt, calculate the tangent for a

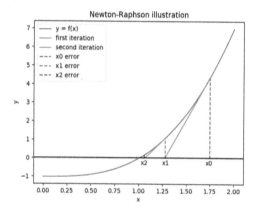

Figure E-1 The Newton-Raphson method

---

1. In this context, y does not refer to the network output, but simply refers to any mathematical function that we want to solve for zero

second iteration (green line), and arrive at a new guess: $x_2 = 1.06$. We insert that value into $f(x)$, see that it is close to 0, and our conclusion is that $x = 1.06$ is an approximate solution to the equation $f(x) = 0$.

Looking at Figure E-1, we can derive a formula for computing the refined value x_{n+1} given a previous x_n. The following equality follows from the figure:

$$f'(x_n) = \frac{f(x_n)}{x_n - x_{n+1}}$$

To understand why, let us assume that $n = 0$. The derivative (left side of equality) is the same as the slope of the orange line. This slope can be computed as $\frac{\Delta y}{\Delta x}$, where Δy is the height of the dashed red line and Δx is the distance between x_0 and x_1. We note that Δy for a given iteration n can be computed as $f(x_n)$, which is the numerator on the right side of the stated equality. Similarly, Δx can be computed as $(x_n - x_{n+1})$, which is the denominator. This explains why the equality holds true. Solving for x_{n+1}, we get

$$x_{n+1} = x_n - \frac{f(x_n)}{f'(x_n)}$$

which is how we iteratively find a solution according to the Newton-Raphson method. The method works even if the initial guess of x results in a negative function value, because the subtraction in the formula in combination with the negative function value will result in x_{n+1} becoming greater than x_n.

NEWTON-RAPHSON APPLIED TO OPTIMIZATION PROBLEMS

We noted in Chapter 2 that, in reality, we want to use an error function that combines the error of multiple training examples into a single metric, such as the MSE:

$$\frac{1}{m} \sum_{i=1}^{m} \left(y^{(i)} - \hat{y}^{(i)} \right)^2 \qquad (mean\ squared\ error)$$

We also described that doing so causes an issue in that there might not exist a solution where the error function is 0. This is illustrated in the upper part of Figure E-2, which plots an error function based on MSE. The initial guess x_0 is fairly close to the minimum value of the error, but because Newton-Raphson tries to find a point where the function is 0, it takes a long step to the left (orange line), followed by a long step to the right (green line), and never converges. It is clear that using a root-finding algorithm on an equation that has no roots is pointless.

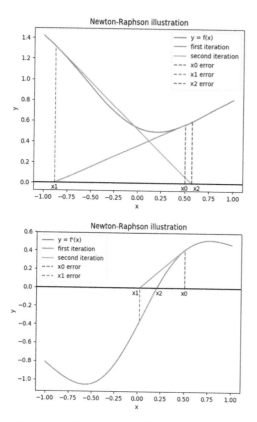

Figure E-2 Top: Newton-Raphson on the original function $f(x)$. The algorithm does not converge because the function has no 0 roots. Bottom: Newton-Raphson on the derivative $f'(x)$. The algorithm finds a point where the derivative is 0, which corresponds to a local minimum for the original function $f(x)$.

Instead, we can use the optimization version of Newton-Raphson. Just like gradient descent, this version aims at minimizing the function instead of solving it for 0. We do this by applying Newton-Raphson to the derivative of the original function, because a derivative of 0 implies an extreme point, such as a local minimum. This is done in the bottom part of Figure E-2, which plots the derivative of the already studied function in the upper part of the figure. We provide an initial guess x_0, and the algorithm takes a step (orange line) to a point x_1 and overshoots the solution. It then takes another step (green line almost exactly on top of the blue function) to x_2, which is very close to the actual solution.

Relationship Between Newton-Raphson and Gradient Descent

One challenge with the optimization version of Newton-Raphson is that we first need to compute the derivative of the error function to arrive at the function to solve for 0, and then we need to compute the derivative of this new function for each step. That is, we need to compute both the derivative and the second derivative of the error function. More formally, the optimization version of Newton-Raphson is a second-order optimization method. Gradient descent, on the other hand, is a first-order optimization method in that it requires only the first derivative. This reduces the amount of both computation and storage needed, which is significant when optimizing a function consisting of millions of parameters.

Appendix F

Matrix Implementation of Digit Classification Network

This appendix is related to Chapter 4, "Fully Connected Networks Applied to Multiclass Classification."

This appendix contains two alternative implementations of the digit classification network. In the first implementation, the idea is to organize the weights for all the neurons in a layer into a single matrix, where each row in the matrix represents a neuron. The weighted sums for an entire layer of neurons can then be computed by multiplying this matrix by the input vector. We then extend it to handle mini-batches as well. We organize all the input examples of a mini-batch into a single matrix. The weighted sums for an entire layer of neurons for all input examples in the mini-batch can then be computed by a single multiplication of these two matrices.

Single Matrix

Starting with the implementation without mini-batches, the only functions that have changed compared to the code example in Chapter 4 are forward_pass, backward_pass, and adjust_weights. They are shown in Code Snippet F-1.

Code Snippet F-1 Functions for Forward Pass, Backward Pass, and Adjusting
Weights

```
def forward_pass(x):
    global hidden_layer_y
    global output_layer_y
    # Activation function for hidden layer.
    hidden_layer_z = np.matmul(hidden_layer_w, x)
    hidden_layer_y = np.tanh(hidden_layer_z)
    hidden_output_array = np.concatenate(
        (np.array([1.0]), hidden_layer_y))
    # Activation function for output layer.
    output_layer_z = np.matmul(output_layer_w,
        hidden_output_array)
    output_layer_y = 1.0 / (1.0 + np.exp(-output_layer_z))

def backward_pass(y_truth):
    global hidden_layer_error
    global output_layer_error
    # Backpropagate error for each output neuron.
    error_prime = -(y_truth - output_layer_y)
    output_log_prime = output_layer_y * (
        1.0 - output_layer_y)
    output_layer_error = error_prime * output_log_prime
    # Backpropagate error for each hidden neuron.
    hidden_tanh_prime = 1.0 - hidden_layer_y**2
    hidden_weighted_error = np.matmul(np.matrix.transpose(
        output_layer_w[:, 1:]), output_layer_error)
    hidden_layer_error = (
        hidden_tanh_prime * hidden_weighted_error)

def adjust_weights(x):
    global output_layer_w
    global hidden_layer_w
    delta_matrix = np.outer(
        hidden_layer_error, x) * LEARNING_RATE
    hidden_layer_w -= delta_matrix
```

```
    hidden_output_array = np.concatenate(
        (np.array([1.0]), hidden_layer_y))
    delta_matrix = np.outer(
        output_layer_error,
        hidden_output_array) * LEARNING_RATE
    output_layer_w -= delta_matrix
```

In these functions, we no longer loop over the individual neurons and do dot products, but instead, we handle an entire layer in parallel using matrix operations.

The forward_pass function is straightforward. We use the NumPy matmul function to multiply the weight matrix by the input vector and then apply the activation function tanh on the resulting output vector. We then append a bias needed for the output layer using the concatenate function and do the matrix multiplication and activation function for the output layer as well.

The backward_pass function is not much more complicated. We compute the derivatives of the error function and the activation function but note that all these computations are done on vectors (i.e., all neurons in parallel). Another thing to note is that the mathematical operators +, −, and * are elementwise operators. That is, there is a big difference between using * and the matmul function. One thing to note is the call to np.matrix.transpose and the indexing we do with output_layer_w[:, 1:]. The transpose operation is needed to make the dimensions of the weight matrix match what is needed for a matrix multiplication with the error vector. The indexing is done to get rid of the bias weights when computing the error terms for the hidden neurons because the bias weight from the output layer is not needed for that operation. All in all, if you are not fluent in matrix algebra, it is hard to see through what is going on in the function. One way to convince yourself that it is doing the right thing is to expand the vector and matrix expressions with a pen and paper for a small-sized problem (like two neurons) and see that it does the same thing as in our previous implementation.

The adjust_weights function is slightly tricky. For each of the two layers, we need to create a matrix with the same dimensions as the weight matrix for that layer but where the elements represent the delta to subtract from the weights. The elements of this delta matrix are obtained by multiplying the input value that feeds into a weight by the error term for the neuron that the weight connects to and finally multiplying by the learning rate. We already have the error terms arranged in the vectors hidden_layer_error and output_layer_error. Similarly, we have the input values for the two layers arranged in the vectors x and hidden_layer_y. For each layer we now combine the input vector with the error vector using the function np.outer which computes the outer product of the two vectors. It results in a matrix where the elements are all the pairwise products from the elements in the two vectors, which is exactly what we want. We multiply the matrix by the learning rate and then subtract from the weight matrix. Again, the best way to convince yourself that it does the right thing is to walk through a small example, possibly in a Python interpreter, to see how the vectors and matrices are combined.

When we run this program, we get very similar output compared to the non-matrix implementation, but it runs faster because of the more efficient implementation using matrix-vector multiplications instead of loops.

Mini-Batch Implementation

We now take this example one step further and introduce mini-batches. We take multiple input examples and organize them into a matrix where each column is an input vector, and the number of columns is the same as the mini-batch size. We can now calculate the weighted sums for all neurons in a layer for all examples in a mini-batch by multiplying these two matrices. The result will be a new matrix with all the weighted sums for that layer for all examples in that mini-batch. We do the same calculation for each layer and then do backpropagation for the entire mini-batch in a similar manner. Finally, we construct N update matrices, where N is the number of examples in the mini-batch. We then calculate the elementwise mean of all of these matrices. This results in a final matrix that we can subtract from the weight matrix to update the weights, using the average gradient computed from the mini-batch. The initialization code and the functions to print progress and plot are unchanged, so we do not repeat them in this example.

The code representing the neurons and connections is shown in Code Snippet F-2. The variables that were previously vector variables have now become matrices where the new dimension is the mini-batch size. The programming example assumes that the variable BATCH_SIZE has been initialized with the value 32.

Code Snippet F-2 **Matrices Representing Weights, Outputs, and Error Terms for the Mini-Batch Implementation**

```
def layer_w(neuron_count, input_count):
    weights = np.zeros((neuron_count, input_count+1))
    for i in range(neuron_count):
        for j in range(1, (input_count+1)):
            weights[i][j] = np.random.uniform(-0.1, 0.1)
    return weights

# Declare matrices and vectors representing the neurons.
hidden_layer_w = layer_w(25, 784)
hidden_layer_y = np.zeros((25, BATCH_SIZE))
hidden_layer_error = np.zeros((25, BATCH_SIZE))

output_layer_w = layer_w(10, 25)
output_layer_y = np.zeros((10, BATCH_SIZE))
output_layer_error = np.zeros((10, BATCH_SIZE))
```

Code Snippet F-3 shows the functions for the forward pass, backward pass, and weight adjustment. The forward_pass function is straightforward. The only difference is that when creating the input to the output layer, we now need to extend it with a vector of bias terms instead of just a single bias term. It is a vector because there needs to be one bias element for each example in the mini-batch. Another difference is that x is now a matrix representing a batch of training examples instead of a vector representing a single example. The code itself has not changed, but it is worth noting that the arguments to matmul are now two matrices instead of a matrix and a vector.

The backward_pass function is unchanged, although the input y_truth now is a matrix. The same applies to the global variables hidden_layer_error and output_layer_error that are used in the function.

In adjust_weights, we need to append a vector of bias terms (technically, a matrix where one dimension is 1) to the outputs from the hidden layer where the vector length represents the mini-batch size. We have added a for loop that loops through all the examples in the mini-batch, accumulates the deltas in the delta_matrix, and then divides by the mini-batch size. This is how we compute the average of the gradient. We then simply do the weight update just as in the previous implementation but now using this averaged matrix instead.

Code Snippet F-3 Functions for Forward Pass, Backward Pass, and Weight Adjustment for the Mini-Batch Implementation

```python
def forward_pass(x):
    global hidden_layer_y
    global output_layer_y
    # Activation function for hidden layer.
    hidden_layer_z = np.matmul(hidden_layer_w, x)
    hidden_layer_y = np.tanh(hidden_layer_z)
    hidden_output_array = np.concatenate(
        (np.ones((1, BATCH_SIZE)), hidden_layer_y))
    # Activation function for output layer.
    output_layer_z = np.matmul(output_layer_w,
        hidden_output_array)
    output_layer_y = 1.0 / (1.0 + np.exp(-output_layer_z))

def backward_pass(y_truth):
    global hidden_layer_error
    global output_layer_error
    # Backpropagate error for each output neuron.
    error_prime = -(y_truth  - output_layer_y)
    output_log_prime = output_layer_y * (
        1.0 - output_layer_y)
    output_layer_error = error_prime * output_log_prime
    # Backpropagate error for each hidden neuron.
    hidden_tanh_prime = 1.0 - hidden_layer_y**2
    hidden_weighted_error = np.matmul(np.matrix.transpose(
        output_layer_w[:, 1:]), output_layer_error)
    hidden_layer_error = (
        hidden_tanh_prime * hidden_weighted_error)

def adjust_weights(x):
    global output_layer_w
    global hidden_layer_w
    delta_matrix = np.zeros((len(hidden_layer_error[:, 0]),
                             len(x[:, 0])))
```

```
for i in range(BATCH_SIZE):
    delta_matrix += np.outer(hidden_layer_error[:, i],
                             x[:, i]) * LEARNING_RATE
delta_matrix /= BATCH_SIZE
hidden_layer_w -= delta_matrix
hidden_output_array = np.concatenate(
    (np.ones((1, BATCH_SIZE)), hidden_layer_y))
delta_matrix = np.zeros(
    (len(output_layer_error[:, 0]),
    len(hidden_output_array[:, 0])))
for i in range(BATCH_SIZE):
    delta_matrix += np.outer(
        output_layer_error[:, i],
        hidden_output_array[:, i]) * LEARNING_RATE
delta_matrix /= BATCH_SIZE
output_layer_w -= delta_matrix
```

Finally, Code Snippet F-4 shows the training loop for the mini-batch implementation. The for loops that loop over the training and test examples are now changed to handle one mini-batch per iteration. This includes logic to collect a number of training examples into a matrix that is then passed to the forward and backward pass functions.

We cheated a little bit in the outer loops (index j) by not properly handling the end of the training and test sets if they are not evenly divisible by the mini-batch size. Instead of worrying about how to use partially filled matrices, we simply skip the final few training and test examples. This would not be acceptable in a production implementation but makes the code shorter and easier to understand.

Code Snippet F-4 Training Loop for the Mini-Batch Implementation

```
index_list = list(range(int(len(x_train)/BATCH_SIZE)))
# Network training loop.
for i in range(EPOCHS): # Train EPOCHS iterations
    np.random.shuffle(index_list) # Randomize order
    correct_training_results = 0
    for j in index_list:
        j *= BATCH_SIZE
```

```
        x = np.ones((785, BATCH_SIZE))
        y = np.zeros((10, BATCH_SIZE))
        for k in range(BATCH_SIZE):
            x[1:, k] = x_train[j + k]
            y[:, k] = y_train[j + k]
        forward_pass(x)
        for k in range(BATCH_SIZE):
            if(output_layer_y[:, k].argmax()
                    == y[:, k].argmax()):
                correct_training_results += 1
        backward_pass(y)
        adjust_weights(x)

    correct_test_results = 0
    for j in range(0, (len(x_test) - BATCH_SIZE),
                BATCH_SIZE): # Evaluate network
        x = np.ones((785, BATCH_SIZE))
        y = np.zeros((10, BATCH_SIZE))
        for k in range(BATCH_SIZE):
            x[1:, k] = x_test[j + k]
            y[:, k] = y_test[j + k]
        forward_pass(x)
        for k in range(BATCH_SIZE):
            if(output_layer_y[:, k].argmax()
                    == y[:, k].argmax()):
                correct_test_results += 1
    # Show progress
    show_learning(i, correct_training_results/len(x_train),
                correct_test_results/len(x_test))
plot_learning() # Create plot
```

When we run this implementation, we will get a different behavior than we got with our previous implementation. Using mini-batches results in the updates being done with different gradients, and there are also fewer total weight updates per epoch. As a result, it can make sense to experiment with different parameter values for our new configuration. Our experiments indicate that, for our mini-batch implementation with a mini-batch size of 32, we see better learning if we increase the learning rate from 0.01 to 0.1.

Appendix G

Relating Convolutional Layers to Mathematical Convolution

This appendix is related to Chapter 7, "Convolutional Neural Networks Applied to Image Classification."

The intent of this appendix is to give a brief description of the mathematical definition of *convolution* and to bridge the gap between the definition and its application in convolutional networks. This description targets readers who already have some familiarity with convolution. If you have not previously encountered the concept, you might first need to consult a more extensive text on convolution, which can typically be found in any book on signals and systems. One such book is written by Balmer (1997). Somewhat counterintuitively, we think it is questionable whether understanding convolution in detail will provide much benefit with respect to basic understanding of convolutional networks.

If you have encountered convolution in the past, chances are that it was 1D convolution in the context of signal processing[1] and most likely was applied

---

1. Chances are that we are wrong and that we are projecting our experience onto you. It might be that convolution was used for analog audio in our days, but nowadays people encounter convolution in digital image processing.

to continuous signals. A common use case for convolution in this context is to establish the impulse response of an audio filter[2] to determine the characteristics of the filter—that is, how much signals of different frequencies will be attenuated. In contrast, in the context of deep learning (DL)-based image classification, we typically use 2D convolution applied to discrete signals. The convolutional kernel is used as a pattern/feature identifier. From an implementation perspective, it is common to do the related operation cross-correlation instead of convolution. We get to that at the end of this description.

A convolution is an operation applied to two functions $f(t)$ and $g(t)$ and results in a new function $(f * g)(t)$, where * is the convolution operator. More specifically, the function resulting from the convolution is defined as

$$(f*g)(t)= \int_{-\infty}^{\infty} f(\tau)g(t-\tau)d\tau$$

Given that convolution is an integral, the value of the convolution represents the area under a curve. The curve that we integrate over is obtained by multiplying f by a mirrored and time-shifted version of g. The variable t determines how much to time-shift the function g.

To make this more concrete,[3] for the example of an audio filter, f would represent the audio signal and g would represent the filter function. See Figure G-1 for a graphical representation. The upper two charts show two functions, f and g. The lower left chart shows how g has been mirrored around the y-axis and time shifted. Over time, we slide this mirrored version of g from left to right. Each time-shifted location of g results in a value of our convolution function. The figure shows how the convolution is calculated for an input value of 2. We first compute the product between f and g (mirrored and time shifted by 2), which results in the red curve in the figure. We then integrate over this function, which results in the green curve. That is, the green curve represents the area under the red curve.

The lower right chart shows the full convolution function for all input values. It peaks at 3.0, which is the area under the red curve when g is in a location where it fully overlaps f.

---

2. Audio filters can be used to control how much to suppress treble versus bass in an audio system.
3. As mentioned earlier, we assume that you have encountered convolution before. If not, this will hardly be concrete to you.

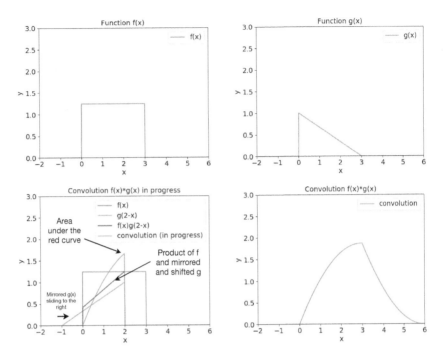

Figure G-1 Upper left: Function *f(x)*. Upper right: Function *g(x)*. Lower left: Convolution process. A mirrored version of *g(x)* is slid from left to right. The red curve represents the product of these two curves. The convolution represents the area under this red curve.

Now consider the case where we apply convolution to a discrete signal instead of a continuous signal—for example, discrete samples of a continuous audio signal. Then the integral is replaced by a sum:

$$(f*g)[i] = \sum_{m=-\infty}^{\infty} f[m]g[i-m]$$

In many cases, it is inconvenient (and unrealistic) to work with infinity, so we fall back on working with finite sequences, and the discrete convolution changes to

$$(f*g)[i] = \sum_{m=-M}^{M} f[m]g[i-m]$$

Figure G-2 shows a graphical representation of discrete convolution, using discrete versions of *f* and *g* from the previous figure. In the lower left chart, we have chosen to time shift g by 1 as opposed to 2, as in the previous example. We

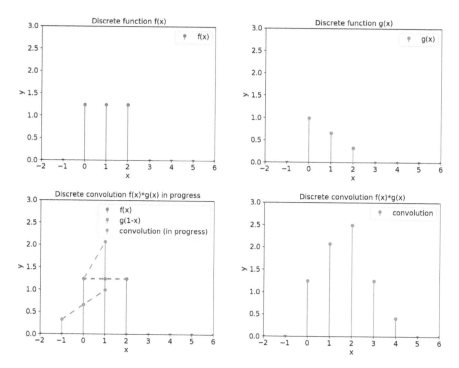

Figure G-2 Discrete convolution. The charts mimic the charts in Figure G-1, but g is shifted by 1 instead of 2.

omitted the red curve and added dashed lines connecting the data points for each function in the lower left chart to make it more readable.

In the case of an audio signal, convolution is done in the time domain where the independent variable is time. The output at time t will be a function of the inputs at times $t, t-1, \ldots, t-n$. A different use case is image processing, where convolution is done in the spatial domain and in two dimensions. Instead of computing an output based on a series of historical values, an image filter computes a pixel value by using a region of pixels as input values. This can be used to blur or sharpen an input image but also to perform edge detection. The latter use case starts to become related to our convolutional networks.

Here is the formula for discrete 2D convolution:

$$(f*g)[i,\,j] = \sum_{m=-M}^{M} \sum_{n=-N}^{N} f[i,j]\; g[i-m,\,j-n]$$

If we inspect the equation, we see that it is almost the same computation as is used when feeding $M{\times}N$ grayscale pixels (a single color channel) as inputs to a neuron, assuming that f represents the pixels and g represents the neuron weights. The two indices i and j represent the location of the pixel in the center of the receptive field. The one complicating factor is the negative signs in the arguments to the g function. These need to be changed to positive signs to match the computations where we fed pixel values to a neuron.

This brings us to the concept of cross-correlation. If we replace the negative signs in the g function by positive signs, then the equation no longer describes a convolution operation. Instead, it describes the related operation *cross-correlation*. In the case of neural networks, this has little significance given that the function g (defined by the neuron weights) is automatically learned during training, so it is just a matter of which weights get what values. From that perspective, it does not matter if the actual implementation of the neural network flips the matrix that holds the weights corresponding to g, or if it keeps the matrix the way it is described in the preceding equation. The result will be the same regardless whether we have implemented a convolutional network or a cross-correlational network. To avoid any confusion, we state the mathematical formula for 2D cross-correlation:

$$(f * g)[i, j] = \sum_{m=-M}^{M} \sum_{n=-N}^{N} f[i, j] \, g[i+m, j+n]$$

Note that the minus signs in the convolution formula are replaced by plus signs in the cross-correlation formula. It is now clear how the convolution operation relates to the pattern identifier that we use in our convolutional network.

Appendix H

Gated Recurrent Units

This appendix is related to Chapter 10, "Long Short-Term Memory."

In Chapter 10, we introduced long short-term memory (LSTM), which was introduced by Hochreiter and Schmidhuber in 1997. In 2014, Cho and colleagues (2014b) introduced the gated recurrent unit (GRU), which was described as "motivated by the LSTM unit but is much simpler to compute and implement." Both LSTM and GRU are frequently used in modern recurrent neural networks (RNNs). To refresh your memory, we start with Figure H-1 of an LSTM-based layer, which was previously shown in Chapter 10, Figure 10-6.

When looking at this network of LSTM cells, a valid question is why we need two different sets of states. It seems like it would be possible to construct a constant error carousel (CEC) with just a single set of states. The GRU does just that, as well as removes the output activation and the output gate. It also combines the remember gate and forget gate into a single update-gate. Two different versions of the GRU are shown in Figure H-2. The reason there are two different versions is that the original version of the paper where the GRU was proposed contained one implementation (Cho et al., 2014a), but this implementation was somewhat revised in a later version (Cho et al., 2014b). We discuss both implementations.

A GRU cell does not have a separate internal state but implements the CEC using the global recurrent connections. It also combines the remember gate and forget gate into a single update gate.

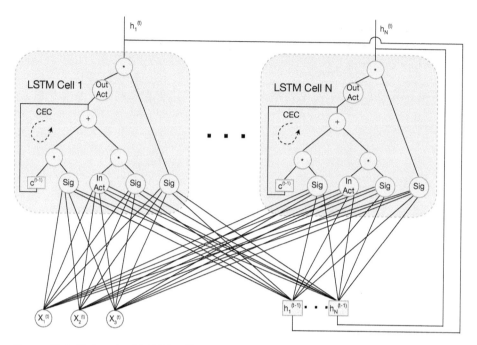

Figure H-1 **Network of LSTM cells**

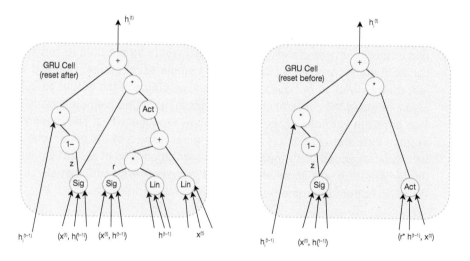

Figure H-2 **Two versions of the GRU. Left: Reset-after implementation. Right: Reset-before implementation.**

The original implementation is shown on the left. The c-state for the CEC has been removed from the cell, and the CEC is now using the output from the previous timestep, indicated by the leftmost input arrow in the figure. This is a single (scalar) value, and each cell receives its own output from the previous timestep. All the other inputs in the figure are vector inputs, corresponding to all x-values for the current timestep as well as all output values from the previous timestep.

The leftmost logistic sigmoid neuron (computing the value z) is known as the *update gate*. It replaces the forget gate and remember gate in the LSTM. As shown in the figure, instead of directly multiplying z by the incoming h-value, the node marked as $1-$ means that we first compute $(1-z)$, which makes the leftmost multiplication in the figure act as a forget gate, whereas the unchanged z-value is used to gate the value coming from the activation function (shown as Act). That is, when the update gate output is 1, the CEC will be updated with the output of the activation function, whereas when the update gate output is 0, it will remember the state from the previous timestep.

Let us now look at what the input to the activation function is (i.e., what will feed into the new value that the cell will remember). The second logistic sigmoid neuron from the left (computing the value r) is known as the reset gate. This gate determines how much the state from the previous timestep should affect the newly computed value. This calculation is done by first computing a weighted sum of the output from the previous timestep by feeding $h^{(t-1)}$ to a neuron with no (linear) activation function (shown as Lin in the figure). We then multiply the two together to form a single value. This value is then added to the output from a weighted sum of the x-inputs (done by the rightmost Lin neuron) for the current timestep. The sum of these two values is then fed into the activation function. All in all, the combination of the set of nodes in the right corner of the GRU can be viewed as a single neuron, which receives inputs $h^{(t-1)}$ that have been scaled by the r-value and inputs $x^{(t)}$ that have not been scaled. Bias terms have been omitted from the figure.

To summarize, the GRU introduces a number of simplifications compared to an LSTM cell. There is no internal cell state. The GRU still has the ability to remember state across many timesteps by computing the output as a weighted sum of the output state from the previous timestep (instead of the internal state) and the input activation function for the current timestep. These two weights are dynamically controlled just as for LSTM, but instead of using two separate gates (remember and forget), it uses a single *update* gate. Finally, the GRU does not have an output gate or output activation function. The output is simply the weighted sum of the input activation from the current timestep and the output state from the previous timestep.

Alternative GRU Implementation

Let us now look at the alternative implementation on the right side of Figure H-2. At a first glance, it looks like a simpler implementation, but note that the input to the activation neuron (the rightmost neuron named Act) receives a vector $r * h^{(t-1)}$. In this expression, r is a vector, and * represents the elementwise product. That is, to use this version of the GRU, we need to first compute a vector of reset values outside of the unit. We will see details of this soon, but first let us consider what this unit does. Just as in the previous version of the GRU, the candidate value that can be remembered by the cell is computed by the activation neuron, which receives inputs $h^{(t-1)}$ that have been scaled elementwise by r-values and inputs $x^{(t)}$ that have not been scaled. In other words, the key difference is that the scaling is done *before* the matrix multiplication of $h^{(t-1)}$ by the weight matrix, whereas in the first version of the GRU, the scaling was done *after* the matrix multiplication.

Network Based on the GRU

Figure H-3 shows an RNN layer built from reset-after GRU. The number of parameters (weights) to learn is three times as many as for a simple RNN. Compared to LSTM, we no longer have two sets of state in the network, and there is only a single activation function and two gate functions.

Figure H-4 shows an RNN layer built from reset-before GRU. We have omitted many connections to focus only on the inputs to the activation neuron. As previously noted, we now need to compute an r-value for each element of $h^{(t-1)}$ outside of the units to first scale each $h^{(t-1)}$ value before feeding it into the cells.

There are two versions of the GRU: **reset-before** and **reset-after.**

This second version (reset-before) is the most common version of GRU (although Keras implements both). According to Chung and colleagues (2014), limited experiments have shown that both alternatives are comparable in their ability to learn (as mentioned in a single footnote in the study). With no significant learning advantage, it might seem odd that one would come up with this second version of the GRU given how it complicates the network topology. The explanation is likely

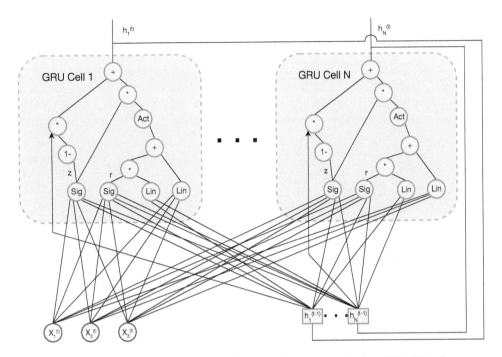

Figure H-3 Recurrent neural network layer built from reset-after GRU. This figure does not show unrolling in time.

that many people do not necessarily think about the units in isolation, but they look at the entire layer of units as a building block. Figure H-5 shows how a GRU layer (bottom) compares to an LSTM layer (top), using the same style as used in *Understanding LSTM Networks* (Olah, 2015).

As you can see in the lower part of the figure, the reset gate (output r) is applied to the vector $h^{(t-1)}$ before it is fed to the *tanh* neurons—that is, this is the reset-before variation (the second version that we studied in this appendix). Clearly, when looking at the entire layer as an entity, this variation does not look as convoluted as when we looked at individual units.

Equation H-1 describes a GRU layer using matrix notation. This is again describing the reset-before variation, where we multiply $h^{(t-1)}$ by $r^{(t)}$ (elementwise) in (3) before doing the matrix multiplication with W.

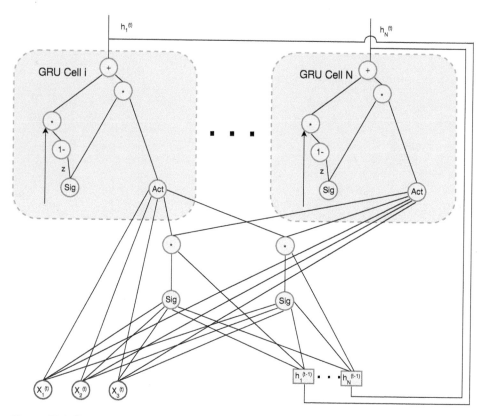

Figure H-4 Recurrent neural network layer built from reset-before GRU. This figure does not show unrolling in time.

Equation H-1 Equations describing a GRU layer

$$z^{(t)} = \sigma\left(W_z\left[h^{(t-1)}, x^{(t)}\right] + b_z\right) \tag{1}$$

$$r^{(t)} = \sigma\left(W_r\left[h^{(t-1)}, x^{(t)}\right] + b_r\right) \tag{2}$$

$$\tilde{h}^{(t)} = \tanh\left(W\left[r^{(t)} * h^{(t-1)}, x^{(t)}\right] + b_{\tilde{h}}\right) \tag{3}$$

$$h^{(t)} = (1 - z^{(t)}) * h^{(t-1)} + z^{(t)} * \tilde{h}^{(t)} \tag{4}$$

If we instead want to describe the version with reset-after, we simply replace (3) with

$$\tilde{h}^{(t)} = \tanh\left(Wx^{(t)} + r^{(t)} * Uh^{(t-1)} + b_{\tilde{h}}\right)$$

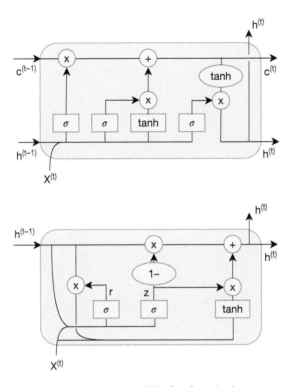

Figure H-5 A layer of LSTM (top) and a layer reset-before GRU (bottom). (Source: Adapted from Olah, C., *Understanding LSTM Networks*, August 2015, https:// colah.github.io/posts/2015-08-Understanding-LSTMs.)

When working at this abstraction level, the two variations are similar to each other.

It turns out that, from an implementation perspective, it can be beneficial to do the reset after the matrix multiplication (Keras Issue Request, 2016).

With respect to deciding between using LSTM or using GRU, we do not know of a way to tell beforehand which unit will be the best choice. LSTM can sometimes do better than GRU because of its larger number of tunable parameters. On the other hand, LSTM can also do worse than GRU. It often makes sense to try both types of units and use the one that works best for the problem in question.

Appendix I

Setting Up a Development Environment

This appendix describes how to set up a suitable development environment to try out the code examples presented throughout this book. The code examples should work on any platform that is capable of running Python 3 and either TensorFlow or PyTorch (depending on which deep learning [DL] framework you like to use), such as Linux, MacOS, and Windows. The examples in the first few chapters are feasible to run on a CPU-only platform, but for the more advanced examples, your experience will be much better if you get access to a graphics processing unit (GPU)-accelerated platform,[1] either by having your own GPU or by renting it by the minute from a cloud service such as Amazon Web Services (AWS).

Similarly, the programming examples in the first four chapters do not require a DL framework but can be run using only Python, some basic libraries, and the Modified National Institute of Standards and Technology (MNIST) dataset. Therefore, if you are eager to get started, then you can begin with the first few sections of this appendix and stop after the section about MNIST. Then get back to installing a DL framework once you are ready to start reading Chapter 5, "Toward DL: Frameworks and Network Tweaks."

---

1. Nothing prevents you from running all programming examples on a CPU, but it will take longer.

If you want to focus on the PyTorch version of the code examples, then consider reading the last section of this appendix, which highlights some key differences between PyTorch and TensorFlow.

Python

All examples in this book are based on Python 3.x. If you are new to Python, you might not be aware that Python 3 is a different language (although similar) than Python 2, so it is key that your Python version is at least 3.0. The exact version does not matter that much as long as it is compatible with the version of the DL framework you are using. Chances are that you already have Python installed on your system, and you can check whether it is installed as well as the version by typing one of the following two command lines in your shell/command prompt:

```
python --version
python3 --version
```

It might be that python is aliased to version 3, or it might refer to version 2, so make sure that you pick the right one. If Python is not installed, it should be straightforward to download and install it from https://www.python.org/downloads.

Once you have Python installed, you should be able to get through the initial examples that do not require a DL framework. Running the examples should be as simple as changing to the directory containing the Python file you want to run, and then providing the filename as an argument when starting Python:

```
python3 my_example.py
```

You will also need the packages numpy, matplotlib, idx2numpy, and pillow, which are used for numerical computations, plotting, reading the MNIST dataset, and images. You can check whether they are installed by typing the following command, which will print all installed packages:

```
pip3 list
```

If not, you will want to install them. First, make sure to upgrade pip3 to the most recent version, and then install the packages:

```
pip3 install pip3
pip3 install numpy
```

```
pip3 install matplotlib
pip3 install idx2numpy
pip3 install pillow
```

Programming Environment

Although it is possible to simply put all code in a text file and run it from the Python interpreter at the command prompt, we strongly believe that a more advanced programming environment improves both debug capability and productivity. We make no claims that what we describe is the best or only environment, but we do find it reasonable. Thus, if you are new to Python and do not want to spend much time researching the best options, we suggest that you simply go with our recommendations.

JUPYTER NOTEBOOK

Jupyter Notebook is an environment where you write and run your programs in a Web browser. If you come from a more traditional programming environment, it might seem odd at first, but if you try it out, you will discover that there are some nice features. One of the more useful features is that you can run, modify, and rerun parts of your program without restarting from the beginning. The declared variables will keep their state. You can try things until you get them right and can easily inspect any variable by adding new print statements. If you come from a more traditional programming environment, you might argue that this can be done with a traditional debugger as well. We still urge you to try it out because we believe that you will see great benefit in Jupyter Notebooks once you get the hang of it. You can also nicely mix and match code and documentation. We have made all the programming examples in this book available as Jupyter Notebook files in addition to providing traditional Python files. More information about how to install Jupyter Notebook can be found on http://jupyter.org.

Depending on your platform and environment, you might have to add the following line at the top of your file to get the plots right with Jupyter:

```
%matplotlib inline
```

This is known as a built-in *magic command* that directs Jupyter how to handle plots.

USING AN INTEGRATED DEVELOPMENT ENVIRONMENT

Although Jupyter Notebooks are good for prototyping, we believe that anytime you get serious about building a larger application, you should be using a proper integrated developer environment (IDE), where you can easily break up and partition your program into multiple files.

Another benefit of an IDE is how it typically comes with a debugger that allows you to set breakpoints and single step into functions deep inside of the DL framework as opposed to just relying on an error message and a stack trace.

There are many popular IDEs. We recommend using PyCharm found at http://www.jetbrains.com/pycharm.

Another alternative is to use Eclipse supplemented by the PyDev extension. This alternative is an easy way of getting started if you are already familiar with Eclipse. Information about how to install Eclipse and PyDev can be found at http://www.eclipse.org/downloads and http://www.pydev.org.

Programming Examples

All programming examples have been tested with TensorFlow 2.4 and PyTorch 1.8.0. Python files and Jupyter notebooks can be downloaded from https://github.com/NVDLI/LDL/ or http://ldlbook.com.

The root of the repository contains four top-level directories:

- `data` is where datasets (see next section) should be downloaded to.

- `stand_alone` contains code examples that do not rely on a DL framework.

- `tf_framework` contains code examples that rely on the TensorFlow framework.

- `pt_framework` contains code examples that rely on the PyTorch framework.

There is a one-to-one mapping between the code examples in the two directories `tf_framework` and `pt_framework`.

The naming of each code example follows the pattern c**X**e**Y**_**DESCRIPTION**.py where **X** represents the chapter number, **Y** the example number in that chapter, and **DESCRIPTION** is a brief description of what the example is doing.

Each code example is expected to be run from within the directory where the code example is located, as it uses a relative path to access the dataset. That is, you first need to change to the stand_alone directory before running code examples located in that directory.

Because of the stochastic nature of DL algorithms, the results may vary from run to run. That is, it is expected that your results will not exactly reproduce the results stated in the book.

SUPPORTING SPREADSHEET

Apart from the described top-level directories, the root of the repository also contains a spreadsheet named network_example.xlsx. The spreadsheet provides additional insight about the basic workings of neurons and the learning process. There are three tabs, each corresponding to a specific section of the initial chapters:

- perceptron_learning corresponds to the section "The Perceptron Learning Algorithm" in Chapter 1, "The Rosenblatt Perceptron."

- backprop_learning corresponds to the section "Using Backpropagation to Compute the Gradient" in Chapter 3, "Sigmoid Neurons and Backpropagation."

- xor_example corresponds to the section "Programming Example: Learning the XOR Function" in Chapter 3.

Datasets

For most of the programming examples in this book, you need access to various datasets or other resources. Some of these are included with the code examples or in the DL framework, and others need to be downloaded to your local computer. We have listed the ones that you need to download. All program examples assume that the downloaded datasets are placed in the directory named data in the root of the code example directory tree.

MNIST

The MNIST Database of handwritten digits can be obtained from http://yann.lecun.com/exdb/mnist.

Download the following files:

train-images-idx3-ubyte.gz

train-labels-idx1-ubyte.gz

t10k-images-idx3-ubyt.gz

t10k-labels-idx1-ubyte.gz

Once downloaded, gunzip them to the `data/mnist/` directory. You need the Python package `idx2numpy` to use this version of the MNIST dataset. This package is not available on all platforms. See the book Web site (http://ldlbook .com) for alternative solutions.

BOOKSTORE SALES DATA FROM US CENSUS BUREAU

Sales data from the United States Census Bureau can be obtained from https:// www.census.gov/econ/currentdata.

Select **Monthly Retail Trade and Food Services** and click the **Submit** button. That should take you to a page where you need to specify five different steps, as shown in Figure I-1. Make the same selections as shown in the figure, and make sure that the checkbox **Not Seasonally Adjusted** is checked. Then click the **GET DATA** button.

That should result in a table with data values. Download it to a comma-separated values (CSV) file by clicking the link **TXT.** Remove the first few lines in the

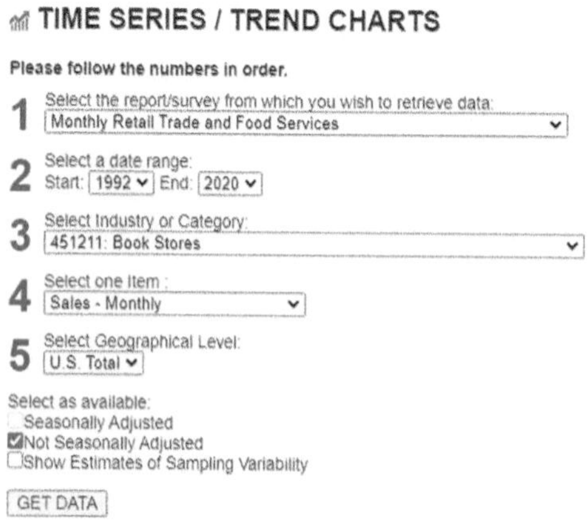

Figure I-1 Fields to populate to download the correct data file

downloaded CSV file so the file starts with a single line containing headings saying "Period,Value" followed by one line for each month. Further, remove any lines with non-numerical values, such as "NA", at the end of the file. Name the file book_store_sales.csv and copy to the data directory.

FRANKENSTEIN FROM PROJECT GUTENBERG

The text of Mary Shelley's *Frankenstein* can be downloaded from https://www.gutenberg.org/files/84/84-0.txt.

Rename the file to frankenstein.txt and copy to the data directory.

GloVe WORD EMBEDDINGS

The GloVe word embeddings file, which is close to 1 GB in size, can be downloaded from http://nlp.stanford.edu/data/glove.6B.zip.

Unzip it after downloading and copy the file glove.6B.100d.txt to the data directory.

ANKI BILINGUAL SENTENCE PAIRS

The Anki bilingual sentence pairs can be downloaded from http://www.manythings.org/anki/fra-eng.zip.

Unzip it after download and copy the file fra.txt to the data directory.

COCO

Create a directory named coco inside of the data directory.

Download the following file:

   http://images.cocodataset.org/annotations/annotations_trainval2014.zip

Unzip it and copy the file captions_train2014.json to the directory coco.

Download the following 13 GB file:

   http://images.cocodataset.org/zips/train2014.zip

Unzip it into the data/coco/ directory so the path to the unzipped directory is data/coco/train2014/.

Installing a DL Framework

There are multiple ways of installing both TensorFlow and PyTorch, and to some extent, it depends on the platform you are using. In this section, we describe some general directions. We distinguish between four different methodologies:

- System installation

- Virtual environment installation

- Running in a Docker container

- Using a cloud service

The code examples for this book have been tested with TensorFlow version 2.4 and PyTorch version 1.8.0.

SYSTEM INSTALLATION

This is the most straightforward way to install a framework in that it does not make use of any mechanisms to isolate it from the rest of the system. You install the framework on your system as well as any packages/libraries that it depends on. If you are lucky, this is simple, but if you are unlucky, you run into problems because you already have some of the libraries installed but you have the wrong versions. You can then decide to upgrade or downgrade to a suitable version, but that might break other pieces of software on your system that depend on a specific installed version. Still, if you do not feel like learning about virtual environments or Docker containers at this point, you can give it a shot. Simply type the following in your shell to install TensorFlow:

```
pip3 install tensorflow
```

If you want to install a specific version that is not the latest version, for example, version 2.4 that the code examples were developed for, then type

```
pip3 install tensorflow==2.4
```

Similarly, use the following command line to install PyTorch:

```
pip3 install torch torchvision
```

If you want to install a specific version that is not the latest version, then you need to find out what versions of torch and torchvision are compatible with each other, and then install the correct versions together. For example, for PyTorch 1.8.0,

```
pip3 install torch==1.8.0 torchvision==0.9.0
```

Pay attention to any error messages that show up as the frameworks are installed. Error messages can indicate dependencies on a missing package or that an already installed package has the wrong version. If the latter is the case, you need to decide whether you are comfortable with starting to tweak the versions of the conflicting package or prefer to move on to a virtual environment.

VIRTUAL ENVIRONMENT INSTALLATION

This is similar to the system installation process, but first you install the `virtualenv` tool. This tool lets you create one or more virtual environments on your system. The benefit from this tool is that each virtual environment can have its own version of a package installed. Thus, if you already have one version of a package installed on your system and your framework requires a different package, then you do not need to remove the existing version. Instead, you install the framework and all the packages that it depends on in its own virtual environment. The details of how to install the `virtualenv` tool and create a virtual environment can be found at https://virtualenv.pypa.io.

GPU ACCELERATION

Additional steps are needed if you want to use GPU acceleration. You need to install CUDA and CuDNN. The details will depend on what system you are running.

For detailed information about TensorFlow installation, with and without GPU acceleration, see tensorflow.org/install.

For PyTorch, the equivalent information can be found at https://pytorch.org/get-started/locally.

However, you do not need GPU acceleration for the first few programming exercises, so you might want to start with a simple setup and worry about GPU acceleration later.

DOCKER CONTAINER

Another option is to use a Docker container. This is a way of getting away from the process of installing the framework altogether. Instead, you first install the Docker Engine on your system. You then download a Docker image, which has everything you need (TensorFlow or PyTorch and any libraries that they depend on) already installed on this image. You then tell the Docker Engine to create a Docker Container based on that image. A Docker Container isolates the software that is running inside it from its environment, somewhat like a virtual machine, but more lightweight, as it does not contain the operating system itself. Using Docker Containers is a popular way of running DL frameworks, and it is perhaps also the simplest way of configuring them to make use of the GPU on your system.

USING A CLOUD SERVICE

Finally, if you do not want to install anything on your system, you can instead use a cloud service. Using a cloud service is also a good alternative if you do not have a system with a GPU but still want to be able to play around with GPU acceleration before deciding to buy one.

One alternative is Google Colab, which provides machine access for free, including GPU acceleration. It already has TensorFlow and PyTorch installed. You will need to learn how to enable access to data on your Google Drive account for any code examples that require datafiles as input.

Another alternative is AWS, where you can rent a machine by the minute. AWS offers preconfigured machines ready to run TensorFlow and PyTorch, but there is a little bit of a learning curve to get started, including setting up an account, deciding what machine to rent, figuring out how to rent persistent storage that does not get wiped when you shut down the machine, and configuring a security group and network access. The benefit is that there is no work of configuring the DL frameworks because they are already set up by AWS.

TensorFlow Specific Considerations

Because TensorFlow is the framework used for all the programming examples in this book, the book is sprinkled with information about TensorFlow. We still figured that it makes sense to specifically spell out here that TensorFlow can be somewhat verbose, especially when using a GPU. If you want to reduce the verbosity when running the programs, you can set the environment variable TF_CPP_MIN_LOG_LEVEL to 2. It can be done with the following command line if you use bash:

```
export TF_CPP_MIN_LOG_LEVEL=2
```

Alternatively, you can add the following code snippet at the top of each program:

```
import os

os.environ['TF_CPP_MIN_LOG_LEVEL'] = '2'
```

Key Differences Between PyTorch and TensorFlow

In this section, we point out some key differences between PyTorch and TensorFlow. We try to highlight these differences in the documentation of each PyTorch programming example as well, but we believe that it is helpful to have them summarized here in a single place. Note that most of what is described here requires skills taught throughout this book, so rather than reading this section up front, we recommend revisiting this section over the course of reading the book.

Overall, when comparing the experience of programming for PyTorch versus TensorFlow with the Keras API, our opinion is that the differences fall into one major and one minor category. The major difference is that some things that are handled by the Keras API need to be explicitly handled in PyTorch. This makes it slightly harder to get started for a beginner but pays off in the long run in terms of providing flexibility when you want to do something slightly off the beaten path. The minor differences simply consist of a number of minor design/API choices that are different between the two frameworks.

Both frameworks are rapidly evolving. Therefore, this section is likely to get outdated over time. We recommend that you consult the most up-to-date documentation for the framework you use.

NEED TO WRITE OUR OWN FIT/TRAINING FUNCTION

In our opinion, for a beginner, one of the bigger obstacles in PyTorch compared to Tensorflow (using the Keras API) is the need to write your own function to train your model. In Tensorflow, once you have defined a model, you simply call the function `fit()` with a set of suitable parameters, and the framework handles a lot of the details, including running the forward pass, running the backward pass, and adjusting the weights. In addition, it computes and prints out a number of useful metrics like loss and accuracy for both the training set and the test set. In PyTorch, you must handle these mechanics yourself.

Although this might seem cumbersome, in reality, it is not that much code to write. In addition, as we show in our code examples, it is simple to write your own library function that can be reused across many models. This is a prime example of where we think it is a little bit harder to get started with PyTorch than with Tensorflow. On the other hand, it is very powerful to be able to easily modify this piece of code. That is illustrated by the natural language translation example (Chapter 14, "Sequence-to-Sequence Networks and Natural Language Translation") and image captioning example (Chapter 16, "One-to-Many Network for Image Captioning"), where our TensorFlow implementations of the training loop are somewhat convoluted.

As a part of writing your own training loop, you will need to include the following steps:

- Call the `zero_grad()` method on the chosen optimizer to inform the optimizer that it should reset all gradients to zero, since the default is to accumulate gradients over multiple steps

- Call to an instance[2] of a `Module` object, which results in a call to the `forward()` method to run the forward pass

- Compute loss and call `backward()` to run the backward pass

- Call the `step()` method on the chosen optimizer to update the weights based on the current gradient

Apart from explicitly handling forward pass, loss computation, backward pass, and weight adjustment, you also need to implement functionality to break up your training and test data into mini-batches. This is typically done using a `DataLoader` object. When using TensorFlow with the Keras API, all this functionality is handled by the `fit()` function.

---

2. In Python 3, you can use the instance variable name of an object as a function name. When you call this function, it will invoke the object's `__call__()` method. In PyTorch, the `__call__()` method for a `Module` object will invoke the `forward()` method.

EXPLICIT MOVES OF DATA BETWEEN NumPy AND PyTorch

The Keras API in TensorFlow uses NumPy arrays as its representation of tensors. For example, when passing a tensor to a model, the format is expected to be in the form of a multidimensional NumPy array. In contrast, in PyTorch you need to explicitly convert data between NumPy arrays and PyTorch tensors.

PyTorch keeps track of information to be able to do automatic differentiation (using backpropagation) on PyTorch tensors. That is, as long as you work on PyTorch tensors, you can use any computation supported by the tensor data type when defining a function, and you will later be able to automatically compute partial derivatives of that function. The explicit move to and from a tensor enables PyTorch to track what variables to provide this functionality for.

There are a few different functions related to this:

- `from_numpy()` converts from NumPy array to PyTorch tensor.

- `numpy()` converts from PyTorch tensor to NumPy array.

- `detach()` creates a PyTorch tensor that shares storage with the original PyTorch tensor but for which automatic differentiation is not supported.

- `clone()` creates a PyTorch tensor from a PyTorch tensor but where storage is not shared between the two tensors.

- `item()` converts a single element in a PyTorch tensor into a NumPy value.

- `with torch.no_grad()` turns off support for automatic differentiation within the scope of this construct.

For a beginner, it can be challenging to understand how these functions and constructs all relate, especially when encountering a combined expression such as `detach().clone().numpy()`. It is like with anything else. It takes some time to get used to, but once you understand it, it is not that complicated.

EXPLICIT TRANSFER OF DATA BETWEEN CPU AND GPU

In addition to explicitly moving data between NumPy and PyTorch, you must explicitly move data (and models) between the CPU and the GPU. It is done using the two functions:

- `to(DEVICE)` moves data to a specific device (typically GPU).

- `cpu()` moves data to the CPU.

In our opinion, this is easier to get familiar with, but it can still trip you in the beginning, especially when combined with the mechanisms given previously, and you might run into a combined expression such as .cpu().detach(). numpy().

EXPLICITLY DISTINGUISHING BETWEEN TRAINING AND INFERENCE

Some types of layers, such as Dropout and BatchNormalization, behave differently during training than during inference. In TensorFlow, this is handled automatically because the framework has explicit functions for training (fit) and inference (predict). As described previously, in PyTorch, you must write these functions yourself. Therefore, you must also explicitly tell a model when it is being used for training or inference. This is done using the following functions:

- train() sets a model in training mode.

- eval() sets a model in inference mode.

For a beginner, it is easy to mix up the functionality of eval() and no_grad(), which was described earlier. Both can make sense to use during inference. The distinction is that eval() is required to get the correct behavior, whereas no_grad() is an optimization to not track the extra state needed for auto-differentiation (which is not needed during inference).

SEQUENTIAL VERSUS FUNCTIONAL API

We are now moving on to the differences that are minor but good to know about. Most of our TensorFlow programming examples use the Keras Sequential API. PyTorch has a very similar concept in the nn.Sequential class.

For the more advanced programming examples, it is a little bit different. For TensorFlow, we use the Keras Functional API where the process of declaring layers is separate from connecting them together. In PyTorch, this is handled differently by instead creating a custom model by inheriting from the nn.Module class and overriding the forward() function.

In our opinion, both methodologies are of a similar complexity level when using supported layer types, but the PyTorch methodology might be somewhat simpler when implementing layers that are not natively supported by the framework. The programming example in Chapter 16 is an example of this, where we implement the functionality of an attention layer in the PyTorch version. As a side note, that highlights another minor difference in that TensorFlow provides an attention layer, whereas PyTorch does not.

LACK OF COMPILE FUNCTION

In TensorFlow, before calling the `fit()` function to train a model, you have to call the `compile()` function to select a loss function and an optimizer. This is not needed in PyTorch and likely follows from the fact that you write your own training loop in PyTorch. As a part of that process, you explicitly invoke your loss function and optimizer, so there is no need to tell the framework up front what functions to use.

RECURRENT LAYERS AND STATE HANDLING

For recurrent layers (e.g., LSTM), there are two key differences to highlight between TensorFlow and PyTorch. First, stacking LSTM layers in PyTorch can be done by simply providing a parameter to the LSTM layer constructor instead of having to declare multiple instances after each other.

Second, in the programming examples that use recurrent layers, we show how TensorFlow has functionality to declare a recurrent layer as either stateful or not, and we make use of this when we build autoregressive models. The stateful concept does not explicitly exist in PyTorch, but we show how to emulate it in our PyTorch versions of the programming examples.

CROSS-ENTROPY LOSS

There are two key differences between the cross-entropy loss implementation in PyTorch compared to Tensorflow. First, in PyTorch, the cross-entropy loss function implicitly also models the logistic sigmoid function of the last neuron, or the softmax in the case of a multiclass classification problem. That is, when defining the network, you should use a linear output unit instead of also defining an activation function. Second, in PyTorch, the cross-entropy loss function expects an integer target instead of a one-hot encoded target. That is, there is no need to one-hot encode the target value. This results in a more efficient implementation from a memory usage perspective.

If you use TensorFlow, there are options to get the same behavior, but they need to be explicitly specified because the default behavior is different.

VIEW/RESHAPE

NumPy provides a function `reshape()` that can be used to change the dimensions of a NumPy array, and TensorFlow has the corresponding function for changing the shape of tensors. PyTorch has the same kind of functionality implemented by a function named `view()`.

Appendix J

Cheat Sheets

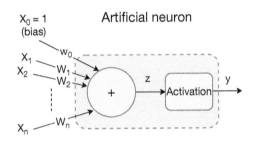

Artificial neuron

$X_0 = 1$
(bias)

X_1
X_2

X_n

w_0
W_1
W_2

W_n

+

z

Activation

y

Feedforward network

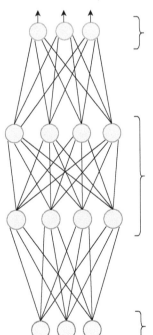

Activation functions for output units

logistic | softmax | linear

Activation functions for hidden units

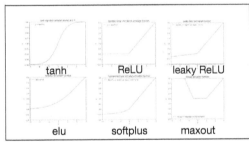

tanh | ReLU | leaky ReLU

elu | softplus | maxout

Input encodings

Standardized numerical values	One-hot encoded classes	Word embeddings from embedding layer

Larger versions of these cheat sheets can be downloaded from http://informit.com/title/9780137470358.

Layer types

Type	Description	Example usage
Fully connected	Each neuron connects to each output in preceding layer. Also known as projection layer if no activation function is used.	Cases where specialized layers do not provide additional value
Convolutional	Sparsely connected. Employs weight sharing. Consists of multiple channels. Each channel is often arranged in two dimensions.	Image processing (2D convolution) and text processing (1D convolution)
Simple recurrent	Recurrent connections. Output from previous timestep is used as input. Weight sharing between timesteps.	Sequential data of variable length, e.g., text processing
Long short-term memory (LSTM)	Recurrent layer with more complex units. Each unit contains an internal memory cell. Gates control when to remember and forget.	Long sequences, e.g., text processing
Gated recurrent unit (GRU)	Simplified version of LSTM. No internal memory cell but still has gates to control when to remember or forget previous output value.	Long sequences, e.g., text processing
Embedding	Converts sparse one-hot encoded data into a dense representation. Implemented as lookup table.	Convert textual input data into word embeddings
Attention	Output vector is a weighted sum of multiple input vectors. The weights are dynamically chosen to attend to the most important vector.	Extract information from long text sequences or images

Linear algebra representation

Weighted sum for single neuron: $z = \mathbf{w}\mathbf{x}$

Weighted sums for fully connected layer: $\mathbf{z} = W\mathbf{x}$

Weighted sums for fully connected layer for mini-batch: $Z = WX$

Recurrent layer: $\mathbf{h}^{(t)} = \tanh(W\mathbf{h}^{(t-1)} + U\mathbf{x}^{(t)} + \mathbf{b})$

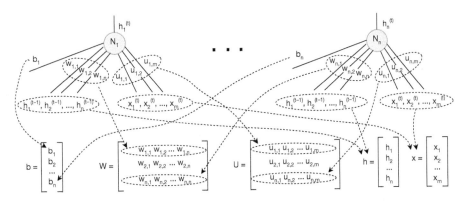

NOTE: Bias term is implicit in all but the recurrent case above

Datasets

Typical splits

Big dataset: 60/20/20 (train/validation/test)

Small dataset: 80/20 (train/test) and k-fold cross-validation

Training algorithm variations

Algorithm	Description
Stochastic gradient descent (SGD)	Gradient is computed based on a mini-batch of training examples.
Momentum	Addition to SGD where weight adjustment depends on gradient from previous adjustments as well as the current gradient.
AdaGrad	Variation on SGD that adaptively adjusts the learning rate during training.
Adam	Variation on SGD with both adaptive learning rate and momentum.
RMSProp	Variation on SGD that normalizes gradient using the root mean square (RMS) of recent gradients.

Regularization techniques

Early stopping

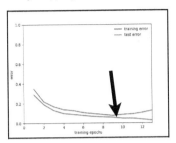

Dropout

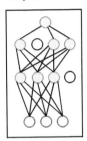

Data augmentation

L1/L2 Regularization

Add a weight penalty to error function:

$$L1 = \lambda w \qquad L2 = \lambda w^2$$

Keeping gradients healthy

Technique	Mitigates vanishing gradients	Mitigates exploding gradients
Glorot or He weight initialization	Yes	No
Batch normalization	Yes	No
Nonsaturating neurons, e.g., ReLU	Yes	No
Gradient clipping	No	Yes
Constant error carousel	Yes	Yes
Skip connections	Yes	No

Problem types

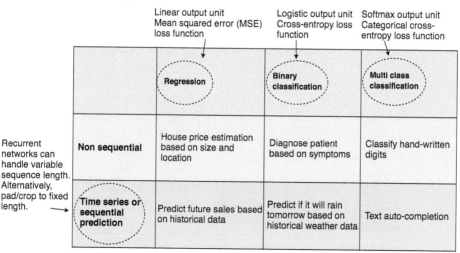

Linear output unit
Mean squared error (MSE)
loss function

Logistic output unit
Cross-entropy loss
function

Softmax output unit
Categorical cross-
entropy loss function

	Regression	Binary classification	Multi class classification
Non sequential	House price estimation based on size and location	Diagnose patient based on symptoms	Classify hand-written digits
Time series or sequential prediction	Predict future sales based on historical data	Predict if it will rain tomorrow based on historical weather data	Text auto-completion

Recurrent networks can handle variable sequence length. Alternatively, pad/crop to fixed length.

Examples of network architectures for different problem types

Generic binary classification

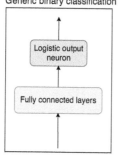

Logistic output neuron

Fully connected layers

Generic regression

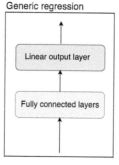

Linear output layer

Fully connected layers

Image classification

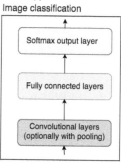

Softmax output layer

Fully connected layers

Convolutional layers (optionally with pooling)

Language model

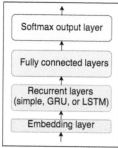

Softmax output layer

Fully connected layers

Recurrent layers (simple, GRU, or LSTM)

Embedding layer

Encoder-decoder for language translation

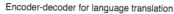
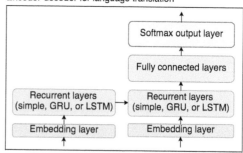

Softmax output layer

Fully connected layers

Recurrent layers (simple, GRU, or LSTM)

Recurrent layers (simple, GRU, or LSTM)

Embedding layer

Embedding layer

Input/output data relationships

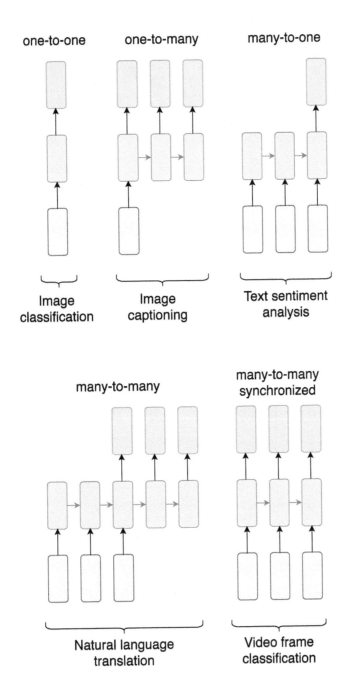

one-to-one

Image
classification

one-to-many

Image
captioning

many-to-one

Text sentiment
analysis

many-to-many

Natural language
translation

many-to-many
synchronized

Video frame
classification

Word embeddings

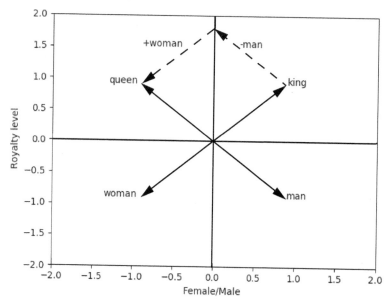

Word vector arithmetic: King – Man + Woman = Queen

Word embedding schemes

Embedding scheme	Notes
word2vec	The "classic," derived using heuristics.
GloVe	Mathematically derived.
wordpieces	Handles out-of-vocabulary words by working on subwords.
FastText	Extension of word2vec to handle out-of-vocabulary words.
ELMo	Same word results in different embeddings depending on context.

Transformer-based NLP architectures

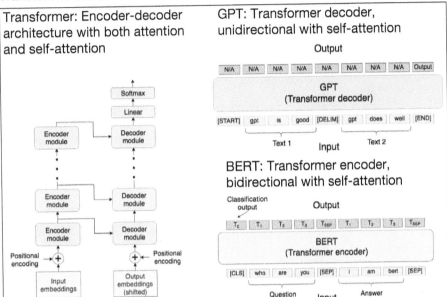

Transformer: Encoder-decoder architecture with both attention and self-attention

GPT: Transformer decoder, unidirectional with self-attention

BERT: Transformer encoder, bidirectional with self-attention

Traditional NLP techniques

Technique	Description	Application examples
n-gram	Simple statistical language model. Computes probability of word sequence.	Find likely sentence candidate in speech recognition. Text auto-completion.
skip-gram	Extension of n-gram model.	See above.
bag-of-words	Unordered document summarization technique.	Building block in sentiment analysis and document comparison.
bag-of-ngrams	Extension of bag-of-words with some notion of word order.	See above.
character-based bag-of-ngrams	Bag-of-word but working on characters instead of words.	Determine similarities between words.

Computer vision

Network	Key properties
LeNet, LeNet-5	CNN before DL boom.
AlexNet	First DL-based ImageNet winner.
VGGNet	Demonstrated importance of depth.
Inception	Complex building block with parallel paths. Used by GoogLeNet.
ResNet	Introduced skip connections. Much deeper than previous networks.
EfficientNet	Explored trade-offs between multiple dimensions for more efficient architecture.
MobileNets, Exception	Depthwise separable convolutions for more efficient implementation.
Inception v2, v3, v4, Inception-ResNet, ResNeXt	Deep hybrid architectures.

Networks for classification; also used as backbone in other models

Detection

Models: R-CNN, Fast R-CNN, Faster R-CNN

Semantic segmentation

Models: Deconvolution network, U-Net

Instance segmentation

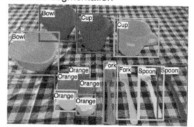

Model: Mask R-CNN

Works Cited

Agarap, A. (2018). "A Neural Network Architecture Combining Gated Recurrent Unit (GRU) and Support Vector Machine (SVM) for Intrusion Detection in Network Traffic Data." In *Proceedings of the 2018 10th International Conference on Machine Learning and Computing,* 26–30. New York: Association for Computing Machinery.

Akenine-Möller, T., E. Haines, N. Hoffman, A. Pesce, M. Iwanicki, and S. Hillaire. (2018). *Real-Time Rendering,* 4th ed. Boca Raton, FL: AK Peters/CRC Press.

Alammar, J. (2018a). "The Illustrated BERT, ELMo, and Co (How NLP Cracked Transfer Learning)" (blog). http://jalammar.github.io/illustrated-bert/.

Alammar, J. (2018b). "The Illustrated Transformer" (blog). http://jalammar.github.io/illustrated-transformer/.

Alammar, J. (2019). "The Illustrated Word2vec" (blog). http://jalammar.github.io/illustrated-word2vec/.

Athiwaratkun, B., A. Wilson, and A. Anandkumar. (2018). "Probabilistic FastText for Multi-Sense Word Embeddings." *Proceedings of the 56th Annual Meeting of the Association for Computational Linguistics* (Volume 1: Long Papers), 1–11. Stroudsburg, PA: Association for Computational Linguistics.

Azulay, A., and Y. Weiss. (2019). "Why Do Deep Convolutional Networks Generalize So Poorly to Small Image Transformations?" *arXiv.org.* https://arxiv.org/pdf/1805.12177v2.

Ba, L., J. Kiros, and G. Hinton. (2016). "Layer Normalization." *arXiv.org.* https://arxiv.org/pdf/1607.06450v1.

Badrinarayanan, V., A. Kendall, and R. Cipolla. (2017). "SegNet: A Deep Convolutional Encoder-Decoder Architecture for Image Segmentation." *IEEE Transactions on Pattern Analysis and Machine Intelligence* 39(12): 2481–2495.

Baer, T. (2019). *Understand, Manage, and Prevent Algorithmic Bias: A Guide for Business Users and Data Scientists.* Berkeley, CA: Apress.

Bahdanau, D., B. Cho, and Y. Bengio. (2014). "Neural Machine Translation by Jointly Learning to Align and Translate." *arXiv.org.* https://arxiv.org/pdf/1607.06450v1.

Balmer, L. (1997). *Signals and Systems.* Hertfordshire, UK: Prentice Hall.

Baltrušaitis T., C. Ahuja, and L. Morency. (2017). "Multimodal Machine Learning: A Survey and Taxonomy." *arXiv.org.* https://arxiv.org/pdf/1705.09406.

Beliaev, S., Y. Rebryk, and B. Ginsburg. (2020). "TalkNet: Fully-Convolutional Non-Autoregressive Speech Synthesis Model." *arXiv.org.* https://arxiv.org/pdf/2005.05514.

Bender E., Gebru T., McMillan A., and Shmitchell S. (2021). "On the Dangers of Stochastic Parrots: Can Language Models Be Too Big?" In *Proceedings of the 2021 ACM Conference on Fairness, Accountability, and Transparency,* 610–623. New York: Association for Computing Machinery.

Bengio, J., R. Ducharme, P. Vincent, and C. Janvin. (2003). "A Neural Probabilistic Language Model." *Journal of Machine Learning Research* 3(6): 1137–1155.

Bengio, Y., P. Simard, and P. Frasconi. (1994). "Learning Long-Term Dependencies with Gradient Descent Is Difficult." *IEEE Transactions on Neural Networks* 5(2): 157–166.

Blum, A., and T. Mitchell. (1998). "Combining Labeled and Unlabeled Data with Co-training." In *Proceedings of the Eleventh Annual Conference on Computational Learning Theory (COLT'98),* 92–100. New York: Association for Computing Machinery.

Bojanowski, P., E. Grave, A. Joulin, and T. Mikolov. (2017). "Enriching Word Vectors with Subword Information." *Transactions of the Association for Computational Linguistics* 5: 135–146.

Bolukbasi, T., K. Chang, J. Zou, V. Saligrama, and A. Kalai. (2016). "Man Is to Computer Programmer as Woman Is to Homemaker? Debiasing Word Embeddings." *Advances in Neural Information Processing Systems* 29: 4349–4357.

Bostrom, N. (2003). "Ethical Issues in Advanced Artificial Intelligence." In *Cognitive, Emotive and Ethical Aspects of Decision Making in Humans and in Artificial Intelligence, Volume 2,* (IIAS-147-2003), edited by I. Smit, W. Wallach, and G. E. Lasker, 12–17. Tecumseh, ON: International Institute of Advanced Studies in Systems Research and Cybernetics.

Brown T., B. Mann, N. Ryder, M. Subbiah, J. Kaplan, P. Dhariwal, A. Neelakantan, et al. (2020). "Language Models Are Few-Shot Learners." *arXiv.org.* https://arxiv .org/pdf 2005.14165.

Buolamwini, J. (n.d.). *Algorithmic Justice League.* https://www.ajl.org/.

Buolamwini, J., and T. Gebru. (2018). "Gender Shades: Intersectional Accuracy Disparities in Commercial Gender Classification." *Proceedings of the 1st Conference on Fairness, Accountability and Transparency, in PMLR* 81: 77–91.

Cho, K., B. van Merrienboer, C. Gulcehre, D. Bahdanau, F. Bougares, H. Schwenk, and Y. Bengio. (2014a, June). "Learning Phrase Representations Using RNN Encoder-Decoder for Statistical Machine Translation" (v. 1). *arXiv.org.* https://arxiv .org/pdf/1406.1078v1.

Cho, K., B. van Merrienboer, C. Gulcehre, D. Bahdanau, F. Bougares, H. Schwenk, and Y. Bengio. (2014b, Sept.). "Learning Phrase Representations Using RNN Encoder-Decoder for Statistical Machine Translation" (v. 3). *arXiv.org.* https://arxiv .org/pdf/1406.1078v3.

Chollet, F. (2016). "Xception: Deep Learning with Depthwise Separable Convolutions." *arXiv.org.* https://arxiv.org/pdf/1610.02357.

Chollet, F. (2018). *Deep Learning with Python.* Shelter Island, NY: Manning Publications.

Chung, J., C. Gulcehre, K. Cho, and Y. Bengio. (2014). "Empirical Evaluation of Gated Recurrent Neural Networks on Sequence Modeling." *arXiv.org.* https://arxiv.org/ pdf/1412.3555.

Ciresan, D., U. Meier, J. Masci, L. Gambardella, and J. Schmidhuber. (2011). "Flexible, High Performance Convolutional Neural Networks for Image Classification." *Proceedings of the Twenty-Second International Joint Conference on Artificial Intelligence (IJCAI'11),* 1237–1242. Menlo Park, CA: AAAI Press/ International Joint Conferences on Artificial Intelligence.

Collobert, R., and J. Weston. (2008)."A Unified Architecture for Natural Language Processing: Deep Neural Networks with Multitask Learning." In *ICML'08: 25th International Conference on Machine Learning,* 160–167. New York: Association for Computing Machinery.

Cordonnier, J., A. Loukas, and M. Jaggi. (2020). "On the Relationship between Self-Attention and Convolutional Layers." *International Conference on Learning Representations (ICLR 2020). arXiv.org.* https://arxiv.org/pdf/1911.03584.

Crawshaw, M. (2020). "Multi-Task Learning with Deep Neural Networks: A Survey." *arXiv.org.* https://arxiv.org/pdf/2009.09796.

Dai, A., and Q. Le. (2015). "Semi-Supervised Sequence Learning." In *Proceedings of the 28th International Conference on Neural Information Processing Systems (NIPS'15).* 3079–3087. Cambridge, MA: MIT Press.

Dai, B., S. Fidler, and D. Lin. (2018). "A Neural Compositional Paradigm for Image Captioning." *Advances in Neural Information Processing Systems* 31: 658–668.

Dai, Z., Z. Yang, Y. Yang, J. Carbonell, Q. Le, and R. Salakhutdinov. (2019). "Transformer-XL: Attentive Language Models Beyond a Fixed-Length Context." In *Proceedings of the 57th Annual Meeting of the Association for Computational Linguistics,* 2978–2988. Stroudsburg, PA: Association for Computational Linguistics.

De-Arteaga, M., A. Romanov, H. Wallach, J. Chayes, C. Borgs, A. Chouldechova, S. Geyik, K. Kenthapadi, and A. T. Kalai. (2019). "Bias in Bios: A Case Study of Semantic Representation Bias in a High-Stakes Setting." *Proceedings of the Conference on Fairness, Accountability, and Transparency.* 120–128. *arXiv.org.* https://arxiv.org/pdf/1901.09451.

Devlin, J., M. Chang, K. Lee, and K. Toutanova. (2018). "BERT: Pre-training of Deep Bidirectional Transformers for Language Understanding." *arXiv.org.* https://arxiv.org/pdf/1810.04805.

Dickson, E. (2019, October 7). "Deepfake Porn Is Still a Threat, Particularly for K-Pop Stars." *Rolling Stone.* https://www.rollingstone.com/culture/culture-news/deepfakes-nonconsensual-porn-study-kpop-895605/

dos Santos, C., and M. Gatti. (2014). "Deep Convolutional Neural Networks for Sentiment Analysis of Short Texts." *Proceedings of the 25th International Conference on Computational Linguistics (COLING'14): Technical Papers,* Vol. 1, 69–78. Dublin, Ireland: Dublin City University and Association for Computational Linguistics.

Duchi, J., E. Hazan, and Y. Singer. (2011). "Adaptive Subgradient Methods for Online Learning and Stochastic Optimization." *Journal of Machine Learning Research* 12: 2121–2159.

Dugas, C., Y. Bengio, F. Bélisle, and C. Nadeau. (2001). "Incorporating Second-Order Functional Knowledge for Better Option Pricing." In *Advances in Neural Information Processing Systems 13 (NIPS'00)*, 472–478. Cambridge, MA: MIT Press.

Elsken, T., Metzen J., and Hutter F. (2019). "Neural Architecture Search: A Survey." *Journal of Machine Learning Research* 20: 1–21.

Fisher, R. (1936). "The Use of Multiple Measurements in Taxonomic Problems." *Annals Eugenics* 7(2): 179–188.

Frome, A., Corrado G., Shlens J., Bengio S., Dean J., Ranzato M., and Mikolov T. (2013). "DeViSE: A Deep Visual-Semantic Embedding Model." In *Proceedings of the 26th International Conference on Neural Information Processing Systems— Volume 2*, edited by C. J. C. Burges, L. Bottou, M. Welling, Z. Ghahramani, and K. Q. Weinberger, 2121–2129. Red Hook, NY: Curran Associates.

Fukushima, K. (1980). "Neocognitron: A Self-Organizing Neural Network Model for a Mechanism of Pattern Recognition Unaffected by Shift in Position." *Biological Cybernetics* 36(4): 193–202.

Gatys L., Ecker A., Bethge M. (2015). "A Neural Algorithm of Artistic Style." *arXiv .org.* https://arxiv.org/pdf/1508.06576.

Gebru, T., J. Morgenstern, B. Vecchione, J. Wortman Vaughan, H. Wallach, H. Daumé III, and K. Crawford. (2018). "Datasheets for Datasets." *arXiv.org.* https://arxiv.org/ pdf/1803.09010.

Gehring, J., M. Auli, D. Granger, D. Yarats, and Y. Dauphin. (2017). "Convolutional Sequence to Sequence Learning." In *Proceedings of the 34th International Conference on Machine Learning (ICML'17)*, edited by D. Precup and Y. W. Teh, 1243–1252. JMLR.org.

Gers, F., J. Schmidhuber, and F. Cummins. (1999). "Learning to Forget: Continual Prediction with LSTM." *Ninth International Conference on Artificial Neural Networks (ICANN 99). IEEE Conference Publication* 2, (470): 850–855.

Gers, F., N. Schraudolph, and J. Schmidhuber. (2002). "Learning Precise Timing with LSTM Recurrent Networks." *Journal of Machine Learning Research* 3: 115–143.

Girshick, R. (2015). "Fast R-CNN." *Proceedings of the 2015 IEEE International Conference on Computer Vision (ICCV'15)*, 1440–1448. Washington, DC: IEEE Computer Society.

Girshick, R., J. Donahue, T. Darrell, and J. Malik. (2014). "Rich Feature Hierarchies for Accurate Object Detection and Semantic Segmentation." *Proceedings of the 2014 IEEE Conference on Computer Vision and Pattern Recognition (CVPR'14)*, 580–587. Washington, DC: IEEE Computer Society.

Glassner, A. (2018). *Deep Learning: From Basics to Practice.* Seattle, WA: The Imaginary Institute,

Glorot, X., A. Bordes, and Y. Bengio. (2011). "Deep Sparse Rectifier Neural Networks." Fourteenth International Conference on Artificial Intelligence and Statistics (AISTATS 2011). *Journal of Machine Learning Research* 15: 315–323.

Glorot, X., and Y. Bengio. (2010). "Understanding the Difficulty of Training Deep Feedforward Neural Networks." Thirteenth International Conference on Artificial Intelligence and Statistics (AISTATS). *Journal of Machine Learning Research* 9: 249–256.

Goodfellow, I., D. Warde-Farley, M. Mirza, A. Courville, and Y. Bengio. (2013). "Maxout Networks." In *Proceedings of the 30th International Conference on Machine Learning (ICML'13),* edited by S. Dasgupta and D. McAllester, III-1319–III-1327. JMLR.org.

Goodfellow, I., Y. Bengio, and A. Courville. (2016). *Deep Learning.* Cambridge, MA: MIT Press.

Goodfellow, I., Pouget-Abadie J., Mirza M., Xu B., Warde-Farley D., Ozair S., Courville A., and Bengio Y. (2014). "Generative Adversarial Nets." *arXiv.org.* https://arxiv.org/pdf/1406.2661.

Graves, A., M. Liwicki, S. Fernandez, R. Bertolami, H. Bunke, and J. Schmidhuber. (2009). "A Novel Connectionist System for Unconstrained Handwriting Recognition." *IEEE Transactions on Pattern Analysis and Machine Intelligence* 31(5): 855–868.

Harrison, D., and D. Rubinfeld. (1978). "Hedonic Housing Prices and the Demand for Clean Air." *Journal of Environmental Economics and Management* 5: 81–102.

Hastie, T., R. Tibshirani, and J. Friedman. (2009). *The Elements of Statistical Learning Data Mining, Inference, and Prediction.* New York: Springer.

He, K., G. Gkioxari, P. Dollár, and R. Girshick. (2017). "Mask R-CNN." 2017 IEEE International Conference on Computer Vision (ICCV). *IEEE Transactions on Pattern Analysis and Machine Intelligence* PP(99): 2980–2988.

He, K., X. Zhang, S. Ren, and J. Sun. (2015a.) "Deep Residual Learning for Image Recognition." *arXiv.org.* https://arxiv.org/pdf/1512.03385.

He, K., X. Zhang, S. Ren, and J. Sun. (2015b). "Delving Deep into Rectifiers: Surpassing Human-Level Performance on ImageNet Classification." In *Proceedings of the 2015 IEEE International Conference on Computer Vision (ICCV),* 1026–1034. Washington, DC: IEEE Computer Society.

He, K., X. Zhang, S. Ren, and J. Sun. (2016). "Identity Mappings in Deep Residual Networks." Computer Vision—ECCV 2016: 14th European Conference. *Lecture Notes in Computer Science* 9908: 630–645.

Heck, J., and F. Salem. (2017). "Simplified Minimal Gated Unit Variations for Recurrent Neural Networks." IEEE 60th International Midwest Symposium on Circuits and Systems (MWSCAS 2017). *arXiv.org.* https://arxiv.org/pdf/1701.03452.

Hinton, G. (n.d.). *Coursera Class Slides.* https://www.cs.toronto.edu/~tijmen/csc321/slides/lecture_slides_lec6.pdf.

Hinton, G., and R. Salakhutdinov. (2006). "Reducing the dimensionality of data with neural networks." *Science* 303(5786): 504–507.

Hinton, G., J. McClelland, and D. Rumelhart. (1986). *Distributed Representations.* Vol. 1, in *Parallel Distributed Processing: Explorations in the Microstructure of Cognition,* edited by D. Rumelhart and J. McClelland, 77–109. Cambridge, MA: MIT Press.

Hinton, G., S. Osindero, and Y. Teh. (2006). "A Fast Learning Algorithm for Deep Belief Nets." *Neural Computation* 18(7): 1527–1554.

Hochreiter, S., and J. Schmidhuber. (1997). "Long Short-Term Memory." *Neural Computation Archive* 9(8): 1735–1780.

Hodosh, M., P. Young, and J. Hockenmaier. (2013). "Framing Image Description as a Ranking Task: Data, Models and Evaluation Metrics." *Journal of Artificial Intelligence Research* 47: 853–899.

Hopfield, J. (1982). "Neural Networks and Physical Systems with Emergent Collective Computational Abilities." *Proceedings of the National Academy of Sciences of the United States of America* 79(8): 2554–2558.

Howard, A., M. Zhu, B. Chen, D. Kalenichenko, W. Wang, T. Weyand, M. Andreetto, and H. Adam. (2017). "MobileNets: Efficient Convolutional Neural Networks for Mobile Vision Applications." *arXiv.org.* https://arxiv.org/pdf/1704.04861.

Howard, J., and S. Gugger. (2020). *Deep Learning for Coders with fastai and PyTorch.* Sebastopol, CA: O'Reilly,

Howard, J., and S. Ruder. (2018). "Universal Language Model Fine-tuning for Text Classification." *Proceedings of the 56th Annual Meeting of the Association for Computational Linguistics,* 328–339. Stroudsburg, PA: Association for Computational Linguistics.

Howley, D. (2015, June 29). *Yahoo Tech.* https://finance.yahoo.com/news/google-photos-mislabels-two-black-americans-as-122793782784.html.

IMDb Datasets. (n.d.). https://www.imdb.com/interfaces/.

Ioffe, S., and C. Szegedy. (2015). "Batch Normalization: Accelerating Deep Network Training by Reducing Internal Covariate Shift." *arXiv.org.* https://arxiv.org/pdf/1502.03167.

Ivakhnenko, A., and V. Lapa. (1965). *Cybernetic Predicting Devices.* New York: CCM Information.

Jin H., Song Q., and Hu X. (2019). "Auto-Keras: An Efficient Neural Architecture Search System." *arXiv.org.* https://arxiv.org/pdf/1806.10282.

Jozefowicz, R., O. Vinyals, M. Schuster, N. Shazeer, and Y. Wu. (2016). "Exploring the Limits of Language Modeling." *arXiv.org.* https://arxiv.org/pdf/1609.02410.

Kärkkäinen, K., and J. Joo. (2019). "FairFace: Face Attribute Dataset for Balanced Race, Gender, and Age." *arXiv.org.* https://arxiv.org/pdf/1908.04913.

Kalchbrenner, N., L. Espehold, K. Simonyan, A. van den Oord, A. Graves, and K. Kavukcuoglu. (2016). "Neural Machine Translation in Linear Time." *arXiv.org.* https://arxiv.org/pdf/1610.10099.

Karpathy, A. (2015, May). *The Unreasonable Effectiveness of Recurrent Neural Networks.* http://karpathy.github.io/2015/05/21/rnn-effectiveness/.

Karpathy, A. (2019a, April). *A Recipe for Training Neural Networks.* April http://karpathy.github.io/2019/04/25/recipe/.

Karpathy, A. (2019b). "Tesla Autopilot and Multi-Task Learning for Perception and Prediction." *Lex Clips.* https://www.youtube.com/watch?v=IHH47nZ7FZU.

Karpathy, A., and F. Li. (2014). "Deep Visual-Semantic Alignments for Generating Image Descriptions." *arXiv.org.* https://arxiv.org/pdf/1412.2306.

Karras, T., S. Laine, and T. Aila. (2019). "A Style-Based Generator Architecture for Generative Adversarial Networks." In *Proceedings of the IEEE/CVF Conference on Computer Vision and Pattern Recognition (CVPR).* 4396–4405. Los Alamitos, CA : IEEE Computer Society.

Karras, T., T. Aila, L. Samuli, and J. Lehtinen. (2018). "Progressive Growing of GANs for Improved Quality, Stability, and Variation." *International Conference on Learning Representations. arXiv.org.* https://arxiv.org/pdf/1710.10196.

Keras Issue Request: Speedup GRU by Applying the Reset Gate Afterwards? (2016, Sept.). https://github.com/keras-team/keras/issues/3701.

Kim, Y., Y. Jernite, D. Sontag, and A. Rush. (2016). "Character-Aware Neural Language Models." In Proceedings of the *Thirtieth AAAI Conference on Artificial Intelligence (AAAI'16),* 2741–2749. Palo Alto, CA: AAAI Press.

Kingma, D., and J. Ba. (2015). "Adam: A Method for Stochastic Optimization." Proceedings of 3rd International Conference on Learning Representations (ICLR'15). *arXiv.org.* https://arxiv.org/pdf/1412.6980.

Kingma, D., Welling M. (2013). "Auto-Encoding Variational Bayes." *arXiv.org.* https://arxiv.org/pdf/1312.6114.

Kiros, R., Y. Zhu, R. R. Salakhutdinov, R. Zemel, R. Urtasun, A. Torralba, and S. Fidler. (2015). "Skip-Thought Vectors." *Advances in Neural Information Processing Systems* 28 (NIPS 2015): 3294–3302.

Krizhevsky, A. (2009). *Learning Multiple Layers of Features from Tiny Images.* Technical report. University of Toronto.

Krizhevsky, A., I. Sutskever, and G. Hinton. (2012). "ImageNet Classification with Deep Convolutional Neural Networks." *Advances in Neural Information Processing Systems* 25 (NIPS 2012): 1106–1114.

Lan, Z., M. Chen, S. Goodman, and K. Gimpel. (2020). "ALBERT: A Lite BERT for Self-supervised Learning of Language Representations." *Proceedings of International Conference on Learning Representations (ICLR 2020).*

Le, Q., and T. Mikolov. (2014). "Distributed Representations of Sentences and Documents." Proceedings of the 31st International Conference on International Conference on Machine Learning (ICML'14). *Journal of Machine Learning Research* 32: 1188–1196.

LeCun, Y., Boser, B. Denker, J. S. Henderson, D. Howard, R. E. Hubbard, W., and Jackel, L. D. (1990). "Handwritten Digit Recognition with a Back-Propagation Network." In *Advances in Neural Information Processing Systems 2*, 396–404. Denver, CO: Morgan Kaufmann.

LeCun, Y., L. Bottou, G. Orr, and K. Müller. (1998). "Efficient BackProp." In *Neural Networks, Tricks of the Trade*, edited by G. Orr, 9–50. London: Springer-Verlag.

LeCun, Y., L. Bottou, Y. Bengio, P. Haffner, and LeCun. (1998). "Gradient-Based Learning Applied to Document Recognition." *Proceedings of the IEEE* 86(11): 2278–2324.

Lenc, K., and A. Vedaldi. (2015). "R-CNN Minus R." In *Proceedings of the British Machine Vision Conference (BMVC)*, 5.1–5.12. Norfolk, UK: BMVA Press.

Lieberman, H., A. Faaborg, W. Daher, and J. Espinosa. (2005). "How to Wreck a Nice Beach: You Sing Calm Incense." In *Proceedings of the 10th International Conference on Intelligent User Interfaces (IUI '05)*, 278–280. New York: Association for Computing Machinery.

Lin, M., Q. Chen, and S. Yan. (2013). "Network In Network." *arXiv.org.* https://arxiv.org/pdf/1312.4400.

Lin, T., M. Maire, S. Belongie, L. Bourdev, R. Girshick, J. Hays, P. Perona, D. Ramanan, C. L. Zitnick, and P. Dollár. (2015). "Microsoft COCO: Common Objects in Context." *arXiv.org.* https://arxiv.org/pdf/1405.0312v3.

Lin, T., P. Doll, R. Girshick, K. He, B. Hariharan, and S. Belongie. (2017). "Feature Pyramid Networks for Object Detection." *2017 IEEE Conference on Computer Vision and Pattern Recognition (CVPR)*. 936–944. Los Alamitos, CA: IEEE Computer Society.

Lin, Z., M. Feng, C. dos Santos, M. Yu, B. Xiang, and B. Zhou. (2017). "A Structured Self-Attentive Sentence Embedding." *arXiv.org.* https://arxiv.org/pdf/1703.03130.

Linnainmaa, S. (1970). "The Representation of the Cumulative Rounding Error of an Algorithm as a Taylor Expansion of the Local Rounding Errors." Master thesis, University of Helsinki.

Lipton, Z., J. Berkowitz, and C. Elkan. (2015). "A Critical Review of Recurrent Neural Networks for Sequence Learning." *arXiv.org*. https://arxiv.org/pdf/1506.00019v4.

Liu, A., M. Srikanth, N. Adams-Cohen, M. Alvarez, and A. Anandkumar. (2019). "Finding Social Media Trolls: Dynamic Keyword Selection Methods for Rapidly-Evolving Online Debates." *arXiv.org*. https://arxiv.org/pdf/1911.05332.

Liu, T., X. Ye, and B. Sun. (2018). "Combining Convolutional Neural Network and Support Vector Machine for Gait-based Gender Recognition." *2018 Chinese Automation Congress (CAC)*, 3477–3481.

Liu, Y., M. Ott, N. Goyal, J. Du, M. Joshi, D. Chen, O. Levy, M. Lewis, L. Zettlemoyer, and V. Stoyanov. (2019). "RoBERTa: A Robustly Optimized BERT Pretraining Approach." *arXiv.org*. https://arxiv.org/pdf/1907.11692.

Liu, Z., P. Luo, X. Wang, and X. Tang. (2015). "Deep Learning Face Attributes in the Wild." In *Proceedings of International Conference on Computer Vision (ICCV)*, 3730–3738.

Long, J., E. Shelhamer, and T. Darrell. (2017). "Fully Convolutional Networks for Semantic Segmentation." *IEEE Transactions on Pattern Analysis and Machine Intelligence* 39(4): 640–651.

Luong, M. (2016). "Neural Machine Translation." Doctoral dissertation, Stanford University.

Luong, T., H. Pham, and C. Manning. (2015). "Effective Approaches to Attention-based Neural Machine Translation." *Proceedings of the 2015 Conference on Empirical Methods in Natural Language Processing*, 1412–1421. Stroudsburg, PA: Association for Computational Linguistics.

Mao, J., W. Xu, Y. Yang, J. Wang, and A. Yuille. (2014). "Explain Images with Multimodal Recurrent Neural Networks." *arXiv.org*. https://arxiv.org/pdf/1410.1090.

Mask R-CNN for Object Detection and Segmentation. (2019). https://github.com/matterport/Mask_RCNN.

McCann, B., J. Bradbury, C. Xiong, and R. Socher. (2017). "Learned in Translation: Contextualized Word Vectors." *Advances in Neural Information Processing Systems 30 (NIPS 2017)*: 6297–6308.

McCulloch, W., and W. Pitts. (1943). "A logical calculus of the ideas immanent in nervous activity." *Bulletin of Mathematical Biophysics* 5: 115–133.

Menon, S., A. Damian, N. Ravi, and C. Rudin. (2020). "PULSE: Self-Supervised Photo Upsampling via Latent Space Exploration of Generative Models." *arXiv.org*. https://arxiv.org/pdf/2003.03808.

Menon, S., A. Damian, S. Hu, N. Ravi, and C. Rudin. (2020). "PULSE: Self-Supervised Photo Upsampling via Latent Space Exploration of Generative Models." *arXiv.org*. https://arxiv.org/pdf/2003.03808v1.

Mikolov, T., I. Sutskever, K. Chen, G. Corrodo, and J. Dean. (2013). "Distributed Representations of Words and Phrases and their Compositionality." In *Proceedings of the 26th International Conference on Neural Information Processing Systems, Volume 2,* edited by C. J. C. Burges, L. Bottou, M. Welling, Z. Ghahramani, and K. Q. Weinberger, 3111–3119. Red Hook, NY: Curran Associates.

Mikolov, T., J. Kopecky, L. Burget, O. Glembek, and J. Cernocky. (2009). "Neural Network Based Language Models for Highly Inflective Languages." In *Proceedings of the 2009 IEEE International Conference on Acoustics, Speech and Signal Processing,* 4725–4728. Washington, DC: IEEE,

Mikolov, T., K. Chen, G. Corrado, and J. Dean. (2013). "Efficient Estimation of Word Representations in Vector Space." *arXiv.org*. https://arxiv.org/pdf/1301.3781.

Mikolov, T., M. Karafiat, L. Burget, J. Cernocky, and S. Khudanpur. (2010). "Recurrent neural network based language model." In *Proceedings of the 11th Annual Conference of the International Speech Communication Association (INTERSPEECH 2010),* 1045–1048. Red Hook, NY : Curran Associates.

Mikolov, T., W. Yih, and G. Zweig. (2013). "Linguistic Regularities in Continuous Space Word Representations." In *Proceedings of the 2013 Conference of the North American Chapter of the Association for Computational Linguistics: Human Language Technologies,* 746–751. Stroudsburg, PA: Association for Computational Linguistics.

Minsky, M., and S. Papert. (1969). *Perceptrons.* Cambridge, MA: MIT Press.

Mitchell, M., S. Wu, A. Zaldivar, P. Barnes, L. Vasserman, B. Hutchinson, E. Spitzer, I. D. Raji, and T. Gebru. (2018). "Model Cards for Model Reporting." *Proceedings of the Conference on Fairness, Accountability, and Transparency, in PMLR* 81: 220–229.

Mnih, V., Kavukcuoglu L., Silver D., Graves A., Antonoglou I., Wierstra D., Riedmiller M. (2013). "Playing Atari with Deep Reinforcement Learning." *arXiv.org*. https://arxiv.org/pdf/1312.5602.

Morin, F., and Y. Bengio. (2005). "Hierarchical Probabilistic Neural Network Language Model." *AISTATS,* 246–252.

Nassif, A., I. Shahin, I. Attili, M. Azzeh, and K. Shaalan. (2019). "Speech Recognition Using Deep Neural Networks: A Systematic Review." *IEEE Access* 7: 19143–19165.

Nesterov, Y. (1983). "A Method of Solving a Convex Programming Problem with Convergence Rate O(1/k^2)." *Soviet Mathematics Doklady* 27: 372–376.

Ng, A. Andrew Ng's Machine Learning Course | Learning Curves. https://www.youtube.com/watch?v=XPmLkz8aS6U.

Nielsen, M. (2015). *Neural Networks and Deep Learning* (ebook). Determination Press.

Nissim, M., R. Noord, and R. Goot. (2020). "Fair is Better than Sensational: Man is to Doctor as Woman is to Doctor." *Computational Linguistics* 03: 1–17.

Noh, H., S. Hong, and B. Han. (2015). "Learning Deconvolution Network for Semantic Segmentation." In *Proceedings of the 2015 IEEE International Conference on Computer Vision (ICCV'15)*, 1520–1528. Piscataway, NJ: IEEE.

Odena, A., V. Dumoulin, and C. Olah. (2016). "Deconvolution and Checkerboard Artifacts." *Distill* 1(10).

Olah, C. (2015). *Understanding LSTM Networks*. https://colah.github.io/posts/2015-08-Understanding-LSTMs.

Olazaran, M. (1996). "A Sociological Study of the Official History of the Perceptrons Controversy." *Social Studies of Science* 26(3): 611–659.

Pagliardini, M., P. Gupta, and M. Jaggi. (2018). "Unsupervised Learning of Sentence Embeddings Using Compositional n-Gram Features." In *Proceedings of the 2018 Conference of the North American Chapter of the Association for Computational Linguistics: Human Language Technologies*, 528–540. Stroudsburg, PA: Association for Computational Linguistics.

Papineni, K., S. Roukos, T. Ward, and W. Zhu. (2002). "BLEU: a Method for Automatic Evaluation of Machine Translation." *Proceedings of the 40th Annual Meeting of the Association for Computational Linguistics*, 311–318. Stroudsburg, PA: Association for Computational Linguistics.

Pennington, J., R. Socher, and C. Manning. (2014). "GloVe: Global Vectors for Word Representations." *2014 Conference on Empirical Methods in Natural Language Processing (EMNLP)*, 1532–1543. Stroudsburg, PA: Association for Computational Linguistics.

Peters, M., M. Neumann, M. Iyyer, M. Gardner, C. Clark, K. Lee, and L. Zettlemoyer. (2018). "Deep Contextualized Word Representations." *2018 Conference of the North American Chapter of the Association for Computational Linguistics: Human Language Technologies*, 2227–2237. Stroudsburg, PA: Association for Computational Linguistics.

Philipp, G., D. Song, and J. Carbonell. (2018). "The Exploding Gradient Problem Demystified—Definition, Prevalence, Impact, Origin, Tradeoffs, and Solutions." *arXiv.org*. https://arxiv.org/pdf/1712.05577v4.

Press, O., and L. Wolf. (2017). "Using the Output Embedding to Improve Language Models." *15th Conference of the European Chapter of the Association for Computational Linguistics*. Association for Computational Linguistics, 157–163.

Puri, R., and B. Catanzaro. (2019). "Zero-Shot Text Classification with Generative Language Models." Third Workshop on Meta-Learning at NeurIPS. *arXiv.org*. https://arxiv.org/pdf/1912.10165.

Radford, A., J. Wu, R. Child, D. Luan, D. Amodei, and I. Sutskever. (2019). *Language Models Are Unsupervised Multitask Learners*. Technical Report, San Francisco: OpenAI.

Radford, A., K. Narasimhan, T. Salimans, and I. Sutskever. (2018). *Improving Language Understanding by Generative Pre-Training*. Technical Report, San Francisco: OpenAI.

Raffel, C., N. Shazeer, A. Roberts, K. Lee, S. Narang, M. Matena, Y. Zhou, W. Li, and P. J. Liu. (2019). "Exploring the Limits of Transfer Learning with a Unified Text-to-Text Transformer." *arXiv.org*. https://arxiv.org/pdf/1910.10683.

Raji, D., and J. Buolamwini. (2019). "Actionable Auditing: Investigating the Impact of Publicly Naming Biased Performance Results of Commercial AI Products." In *Proceedings of the 2019 AAAI/ACM Conference on AI, Ethics, and Society*, 429–435. New York : Association for Computing Machinery.

Ren, P., Xiao Y., Chang X., Huang P., Li Z., Chen X., Wang X. (2020). "A Comprehensive Survey of Neural Architecture Search: Challenges and Solutions." *arXiv.org*. https://arxiv.org/pdf/2006.02903.

Ronneberger, O., P. Fischer, and T. Brox. (2015). "U-Net: Convolutional Networks for Biomedical Image Segmentation." *Medical Image Computing and Computer-Assisted Intervention (MICCAI 2015), Lecture Notes in Computer Science* 9351: 234–241.

Rosenblatt, Frank. (1958). "The Perceptron: A Probabilistic Model for Information Storage and Organization in the Brain." *Psychological Review* 65(6): 386–408.

Ruder S. (2017). "An Overview of Multi-Task Learning in Deep Neural Networks." *arXiv.org*. https://arxiv.org/pdf/1706.05098.

Rumelhart, D., G. Hinton, and R. Williams. (1986). *Learning Internal Representations by Error Propagation*. Vol. 1, in *Parallel distributed processing: explorations in the microstructure of cognition*, by D. Rumelhart and J. McClelland, 318–362. Cambridge, MA: MIT Press.

Russakovsky, O., J. Deng, H. Su, J. Krause, S. Satheesh, S. Ma, Z. Huang, et al. (2015). "ImageNet Large Scale Visual Recognition Challenge." *International Journal of Computer Vision* 115: 211–252. https://doi.org/10.1007/s11263-015-0816-y.

Salminen, J., S. Jung, S. Chowdhury, and B. Jansen. (2020). "Analyzing Demographic Bias in Artificially Generated Facial Pictures." *Extended Abstracts of the 2020 CHI Conference on Human Factors in Computing Systems*, 1–8.

Sample, I. (2020, January 13). "What Are Deepfakes—And How Can You Spot Them?" *The Guardian*. https://www.theguardian.com/technology/2020/jan/13/what-are-deepfakes-and-how-can-you-spot-them

Santurkar, S., D. Tsipras, A. Ilyas, and A. Mądry. (2018). "How Does Batch Normalization Help Optimization?" In *Proceedings of the 32nd International Conference on Neural Information Processing Systems (NIPS 18)*, 2488–2498. Red Hook, NY: Curran Associates.

Schmidhuber, J. (2015). "Deep Learning in Neural Networks: An Overview." *Neural Networks* 61: 85–117.

Schuster, M., and K. Nakajima. (2012). "Japanese and Korean Voice Search." *International Conference on Acoustics, Speech and Signal Processing*, 5149–5152. Piscataway, NJ: IEEE.

Schuster, M., and K. Paliwal. (1997). "Bidirectional Recurrent Neural Networks." *IEEE Transactions on Signal Processing* 45(11): 2673–2682.

Sennrich, R., B. Haddow, and A. Birch. (2016). "Neural Machine Translation of Rare Words with Subword Units." *Proceedings of the 54th Annual Meeting of the Association for Computational Linguistics (Volume 1: Long Papers)*. 1715–1725. Red Hook, NY: Curran Associates.

Shah, A., E. Kadam, H. Shah, S. Shinde, and S. Shingade. (2016). "Deep Residual Networks with Exponential Linear Unit." *Proceedings of the Third International Symposium on Computer Vision and the Internet (VisionNet'16)*, 59–65. New York: Association for Computing Machinery.

Shaoqing, R., K. He, R. Girshick, and J. Sun. (2015). "Faster R-CNN: Towards Real-time Object Detection with Region Proposal Networks." In *Proceedings of the 28th International Conference on Neural Information Processing Systems—Volume 1 (NIPS'15)*, 91–99. Cambridge, MA: MIT Press.

Sharma, P., N. Ding, S. Goodman, and R. Soricut. (2018). "Conceptual Captions: A Cleaned, Hypernymed, Image Alt-text Dataset for Automatic Image Captioning." In *Proceedings of the 56th Annual Meeting of the Association for Computational Linguistics*. Stroudsburg, PA: Association for Computational Linguistics, 2556–2565.

Shelley, M. (1818). *Frankenstein; or, The Modern Prometheus*. Lackington, Hughes, Harding, Mavor & Jones.

Shen, J., R. Pang, R. J. Weiss, M. Schuster, N. Jaitly, Z. Yang, Z. Chen, et al. (2018). "Natural TTS Synthesis by Conditioning Wavenet on MEL Spectrogram Predictions." *2018 IEEE International Conference on Acoustics, Speech and Signal Processing (ICASSP)*, 4779–4783. Piscataway, NJ: IEEE.

Sheng, E., K. Chang, P. Natarajan, and N. Peng. (2019). "The Woman Worked as a Babysitter: On Biases in Language Generation." In *Proceedings of the 2019 Conference on Empirical Methods in Natural Language Processing and the 9th International Joint Conference on Natural Language Processing*, 3405–3410. Stroudsburg, PA: Association for Computational Linguistics.

Sherman, Richard, and Robert Sherman. (1963). "Supercalifragilisticexpialidocious." From Walt Disney's *Mary Poppins*.

Shoeybi, M., M. Patwary, R. Puri, P. LeGresley, J. Casper, and B. Catanzaro. (2019). "Megatron-LM: Training Multi-Billion Parameter Language Models Using Model Parallelism." *arXiv.org*. https://arxiv.org/pdf/1909.08053.

Simonyan, K., and A. Zisserman. (2014). "Very Deep Convolutional Networks for Large-Scale Image Recognition." *arXiv.org*. https://arxiv.org/pdf/1409.1556.

Sorensen, J. (n.d.). *Grounded: Life on the No Fly List*. https://www.aclu.org/issues/national-security/grounded-life-no-fly-list.

Srivastava, N., G. Hinton, A. Krizhevsky, I. Sutskever, and R. Salakhutdinov. (2014). "Dropout: A Simple Way to Prevent Neural Networks from Overfitting." *Journal of Machine Learning Research* 15: 1929–1958.

Srivastava, R., K. Greff, and J. Schmidhuber. (2015). "Highway Networks." *arXiv.org*. https://arxiv.org/pdf/1505.00387.

Sun, Y., S. Wang, Y. Li, S. Feng, H. Tian, H. Wu, and H. Wang. (2020). "ERNIE 2.0: A Continual Pre-Training Framework for Language Understanding." *Thirty-Fourth AAAI Conference on Artificial Intelligence.* New York: Association for the Advancement of Artificial Intelligence.

Sun, Y., S. Wang, Y. Li, S. Feng, X. Chen, H. Zhang, X. Tian, D. Zhu, H. Tian, and H. Wu. (2019). "ERNIE: Enhanced Representation through Knowledge Integration." *arXiv.org*. https://arxiv.org/pdf/1904.09223.

Sun, Y., X. Wang, and X. Tang. (2013). "Hybrid Deep Learning for Face Verification." *Proceedings of International Conference on Computer Vision.*

Suresh, H., and J. Guttag. (2019). "A Framework for Understanding Unintended Consequences of Machine Learning." *arXiv.org*. https://arxiv.org/pdf/1901.10002.

Sutskever, I., O. Vinyals, and Q. Le. (2014). "Sequence to Sequence Learning with Neural Networks." In *Proceedings of the 27th International Conference on Neural Information Processing (NIPS'14).* Cambridge, MA: MIT Press, 3104–3112.

Szegedy, C., Liu, W., Jia, Y., Sermanet, P., Reed, S., Anguelov, D., Erhan, D., Vanhoucke, V., and Rabinovich, A. (2014). "Going Deeper with Convolutions." *28th IEEE Conference on Computer Vision and Pattern Recognition (CVPR)*, 1–9. Piscataway, NJ: IEEE.

Szegedy, C., Zaremba, W., Sutskever, I., Bruna, J., Erhan, D., Goodfellow, I., and Fergus, R. (2014). "Intriguing Properties of Neural Networks." *International Conference on Learning Representations.*

Szegedy, C., S. Ioffe, V. Vanhoucke, and A. Alemi. (2017). "Inception-v4, Inception-ResNet and the Impact of Residual Connections on Learning." In *Proceedings of the Thirty-First AAAI Conference on Artificial Intelligence (AAAI-17)*, 4278–4284. Palo Alto, CA: AAAI Press.

Szegedy, C., V. Vanhoucke, S. Ioffe, J. Shlens, and Z. Wojna. (2016). "Rethinking the Inception Architecture for Computer Vision." In *Proceedings of IEEE Conference on Computer Vision and Pattern Recognition.* Piscataway, NJ: IEEE.

Tan, M., and Q. Le. (2019). "EfficientNet: Rethinking Model Scaling for Convolutional Neural Networks." *36th International Conference on Machine Learning*, 6105–6114. Red Hook, NY: Curran Associates.

Tang, Y. (2013). "Deep Learning Using Linear Support Vector Machines." *Challenges in Representation Learning, Workshop in Conjunction with the 30th International Conference on Machine Learning (ICML 2013)*.

TensorFlow. (n.d.). *Text Classification with Movie Reviews*. https://www.tensorflow .org/hub/tutorials/tf2_text_classification

Thomas, R. (2018). "An Opinionated Introduction to AutoML and Neural Architecture Search." *fast.ai*. https://www.fast.ai/2018/07/16/auto-ml2/.

Thomas, R. (2019). "Keynote at Open Data Science Conference West."

Thomas, R., J. Howard, and S. Gugger. (2020). "Data Ethics." In *Deep Learning for Coders with fastai and PyTorch*, edited by J. Howard and S. Gugger. Sebastopal, CA: O'Reilly Media.

Vahdat, A., Kautz J. (2020). "NVAE: A Deep Hierarchical Variational Autoencoder." *arXiv.org*. https://arxiv.org/pdf/2007.03898.

Valle, R., K. Shih, R. Prenger, and B. Catanzaro. (2020). "Flowtron: An Autoregressive Flow-Based Generative Network for Text-to-Speech Synthesis." *arXiv.org*. https://arxiv.org/pdf/2005.05957.

Vallor, S. (2018). "Ethics in Tech Practice: A Toolkit." Markkula Center for Applied Ethics, Santa Clara University.

Vaswani, A., N. Shazeer, L. Kaiser, I. Polosukhin, N. Parmar, J. Uszkoreit, L. Jones, and A. N. Gomez. (2017). "Attention Is All You Need." *Proceedings of the 31st International Conference on Neural Information Processing (NIPS'17)*, edited by U. von Luxburg, I. Guyon, S. Bengio, H. Wallach, and R. Fergus, 6000–6010. Red Hook, NY: Curran Associates.

Vinyals, O., A. Toshev, S. Bengio, and D. Erhan. (2014). "Show and Tell: A Neural Image Caption Generator." *arXiv.org*. https://arxiv.org/pdf/1411.4555.

Wang, Y., R. J. Skerry-Ryan, D. Stanton, Y. Wu, R. J. Weiss, N. Jaitly, Z. Yang, et al. (2017). "Tacotron: Towards End-to-End Speech Synthesis." *INTERSPEECH 2017*, 4006–4010.

Werbos, P. (1981). "Applications of Advances in Nonlinear Sensitivity Analysis." *Proceedings of the 10th IFIP Conference,* 762–770. Berlin: Springer-Verlag.

Werbos, P. (1990). "Backpropagation Through Time: What It Does and How to Do It." *Proceedings of the IEEE* 78 (10): 1550–1560.

Wieting, J., M. Bansal, K. Gimpel, and K. Livescu. (2016). "Charagram: Embedding Words and Sentences via Character n-grams." *Proceedings of the 2016 Conference on Empirical Methods in Natural Language Processing,* 1504–1515. Stroudsburg, PA: Association for Computational Linguistics.

Wojcik, S., S. Messing, A. Smith, L. Rainie, and P. Hitlin. (2018). "Bots in the Twiitersphere." *Pew Research Center.* https://www.pewresearch.org/internet/2018/04/09/bots-in-the-twittersphere/

Wu, H., and X. Gu. (2015). "Towards Dropout Training for Convolutional Neural Networks." *Neural Networks* 71 (C): 1–10.

Wu, Y., Y. Wu, M. Schuster, Z. Chen, Q. V. Le, M. Norouzi, W. Macherey, et al. (2016). "Google's Neural Machine Translation System: Bridging the Gap between Human and Machine Translation." *arXiv.org.* https://arxiv.org/pdf/1609.08144.

Xiao, H., Rasul, K., and Vollgraf, R. (2017). "Fashion-MNIST: a Novel Image Dataset for Benchmarking Machine Learning Algorithms." *arXiv.org.* https://arxiv.org/pdf/1708.07747.

Xie, S., R. Girshick, P. Dollár, Z. Tu, and K. He. (2017). "Aggregated Residual Transformations for Deep Neural Networks." *2017 IEEE Conference on Computer Vision and Pattern Recognition (CVPR).* IEEE, 5987–5995.

Xu, B., N. Wang, T. Chen, and M. Li. (2015). "Empirical Evaluation of Rectified Activations in Convolutional Networks." *Deep Learning Workshop held in conjunction with International Conference on Machine Learning.*

Xu, K., J. Ba, R. Kiros, K. Cho, A. Courville, R. Salakhutdinov, R. Zemel, and Y. Bengio. (2015). "Show, Attend and Tell: Neural Image Caption Generation with Visual Attention." *Proceedings of the 32nd International Conference on International Conference on Machine Learning (ICML'15),* edited by F. Bach and D. Blei, 2048–2057. JMLR.org.

Yang, Z., Z. Dai, Y. Yang, J. Carbonell, R. Salakhutdinov, and Q. Le. (2019). "XLNet: Generalized Autoregressive Pretraining for Language Understanding." *Advances in Neural Information Processing Systems 32 (NIPS 2019),* 5753–5763. Red Hook, NY: Curran Associates.

Zaremba, W., I. Sutskever, and O. Vinyals. (2015). "Recurrent Neural Network Regularization." *arXiv.org*. https://arxiv.org/pdf/1409.2329v5.

Zeiler, M., and R. Fergus. (2014). "Visualizing and Understanding Convolutional Networks." *Computer Vision–ECCV 2014*, 818–833. Cham, Switzerland: Springer.

Zeiler, M., D. Krishnan, G. Taylor, and R. Fergus. (2010). "Deconvolutional Networks." *2010 IEEE Computer Society Conference on Computer Vision and Pattern (CVPR'10)*, 2528–2535. Piscataway, NJ: IEEE.

Zeiler, M., G. Taylor, and R. Fergus. (2011). "Adaptive Deconvolutional Networks for Mid and High Level Feature Learning." *Proceedings of the 2011 International Conference on Computer Vision (ICCV'11)*, 2018–2025. Washington, DC: IEEE Computer Society.

Zhang, S., L. Yao, A. Sun, and Y. Tay. (2019). "Deep Learning Based Recommender System: A Survey and New Perspectives." *arXiv.org*. https://arxiv.org/pdf/1707.07435.

Zhuang F., Qi Z., Duan K., Xi D., Zhu Y., Zhu H., Xiong H., and He Q. (2020). "A Comprehensive Survey on Transfer Learning." *arXiv.org*. https://arxiv.org/pdf/1911.02685.

Index

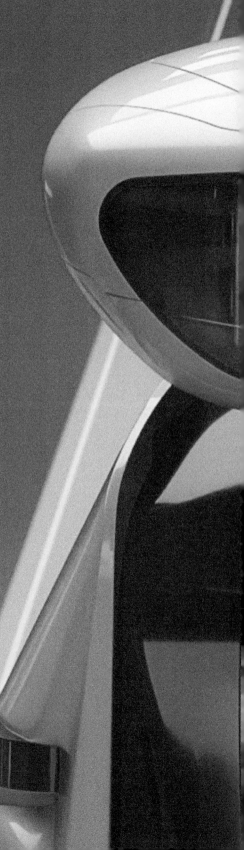

Register Your Product at informit.com/register

Access additional benefits and **save 35%** on your next purchase

- Automatically receive a coupon for 35% off your next purchase, valid for 30 days. Look for your code in your InformIT cart or the Manage Codes section of your account page.

- Download available product updates.

- Access bonus material if available.*

- Check the box to hear from us and receive exclusive offers on new editions and related products.

Registration benefits vary by product. Benefits will be listed on your account page under Registered Products.

InformIT.com—The Trusted Technology Learning Source

InformIT is the online home of information technology brands at Pearson, the world's foremost education company. At InformIT.com, you can:

- Shop our books, eBooks, software, and video training
- Take advantage of our special offers and promotions (informit.com/promotions)
- Sign up for special offers and content newsletter (informit.com/newsletters)
- Access thousands of free chapters and video lessons

Connect with InformIT—Visit informit.com/community

the trusted technology learning source

Addison-Wesley • Adobe Press • Cisco Press • Microsoft Press • Pearson IT Certification • Que • Sams • Peachpit Press

Ⓟ Pearson